Managerial Accounting
14th Edition

TO THE STUDENT

A Study Guide, Working Papers, and Student Solutions Manual are available through your bookstore. The purpose of the Study Guide is to assist you in studying and reviewing the text material and provide you with a means of diagnosing your understanding of underlying concepts by studying the detailed outlines and using true-false questions, multiple choice questions, matching and completion statements, and exercises included in the Study Guide. These may be used both in your initial study of the chapter material and in your subsequent review. The Working Papers have prepared forms and check figures for your problem assignments. The Student Solutions Manual has complete solutions for the even–numbered problems, check figures for the odd–numbered problems, and sample examinations with answers. If the Study Guide, Working Papers, or Student Solutions Manual is not in stock in your bookstore, ask the bookstore manager to order copies for you.

MANAGERIAL ACCOUNTING

14th Edition

Paul E. Dascher
Stetson University

Jeffrey W. Strawser
Sam Houston State University

Joyce A. Strawser
Seton Hall University

Managerial Accounting—14th Edition, by Paul E. Dascher, Jeffrey W. Strawser, and Joyce A. Strawser

Project Coordinator: Brian Schaefer
Editor: Staci Powers
Cover Design: Krista Pierson
Printer: West

COPYRIGHT ©2005 by Dame, a division of Thomson Learning. The Thomson Learning logo is a registered trademark used herein under license.

All Rights Reserved. No part of this work covered by the copyright hereon may be reproduced or used in any form or by any means-graphic, electronic, or mechanical, including photocopying, recording, taping, or information storage and retrieval systems-without the written permission of the publisher.

Printed in the United States of America
12 13 14 15 07 06 05 04

For more information contact Thomson Custom Publishing,
5191 Natorp Blvd., Mason, Ohio, 45040,1-800-355-9983 or find us on the Internet at http://www.custom.thomsonlearning.com

For permission to use material from this text or product, contact us by:
- **telephone: 1.800.730.2214**
- **fax: 1.800.730.2215**
- **web: http: www.thomsonrights.com**

Library of Congress Cataloging-in-Publication Data: 01-131651 ISBN 0759338175

Preface

The 14th edition of this text, like its predecessors, was written as an integrated work in managerial accounting, and is intended for use as a basic text for students completing a first semester or quarter course in financial accounting at either the undergraduate or graduate level. This text is organized around the following major areas of managerial accounting:

- **An Overview of Managerial Accounting.** In this section, the text discusses the uses of managerial accounting and contrasts the type and use of information provided by managerial accounting and financial accounting (Chapter 1). Chapter 2 focuses on basic cost information and behavior. In this chapter we distinguish between the different types of costs incurred by organizations. In addition, this chapter discusses the behavior of these costs with changes in activity as well as the effect of cost behavior on managerial decisions.

- **Cost Accumulation.** Chapters 3 through 5 illustrate the process through which the organization accumulates costs with its inventory products and services. In Chapter 3, we focus on production and service processes that require different levels of effort across individual jobs (job-order costing). Chapter 4 illustrates the cost accumulation process for manufacturing environments characterized by the production of a large number of similar products (process costing). Chapter 5 focuses on the process through which overhead costs are accumulated with the organization's inventory and services. The dedication of an entire chapter to overhead costs represents a significant change from the prior editions of this text and is considered necessary given the importance of controlling overhead costs to organizations in manufacturing inventory and providing services.

- **The Use of Managerial Accounting Information.** Chapters 6 through 11 describe various uses of managerial accounting information. Topics discussed in these chapters include variable costing and cost-volume-profit analysis (Chapter 6), standard costing and determination of variances (Chapter 7), budgeting (Chapter 8), responsibility accounting (Chapter 9), short-term managerial decisions (Chapter 10), and capital budgeting (Chapter 11). In these chapters, the basic principles of cost behavior and cost accumulation discussed in the preceding two sections are applied to important decisions facing managers in today's business world.

In addition, Chapters 12 and 13 provide discussions of The Statement of Cash Flows and Financial Statement Analysis, respectively (if coverage of these topics is desired).

Several pedagogical improvements initiated in previous editions are continued in this edition. These include:

1. The use of illustrations and diagrams to provide students with a conceptual "picture" of many important concepts associated with managerial accounting. For example, in discussing cost flows and the allocation of service department costs, pictorial representations are used to accompany textual discussion.

2. Additional "real-world" examples have been added throughout the text to allow students to see how managerial accounting topics apply in today's business environment. Included are a wealth of excerpts from articles in such publications as *Business Week*, *Forbes*, and *The Wall Street Journal*.

3. A variety of hypothetical corporations are used to illustrate basic managerial accounting concepts. The use of a number of examples allows students to approach each concept with a "fresh" perspective. In addition, this also illustrates the wide variety of situations in which managerial accounting concepts are commonly applied.

Numerous end-of-chapter materials (Questions, Exercises, and Problems) allow instructors maximum flexibility in tailoring the course to fit their students' needs. These materials are identified by topic area to allow instructors to include all major concepts and issues in their assignments. Questions are designed to focus on concepts, definitions, and descriptions introduced in that chapter. Exercises and Problems usually require analytical analysis of chapter concepts.

The 14th edition includes over 700 questions, exercises, and problems and provides the student and instructor with additional opportunities to apply the concepts described and illustrated in the chapters.

Numerous appendices are included throughout the text in proximity to the relevant chapters of interest. The use of appendices is designed to allow instructors the maximum amount of flexibility in tailoring the course to suit their students' needs. These appendices can be assigned as instructors see fit without disrupting the main concepts embodied in the chapters.

In addition to the text, a *Study Guide*, *Working Papers*, and *Student Solutions Manual* have been prepared by the authors and are readily available. The Study Guide contains an outline of key text concepts along with extensive self-testing materials. These materials include true-false questions, completion exercises, multiple choice questions, and short exercises. The purpose of the *Study Guide* is to provide students with additional exposure to concepts discussed in each text chapter and practice in their application to singular cases. The *Working Papers* contain prepared forms and check figures for problem assignments. The *Student Solutions Manual* has complete solutions for the even-numbered problems, check figures for the odd-numbered problems, and sample examinations with answers.

We are indebted to many people for their ideas and assistance. The following professors made constructive comments on the manuscript: Natalie Allen (Texas A&M University), Kathryn Lancaster (California Polytech State University-San Luis Obispo), and Haresh Sapra (University of Minnesota). Additional thanks are due to N. Ross Quarles and R. Dean Lewis of Sam Houston State University, Jerry R. Strawser, A. Benton Cocanougher, and James J. Benjamin (of Texas A&M University) for providing the environment for this effort.

We also appreciate the permission received from the American Institute of Certified Public Accountants and the Institute of Management Accountants for allowing us to use problem materials from past Uniform CPA and CMA Examinations, respectively.

Finally, we acknowledge a special thanks to Natalie Allen, William Fishkin, Billy Strawser, Carol Strawser, and Jan Tiefel for their help in turning our draft materials into the finished product. Without their valuable assistance, the final output would not have been possible. These individuals made the entire process truly enjoyable and ensured a timely completion of all necessary steps. Of course, the authors are solely responsible for any shortcomings of this text.

July 2004

Paul E. Dascher
Jeffrey W. Strawser
Joyce A. Strawser

Table of Contents

Part I
Introduction to Managerial Accounting

**1 Introduction
Managerial Accounting**...1-1

LEARNING OBJECTIVES. INTRODUCTION. THE NEED FOR MANAGERIAL ACCOUNTING INFORMATION. ACCOUNTING SYSTEMS AND THE MANAGEMENT PROCESS. Identifying and Gathering Information on Transactions. Preparing Reports. Using Reports for Decisions and Activities. Feedback. The Role of Accountants in the Management Process. LOCATION OF THE ACCOUNTING FUNCTION. OVERVIEW OF THE MANAGERIAL ACCOUNTING FUNCTION. Preparing Budgets and Devising Standards. Accumulating Data on Costs and Profits. Comparing Actual Activity with Plans or Budgets. Advising Management About Nonroutine Decisions. SUMMARY. KEY DEFINITIONS. QUESTIONS.

2 Analyzing Cost Behavior..2-1

LEARNING OBJECTIVES. INTRODUCTION. TYPES OF COSTS. Direct Materials. Direct Labor. Manufacturing Overhead. OVERVIEW OF COST BEHAVIOR. Level of Activity (Cost Driver). Relevant Range. ILLUSTRATION OF COST BEHAVIOR. Fixed Costs. Variable Costs. Step Costs. Semi-Variable (Mixed) Costs. ANALYZING COST BEHAVIOR. The Graphical Method. The Two-Point Method. Semi-Averages Method. Least Squares Regression Method. COST BEHAVIOR FOR RETAIL AND SERVICE COMPANIES. USING MANAGERIAL ACCOUNTING INFORMATION: BETTER BOOKS. SUMMARY. KEY DEFINITIONS. QUESTIONS. EXERCISES AND PROBLEMS.

Part II
Cost Accumulation

3 Job-Order Costing 3-1

LEARNING OBJECTIVES. INTRODUCTION. IMPORTANCE OF COST ACCUMULATION. Preparation of Financial Statements. Internal Decision-Making Process. INTRODUCTION TO JOB-ORDER COSTING: THE ACE CONSTRUCTION COMPANY. Obtain Direct Materials. Incur Manufacturing Costs. Completion of Production. Sale of Inventory. PREPARATION OF FINANCIAL STATEMENTS. Cost of Goods Manufactured Statement. Cost of Goods Sold Statement. SUMMARY: THE ACE CONSTRUCTION COMPANY. USING MANAGERIAL ACCOUNTING INFORMATION: ACE CONSTRUCTION COMPANY. SUMMARY. KEY DEFINITIONS. QUESTIONS. EXERCISES AND PROBLEMS.

4 Process Costing 4-1

LEARNING OBJECTIVES. INTRODUCTION. AN OVERVIEW OF PROCESS COSTING. COMPREHENSIVE EXAMPLE: THE AMERICAN VEGETABLE COMPANY. Account for Units Produced. Determine Total Manufacturing Costs. Determine Equivalent Units of Production. Calculate the Cost per Unit. Accumulate Costs with Inventory Units. Transfer and Completion of Production. JOINT MANUFACTURING PROCESSES. COST ACCUMULATION FOR SERVICE ORGANIZATIONS. JUST-IN-TIME INVENTORY AND PRODUCTION MANAGEMENT. USING MANAGERIAL ACCOUNTING INFORMATION: THE AMERICAN VEGETABLE COMPANY. SUMMARY. KEY DEFINITIONS. QUESTIONS. EXERCISES AND PROBLEMS. *Appendix A-Process Costing Using the FIFO Method. Appendix B-Cost Accumulation and Cost Flows in a Just-in-Time Costing System. Appendix C-Production Processing Having Multiple Departments.* Production Costs-Canning Department. Completion of Production-Canning Department. Production Costs-Packaging Department. Completion of Production. Work-in-Process in Subsequent Production Departments.

5 Overhead Costs and Activity-Based Costing 5-1

LEARNING OBJECTIVES. INTRODUCTION. THE NATURE OF MANUFACTURING OVERHEAD COSTS. Applying Overhead Cost to Production. Recording Overhead Costs. TWO-STAGE ALLOCATIONS OF SERVICE DEPARTMENT COSTS. Determining Departmental Overhead Rates. Allocating Service Department Costs to Operating Departments (Stage 1 Allocations). ACTIVITY-BASED COSTING. Step 1: Identify Overhead Costs Pools. Step 2: Identify Cost Drivers. Step 3: Allocate Costs to Inventory Items. Other Issues Involved with Activity-Based Costing. USING MANAGERIAL ACCOUNTING DATA: THE AMERICAN VEGETABLE COMPANY. SUMMARY. KEY DEFINITIONS. QUESTIONS. EXERCISES AND PROBLEMS.

Part III
Management's Use of
Managerial Accounting Information

6 Cost Behavior–Cost-Volume-Profit Analysis and Variable and Absorption Costing 6-1

LEARNING OBJECTIVES. INTRODUCTION. CVP ANALYSIS: GRAPHICAL APPROACH. CVP ANALYSIS: EQUATION APPROACHES. General Equation Approach. Unit Contribution Margin Approach. Contribution Margin Ratio Approach. OTHER USES OF CVP ANALYSIS. Desired Level of Profit (Before Taxes). Desired Profit (After Taxes). Variable Levels of Profit. Change in Variable Costs/Contribution Margin. Change in Fixed Costs. Calculating Necessary Selling Prices. CVP for Multiple Products. OPERATING LEVERAGE AND AUTOMATED MANUFACTURING PROCESSES. ASSUMPTIONS OF CVP ANALYSIS. PRACTICAL APPLICATION OF CVP ANALYSIS. INCOME DETERMINATION: ABSORPTION AND VARIABLE COSTING. Absorption (Full) Costing. Variable (Direct) Costing. Comparing Absorption and Variable Costing. USING MANAGERIAL ACCOUNTING INFORMATION: GOLDEN MUSIC PRODUCERS. SUMMARY. KEY DEFINITIONS. QUESTIONS. EXERCISES AND PROBLEMS. Appendix Probabilistic Estimates for CVP Analysis.

Table of Contents ix

7 Standard Costing and Variance Analysis 7-1

LEARNING OBJECTIVES. INTRODUCTION. PERFORMANCE STANDARDS. Direct Materials and Direct Labor Costs. Manufacturing Overhead Costs. VARIANCE ANALYSIS: DIRECT MATERIALS AND DIRECT LABOR COSTS. Direct Material Variances. Direct Labor Variances. COST ACCUMULATION IN A STANDARD COSTING SYSTEM. RECENT DEVELOPMENTS IN THE MANUFACTURING ENVIRONMENT. BENEFITS OF PERFORMANCE STANDARDS AND STANDARD COSTING. USING MANAGERIAL ACCOUNTING INFORMATION: SPORTSWORLD. SUMMARY. KEY DEFINITIONS. QUESTIONS. EXERCISES AND PROBLEMS. Appendix-Variance Analysis: Manufacturing Overhead Costs. VARIABLE OVERHEAD COSTS. Variable Overhead Efficiency Variance. Variable Overhead Spending Variance. Summary: Variable Overhead Variances. FIXED OVERHEAD COSTS. Fixed Overhead Volume Variance. Fixed Overhead Spending Variance. Summary: Fixed Overhead Variances. OVERALL ANALYSIS OF OVERHEAD VARIANCES. ACCUMULATION OF MANUFACTURING OVERHEAD COSTS WITH PRODUCTION.

8 Budgeting 8-1

LEARNING OBJECTIVES. INTRODUCTION. PURPOSES OF BUDGETING. THE BUDGETING PROCESS. COMPREHENSIVE EXAMPLE: OPERATING BUDGETS. Sales Budget. Production Budget. Direct Materials Purchases and Usage Budgets. Direct Labor and Manufacturing Overhead Budgets. Nonmanufacturing Expense Budget. BUDGETED FINANCIAL STATEMENTS-OPERATIONS. FINANCIAL AND RESOURCE BUDGETS. Cash Budget. Accounts Receivable Budget. Inventory Budgets. Property, Plant and Equipment Budget. Accounts Payable Budget. Notes Payable Budget. Budgeted Shareholders' Equity. NONQUANTITATIVE ASPECTS OF BUDGETING. The Difficulty of Budget Standards. Participative Budgeting and Slack. BUDGETS FOR MERCHANDISING AND SERVICE ORGANIZATIONS. USING MANAGERIAL ACCOUNTING INFORMATION: TOY CONCEPTS, INC. SUMMARY. KEY DEFINITIONS. QUESTIONS. EXERCISES AND PROBLEMS.

9 Control of the Organization—Responsibility Accounting 9-1

LEARNING OBJECTIVES. INTRODUCTION. MANAGEMENT CONTROL SYSTEMS. RESPONSIBILITY CENTERS. RESPONSIBILITY ACCOUNTING AT BLAST! SNACK FOODS. COST CENTERS. PROFIT CENTERS. INVESTMENT CENTERS. Return on Investment (ROI). Residual Income. ISSUES IN EVALUATING INVESTMENT CENTERS. Assets. Net Income. Life of Investment. Transfer Pricing. TOTAL QUALITY MANAGEMENT. NONFINANCIAL PERFORMANCE AND THE BALANCED SCORECARD. USE OF MANAGERIAL ACCOUNTING INFORMATION: BLAST! SNACK FOODS. SUMMARY. KEY DEFINITIONS. QUESTIONS. EXERCISES AND PROBLEMS.

10 The Use of Managerial Accounting Data in Making Short-Term Decisions 10-1

LEARNING OBJECTIVES. INTRODUCTION. TERMINOLOGY FOR SHORT-TERM DECISIONS. Decisions. Relevant Costs. Opportunity Costs. Sunk Costs. Summary. THE USE OF MANAGERIAL ACCOUNTING DATA IN MAKING SHORT-TERM DECISIONS. Product Pricing Decisions. Contribution Margin (Variable) Approach. Full-Cost (Absorption) Approach. Setting Prices to Earn a Profit. Elasticity of Demand. SPECIAL ORDERS. No Excess Capacity. Qualitative Considerations. Summary: Special Orders. CONTINUATION OF A SEGMENT OR PRODUCT LINE. Other Considerations-Resource Constraints. Summary: Continuation of a Segment or Product Line. ADDITIONAL PROCESSING. MAKE-OR-BUY DECISIONS. Alternative Use of Capacity. Qualitative Considerations. Other Considerations. SUMMARY. KEY DEFINITIONS. QUESTIONS. EXERCISES AND PROBLEMS.

11 Capital Budgeting: Search for Long-Run Alternatives 11-1

LEARNING OBJECTIVES. INTRODUCTION. AN INTRODUCTION TO CAPITAL BUDGETING. Types of Capital Budgeting Decisions. Capital Budgeting-Quantitative Factors. Capital Budgeting- Qualitative Factors. CAPITAL BUDGETING TECHNIQUES THAT IGNORE THE TIME VALUE OF MONEY. Payback Period. Average Rate of Return (Accounting Rate of Return). CAPITAL BUDGETING TECHNIQUES THAT CONSIDER THE TIME VALUE OF MONEY. NET PRESENT VALUE. Future Cash Inflows and Outflows-Basic. Evaluating Competing Projects Using Net Present Value. Additional Complexities Using Net Present Value. Limitations of the Net Present Value Method. Advantages of the Net Present Value Method. Summary-Net Present Value. INTERNAL TIME-ADJUSTED RATE OF RETURN. SUMMARY: TECHNIQUES THAT CONSIDER THE TIME VALUE OF MONEY. SUMMARY OF CAPITAL BUDGETING TECHNIQUES. POSTAUDIT OF CAPITAL INVESTMENTS. CAPITAL BUDGETING FOR HIGH-TECHNOLOGY ASSETS. THE USE OF CAPITAL BUDGETING TECHNIQUES IN PRACTICE. SUMMARY. KEY DEFINITIONS. QUESTIONS. EXERCISES AND PROBLEMS. *Appendix-Present Value (The Time Value of Money).* Determining Present Value-Single Sum. Determining Present Value-Annuities.

Part IV
The Statement of Cash Flows and Financial Statement Analysis

12 The Statement of Cash Flows 12-1

LEARNING OBJECTIVES. INTRODUCTION. IMPORTANCE OF CASH FLOWS. A BRIEF HISTORY. CASH FLOW CONCEPT. THE STATEMENT OF CASH FLOWS. CASH FROM OPERATIONS. Direct Method. Indirect Method. PREPARATION OF THE STATEMENT OF CASH FLOWS. Change in Cash. Changes in Noncash Accounts. The Statement of Cash Flows. ADDITIONAL PROBLEMS IN THE ANALYSIS OF THE STATEMENT OF CASH FLOWS. Uncollectible Accounts. Dividends. Income Tax Expense. Stock Dividends and Conversions. Significant Noncash Transactions. Multiple Changes Affecting Specific Accounts. CASH FLOW INFORMATION FOR ANALYSIS. SUMMARY. KEY DEFINITIONS. QUESTIONS. EXERCISES. PROBLEMS. *Appendix—Worksheet Approach.*

13 Financial Statement Analysis 13-1

LEARNING OBJECTIVES. INTRODUCTION. COMPARATIVE FINANCIAL STATEMENTS. BASIC ANALYTICAL PROCEDURES. Horizontal Analysis. Vertical Analysis. Common-Size Statements. RATIO ANALYSIS. Comparison with Standards. USERS OF FINANCIAL STATEMENT. ANALYSIS FOR COMMON STOCKHOLDERS. Rate of Return on Total Assets. Rate of Return on Common Stockholders' Equity. The Relationship between ROA and ROCS. Earnings Per Share of Common Stock. Price-Earnings Ratio on Common Stock. OTHER INVESTOR RATIOS. ANALYSIS FOR LONG-TERM CREDITORS. How Much Long-Term Debt? Debt-to-Equity Ratio. Interest Coverage Ratios. Continued Existence of the Company. ANALYSIS FOR SHORT-TERM CREDITORS. The Nature of Short-Term Liquidity Analysis. Working Capital. Current Ratio. Acid-Test or Quick Ratio. Analysis of Key Current Assets and Liabilities. Analysis of Accounts Receivable. Analysis of Inventories. Operating Cycle. INTERPRETATION OF ANALYSES. SUMMARY. KEY DEFINITIONS. QUESTIONS. EXERCISES AND PROBLEMS. *Appendix-An Annual Report to Shareholders.* Questions.

Index I-1

Part I

Introduction to Managerial Accounting

The initial section of this text introduces the students to managerial accounting and the basic purposes of managerial accounting. In addition, important terminology related to managerial accounting and cost behavior is discussed. The chapters comprising this initial section are:

Chapter 1: *Introduction to Managerial Accounting*

Chapter 2: *Analyzing Cost Behavior*

Learning Objectives

Chapter 1 introduces managerial accounting and the role of the managerial accountant in the organization. Studying this chapter should enable you to:

1. Identify the major purposes of managerial accounting.
2. Contrast managerial accounting with financial accounting.
3. Describe the steps in an accounting system and the interrelationships within the system.
4. Portray the accountant's role in the managerial process.
5. Determine where managerial accountants gather source data and to whom they issue final reports.

Introduction to Managerial Accounting

INTRODUCTION

At the beginning of their second accounting class, two students (Rick James and Mike Hammer) were discussing the class in financial accounting they had just completed:

Rick: You know, that accounting class was really interesting. It's amazing how accounting can take so much information and summarize it in financial statements. How in the world would bankers and investors ever know about a company without accounting?

Mike: I agree. Something bothered me, though. All we talked about in financial accounting was how information can be summarized and communicated to external users. What about the management of the company? Surely they need to have information to make decisions about what products to produce, how many employees to hire, and how much to charge for their products. We didn't even discuss the need for information by the company's management.

Rick: I never thought about that. Surely there must be some way to provide management with information for decision-making purposes.

Mike: Shhh. I think class is about to start...

Information is a truly irreplaceable commodity in today's business world. In order to manage and plan for various organization activities, upper management needs to have a vast amount of information available in a timely fashion. For example, when producing automobiles, the following are examples of some of the types of questions that must be answered by the management of General Motors:

- What are expected sales during the year?
- How much does it cost to manufacture a certain type of automobile?
- How many automobiles need to be produced to meet quarterly demand?
- How much over or under budget are labor costs?
- Did we use greater or fewer pounds of steel in producing automobiles than expected?
- How profitable are the various makes of automobiles?

These are just a sample of questions that face the management of General Motors. As you will see throughout this text, the answers to these and many more questions will be provided through the process of managerial accounting.

Accounting may be defined as "... the art of recording, classifying, and summarizing ... transactions and events ... and interpreting the results thereof."[1] In addition to the above tasks, the process of accounting is also concerned with communicating relevant information about an entity to interested users. This information is used by these parties in making economic decisions related to the entity in question, and as such accountants have often been referred to as "information engineers."

These "interested users" may be parties who are external to the entity, such as potential creditors and investors. For these parties, *financial accounting* describes the process through which the entity's historical transactions and events are recorded, classified, and summarized in the form of financial statements (the balance sheet, income statement, statement of retained earnings, and statement of cash flows). These financial statements are used by external third parties (potential creditors and investors) to make economic decisions (i.e., decisions to lend money to or invest money in a given entity).

Managerial accounting, on the other hand, is concerned with "interested users" who are internal to (i.e., employed by) the entity. These individuals include managers and other personnel who are involved in the day-to-day operations of the entity. It is important to note that the basic purposes of accounting are unchanged: to record, summarize, interpret, and communicate information to interested users. The primary differences relate to the individual needing the information and the type of information needed. The purpose of managerial accounting is to provide information to internal users for the purpose of allowing them to make various decisions concerning the operations of the entity.

Illustration 1 provides a brief comparison of financial and managerial accounting. It is important to note that both types of accounting involve the communication of information to users for decision-making purposes; this information is normally summarized in the form of a report or analysis. However, as shown in Illustration 1, these two classes of accounting can be distinguished along several dimensions. For example, while financial accounting is governed by specific rules and conventions (generally accepted accounting principles), no such body of generalized rules exists for managerial accounting. Also, financial accounting is primarily concerned with *historical* (or past) financial information; in contrast, managerial accounting uses both past information and *future* information.

As noted earlier, one significant difference between financial and managerial accounting is in the intended user of the reports. Financial accounting provides information to decision-makers external to the firm (such as investors and creditors); managerial accounting provides its information to users internal to the firm (such as management). As noted on the previous page, one difference in the two types of accounting is in the types and formats of reports. An example of the flexibility permitted in reports prepared by managerial accountants is shown below.

> **Motorola's managerial accountants use "Mr. Overhead" (a cartoon figure shaped like a cloud) to reduce the boredom of examining lengthy computer reports and enable managers to concentrate on results. Mr. Overhead is shown in a variety of moods: a smiling Mr. Overhead is used to indicate favorable results, a frowning Mr. Overhead suggests unfavorable results, and a perplexed Mr. Overhead indicates unusual results.[2]**

---

[1] *Accounting Terminology Bulletin No. 1–Review and Resume* (New York: American Institute of Certified Public Accountants), 9

[2] Douglas A. Johnson, Steven Kaplan, and Bill B. Hook, "Looking for Mr. Overhead: An Expanded Role for Management Accountants," *Management Accounting* (November 1983), 65-68.

Illustration 1
Comparison of Financial and Managerial Accounting

	Financial Accounting	**Managerial Accounting**
Underlying Authority	Generally Accepted Accounting Principles	No required rules or conventions
Types of Reports Issued	Financial statements in a prescribed format (balance sheet, income statement, and statement of cash flows)	Budgets, cost reports, performance reports, and special analysis in the form desired by management
Types of Data	Normally limited to historical data	Includes both historical and forecasted data
Users of the Reports	Investors, creditors, and others external to the firm	Top management and others internal to the firm

The focus of managerial accounting (and managerial accounting reports) on internal decision-making is illustrated by the following example from practice.

> **Borg-Warner Automotive, a manufacturer of transmissions and other products for the automotive industry, has recently revised the content of the internal reports prepared by managerial accountants for Borg-Warner's management. One major criticism of the previous internal reports is that managerial accountants did not understand what information was needed by managers. As a result, Borg-Warner's accounting department now assigns a cost analyst to work in different parts of the plant. This approach will allow the accounting department to integrate the needs of the manufacturing managers with the capabilities of the existing accounting system.[3]**

While some significant differences exist between managerial and financial accounting (as noted above), there is one distinct similarity—the basic purpose of accounting. Both classes of accounting attempt to summarize a wide body of information (in the form of an accounting report or other analysis) to allow users to make decisions. The type of information and user differs between the two types of accounting, as summarized above.

THE NEED FOR MANAGERIAL ACCOUNTING INFORMATION

The demand for managerial accounting has increased dramatically as the nature of the business entity has evolved into today's large, geographically dispersed, and complex organization. Consider, for example, the different information needs of the owner/manager of a sole proprietorship and the manager of a large organization. The owner/manager of a sole proprietorship is usually heavily involved with the day-to-day operations of the business. They often make most (if not all) of the operating decisions and generally observe most of the transactions (such as purchases of inventory and receipt of customer orders) that affect their business. Through this involvement, they acquire a great deal of firsthand knowledge about the events and transactions that affect the entity. As a result, this owner/manager has very limited information needs with respect to the entity.

In contrast, the manager of a large organization has only limited firsthand knowledge of the day-to-day operations of the entity. The large size, increased complexity, and geographic location of the entity makes it almost impossible for the manager of a large organization to operate the entity based on personal, firsthand

---

[3] G.F Hanks, M.A. Fried, and J. Huber, "Shifting Gears at Borg-Warner Automotive," *Management Accounting* (February 1994), 25–29.

knowledge. Therefore, he or she must rely on summaries and reports of relevant information prepared by other individuals within the organization. Thus, in making operating decisions concerning the entity, it can be said that this manager has a greater need for information provided through the process of managerial accounting. This need is illustrated by the following excerpts concerning Sears, Roebuck & Co. and Wal-Mart:

> ...[Sears'] decentralized accounting methods made it difficult for buyers sitting in Chicago to track merchandise. Finding out how screwdrivers were selling in Albuquerque, for instance, was nearly impossible. The bottom line: Merchandisers had little information to work with, which made the huge retailer slow to react to its own sales patterns and larger consumer trends.[4]
>
> Wal-Mart is a giant in more than retailing. The world's largest retailer spends half a billion dollars annually on information technology and maintains a level of data storage capacity that is second only to that of the U.S. government. More importantly, the company is unparalleled in its ability to use the data it gathers to motivate its suppliers, employees, and customers. Computers at Wal-Mart record sales of each item and automatically alert Wal-Mart's warehouses when items are in short supply. This allows Wal-Mart employees to spend more time with customers and less time scanning shelves and manually placing orders for depleted items.[5]

Throughout this text, we will discuss the need for managerial accounting information for three major types of organizations. The distinguishing characteristic of these organizations is the process through which they generate their revenues. A *manufacturing company* is an organization that utilizes materials to manufacture (or produce) inventory that is eventually sold to customers. Compaq Computer Corporation, General Motors, and Exxon are examples of manufacturing companies who produce the inventory that is sold to their customers. A *retail company* is an organization that purchases its inventory from suppliers in final form and subsequently sells this inventory to its customers; Wal-Mart, Blockbuster Entertainment, and Toys "R" Us are examples of retail companies. Finally, a *service company* does not generate revenue through the sale of inventory; rather, this type of company earns revenues by providing services to its customers. Federal Express, Union Pacific Railroad and H&R Block are examples of service companies. Illustration 2 presents examples of the types of decisions facing Compaq Computer as well as the information required by Compaq's management to make those decisions. While Compaq is a manufacturing company, many of these same decisions are applicable to retail and service companies.

Illustration 2
Common Management Decisions for Compaq Computer

Decision	Relevant Information
1. Should the production of laptop computers be continued?	• Anticipated demand for laptops • Costs of producing laptops • Anticipated revenues from the sale of laptops
2. What price should be charged for monitors?	• Cost of producing monitors • Desired level of profit from sale of monitors
3. How much plastic should be purchased to meet production needs?	• Number of computers to be manufactured • Amount of plastic required per computer
4. How well did assembly workers perform in producing computers?	• Actual hours worked by assembly workers • Number of computers manufactured • Budgeted or standard hours required to manufacture computers

ACCOUNTING SYSTEMS AND THE MANAGEMENT PROCESS

In order to provide the necessary information to managers for internal decision-making, entities develop detailed *accounting systems*. These systems are designed in such a way as to ensure that the relevant information

---

[4] "The Big Store's Big Trauma," *Business Week* (July 10, 1989), 5.

[5] Christopher Palmeri, "Believe in Yourself, Believe in the Merchandise," *Forbes* (September 8, 1997), 122; "Why Wall Street's Buying Wal-Mart Again," *Fortune* (February 16, 1998), 92–94.

needed by individuals within the firm is provided in a timely and accurate manner. The primary purposes of an accounting system are to record, classify, and summarize relevant information in the form of an *accounting report*.

The major events occurring in a typical accounting system are shown in Illustration 3. These events are discussed in detail in the following paragraphs.

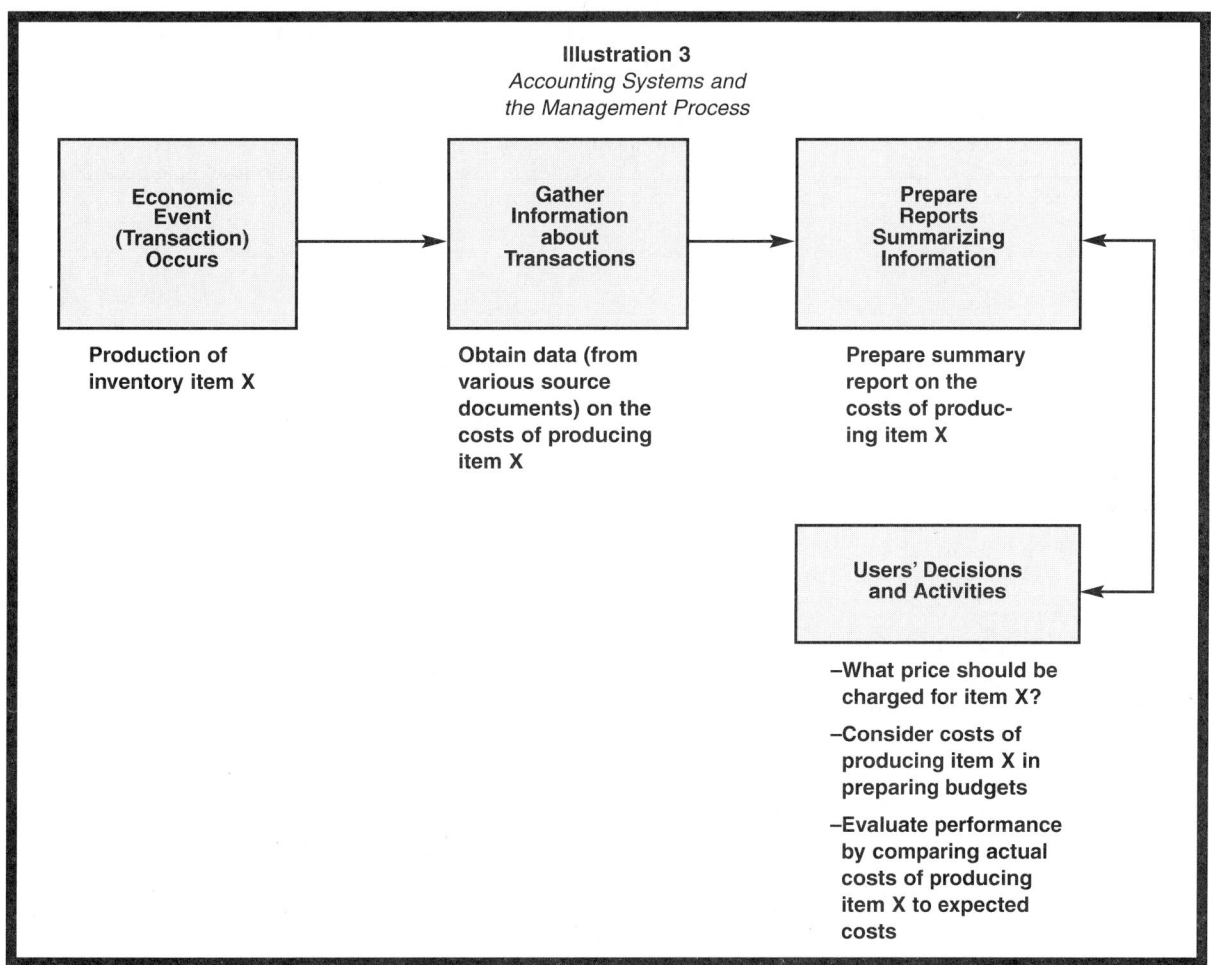

Identifying and Gathering Information on Transactions

The first two steps in Illustration 3 deal with identifying transactions that occur and gathering information about these transactions. Transactions are those activities that are undertaken by organizations as part of their normal operations. For example, General Motors manufactures and sells automobiles; both of these activities would be considered transactions. Service organizations (such as FedEx) provide services to customers and subsequently bill customers for these services; these actions would also be considered as transactions. Transactions are the basic lifeblood of the organization and are necessary for the short- and long-term survival of the organization.

Once transactions occur, they are usually summarized by accounting personnel through the preparation of source documents. A *source document* allows individuals who do not personally observe the transaction to have an understanding of the transaction that has taken place. Most large organizations have formal procedures for producing source documents at the point where transactions occur. For example, General Motors will use source documents to accumulate the actual materials (steel) and labor (wages paid to machine operators) inputs required to manufacture an automobile. FedEx uses source documents to record the fees charged to customers for delivery of merchandise. The lack of firsthand knowledge of transactions in most large organizations makes the preparation of source documents a critical component in their accounting systems. In performing the accounting process, these source documents enable accounting personnel to gather information about transactions.

The following excerpt describes a recent technological development that greatly automates the collection of certain transaction data.

> A new tracking and identification system called Radio Frequency Identification (RFID) is expected to provide enormous cost savings to distributors and retailers. An RFID system consists of microchip smart tags that contain product identification information and tag readers, which can be located in warehouse receiving areas, store shelves, and customer checkout counters. Tag readers will automatically scan the smart tags on pallets of incoming goods as they pass by on conveyor belts, saving billions of dollars in labor costs associated with manually scanning bar codes. In addition, smart shelves equipped with tag readers can alert systems as they become empty, avoiding a stock-out situation. Smart shelves can also be programmed to signal when many units are taken at once, a sign that a theft may be in process. Wal-Mart plans to require its suppliers to attach RFID tags to boxes and pallets of goods it sells to Wal-Mart, practically mandating the implementation of RFID for all companies that want to do business with the world's largest retailer.[6]

Preparing Reports

Once information about transactions has been gathered (through source documents), reports are prepared by recording, classifying, summarizing, and interpreting transactions—all important elements in the process of accounting. These reports attempt to summarize a large amount of information in an orderly fashion to allow users to make decisions relating to the organization. In financial accounting, these reports take the form of the traditional financial statements (balance sheet, income statement, and statement of cash flows).

Managerial accounting reports can assume a variety of forms, such as budgets, analysis, and cost summaries. In addition, while financial accounting reports reflect solely historical information, managerial accounting reports may include historical information, future information, or both. For example, the management of General Motors may request an estimate of the amount of materials and labor inputs necessary to meet anticipated production during the first quarter of the year. In preparing this report, General Motors needs to consider both historical (e.g., the amount of steel and labor inputs required for the production of an automobile) and future (e.g., anticipated level of demand and production) information.

An example of the use of historical information and sophisticated forecasting techniques to support inventory acquisition decisions is summarized below.

> The Longs Drug Stores chain uses "demand chain science" to cut costs related to inventory acquisition and replenishment. Each day, using application software developed by Nonstop Solutions (now named Evant), pharmacy managers generate a 90-day inventory replenishment plan based on a statistical analysis of more than 150 variables for each product. In addition to the daily replenishment plan, pharmacy managers also get a biweekly top-ten list of how much money they can save by returning unneeded drugs to their manufacturers.[7]

Using Reports for Decisions and Activities

Finally, after reports have been prepared, these reports are used by third parties to make economic decisions related to the company. Users external to the entity, such as creditors and investors, rely on these reports (in the form of financial statements) to make lending and investing decisions with respect to the organization. This text focuses on the use of accounting reports for internal purposes. Summary reports are prepared for managers to allow them to perform the following basic activities:

1. Decision-Making
2. Planning
3. Directing Operations
4. Controlling

---

[6] "The Best Thing Since the Bar-Code," *The Economist* (February 8, 2003), 72 and Matthew Boyle, "Wal-Mart Keeps the Change," *Fortune* (November 10, 2003), 46.

[7] Amy Doan, "Vitamin Efficiency," *Forbes* (November 1, 1999), 176–186.

The process of *decision-making* requires management to select from among various alternatives. For example, General Motors (GM) must decide what types of automobiles to manufacture and the quantities of those automobiles to manufacture. Once these decisions have been made, they must establish a selling price for the automobiles to provide an adequate profit margin. All of these choices represent decisions that require information from both accountants and other sources. In deciding the type and quantities of automobiles to manufacture, GM will undoubtedly rely on both historical and forecast sales data. In establishing the price of its automobiles, one important piece of information of interest to GM is the costs it incurs in manufacturing those automobiles. Managerial accountants will provide management with this and other important information needed in making decisions.

Planning requires goals to be established in order to achieve certain objectives. These objectives are normally closely related to the decisions made by the organization, as discussed above. After GM has determined the quantity of automobiles to manufacture, it must acquire sufficient materials and labor inputs to complete that level of production. Further, GM should commence production to allow the automobiles to be completed in a timely fashion for distribution to its dealers. As each of these actions is taken to achieve objectives (completing and distributing automobiles), collectively, they are integral parts of the planning process.

Directing operations requires oversight of the day-to-day operations of the entity. One very important aspect for manufacturing companies is ensuring that production is completed on a timely basis. In directing operations for GM, the need for additional materials and labor inputs should be periodically monitored to reduce "down time" (a period during which operations must cease). For a service-oriented entity (such as a restaurant), directing operations may include such diverse activities as ensuring that customers are served promptly and efficiently, providing complementary meals for customers experiencing excessively long waits for service, and identifying the number of kitchen and wait personnel required during "peak" dining times. The distinguishing feature of directing operations is that this type of activity requires "hands on" attention from company personnel.

The critical role that a company's information system plays in the process of directing operations and the devastating consequences that can result from an information system failure are illustrated in the following excerpts from practice.

> **Hershey Foods Corporation experienced a gigantic Halloween scare when complications associated with the implementation of its new inventory ordering and distribution system resulted in nationwide shortages of Kisses, Kit Kats and other Hershey staples right before the start of the trick-or-treat season—the single biggest candy-consuming holiday. System-related problems in inputting order data and transmitting it to warehouses resulted in Hershey's inability to meet customer delivery deadlines, despite the fact that the company had plenty of candy on hand to fill all of its orders.[8]**
>
> **A breakdown in communications in its extensive supply chain contributed to Cisco System's May 2001, $2.2 billion inventory write-down. Cisco's supply-chain system failed because it provided information only to contract manufacturers. Multiple manufacturers competing for a specific contract ordered the necessary component parts in anticipation of being awarded the contract. Suppliers of component parts were then swamped with multiple orders from the competing manufacturers and believed that demand for parts was two to three times the actual demand. A new communications system called eHub is being implemented to correct the disconnect in the system. eHub communicates the demand originating from Cisco to all members of the supply chain, allowing both suppliers and manufacturers to anticipate orders and eliminating double ordering, parts shortages and other inefficiencies.[9]**

The final activity performed by management is *controlling*. Controlling is the process of determining whether the organization's operations are being conducted in a manner consistent with its goals. This process involves comparing *actual* operating results to *expected* (or *budgeted*) operating results. For example, GM may compare actual production, revenue, and profit information with expected information for the same time period. An additional comparison of special interest to manufacturing companies (such as GM) involves the actual inputs required for a given quantity of production. That is, did GM use a greater amount of materials, labor, and other inputs in producing automobiles than planned? Comparisons of this nature require the company to develop standards against which performance can be measured. These standards will be discussed in detail later in this text.

---

[8] Emily Nelson and Evan Ramstad, "Hershey's Biggest Dud Has Turned Out to Be Its New Technology," *The Wall Street Journal* (October 29, 1999), A1, A6.

[9] Paul Kaihla, "Inside Cisco's $2 Billion Blunder," *Business 2.0* (March 2002), 88-90.

Feedback

The final step in the accounting system depicted in Illustration 3 involves receiving and using feedback. This feedback provides management with information regarding the effectiveness and efficiency of its decisions and activities. For example, assume that previous experience suggested that GM needed eight hours of machine time and fifty hours of human labor time to produce a particular type of automobile. Based on this information, GM began production of a series of 100 of these automobiles. If a total of 600 machine hours and 6,000 labor hours were required to complete production, one of two possibilities exists. First, GM's production personnel may have performed more or less efficiently than planned. Alternatively, GM may wish to consider revising its production requirements to six machine hours (600 hours ÷ 100 automobiles = 6 hours) and sixty labor hours (6,000 hours ÷ 100 automobiles = 60 hours) for subsequent production runs.

The importance of timely information regarding the company's operations is illustrated in the following example from practice.

> The inability of employees to provide information about the costs invested in a work-in-process plane lead Boeing's President Harry Stonecipher to revamp the aircraft manufacturer's accounting system to provide more timely information. "Here's a company that's doing better than $50 billion a year. That's a billion dollars a week! And we're rolling this dude up once a quarter? Folks, there's a lot of money going by here." Stonecipher's initiative has resulted in Boeing closing its quarterly accounts in 10 days, as opposed to the three weeks it took previously. Stonecipher's ultimate goal: three days.[10]

The Role of Accountants in the Management Process

As noted above, managers engage in decision-making, planning, monitoring operations, and controlling. because of the large size of most organizations, they must rely on information supplied by management (or managerial accountants in performing these activities. The relationships between the activities of management and managerial accountants are shown in Illustration 4. As can be seen herein, the activities of managerial accountants involve the traditional responsibilities associated with accounting—recording, classifying, summarizing, and interpreting information. From our earlier discussion of the accounting system, this information will be summarized in the form of reports that will be used by management, an internal user of the organization.

Three examples of accounting systems used by well-known companies are summarized below.

> The manager of a 7-Eleven outlet in Tokyo, Japan relies heavily on a computerized management information system to provide him with information about the purchasing habits of his customers and the items stocked in his store. This information shows what products are selling at various times of the day. This allows the manager to restock shelves with rice dishes that are popular with salarymen who shop between 7 and 9 p.m. and potato chip snacks that children buy on their way home from school.[11]
>
> Pizza Hut spent over $20 million in 1993 to create electronic profiles of its customers. This system attempts to match the tastes of Pizza Hut's customers to the coupons sent to those customers. For example, individuals who normally ordered Neapolitan style pizza received coupons for that type of pizza. Also, customers who had not ordered pizza for relatively long time periods received larger discounts than others. Pizza Hut has found that matching customers and their buying habits is more effective than sending uniform coupons to all of its customers.[12]
>
> Blockbuster Entertainment, the world's largest video rental and entertainment chain, has a customer card carried by over 40 million Americans, making it more widely held than the American Express card. When customers make purchases or rent videos, this card is used to provide customers with discounted merchandise. Each time the card is scanned, Blockbuster's database knows more about its customers' buying habits. For example, when country-western star Garth Brooks comes to Blockbuster's Phoenix (Arizona) amphitheater, the company can target a mailing to all of its Arizona cardholders who have purchased Garth Brooks recordings.[13]

---

[10] Jerry Useem, "Boeing vs. Boeing," *Fortune* (October 2, 2000), 155-156.

[11] "Information Power," *Forbes* (June 21, 1993), 44.

[12] "How to Get Closer to Your Customers," *Business Week: Enterprise Edition* (1993), 44.

[13] "Pressing Fast-Forward," *US News & World Report* (May 16, 1994), 55.

Illustration 4
Activities of Managers and Managerial Accountants

Management Activity	Example(s)	Managerial Accounting Activity
Decision-Making	• Determine the quantity of desired production	• Accumulate data on historical and anticipated demand
	• Establish the price of the organization's product or service	• Accumulate data on costs of producing product or providing service
Planning	• Determine quantities of inputs required for production	• Develop performance standards based on previous input requirements
Directing Operations	• Identify expected operating results	• Prepare budgets or forecasts
	• Ensure that sufficient inputs exist to continue production	• Accumulate data on inputs used and inputs needed In production
	• Ensure that staffing is sufficient to meet customer needs during peak demand periods	• Accumulate data on personnel needs for these time periods
Controlling	• Compare actual activity with anticipated activity	• Accumulate data on actual activity
		• Develop performance standards or other measures of anticipated activity
		• Assist in comparing actual activity to anticipated activity
		• Identify possible explanations for differences in actual and anticipated activity

LOCATION OF THE ACCOUNTING FUNCTION

Where in the typical organization do managerial accountants gather the data for their reports? They must gather information on activities in all parts of the the organization; thus all departments are potential subjects of the managerial accountant's attention.

Most manufacturing concerns recognize each major business function as a separate area of responsibility and structure their organizations accordingly. Each rectangle in the organization chart in Illustration 5 represents a separate function in the organization. The overall management function is the responsibility of the board of directors and the president of the corporation. At the next level, responsibility is separated for finance, manufacturing, and sales, the three major subfunctions of many firms.

The managers of the three major subfunctions are directly responsible to higher management for their operations and performance; that is, they serve in a *line relationship* to top management. The vice president in charge of sales is directly responsible for maintaining and increasing sales activities; the vice president in charge of manufacturing is responsible for maintaining production at levels established or projected by top management. *Line relationships* indicate that one party (a superior) directly or indirectly supervises the work of a second party (the subordinate).

Staff relationships, on the other hand, exist when one department serves in an advisory capacity and provides services to other departments upon request. Therefore, no direct supervision or responsibility exists in a *staff relationship*. On most organizational charts, staff relationships are presented in a horizontal relationship to the line functions that they service, whereas line functions are represented by vertical connectors between subordinates and their immediate supervisors. Line and staff relationships are portrayed by solid and broken connectors, respectively, in Illustration 5. Although the distinction between line and staff may be hazy, it is generally agreed that line authority is exerted downward over subordinates, whereas staff authority is exercised laterally or upward. Managerial accountants perform a staff function by providing line managers and other staff managers with specialized information. Accordingly, the accounting function in Illustration 5 is related to other

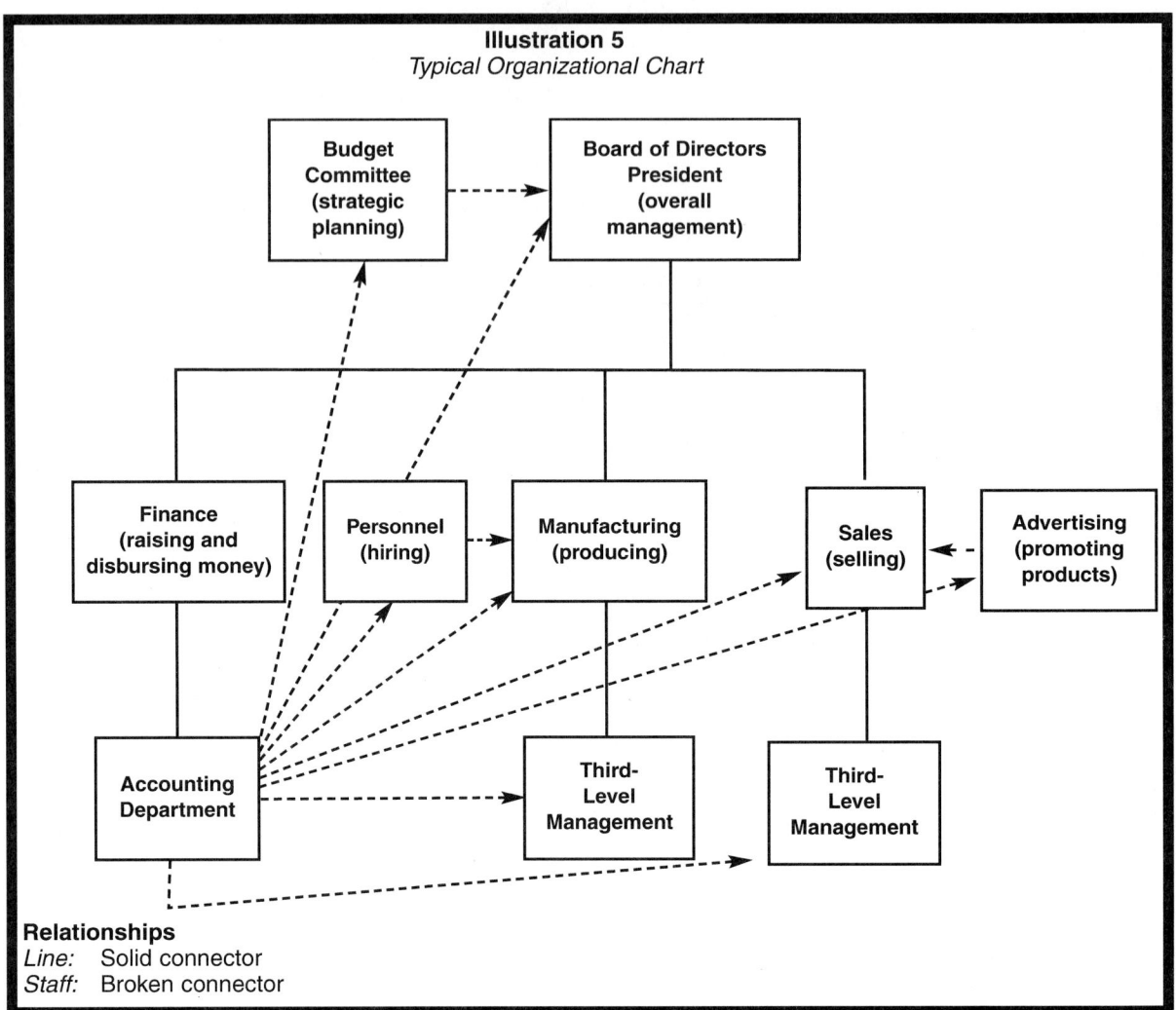

functions by broken-line connectors. Accountants provide advice and help in planning operations, determining actual costs, developing controls, and making special decisions. After the information is collected, reports are prepared and distributed both to the line or staff functions from whom information was gathered and to the manager who requested it.

The typical accounting department is headed by a controller. The immediate supervisor of the controller is generally an officer in the finance division, often the vice president in charge of finance. To summarize, the controller and his or her accountants are directly responsible to the vice president of finance, but they also act in a staff capacity to the rest of the organization.

OVERVIEW OF THE MANAGERIAL ACCOUNTING FUNCTION

Illustration 4 suggests that managerial accountants perform several functions in providing assistance to management. These functions are briefly discussed to provide an overview of the managerial accountant's responsibilities. These responsibilities are discussed in further detail in subsequent chapters of this text.

Preparing Budgets and Devising Standards

A basic managerial accounting activity relates to the preparation of budgets. *Budgets* are formal plans expressing courses of action in quantitative terms. Budgets can encompass either a short- term or long-term period of time. For example, accountants often prepare budgets for management which determine how many units of inventory need to be produced in a given period of time (usually a month) in order to meet that period's expected demand. Accountants can also prepare budgets encompassing longer periods of time. For potential capital expenditures, accountants identify the expected costs and cash savings associated with the expenditure to provide management with an indication of the desirability of the expenditure. This type of budgeting is referred to as *capital budgeting*.

Performance standards are used by management to identify areas where potential inefficiencies may exist. For example, assume that performance standards suggest that 100 hours of labor are required to produce a given number of units; if 200 hours are actually used to produce this quantity, the difference may suggest that workers are not performing up to their capabilities. Managerial accountants often help establish performance standards for the entity and assist management in interpreting the relationship between actual performance and these standards.

Accumulating Data on Costs and Profits

When an entity manufactures the inventory it sells to its customers, a critical requirement of the accounting system is that all costs associated with the production of the inventory (referred to as product costs) are accurately accumulated. These costs should be included with the inventory as it moves through the various stages of production and are expensed (as cost of goods sold) when the inventory is sold to customers. Accumulating the costs associated with inventory is a central activity performed by managerial accounting. In addition, managerial accountants also accumulate data on profits. These data are used to provide reports on the profitability of the entity. Information in these reports is used in making both pricing decisions (how much do we need to charge for unit X to "break even" if we sell 100 units?) as well as evaluation decisions (does segment Y earn enough to cover its variable costs?). This latter type of analysis is referred to as *cost-volume-profit analysis* and is an important consideration in the organization's decision to sell its products and/or services.

Comparing Actual Activity with Plans or Budgets

In many instances, accounting data are used to evaluate personnel and/or pinpoint areas that may require additional attention. Once actual results have been achieved, they can be compared to planned or budgeted results. Any unexpected differences between actual and budgeted results may suggest the need for increased managerial attention. In addition to identifying areas where additional attention may be needed, individuals and/or departments within the organization are often evaluated based upon how they perform in relation to the budget. The managerial accountant often gathers this information and prepares summary reports that present how actual performance differs from planned (or budgeted) performance.

Advising Management About Nonroutine Decisions

The three functions discussed above are related to the normal day-to-day operations of the company. As a result, managerial accountants frequently gather and summarize information related to those types of activities. In other cases, management may request assistance in making decisions of a less routine nature. Some of these decisions include: (1) discontinuing an industry segment or product line, (2) manufacturing components used in producing inventory versus purchasing components from an external supplier, and (3) purchasing long-term assets for use in production (capital budgeting). The managerial accountant will gather information about the consequences of alternatives in these decisions.

SUMMARY

Chapter 1 introduces managerial accounting and contrasts this form of accounting with financial accounting. In addition, the basic functions performed by managerial accountants are discussed. Some of the more important concepts in this chapter are summarized below.

1. *Accounting* is defined as the process in which transactions and events are recorded, classified, summarized, and interpreted. *Financial accounting* is concerned with the information needs of users external to the entity, such as potential investors and creditors. *Managerial accounting* is concerned with the information needs of users internal to the entity, such as managers and other personnel.
2. Financial and managerial accounting differ along several dimensions, including: (1) the presence of an underlying authority, (2) the types of reports issued, (3) the types and nature of data considered, and (4) the users of the reports. However, both types of accounting require information to be summarized, classified, interpreted, and recorded for users' decisions.

3. The accounting system is intended to provide management with information necessary to conduct its four major types of activities. These activities include decision-making, planning, directing operations, and controlling.

4. *Managerial accountants* perform several types of activities in order to provide information needed for managerial decisions and activities. These activities include: (1) *preparing budgets and devising standards,* (2) *accumulating data on costs and profits,* (3) *comparing actual activity with plans or budgets,* and (4) *advising management about nonroutine decisions.* In all of these activities, managerial accountants prepare accounting reports for management which contain relevant information and/or assist management in interpreting these reports.

5. Within an organization, the relationship between various departments and/or functions can be described based on whether the department has responsibility to other department(s). When one department has direct responsibility to another department, it is said that a *line relationship* exists. In a *staff relationship*, one department serves in an advisory capacity and provides services to other departments when requested to do so. The accounting department is typically located as a staff relationship within the organization.

KEY DEFINITIONS

Accounting—the process of recording, classifying, summarizing, and communicating economic information about an entity to a particular group of users. This information is used by these individuals to make decisions concerning the entity.

Accounting report—the output of an accounting system which is used by the accountant to communicate information about an entity to interested users.

Accounting system—a series of tasks and activities developed by an entity to record, classify, summarize, and communicate information about an entity's activities.

Budget—a formal plan of action expressed in quantitative terms.

Controller—the executive responsible for managing the accounting function (sometimes spelled as "comptroller").

Financial accounting—the class of accounting interested in providing information about the transactions and activities of an entity to users who are external to an entity. These users include creditors and investors.

Line relationship—a type of relationship in which one party (the superior) directly or indirectly supervises the work of a second party (the subordinate).

Managerial accounting—the class of accounting that is concerned with recording, summarizing, interpreting, and communicating information to interested users who are internal to the entity.

Manufacturing company—a company whose primary revenue-generating activity is through the sale of inventory to its customers. A manufacturing company manufactures (or produces) its inventory using materials purchased from outside vendors.

Retail company—a company whose primary revenue-generating activity is through the sale of inventory to its customers. Retail companies do not manufacture their inventory but purchase it in salable form from outside vendors.

Service company—a company whose primary revenue-generating activity is through providing services to its customers.

Source document—an internal document used by accounting personnel to summarize a transaction that has occurred.

Staff relationship—a relationship in which one party serves in an advisory capacity and provides services to other departments only when they are requested to do so.

QUESTIONS

1. "Decision-makers require quantitative information to make optimal decisions." List reasons why this statement might be true.

2. Define accounting. In your definition, indicate major activities that characterize the process of accounting.

3. How does the process of accounting allow decisions to be made by individuals who are less familiar with the activities of the company?

4. Distinguish between financial accounting and managerial accounting.

5. How are financial accounting and managerial accounting similar?

6. Who are the primary users of financial accounting information? Managerial accounting information?

7. What are the major steps in a typical accounting system?

8. Define the three major types of companies (based on their revenue-generating activities). Which of these types of companies utilize managerial accounting information?

9. How are the reports prepared in an accounting system different for financial accounting information and managerial accounting information?

10. List and briefly describe the four functions normally performed by management. How does the managerial accountant assist management in performing these functions?

11. What is a budget? What time frames can be encompassed by budgets?

12. Define controlling. How does management attempt to perform this function?

13. Differentiate between line and staff authority. Which type of authority does the controller have?

14. Describe the role of accountants in the management process.

15. Michael Johnson, the sales manager of Computation, Inc., is discussing the pricing of a new product soon to be placed on the market with the president, Thomas Samisen:

    Tom, we have to set the price on our new calculator before the end of the day so that we can order the sales brochures.

    I thought that question was settled at the weekly executive meeting yesterday, Mike. According to the cost figures prepared by our new accountant, yesterday's decision seems perfectly reasonable.

    But what does an accountant know about trying to sell a product against stiff competition?

    Well, Mike, why don't you write out your objections and present them at next week's meeting?

    What problem do you observe in this organization?

16. In the following examples, identify the problem that may exist in either the accountant's role, the decision-making process, or the purposes of the managerial accounting system.

    a. The logistics department manager schedules truck departures on the basis of information he receives from the production department manager, whom he has known for twelve years. The shipping clerk is complaining because backlogs have built up.
    b. The sales projection committee meets on the last working day of each month to update the monthly projected sales quota for the next twelve-month period. The sales figures employed at this meeting are furnished by the assistant vice president of sales. The accounting department's monthly performance reports are issued on the 10th of the following month.
    c. The Cord Tire Company has a flexible pricing structure. The sales department uses the production cost sheets as prepared by individual machine operators to price each order. The accounting department manager has argued that the pricing policy does not include charges for administrative expenses. The sales manager says that he is using last year's figures to approximate the administrative and sales expenses.
    d. John Thompson, a lathe operator for the Twilight Lamp Company, has complained to his line foreman that the performance standards set by the accounting department are too stringent. Furthermore, John asks, "How does that accountant know what it's like to work down here on the production line? He never leaves his plush office." The line foreman agrees with John but says that he has no control over upper management.

17. Define feedback. In addition to helping managers improve their view of the real world, how can feedback improve the managerial process?

18. Both the managerial accountant and the manager are involved in the decision-making process. How do their roles differ?

19. Does management or the managerial accountant set the goals and objectives of the organization? Does management or the managerial accountant determine the means by which the chosen goals and objectives will be achieved? Does management or the managerial accountant determine what information should be reported, when it should be reported, and how it should be reported?

20. When management wishes to plan or forecast to achieve organizational coordination or motivation, what action does the managerial accountant take?

21. How can a managerial accountant help management ascertain the status of current operations or the organization's financial position?

22. The managerial accountant may compare data on actual activities with plans or budgets so that management will be better able to engage in what type of activity?

23. List four activities commonly performed by managerial accountants.

24. *Classes of Accounting.* Indicate whether each of the following terms is most closely related to financial accounting or managerial acounting. Use "F" for financial accounting and "M" for managerial accounting. A particular term may relate to both financial accounting and managerial accounting.

   _____ Balance sheet

   _____ Budget Control

   _____ Cost accumulation

   _____ Forecast information

   _____ Decision-making

   _____ Generally accepted accounting principles

   _____ Income statement

   _____ Planning

   _____ Historical information

25. *Classes of Accounting.* The Ways Company has suffered a terrible year. Sales dropped 40 percent, cost increased 5 percent, income went from a profit of $1,500,000 to a $5,000,000 loss, and the president's wife told him her brother wanted to enter the business. The company was listed on the New York Stock Exchange and wished to remain there. When asked for cost-reduction ideas, the production manager recommended reducing the accounting costs. The accounting department has four major cost segments: financial accounting, tax reporting, the auditor's bill, and managerial accounting. The controller determined that no excess cost could be cut from any of these segments without the loss of that function.

   a. If the production manager is right, which accounting function could be eliminated by this company? Why?

   b. What arguments could be used for keeping all the accounting functions at operating strength?

   c. Which accounting function would be the hardest to defend? Why?

   d. In periods of financial difficulty, would the accounting department be one of the first areas to contract? In actual practice, which other functions or departments are more likely candidates for contraction than accounting?

26. *Managerial Accounting–General.* A small company producing parts for the automobile industry is taking a hard look at its staff functions to determine whether they have "grown beyond their worth." The standard functions of financial, tax, and managerial accounting are performed by three men. The reason for having a managerial segment seems hazy. As the president states, "I handle any control problems. If someone needs a push, I know it before the accountants tell me. All the accounting people do is confirm that I push the right one."

   a. If the president is right, should the managerial segment be abolished?

   b. What could be done to improve the existing control function?

   c. If the president believes control is the only function of managerial accounting, what could be done to expand his viewpoint?

   d. Do you think the president worked his way up to his position through the financial side of the business? Is the president's background of any importance in ascertaining possible problems between the financial side of the business and top management? Explain.

27. *Managerial Accounting Activities.* The four major activities performed by the managerial accounting function are: (1) preparing budgets and devising standards, (2) accumulating data on costs and profits, (3) comparing actual activity with plans or budgets, and (4) advising management on nonroutine decisions. Indicate (by using the numbers 1-4) which activity is associated with each of the following questions. Each question may be associated with more than one activity.

　　_____ 1. How long should it take employees to produce one unit of inventory?

　　_____ 2. Should this particular component be purchased from an external supplier or manufactured internally?

　　_____ 3. Were last period's operating results consistent with our expectations?

　　_____ 4. What was the actual cost of producing our inventory?

　　_____ 5. How much inventory should be purchased to meet next period's production needs?

　　_____ 6. Should we discontinue this product line?

　　_____ 7. How efficient were we in using direct materials in the production of inventory?

　　_____ 8. How many units of our new product need to be sold to recover our costs of production?

28. *Management Functions.* Indicate which of the following management functions is most closely related to each of the following terms or statements. Each statement can be related to more than one management function. Use the following abbreviations in your answer:

　DM = Decision-making

　P = Planning

　DO = Direct operations

　C = Controlling

　　_____ 1. Preparing and evaluating budgets.

　　_____ 2. Responding to unexpected shutdowns or delays in production.

　　_____ 3. Establishing the selling price for one of the organization's products.

　　_____ 4. Investigating the efficiency of production operations.

　　_____ 5. Determining the production levels necessary to satisfy future levels of demand.

　　_____ 6. Ensuring that customers are serviced promptly and efficiently.

　　_____ 7. Comparing actual revenues to anticipated revenues.

　　_____ 8. Acquiring sufficient direct materials inputs to ensure that production needs can be met.

29. *Organizational Relationships.* One of the first steps in management control is to produce an organizational chart. Producing an accurate chart may be difficult if job performance does not conform to the sphere of activity implied by the job title. Strong employees tend to view their jobs and spheres of activity broadly, whereas others view their jobs narrowly.

For the following problem, assume that each job is exactly what its title implies. Identify any title that might be ambiguous. Next, draw an organizational chart using the same job titles.

- **a.** Controller
- **b.** President
- **c.** Head Designer
- **d.** Vice President of Manufacturing
- **e.** Vice President of Personnel
- **f.** Manager of Accounting
- **g.** Manager of Salary Personnel
- **h.** Manager of Hourly Personnel
- **i.** Vice President of Sales
- **j.** Manager of Budgeting
- **k.** Manager of General Accounting
- **l.** Production Superintendent
- **m.** Sales Manager
- **n.** Assembly Line Foreman
- **o.** Maintenance Foreman
- **p.** Production Control Foreman

Learning Objectives

Chapter 2 provides an overview of the types of costs incurred by organizations and how these costs change with changes in the level of activity. Studying this chapter should enable you to:

1. Define and provide examples of different types of costs incurred by organizations.
2. Distinguish between product and period costs and understand how these costs are treated for financial reporting purposes.
3. Define the relevant range and understand its importance in discussing cost behavior.
4. Identify how variable costs, fixed costs, step costs, and semi-variable costs behave over changes in activity.
5. Use the graphical method, two-point method, semi-averages method, and least squares regression method to identify the fixed and variable components of semi-variable costs.

2

Analyzing Cost Behavior

INTRODUCTION

Two college roommates, John Metcalf and Jay Evans, just received their bank statements in the mail. You overheard them discussing their cash balances:

John: I just don't understand why I never have any money saved. It seems like I never go anywhere—how can I spend so much?

Jay: Me too. I've really got to get a good handle on my expenditures. That way, I'll have enough cash on hand to make it through the end of the semester.

John: Why don't we just decide to eat out less often? Let's see—right now, we eat out four nights a week. If we only eat out two nights, our expenses will be cut in half.

Jay: That's only true for the costs of going to restaurants. What about rent and utilities? We have to pay the same amount for these items whether we go out one night or seven nights. Also, while we'll save on gasoline costs by eating out less often, it won't be exactly one-half, since we still need to drive to go to other places.

John: You're right. I guess we should see what costs we can reduce and what costs we can't reduce. Eating out less often won't help us save on all of our costs.

In the previous chapter, we introduced the concept of managerial accounting and discussed the basic function of the managerial accountant. One of the most important roles of the managerial accountant is to obtain and analyze data related to the costs incurred by the organization. Management uses information about costs in a variety of ways. For example, when establishing a selling price for the organization's inventory products or services, management uses information about the costs of manufacturing that inventory or providing that service.

A *cost* is an expenditure or allocation of a previous expenditure made by the organization. Many students use the terms *cost, expenditure*, and *expense* interchangeably. In distinguishing between these terms, it is important to note that costs are more inclusive in nature than either expenditures or expenses. An expenditure is an actual outlay of funds for some purpose. While costs include outlays of funds, they also include allocations of previous outlays of funds (such as depreciation expense on manufacturing facilities). Expenses are limited to costs that are recognized and matched with revenues under generally accepted accounting principles. While some costs are considered to be expenses, others are not. For example, when manufacturing inventory, companies incur direct materials and direct labor costs; however, as noted in the following section, these costs are not expensed unless the units of inventory are sold to customers.

This chapter introduces the concept of a cost and defines the two major categories of costs incurred by organizations (product costs and period costs). Then the discussion turns to the different manner in which costs vary over changes in some level of activity (known as *cost behavior*).

TYPES OF COSTS

Prior to discussing cost behavior, it is important to distinguish between two major categories of costs incurred by companies in manufacturing inventory or providing services. *Product costs* are those costs that are related to purchasing inventory (for a retail company), manufacturing inventory (for a manufacturing company), or providing services (for a service company). For example, when Compaq Computer Corporation manufactures personal computers and monitors, the costs of manufacturing these items are product costs. For retailers (such as Wal-Mart), the costs of purchasing inventory from suppliers are examples of product costs. Finally, while service organizations do not sell "products," they do incur costs in providing services to their customers. When FedEx provides delivery services, the costs of packaging materials, wages paid to delivery personnel, and depreciation of delivery equipment are all examples of product costs.

The important characteristic of a product cost is that it is incurred when manufacturing or purchasing inventory or providing services. When incurred, product costs should be considered an asset until the time that the inventory or product is sold or the service is provided. Product costs are then expensed and matched against revenue to determine the income from the sale or service.

Period costs are those costs which are related to activities other than the purchase or manufacture of an organization's inventory or provision of an organization's services. Period costs are often classified as selling, general, and administrative (SG&A) expenses by companies. While these costs are important to the overall activities of the organization, they are not directly related to the production or manufacture of the organization's inventory or the provision of the organization's services. Examples of period costs include salaries paid to an organization's management executives and costs associated with the overall operations of the organization (administrative costs), the costs of selling and distributing goods and services (marketing and distribution costs), and costs associated with developing new products and services (research and development costs).

The important distinction between product and period costs is how they are presented in the financial statements. As indicated above, product costs are initially accumulated and recorded or classified as assets (inventory) until the inventory is sold. Once sold, these costs are recognized as an expense (cost of sales or cost of goods sold) that is "matched" against the organization's sales revenue. For example, when Wal-Mart purchases inventory for resale to its customers, the cost of the items purchased is originally included in inventory. Once these items have been sold to Wal-Mart's customers, the costs are then expensed as the cost of goods sold. Similarly, as Compaq manufactures computers for sale to its customers, the cost of manufacturing the computers is accumulated as inventory until the computers are sold to Compaq's customers.[1]

In contrast, period costs are either expensed as they are incurred or allocated to expense over future periods of time. If period costs provide future benefits that can be measured, these costs are expensed using a systematic and rational method of allocation. For example, the costs incurred in constructing WalMart's distribution centers are initially capitalized as assets (property, plant and equipment); these costs are then expensed (through depreciation) over the estimated useful life of the distribution centers. On the other hand, if period costs do not provide future benefits to the organization, these costs are expensed as incurred. The salaries paid to Wal-Mart's clerical staff are an example of this latter type of period cost. Illustration 1 summarizes the basic methods used in accounting for product and period costs.

Three major types of product costs incurred by a manufacturing company are direct materials costs, direct labor costs, and manufacturing overhead costs. Each of these cost categories is briefly discussed in the following sections.

Direct Materials

Direct materials (sometimes called raw materials) represent the cost of physical inputs used in the manufacture of the inventory. Direct materials become a part of the completed product and may be thought of as the identifiable components of the final inventory product. Indeed, the distinguishing feature of direct materials is that these materials are a part of and can be readily identified with the final inventory product. For example, when DaimlerChrysler Corporation manufactures automobiles, the steel (chassis), leather (upholstery), plastic (dashboard and interior), and glass (windows and windshield) are examples of direct materials. Direct materials

---

[1] Theoretically, service organizations would also accumulate product costs with inventory as the costs are incurred and expense these costs as revenues are earned. However, because service organizations generally recognize revenues as soon as services are rendered (and costs are being incurred), these costs are normally expensed as they are incurred.

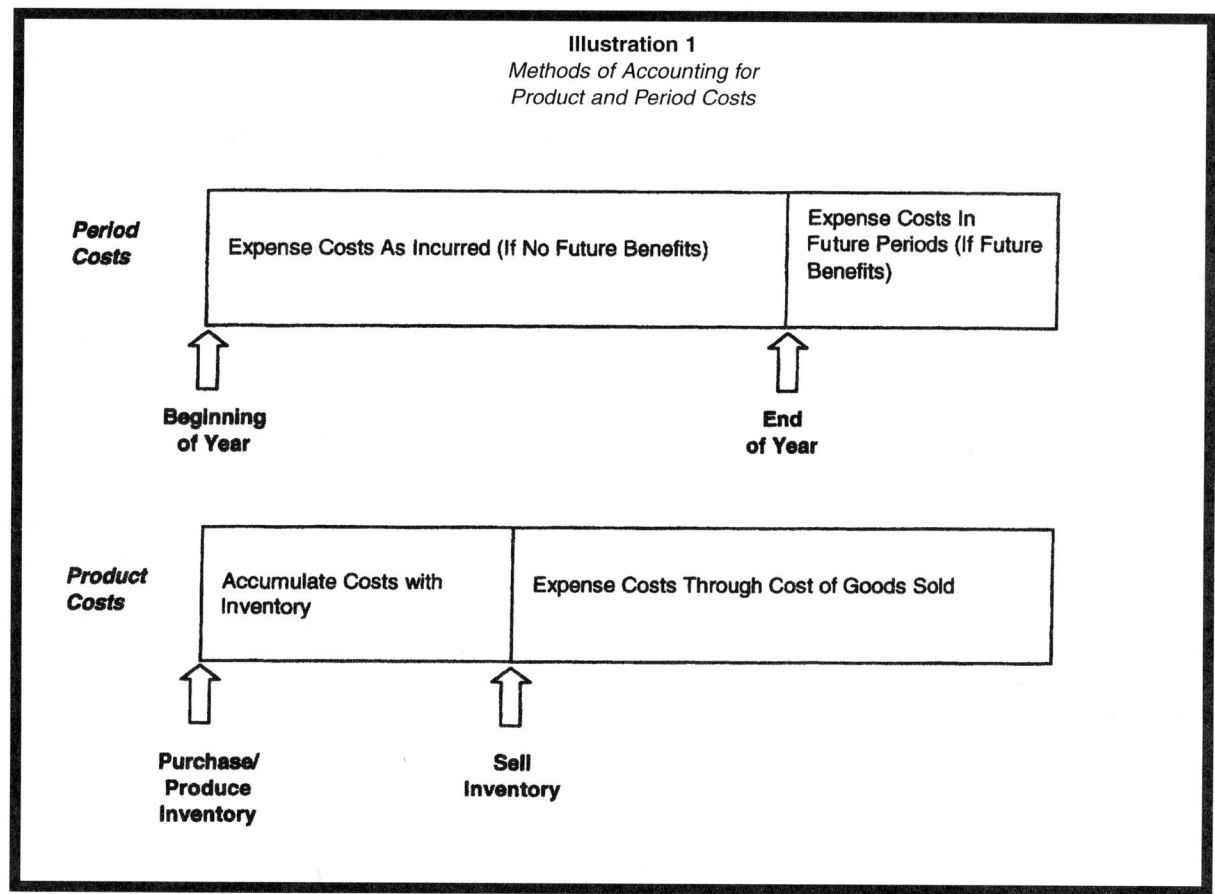

normally represent a relatively large portion of the total cost of materials used to manufacture inventory products for most manufacturing companies.

In addition to direct materials, other materials costs are incurred as inventory is manufactured. For example, in manufacturing automobiles, DaimlerChrysler Corporation utilizes a number of small parts such as screws, bolts, and other materials to assemble the automobiles. The cost of these materials is referred to as an *indirect material cost*. Indirect materials represent items that cannot easily be identified with the final inventory product. In addition, indirect materials ordinarily represent a much smaller portion of the total materials costs than do direct materials. It is ordinarily not cost-efficient to identify indirect materials cost with individual units of production. (Imagine the effort required to determine the costs of screws and bolts used by DaimlerChrysler in manufacturing automobiles!) While indirect materials are considered to be product costs, they are not ordinarily included with direct materials costs. The cost of indirect materials is included as a component of manufacturing overhead, another type of product cost discussed later in this chapter.

Of the three major types of companies introduced earlier (retail companies, manufacturing companies, and service companies), direct materials costs are incurred only by manufacturing companies. Retail companies (such as Wal-Mart) purchase their inventory in final form from outside suppliers and do not incur direct materials costs. Service companies (such as FedEx) do not earn revenues through the sale of inventory and, as a result, have no direct materials costs.

Direct Labor

Direct labor represents the cost of wages (and fringe benefits) paid to individuals whose work is directly related to the completion of the final inventory product. Examples of direct labor costs are the wages paid to individuals assembling the inventory product or operating machinery that assembles the inventory product. For a service organization, direct labor costs are the costs paid to employees who directly provide the services to customers. For DaimlerChrysler Corporation, direct labor costs would include wages paid to assembly-line workers who assemble its automobiles. Since both direct materials and direct labor are identifiable with the finished product, the sum of these two costs is often referred to as *prime costs*.

As with materials costs, other labor costs are required to manufacture the finished inventory product but these costs cannot easily be identified with that product. These costs include the wages paid to supervisory personnel (such as foremen) and the maintenance personnel who service the manufacturing department. Costs of this nature are also product costs and are referred to as indirect labor costs. For DaimlerChrysler Corporation, the wages paid to individuals who supervise assembly line workers or who inspect automobiles after they are manufactured are examples of *indirect labor costs*. Like indirect materials costs, indirect labor costs are included as part of manufacturing overhead.

Manufacturing Overhead

Manufacturing overhead costs (or factory overhead costs) include all of the costs related to the organization's inventory and/or services that are not classified as either direct materials costs or direct labor costs. Overhead costs include indirect material and supply costs, indirect labor costs, depreciation on manufacturing plant and equipment, and utilities and maintenance costs. For example, the depreciation on DaimlerChrysler's manufacturing facilities and the utility costs associated with its manufacturing activities are manufacturing overhead costs. The basic test for classifying a cost as overhead is as follows: is the cost something other than direct materials or direct labor, but incurred primarily in manufacturing the organization's inventory or providing its services? If the answer to this question is "yes," the cost is considered an overhead cost. As a result, the insurance and property taxes paid on manufacturing facilities are overhead costs (product costs); however, the insurance and property taxes related to sales or administrative facilities are not. These latter costs are treated as period costs.

As it manufactures its inventory, the organization incurs direct labor and overhead costs in order to "convert" direct materials into a finished inventory product. Therefore, the sum of direct labor and manufacturing overhead costs is often referred to as conversion costs. The three basic types of product costs are summarized below.

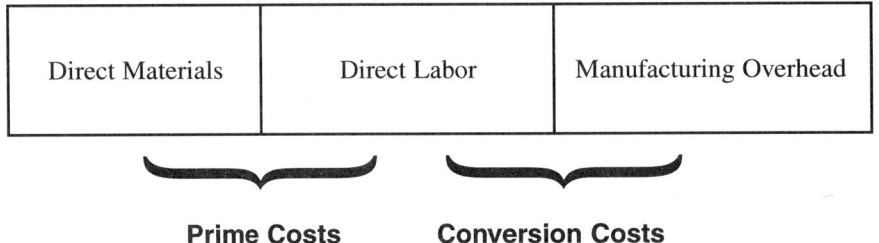

An important recent development in the manufacturing environment is the use of robots and other motorized manufacturing techniques in the production process. As these methods are substituted for direct labor, the importance of overhead costs increases. For example, General Motors' assembly plants have increasingly replaced the traditional assembly line of human workers with motorized, unmanned carriers that move cars through successive stages of assembly. This manufacturing process represents a basic shift from direct labor costs (cost of wages paid to assemblyworkers) to overhead costs (costs of motorized carriers).

Similar improvements that Dell Computer is making in its production process are summarized in the following excerpt.

> **Dell Computer continuously updates and reorganizes its manufacturing and assembly process to increase production velocity. Currently, workers assemble computers in six-person cells from batches of parts that arrive via a computer-directed conveyor system. Problem batches can instantly be shifted to another cell to avoid the stoppages that would result in a conventional assembly-line system. Dell is now working to automate the packaging of finished computers, which would eliminate a human-staffed assembly line and free up space for more assembly cells. By implementing subtle changes in product design and factory layout, Dell has "upgraded" its production per square foot threefold over the past five years.[2]**

Illustration 2 provides examples of direct materials costs, direct labor costs, and manufacturing overhead cost associated with the products or services provided by a manufacturing company (Compaq Computer Corporation), a retail company (Wal-Mart), and a service company (FedEx). Note that since retailers purchase inventory from

---
[2] Daniel Fisher, "The Best Little Factory in Texas," *Forbes* (June 10, 2002), 110.

Illustration 2
Examples of Product Costs for Different Organizations

	Compaq Computer	**Wal-Mart**	**FedEx**
Direct Materials	Plastic, Hard Disk Drive CD-ROM Player, Microchip	None (final total cost is the purchase price of inventory from vendors)	None
Direct Labor	Wages paid to assembly workers and machine operators	None (final total cost is the purchase price of inventory from vendors)	Wages paid to deliverypersons
Manufacturing Overhead	Depreciation on manufacturing equipment	None (final total cost is the purchase price of inventory from vendors)	Depreciation of delivery equipment

vendors in final (saleable) form, the cost of inventory for Wal-Mart is simply the purchase price of this inventory from vendors. Thus, Wal-Mart does not incur direct materials, direct labor, or manufacturing overhead costs in acquiring its inventory. Also, note that service organizations (such as FedEx) do not incur costs of direct materials, since they do not manufacture inventory as part of their revenue-generating process.

The following excerpt about the production and sale of sneakers illustrates the application of several of the cost terms that have been discussed thus far.

> **How profitable is the sneaker business?** Generally, the actual cost of a shoe is split evenly in terms of materials, labor and overhead (marketing, packaging and shipping) and represents 25% of its retail price. A gross margin of 50% is typical. The specific breakdown for a pair of $120 "kicks" is as follows:
>
> - materials: $10
> - labor: $10
> - overhead: $10
> - manufacturer pays: $30
> - retailer pays: $60
> - customer pays: $120[3]

OVERVIEW OF COST BEHAVIOR

Cost behavior is defined as how costs react when the *level of activity* (or *volume*) changes. Identifying how different costs react as the level of activity changes is very important, since it allows management to determine how the total costs will be affected by planned levels of activity. While many costs vary directly with changes in activity, others are not affected. In order to make various operating decisions, management must consider how the level of activity will affect the total costs incurred by the organization.

For example, consider two separate scenarios for the costs of renting an automobile. Assume that you are planning a three-day vacation and have two choices for renting an automobile. Company A will charge you a flat rate of $100 per day with no charge for mileage. Company B charges a flat rate of $50 per day and an additional charge of $0.60 per mile driven. Based on this information, which option would you choose?

The choice you make depends on the expected level of activity. The total costs associated with two levels of activity (200 total miles driven and 300 total miles driven) are presented in Illustration 3. As shown in Illustration 3, the total cost of renting from Company A ($300) is less than the cost of renting from Company B ($330) provided that you drive 300 miles. If you drive more than 300 miles, this difference will become larger as the additional mileage charged by Company B increases. On the other hand, if you plan on driving 200 miles, it would be cheaper to rent the car from Company B. This outcome occurs because the additional mileage charges are not large enough to exceed the additional cost per day charged by Company A.

---

[3] Leigh Gallagher, "Fancy Footwork," *Forbes* (January 8, 2001), 210.

> **Illustration 3**
> *Cost Behavior Example*
>
> | | Level of Activity (Miles Driven) | |
> | --- | ---: | ---: |
> | | 200 Miles | 300 Miles |
> | **Company A:** | | |
> | Flat Rental Charge (3 days × $100/day)........... | $300 | $300 |
> | **Company B:** | | |
> | Flat Rental Charge (3 days × $50/day) .... | $150 | $150 |
> | Mileage Charge (at $0.60 per mile)............... | 120 | 180 |
> | Total Charge................................... | $270 | $330 |

Notice that in the above example some of the costs (additional mileage charges) vary with changes in the level of activity (miles driven) and other costs do not vary with changes in the level of activity (daily rental charge). The differences in the behavior of these types of costs illustrate the concept of cost behavior.

Two important concepts in evaluating cost behavior are the level of activity (or cost driver) and the relevant range. These concepts are briefly discussed below.

Level of Activity (Cost Driver)

The level of activity (or cost driver) is the item or factor that causes one or more cost(s) to change. For example, as the number of automobiles manufactured by DaimlerChrysler Corporation increases, the amount and cost of raw steel (direct materials) and wages paid to assemblyworkers (direct labor) also increases. Therefore, the number of automobiles manufactured is the *cost driver* for DaimlerChrysler's raw steel and direct labor costs. Identifying the appropriate cost driver is important because this cost driver will be used to determine the behavior of costs.

Illustration 4 provides an example of several cost drivers that should be familiar to most students. Note, that in each case, a cost driver is the activity that causes a particular type of cost to change. Also notice that each type of cost has a different cost driver.

> **Illustration 4**
> *Examples of Cost Drivers*
>
> | Cost | Cost Driver |
> | --- | --- |
> | Tuition costs at a university | Hours of coursework for which student is enrolled |
> | Gasoline costs (for automobile) | Number of miles driven |
> | Costs of washing laundry | Number of loads of clothing laundered |
> | Costs of long-distance telephone service | Minutes of long-distance calls made |
> | Utility costs | Number of kilowatt hours used |

It is important to note that for a given cost any number of cost drivers can be identified, and that the behavior of the cost depends upon the cost driver selected by the organization. For example, since DaimlerChrysler's assembly workers are paid hourly wages, the most appropriate cost driver for DaimlerChrysler's direct labor costs is the number of direct labor hours worked. However, organizations often require information related to their primary revenue-generating activity (for DaimlerChrysler, the number of automobiles manufactured) for planning purposes. Thus, important cost drivers used by organizations are the number of units manufactured (for manufacturing companies), the number of units sold (for retail companies), and the level of services provided (for service companies). In this chapter, we illustrate cost behavior through the use of a single cost driver (number of textbooks manufactured by Better Books Company). The use of multiple cost drivers is discussed in a subsequent chapter.

The importance of correctly identifying cost drivers is illustrated in the following examples from practice.

> A regional bank originally used the number of telephone calls as its cost driver for the cost of providing telephone services to customers. One problem with this cost driver is that, while fewer customers have variable rate mortgages, these customers require more service time than fixed-rate customers (15 minutes per call versus 7 minutes per call). When the bank changed its cost driver from number of calls to number of minutes of calls, the "costs" of servicing fixed-rate mortgages decreased by 43 percent and the "costs" of servicing variable-rate mortgages increased by 36 percent.[4]
>
> Bachman Foods, a large producer of snack foods (pretzels, popcorn, etc.), originally used the total weight of products shipped as its cost driver for delivery costs. However, since most of the products are light (in terms of weight), they discovered that weight has little effect on delivery costs. A subsequent analysis resulted in the identification of four cost drivers: (1) the number of miles traveled; (2) the number of boxes unloaded; (3) the number of stops made by drivers; and (4) the requirement for drivers to obtain overnight lodging.[5]

Relevant Range

The relevant range may be defined as the operating range or activity level over which a firm finds it practical to operate in the short-run. For each firm, there is a floor of activity below which it is impractical to operate. These levels are either unrealistic (for example, firms cannot operate using less than some minimum number of kilowatt hours of electricity) or would not allow for adequate profits (firms could not manufacture less than some minimum number of inventory units). In addition, because of limited operating capacity, most firms have an upper level of activity above which they cannot operate without significantly expanding their current facilities. The unique characteristic of the relevant range is that costs assume a linear (or nearly linear) relationship over that level of activity. Illustration 5 shows a graph plotting the total costs of manufacturing inventory against the number of units manufactured.

The number of units manufactured on the horizontal axis of Illustration 5 can be classified into three basic categories. First are all levels below a specified *minimum level of activity* [part (a) of Illustration 5]. Note that total manufacturing costs rise sharply with the first units of production. This represents the high initial (or start-up) costs of manufacturing inventory. For example, consider three main costs of manufacturing automobiles by DaimlerChrysler Corporation: (1) raw steel (direct materials), (2) wages paid to assembly workers (direct labor), and (3) depreciation on manufacturing facilities (manufacturing overhead). If only one automobile is manufactured, the cost of that automobile includes the cost of steel for that automobile, the wages paid to assembly workers for manufacturing that automobile, and the *entire amount of depreciation* on the manufacturing facilities. As additional automobiles are manufactured, the cost of these automobiles rises slightly to reflect additional material and labor costs; however, no additional depreciation costs are incurred. As discussed later in this chapter, the depreciation cost is classified as a fixed cost, since it does not change with changes in activity. The materials and labor costs are known as variable costs because they vary directly and proportionately with changes in activity.

Above this minimum level of activity, the total cost curve approximates a straight line. At this point, each additional automobile manufactured results in an increase in total costs of the same amount. Part (b) on the graph in Illustration 5 is known as the relevant range. Because costs are assumed to have a linear (or nearly linear) relationship with activity within the relevant range, the behavior of these costs can be estimated for those levels of activity within that range.

The upper bound of the relevant range represents a limitation based on practical operating capacity. Any levels of activity above this upper bound will require additional capacity to be obtained, resulting in another large increase in total fixed costs. For example, if DaimlerChrysler decided to dramatically increase its production of automobiles, it would need to obtain additional manufacturing facilities, resulting in a further increase in total

---

[4] G.Y. Yang and R.C. Wu, "Strategic Costing & ABC," *Management Accounting* (May 1993), 33–37.

[5] R.D. Enright, "Standard Costs for Delivery Systems," *Management Accounting* (January 1974), 34–36.

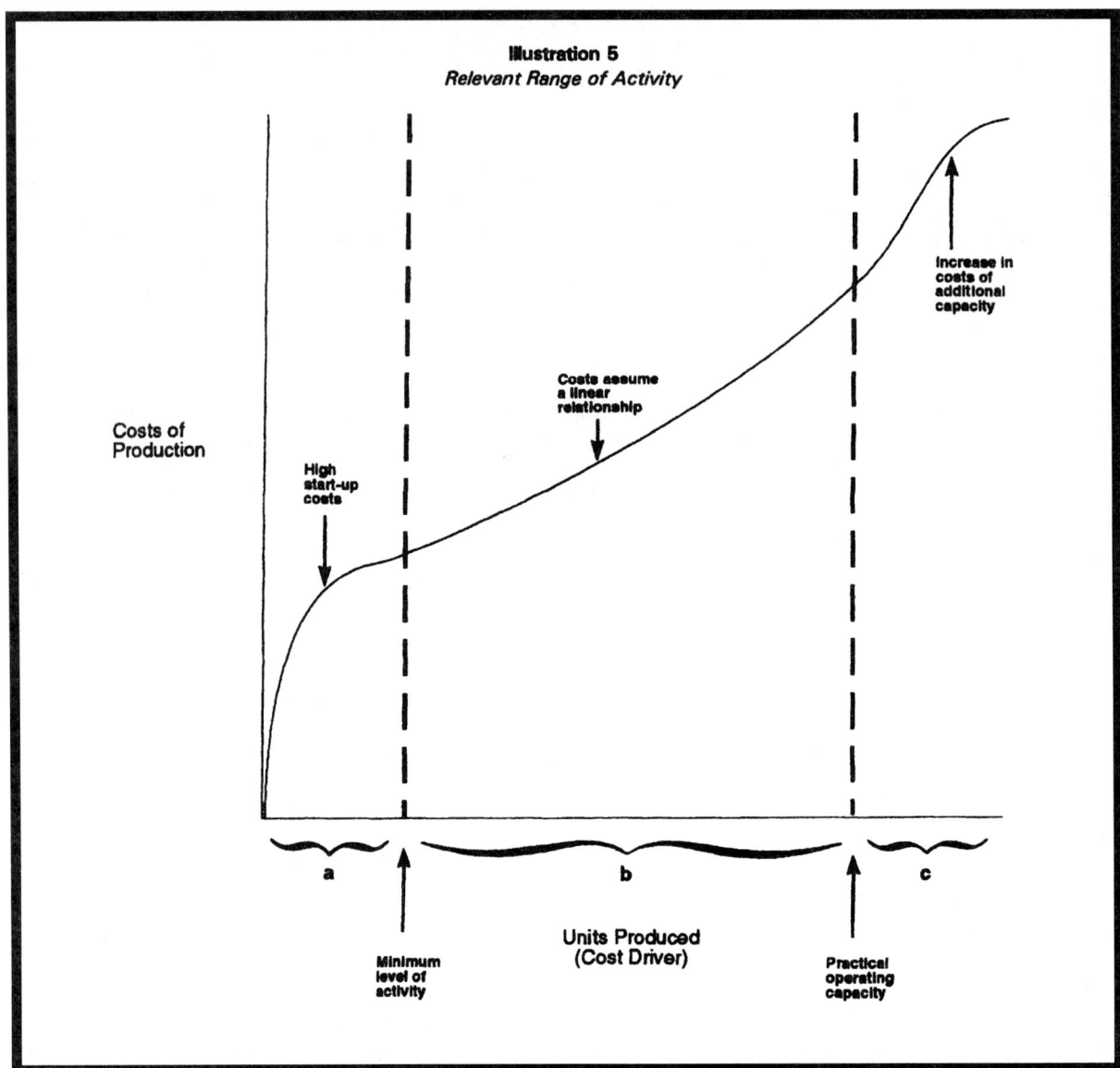

costs. This can be evidenced by the sharp increase in total manufacturing costs above the upper bound [part (c) on the graph in Illustration 5].

The importance of the relevant range can be summarized by one statement: the relationship between costs and activity is assumed to be linear within the relevant range. As a result, management can estimate the total costs associated with any level of activity within the relevant range. Conversely, because of different conditions and uncertainty, similar estimates cannot be made for levels of activity less than or greater than those that fall within the relevant range.

ILLUSTRATION OF COST BEHAVIOR

To illustrate cost behavior, assume that you are asked to identify the budgeted level of costs for Better Books Company, a publisher of high school and college textbooks. To assist you, Better Books has accumulated manufacturing cost data from 20x1, which will be used to determine estimated manufacturing costs for the first quarter of 20x2. While numerous costs exist, Better Books is interested in determining the expected level of the following costs:

1. Manufacturing equipment and facilities.
2. Paper and ink used in production.
3. Wages paid to machine operators.

4. Utility costs.
5. Wages paid for inspection of completed textbooks.

Better Books has identified the number of textbooks manufactured as its cost driver. More appropriate cost drivers may exist for some of the above costs. For example, utility costs vary more closely with the number of kilowatt hours used than with the number of textbooks manufactured. However, manufacturing companies must often make important decisions that are influenced by the level of manufacturing activity. For example, before trying to set a selling price for its textbooks, Better Books needs to know the cost associated with manufacturing these textbooks. Thus, Better Books is interested in determining how the five costs shown above vary with changes in manufacturing volume (number of textbooks manufactured).

These costs can be classified into one of four categories, depending on how they fluctuate with changes in the level of activity. If the number of textbooks (units) manufactured is utilized as Better Books' cost driver, the above costs can have one of four relationships to activity: (1) fixed, (2) variable, (3) step, or (4) semi-variable (or mixed).

Fixed Costs

Fixed costs do not change (in total) with changes in the organization's level of activity. For example, assume that the depreciation on Better Books' typesetting and manufacturing equipment is $75,000 per month. In addition, suppose that Better Books pays monthly rent on its manufacturing facilities of $25,000. Thus, the total monthly costs of Better Books' manufacturing facilities are $100,000. Since Better Books uses the number of textbooks manufactured as its cost driver, these costs are classified as fixed costs, since they are not expected to change with changes in the number of textbooks manufactured (within the relevant range).

Parts A and B of Illustration 6 reveal the basic relationship between fixed costs and activity; as activity increases, fixed costs in total remain unchanged. However, as activity increases, the fixed costs per unit of activity decrease. This decrease reflects spreading a constant level of fixed costs over a greater number of units. For example, if Better Books Company manufactured 10,000 textbooks during the month, the fixed cost per textbook equals $10 ($100,000 ÷ 10,000 textbooks = $10 per textbook). If production were increased to 20,000 texts, fixed costs per textbook equal $5 ($100,000 ÷ 20,000 textbooks = $5 per textbook). For either level, note that total fixed costs equal $100,000.

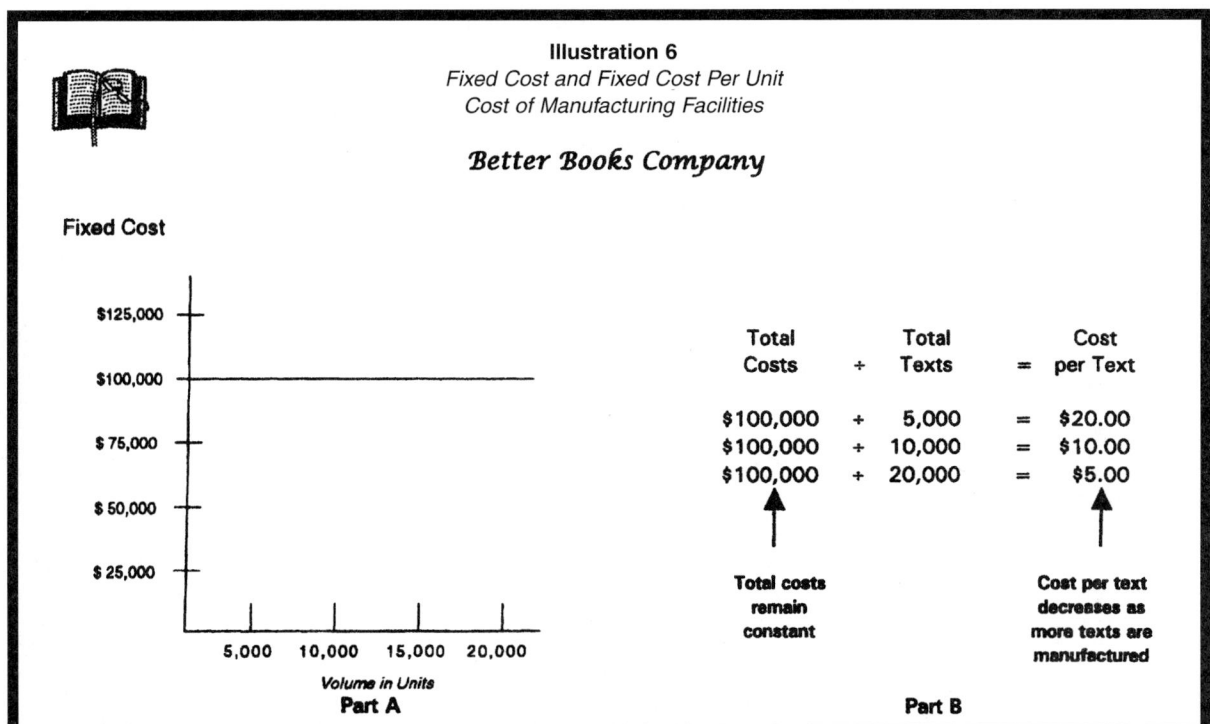

Fixed costs may be classified as one of two types. *Committed fixed costs* are those costs that are incurred on a long-term basis and cannot be reduced in the short-term without impairing the organization's ability to operate at current levels. For example, if the organization wishes to reduce the depreciation costs associated with its manufacturing facilities, it could sell its facilities; however, doing so would require its operating activities to be limited. In contrast, *discretionary fixed costs* are costs that result from short-term management decisions to undertake activities such as research and development, training programs, advertising, and sales promotions. Unlike committed fixed costs, discretionary fixed costs may be modified in the short-term without impairing the organization's operating activities to a great extent.

Recent developments in the automobile industry illustrate the concept of a fixed cost and how this cost remains constant over various levels of activity. For example, both Chrysler and General Motors have recently added additional shifts, which increases their production of automobiles without increasing the level of investment in plant and equipment. These decisions have resulted in decreases in the cost per automobile manufactured.[4]

Variable Costs

Variable costs change in direct proportion to changes in some level of activity. That is:

1. As activity increases, variable costs increase (or conversely, as activity decreases, variable costs decrease).

2. The increase or decrease in variable costs is the same for each unit of change in activity.

To illustrate the behavior of a variable cost, assume that the cost of paper and ink for Better Books averaged $20 per textbook in 20x1. Since the costs of paper and ink increase directly and proportionately with increases in activity, this is an example of a variable cost. Illustration 7 summarizes the relationship between the costs of paper and ink and levels of activity. As shown therein, if zero textbooks are manufactured, the total costs of paper and ink are zero. Also note that each textbook results in an additional $20 of paper and ink costs. The slope of the cost line in Illustration 7 equals the variable cost per unit ($20 per textbook).

In classifying costs as either fixed or variable, it is important to recall the concept of the relevant range of activity. For example, the depreciation costs of DaimlerChrysler's manufacturing facilities are generally considered a fixed cost. However, if production is increased beyond current capacity, additional facilities must be acquired, resulting in an increase in depreciation costs. Thus, costs may not be fixed if DaimlerChrysler operates at levels of activity beyond the relevant range. Further, while the wages paid to assembly workers is ordinarily considered to be variable in nature, this classification assumes that DaimlerChrysler would dismiss their assembly workers in response to short-run shutdowns in production. This latter example illustrates how costs may be affected when DaimlerChrysler operates at levels of activity below the relevant range.

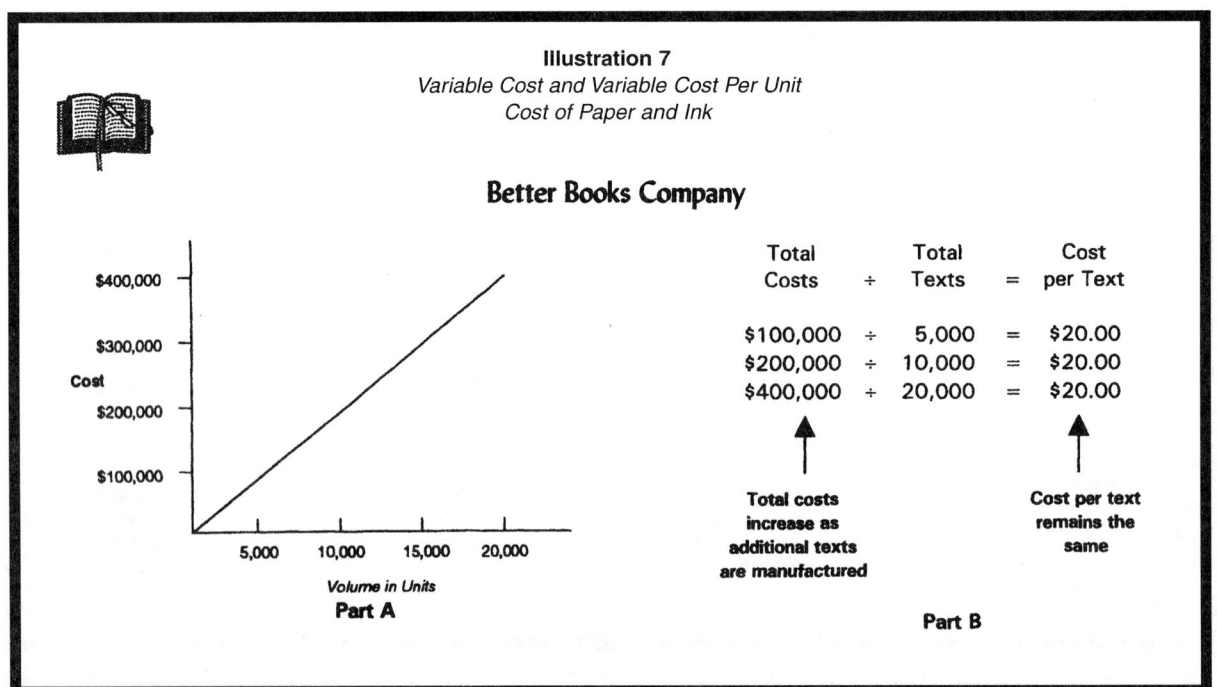

[4] "Chrysler's Star Keeps Rising," *U.S. News & World Report* (February 28, 1994), 51 and "Detroit: Hiballing It into Trucks," *Business Week* (March 7, 1994), 46.

> A trend that affects the cost structure of many large corporations is the decision to have outside companies provide services formerly performed internally (known as outsourcing). Kenneth Tuchman, CEO of TeleTech Holdings (which provides customer-service outsourcing for AT&T), notes that these arrangements "...turn fixed costs into variable costs."[5]

Step Costs

A *step cost* is a cost that remains constant over a given range of activity and increases or decreases in fixed incremental amounts within the relevant range. Step costs are similar to fixed costs in that they do not vary over a given level of activity. However, these costs will increase and decrease as various levels of activity are attained within the relevant range.

Assume that Better Books Company hires machine operators based on anticipated monthly production and pays these operators a fixed salary of $3,000 per month. Based on a normal work schedule, each operator can manufacture approximately 5,000 textbooks per month. The wages paid to machine operators is an example of a step cost. This step cost is presented in Illustration 8.

Notice that the total costs of wages paid to machine operators for Better Books is $3,000 for levels of manufacturing activity less than or equal to 5,000 texts. But if Better Books increases production beyond 5,000 texts, additional machine operators must be hired and total costs will increase. Note that these costs are fixed over subsets of the relevant range. For example, the total cost of wages paid to machine operators is $6,000, regardless of whether 5,001 or 10,000 texts are manufactured. Similarly, for levels of activity between 10,001 and 15,000 texts, the total cost of wages paid to machine operators is $9,000.

Illustration 8 represents a step *fixed* cost, since the wages paid to machine operators are fixed over relatively large ranges of activity. Other types of step costs are fixed over much smaller ranges of activity. For example, if

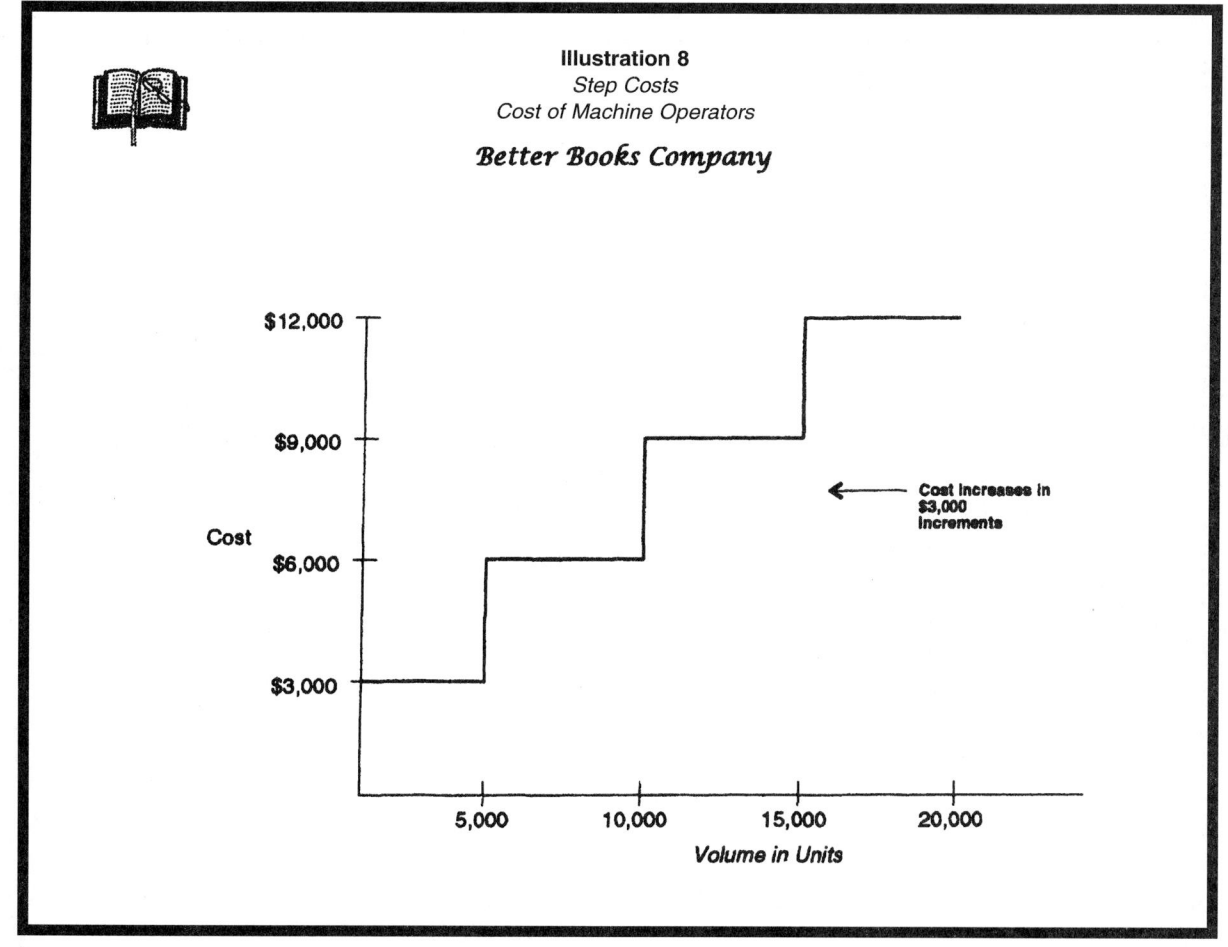

Illustration 8
Step Costs
Cost of Machine Operators
Better Books Company

---

[5] "Has Outsourcing Gone Too Far?," *Business Week* (April 1, 1996), 27.

Better Books ships its products in cartons that hold ten textbooks, the costs of packaging would be classified as a step cost, since the costs would remain constant for each group of ten textbooks. If the cost of packaging is $1.00 per carton, the total packaging costs for selected levels of activity would be as follows:

```
0–10 textbooks ...................................... $1.00
11–20 textbooks .................................... $2.00
21–30 textbooks .................................... $3.00
```

The costs of packaging would be considered a step *variable* cost, since these costs are constant over relatively small ranges of activity. Viewed from another standpoint, a variable cost is one that varies over individual units of activity whereas a step variable cost varies over small "groups" of units of activity. In many instances, step variable costs are approximated as a variable cost. For the above example, Better Books may classify the costs of packaging as a variable cost of $0.10 per textbook ($1.00 ÷ ten textbooks = $0.10 per textbook).

Semi-Variable (Mixed) Costs

Semi-variable (or mixed) costs are composed of both fixed and variable elements. Using textbooks manufactured as the cost driver, the utility cost of Better Books is an example of a semi-variable cost. For example, some components of the costs of heating, cooling, and lighting the manufacturing facilities will be incurred regardless of the level of manufacturing activity. However, other components will increase as the number of textbooks manufactured increases, since the increased utilization of manufacturing equipment will increase utility costs.

Based on past experience, Better Books estimates a "fixed" utility cost of $5,000 per month. This portion of the utility cost relates to the heat, light, and power used in the manufacturing facilities without considering the actual utility costs incurred in operating the manufacturing equipment. Thus, if production during a month is zero textbooks, total utility costs are $5,000. If Better Books determines that the cost of operating manufacturing

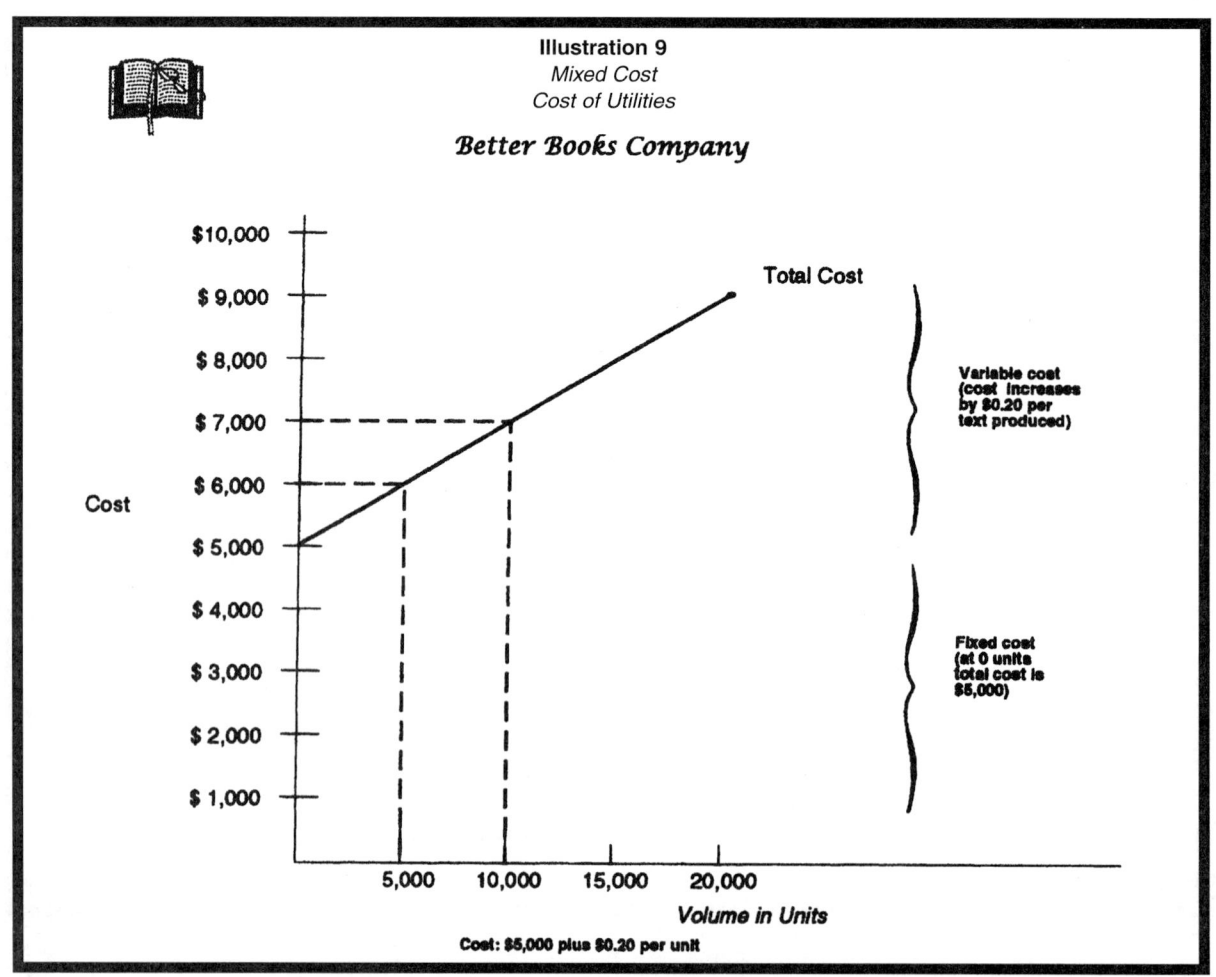

equipment is $0.20 per textbook, the behavior of utility costs is summarized in Illustration 9. The following section illustrates how this cost is decomposed into its fixed and variable components.

Illustration 9 shows the relationship between fixed costs, variable costs, and total costs. Notice that the total utility cost includes two components: (1) a fixed cost of $5,000, and (2) a variable cost of $0.20 per textbook manufactured. The total cost line in Illustration 9 intersects the vertical axis at $5,000. This implies that, if activity (textbooks manufactured) is zero, the utility cost is $5,000. This represents the fixed cost portion of the total cost. Beginning with zero activity, notice that, as activity increases, the total cost line slopes upward. This indicates that total utility costs increase with the increases in the production of textbooks. The increase in total costs reflects the variable cost of $0.20 per textbook manufactured. Because the slope of any line (as defined by two points on that line) is the change in the vertical distance divided by the change in the horizontal distance, the slope of the total cost line represents the variable cost per text manufactured.

To illustrate how the total cost line reflects the variable cost per text, refer to the two dashed lines in Illustration 9. At 5,000 texts, total utilities costs are $6,000; at 10,000 texts, total utilities costs are $7,000. The variable costs per unit can be calculated as follows:

Total Costs	-	Fixed Costs	=	Variable Costs	÷	Activity (Texts)	=	Variable Cost Per Unit
$6,000	-	$5,000	=	$1,000	÷	5,000	=	$0.20
$7,000	-	$5,000	=	$2,000	÷	10,000	=	$0.20

ANALYZING COST BEHAVIOR

In the above example regarding semi-variable costs, information was provided regarding the fixed and variable components of Better Books' utility cost. To estimate these components, Better Books analyzes the historical relationship between semi-variable costs and levels of activity. To illustrate, assume that Better Books hires part-time workers to inspect a sample of textbooks from each manufacturing run for defects and mistakes. The total inspection costs for the last six months of 20x1 are shown in Illustration 10, along with the number of textbooks manufactured during that period.

These historical data are used to estimate the fixed and variable components of Better Books' inspection costs. This section discusses four methods of cost analysis: (1) the graphical method, (2) the two-point method, (3) the semi-averages method, and (4) the least squares regression method.

The Graphical Method

One technique for analyzing semi-variable costs relies upon a graphical analysis of the relationship between activity and total costs. The inspection cost data from Illustration 10 have been plotted on a scattergraph and are shown in Illustration 11. Each point on the scattergraph represents the cost and activity for a month. For example, the point labeled "July" represents the total inspection costs ($950) for the level of manufacturing activity (9,000 textbooks) in July 20x1.

Once the historical data have been plotted, a line can be fitted to minimize the total distance between the data points and the line. Assuming that line AB has been fitted, we can see that the total fixed cost using the graphical method is approximately $700. This is determined by observing the point at which line AB intersects the vertical

Illustration 10
Inspection Costs: 20x1

Better Books Company

	Total Inspection Costs	Textbooks Manufactured
July	$950	9,000
August	1,200	14,000
September	1,050	12,000
October	1,000	11,000
November	1,150	13,000
December	1,250	15,000

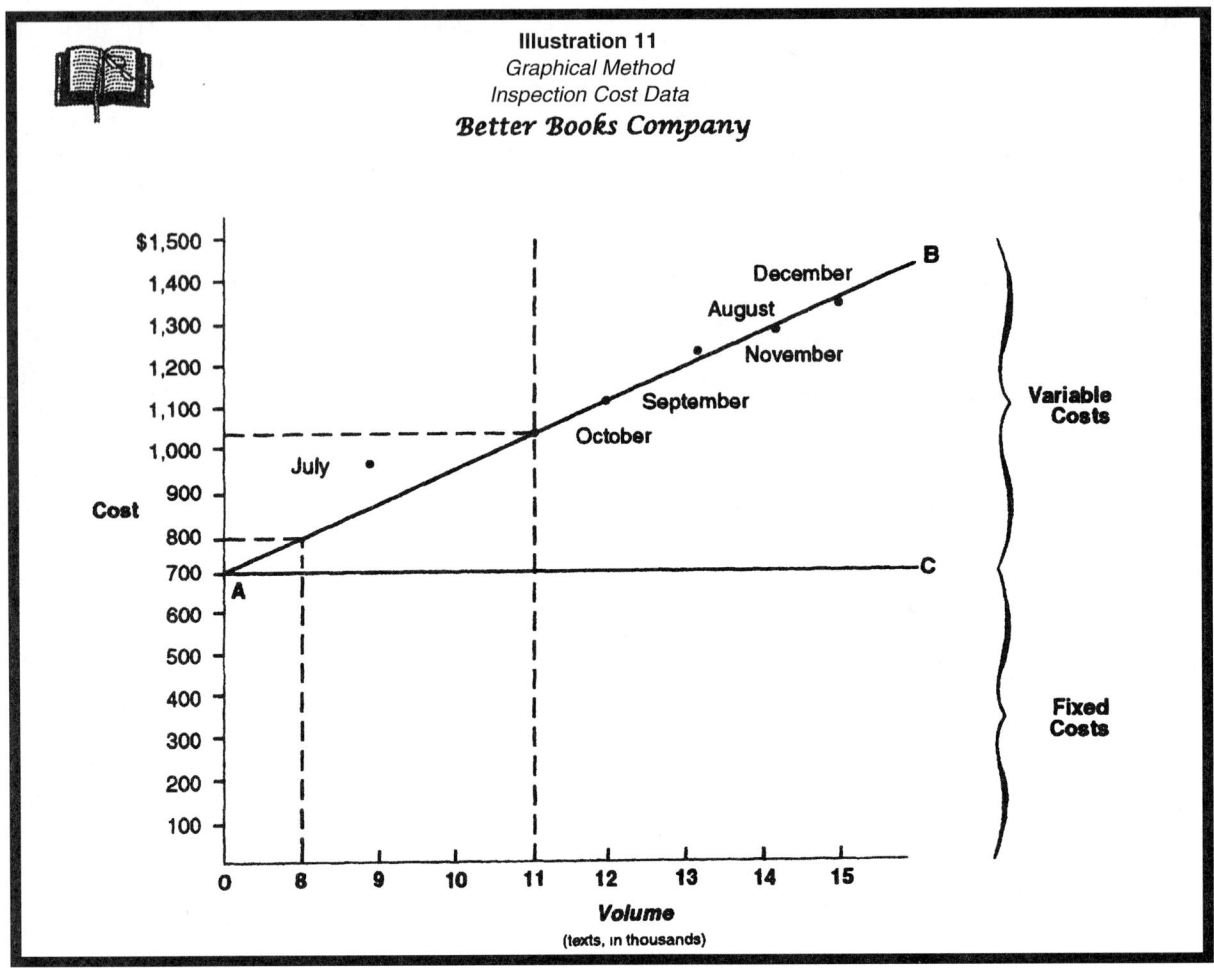

cost axis (i.e., the point at which the level of activity is zero). Thus, line AC represents the total fixed cost component of the inspection cost using the graphical method.

To determine the variable component, the "slope" (the change in costs divided by the change in activity) of the line AB is calculated. This is done by selecting two points on line AB and noting the level of activity and costs associated with these two points. Assume that the two levels of activity selected are 8,000 textbooks and 11,000 textbooks (see the dashed lines in Illustration 11). The total costs associated with these two levels of activity are $800 and $1,020, respectively. To calculate the variable cost per unit (slope), we simply divide the change in costs by the associated change in activity, as follows:

$$\frac{\text{Change in Costs}}{\text{Change in Activity}} = \frac{\$1{,}020 - \$800}{11{,}000 \text{ texts} - 8{,}000 \text{ texts}} = \$0.073 \text{ per textbook (rounded)}$$

Thus, using the graphical method, Better Books estimates its variable inspection cost per text at $0.073 and its fixed inspection costs to be $700.

The Two-Point Method

The *two-point method* (also referred to as the *high-low method*) attempts to analyze costs by "fitting" a line between two extreme historical levels of cost and activity. To illustrate the two-point method, consider the historical cost and activity data from Illustration 10. Notice that the month of July had the lowest levels of cost and activity ($950 and 9,000 textbooks), while the month of December had the highest levels ($1,250 and 15,000 textbooks). Under the two-point method, the variable cost per textbook can be determined by dividing the dollar change in total costs by the change in activity, thus similar to the graphical method. This relationship is shown as follows:

$$\frac{\text{High Cost - Low Cost}}{\text{High Activity - Low Activity}} = \text{Variable cost per unit of activity}$$

For Better Books:

$$\frac{\$1,250 - \$950}{15,000 \text{ texts} - 9,000 \text{ texts}} = \$0.05 \text{ per textbook}$$

Since total costs equal fixed costs plus variable costs, Better Books can calculate fixed costs by using the variable cost per unit calculated above along with information relating to total costs and levels of activity for either of the two data points used to calculate the variable cost per unit. Using December's total inspection costs of $1,250, manufacturing activity of 15,000 textbooks, and the $0.05 variable cost per textbook, the total fixed costs are estimated at $500.

Total Costs	=	Fixed Costs	+	(Variable Cost x Textbooks)
$1,250	=	Fixed Costs	+	($0.05 x 15,000 texts)
$1,250	=	Fixed Costs	+	$750
Fixed Costs	=	$500		

In summary, the two-point method first calculates the "slope" of the total cost line for inspection costs. As noted earlier, this slope represents the variable cost per unit. Then, the total cost equation is solved to determine the level of fixed costs utilizing either the high or low point.

Semi-Averages Methods

A method similar in nature to the two-point method is the *semi-averages method*. Like the two-point method, the semi-averages method decomposes the fixed and variable components of a semi-variable cost using historical levels of cost and activity. The primary difference between this method and the two-point method described above is that the semi-averages method uses a greater amount of historical data.

Once a period of time is selected, the levels of cost and activity are divided into high levels (levels above the median observation) or low levels (levels below the median observation). The high and low levels are then averaged to determine "average" high and low levels of cost and activity, with the resulting averages used in the equations illustrated in the preceding discussion of the two-point method.

To illustrate the use of the semi-averages method, consider the data presented earlier in Illustration 10. The average levels of activity and cost for the high three months and the low three months are calculated below.

Highest Three Months:

	Cost	Textbooks
August	$1,200	14,000
November	1,150	13,000
December	1,250	15,000
Totals	$3,600	42,000
	÷ 3	÷ 3
Averages	$1,200	14,000

Lowest Three Months:

	Cost	Textbooks
July	$950	9,000
September	1,050	12,000
October	1,000	11,000
Totals	$3,000	32,000
	÷ 3	÷ 3
Averages	$1,000	10,667

As shown below, applying the two-point method to the averages calculated above provides a variable cost of $0.06 per text and a fixed cost of $360.

$$\frac{\$1,200 - \$1,000}{14,000 \text{ texts} - 10,667 \text{ texts}} = \$0.06 \text{ per textbook (rounded)}$$

Total Costs	=	Fixed Costs	+	(Variable Cost x Textbooks)
$1,200	=	Fixed Costs	+	($0.06 x 14,000 texts)
$1,200	=	Fixed Costs	+	$840
Fixed Costs	=	$360		

Comparing the results obtained using the semi-averages method with those obtained using the two-point method reveals differences between the calculation of fixed and variable costs. Since the semi-averages method utilizes a larger amount of historical data, it is generally perceived to provide a more reliable analysis of semi-variable costs. The two-point method may result in undue influence being placed on abnormally high or low levels of cost and activity.

Least Squares Regression Method

As discussed above, the graphical method analyzes costs by "fitting" a line through points representing historical levels of costs and activity on a scatterplot. One weakness of this method is that the line is constructed by attempting to minimize the distance of the points from this line by visual inspection. While this line represents an approximation of the behavior of a given cost, it suffers from imprecision. One method of overcoming this imprecision is through the use of the *least squares regression method*.

The least squares regression method mathematically "fits" a line through scatterplot points in such a way as to minimize the total deviation from the points to the line. Thus, this method attempts to find the "best fit" of a line through a series of points representing cost and activity. Once the line has been fitted, the analysis of the cost behavior is identical to that used in the graphical analysis discussed earlier.

The least squares regression method uses the following formula to define the total cost relationship:

$$y = a + bx$$

y = Total Costs
a = Fixed Costs
b = Variable Cost per Unit of Activity
x = Level of Activity

Based on the above formula, the least squares regression method can be used to calculate either the fixed costs or variable costs for a given set of cost data. As with the other methods illustrated in this chapter, once either the fixed or variable costs are known, we can solve to find the remaining component of total cost. The constants a and b in the equation for a straight line can be determined by solving the following two simultaneous equations:

(1) $na + b(\Sigma x) = \Sigma y$
(2) $a(\Sigma x) + b(\Sigma x^2) = \Sigma xy$

where a, b, x, and y are defined as above, n is the number of (x, y) observations for costs and activity, and Σ is used to designate the sum for all observations. For example, the term Σx indicates the sum (total) of units of activity for all months in the sample.

To illustrate the use of the least squares regression method, consider the data presented earlier relating to total inspection costs. These data are presented again in Illustration 12. For computational convenience, a column for

Illustration 12
Inspection Cost Data
Method of Least Squares Regression
(in thousands)

Better Books Company

Month	Textbooks Manufactured (x)	Total Costs (y)	x^2	xy
July	9	$0.95	81	8.55
August	14	1.20	196	16.80
September	12	1.05	144	12.60
October	11	1.00	121	11.00
November	13	1.15	169	14.95
December	15	1.25	225	18.75
Total (Σ)	74	$6.60	936	82.65

the sum of the activity squared (Σx^2) and the activity multiplied by the cost (Σxy) have been added. The data have been restated in thousandths (divided by one thousand) for ease of exposition.

Substituting the values calculated in Illustration 12 into equations (1) and (2) yields the following two simultaneous equations:

(1) 6a + 74b = 6.60
(2) 74a + 936b = 82.65

To solve this pair of equations, one of the original equations must be restated in such a manner so that either the a or b terms is of equal value. Then one equation is subtracted from the other. To solve the above simultaneous equations, the "a" term can be converted to 222 by multiplying equation (1) by 37 and multiplying equation (2) by 3. Subtracting equation (1) from equation (2) yields the following results:

(2) 222a + 2808b = 247.95
(1) 222a + 2738b = 244.20
            70b = 3.75
              b = 0.05 (rounded)

Substituting 0.05 for b in the first equation yields 0.48 (or $480), as shown below:

6a + 74(0.05) = 6.60
6a +   3.70 = 6.60
         6a   = 2.90
          a   = 0.48

Thus, cost analysis using the least squares regression method indicates that the variable costs per unit are $0.05 and the fixed costs are $480 (recall that the data were stated in thousands; thus $0.48 equals $480).

COST BEHAVIOR FOR RETAIL AND SERVICE COMPANIES

The preceding example focused on the behavior of costs incurred by a manufacturing company. However, it is important to note that similar relationships between costs and activity exist for retail companies and service companies. For example, consider the following types of costs incurred by FedEx (a service company) and their relationship to activity levels (using number of parcels delivered as a cost driver).

- Variable costs: Packaging, Order processing
- Fixed costs: Depreciation on delivery vehicles
- Step costs: Wages paid to delivery persons
- Semi-variable costs: Delivery vehicle fuel

As with the Better Books Company example illustrated throughout this chapter, the classification of the above costs depends upon the cost driver selected. For example, while the costs of fuel for delivery vehicles behaves as a semi-variable cost using the number of parcels delivered as a cost driver, it would behave as a variable cost if the number of miles driven were used as the cost driver. However, because of the importance of revenue-generating activities in various organization decisions (discussed in the following section), organizations are interested in identifying how costs behave over activity levels related to their primary revenue-generating transactions (for FedEx, the number of parcels delivered). Thus, the behavior of the above costs over different levels of parcels delivered would be important information to FedEx's management.

USING MANAGERIAL ACCOUNTING INFORMATION: BETTER BOOKS

Based on the preceding discussion, the behavior of costs with changes in manufacturing activity (the cost driver) has been identified. This information is summarized below:

	Fixed	Variable
Manufacturing equipment and facilities	$100,000	$ 0.00
Paper and ink	0	20.00
Utility costs	5,000	0.20
Inspection costs (semi-averages method)	360	0.06

In addition, recall that the wages paid to machine operators is a step cost. This cost is fixed at $3,000 and increases in increments of $3,000 as manufacturing activity reached 5,000 texts, 10,000 texts, and 15,000 texts.

Once the behavior of these costs has been analyzed, Better Books can now use this information to budget (or determine) the expected costs that would be incurred for given levels of activity. If Better Books is considering manufacturing 6,500, 13,000, and 14,000 texts in the first three months of 20x2, the expected costs are summarized in Illustration 13.

Illustration 13
Budgeted Manufacturing Costs

Better Books Company

	January (6,500 texts)	February (13,000 texts)	March (14,000 texts)
Manufacturing equipment and facilities	$100,000	$100,000	$100,000
Paper and ink	130,000	260,000	280,000
Wages paid to machine operators	6,000	9,000	9,000
Inspection costs	750	1,140	1,200
Utility costs	6,300	7,600	7,800
Total costs	$243,050	$377,740	$398,000

The cost of manufacturing equipment and facilities are unaffected by levels of manufacturing activity, held constant at $100,000 per month. The costs of paper and ink average $20 per text. As a result, these costs increase directly and proportionately with increases in manufacturing activity. To determine the total costs of paper and ink, the expected manufacturing activity for a particular month is multiplied by the variable cost per text of $20. Recall that these two costs are classified as fixed and variable costs, respectively.

The cost of wages paid to machine operators is a step cost, since it is fixed over subsets of the relevant range but will increase as certain levels of activity are attained. In this example, one machine operator is capable of manufacturing up to 5,000 texts. Since machine operators are paid $3,000 per month, a total of two operators are required for January's level of manufacturing activity and three operators for February and March. Thus, total wages paid to machine operators would be $6,000 for January and $9,000 for February and March.

Inspection costs are a semi-variable cost. Semi-variable costs contain both fixed and variable components. Once the behavior of these costs has been identified, the costs may be budgeted. To estimate the variable component, Better Books multiplies the variable cost per unit by the level of activity. For example, using the method of semi-averages, the variable component of inspection costs was calculated as $0.06 per text. Once it has been determined, the total variable cost is then added to the fixed cost to determine the total cost. Recalling that the fixed cost of inspection was determined to be $360, the total inspection costs can be calculated as follows:

January (6,500 textbooks x $0.06) + $360	$750
February (13,000 textbooks x $0.06) + $360	$1,140
March (14,000 textbooks x $0.06) + $360	$1,200

Utility costs are also a semi-variable cost. Once the fixed ($5,000) and variable ($0.20 per textbook) components of the utility costs are known, they would be estimated in a similar manner to inspection costs. The estimated utility costs for January, February, and March would be $6,300, $7,600, and $7,800, respectively.

Once the total expected manufacturing costs have been identified, how would the management of Better Books use this information? While this aspect of managerial accounting is discussed throughout the remainder of this text, some uses include:

1. Establishing textbook prices to achieve desired levels of profit. Once the costs of manufacturing textbooks have been determined, Better Books can establish a selling price for its texts to provide some desired level of profit. This type of activity is often referred to as cost-volume-profit analysis and is discussed later in this text.

2. Ensuring that sufficient levels of cash are maintained in order to reduce interest costs (for borrowed funds) or the opportunity costs associated with failing to invest cash (for idle funds). By estimating the level of expected costs during a future period, the management of Better Books Company can identify the amount

of cash needed to meet expected costs so that excess revenue may be promptly reinvested. Budgeting costs for purposes such as these is discussed further in a subsequent chapter of this text.

3. Allowing management to identify favorable or unfavorable levels of performance. Once information on expected costs has been identified, Better Books' management can compare the actual costs incurred for various activities to the budgeted costs. Instances where actual costs are significantly different (either higher or lower) than budgeted costs may reveal areas of superior or substandard performance. Using performance standards and evaluating the performance of individuals and divisions is discussed in subsequent chapters.

SUMMARY

This chapter provides an overview of different types of costs and the behavior of these costs. In addition, methods of analyzing the costs incurred by organizations are discussed. Knowledge about how costs behave as the level of activity changes is important in both accounting for these costs as well as planning for the organization's operating activity.

1. Manufacturing companies incur two major types of costs. *Product costs* are those costs incurred by an organization related to the manufacture of that organization's inventory. Examples of product costs include direct materials costs, direct labor costs, and manufacturing overhead costs. Product costs are accumulated with inventory and expensed upon the sale of the inventory to the organization's customers (as cost of goods sold).

2. *Period costs* are those costs not related to the manufacture of the organization's inventory. Major classifications of period costs include administrative costs, marketing and distribution costs, and research and development costs. Depending on whether the cost provides future benefits to the organization, period costs are either expensed as they are incurred or allocated over future time periods using a systematic and rational allocation method.

3. *Cost behavior* is defined as the manner in which costs react to changes in a given level of activity within the relevant range (the operating range or span over which a firm finds it practical to operate in the short run). The level of activity that causes costs to change (or vary) is known as a *cost driver*.

4. *Fixed costs* do not fluctuate in response to changes in the level of activity. Examples of fixed costs include depreciation, property insurance, executive salaries, and rent. While the total fixed costs remain constant as activity increases, the fixed cost per unit decreases as activity increases. Two types of fixed costs are *committed fixed costs* and *discretionary fixed costs*.

5. *Variable costs* fluctuate directly and proportionally with changes in the level of activity. While total variable costs increase as activity increases, the variable cost per unit remains the same within the relevant range. Examples of variable costs include the cost of materials and labor used in manufacturing the organization's inventory.

6. A *step cost* is a cost that remains constant over a given range of activity and increases or decreases in fixed incremental amounts within the relevant range. An example of a step cost is the additional salary incurred when additional personnel are hired because of increases in activity. Step costs can either be fixed (if they remain constant over relatively large levels of activity) or variable (if they remain constant over relatively small levels of activity).

7. A *semi-variable* (or *mixed*) cost is a cost containing both fixed and variable components. Utility costs are an example of a semi-variable cost.

8. In analyzing cost behavior, it is often necessary to decompose costs into their fixed and variable components. In doing so, the organization utilizes historical cost data in an effort to identify the fixed and variable components. Methods of analyzing cost behavior include the *graphical method*, the *two-point method*, the *semi-averages method*, and the *least squares regression method*.

KEY DEFINITIONS

Cost–expenditures (or allocation of previous expenditures) necessary in conducting the activities of the organization.

Cost behavior–the manner in which costs react when the level of activity changes.

Cost driver–that level of activity, or element, that causes costs to change within the relevant range.

Committed fixed costs–fixed costs associated with the firm's capacity to manufacture inventory or provide services. Committed fixed costs reflect the capability for sustaining a planned volume of activity and generally arise from factors such as the acquisition of plant and equipment.

Discretionary fixed costs–fixed costs that are usually incurred on a relatively short-term basis and can be modified without impairing the organization's operating capacity to a great extent. Discretionary fixed costs are also referred to as managed or programmed fixed costs.

Fixed cost–costs that do not fluctuate in response to changes in the organization's activity within the relevant range.

Graphical method–a method of estimating the fixed and variable components of a semi-variable cost in which a visual plot of costs and activity is relied upon.

Least squares regression (method of least squares regression)–a form of regression in which a straight line is mathematically fitted to describe costs (y) according to the formula $y = a + bx$, where a represents fixed costs, b is the variable cost per unit of activity, and x is the activity.

Relevant range–the range or span of activity over which a firm finds it practical to operate in the short run. Conclusions about cost behavior are generalizable only within the relevant range of activity.

Semi-averages (method of semi-averages)–a method of estimating the fixed and variable components of a semi-variable cost in which historical data are classified into high and low levels of cost and activity.

Semi-variable costs (mixed costs)–costs containing both fixed and variable components. Semi-variable costs must be analyzed in order to identify the fixed and variable components of these costs.

Step costs–costs that remain constant over a given range of activity and increase or decrease in fixed incremental amounts within the relevant range. Step costs remaining constant over relatively large levels of activity are step fixed costs. Those remaining constant over relatively small levels of activity are step variable costs.

Two-point method–a method of estimating the fixed and variable components of a mixed cost using the high and low measures of cost and activity for a given period of time. Also known as the "high-low" method.

Variable cost–costs that fluctuate in direct proportion to changes in volume within the relevant range.

QUESTIONS

1. Define product costs and period costs. How is each of these types of costs treated for income determination?

2. Briefly define and provide examples of each of the three major categories of product costs.

3. What are prime costs? What are conversion costs?

4. Define cost behavior. Why is cost behavior important to the organization?

5. Define relevant range and cost driver. How do these concepts influence cost behavior?

6. Describe and provide examples of fixed costs, variable costs, and semi-variable costs. What are the planning implications of each type of cost?

7. How can increases in activity reduce the fixed cost per unit of activity?

8. What is the relationship between fixed costs and levels of activity? Variable costs and levels of activity?

9. Distinguish between committed fixed costs and discretionary fixed costs.

10. Define step costs. Distinguish between step fixed costs and step variable costs.

11. Describe the graphical method. How are fixed costs determined using this method? How is the variable cost per unit determined using this method?

12. What information is required when the two-point method is used to identify the fixed and variable components of a semi-variable cost? Is this information different when the semi averages method is used?

13. How is the least squares regression method related to the graphical method?

14. Once the fixed and variable components of a semi-variable cost are identified, how does the organization estimate total costs?

EXERCISES AND PROBLEMS

15. *Basic Definitions.* After reading an article you recommended on cost behavior, your client asks you to explain the following excerpts from it:

    1. "*Fixed costs* are variable per unit of output and *variable costs* are fixed per unit of output (though in the long run all costs are variable)."
    2. "*Depreciation* may be either a fixed cost or a variable cost, depending on the method used to compute it."

    For each excerpt:
    a. Define the italicized terms, and give examples where appropriate.
    b. Explain the meaning of the excerpt to your client.

    (AICPA adapted)

16. *Classification of Fixed Costs.* For each of the following types of fixed costs, identify whether the cost would usually be considered a discretionary fixed cost or a committed fixed cost.

    a. Depreciation on existing building
    b. Research and development costs
    c. Training costs
    d. Salaries of executive personnel
    e. Property taxes
    f. Costs of building modifications

17. *Costs—General Classification.* Costs may be classified in several ways such as: fixed, variable, or semi-variable. Some fixed costs are classified for planning purposes as committed costs and others as discretionary.

    Required:

    a. What determines whether a cost is classified as fixed, variable, or semi-variable?
    b. What determines whether a fixed cost is committed or discretionary?
    c. All costs can be variable, depending on the volume or type of company. Specify whether each cost from the following list is normally fixed, variable, or semi-variable. For costs classified as fixed costs, indicate whether they are discretionary or committed fixed costs.

    1. Plant depreciation
    2. Advertising expense
    3. Indirect labor
    4. Superintendent's salary
    5. Foreman's salary
    6. Electricity and heat
    7. President's salary
    8. Rent
    9. Research and development

18. *Cost-Volume Relationship.* The cost of telephone services is a semi-variable cost in most cases. A technique referred to as "the graphical approach" can be used to determine budgeted costs. The following minutes of telephone usage are listed along with the telephone costs that relate to recent periods.

	Telephone Usage (minutes)	Telephone Costs
January	20,000	$15,500
February	21,000	15,950
March	17,000	13,900
April	19,000	14,900
May	23,000	16,400
June	25,000	17,000

Required:

Produce a scatterplot with the vertical axis measuring costs and the horizontal axis measuring telephone usage.

19. *Estimating Costs.* Based on an analysis of historical cost relationships, Stewart Company has determined that its fixed operating costs are $10,000, and its variable costs are $3.50 per unit produced. Compute the total costs incurred by Stewart for expected production of 1,000 units, 5,000 units, and 10,000 units.

20. *Estimating Costs.* Assume that Ralph Company's telephone charge consists of both a fixed monthly charge of $25.00 and a $0.10 per minute charge for telephone usage. Given the expected utilization below, estimate Ralph's telephone expense for the first six months of 20x1.

	Minutes of Telephone Usage
January	1,500
February	900
March	1,100
April	800
May	2,000
June	650

21. *Estimating Costs—Two-Point Method.* During the first week in August, direct labor costs were $66,000 and production equalled 100,000 units. During the second week, direct labor costs were $61,000 and production equaled 75,000 units. During the third week, the budget calls for the production of 80,000 units. Estimate the costs at this level of production.

22. *Estimating Costs—Two-Point Method.* When Copen Co. produced a volume of 100,000 units, it incurred mixed costs of $100,000. When 120,000 units were produced, mixed costs equaled $101,000.

Required:

a. Estimate the fixed costs.
b. Compute the variable cost per unit.
c. If production rose to 90,000 units, what amount would be expected for mixed costs?

23. *Cost Analysis—Graphical.* The travel expenses and other related data for the sales force of Acme are listed below.
Required:

Week	Travel Expenses	Number of Calls	Number of Miles	Number of Customers
1	500	50	1,800	125
2	300	30	900	215
3	800	80	1,600	140
4	300	30	5,600	115
5	500	50	1,000	225
6	300	30	300	115
7	800	80	1,800	140
8	900	90	1,900	145
9	700	70	1,600	135

a. Using graphical analysis, which measure (calls, miles, or customers) provides the best basis for estimating travel expense?
b. Estimate travel expense for sixty calls, using the cost driver you selected in part a.

24. *Cost Analysis—Graphical.* For each of the costs illustrated below, use graphical analysis to determine whether the costs are fixed, variable, semi-variable, or step costs.

Production	Depreciation	Materials Cost	Maintenance Cost	Training Cost
5,000 units	$10,000	$ 5,000	$ 3,000	$4,000
6,000 units	10,000	6,000	4,500	4,000
8,000 units	10,000	8,000	7,000	5,000
10,000 units	10,000	10,000	8,500	5,000
15,000 units	10,000	15,000	13,500	6,000

25. *Cost Analysis and Estimation—Two-Point Method.* Shown below are historical data for the relationship between monthly automobile operating expenses and mileage driven. Using the two-point method, identify the fixed and variable components of the operating expense. Given this answer, what would be the estimated cost for driving 10,000 miles?

Operating Cost	Mileage Driven
$16,000	11,000
18,000	12,000
9,000	4,500
11,500	8,000

26. *Cost Analysis and Estimation—Two-Point (Multiple Costs).* Jax has collected the following cost data for your use in analyzing cost behavior:

	1,000 Units Produced	3,000 Units Produced
Materials	$5,000	$15,000
Labor	8,000	12,000
Depreciation	1,000	1,000
Property taxes	500	500
Supplies	500	1,000

Using the two-point method, determine the fixed and variable components of the above costs. What are the expected production costs if Jax produces 5,000 units?

27. *Cost Analysis–Semi-Averages.* Using the method of semi-averages, determine the fixed and variable components of the following labor costs during the previous two years.

	Hours Worked	Labor Costs
Year 1, Quarter 1	15,000	$105,000
Year 1, Quarter 2	22,000	160,000
Year 1, Quarter 3	20,000	135,000
Year 1, Quarter 4	10,000	81,000
Year 2, Quarter 1	12,000	100,000
Year 2, Quarter 2	30,000	200,000
Year 2, Quarter 3	28,000	180,000
Year 2, Quarter 4	19,000	128,000

28. *Cost Analysis—Semi-Averages.* Using the method of semi-averages, determine the fixed and variable components of the following indirect labor costs.

Month	Indirect Labor Cost	Labor Hours
January	$15,000	3,500
February	30,000	9,500
March	28,000	7,500
April	21,000	5,500
May	24,000	6,000
June	32,000	10,000

29. *Cost Analysis—Least Squares Regression.* Labor hours and production costs for the last four months of 20x9, which you believe are representative for the year, were as follows:

Month	Labor Hours	Total Production Costs
September	2,500	$ 20,000
October	3,500	25,000
November	4,500	30,000
December	3,500	25,000
Total	14,000	$ 100,000

Required:
a. Using the least squares regression method, estimate the fixed monthly production cost.
b. Using the least squares regression method, estimate the variable production cost per labor hour.
c. Compute total production costs for 4,000 labor hours.

(AICPA adapted)

30. *Cost Analysis—Two-Points and Semi-Averages.* Jefferson, Inc. plans to produce the following number of units in the first quarter of 20x2:

January	10,000
February	8,000
March	12,000

These levels of production are all within Jefferson's relevant range. Jefferson wishes to determine the total expected production costs during the first quarter of 20x2. The following historical data concerning production activity and costs is available for your analysis.

Units Produced	Costs
4,000	$ 8,000
7,000	15,000
9,000	22,000
13,000	29,000
15,000	32,000
20,000	39,000

Required:

a. Using the two-point method, estimate the fixed and variable costs of production.
b. Using the rates calculated above, estimate the costs of production for the first quarter of 20x2.
c. Repeat (a) and (b) using the semi-averages method.

31. *Cost Analysis—Two-Point and Graphical.* To enable Alexis Corp. to estimate its cost for budgeted levels of activity during the first quarter of 20x2, you have been asked to analyze the behavior of total production costs. Alexis has provided you with the following data concerning the relationship between total production costs and direct labor hours worked:

Total Costs	Direct Labor Hours Worked
$ 6,000	1,000
10,000	2,000
28,000	6,000
8,000	1,500
18,000	4,000
23,000	5,000

Assume that Alexis wishes to produce 200 units in January, 150 units in February, and 300 units in March with each unit requiring ten direct labor hours.

Required:

a. Using the two-point method and the method of semi-averages, identify the fixed and variable components of total production costs.
b. Using the graphical method, identify the components noted in (a) above.
c. For each case, estimate total production costs for Alexis Corp. in the first quarter of 20x2.

32. *Cost Analysis—Two-Point and Least Squares.* Below are cost and volume data for two independent cases (X equals the total volume and Y equals total costs).

Case 1					Case 2			
X	Y$	X^2	XY		X	Y$	X^2	XY
0	1	0	0		1	2	1	2
1	4	1	4		2	9	4	18
3	8	9	24		4	12	16	48
4	9	16	36		5	14	25	70
Σ 8	22	26	64		Σ 12	37	46	138

Required:

a. Using the two-point method, determine the fixed and variable components of cost for each case.
b. Using the least squares regression method, determine the fixed and variable components of cost for each case (i.e., substitute data for each case in the formula):

$$na + b(\Sigma x) = \Sigma y$$
$$a(\Sigma x) + b(\Sigma x^2) = \Sigma xy$$

c. Describe the conditions under which the two methods would produce substantially similar results.

33. *Cost Analysis—Two-Point and Least Squares.* The Ramon Co. manufactures a wide range of products at several different plant locations. Its Franklin Plant, which manufactures electrical components, has been experiencing some difficulties with fluctuating monthly overhead costs. The fluctuations have made it difficult to estimate the level of overhead that will be incurred for any one month.

Management wants to estimate overhead costs accurately in order to plan its operation and financial needs better. A trade association publication to which Ramon Co. subscribes indicates that for companies manufacturing electrical components overhead tends to vary with direct labor hours.

One member of the accounting staff has proposed that the cost behavior pattern of the overhead costs be determined. Then overhead costs could be predicted from the budgeted direct labor hours.

Another member of the accounting staff suggested that a good starting place for determining the cost behavior pattern of overhead costs would be an analysis of historical data. The historical cost behavior pattern would provide a basis for estimating future overhead costs. Ramon Co. decided to employ the two-point method, the graphical method, and the least squares regression method. Data on direct labor hours and the respective overhead costs incurred were collected for the past two years. The raw data and scatterplot prepared from the data are presented below.

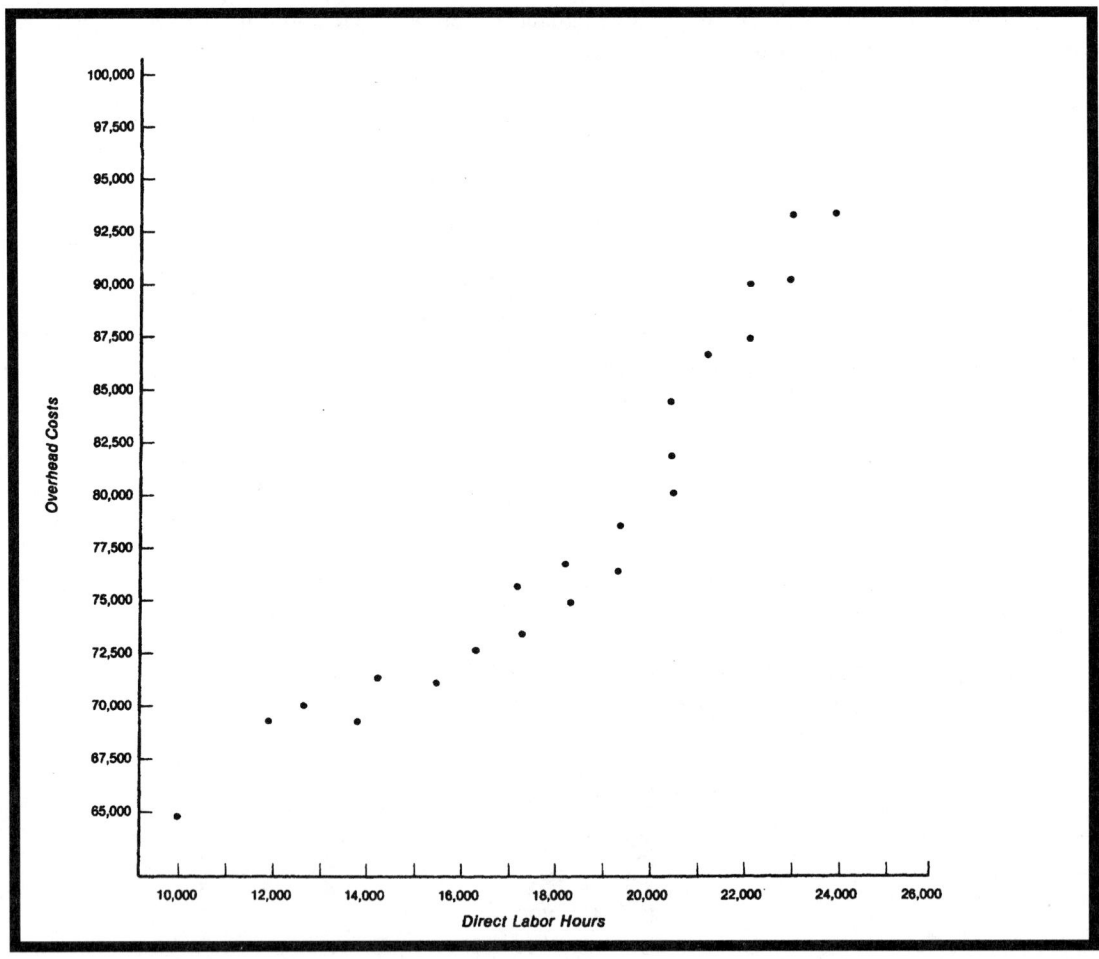

Using linear regression, the constant term a of the regression equation Y = a + bx was found to be 39.859, and the slope, b, was found to be 2.1549.

20x3	Direct Labor Hours	Overhead Costs	20x4	Direct Labor Hours	Overhead Costs
January	20,000	$84,000	January	21,000	$86,000
February	25,000	99,000	February	24,000	93,000
March	22,000	89,500	March	23,000	93,000
April	23,000	90,000	April	22,000	87,000
May	20,000	81,500	May	20,000	80,000
June	19,000	75,500	June	18,000	76,500
July	14,000	70,500	July	12,000	67,500
August	10,000	64,500	August	13,000	71,000
September	12,000	69,000	September	15,000	73,500
October	17,000	75,000	October	17,000	72,500
November	16,000	71,500	November	15,000	71,000
December	19,000	78,000	December	18,000	75,000

Required:

a. Using the two-point method, determine the cost behavior pattern of the overhead costs for the Franklin Plant.
b. Using the results of the regression analysis, calculate the estimated overhead costs for 22,500 direct labor hours.
c. Which of the three proposed methods (two-point method, graphical method, least squares regression method) should Ramon Co. employ to determine the historical cost behavior pattern of Franklin Plant's overhead costs? Explain your answer completely, indicating the reasons why the other methods should not be used.

(CMA adapted)

34. *Cost Behavior—Graphical.* Identify the graph that best illustrates the cost volume relationship for each factory cost or expense element listed below. The vertical axes of the graphs represent total dollars of expense and the horizontal axes represent production. In each case, the zero point is at the intersection of the two axes. The graphs may be used more than once.

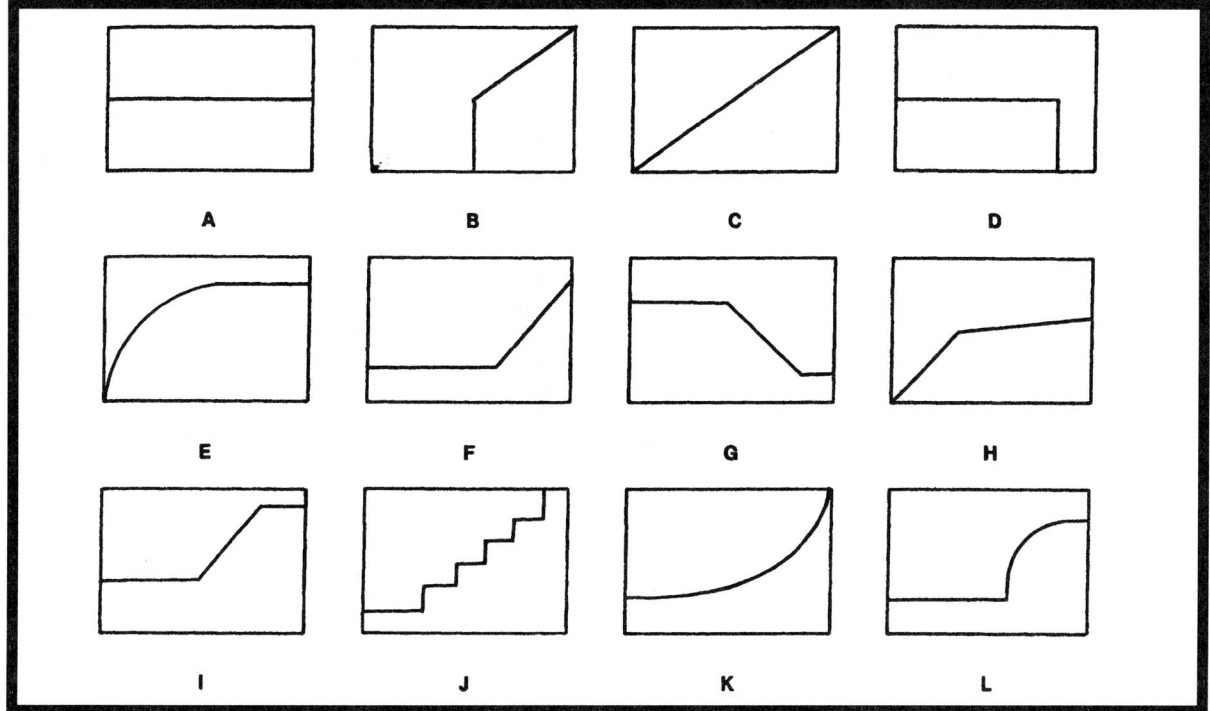

Required:

a. Depreciation of equipment, where the amount of depreciation charged is computed based on the number of machine-hours used.
b. Utilities cost comprised of a fixed charge and a variable cost after a certain number of kilowatt hours are used.
c. Water costs, which are determined as follows:

First 1,000,000 gallons or less	$1,000 flat charge
Next 10,000 gallons	$0.003 per gallon used
Next 10,000 gallons	$0.006 per gallon used
Next 10,000 gallons, etc.	$0.009 per gallon used

d. Cost of lubricant for machines, where cost per unit decreases with each pound of lubricant used. For example, if one pound is used, the cost is $10.00; if two pounds are used, the cost is $19.98; if three pounds are used, the cost is $29.94. This cost decreases until a minimum cost per pound of $9.25 is reached.
e. Depreciation of equipment, where the asset is depreciated by the straight-line method. When the depreciation rate was established, it was anticipated that the obsolescence factor would be greater than the wear and tear factor.
f. Rent on a factory building donated by the city, where the agreement calls for a fixed-fee payment unless 200,000 man-hours are worked, in which case no rent need be paid.
g. Salaries of repairmen, where one repairman is needed for every 1,000 hours of machine usage (that is, 1,000 hours or less requires one repairman, 1,001 to 2,000 hours requires two repairmen, etc.).
h. Federal unemployment compensation taxes for the year, where labor force is constant throughout year (average salary is $26,000).
i. Cost of direct materials used.
j. Rent on a factory building donated by county, where the rental agreement calls for rent of $100,000 less $1 for each direct labor hour worked in excess of 200,000 hours; however, a minimum rent of $20,000 must be paid.

(AICPA adapted)

35. *Cost Analysis—Comprehensive.* Rypien Company wants to analyze the behavior of its utilities expense and selects units produced as the appropriate cost driver. Rypien has collected the following cost data with respect to its utilities expense for the past year. Using this data and (a) the two-point method, (b) the semi-averages method, and (c) the least squares regression method, determine the fixed and variable components of Rypien's utilities expense.

Month	Units Produced	Cost
January	1,500	$ 900
February	2,000	1,100
March	1,200	800
April	800	650
May	1,700	1,000
June	2,200	1,200
July	1,000	700
August	1,800	1,050
September	2,100	1,150
October	1,550	910
November	2,500	1,400
December	850	660

Hint: For ease of computation, you may wish to convert the data to hundredths (divided by 100) before analysis using the least squares regression method.

Part II

Cost Accumulation

This section of this text examines accumulating manufacturing costs with inventory, a major activity performed by managerial accountants. Chapters 3 and 4 examine the basic accumulation of manufacturing costs with inventory for companies using two different types of manufacturing processes and costing systems: job-order costing (Chapter 3) and process costing (Chapter 4). In these chapters, the focus is on the accumulation of costs with inventory as it moves through the various stages of the manufacturing/sales process. Chapter 5 discusses the nature of overhead costs and illustrates methods of accumulating and allocating overhead costs with inventory.

Chapter 3:   *Job-Order Costing*

Chapter 4:   *Process Costing*

Chapter 5:   *Overhead Costs and Activity-Based Costing*

Learning Objectives

Chapter 3 introduces the concept of cost accumulation. In this chapter, the accumulation of the costs of manufacturing inventory in a job-order costing system is illustrated. Cost accumulation in a process costing system is discussed and illustrated in Chapter 4. Studying Chapter 3 should enable you to:

1. Identify the objectives and importance of cost accumulation.
2. Discuss two basic types of manufacturing processes and understand the methods of accumulating costs under each process.
3. Understand the manufacturing process and the flow of costs in a manufacturing environment.
4. Understand how the costs of manufacturing inventory are accumulated in a job-order costing system.
5. Prepare a Cost of Goods Manufactured Statement, Cost of Goods Sold Statement, and Income Statement for a manufacturing company.

3

Job-Order Costing

INTRODUCTION

John Salvaggio is the manager of Ace Construction Company. Ace Construction builds wooden decks and other home improvements for customers on an individual order basis. John was concerned that he wasn't pricing Ace's construction jobs properly and decided that he needed better information about the actual costs required to complete Ace's construction jobs. John had the following discussion with one of his foremen, Carl Briggs:

John: We've really got to do a better job of determining how much it costs us to complete a construction project. Unless we know the correct amounts, how can we determine what to bid for a job?

Carl: That shouldn't be too difficult. Our two major costs are materials and labor. All we need to do is identify how much material will be used and the cost of that material. The same goes for labor.

John: You're overlooking a number of costs. For example, we have utility costs, costs of our construction tools, and your salary. There are several other costs, too. The problem is that we can't associate most of these costs with a particular job. For example, you spend time at five or six job sites a day. How can we identify your salary with each of these projects?

Carl: Boy, that would take a lot of recordkeeping. I see your point. We do need to consider these costs, or we won't be able to earn a decent profit. But is it really worthwhile to identify all of these costs for a particular project?

John: It doesn't seem like it would be practical, but we have to do something. Do you have any ideas?

Some very basic, yet important, information for companies selling inventory or providing services is the cost of manufacturing or purchasing that inventory or the cost of providing those services. The process of identifying the costs associated with various organization activities is referred to as *cost accumulation*. When these activities are related to the purchase or production of the company's inventory products, this process is also known as *product costing*. Cost accumulation was introduced and discussed earlier in Chapter 1. In this and the following two chapters, the process of accumulating costs and associating these costs with inventory items is discussed in greater detail.[1]

IMPORTANCE OF COST ACCUMULATION

Prior to discussing cost accumulation in a job-order costing system, we will first briefly describe the importance of cost accumulation to the organization. Cost accumulation is an important process in both (1) the preparation of financial statements (financial accounting) and (2) the internal decision-making process (managerial accounting).

Preparation of Financial Statements

For organizations whose primary operating activity represents the sale of inventory to customers, two significant components of their financial statements are the cost of inventory shown on their balance sheets and the cost of goods sold expense shown on their income statements. As discussed in the preceding chapter, product costs (direct materials costs, direct labor costs, and manufacturing overhead costs) are accumulated with the organization's inventory until the items are sold to customers. At that time, these costs are then expensed (as cost of goods sold) to "match" these costs with the related sales revenue. Therefore, in order to determine the total cost of manufacturing inventories (and ultimately the cost of goods sold associated with those inventories), it is necessary that manufacturing organizations accurately accumulate the costs of manufacturing their inventory with the related items.

To illustrate the importance of cost accumulation in the preparation of financial statements, assume that LLED Computer Corporation began 20x2 with no inventory of personal computers. During January 20x2, LLED manufactured 100,000 personal computers and sold 60,000 of these computers to customers for $1,200 each. As a result, LLED had a total of 40,000 computers in inventory at the end of January 20x2. LLED determined that the average cost of manufacturing a computer (product cost per computer) was $650.

Illustration 1 presents the partial financial statements for LLED Computer Corporation for January 20x2. As shown therein, the total costs of inventory shown in LLED's balance sheet equal the manufacturing cost per unit ($650) multiplied by the number of computers in ending inventory (40,000), or $26,000,000 ($650 x 40,000 computers = $26,000,000). Similarly, the cost of goods sold recognized by LLED Computer Corporation equals the number of computers sold by LLED multiplied by the manufacturing cost per computer, or $39,000,000 ($650 x 60,000 computers = $39,000,000).

Illustration 1

Partial Financial Statements: LLED Computer Corporation

Partial Income Statement
for the month ended January 31, 20x2

Sales (60,000 computers x $1,200) $72,000,000
Cost of Goods Sold (60,000 computers x $650) ....(39,000,000)

Partial Balance Sheet
As of January 31, 20x2

Assets:

Inventory (40,000 computers x $650) $26,000,000

---

[1] Cost accumulation is important for companies that produce inventories (manufacturing companies) as well as those that provide services (service companies). While many of the references in this and subsequent chapters illustrate cost accumulation for manufacturing companies, the student should recognize the importance of this concept for all types of companies.

The above example is concerned with illustrating how the cost accumulation process influences the preparation of the organization's financial statements. Because the cost per unit of $650 was provided, the example above did not reflect the complexity involved with accumulating manufacturing costs with inventory. As you will see in this and the following two chapters, it is often quite difficult (and costly) for organizations to determine the costs required to manufacture their inventories or provide their services. This process serves as the focus of this section of the text.

Internal Decision-Making Process

In addition to the preparation of financial statements, the cost accumulation process is critical in allowing the organization's management to make several important decisions. One particularly important decision that requires information on the costs of manufacturing inventory is the price at which the organization sells its inventory. Clearly, the organization should price its inventory at a sufficient amount to recover manufacturing costs and earn a desired level of profit. While product pricing decisions are discussed later in this text, these decisions consider, among other information, the costs of manufacturing inventory.

> A humorous example of how cost accumulation affects pricing decisions is reflected in a letter written by a former patient of a California hospital to advice columnist Ann Landers. This person was complaining about being charged $7 for a single aspirin tablet. In her response, Ms. Landers noted that the cost of this aspirin included wages paid to the: (1) physician (who prescribed the aspirin), (2) pharmacist (who dispensed the aspirin), (3) nurse (who administered the aspirin to the patient), and (4) medical records personnel (who recorded the prescription, dispensing, and administration of the aspirin). Another author noted that this cost could theoretically include the costs of malpractice insurance and costs associated with uncollectible accounts receivable of the hospital.[2]

The cost accumulation process is also important in evaluating the performance of individuals within the organization. As will be seen in this chapter, cost accumulation involves identifying both the total amounts and total costs of materials, labor, and other inputs used to manufacture inventory. One method of evaluating performance is to compare the actual cost and quantities of inputs to *expected* (or *standard*) costs and quantities. This comparison involves establishing performance standards and will be discussed later in this text.

Finally, cost accumulation data can be used to provide management with information about the effect of continuing or discontinuing a product line on overall organization profits. An important factor in making this type of decision is whether the organization can earn an appropriate return on the sale of specific products or product lines. To make this determination, information about the costs of manufacturing inventory is required. The process of cost accumulation provides management with this information.

INTRODUCTION TO JOB-ORDER COSTING: THE ACE CONSTRUCTION COMPANY

The manufacturing process used by an organization normally can be categorized as one of two types depending on the nature of inventory produced. Contrast the inventory produced by a construction company with that produced by a chemical company. A construction company produces (builds) homes and home improvement projects on an individual basis, as each home requires unique materials and labor inputs that are readily identifiable with that particular home. This type of manufacturing activity is commonly referred to as a *discrete manufacturing process*. Because each "product" requires different amounts of materials and labor inputs, it is desirable to separately accumulate the materials and labor costs of producing each home. In cases such as this, companies accumulate the costs of producing inventory by product (or job); this method of cost accumulation is referred to as *job-order costing*. Examples of companies with discrete manufacturing processes that use job-order costing (along with the type of inventory produced by these companies) include Compaq Computer and Dell Computer (personal computers), General Motors (automobiles), Walt Disney (motion pictures), and Boeing (aircraft). Each of these companies manufactures products with different amounts and types of materials, labor, and overhead costs.

---

[2] D.W. McFadden, "The Legacy of the $7 Aspirin," *Management Accounting* (April 1990), 38–41.

> The process used to craft the world-renowned Steinway piano is a "note" worthy example of job order production. Building a single Steinway can take up to a year, and the assembly requires 12,000 parts, most of which are handmade by craftsmen. Hand-bent rims made of laminated maple must be stabilized in a temperature-controlled room for up to ten weeks. Eight different species of wood are used, and the piano's mechanism is assembled at 30 different desks.[3]

In contrast, a chemical company does not produce chemicals on an individual or a gallon-by-gallon basis. Instead it normally manufactures a "batch" of chemicals at one time. The materials and labor inputs cannot be clearly associated with any individual gallon of chemicals; however, they can be identified with a "batch" of production. This type of manufacturing process is referred to as a *continuous manufacturing process*. In a continuous manufacturing process, the organization utilizes *process costing* to accumulate costs with the inventory manufactured. This chapter discusses job-order costing, while process costing is discussed in the next chapter.

The following excerpts from the business press describe how automakers are attempting to move toward the build-to-order methodology that has become the hallmark of Dell Computer.

> General Motors and its rivals want to do with cars what Dell Computer does with computers—take orders online, custom build the product and deliver it on a promised date. Unfortunately, the cars we drive are more complex to manufacture than hard drives. An automaker must coordinate the delivery of 3,000 or more parts, many of which are too big and expensive to stockpile in warehouses. Painting each car takes a relatively long period of time, and many car parts have to be color-coordinated. Also, while Dell can arrange for overnight shipping of a PC, Ford cannot FedEx a two-ton vehicle. Nonetheless, Harold Kutner, GM's group vice president of worldwide purchasing, has articulated a goal of cutting the normal shipping time in the United States down to a range of one to eight days.[4]
>
> In a surprising move for its industry, Toyota Motor Corporation announced its intention to custom-build its Camry Solara coupe within five days of customer order. Automakers typically "build to stock" on the basis of educated guesses about consumer demand, leaving many car buyers not completely satisfied with available options. However, the widespread use of the Internet has produced a new breed of consumer—one who is more educated in terms of options and prices and who is easily able to comparison-shop among a broad range of dealers. Toyota leadership believes that the move to build-to-order will result in several benefits, including the development of a high-velocity supply chain, improved relations with dealers, and increased customer satisfaction and loyalty.[5]

Illustration 2 summarizes the major steps undertaken and the flow of costs in a typical manufacturing/sales process. These steps and cost flows are discussed in the following subsections.

Obtain Direct Materials

To illustrate the accumulation and flow of costs in a job-order costing system, we will examine various construction projects of the Ace Construction Company. Ace Construction builds wooden decks and other home improvements for customers on an individual order basis. Because each of Ace's construction jobs requires different material and labor inputs, Ace Construction uses a job-order costing system.

A common type of home improvement built by Ace Construction Company is a wooden deck. Wooden decks use treated lumber with dimensions of 1" (thick) x 2" (width) x 48" (length). At the beginning of 20x1, Ace has a total of 5,000 pieces of this lumber on hand, at a cost of $5 per piece. This lumber is an example of direct materials inventory. *Direct materials inventory* represents items that are used in the manufacturing process and have not yet been issued into production. At the end of the period, the cost of direct materials inventory on hand is included in the balance sheet as an asset (a component of Ace Construction's inventories).

---

[3] Andy Serwer, "Happy Birthday, Steinway," *Fortune* (March 17, 2003), 94–97.

[4] Robert L. Simison, "GM Aims to Become Build-to-Order Business—But Custom Online Sales are a Daunting Task for Car Makers," *The Wall Street Journal* (February 22, 2000), A1.

[5] Jeffrey Bodenstab, "An Automaker Tries the Dell Way," *The Wall Street Journal* (August 30, 1999), A26.

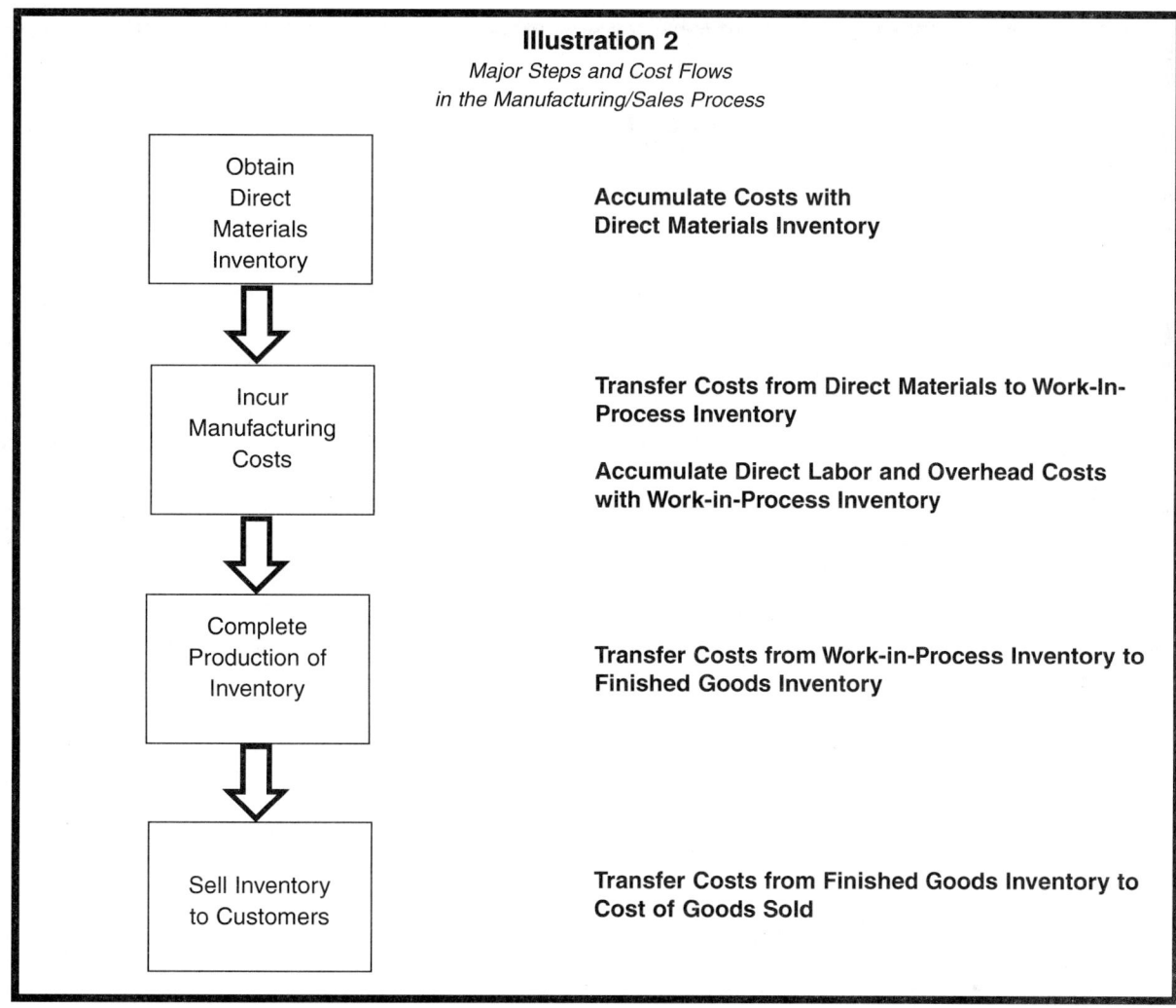

Illustration 2
Major Steps and Cost Flows in the Manufacturing/Sales Process

The initial step in the manufacturing/sales process is the acquisition of direct materials inventories for use in production. If Ace Construction acquired an additional 4,000 pieces of lumber for its scheduled construction jobs and paid $5 per piece for this lumber, the following journal entry would be prepared.

    Direct Materials-Control 20,000
        Accounts Payable   20,000

Notice that this entry accumulates the cost of the lumber using an inventory account (direct materials).

Incur Manufacturing Costs

Use of Direct Materials. The second step in the manufacturing/sales process is issuing direct materials inventory to production. While direct materials may be issued at numerous times during the manufacturing process, at least some quantity of materials is issued as production commences. Assume that Ace Construction received an order from John Guerra to construct a wooden deck on January 5, 20x1. Ace assigns each of its jobs an identification number based on the customer's initials and the date of the order. This particular job was assigned job number JG-0105. Throughout this example, we will record all of Ace Construction Company's manufacturing costs; however, we separately identify the manufacturing costs associated with Job JG-0105 to illustrate how costs flow as inventory moves through various stages of the manufacturing/sales process.

Assume that during January a total of 6,000 pieces of lumber were issued into production. To record the issuance of these materials into production, companies utilize a document known as a *Materials Requisition*. The Materials Requisition authorizes the issuance of direct materials to manufacturing jobs and serves as a record of the amount (and cost) of materials issued to various individual jobs. Of the 6,000 pieces of lumber issued to production, 200 were used for Job JG-0105. Therefore, the total materials costs incurred in January production were $30,000 (6,000 pieces x $5 per piece = $30,000), $1,000 of which were related to Job JG-0105 (200 pieces

**Illustration 3
Ace Construction Company**
Materials Requisition

Number: 106-04
Approved by: JRS
Received by: RHS

Date	Job Number	Description	Quantity	Cost	Total Cost
1-07-x1	JG-0105	1" x 2" x 48" treated lumber	200 pieces	$5.00	$1,000

x $5 per piece = $1,000). The total costs of direct materials associated with manufacturing jobs are referred to as the *cost of direct materials* used. A sample Materials Requisition authorizing the issuance of direct materials to Job JG-0105 is shown in Illustration 3.

Initially, direct materials costs are accumulated in the work-in-process inventory account as the items are produced. *Work-in-process inventory* represents the manufacturing costs of items on which production has begun but is not yet complete. Similar to direct materials inventory, work-in-process inventory is shown on the balance sheet as an asset (component of the Ace Construction's inventories at year-end). Based on Materials Requisition 106-04 (see Illustration 3), 200 pieces of lumber (at a cost of $5.00 per piece) were used in manufacturing Job JG-0105. Thus, the total materials costs accumulated in work-in-process inventory for this job are $1,000 (200 pieces x $5.00 per piece = $1,000). Similarly, other Materials Requisitions (not shown) would support the $29,000 of direct materials costs accumulated with other manufacturing jobs. The journal entry prepared to record the issuance of direct materials inventory to production is shown below. This entry transfers costs from one inventory account (direct materials) to another (work-in-process) to recognize the fact that materials have been issued into production.[6]

Work-in-Process-Control (Job JG-0105)	1,000	
Work-in-Process-Control (other jobs)	29,000	
Direct Materials-Control		30,000

Use of Direct Labor. The next step in the manufacturing/sales process is accumulating direct labor and overhead costs as the items are produced. In a job order costing system, direct labor costs are accumulated in work-in-process inventory in a manner similar to that used for direct materials costs. As employees work on a particular construction job, the costs of their wages (including fringes) are accumulated with that job. For example, assume that Ace Construction's employees earn an average of $20 per hour (including fringe benefits) and a total of 580 labor hours are worked during the month; total direct labor costs in January 20x1 were $11,600 ($20 per hour x 580 hours = $11,600). Of these, 16 hours were worked on Job JG-0105. Thus, a total of $320 ($20 per hour x 16 hours = $320) of direct labor costs would be accumulated with this job. As with direct materials costs, direct labor costs are accumulated in work-in-process inventory as the items are produced. The journal entry used to record the direct labor costs is shown below.

Work-in-Process-Control (Job JG-0105)	320	
Work-in-Process-Control (other jobs)	11,280	
Wages Payable		11,600

---

[6] The two separate entries to work-in-process inventory in this and subsequent examples are made to highlight the flow of manufacturing costs associated with Job JG-0105. For ease in recordkeeping, companies often accumulate manufacturing costs with inventory using a single journal entry in work-in-process inventory.

As with direct materials costs, Ace Construction Company would use an internal document to accumulate its direct labor costs with production. This document is referred to as a *Work Ticket*. A Work Ticket summarizes an employee's hours worked over a specified period of time and the individual job(s) on which he or she has worked. Assuming that a single employee worked the 16 hours on Job JG-0105 during the period January 7, 20x1 through January 10, 20x1, the Work Ticket for this employee's activity is shown below. Notice that this Work Ticket summarizes the work of this employee on all job(s) on which he or she has participated during the time period.

**Illustration 4
Ace Construction Company**
Work Ticket

Number   106-JS
Approved by   JRS
Time Period   1-7 to 1-11

Date	Job Number	Description	Quantity	Rate	Total Cost
1-07-x1/ 1-10-x1	JG-0105	Labor on wooden deck	16 hrs.	$20.00	$320
1-10-x1/ 1-11-x1	DH-0110	Labor on fence	24 hrs.	$20.00	$480

Applying Overhead Costs. In addition to direct materials and direct labor costs, Ace Construction incurs other construction costs; however, these costs are difficult to associate with any single job. For example, Ace must furnish its employees with tools and supplies for use in their work. In addition, Ace Construction also incurs costs in operating its vehicles (such as gasoline, repairs, and depreciation on trucks). These costs are referred to as overhead costs. Like direct materials and direct labor costs, overhead costs are necessary to manufacture Ace Construction Company's inventory. However, unlike direct materials and direct labor costs, overhead costs are difficult to identify with any particular construction job or item of inventory.

To illustrate the difficulty of accumulating overhead costs with production, consider the monthly depreciation recorded on Ace Construction Company's equipment. If monthly depreciation on this equipment is $6,000, Ace Construction Company could attempt to determine the monthly utilization of its equipment on different jobs and allocate the depreciation based on the relative utilization for each of its construction jobs. For example, if the equipment were used on Job JG-0105 for four hours, Ace could determine the total utilization of this equipment for January and allocate the appropriate cost to Job JG-0105. However, this introduces at least two difficulties. First, Ace Construction Company must identify overhead costs with production as jobs are completed, since it needs information on the cost of completing these jobs on a timely basis. Simply stated, Ace cannot wait until the end of the month to allocate the depreciation costs of the equipment to the various jobs that have been completed during this month. Second, even if the utilization of its construction equipment could be identified on a timely basis, the cost of doing so for all of the components of overhead would likely be excessive.

To provide management with timely information concerning the overhead costs associated with a particular job, companies calculate a predetermined overhead rate by estimating total overhead costs and dividing this by some expected level of activity (or cost driver). The cost driver represents the activity that causes overhead costs to change within the relevant range.

To illustrate the calculation of a predetermined overhead rate, assume that Ace Construction uses direct labor hours as a cost driver. Ace estimates that its employees will work 500 labor hours during the month of January

20x1. In addition, Ace estimates that it will incur a total of $15,000 in overhead costs in January. This estimate is based on the average monthly overhead costs incurred during 20x0 and is comprised of the following:

Indirect Materials	$1,000
Supervisors' Salaries (including fringe benefits)	5,500
Depreciation on Construction Equipment	6,000
Utilities, Repairs, and Other	2,500
Total	$15,000

Dividing the $15,000 of estimated overhead costs by 500 estimated direct labor hours results in a predetermined overhead rate of $30 per direct labor hour, as shown below:

$$\text{Overhead Rate} = \frac{\$15,000}{500 \text{ labor hours}} = \$30 \text{ per direct labor hour}$$

Once calculated, this overhead rate is used to apply overhead costs to inventory as it is produced. Recall that Ace Construction Company worked a total of 580 direct labor hours during January. Therefore, it would apply a total of $17,400 (580 hours x $30 per hour = $17,400) to its January production. Since Ace worked a total of 16 direct labor hours on Job JG-0105, it would accumulate $480 (16 hours x $30 per hour = $480) of overhead costs with this job. While this is a fairly simple example, other methods of applying overhead and determining the overhead rate are illustrated and discussed in Chapter 5.

The journal entry prepared by Ace Construction Company to accumulate overhead costs with Job JG-0105 is shown below. Unlike direct materials costs and direct labor costs, which are accumulated with work-in-process inventory at various intervals throughout the manufacturing process, overhead costs usually are applied either (1) upon completion of production or (2) at the end of the accounting period to facilitate the preparation of financial statements.

Work-in-Process-Control (Job JG-0105)	480
Work-in-Process-Control (other jobs)	16,920
Factory Overhead-Control	17,400

> **For companies with relatively small levels of direct labor costs, an alternate method of cost accumulation is to include direct labor costs as part of manufacturing overhead and apply these costs to inventory as it is produced. To illustrate, Hewlett-Packard's (HP's) direct labor costs average only 3 to 5 percent of the total costs of manufacturing its inventory. As a result, HP recently modified its accounting system to include direct labor costs with overhead and apply these costs to production. This one simplification is estimated to have eliminated over 100,000 journal entries per month.[7]**

The above journal entries are used to record the accumulation of manufacturing costs in the accounting records. While these records are sufficient for the preparation of financial statements, the management of Ace Construction Company needs to have more timely information regarding the cost and details of its various construction projects. For example, if Job JG-0105 is expected to require 250 pieces of lumber, Ace's management may wish to determine the quantity of lumber that has been issued to this job in order to determine if additional lumber needs to be delivered to the job site. However, this information would be difficult (if not impossible) to determine strictly from Ace Construction Company's accounting records.

To provide management with assistance in these and other situations, information regarding the manufacturing costs is accumulated using a *Job Cost Sheet*. An example of a Job Cost Sheet that should be familiar to most students is an automobile repair ticket. Automobile repair tickets list all parts provided by the garage (direct materials costs) and specifically indicate the number of labor hours worked and the labor rate (direct labor costs). While overhead costs are not ordinarily identified separately on an automobile repair ticket, the labor rate shown on automobile repair tickets includes wages paid to workers, an allowance for estimated overhead costs, and a desired profit margin for the garage.

The Job Cost Sheet for Job JG-0105 is shown in Illustration 5. Notice that this document includes references to individual Materials Requisitions and Work Tickets related to that job. From the Job Cost Sheet, the management of Ace Construction Company can determine the following information:

---

[7] R. Hunt and L. Garret, "Direct Labor Cost Not Always Relevant at H-P," *Management Accounting* (February 1985), 58–62.

Illustration 5
Ace Construction Company
Job Cost Sheet

Job Number: JG-0105
Date Started: January 7, 20x1
Description: Wooden Deck
Job Status: Completed (1-11-x1)

DIRECT MATERIALS COSTS

Date	Requisition	Quantity	Unit Cost	Total Cost
1-07-x1	MR 106-04	200 pieces	$5.00	$1,000

DIRECT LABOR COSTS

Date	Work Ticket	Hours	Rate	Total Cost
Various	WT 106-JS	16 hours	$20.00	$320

OVERHEAD COSTS

Date	Activity Base	Level of Activity	Rate	Total Costs
1-11-x1	Labor Hours	16 hrs.	$30.00	$480

COST SUMMARY

Direct Materials............................	$1,000
Direct Labor.................................	320
Manufacturing Overhead................	480
Total Cost	$1,800

- The total cost of producing Job JG-0105 was $1,800.
- A total of 200 pieces of lumber (with a cost of $5 per piece) was used on Job JG-0105.
- A total of 16 hours of direct labor (with a cost of $20 per hour) was worked on Job JG-0105.
- Overhead was applied to Job JG-0105 at a rate of $30 per direct labor hour.

As illustrated in the following section, as the items move through the various stages of the manufacturing and sales processes, information from the Job Cost Sheet can be used to transfer the costs of producing inventory. Job Cost Sheets are internal documents used by management in making various decisions and are not normally viewed by external parties. After all, most companies would not want their customers to know the amount of the profit made on their purchases!

Completion of Production

The first three steps in the manufacturing/sales process are obtaining direct materials inventory, issuing direct materials to production, and accumulating direct labor and overhead costs with the items manufactured. The next step in the manufacturing/sales process is the completion of production. Upon completion, the costs accumulated with the inventory are transferred from work-in-process inventory to finished goods inventory. *Finished goods inventory* is comprised of inventory jobs (or items) that are completed but are not yet sold to customers. Like direct materials inventory and work-in-process inventory, finished goods inventory is shown on the balance sheet as an asset (a component of Ace Construction Company's inventories at year-end). Thus, a manufacturing company has three types of inventories: direct materials inventory, work-in-process inventory, and finished goods inventory.

The cost of units transferred from work-in-process to finished goods is referred to as the *cost of goods manufactured*. The total cost of goods manufactured for an organization is the total costs associated with inventory that has been completed during the period. From the previous section, we can determine the total cost of constructing the wooden deck for John Guerra (Job JG-0105) as follows (this information could also be determined from the Job Cost Sheet shown in Illustration 5):

Direct Materials	$1,000
Direct Labor	320
Manufacturing Overhead	480
Total Cost of Job JG-0105	$1,800

Assume that, in addition to Job JG-0105, other jobs with a cost of $47,800 were completed during January. These costs were obtained by summing the Job Cost Sheets for all jobs completed during the month. The journal entry to record the completion of these jobs is shown below. This entry transfers the cost of completed jobs from one inventory account (work-in-process inventory) to another (finished goods inventory) to recognize the fact that production on the jobs is completed.

Finished Goods-Control (Job JG-0105)	1,800	
Finished Goods-Control (other jobs)	47,800	
Work-in-Process-Control		49,600

Sale of Inventory

The final step in the manufacturing/sales process depicted in Illustration 2 is the sale of inventory to the organization's customers. When inventory is sold, the costs associated with producing the inventory must be transferred from an inventory account (finished goods inventory) to an expense account (cost of goods sold). This transfer represents the "matching" of revenues (sales revenue) with the expenses necessary to earn those revenues (cost of goods sold).

Concluding our example for Job JG-0105, assume that Ace Construction Company's policies do not permit revenue to be recognized until one week after the completion of its jobs. This policy provides Ace's customers with time to inspect the job and request any additional work prior to final approval. Once the customer has approved a job, Ace Construction does not provide any refunds or incur any obligations beyond its warranty work.

Assume that the total cost of jobs receiving final approval from customers (including Job JG-0105) during January was $52,300. Included in this total is the $1,800 cost of Job JG-0105 (see the Job Cost Sheet in Illustration 5). If customers were charged a total of $68,500 for these jobs, the following journal entries would be prepared to recognize the revenues and expenses associated with these jobs.

Accounts Receivable	68,500	
Sales Revenue		68,500
Cost of Goods Sold	52,300	
Finished Goods-Control (Job JG-0105)		1,800
Finished Goods-Control (other jobs)		50,500

In this section, we have illustrated the major steps in the manufacturing/sales process as well as the cost flows associated with these steps. These steps are summarized below:

- Ace Construction purchased direct materials inventories for use in production.
- Upon receipt of the customer's order, direct materials, direct labor, and manufacturing overhead costs were incurred to produce the inventory. These costs are accumulated in work-in-process inventory as the inventory is produced.
- Once the production of inventory is completed, costs are transferred from work-in-process inventory to finished goods inventory. The amount of this cost is referred to as cost of goods manufactured.
- Upon sale of the inventory to the organization's customers, the costs are transferred from finished goods inventory to cost of goods sold.

PREPARATION OF FINANCIAL STATEMENTS

As with other publicly-traded companies, Ace Construction Company would prepare a basic set of financial statements (Balance Sheet, Income Statement, Statement of Cash Flows, and Statement of Shareholders' Equity) for use by external parties. However, manufacturing companies often find it useful to prepare at least two additional financial statements for internal purposes. These statements allow organizations to identify activity in their work-in-process inventory and finished goods inventory accounts and provide the answers to questions such as:

- What was the total cost of inventory completed (cost of goods manufactured) during the period?
- What were total manufacturing costs during the period?
- What was the total cost of items sold to customers during the period?

To illustrate the preparation of financial statements for Ace Construction Company, assume the following inventory balances at January 1, 20x1 and January 31, 20x1. These balances were determined by taking a physical count of direct materials inventories (direct materials inventory) and totaling job cost sheets for items in process (work-in-process inventory) and completed (finished goods inventory) at each date.

	January 1, 20x1	January 31, 20x1
Direct Materials	$25,000	$15,000
Work-in-Process	3,600	13,000
Finished Goods	5,000	2,300

Cost of Goods Manufactured Statement

To analyze changes in the work-in-process inventory during a period, organizations may prepare a *Cost of Goods Manufactured Statement*. This statement, which is prepared for internal use by management, details the total manufacturing costs incurred during the period as well as the cost of items completed during the period and transferred to finished goods inventory. Essentially, the Cost of Goods Manufactured Statement represents a reconciliation of the company's beginning and ending work-in-process inventories and includes the following information:

- Beginning and ending balances in work-in-process inventory.
- Total manufacturing costs (direct materials, direct labor, and manufacturing overhead) incurred during the period.
- Cost of goods manufactured.

Prior to preparing the Cost of Goods Manufactured Statement, the organization must determine its total manufacturing costs. First, consider the cost of direct materials used. Continuing the Ace Construction Company example, recall that Ace purchased a total of $20,000 of direct materials inventory during January 20xl. Using this information, along with the beginning ($25,000) and ending ($15,000) direct materials inventory balances shown above, the total cost of direct materials used ($30,000) can be determined as follows (a previous journal entry also recorded the cost of direct materials issued to production of $30,000):

Direct Materials Inventory		Beginning Direct Materials Inventory	$25,000
25,000		Purchases	20,000
		Direct Materials Available	$45,000
20,000	30,000	Ending Direct Materials Inventory	(15,000)
15,000		Direct Materials Used	$30,000

The direct materials used represents the cost of the direct materials inventory that has been issued into production (i.e., the costs have been accumulated with work-in-process inventory). Once the cost of the direct materials used has been determined, Ace Construction would identify the total cost of its direct labor and overhead from its accounting records. Recall from previous journal entries that total direct labor and overhead costs for January 20x1 were $11,600 and $17,400, respectively. At this point, Ace Construction Company can prepare the Cost of Goods Manufactured Statement shown in Illustration 6. Note that this statement reflects an analysis of the Work-in-Process-Control account, as shown below:

Illustration 6
Ace Construction Company
Cost of Goods Manufactured Statement
for the Month Ended January 31, 20x1

Beginning Work-in-Process Inventory		$ 3,600
Total Manufacturing Costs:		
Beginning Direct Materials	$ 25,000	
Direct Materials Purchases	20,000	
Direct Materials Available	45,000	
Ending Direct Materials	(15,000)	
Direct Materials Used	30,000	
Direct Labor Costs	11,600	
Manufacturing Overhead Costs	17,400	59,000
Goods Available for Completion		$62,600
Less: Ending Work-in-Process Inventory		(13,000)
Cost of Goods Manufactured		$49,600

As noted earlier, the cost of goods manufactured represents the cost of units completed during the period by the organization and transferred to finished goods inventory.

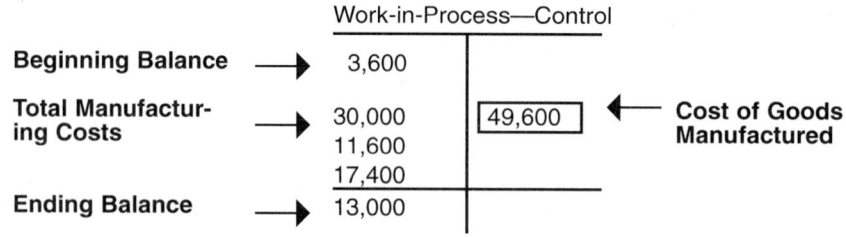

Cost of Goods Sold Statement

Analogous to the Cost of Goods Manufactured Statement, Ace Construction Company can prepare a *Cost of Goods Sold Statement* to analyze changes in its finished goods inventory account during the month of January 20x1. The transactions that affect finished goods inventory include:

- Beginning and ending balances in finished goods inventory.
- The cost of goods manufactured (transfers from work-in-process inventory to finished goods inventory).
- The cost of items sold to the organization's customers.

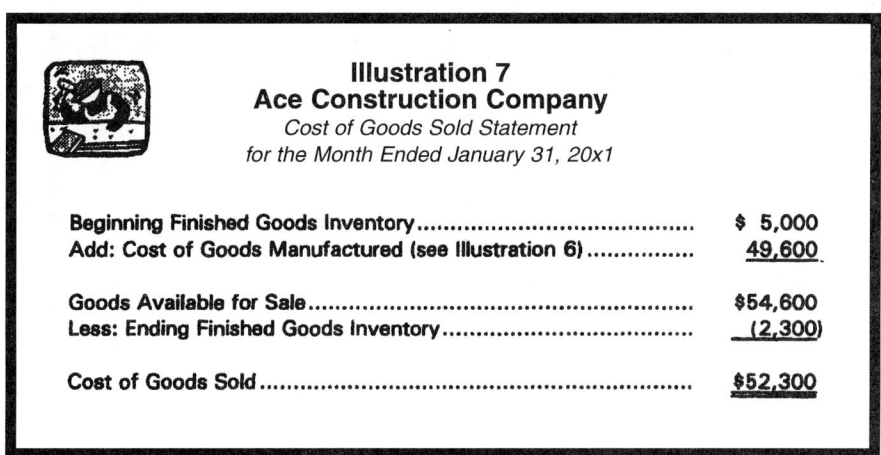

Illustration 7
Ace Construction Company
Cost of Goods Sold Statement
for the Month Ended January 31, 20x1

Beginning Finished Goods Inventory	$ 5,000
Add: Cost of Goods Manufactured (see Illustration 6)	49,600
Goods Available for Sale	$54,600
Less: Ending Finished Goods Inventory	(2,300)
Cost of Goods Sold	$52,300

The Cost of Goods Sold Statement for Ace Construction Company for the month of January 20x1 is shown in Illustration 7. This statement summarizes the total costs of producing items sold to Ace's customers and mirrors the Finished Goods Inventory-Control account as follows.

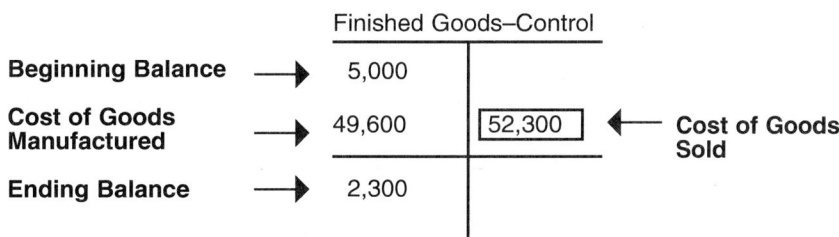

Once the cost of goods sold has been determined, Ace Construction Company can prepare its Balance Sheet and Income Statement for the month of January. Unlike the Cost of Goods Manufactured and Cost of Goods Sold Statements illustrated earlier, these statements are provided to external users (such as creditors and investors) for their use in making decisions with respect to Ace Construction Company. Assume that in addition to the cost of goods sold of $52,300 Ace Construction Company had nonmanufacturing expenses (period costs) totaling $10,000. Recalling that total sales revenue for Ace Construction Company during January 20x1 was $68,500, the Income Statement and partial Balance Sheet for Ace Construction Company are shown in Illustration 8.

> **Illustration 8**
> *Ace Construction Company*
> *Income Statement*
> *For the Month Ended January 31, 20x1*
>
> | | |
> |---|---:|
> | Sales Revenue .... | $ 68,500 |
> | Less: Cost of Goods Sold (see Illustration 7) .... | (52,300) |
> | Gross Profit .... | $ 16,200 |
> | Less: Nonmanufacturing Costs .... | (10,000) |
> | Net Income .... | $ 6,200 |
>
> *Ace Construction Company*
> *Balance Sheet (partial)*
> *At January 31, 20x1*
>
> **Current Assets:**
>
> **Inventories:**
>
> | | | |
> |---|---:|---:|
> | Direct Materials .... | $ 15,000 | |
> | Work-in-Process .... | 13,000 | |
> | Finished Goods .... | 2,300 | $30,300 |

SUMMARY: THE ACE CONSTRUCTION COMPANY

Illustration 9 summarizes the cost flows for Ace Construction Company during the month of January 20x1. It is important to summarize the major steps and cost flows in the manufacturing/sales process.

1. The organization purchases direct materials inventory and accumulates these costs in the direct materials inventory account.
2. The organization issues direct materials to production upon receipt of a customer order. The cost of the direct materials used is transferred from the direct materials inventory account to the work-in-process inventory account.
3. Direct labor and overhead costs are incurred and accumulated with the work-in-process inventory account.
4. As production is completed, costs are transferred from work-in-process inventory to finished goods inventory. The total cost of units completed during a period is known as the cost of goods manufactured.
5. When inventory is sold to the organization's customers, the costs are transferred from finished goods inventory to cost of goods sold.

In this chapter, we illustrated the use of job-order costing for a manufacturing company (Ace Construction Company). As noted throughout, the key characteristic of a company using job-order costing is that its products require different amounts of materials, labor, and overhead costs. In addition to manufacturing companies, service companies may also use job-order costing to determine the costs required to provide services to their customers. For example, automobile garages require different amounts of direct labor (from service technicians) and supplies on their different repair jobs. Similarly, law firms require their employees to track the hours they work serving various clients to ensure that these clients are billed for all services worked on their behalf. While neither of these types of organizations manufactures inventory (or products), it is critical that they identify the costs of providing services to their customers. Since each service requires different amounts and types of labor and other inputs, job-order costing would be appropriate in these instances as well.

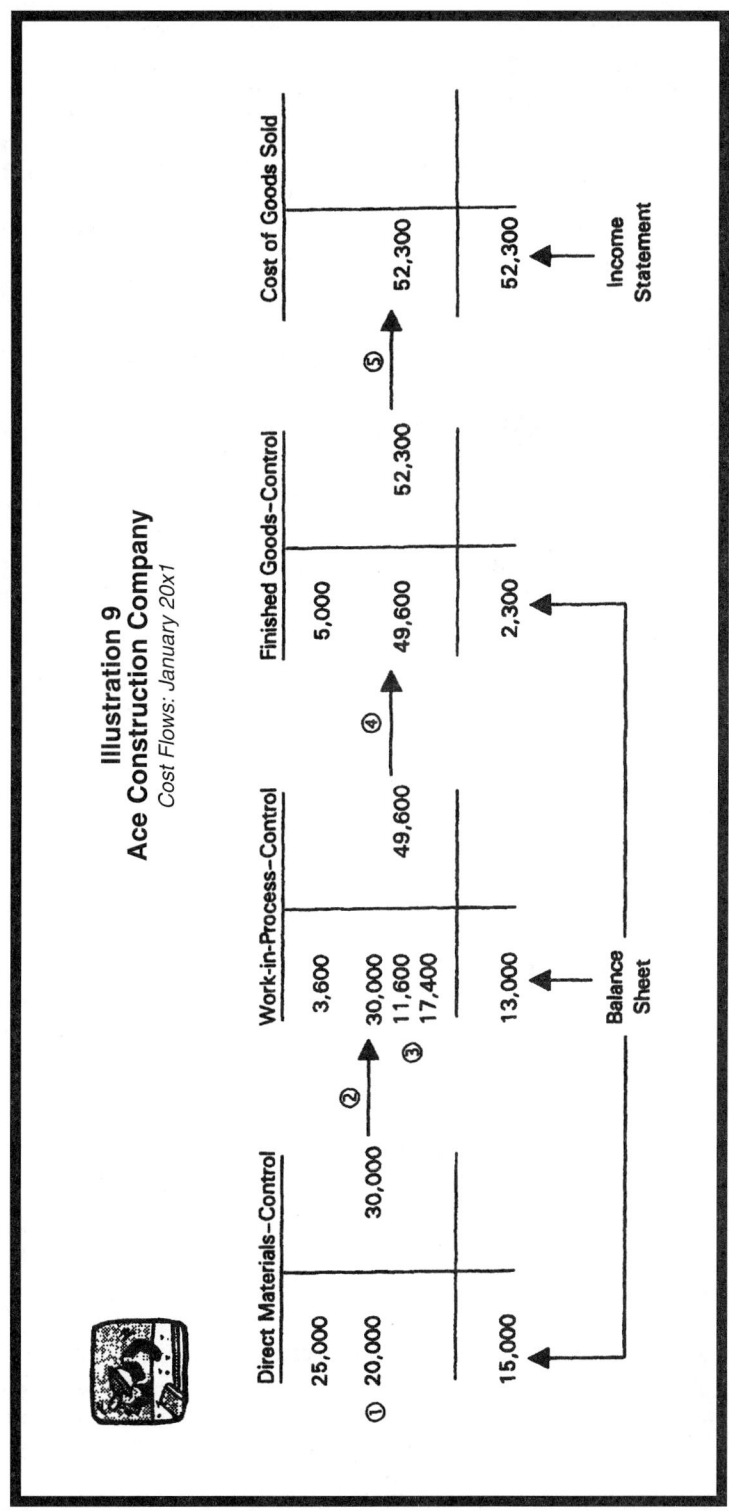

Job-order companies may find that their production systems become "overstressed" by the myriad product variations that customers demand. The following excerpt describes how Boeing is attempting to limit the options it provides to customers in an effort to increase its operating efficiency.

> An airplane has over 4 million parts and 170 miles of wiring, making its production highly complex. Prior to the implementation of a new manufacturing process, Boeing's assembly lines could only be characterized as inefficient. Airplanes were built like customized houses, with airlines having a choice of 109 shades of white paint and 20,000 galley and lavatory arrangements. In addition, because of these highly customized options, Boeing had to maintain millions of dollars of spare parts to accommodate the large number of possible configurations.
>
> Recent changes in Boeing's manufacturing process (an unnamed acronym DCAC/MRM) created a more limited set of standardized customer options. The reduction in these options has reduced the number of parts that Boeing needs to stock and has also decreased the man-hours per aircraft from 30,000 to 6,500.[8]

USING MANAGERIAL ACCOUNTING INFORMATION: ACE CONSTRUCTION COMPANY

In this chapter, the cost accumulation and cost flows for Ace Construction Company were summarized. The purpose of cost accumulation is to allow Ace Construction Company to determine the cost of producing or manufacturing its inventory. This cost is summarized in the Job Cost Sheet shown earlier in Illustration 5. How can Ace Construction's management use the information in Illustration 5? While several possibilities exist, two are:

1. Ace Construction Company can use this information in its product pricing decisions. For example, assume that Ace wishes to earn a 10 percent return on its construction jobs. If so, Ace would charge John Guerra $1,980 ($1,800 x 1.10 = $1,980) for Job JG-0105. Since the Job Cost Sheet is an internal source document, the customer would not be aware of Ace Construction Company's actual manufacturing costs.

2. Once the above cost information has been accumulated, Ace can use it to evaluate the performance of its personnel. For example, assume that Ace expected Job JG-0105 to require 210 pieces of lumber at a cost of $4.80 per piece. If so, Ace's laborers appeared to perform efficiently, as the job was completed using 10 fewer pieces of lumber (200 pieces used versus 210 pieces expected) than planned. Conversely, it appears that Ace Construction Company's purchasing personnel paid an excessive amount for its materials inputs ($5.00 per piece versus $4.80 per piece). The labor and overhead costs incurred by Ace on this job can be evaluated in a similar manner. This is an example of the control function of management. The use of performance standards and budgets for control purposes is discussed further in subsequent chapters.

SUMMARY

Chapter 3 introduces the concept of cost accumulation and discusses the types of costs incurred by a manufacturing organization. In addition, a job-order costing system is introduced and illustrated. Some important concepts presented in this chapter are summarized below:

1. *Cost accumulation* is the process through which the organization identifies and determines the costs associated with manufacturing its inventory or providing its services. Cost accumulation is important in both allowing the organization to prepare its financial statements and providing management with important information to make decisions relating to the organization's products.

2. There are two main types of cost accumulation systems. In a *job-order costing* system, manufacturing costs are accumulated with individual jobs or units of inventory. In contrast, *process costing* systems accumulate manufacturing costs with batches (or larger quantities) of inventory. Job-order costing is normally used when inventory items require different amounts and types of materials and labor inputs.

3. The major steps in the manufacturing/sales process include: (1) obtaining direct materials inventory, (2) incurring manufacturing costs, (3) completing production, and (4) selling inventory to customers. When

---

[8] Jerry Useem, "Boeing vs. Boeing," *Fortune* (October 2, 2000), 152, 160.

purchased from vendors, the cost of direct materials is initially accumulated in the *Direct Materials-Control* account. Direct materials inventories represent the cost of materials inputs that have not been issued into production.

4. Upon the initiation of the manufacturing process, direct materials are issued to production. In addition to direct materials costs, other manufacturing costs (such as direct labor costs and manufacturing overhead costs) are initially accumulated in the *Work-in-Process-Control* account. Work-in-process inventory represents items that have been started in production but have not yet been completed.

5. As inventory is completed, the cost of the inventory is transferred from work-in-process to the *Finished Goods-Control* account. Finished goods inventory represents items that have been completed but are not yet sold to customers. Thus, a manufacturing company has three types of inventories: direct materials, work-in-process, and finished goods. The cost of goods completed during any period is referred to as the cost of goods manufactured.

6. Finally, when inventory is sold to customers, the matching principle dictates that the cost of the inventory is expensed in the period of the sale. These costs are expensed by transferring them from the Finished Goods-Control account to *Cost of Goods Sold*. Cost of Goods Sold represents the cost of manufacturing items (or providing services) that have been sold to customers during the period.

KEY DEFINITIONS

Cost of goods manufactured–the total cost of inventory completed during a specific period. The cost of goods manufactured represents the costs transferred from work-in-process inventory to finished goods inventory.
Cost of goods sold–the cost of inventory sold (or services provided) to the organization's customers during a specific period. The cost of goods manufactured represents the cost transferred from finished goods inventory upon sale of the inventory.
Finished goods inventory–inventory that is totally complete in the manufacturing process and is ready for sale to the organization's customers.
Job-order costing–a cost accumulation process in which manufacturing costs are accumulated with individual units of inventory (or individual jobs).
Overhead rate–a rate calculated by dividing expected overhead costs by an expected volume of activity (or cost driver). This rate is used to apply overhead to inventory as it is being manufactured.
Process costing–a cost accumulation system that accumulates manufacturing costs by manufacturing process (or batch of units).
Work-in-process inventory–inventory on which production has begun but is not yet completed.

QUESTIONS

1. Is cost accumulation important for external reporting purposes? For internal decision-making purposes?

2. Indicate whether each of the following businesses would use a job order costing system or a process costing system:

    a. A house-painting firm
    b. A shipbuilding company
    c. A toy manufacturer
    d. A gasoline filling station
    e. A custom home builder
    f. A book publisher
    g. A salt producer
    h. An automobile manufacturer
    i. An architectural firm

3. What internal decisions would rely on the process of cost accumulation?

4. How is cost accumulation necessary for the preparation of an organization's financial statements?

5. At what point in the manufacturing/sales process does the organization expense the costs of manufacturing its inventory?

6. Briefly describe each of the major steps in the manufacturing process. In doing so, indicate any cost accumulations or cost flows associated with that step.

7. Costs that cannot be directly traced (related) to a product (for example, building depreciation) are classified as overhead. Does it follow then that all costs that can be directly traced (related) to a product are not overhead?

8. Why is it difficult to accumulate actual overhead costs with the inventory manufactured by the organization?

9. How does the organization accumulate overhead costs with inventory as it is manufactured?

10. Define cost of goods manufactured and cost of goods sold. In terms of cost flows, what do each of these amounts represent?

11. What information appears on a Cost of Goods Manufactured Statement? On a Cost of Goods Sold Statement?

12. What are the three types of inventory accounts used by a manufacturing company? Define each type of inventory.

13. What is the general flow of costs through the three types of inventory accounts in a cost accounting system?

14. On what basis are costs accumulated in a job-order costing system? What is the primary document used to accumulate these costs?

EXERCISES AND PROBLEMS

15. *Traceable Costs vs. Nontraceable Costs.* Overhead costs arise because: (1) costs cannot be physically traced to factory jobs, or (2) costs can be traced but the expense of monitoring them is prohibitive. For each of the following manufacturing costs indicate: (1) if it is traceable or not traceable, and (2) if it is traceable, whether it is justifiable in terms of cost. Use the terms *traceable* or *not traceable* and *justifiable* or *not justifiable* as your answer.

    a. Direct materials
    b. Maintenance on the factory building
    c. Packing tape used in wrapping the product
    d. Electricity used for lighting the factory
    e. Electricity used to operate power tools
    f. A foreman's salary
    g. The corporate president's salary
    h. The salary of a craftsman working in the factory
    i. The time that a craftsman spends between factory jobs on a coffee break
    j. The salary of a managerial accountant working in the factory

16. *Cost Accumulation—General.* The Wayco Company has received an order to build some large concrete ducks for a contractor who wants to place them in the lake of a housing development so that boat owners have a place to anchor in the lake to fish. The order should take two months to complete. During the first month, $600 worth of material and $700 worth of labor are used. During the next month, $800 in material and $900 in labor are used. The factory overhead rate is 100 percent of direct labor and it is applied whenever direct labor is used.

Required:

a. What type of cost accumulation system should be used by the Wayco Company? Briefly explain why.
b. What amount should appear in the total column of the cost sheet at the end of the first month?
c. What amount should appear in the total column of the cost sheet at the end of the second month? Prepare a sample cost sheet for the second month.
d. If the other type of cost accounting system were used, what would be the amount in the total column at the end of the second month?

17. *Cost Accumulation—Inventories.* A clerk in a job shop was told to verify that all source documents were accounted for. He thereupon unstapled all documents from the Job Cost Sheets, placed the Work Tickets and Material Requisitions in descending numerical order, and promptly lost the Job Cost Sheets. The clerk did know, however, that overhead was applied at the rate of $2 for every $1 of direct labor cost. The clerk produced the following summary report on his verification task:

Material Requisitions			Work Tickets		
Number	Amount	Job	Number	Amount	Job
MR455	$230	#104	WT 56	$90	#105
MR456	$130	#105	WT 57	$20	#104
MR457	$100	#105	WT 58	$70	#106
MR458	$200	#103	WT 59	$60	#104
MR459	$170	#103	WT 60	$40	#103
MR460	$110	#104	WT 61	$50	#106
MR461	$100	#106	WT 62	$10	#103

At the end of the month, Job No. 105 is still in the shop. Job Nos. 103 and 104 are in the finished-goods storeroom, and Job No. 106 has been delivered to the customer.

Determine the ending balances for work-in-process inventory, finished-goods inventory, and cost of goods sold.

18. *Cost Flows—Cost of Goods Manufactured.* The work-in-process account for Rudi, Inc. had a $25,000 balance on June 1, 20x2. During June, Rudi incurred $40,000 of direct materials costs and $60,000 of direct labor costs. Overhead was applied at a rate of 50 percent of direct labor costs.

Assuming that the balance in the work-in-process account was $40,000 at June 30, 20x2, what is the cost of goods manufactured for June?

19. *Cost Flows—Cost of Goods Manufactured.* The cost of goods manufactured calculation follows a known relationship. In each of the following four independent cases, determine the missing numbers for each of the letters A through G.

	Case 1	Case 2	Case 3	Case 4
Cost in Beginning Inventory	$1,000	$ C	$2,000	$2,000
Costs Added to Production	8,000	6,000	E	9,000
Costs Available for Manufacturing	$9,000	$9,000	D	F
Cost in Ending Inventory	2,000	B	$1,000	G
Cost of Goods Manufactured	$ A	$7,000	$8,000	$6,000

20. *Cost Flows—Cost of Goods Sold.* Complete each of the following partial Cost of Goods Sold Statements for Aaron Company:

	Case 1	Case 2	Case 3
Beginning Finished Goods	$15,000	B	$10,000
Add: Cost of Goods Manufactured	28,000	$40,000	D
Goods Available for Sale	A	$70,000	E
Less: Ending Finished Goods	(20,000)	C	(25,000)
Cost of Goods Sold	$23,000	$50,000	$70,000

21. *Cost Flows—Cost of Goods Manufactured and Cost of Goods Sold.* Assume that Dolphin Corporation had the following beginning inventory balances: work-in-process, $10,000, and finished goods, $20,000. During 20x2, Dolphin incurred $70,000 of production costs. Its ending balances were as follows: work-in-process, $25,000 and finished goods, $15,000. What were cost of goods manufactured and cost of goods sold for Dolphin Corporation during 20x2?

22. *Cost Flows—Materials Used and Cost of Goods Manufactured.* At the beginning of 20x1, White Company had direct materials inventories totaling $10,000 and work-in-process inventory with an accumulated cost of $15,000. During 20xl, White purchased $60,000 of direct materials and incurred total production costs (including direct materials costs, direct labor costs, and applied overhead costs) of $140,000. At the end of 20x1, White's physical inventories revealed that direct materials costing $12,000 and work-in-process with an accumulated cost of $30,000 were on hand at year-end.

    Required: Determine the following subtotals:

    a. The cost of direct materials used in production during 20x1.
    b. The cost of goods manufactured for White Company during 20x1.

23. *Cost Flows—Various.* The beginning and ending inventories for Blake Company are as follows:

	January 1	December 31
Direct Materials	$15,000	$22,000
Work-in-Process	20,000	17,500
Finished Goods	12,000	18,000

    The cost of goods sold during the year is $58,000. Direct labor costs are $20,000 and overhead of $10,000 is applied during the year.

    Required: Compute the following totals:

    a. Cost of goods manufactured
    b. Total manufacturing costs
    c. Cost of direct materials used during the year
    d. Direct materials purchased during the year

24. *Cost Flows—Production Costs, Cost of Goods Manufactured, Cost of Goods Sold.* Schroeder Company had the following balances in its inventory accounts as of January 1, 20x2:

Direct Materials	$20,000
Work-in-Process	30,000
Finished Goods	45,000

    Direct material purchases during 20x2 amounted to $55,000. In addition, Schroeder sold inventory costing $100,000 for $120,000 to its customers during 20x2.

    At December 31, 20x2, a physical inventory and summation of the Job Cost Sheets revealed that Schroeder had the following inventory balances:

Direct Materials	$30,000
Work-In-Process	50,000
Finished Goods	75,000

    Required:

    a. What were cost of goods manufactured during 20x2?
    b. Given your answer to (a) above, what were total production costs during 20x2?
    c. Prepare a Cost of Goods Manufactured Statement and a Cost of Goods Sold Statement for Schroeder Company for the year ended December 31, 20x2.

25. *Cost Flows—Cost of Goods Manufactured.* The Burro Excavating Company uses a job-order costing system to account for its customer orders. At the beginning of the current year, the company had an inventory of direct materials valued at $102,000. Purchases of materials (mostly shoring timbers) during the year totaled $56,000. During the year, $6,000 of materials and $10,000 of labor were used to constrict an executive swimming pool at the main office of Burro Excavating. It was estimated that the pool would last for ten years and would provide a valuable service to the company by enabling the executives to stay in good physical condition.

During the year, total direct labor costs were $415,000. Materials valued at $14,000 were used in overhead operations during the year. Maintenance employees were paid $39,000, and the executives' salaries, including bonuses, were $142,000. Miscellaneous overhead expenses totaled $73,000. The year-end inventory revealed that the direct materials inventory was $84,000. At the beginning of the year, two jobs were in process; Job Order No. 916, which had costs of $47,000, and Job Order No. 917, which had a total cost of $87,000. During the year, Job Order Nos. 917, 918, and 919 were completed, leaving Job Order No. 916 in process at year's end, with $93,000 of associated costs.

Using the information above, construct a Cost of Goods Manufactured Statement for the Burro Excavating Company. Of what use is this statement to the company?

26. *Cost Flows—Account Balances and Journal Entries.* The Hawley Manufacturing Company, which custom-builds boats, is currently processing two major orders for which it is using job-order costing. Job Order No. 100 is assigned to the first boat and Job Order No. 101 to the second boat. The following transactions occurred during the first month of production on these orders:

1. Wood and metal fittings were purchased for $4,000 and $5,000, respectively.
2. Metal fittings totaling $1,000 were issued to Job Order No. 100 and $2,500 of metal fittings to Job Order No. 101.
3. The total payroll was $4,000, incurred as follows: Job Order No. 100, $2,000; Job Order No. 101, $1,000; overhead, $600; and selling expense, $400.
4. Sail cloth was purchased for $3,000. All sail cloth was required for Job Order No. 100 except for $500 worth, which was kept in the inventory for future use.
5. Issued $500 of wood to Job Order No. 100 and $600 of metal fittings to Job Order No. 101.
6. Various additional indirect factory costs amounted to $5,000.
7. Overhead is allocated to both Job Order Nos. 100 and 101 at the predetermined rate of 100 percent of direct labor costs.
8. Job Order No. 100 is finished and delivered to the customer.

27. *Cost Flows—Various.* The following inventory data relate to the Shober Corporation.

	Inventories	
	Ending	Beginning
Finished Goods	$95,000	$110,000
Work-in-Process	80,000	70,000
Direct Materials	95,000	90,000

In addition, the following information is known.

Cost of Goods Available for Sale	$684,000
Total Manufacturing Costs to Account for	654,000
Applied Factory Overhead	167,000
Direct Materials Used	193,000

Required: Determine the following amounts:

a. Direct materials purchased during the year.
b. Direct labor costs incurred during the period.
c. The cost of goods sold during the period.

28. Journal Entries.

a. Make the appropriate journal entry to record each of the following events relating to the Bright Idea Lamp Company.

June 1   Purchased direct materials on account. The invoice price was $17,400.
June 10   The factory payroll of $4,210 was paid in cash. A foreman estimated that 20 percent of the payroll related to overhead tasks.
June 16 $6,230 of material was released directly into production. Also, $2,910 of material was used in an overhead operation.
June 17   Overhead, which is assigned at a rate of 10 percent of direct labor cost, was allocated to production.

b. Refer again to part (a). What source or support documents would you look for to document the events that occurred on each date?

29. Journal Entries.
Devon Corporation entered into the following transactions during 20x2, its first year of operations:

1. Devon purchased 5,000 pounds of direct materials for use in production. The purchase price of $15,000 was paid for in cash.
2. Three thousand pounds of direct materials were issued to production for the following jobs: Job No. 101 (2,000 pounds) and Job No. 102 (1,000 pounds).
3. Devon incurred direct labor costs in producing Job Nos. 101 and 102. Devon's employees worked a total of 100 hours on Job No. 101 and 50 hours on Job No. 102. The charge for direct labor was $10 per hour.
4. Devon allocated overhead to the production based on 50 percent of the direct labor costs.
5. Job No. 101 was completed and transferred to finished goods.

Required.
a. Prepare all necessary journal entries for Devon Corporation.
b. What is the total cost accumulated with Job No. 101? Job No. 102?

30. Journal Entries.
Wally, Inc. is a manufacturer of custom-made furniture. The following information is available concerning the transactions of Wally during January 20x2, its first month of operations.

1. Purchased direct materials for use in production. The total purchase price of $20,000 was paid in cash.
2. Direct materials costing $9,000 were issued into production.
3. Wally incurred direct labor costs of $10,000 during January of 20x2. Also, assume that Wally applies overhead costs at a rate of 200 percent of direct labor costs.
4. Wally completed Job No. 1000, which had a total accumulated cost of $16,000. This job was transferred to finished goods inventory.
5. Wally sold Job No. 1000 for $28,000. The proceeds were received in cash.

Required:
Prepare journal entries for Wally, Inc. for the month of January.

31. Journal Entries and Account Balances.
During its first month of operations, Suns Corporation had the following transactions.

1. Purchased raw materials for $15,000.
2. Transferred $5,000 of raw materials to production.
3. Direct labor costs totaling $14,000 were paid in cash; total overhead costs applied to work-in-process (which were based on direct labor costs) were $5,000.
4. Total cost of goods completed and transferred to finished goods was $13,000.
5. Total cost of goods sold was $8,000.

Required:
a. Prepare the necessary journal entries for the above transactions.
b. Determine the ending balances in the work-in-process and finished goods inventory accounts at the end of the month.

32. *Job Order Cost Documents.* Part of the managerial accounting reporting system for Permanent Design, Inc., is diagramed below.

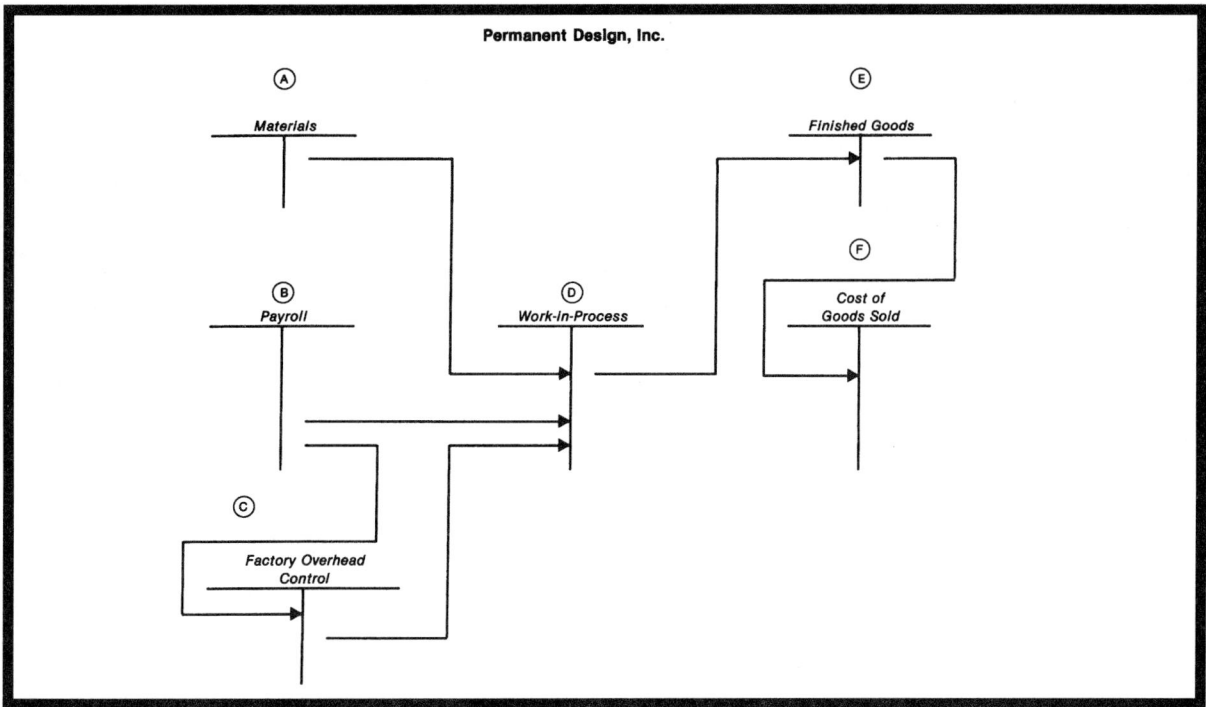

Required:
a. What documentation authorizes the flow from A to D? What documentation authorizes the flow from B to D? From C to D?
b. Why is factory overhead (C) handled differently from payroll or material? What happens when factory overhead applied is different from factory overhead control?
c. What documentation authorizes the flow from D to E? From E to F? Which individual could authorize these flows?
d. Manufacturing companies usually have three inventories. What are they called? Why are three inventories needed? Why isn't payroll considered an inventory (or is it)?

33. *Job Cost Sheet.* The Stor Moore Company manufactures custom-made cabinets on order for a select clientele. Since the underlying production processes are uniform (although each customer order is unique), manufacturing operations are organized into departments. A Job Cost Sheet is used to record the manufacturing costs associated with each job. One such sheet is exhibited on page 3-24.

Required:
a. Which of the departments in the Stor Moore Company has the highest direct labor cost? Which department has the greatest prime cost?
b. How can direct material be requisitioned for Department C on 9/11/x4, when no direct labor was reported on that date? Doesn't it take some labor to transport material?
c. What overhead rate and base were used to assign overhead costs to factory orders? Can this procedure cause problems in projecting future costs? What happens when the firm's accountant attempts to match costs to the time periods in which they were incurred?
d. What documentation supports the direct material amounts entered on the Job Cost Sheet? What documentation supports the direct labor figures entered on the job cost sheet?
e. Is $25,000 a good selling price for this product? Why or why not?

Stor Moore Company
Job Cost Sheet

Job Order No.: 152
Date Started: 9/7/x4
Date Completed: 12/15/x4

Date	Department A	Department B	Department C	Total
Direct Materials				
9/1/x4	$ 2,407.50	$1,504.50	$ 705.40	$ 4,617.40
10/1/x4	1,600.20	1,210.00	501.50	3,311.70
Totals	$ 4,007.70	$2,714.50	$1,206.90	$ 7,929.10
Direct Labor				
9/30/x4	$ 500.42			$ 500.42
10/28/x4	700.50	$ 500.50		1,201.00
11/30/x4	800.00	1,142.00	$1,500.42	3,442.42
Totals	$ 2,000.92	$1,642.50	$1,500.42	$ 5,143.84
Factory Overhead				
9/30/x4	$ 1,000.84			$ 1,000.84
10/28/x4	1,401.00	$1,001.00		2,402.00
11/30/x4	1,600.00	2,284.00	$3,000.84	6,884.84
Totals	$ 4,001.84	$3,285.00	$3,000.84	$10,287.68

Summary

	Department A	Department B	Department C	Total
Selling Price				$25,000.00
Cost:				
Direct Materials	$ 4,007.70	$2,714.50	$1,206.90	$ 7,929.10
Direct Labor	2,000.92	1,642.50	1,500.42	5,143.84
Factory Overhead	4,001.84	3,285.00	3,000.84	10,287.68
	$10,010.46	$7,642.00	$5,708.16	$23,360.62
Gross Profit				$ 1,639.38

34. *Job-Order Costing—Basic Product Costs.* The Schrader Company builds modular houses. Three models are currently being built: Job Order Nos. 251, 252, and 253. The following information relates to these job orders:

	Job No. 251	Job No. 252	Job No. 253
Materials Requisitioned	$4,500	$3,200	$3,500
Units Completed	10	8	7
Labor Hours	1,000	900	750

The company pays the workers $10 an hour and assigns overhead on the basis of direct labor hours. The Schrader Company expects to have a labor payroll of $500,000 this year and $1,000,000 in overhead costs.

Required:

Using this information, calculate the following:

a. The total cost of each job order.
b. The per-unit cost of each job order.
c. The per-unit selling price of each job order, if the company intends to set a price equal to 200 percent of cost.

35. *Entries and Income Statement Preparation.* Delta, Inc. had the following inventories at the beginning of 20x2:

Direct Materials:	10,000 pounds of A (cost of $5 per pound)	
Work-in-Process:	Job No. 101	$15,000
	Job No. 102	6,000
	Job No. 103	4,000
		$25,000
Finished Goods:	Job No. 99	$13,000
	Job No. 100	8,000
		$21,000

The following transactions occurred during January of 20x2:

January 2	Purchased an additional 4,000 pounds of direct materials. The invoice price of $20,000 was paid in cash.
January 8	Issued 7,000 pounds of direct materials into production. These materials were allocated as follows: Job No. 101 (2,000 pounds) and Job No. 104 (5,000 pounds).
January 15	Incurred total direct labor costs of $10,000 (2,000 hours at $5 per hour). The labor costs were allocated as follows: Job No. 101 (200 hours); Job No. 102 (500 hours); and Job No. 104 (1,300 hours). Assume that overhead was also applied at the rate of $2 per direct labor hour.
January 16	Transferred Job Nos. 101 and 102 (which were completed) to finished goods inventory.
January 20	Sold Job Nos. 99, 100, and 101 for a total of $75,000. The sale was made on account.
January 31	Direct labor costs for the last half of January were $4,000. These costs were all incurred to continue work on Job No. 103. Overhead for the 800 direct labor hours worked in the last half of January was also applied to Job No. 103 at the predetermined rate of $2 per direct labor hour.

Required:

a. Prepare journal entries to record the above transactions.
b. Prepare an Income Statement (in good form) for Delta, Inc, for the month ended January 31, 20x2.

36. *Comprehensive—Journal Entries and Statement Preparation.* Jones Star, Inc. manufactures custom-made furniture based on orders taken from its customers. On October 3 its inventories were as follows: direct materials, $30,000; work-in-process (Job No. 1000), $18,000; and finished goods (Job No. 999), $28,000. Jones began production of Job Nos. 1001, 1002, and 1003 during November. Direct materials costs and direct labor costs incurred during November were as follows:

	Direct Materials	Direct Labor
Job No. 1000	$1,000	$2,000
Job No. 1001	2,000	5,000
Job No. 1002	3,000	7,500
Job No. 1003	8,000	4,000

Jones Star, Inc. applies overhead costs at a rate of $10 per direct labor hour. Direct labor costs during November were $5 per hour. During November, Job Nos. 1000, 1002, and 1003 were completed and transferred to finished goods. Job Nos. 999, 1000, and 1002 were sold for a total of $75,000, which was received in cash.

Required:

a. Prepare journal entries to record the following events:

1. Production costs incurred during November.
2. Transfer of completed jobs to finished goods.
3. Sale of Job Nos. 999, 1000, and 1002.

b. Assuming that there were no purchases of direct materials during November, prepare the following statements for Jones Star, Inc. for the month of November, 20x2.

1. Cost of Goods Manufactured Statement
2. Cost of Goods Sold Statement
3. Income Statement

Learning Objectives

In Chapter 3, cost accumulation for companies using a job-order costing system was introduced. Chapter 4 illustrates cost accumulation for companies with continuous manufacturing processes. The method of cost accumulation used by these companies is referred to as process costing. Studying this chapter should enable you to:

1. Distinguish between the nature of continuous manufacturing processes and discrete manufacturing processes.
2. List the basic steps in a process costing system.
3. Calculate equivalent units of production.
4. Determine a cost per unit and accumulate manufacturing costs with inventory as it moves through various stages of the manufacturing/sales process.
5. Allocate manufacturing costs among different inventory products manufactured in a joint manufacturing process.
6. Discuss the just-in-time manufacturing philosophy and identify the major characteristics of a just-in-time manufacturing philosophy.

4

Process Costing

INTRODUCTION

After studying the previous chapter on cost accumulation, Jeffrey Jones (an accounting major) understood why manufacturing companies accumulated their manufacturing costs with inventory. Jeffrey worked part-time for The American Vegetable Company, a regional manufacturing company that produces vegetables for sale to grocery stores, restaurants, and other dining establishments in the northwest United States. Jeffrey had the following conversation with his boss, Jack Evans, about what he had learned in his accounting courses:

Jeffrey: We just learned about cost accumulation in class. You know, if we knew the costs of producing our vegetable products, we'd have a much better idea of how much we should charge our customers. We could also use that information to see if we are using excess vegetables in production or not working efficiently in producing vegetable products.

Jack: That sounds like a good idea, but there's one catch—we don't produce vegetables on a can-by-can basis. There's just no way we can identify the costs of producing a can of vegetables. It's simply too difficult.

Jeffrey: You know, I didn't think about that. We talked about a construction company in class. Each of its jobs was done on a one-by-one basis and costs could be specifically identified with a particular job. Also, because each job was so different, it was really important for the company to determine the actual cost of a job so that it would know how much to charge its customers.

Jack: Well, that's a lot different from our situation. A can of peas is a can of peas. I'm really not too worried about how much it costs to produce a specific can of peas. But it would be useful for us to know some average cost per can. Why don't you ask your accounting professor how we can track our manufacturing costs?

AN OVERVIEW OF PROCESS COSTING

Consider the type of manufacturing process described in the opening dialogue between Jeffrey Jones and Jack Evans, both of whom work for The American Vegetable Company. In producing canned vegetable products, American Vegetable obtains raw vegetables (direct materials) and then incurs direct labor costs and overhead costs in producing its inventory. An important difference between this type of process and that used by Ace Construction Company (described in the preceding chapter) is that Ace's production occurs over a number of different jobs that require substantially different materials, labor, and overhead costs. In contrast, The American Vegetable Company's production is done continuously (or semicontinuously) in "batches" of items (cans of vegetables), each of which requires approximately the same materials, labor, and overhead costs. The manufacturing process used by Ace Construction is referred to as a *discrete manufacturing process*, whereas the process used by American Vegetable is known as a *continuous manufacturing process*.

Ace Construction's manufacturing process lends itself to the use of a job-order costing system. In that system, manufacturing costs are accumulated with individual inventory items as they are manufactured. Because of the differences discussed above, The American Vegetable Company's manufacturing process utilizes a process costing system. *Process costing* systems accumulate manufacturing costs with items by manufacturing process (or "batch" of inventory) and not on an individual item-by-item basis. Process costing systems are more feasible for certain types of companies for at least two reasons. First, the production of certain types of inventory does not allow manufacturing costs to be accumulated with individual items in an efficient manner. For example, ExxonMobil Corporation does not refine crude oil to produce gasoline in single gallons. Instead, a large quantity of gasoline is produced at one time. Similarly, Intel Corporation produces numerous computer microchips in one production run. Therefore, the materials, labor, and overhead costs of a single unit of inventory (gallon of gasoline or computer microchip) cannot be easily identified with that individual item.

In addition to the nature of the manufacturing process, the homogeneous nature of certain inventory products makes the accumulation of costs on an item-by-item basis less useful for management. Continuing with the above examples, since gasoline and computer microchips are produced in large quantities, it is not necessary for management to know the cost of a particular *individual gallon of gasoline* or *individual microchip*, since each item should have approximately the same cost. In these situations, a process cost accumulation system is normally more appropriate.

Illustration 1 summarizes the differences in the job-order costing system introduced in Chapter 3 and the process costing systems that are the focus of this chapter.

Illustration 1
Comparison of Job-Order Costing and Process Costing

	Job-Order Costing	Process Costing
Nature of Production Effort	Production occurs separately over multiple jobs	Production occurs continuously in large batches
Amounts and Costs of Materials, Labor, and Overhead	Differ across products	Similar across products
Examples of Companies	Dell Computer Walt Disney General Motors Boeing Company	Coca-Cola ExxonMobil Ben & Jerry's Ice Cream Johnson & Johnson

> Dell Computer Corp. has a manufacturing system that combines the efficiencies of process coating with the customized nature of job-order costing. As partially assembled personal computers move down an assembly line, green and red lights on drawers containing computer components (drives, chips, and boards) let workers know whether parts are installed on the machine. This allows Dell to produce customized products on a continuous basis.[1]

---

[1] A. Serwer, "Michael Dell Rocks," *Fortune* (May 11, 1998), 66.

Despite the differences between process and job-order costing noted above, an important similarity does exist. The cost flows in both types of systems are the same. Therefore, the preparation of journal entries and financial statements discussed in Chapter 3 is identical to that in a process costing system. The only difference is the method of accumulating manufacturing costs with inventory as it is manufactured.

To illustrate cost accumulation in a process costing system, we will describe the production of vegetable products by The American Vegetable Company. American Vegetable produces canned vegetables for sale to grocery stores, restaurants, and other dining establishments in the northwest United States. Its manufacturing process requires activities in two separate departments, the Canning Department and the Packaging Department. The company's manufacturing process is illustrated as follows:

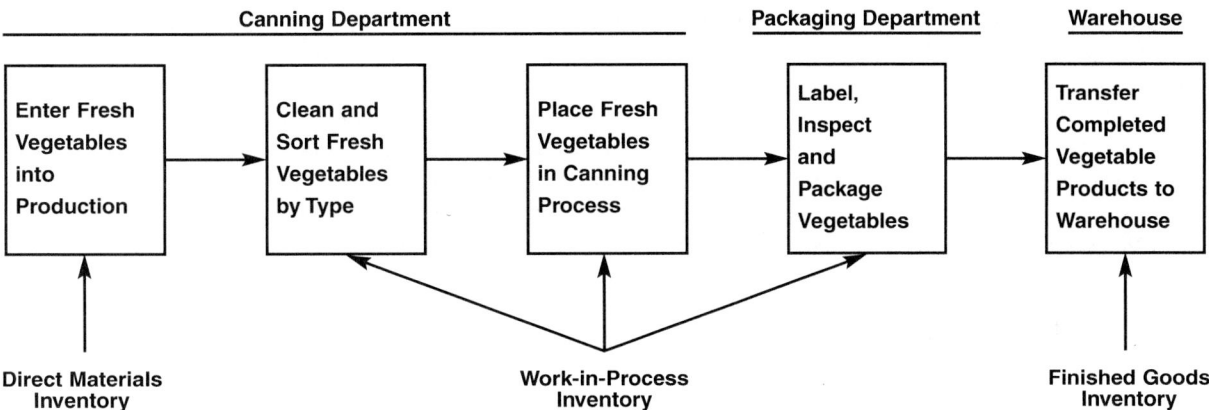

The above process may be summarized as follows:

- Fresh vegetables are purchased from suppliers as direct materials inputs. The cost of these vegetables is a direct material cost. As shown in the above summary, direct materials costs are incurred at the beginning of production in the Canning Department prior to incurring any direct labor or overhead costs.
- Vegetables are cleaned, sorted, and prepared for production by workers at a conveyer belt. The wages paid to these individuals are direct labor costs, since their activities are directly involved in the production of inventory. Costs related to the operation of the conveyer belt (depreciation, repairs, and utilities) as well as the costs of equipment used by employees to clean and prepare the vegetables are overhead costs. In the Canning Department, labor and overhead costs are incurred continuously during the manufacturing process.
- After vegetables are cleaned, sorted, and prepared, they are placed in a mechanized manufacturing process that adds preservatives to the vegetables and prepares them for canning. All three types of manufacturing costs are incurred during this stage of production. The cost of cans is a direct materials cost that is incurred continuously throughout the manufacturing process. In addition, both direct labor costs (the costs of wages paid to personnel operating the canning machinery) and overhead costs (all other manufacturing costs including such costs as the cost of preservatives added to vegetables and costs associated with the production machinery) are incurred continuously throughout the manufacturing process in the Canning Department.
- Once the vegetables have been canned and sealed, they are transferred to the Packaging Department, where they are inspected, labeled, and packaged for delivery to customers. In the Packaging Department, the direct materials costs (cost of labels and packaging),[2] direct labor costs (wages paid to individuals who operate machinery that labels and packages the vegetables) and overhead costs (wages paid to individuals who perform quality inspection and costs associated with machinery and facilities) are incurred throughout the manufacturing process.
- Once completed in the Packaging Department, canned vegetables are transferred to American Vegetable's warehouse for storage until they are sold and delivered to customers.

To determine the cost of producing a can of vegetables, The American Vegetable Company determines the total costs of manufacturing a "batch" of its inventory (materials, labor, and overhead) and then divides this cost by the number of units (cans of vegetables) produced. For example, assume that American Vegetable began a

---

[2] Alternatively, these costs could be considered as indirect materials costs and accumulated with inventory as a type of overhead cost.

production run of 100,000 cans of mixed vegetables. A total of $75,000 of manufacturing costs were incurred in producing this 100,000 can batch, as shown below:

Direct Materials	$30,000
Direct Labor	30,000
Manufacturing Overhead	15,000
	$75,000

Production of all 100,000 cans was completed. Thus, no work-in-process existed at the end of the period. Of the 100,000 cans of vegetables completed, 60,000 were sold to grocery stores at a price of $1.20 per can. Thus, 40,000 cans of vegetables remain in finished goods inventory at the end of the period (100,000 cans – 60,000 cans = 40,000 cans).

The major difference between job-order costing and process costing is the method of accumulating manufacturing costs with inventory. In job-order costing, the cost of inventory was accumulated by each individual product. As that product was completed, its cost (determined from the Job Cost Sheet) was transferred from work-in-process inventory to finished goods inventory. When that product was sold, the cost was then transferred from finished goods inventory to cost of goods sold. In a process costing setting, a *cost per unit* is determined and used to transfer costs as inventory moves through the various stages of the manufacturing/sales process. For The American Vegetable Company, this cost per unit is $0.75 per can, as shown below:

Total Manufacturing Costs	$ 75,000
Number of Cans Produced	÷ 100,000
Manufacturing Cost per Can	$0.75

An overview of the cost flows for The American Vegetable Company is summarized in Illustration 2. From a review of Illustration 2, it is evident that these cost flows are identical to those discussed in the previous chapter for job-order costing. As inventory is produced, the manufacturing costs are accumulated in work-in-process inventory. Once production is completed, these costs are then transferred to finished goods inventory. Finally, upon sale of the inventory to customers, the costs are transferred from finished goods inventory to cost of goods sold.

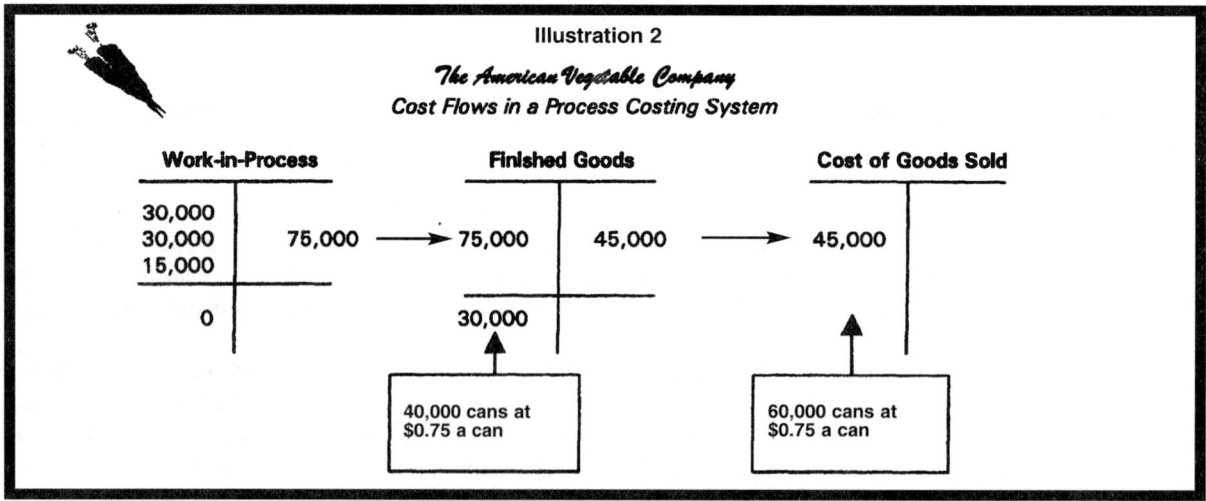

The above example was somewhat simplified as it assumed that no work-in-process inventory existed at either the beginning or end of the period. In reality, these inventories do exist and present certain issues to the managerial accountant in identifying the manufacturing costs of inventory and transferring costs as inventory moves through various stages of the manufacturing/sales process. These issues are discussed in the comprehensive example discussed in the next section of this chapter.

COMPREHENSIVE EXAMPLE: THE AMERICAN VEGETABLE COMPANY

Accumulating costs with products in a process costing system involves a basic five-step procedure that will be illustrated using the production of canned vegetables by The American Vegetable Company. In this example, we focus on the activities of the Canning Department. Assume that American Vegetable produces large, industrial-sized cans of vegetables for sale to restaurants and other dining establishments. These larger cans are produced in smaller batches than American Vegetable's individual-sized cans sold to grocery stores. American Vegetable normally produces these larger-sized cans in batches of 5,000 to 8,000 cans.

At the beginning of January 20x2, The American Vegetable Company had total inventories of $15,120 in its Canning Department, as follows:

Direct Materials inventory	$ 8,000
Work-in-Process Inventory	7,120
	$15,120

The work-in-process inventory at January 1, 20x2 consisted of a 6,000 can batch of vegetables. Because American Vegetable adds all of its materials (vegetables) at the beginning of the manufacturing process in the Canning Department, these 6,000 cans were 100 percent complete with respect to direct materials costs. Based on the costs incurred to date for labor and overhead, American Vegetable estimated that the cans were 30 percent complete with respect to direct labor and manufacturing overhead costs. A total of $7,120 of manufacturing costs have been incurred for the beginning work-in-process inventory as of January 1, 20x2. The composition of these costs is shown in Illustration 3.

Illustration 3

The American Vegetable Company
Beginning Work-in-Process
(6,000 cans)

	Completion	Costs
Direct Materials	100%	$ 5,800
Direct Labor	30%	580
Manufacturing Overhead	30%	740
		$ 7,120

To determine the cost per unit of a can of vegetables, The American Vegetable Company follows the following steps. These steps are discussed in the following subsections:

1. Account for units produced.
2. Determine total manufacturing costs.
3. Determine equivalent units of production.
4. Calculate the cost per unit.
5. Accumulate costs with inventory units.
6. Transfer and completion of production.

Account for Units Produced

When accounting for units produced, the managerial accountant analyzes the flow of production to and from the work-in-process inventory account. Accounting for units produced recognizes that two possibilities exist with respect to items in work-in-process during the period. First, if units are completed, the items themselves (and the costs incurred in manufacturing the items) are transferred from work-in-process inventory to finished goods inventory. Alternatively, if units are not completed, the costs of these items remain in work-in-process inventory at the end of the period. It is important to note that this logic parallels that discussed in the previous chapter for job-order costing.

The basic equation used in accounting for units produced is as follows:

$$\text{Beginning Work-in-Process} + \text{Units Started} - \text{Units Completed} = \text{Ending Work-in-Process}$$

Rearranging the above equation, we obtain

$$\text{Beginning Work-in-Process} + \text{Units Started} - \text{Ending Work-in-Process} = \text{Units Completed}$$

In The American Vegetable Company example, a total of 6,000 cans were in beginning work-in-process inventory. Assume that during January 20x2, an additional 8,000 cans were entered into production. Thus, a total of 14,000 (6,000 + 8,000 = 14,000) cans were worked on and available for completion. Of these, American Vegetable completed production of 11,000 cans during January and the remaining 3,000 cans were in process at the end of January.[3] These activities are summarized below:

Units in Beginning Work-in-Process	6,000	Units Completed	11,000
Units Started in January	8,000	Units in Ending Work-in-Process	3,000
Units Available for Completion	14,000	Total Units Accounted For	14,000

A subtotal of interest is the number of units completed during January that were also entered into production during January. For example, as shown above, American Vegetable completed 11,000 cans of vegetables during January. If we assume that the beginning work-in-process of 6,000 cans were completed during January (a logical assumption), then an additional 5,000 cans (11,000 cans – 6,000 cans = 5,000 cans) were completed. These cans were entered into production during January, thus 5,000 cans of vegetables were both *started and completed in January*.

Determine Total Manufacturing Costs

The second step in accumulating costs with production in a process costing system is determining the total manufacturing costs. In a process costing system, the manufacturing costs are accumulated by manufacturing process (i.e., "batch" of inventory) and not by individual inventory items. Costs are separately accumulated in both the Canning Department and Packaging Department using the same type of source documents discussed in the preceding chapter (Materials Requisitions and Work Tickets). Ultimately, the total manufacturing costs will be summarized in a Production Cost Report (illustrated later in this chapter).

When beginning work-in-process inventory exists, it is important to consider both the current manufacturing costs and the costs associated with the beginning work-in-process inventory. The sum of these two costs will ultimately be allocated between units completed and those that remain in ending work-in-process inventory. Illustration 3 summarized the manufacturing costs associated with the beginning work-in-process inventory. In addition to these costs, American Vegetable incurred $22,200 of manufacturing costs during January 20x2. These costs are summarized below:

Direct Materials	$ 4,000
Direct Labor	10,400
Manufacturing Overhead	7,800
	$22,200

The journal entry used to record manufacturing costs during January 20x2 is shown below. Note that this journal entry is similar to the one prepared for Ace Construction Company using the job-order costing system discussed in the preceding chapter. The only difference is that since the production of vegetables requires

---

[3] It is important to note that these units are completed only with respect to the Canning Department; once completed in this department, they are transferred to the Packaging Department for further processing. For purposes of brevity, we will use the term "completed" to refer to completion of manufacturing in the Canning Department.

multiple manufacturing processes, the work-in-process and direct materials inventories are identified with the appropriate department.

Work-in-Process—Canning	22,200	
Direct Materials—Canning		4,000
Wages Payable		10,400
Factory Overhead—Control		7,800

Total manufacturing costs of $29,320 incurred by the Canning Department must be allocated by American Vegetable. These costs include January's manufacturing costs of $22,200 and the costs of beginning work-in-process inventory of $7,120 (from Illustration 3).

Determine Equivalent Units of Production

As noted earlier, the initial step in process costing is accounting for units produced. From our previous discussion, recall that 14,000 units were available for completion (6,000 units included in beginning work-in-process and 8,000 units entered into production during January). Also recall that of these 14,000 units, 11,000 were completed during January and 3,000 remain in work-in-process at the end of January. This raises the following question: how many units were started and completed in January? If no beginning work-in-process were on hand, we could conclude that between 11,000 and 14,000 units were produced during January. However, the existence of beginning work-in-process introduces additional complexity into the determination of January production. In cases where work-in-process inventories exist at the beginning of the period, end of the period, or both, equivalent units of production must be calculated.

An *equivalent unit of production* is a single quantity that represents the number of units that would have been produced if units were manufactured on an individual unit basis. That is, if a unit was worked on until it was completed and then, and only then, work was begun on the next unit. The concept of equivalent units assumes that, instead of producing a batch of 500 units that are one-half complete, a company could produce 250 fully completed units. Calculating equivalent units of production allows companies to determine the number of "whole" units that could have been completed given the overall production effort expended.

From our earlier analysis of American Vegetable Company's production in the Canning Department during January 20x2, the beginning work-in-process of 6,000 cans was 100 percent complete with respect to materials costs and 30 percent complete with respect to labor and overhead costs (see Illustration 3).[4] An additional 8,000 cans of vegetables were entered into production during January. Of these, 5,000 were completed and 3,000 were in work-in-process inventory at the end of January. Assume that you have examined the ending work-in-process inventory and determined it to be 100 percent complete with respect to materials costs and 40 percent complete with respect to labor and overhead costs. Since all direct materials are added at the beginning of the manufacturing process, American Vegetable's inventories are always 100 percent complete as to direct materials. The percentage of completion for labor and overhead costs is estimated based on time spent in production, stage in the manufacturing process, or some other measure. Shown below is the production data for materials and conversion costs during January 20x2.

	Beginning Work-in-Process Inventory	Units Started and Completed	Ending Work-in-Process Inventory
Direct Materials	**20x1**: 6,000 cans (6,000 x 1.00)	**20x2**: 5,000 cans	**20x2**: 3,000 cans (3,000 x 1.00)
Direct Labor and Overhead	**20x1**: 1,800 cans (6,000 x 0.30) | **20x2**: 4,200 cans (6,000 x 0.70)	**20x2**: 5,000 cans	**20x2**: 1,200 cans (3,000 x 0.40)

---

[4] Whenever overhead is applied as a percentage of direct labor costs or based on direct labor hours, it is normally easier to combine the calculation of equivalent units for labor and overhead. As a result, only a single calculation of equivalent units for these two inputs is made. As noted in Chapter 2, the sum of labor and overhead costs is referred to as conversion costs. In cases where overhead is applied using a cost driver not related to direct labor, separate calculations of equivalent units for direct labor and overhead costs are necessary.

In terms of actual production effort, the number of cans of vegetables produced in the Canning Department is summarized as follows:

	Direct Materials		Labor and Overhead	
	20x1	20x2	20x1	20x2
Beginning Work-in-Process	6,000	0	1,800	4,200
Units Started and Completed	0	5,000	0	5,000
Ending Work-in-Process	0	3,000	0	1,200
Total Production	6,000	8,000	1,800	10,400

In cases where manufacturing costs do not vary significantly from one period to another, companies may "average" the costs and units from beginning work-in-process inventory with current production to determine an average cost per unit. This process is referred to as the *weighted-average* method. Under the weighted-average method, the equivalent units of production for a period equals the sum of the:

- Production effort related to beginning work-in-process inventory at January 1, 20x2. This effort relates to work actually done in one or more prior periods.
- Production effort during the current period.

Since the weighted-average method considers work done in the one or more prior periods on beginning work-in-process inventory, "equivalent units" are merely a measure of production used to accumulate costs with inventory and not an exact measure of actual production activity during the current period. By adding the columns for 20x1 and 20x2, we could determine equivalent units for materials of 14,000 (6,000 in 20x1 + 8,000 in 20x2 = 14,000) and labor and overhead of 12,200 (1,800 in 20x1 + 10,400 in 20x2 = 12,200).

Alternatively, since the units in beginning work-in-process inventory and those entered into production during the period will either be (1) completed or (2) included in ending work-in-process inventory. A shortcut for calculating equivalent units of production focuses on the output of the manufacturing process, as shown below:

	Materials	Labor and Overhead
Units Completed	11,000	11,000
Ending Work-in-Process:		
(3,000 x 1.00)	3,000	
(3,000 x 0.40)		1,200
Total Equivalent Units	14,000	12,200

The above analysis indicates that for the 14,000 units available for completion in January 20x2 all units were complete with respect to material at the end of January, and 12,200 units were complete with respect to labor and overhead. Once again, it is important to note that this calculation includes both work done in January 20x2 and work in one or more prior periods for the beginning work-in-process inventory.

An alternative method of calculating equivalent units of production and accumulating costs with inventory in a process costing system is the first-in, first-out (FIFO) method. Unlike the weighted-average method, the FIFO method calculates a current period cost per unit which excludes prior period costs and the production related to the beginning work-in-process inventory. The FIFO method is illustrated in Appendix A to this chapter.

Calculate the Cost per Unit

Once the equivalent units of production have been calculated, the total manufacturing costs are divided by equivalent units to determine a cost per unit. This cost per unit is then used to transfer costs as inventory moves through the various stages of the manufacturing/sales process. That is, as units are completed, the costs are transferred from work-in-process inventory in Canning to work-in-process inventory in Packaging. Then, when units are completed in Packaging, the costs are transferred to finished goods inventory and ultimately to cost of goods sold. With the exception of the existence of a second manufacturing department, this transfer of costs is identical to that shown in the previous chapter in Ace's job-order costing system.

In determining equivalent units of production, the weighted-average method includes both (1) production effort on the beginning work-in-process inventory in one or more prior periods and (2) production effort of the current period. Therefore, to determine the cost per equivalent unit, the manufacturing costs associated with both the beginning work-in-process inventory and the units started during the current period are considered. The cost per can of vegetables in the Canning Department for American Vegetable under the weighted-average method is shown in the Production Cost Report in Illustration 4. As shown in Illustration 4, the total cost per can of vegetables is $2.30, consisting of $0.70 per can of direct materials costs, $0.90 per can of direct labor costs, and $0.70 per can of manufacturing overhead costs.

Illustration 4

The American Vegetable Company
Production Cost Report: Canning Department
January 20x2

	Direct Materials	Direct Labor	Overhead	Total
Beginning WIP	$5,800	$ 580	$ 740	$ 7,120
January Costs	4,000	10,400	7,800	22,200
Total Costs	$9,800	$10,980	$8,540	$29,320
Equivalent Units	14,000	12,200	12,200	
Cost per Unit	$0.70	$0.90	$0.70	$2.30

Allocation of Manufacturing costs:

Completed and Transferred to Packaging (11,000 cans x $2.30)		$25,300
Ending Work-in-Process:		
Direct Materials (3,000 cans x 1.00 x $0.70)	$2,100	
Direct Labor (3,000 cans x 0.40 x $0.90)	1,080	
Overhead (3,000 cans x 0.40 x $0.70)	840	4,020
Total Costs Accounted For		$29,320

Accumulate Costs with Inventory Units

In the previous step, a total manufacturing cost per can of vegetables of $2.30 was calculated (see the Production Cost Report in Illustration 4). Once this cost has been determined, the accumulation of costs with inventory is relatively straightforward and is similar to the approach used in Chapter 3 for job-order costing. For example, the cost of the 11,000 cans of vegetables completed in January would be transferred from work-in-process inventory in the Canning Department to work-in-process inventory in the Packaging Department. The amount of this transfer is determined by multiplying the number of cans of vegetables completed by the $2.30 cost per can (11,000 cans x $2.30 = $25,300) and can be obtained from Illustration 4. The journal entry prepared to record the completion of the 11,000 cans of vegetables in the Canning Department and the transfer to Packaging follows below. If American Vegetable did not have processing in an additional manufacturing department, the transfer would have been made to finished goods inventory. Instead, the costs are transferred from work-in-process inventory in one manufacturing department (Canning Department) to another (Packaging Department).

Work-in-Process—Packaging	25,300	
Work-in-Process—Canning		25,300

The Production Cost Report shown in Illustration 4 reveals that a total of $4,020 of costs is included in ending work-in-process inventory. This represents the total cost to produce 3,000 cans of vegetables that are 100 percent complete for materials costs and 40 percent complete as to labor and overhead costs.

Transfer and Completion of Production

At this point, 11,000 cans of vegetables with a total cost of $25,300 have been transferred to the Packaging Department (see Illustration 4). The cans are now ready for labeling, inspection, and packaging in the Packaging Department. The accumulation of additional manufacturing costs, determination of equivalent units of production, and calculation of a cost per unit would proceed as it was done in the Canning Department. If additional materials, labor, and overhead costs incurred in the Packaging Department for these 11,000 cans were $330, $550, and $770 respectively, the following journal entry would be prepared.

Work-in-Process—Packaging	1,650	
Direct Materials—Packaging		330
Wages Payable		550
Factory Overhead—Control		770

At this point, the total cost of producing a can of vegetables can be determined as shown below:

Direct Materials (Packaging)	$ 330
Direct Labor (Packaging)	550
Manufacturing Overhead (Packaging)	770
Costs Incurred in Canning	25,300
Total Costs	$26,950
Number of Cans Produced	÷11,000
Cost per Can	$ 2.45

The Production Cost Report for The American Vegetable Company's Packaging Department (not shown) would indicate a total manufacturing cost of $2.45 per can. Of this, $2.30 per can was transferred from the Canning Department (see the Production Cost Report in Illustration 4), and an additional $0.15 per can was incurred in the Packaging Department ($2.45 per can − $2.30 per can = $0.15 per can). The $0.15 per can can be further disaggregated to reflect materials costs of $0.03 per can ($330 ÷ 11,000 cans = $0.03), direct labor costs of $0.05 per can ($550 ÷ 11,000 cans = $0.05), and overhead costs of $0.07 per can ($770 ÷ 11,000 cans = $0.07). This $2.45 cost per can would be used to transfer manufacturing costs to finished goods inventory (upon completion of production in the Packaging Department). For example, once all 11,000 cans have been completed in the Packaging Department, a total of $26,950 (11,000 cans x $2.45 per can = $26,950) would be transferred to finished goods inventory. The following journal entry reflects this transfer:

Finished Goods—Control	26,950	
Work-in-Process—Packaging		26,950

Finally, the $2.45 cost per unit is used to transfer costs from finished goods inventory to cost of goods sold upon the sale of these items to customers. If 6,000 cans of vegetables were sold to The American Vegetable Company's customers during January, the cost of goods sold would equal $14,700 (6,000 cans x $2.45 = $14,700). The following journal entry would be prepared to record cost of goods sold for January.

Cost of Goods Sold	14,700	
Finished Goods—Control		14,700

Assuming that no beginning work-in-process exists in the Packaging Department and that $4,000 of direct materials inventory is on hand at January 31, 20x2, Illustration 5 summarizes the cost flows and partial financial statements for the American Vegetable Company for January 20x2.

JOINT MANUFACTURING PROCESSES

Certain manufacturing processes result in the production of several different products. For example, consider The American Vegetable Company's production of carrot products. American Vegetable purchases carrots for use in producing two primary products: bagged carrots and canned carrots. Upon receipt, the carrots are cleaned and sorted by size. Larger carrots are sorted into breathable plastic bags (six carrots per bag) and placed in refrigerated storage. These bagged carrots are sold to grocery stores and specialty produce and fruit stands. Smaller carrots are sliced, cooked, and canned after adding water and preservatives in an automated manufacturing process; these canned carrots are sold exclusively to grocery stores and restaurants. In addition to

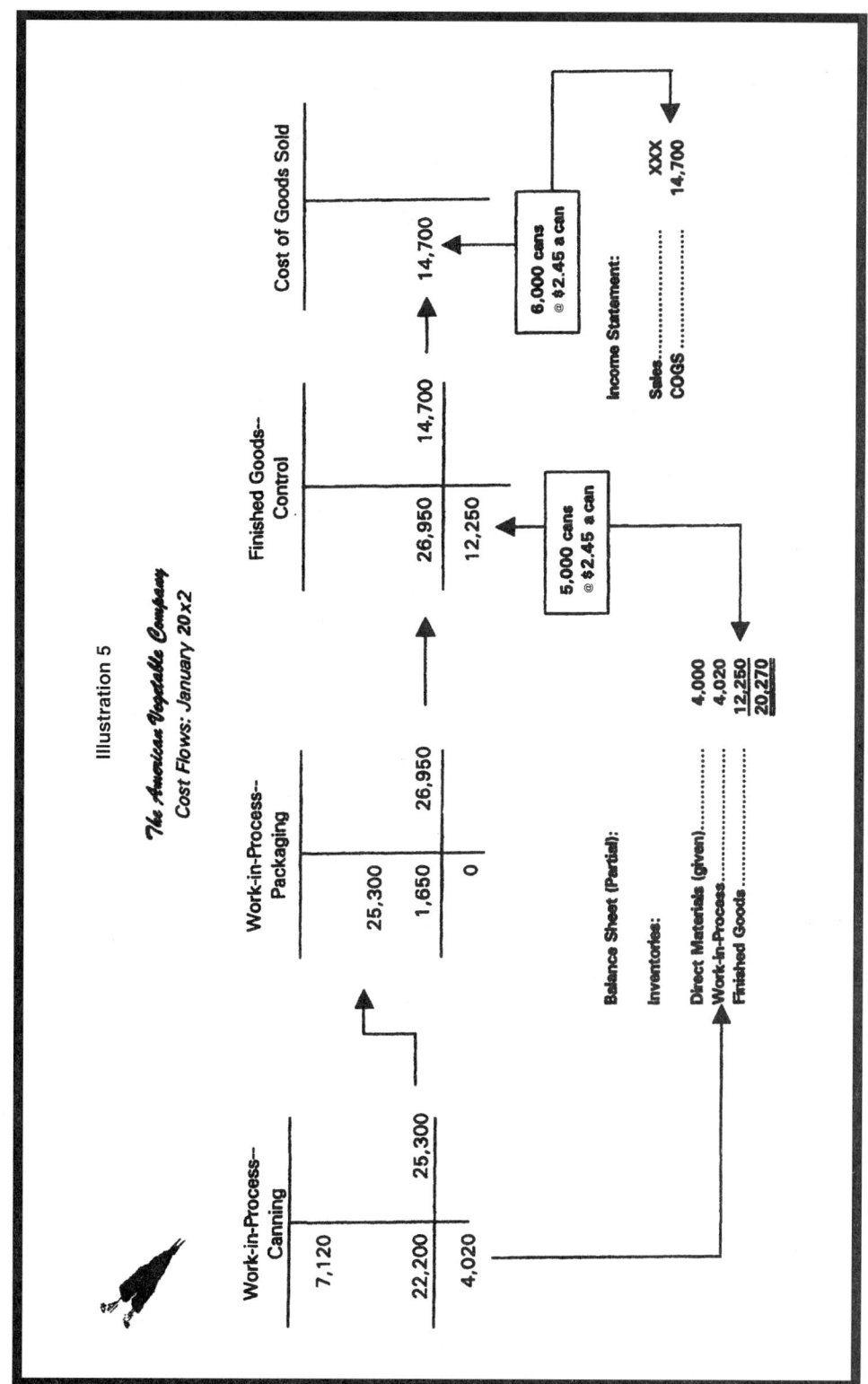

these primary products, any excess carrot pieces are shredded and bagged for sale to grocery stores. Finally, the carrot stems that are removed in the initial cleaning of the carrots are collected and sold to the local zoo as animal feed.

The above process reveals three major types of products. The bagged carrots and canned carrots are referred to as *joint products* (or *major products*). The distinguishing feature of a joint or major product is that it makes a substantial contribution to revenues and is the primary objective of the manufacturing process. In contrast, while the shredded carrots and carrot stems produce revenue for American Vegetable, the amount of this revenue is significantly less than that generated by the joint products. These products are referred to as either *by-products* or *scrap*. The primary difference between by-products and scrap is that by-products: (1) make a greater contribution to revenues than scrap and (2) may require additional processing. Since the excess carrot pieces must be shredded and bagged, this product would be considered a by-product. Conversely, since carrot stems are not processed further prior to their sale, this product would ordinarily be considered as scrap.

The primary issue introduced in a joint manufacturing process is allocating manufacturing costs to the products obtained from that process. The costs incurred in a joint manufacturing process can be classified into two categories. *Joint manufacturing costs* (or *common manufacturing costs*) are those manufacturing costs that are incurred to produce more than one inventory item. Joint manufacturing costs cannot be associated exclusively with any one item and must be allocated to each of the joint products being produced. For American Vegetable's production of carrot products, the cost of carrots and the costs of cleaning and sorting carrots are examples of joint (or common) manufacturing costs.

In addition to joint manufacturing costs, other costs are necessary for the production and sale of the organization's products; however, these costs are associated with, and can be traced to, individual products. Costs of this nature are known as *separable costs*. For example, the costs of the plastic bags and the wages paid to workers are incurred solely for the production of bagged carrots. Similarly, the costs of cutting, cooking, and canning carrots are strictly related to canned carrot products. Finally, the costs of shredding and bagging excess carrot pieces are associated only with American Vegetable's shredded carrot products. Because separable manufacturing costs are associated with a single type of product, there is no need to allocate these costs among different products.

The American Vegetable Company's joint manufacturing process for carrot products is summarized below. This process begins with the purchase of carrots (direct materials) and payment of wages to employees who clean and sort carrots (direct labor). Once the carrots have been purchased, cleaned, and sorted, production of the individual products begins. The point at which joint processing stops and the separate processing of individual products begins is referred to as the *split-off point*. At the split-off point, American Vegetable has four potential products; three of these products are in partial stages of completion (bagged carrots, canned carrots, and shredded carrots) and one is complete (carrot stems).

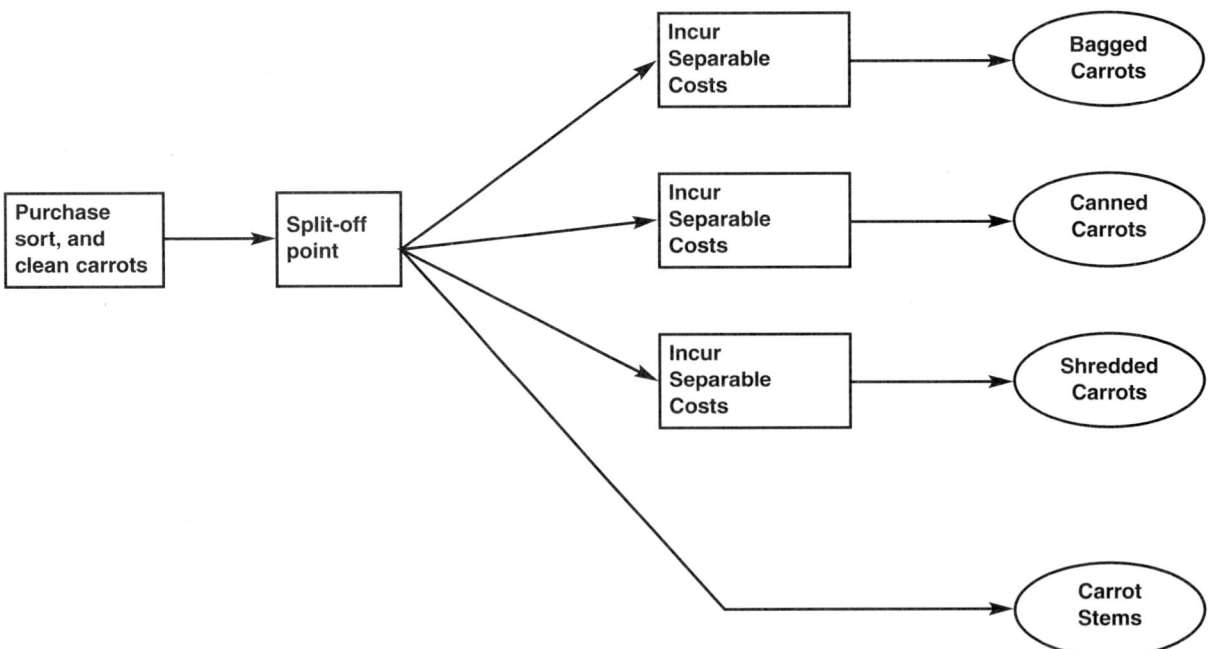

Because joint products are the primary objectives of the manufacturing process and contribute the most to organization revenues, it is common practice to allocate joint manufacturing costs only to these products. That is, joint manufacturing costs normally are not allocated to either by-products or scrap. Thus, the total cost of producing a joint product consists of: (1) the separable manufacturing costs associated with that product and (2) an allocated portion of the joint manufacturing costs. The costs of producing by-products and scrap usually include only the separable manufacturing costs (if any) incurred to produce those products.

Joint manufacturing costs may be allocated to joint products based on either relative physical measures or market values of the joint products. To illustrate the allocation of joint manufacturing costs, we will examine the production of carrot products by American Vegetable. Assume that The American Vegetable Company incurred a total of $200 in costs for purchasing, cleaning, and sorting carrots prior to the split-off point. These costs are examples of joint manufacturing costs. After the carrots were cleaned and sorted, American Vegetable estimated that 400 pounds of carrots would be used for bagged carrot products and 600 pounds of carrots would be used for canned carrot products.

After the split-off point, American Vegetable estimated that it would incur an additional $50 and $250 of separable costs to produce bagged carrot products and canned carrot products, respectively. The final estimates of production volumes and revenues were as follows:

Bagged Carrots (400 bags selling at $2.25 per bag)	$900
Canned Carrots (1,000 cans selling at $0.40 per can)	400

Illustration 6 summarizes the allocation of joint manufacturing costs to bagged and canned carrot products using both physical measures and market values. Notice that the costs allocated to each product are influenced by the method of allocation chosen. Using physical measures, a relatively higher allocation of the $200 joint manufacturing cost is made to canned carrots, since a greater quantity of carrots is used for canned carrots (600 pounds) compared to bagged carrots (400 pounds). However, the higher market value for bagged carrots results in a greater allocation of joint manufacturing costs to bagged carrots if market values are utilized. Notice that the market value of the bagged and canned carrots at the split-off point is estimated by subtracting separable manufacturing costs from the final sales values of the products.

Illustration 6

The American Vegetable Company
Allocation of Joint Manufacturing Costs

Panel A: Physical Measures

	Quantity	Percentage	Allocation
Bagged Carrots	400 lbs.	0.40[a]	0.40 × $200 = $ 80
Canned Carrots	600 lbs.	0.60[a]	0.60 × $200 = 120
	1,000 lbs.	1.00	$200

Panel B: Market Values

	Market Value		Percentage	Allocation
Bagged Carrots	$900 - $50 =	$ 850	0.85[b]	0.85 × $200 = $170
Canned Carrots	$400 - $250 =	$ 150	0.15[b]	0.15 × $200 = 30
		$1,000	1.00	$200

[a] Bagged Carrots = 400 lbs. ÷ 1,000 lbs. = 0.40
Canned Carrots = 600 lbs. ÷ 1,000 lbs. = 0.60

[b] Bagged Carrots = $850 ÷ $1,000 = 0.85
Canned Carrots = $150 ÷ $1,000 = 0.15

Once the joint manufacturing costs are allocated in the above manner, the cost per unit may be determined by adding the separable costs of production to the costs obtained by the allocation of joint manufacturing costs. For example, if joint manufacturing costs were allocated using the relative sales values of the joint products, the cost per unit for bagged carrots would be $0.55, as determined below:

Allocation of Joint Costs (see Illustration 6)	$170.00
Separable Costs	$ 50.00
Total Manufacturing Costs	$220.00
Bags of Carrots Produced	÷ 400
Manufacturing Cost per Bag	$ 0.55

Once determined, the manufacturing cost of $0.55 per bag of carrots is accumulated with the inventory items and transferred as the items move through the manufacturing/sales process. The only difference introduced in this instance is that these items were produced in a joint manufacturing process along with other items.

COST ACCUMULATION FOR SERVICE ORGANIZATIONS

While the focus on this chapter is on the manufacturing process used by The American Vegetable Company, it is important to note that the concepts discussed also apply to service organizations. Two examples are discussed below:

- Delivery services (such as FedEx and United Parcel Service) incur costs in transporting parcels to various destinations. Once these parcels reach a general distribution point for a certain geographic area, additional costs are incurred in delivering parcels to their intended recipients. The delivery of each parcel generally requires similar levels of cost and effort. To determine the cost of delivering an individual parcel, delivery companies can determine the total costs of delivering a group of parcels and divide this cost by the number of parcels in each delivery.
- Companies performing yard maintenance services incur labor costs, depreciation on equipment, and fertilizer costs in servicing their customers' lawns. While larger lawns may require greater effort (and costs) to maintain than do smaller lawns, it is normally not cost-efficient to calculate a cost per yard on an individual basis. Instead, yard maintenance companies usually determine the total costs incurred over some period of time (a day, a week, or a month) and divide this cost by the total number of yards maintained during that period.

JUST-IN-TIME INVENTORY AND PRODUCTION MANAGEMENT

An important decision made by companies is the quantity of inventory maintained on hand for sale to customers. Significant trade-offs exist between maintaining excessive quantities of inventory and maintaining insufficient quantities of inventory. For example, when shopping at a grocery store, if insufficient quantities of inventory are on hand, the store will lose sales on those items and may lose the patronage of customers if stock-outs are frequent. Conversely, maintaining larger quantities of inventory requires the grocery store to invest additional capital in those items, possibly resulting in insufficient capital to meet its other needs. Also, if inventory is perishable, the costs resulting from spoilage may become significant. In the current manufacturing environment, the large costs (insurance costs, storage costs, and cost of capital) associated with maintaining inventory have led to a movement away from stockpiling excessive quantities of inventory.

A philosophy of inventory production that is consistent with this movement is referred to as *just-in-time manufacturing (JIT)*. The JIT philosophy originated in Japan by Toyota and Kawasaki and is being increasingly used by U.S. manufacturing companies (such as Hewlett-Packard).[5] The concept of JIT manufacturing is perhaps best illustrated by the following description of Toyota's manufacturing process:

> At Toyota, overproduction is considered one of the worst forms of waste. The company designs the work to flow from process to process without peaks or valleys and still arrive in just the right quantity for the customer.[6]

Under JIT production, companies attempt to minimize the time period between the receipt of direct materials inventory to the delivery of inventory to customers; that is, inventory is produced "just in time" for delivery to customers. The major steps involved in this cycle are summarized below:

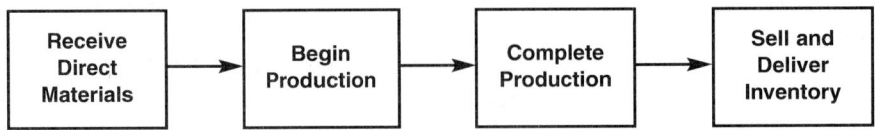

---

[5] S.A. Moscove and A. Wright, *Cost Accounting with Managerial Applications* (Boston: Houghton Mifflin, 1990). For a thorough discussion of Toyota's use of JIT, see J.Y. Lee, *Managerial Accounting Changes for the 1990s* (New York: Addison-Wesley, 1987).

[6] "How Toyota Defies Gravity," *Fortune* (December 8, 1997), 102.

The following excerpts from the business press provide additional examples of the application of a just-in-time philosophy.

> Dell Computer makes its PCs to order, with the elapsed time from a customer's phone call to loading the finished product onto a delivery truck generally equal to 36 hours. Customer orders are instantly relayed to one of Dell's three plants (located in Austin, Texas; Penang, Malaysia; or Limerick, Ireland), where suppliers are expected to make component deliveries within an hour. Computer chips, boards, and drives are stored in trucks that are parked in bays just 50 feet from the beginning of the assembly line. Completed computers are immediately shipped to customers—Dell carries no finished goods inventory.[7]
>
> Netflix, an online DVD rental company, charges its subscribers $20 per month and allows them to make an unlimited number of rentals, so long as they have no more than three DVDs out at any one time. High demand levels created chaos in managing its DVD inventories, until Netflix came up with the ultimate just-in-time system. Customers return DVDs in preaddressed mailers. Immediately upon a DVD's return, a Netflix employee scans the disc's bar code, retrieves and prints a mailing label for the next subscriber on the waiting list for that DVD, and makes sure that the disc is sent out in the afternoon mail. The new system has reduced labor costs by about 15 percent, and the vast majority of DVDs never touch the shelf before they go out to the next viewer.[8]

To illustrate the use of JIT manufacturing techniques, assume that The American Vegetable Company receives an order for 10,000 cans of its vegetable products to be delivered to the customer in 30 days. The American Vegetable Company has estimated the following time required for important events relating to this order:

- Lead time from ordering materials to receiving materials from vendors: four days.
- Time required to complete production of 10,000 cans: one day (in both the Canning Department and Packaging Department).
- Time required to deliver inventory to customer: four days.

Given the above information, The American Vegetable Company should order the materials in 21 days, as follows:

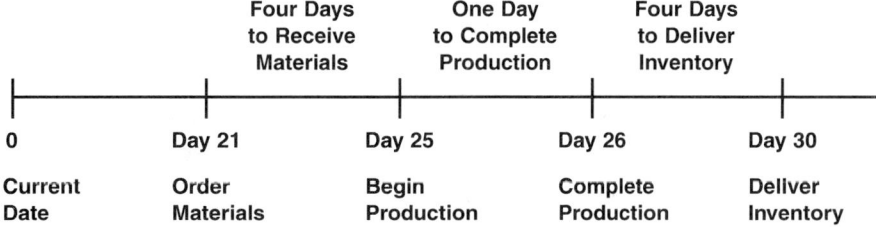

Contrast this manufacturing process to the following schedule for a similar production run:

Order Direct Materials	Day 0
Receive Direct Materials	Day 4
Inspect Direct Materials	Day 5
Transfer Direct Materials to Warehouse	Day 6
Store Direct Materials	Days 7–9
Issue and Deliver Direct Materials	Day 10
Begin and Complete Production in Canning	Day 11
Await Availability of Machinery in Packaging	Days 12–13
Complete Production in Packaging	Day 14
Inspect Production	Days 15–16
Transfer Finished Goods to Warehouse	Day 17
Store Finished Goods	Days 18–25
Sell Finished Goods to Customer	Day 26
Deliver Finished Goods to Customer	Days 27–30

---

[7] Andrew E. Serwer, "Michael Dell Turns the PC World Inside Out," *Fortune* (September 8, 1997), 86.

[8] Christopher Null, "How Netflix is Fixing Hollywood," *Business 2.0* (July 2003), 41–43.

Notice that the same time constraints regarding the major manufacturing events are reflected in the above production schedule as in the JIT production schedule shown earlier. That is, a total of four days are still required from the date direct materials are ordered until they are received. In addition, four days are required to deliver the inventory to the organization's customers. Recall that the JIT production schedule required only five days from receipt of the direct materials (day 25) until the finished products are delivered to customers (day 30). In contrast, the above production schedule requires a total of 26 days from receipt of the materials (day 4) until the delivery of finished products to customers (day 30). Where do the differences occur?

The above differences reflect the existence of non-value-added activities in the latter manufacturing process. *Non-value-added activities* are those activities that increase the length of time in the manufacturing/sales process without increasing the value of the product to the customer. Non-value added activities typically represent delays that occur in the manufacturing process from the time direct materials are received until the finished inventory is ready for sale to the organization's customers. In the above example, the non-value-added activities include the time associated with inspection, transfer, waiting, and storage of direct materials, work-in-process, and finished goods inventory. The basic objective of JIT is to reduce the time spent by the organization on non-value-added activities.

The following excerpts from practice describe actions that companies have taken to eliminate non-value-added activities and associated costs.

> **When Alexander Doll Company, maker of the coveted Madame Alexander doll, was on the brink of bankruptcy, TBM Consulting applied Toyota's lean production techniques to bring it back to profitability. The doll-making process, where costumes can contain more than 20 separate pieces and must go through as many as 30 production steps, was originally organized as a batch manufacturing system. The result was an excessive work-in-process inventory and waiting periods for customers that could sometimes last as long as 16 weeks. TBM reorganized operations by creating seven- or eight-person teams that were responsible for completing approximately 300 doll or wardrobe assemblies per day. The result: work-in-process was cut by 96% and orders were filled in one to two weeks.[9]**
>
> **IBM found that little changes in design and packaging can lead to enormous cost savings without decreasing customer value. When IBM replaced its four-color packaging box with a two-color blue-and-black box that costs 5 cents less, annual savings of $350,000 resulted. IBM engineers redesigned LCD monitors so that they would fit into smaller boxes, reducing shipping costs by $1.6 million.[10]**

In contrast, *value-added activities* represent those activities that increase the value of the product to the organization's customers. In this example, the production times in the Canning and Packaging Departments are the sole value-added activities for The American Vegetable Company.

JIT production systems reduce the levels of inventory maintained by the organization (and the non-value-added activities described above) through some of the following methods or techniques.

1. Purchasing direct materials inventory in smaller quantities. By purchasing smaller quantities of direct materials inventory, the organization reduces the amount of these inventories maintained on hand. Ideally, materials should be purchased only as they are required to fill customer orders. If the organization maintains excessive direct materials inventory, it incurs greater levels of non-value-added costs in the form of storage costs and waiting time.

> **In order to be successful, just-in-time or build-to-order companies must simplify the purchasing process. One approach to simplification is to reduce the number of different parts purchased; this is often accomplished by redesigning products so that one component part can be used in many different configurations. Lexmark International, a manufacturer of laser printers, cut the number of different fuses it stocks from 14 down to 4. Hoffman Enclosures, which makes large metal boxes for industrial supplies, purchases and stocks only one size of hinge and cuts it to length to suit a particular order.[11]**

---

[9] Alex Taylor III, "It Worked for Toyota. Can It Work for Toys?" *Fortune* (January 11, 1999), 36.

[10] Daniel Lyons, "Back on the Chain Gang," *Forbes* (October 13, 2003), 119.

[11] Philip Siekman, "Where 'Build to Order' Works Best," *Fortune* (April 26, 1999), 160[C]-160[V]

> **International Truck & Engine Corporation** pared down its purchasing and inventory costs by greatly reducing the complexity of its product line. While its current "medium" truck line has more than 800 combinations of engines and transmissions, the company is unveiling a new medium truck that has only 34 such combinations. What's more, the company claims that each of the new combinations is superior because engineers took the time and effort to develop them in response to the needs of drivers.[12]

2. Maintaining favorable relationships with suppliers and other vendors. If favorable relationships are maintained with suppliers and vendors, unanticipated shortages of direct materials inventory can be filled more easily.
3. Using a "pull" method of manufacturing. Under "pull" manufacturing, inventory in a given stage is produced only when required by the following manufacturing stage. For example, if The American Vegetable Company utilized a "pull" method of manufacturing, no inventory would be produced in the Canning Department until the production machinery was available for use in the Packaging Department. By using this manufacturing technique, the amount of work-in-process inventory maintained on hand is reduced.

The following excerpt from the business press describes a form of "pull" manufacturing.

> **"Demand-flow manufacturing,"** the brain child of John Costanza, founder of the John Costanza Institute of Technology, is a system of manufacturing that departs from the repetitive-processing approaches that have previously dominated American manufacturing. In demand-flow manufacturing, supplies of raw materials are replenished as necessary to meet changing customer demands for varied products. In addition, workers shift from one task to the next to avoid stockpiling of work-in-process, and finished goods move directly from assembly lines to delivery trucks. Companies that have adopted the demand-flow methodology have been able to dramatically reduce the size of their finished goods inventory. They have, as a result, realized the benefits of decreased working capital requirements and increased inventory turnover rates.[13]

4. Establishing high quality standards for finished goods inventory. One important limitation of maintaining relatively small levels of inventories is that very little margin for error exists for substandard finished goods inventories. If substandard finished goods inventories exist, delays will occur as products must be reworked prior to their delivery to the customer. Thus, it is important that the organization establish high quality control standards to ensure high quality production.
5. Producing finished goods inventory in smaller quantities. Similar to direct materials inventories, finished goods inventories should be produced only as required for sale to the organization's customers. As with direct materials inventories, maintaining excessive levels of finished goods inventory causes the organization to incur greater levels of non-value-added costs in the form of storage and waiting time.

One limitation associated with JIT production is that it provides little room for unanticipated shutdowns or shortages in production. Three examples of this limitation are shown in the following recent excerpts from the business press.

> **General Motors Corp. (GM)** fell short of its production goal of 90,000 cars and trucks because of problems at one of its engine plants. The production shortage was magnified by the shortage of existing automobile inventory created by GM's decision to adopt a JIT inventory approach. However, Alan Dawes, executive in charge of operations at GM's auto components group noted that "There's no way we're going away from just-in-time."[14]

---

[12] Stuart F. Brown, "International's Better Way to Build Trucks," *Fortune* (February 19, 2001), 210[L].

[13] Gene Bylinsky, "Heroes of U.S. Manufacturing," *Fortune* (March 20, 2000), 192[B].

[14] "A Tonic for the Business Cycle," *Business Week* (April 4, 1994), 57.

> Boeing's production process requires extensive cooperation between Boeing and its suppliers. In October 1997, late shipment of parts from Boeing's suppliers did not permit workers to perform their assembly tasks in the proper order. As a result, overhead costs soared to 30% of total labor costs and Boeing was forced to halt production at two of its facilities.[15]
>
> The January 1998 ice storms in eastern Canada were one of the worst natural disasters in that country's history. These storms resulted in numerous power outages and delayed delivery of important materials components, significantly impacting manufacturing processes throughout Canada. Companies operating on a JIT process rented generators to reduce the disruption of their manufacturing processes. As the plant manager for Mitel Corp. (a manufacturer of semiconductor chips) noted, "we don't produce to inventory; we produce to order only."[16]

The risks associated with a just-in-time inventory philosophy were highlighted in the wake of the September 11th terrorist attacks on New York City and Washington, D.C.

> The grounding of air-freight carriers in response to the September 11th attacks had a significant disruptive effect on the U.S. manufacturing economy, which increasingly relies on just-in-time shipments. The resulting delivery interruptions, which translated into inventory stock-outs and production shutdowns, illustrate the risks of just-in-time methods, "where parts often arrive only hours before they're needed, and a single missing part can shut down an assembly line."[17]
>
> Heightened security at U.S. Customs checkpoints, as well as ports and airports, resulted in delays in transport and delivery of critical parts and components from abroad. While delays were inconvenient for all purchasers, companies with just-in-time purchasing practices were most severely impacted. A case in point: shortly after the attacks took place, inadequate supplies of component parts from Canada contributed to the closure of five of Ford's U.S. manufacturing plants.[18]

Four examples of the application of JIT production systems in practice follow below. Two of these systems appear to have been successful (Dell Computer and Oregon Cutting Systems); the other two were not (Allen-Edmonds and Bandai Co.). These examples illustrate one important point—despite their reported popularity in the business media, JIT production systems are not advantageous for all companies.

> Dell Computer Corp., a computer retailer headquartered in Austin, Texas has taken the notion of just-in-time manufacturing further by warehousing its component parts within fifteen minutes of a Dell factory and utilizing electronic commerce to receive customer payments. Unlike other manufacturers, Dell does not begin ordering component parts or assembling computers until an order is booked. Because the price of computer components may fall rapidly in just a few months, Dell's component parts are newer (and cheaper) than those used in machines sold at the same time by its rivals. This can translate into a six-percent profit advantage in terms of the cost of component parts alone. This strategy puts pressure on suppliers to provide parts to Dell on a timely basis. Says Andrew Grove, CEO of Intel (Dell's chief supplier of microprocessor chips), "I have bruises on my back from [Dell] when we can't keep up with them."[19]
>
> As a result of JIT, Oregon Cutting Systems, a manufacturer of cutting chains for chain saws, timber harvesting equipment, and sporting goods, realized the following benefits: (1) lead times for production were reduced from 21 days to 3 days; (2) productivity increased by 10 percent; (3) manufacturing costs were reduced by 35 percent; and (4) work-in-process and direct materials inventories were reduced by 50 percent.[20]

---

[15] "Boeing's Big Problem," *Fortune* (January 12, 1998), 98.

[16] Christopher J. Chipello, "Canadian Ice Storm Provided Stern Test of Popular Just-in-Time Supply Method," *The Wall Street Journal* (January 26, 1998), A2, A6.

[17] Jeffrey Ball, Rick Brooks and Scott Thurm, "Flight Ban Slows 'Just in Time' Factories," *The Wall Street Journal* (September 13, 2001), B3.

[18] Joseph Martha and Sunil Subbakrishna, "When Just-in-Time Becomes Just-in-Case," *The Wall Street Journal* (October 22, 2001), A18.

[19] "Whirlwind on the Web," *Business Week* (April 7, 1997), 133.

[20] "J.C. Baffles and I.K. Kleinsorge, "Cutting Waste with JIT," *Management Accounting* (May 1992), 28–32.

> Allen Edmonds Shoe Corp. is an example of a company whose experience with JIT production was not successful. Because it manufactures 41,000 varieties of shoes in limited production runs, Allen-Edmonds had to continually switch product lines under its JIT system, resulting in reduced levels of efficiency. In addition, the European tanneries supplying calfskin hides to Allen-Edmonds refused to provide their direct materials inputs on a demand basis, an important characteristic of JIT. In all, Allen-Edmonds estimates that its three-year experiment with JIT production resulted in a loss of $1 million.[21]
>
> The existence of JIT systems created havoc during the Christmas season of 1993 when unexpected demand for "Power Rangers" (an action figure produced by Bandai Co.) led to short supply of this product. As Alan Hassenfeld, chairman of Hasbro noted, toy manufacturers "...must and are becoming partners with [vendors]."[22]

A final comment on the JIT inventory method identifies a negative economic consequence of its growing popularity.

> The widespread adoption of just-in-time inventory techniques may have the unintended consequence of making economic recoveries more difficult. As more companies embrace a just-in-time inventory philosophy, the volatility of traditional economic indicators, such as capital goods orders, increases. This increased volatility makes the economy less predictable and reduces investor confidence, slowing the prospects for general recovery.[23]

Appendix B illustrates the method of accumulating manufacturing costs with inventory in a JIT system.

USING MANAGERIAL ACCOUNTING INFORMATION: THE AMERICAN VEGETABLE COMPANY

In this chapter, we illustrated the accumulation of manufacturing costs and determination of a cost per unit for The American Vegetable Company, a manufacturer of vegetable products using a process costing system. The cost accumulation process ultimately allows American Vegetable to prepare its financial statements by apportioning the costs of producing inventory between asset accounts (work-in-process inventory and finished goods inventory) and expense accounts (cost of goods sold). The preparation of financial statements is the primary objective of financial accounting. Partial financial statements for The American Vegetable Company (based on the weighted-average method of cost determination) were shown earlier in Illustration 5.

As discussed in Chapter 3, cost accumulation also provides management with the information necessary to make numerous decisions. For example, consider the following managerial decisions that may use information discussed in this chapter.

1. The total cost of producing a can of industrial-sized vegetables (in both the Canning and Packaging Departments) was $2.45. If American Vegetable wishes to earn a 20 percent return on its operating activities, it should charge $2.94 for its canned vegetable products ($2.45 x 1.20 = $2.94). Since cost data are maintained on internal documents, American Vegetable's customers would not be aware of the actual costs of production.
2. Once information about manufacturing costs has been accumulated, American Vegetable can use this information to evaluate the performance of its personnel. For example, assume that the standard materials cost per can in the Canning Department was $0.60. Referring to the Production Cost Report included in Illustration 4, American Vegetable's actual direct materials cost ($0.70) exceeded the standard cost. Two possibilities exist: (1) the price of vegetables has increased from previous periods and/or (2) American Vegetable's production personnel are using excessive quantities of vegetables. This is an example of the control function of management. The use of performance standards and performance evaluation for control purposes is discussed further in subsequent chapters of this text.

---

[21] "Allen-Edmonds Shoe Tries 'Just-in-Time' Production," *The Wall Street Journal* (March 4,1993), B2.

[22] "Toy Industry Finds It's Harder and Harder to Pick the Winners," *The Wall Street Journal* (December 21, 1993), A1, A5.

[23] Clare Ansberry, "A New Hazard for Recovery: Last-Minute Pace of Orders," *The Wall Street Journal* (June 25, 2002), A1, A12.

SUMMARY

In Chapter 4, we illustrate how organizations with a continuous manufacturing process record the costs of producing their inventory. This type of costing system is referred to as a process costing system. Some of the important concepts discussed in this chapter are summarized below.

1. For certain types of manufacturing processes, the use of a job-order costing system is simply not feasible. These types of manufacturing processes (referred to as continuous manufacturing processes) use process costing systems to accumulate the costs of manufacturing inventory. As discussed in Chapter 3, job-order costing systems accumulate costs with a given item of production (unit). In a process costing system, costs are accumulated with a given manufacturing process (or batch of units).
2. Job-order costing is appropriate when production occurs across multiple jobs requiring different amounts and costs of direct materials, direct labor, and manufacturing overhead. In contrast, process costing is normally used when production occurs continuously in large batches that require similar amounts and costs of direct materials, direct labor, and manufacturing overhead per unit.
3. In process costing, the total cost of manufacturing a number of units is divided by the number of units produced to obtain a cost per unit. This cost per unit is then used to accumulate costs with inventory as items move throughout the manufacturing/sales process.
4. Process costing involves the following procedures: (a) account for units produced; (b) determine total manufacturing costs; (c) determine equivalent units of production; (d) calculate the cost per unit; and (e) accumulate costs with inventory units.
5. To account for units that are partially complete at the end of the period, equivalent units of production are calculated. Equivalent units of production represent a production level that assumes items are produced on a one-by-one basis. For example, if a company had 100 units that were one-fourth finished, the equivalent units of production would be 25 (100 units x 0.25 = 25 units).
6. The weighted-average method of cost determination calculates a cost per unit that reflects both: (a) the costs and equivalent units included in the beginning work-in-process inventory, and (b) the costs and equivalent units produced in the current period.
7. In a joint manufacturing process, manufacturing costs are incurred to produce more than a single type of inventory product. These costs should be allocated among the primary products (joint products) produced using some measure of either relative physical quantities or relative market values.

KEY DEFINITIONS

By-product–product that results from a joint manufacturing process and that is of minor importance to the organization. Joint manufacturing costs are not ordinarily allocated to by-products. By-products sometimes require further processing prior to their sale.

Continuous manufacturing process–type of manufacturing process in which many identical units are produced, each requiring approximately the same amount and costs of direct materials, direct labor, and manufacturing overhead.

Equivalent units of production–measure that expresses production in "whole" units. Determining equivalent units allows an accountant to calculate a cost per unit in cases where units are only partially completed.

First-in, First-out method (FIFO)–method of allocating manufacturing costs that assumes that the beginning work-in-process inventory is completed prior to the start of any additional production. Under FIFO, a cost per unit is calculated that considers only the current period's manufacturing cost and activity (i.e., costs and activity associated with the beginning work-in-process inventory are ignored).

Joint manufacturing costs (or common manufacturing costs)–manufacturing costs that are incurred for the production of more than one type of inventory product. Joint manufacturing costs are allocated among the joint products produced based on some measure of relative volume or relative market values.

Joint products–products resulting from a joint manufacturing process. Unlike by-products, the sale of joint products provides a relatively major source of revenue to the organization. Joint manufacturing costs must be allocated among these products.

Just-in-Time (JIT) Manufacturing–philosophy of manufacturing inventory that attempts to reduce the quantities of inventory maintained on hand by the organization and complete production "just in time" for sale to the organization's customers.

Non-value-added activities–activities that increase the length of time in the manufacturing/sales process without increasing the value of the product to the customer. Examples of non-value-added activities include inspection, transfer, waiting, and storage times.

Process costing–cost accumulation system used by companies with a continuous manufacturing process. In process costing, the costs are accumulated by the manufacturing process and not individual units of inventory.

Scrap–product resulting from a joint manufacturing process that is of minor importance to the organization. Joint manufacturing costs are not ordinarily allocated to scrap, and scrap is normally not processed further prior to its sale.

Separable manufacturing costs–costs which are incurred after the split-off point and are associated with the production of only a single inventory product.

Split-off point–the point in a joint manufacturing process where joint processing ends and the separate processing of individual products begins.

Value-added activities–activities in the manufacturing/sales process that increase the value of the organization's products to its customers. Examples of value-added activities include production activities and packaging activities.

Weighted-average method–method of allocating manufacturing costs that assumes the units completed during a given period represent a mix of: (1) beginning work-in-process inventory, and (2) units started in production during the current period. Under the weighted average method, a cost per unit is calculated that considers the costs and production activity both during the current period and associated with the beginning work-in-process inventory.

QUESTIONS

1. Why must the managerial accountant use the concept of equivalent units?

2. How does cost accumulation differ in a job-order costing system and a process costing system?

3. What is the difference between a Production Cost Report and a Job Cost Sheet? What are the similarities between these two documents?

4. What differences in information needs exist between a firm using continuous manufacturing processes and one using discrete manufacturing processes?

5. Which of the following firms will generally use job-order costing and which will generally use process costing methods for collecting manufacturing cost information? Use the terms "job order" or "process" as your answer.
    a. A distillery
    b. A manufacturer of large airplanes
    c. A pencil manufacturer
    d. A construction firm
    e. A chemical company
    f. An aluminum rolling mill
    g. A custom catering service
    h. A fertilizer factory

6. What are the basic steps in allocating manufacturing costs in a process costing system?

7. What production activity and manufacturing costs are considered in determining a cost per unit under the weighted-average method?

8. In a manufacturing process involving two manufacturing departments, describe the flow of costs throughout the manufacturing/sales process.

9. Define the following terms:
   a. Common cost
   b. Joint product
   c. By-product

10. Discuss the concept of the common cost and explain its relationship to joint products.

11. Which basic types of managerial decisions must be made in joint-product situations? Explain how these are related to characteristics of the inputs into manufacturing.

12. Common costs are also referred to as non-traceable and non-separable costs. Why?

13. Suppose that a firm produces two joint products and wants to use the ultimate market value technique for allocating common costs. If an intermediate market exists for one of the products and not for the other, how should the managerial accountant determine the allocation basis? Briefly defend the reasoning underlying your answer.

14. Why are by-products treated differently from joint products?

15. a. Differentiate between joint products and by-products. List one criterion for making such a differentiation.
    b. By-products that require no additional processing after the point of separation are often accounted for by assigning them a value of zero at the product separation and reducing cost of production as sales are made. Justify the treatment. Discuss the possible shortcomings of the treatment.

    (AICPA adapted)

16. What is *allocation*? In what situations can allocation techniques provide cost information for joint products?

17. What is the difference between joint products, by-products, and scrap? To which of these products are joint manufacturing costs allocated?

18. What is the split-off point? How are manufacturing costs incurred before and after the split-off point accumulated with inventory in a joint manufacturing process?

19. Define the just-in-time manufacturing philosophy. List several characteristics of the just-in-time manufacturing philosophy.

*20. What are the basic differences in the assumptions of the FIFO method and weighted-average method in determining equivalent units and cost per unit?

EXERCISES AND PROBLEMS

21. *Equivalent Units—Basic.* Calculate the equivalent units of production for the current period in each of the following situations. Assume that all product costs are in the same stage of completion.

		Units
a.	Beginning Inventory—20% Complete	10,000
	Ending Inventory—20% Complete	10,000
b.	Started during the Period	80,000
	Completed during the Period	72,000
	Beginning Inventory—50% Complete	22,000
	Started during the Period	60,000
c.	Ending Inventory—30% Complete	?
	Ending Inventory—25% Complete	28,000
	Completed during the Period	52,000
	Started during the Period	68,000
d.	Beginning Inventory—40% Complete	?
	Beginning Inventory—10% Complete	12,000
	Ending Inventory—80% Complete	15,000
	Completed during the Period	50,000

22. *Equivalent Units—Basic.* Calculate the equivalent units of production in the current period from the following data:

Beginning Inventory	10,000 units
	(100 percent complete for materials, 60 percent complete for labor and overhead)
Units Completed and Transferred	60,000 units
Ending Inventory	6,000 units
	(100 percent complete for materials, 30 percent complete for labor and overhead)

23. *Equivalent Units—Multiple Production Processes.* The Jorcano Manufacturing Company uses a process costing system to account for the costs of its only product: Product D. Production begins in the Fabrication Department, where units of direct material are molded into various connecting parts. After fabrication is complete, the units are transferred to the Assembly Department. No material is added in the Assembly Department. After assembly is complete, the units are transferred to the Packaging Department, where packing material is placed around the units. After the units are ready for shipping, they are sent to the shipping area.

At year end, June 30, 20x3, the following inventory of Product D is on hand:

- No unused direct material or packing material.
- Fabrication Department: 300 units, one-third complete as to direct material and one half complete as to direct labor.
- Assembly Department: 1,000 units, two-fifths complete as to direct labor.
- Packaging Department: 100 units, three-fourths complete as to packing material and one-fourth complete as to direct labor.
- Shipping area: 400 units.

Required:
a. How many equivalent units of direct material and direct labor are in the Fabrication Department inventory on June 30?
b. How many equivalent units of direct material and direct labor are in the Assembly Department inventory on June 30?
c. How many equivalent units of direct material, direct labor, and packing material are in the Packing Department inventory on June 30?
d. How many equivalent units of direct material, direct labor, and packing material are in the shipping area inventory on June 30?

(AICPA adapted)

24. *Basic Calculations—Units Completed and Transferred.* In each of the following independent situations, determine the number of units completed and transferred to finished goods inventory during the period.

	Units
a. Beginning Inventory	20,000
Ending inventory	10,000
Units Started	100,000
b. Beginning Inventory	15,000
Ending inventory	35,000
Units Started	60,000
c. Beginning Inventory	5,000
Ending Inventory	25,000
Units Started	120,000

25. *Ending Inventory—Basic.* In each of the following independent scenarios, determine the number of units on hand in ending work-in-process inventory.

	Units
a. Beginning Inventory	27,000
Units Started	50,000
Units Completed and Transferred	56,000
b. Beginning Inventory	7,000
Units Started	54,000
Units Completed and Transferred	40,000
c. Beginning Inventory	20,000
Units Started	20,000
Units Completed and Transferred	16,000

26. *Basic Calculations—Beginning Inventory.* In each of the following independent cases, determine the number of units on hand in beginning work-in-process inventory.

	Units
a. Units Started	106,000
Units Completed and Transferred	98,000
Ending Inventory	27,000
b. Units Started	86,000
Units Completed and Transferred	98,000
Ending Inventory	20,000
c. Units Started	36,000
Units Completed and Transferred	45,000
Ending Inventory	10,000

27. *Basic Inventory Calculations.* Your company has three departments. Costs incurred directly by each department are called "directly traceable costs" and are determined by using the FIFO method. None of the three departments has beginning inventories. Determine the missing data (indicated by a question mark) for each department.

	Department 1	Department 2	Department 3
Directly Traceable costs	$100,000	$200,000	$150,000
Transfer in Costs	0	?	245,000
Transfer out Costs	?	245,000	345,000
Ending Inventory	10,000	45,000	?

28. *Cost per Unit Calculation—Basic.* Diamond Company manufactures jewelry in a continuous production process. Diamond began its operations in January, 20x1. During that month, a total of 100,000 rings were entered into production, of which 80,000 were completed. The ending work-in-process inventory was 100 percent complete for materials and 80 percent complete with respect to conversion costs. Total production costs incurred in January are summarized below:

Direct Materials	$1,000,000
Direct Labor	1,440,000
Manufacturing Overhead	720,000

Calculate the production cost per unit.

29. *Cost Per Unit and Cost Allocation—Basic.* Iron Works manufactures cement in a continuous production process and, accordingly, uses process costing. No cement was in-process at the beginning of June, 20x0. During that month, 50,000 pounds of cement were entered into production, of these 40,000 were completed. The following production costs were incurred during June.

Direct Materials	$100,000
Direct Labor	25,000
Overhead	65,000

The ending work-in-process is 100 percent complete for materials costs and 50 percent complete for labor and overhead costs.

Required:

a. Calculate the cost per pound of cement for Iron Works during June.
b. Determine the dollar amounts of: (1) cost of goods manufactured and (2) ending work-in-process inventory for June.

30. *Cost Per Unit and Journal Entries.* The Incredible Gadget Corp. manufactures a single product in its Machining Department. In the month of May 20x6, the records showed that 75,000 units were entered in production in the Machining Department. Of these units, 60,000 were completed and transferred to Finished Goods, and 15,000 were left in the process with all materials applied but with only one-third of the required labor and overhead.

There was no work-in-process in either department at the first of the month. Cost records showed the following charges during the month:

	Materials	Labor	Overhead
Machining Department	$120,000	$87,100	$39,000

Required:

a. Prepare in good form a statement showing the unit cost for the month.
b. Prepare a schedule showing the details of the ending work-in-process inventory.
c. Determine the costs transferred from the Machining Department to Finished Goods Inventory.
d. Prepare journal entries to record all of the transactions in May 20x6.

(AICPA adapted)

31. *Cost Allocation—Weighted Average.* The fender welding department of an automobile assembly plant reported $60,000 of costs for 20,000 equivalent units in the beginning inventory. Costs added during the current production period were $160,000 for 40,000 equivalent units of production. Ending inventory consisted of 10,000 equivalent units, and 50,000 units were transferred out. Using the weighted-average method, determine the cost of units transferred and the cost of ending inventory.

*32. *Cost Allocation—FIFO.* Using the first-in, first-out (FIFO) method, recalculate the cost of units transferred and the cost of ending inventory for the data in 31.

*33. *Cost Allocation—FIFO and Weighted Average.* An auto assembly production line manufactures chassis through a fender welding department on an endless conveyor belt. Physical counts of chassis are taken in the morning as the line is about to start up (beginning inventory), as the chassis are transferred out of this department to the next department, and at the end of the day (ending inventory). Four fenders are welded to each chassis. A chassis with only one fender welded at the end of the day is considered to be one-fourth complete in terms of fender welding. The fender welding department accounts for the flow of chassis in terms of equivalent units of completed chassis.

Costs in Beginning Inventory	$ 34,000
Costs Added this Period	120,000
Incomplete Units In Ending Inventory, One-Half Completed	40,000
Incomplete Units in Beginning Inventory, One-Fourth Completed	40,000
Units Transferred out	50,000
Equivalent Units Produced this Week	60,000

Required:

a. Determine the cost of ending inventory and the cost of units transferred under the FIFO cost flow assumption.
b. Determine the cost of ending inventory and the cost of units transferred under the weighted-average cost flow assumption.

34. *Cost Allocation—Weighted-Average (Product Costs in Different Stages of Completion).* Department 9 had beginning work-in-process inventory of 2,000 units. These units were 100 percent complete with respect to direct materials costs and 50 percent complete with respect to labor and overhead costs.

Costs incurred during the period as well as the cost of the beginning work-in-process inventory are shown below:

	Beginning Work-in-Process	Current Costs
Materials	$2,000	$ 5,000
Labor	2,000	12,000
Overhead	1,000	6,000

A total of 8,000 units were completed and transferred to Department 10. Ending work-in-process consisted of 4,000 units, which were 100 percent complete with respect to materials and 30 percent complete with respect to labor and overhead.

Required:

Determine: (1) the cost of the units transferred to Department 10 during the period and (2) the cost of the ending work-in-process inventory in Department 9 using the weighted-average method.

*35. *Cost Allocation—FIFO (Product Costs in Different Stages of Completion).* Using the FIFO method, recalculate the cost of units transferred and the cost of ending inventory for 34.

36. *Cost Allocation–Weighted-Average with Journal Entries (Product Costs in Different Stages of Completion).* Luis Corporation produces a chemical product (Tsoc) in a continuous production process. At the beginning of 20x1, there are no units of Tsoc in work-in-process inventory. A total of 10,000 gallons of Tsoc are started into production during January. Of these, 8,000 gallons are completed. Luis' ending work-in-process inventory is 100 percent complete with respect to materials costs and 60 percent complete with respect to labor and overhead costs.

Luis incurred the following costs during January of 20x1:

Materials	$ 5,000
Labor	16,100
Overhead	8,096

Required:

a. Allocate the production costs of Luis between goods completed and transferred and ending work-in-process inventory using the weighted-average method.
b. Prepare all necessary journal entries, assuming that these costs are incurred in Luis' only production department and the gallons of Tsoc are transferred to finished goods upon completion in this department.
c. Prepare all necessary journal entries, assuming that these costs are incurred in Department A and the gallons of Tsoc are transferred to Department B for further processing.

*37. *Cost Allocation—FIFO (Product Costs in Different Stages of Completion).* The Puck Company uses a single manufacturing process to produce hockey pucks. The process is highly mechanized and the costs stem primarily from materials. Since Puck has an exclusive contract to produce pucks for the National Hockey League for the next five years and foresees no developing competition, they have adopted the process cost method of cost accumulation. The vulcanizing department incurred $34,500 of production costs during the month of November. Rubber costing $25,000 was introduced to the process at the start. Labor and overhead totaling $9,500 were incurred evenly throughout the production cycle. Fifty-thousand units were started in production and 5,000 are still in production at the end of the month. Work-in-process is half completed for labor and overhead and 100 percent complete for material.

Required:

a. What is the unit cost of goods transferred to the finished goods inventory if the FIFO method of cost assignment is used?
b. Would there be a difference in unit cost if the weighted-average method were used? Why or why not?
c. What is the dollar amount in the finished goods inventory under the FIFO method?
d. What is the dollar amount in the work-in-process inventory under the FIFO method?

*38. *Cost Allocation—FIFO and Weighted-Average (Product Costs in Different Stages of Completion).* The Scotch Review Company makes large decorator bottles in a single glass-blowing process. The beginning work-in-process inventory included 25,000 bottles, completed as to the glass but only half complete as to labor and overhead. The value of the material input was $91,000, direct labor was $52,000, and overhead was assigned at a rate of 75 percent of direct labor dollars. During the year, 200,000 bottles were completed, and 20,000 bottles were still in-process at the end of the year. The ending inventory for material was complete, but labor and overhead were only three-fourths complete. The following costs were charged to the production department during the year: material, $900,000; labor, $250,000; and overhead, $187,500.

Required:
a. Using the FIFO method, calculate the unit cost of goods transferred to finished goods inventory.
b. Using the weighted-average method, calculate the unit cost of goods transferred to finished goods inventory.
c. If there is a difference between (a) and (b) above, what accounts for the difference?
d. What are the dollar amounts of the ending work-in-process inventory under both methods?

39. *Comprehensive—FIFO (Product Costs in Different Stages of Completion).* Zeus Company has two production departments (Fabricating and Finishing). In the Fabricating Department, polyplast is prepared from miracle mix and bypro. In the Finishing Department, each unit of polyplast is converted into six tetraplexes and three uniplexes.

The Fabricating and Finishing Departments use process cost-accounting systems. Actual production costs, including overhead, are allocated monthly. Direct materials inventory and work-in-process are priced on a FIFO basis.

The following data were taken from the Fabricating Department's records for December 20x1:

Quantities (units of polyplast):	
In-Process, December 1	3,000
Started in-Process during Month	25,000
Total Units to be Accounted for	28,000
Transferred to Finishing Department	22,000
In-Process, December 31	6,000
Total Units Accounted for	28,000
Cost of Work-in-Process, December 1:	
Materials	$ 13,000
Labor	17,500
Overhead	21,500
	$ 52,000
Direct Labor Costs, December	$154,000
Department Overhead, December	$198,000

Polyplast work-in-process at the beginning and end of the month was partially completed as follows:

	Materials	Labor and Overhead
December 1	66⅔%	50%
December 31	100	75

The following data were taken from direct materials inventory records for December:

	Miracle Mix		Bypro	
	Quantity	Amount	Quantity	Amount
Balance, December 1	62,000	$62,000	265,000	$18,550
Purchases:				
December 12	39,500	49,375		
December 20	28,500	34,200		
Fabricating Department Usage	83,200		50,000	

Required:

a. Compute the equivalent number of units of polyplast, with separate calculations for materials and conversion cost (direct labor plus overhead), manufactured during December.

b. Compute the following items to be included in the Fabricating Department's production report for December 20x1, with separate calculations for materials, direct labor, and overhead. Prepare supporting schedules.

1. Total costs to be accounted for.
2. Unit costs for equivalent units manufactured.
3. Transfers to Finishing Department during December and work-in-process at December 31. Reconcile your answer to (1) of part (b).

(AICPA adapted)

*40. *Cost Allocation with Journal Entries—Weighted Average (Multiple Processes).* Olaf, Inc. produces a single product (DPM), which requires processing in two separate production departments. In each department, materials are introduced at the beginning of the production process. Beginning work-in-process is 50 percent complete with respect to labor and overhead costs in Department A and 25 percent complete with respect to labor and overhead costs in Department B. Total Department A costs associated with the beginning work-in-process in Department B are $60,000. Information concerning the beginning work-in-process in each department is shown below:

	Department A		Department B	
	Units	Cost	Units	Cost
Materials	5,000	$ 2,000	4,000	$10,000
Labor	2,500	25,000	3,000	42,000
Overhead	2,500	12,500	3,000	21,000

During the period, Olaf's production resulted in 10,040 units being completed in Department A, and these were transferred to Department B for further processing. A total of 8,000 units were transferred from Department B during the period to finished goods inventory. Total processing costs for the period are shown as follows:

	Department A	Department B
Materials	$ 3,000	$10,000
Labor	88,000	24,000
Overhead	44,000	12,000

Ending work-in-process inventory consisted of 1,000 units in Department A and 6,000 units in Department B. the Equivalent units associated with each department's ending work-in-process is shown below:

	Department A	Department B
Materials	1,000	6,000
Labor	500	3,000
Overhead	500	3,000

Required:

a. Determine the allocation of costs between units completed and transferred and ending work-in-process for each department using the weighted-average method.

b. Prepare journal entries for Department A based on the above cost allocations.

c. Prepare journal entries for Department B based on the above cost allocations.

*41. *Cost Allocation (Multiple Process) with the Journal Entries—FIFO.*   Repeat 40 using the FIFO method.

*42. *Process Costing System—Reports for Multiple Processes.* Ballinger Paper Products manufactures a high-quality paper box. The box department applies two separate operations—cutting and folding. The paper is first cut and trimmed to the dimensions of a box by one machine group. One square foot of paper is equivalent to four boxes. The trimmings from this process have no scrap value. Box forms are then creased and folded (i.e., completed) by a second machine group. Any partially processed boxes in the department are cut box forms that are ready for creasing and folding. These partly processed boxes are considered 50 percent complete as to labor and overhead. The materials department maintains an inventory of paper in sufficient quantities to permit continuous processing, and transfers to the box department are made as needed. Immediately after folding, all good boxes are transferred to the finished goods department.

During June 20x1 the materials department purchased 1,210,000 square feet of unprocessed paper for $244,000. Conversion costs (direct labor and overhead) for the month were $226,000. Ballinger applies the weighted average cost method to all inventories. Following are the inventory data for June.

		June 30, 20x1	June 1, 20x1	
Inventory	Physical Unit	Units on Hand	Units on Hand	Cost
Materials Department:				
Paper	square feet	200,000	390,000	$76,000
Box Department:				
Boxes Cut, not Folded	number	300,000	800,000	55,000*
Finished Goods Department:				
Completed Boxes on Hand	number	50,000	250,000	18,000
* Materials	$35,000			
Conversion Cost	20,000			
	$55,000			

Required:

Prepare the following for the month of June 20x1:

a. A report of the cost of paper used for the materials department.
b. A schedule showing the physical flow of units (including beginning and ending inventories) in the materials department, in the box department, and in the finished goods department.
c. A schedule showing the computation of equivalent units produced for materials and conversion costs in the box department.
d. A schedule showing the computation of unit costs for the box department.
e. A report of inventory valuation and the cost of completed units for the box department.
f. A schedule showing the computation of unit costs for the finished goods department.
g. A report of inventory valuation and cost of units sold for the finished goods department.

(AICPA adapted)

43. *Cost Allocation—General.* The Morey Company has completed its first year of operations. There were no partially finished goods in the Assembly Department at the beginning of the year, but there are partially finished goods at the close of the first year. Three materials are used in the assembly process: steel to start the process and to be tumbled, bronze that is added halfway through the process, and a clear, protective paint applied as the last step in assembly. Labor and overhead are applied evenly throughout the assembly process. The Morey Company started 100,000 units and completed 80,000 of them by the end of the year. Exactly $400,000 worth of steel, $200,000 worth of bronze, and $10,000 worth of clear paint were used. The overhead was applied proportionally with labor and combined labor and overhead costs amounted to $800,000.

Required:

a. If the work-in-process is one-fourth finished at the end of the year, what cost is transferred to the finished goods inventory? What amount is still associated with the work-in-process inventory?
b. If the work-in-process inventory is three-fourths finished, what cost is transferred to the finished goods inventory? What amount is still associated with the in-process inventory?
c. In part (a) above, are all the units that remain unfinished located at exactly one-fourth of the production cycle? Who made the estimate that work-in-process was one-fourth completed? How was this estimate made?

*44. *Cost Allocation and Journal Entries—Weighted Average (Multiple Departments).* Crews Company produces a chemical agent for commercial use. The company accounts for production in two cost centers: (1) Cooking and (2) Mix-Pack. In the first cost center, liquid substances are combined in large cookers and boiled; the boiling causes a normal decrease in volume from evaporation. After the "batch" is cooked, it is transferred to Mix-Pack, the second cost center. A quantity of alcohol is added equal to the liquid measure of the "batch," that is then mixed and bottled in one-gallon containers.

Material is added at the beginning of production in each cost center and labor is added equally during production in each cost center. Overhead is applied on the basis of 80 percent of labor cost.

The following information is available for the month of October 20x7:

Cost Information	Cooking	Mix-Pack
Work-in-Process, October 1, 20x7:		
Materials	$990	$120
Labor	100	60
Prior Department Cost		426
Month of October		
Materials	$39,600	$15,276
Labor	10,050	16,000

Inventory and production records show that Cooking had 1,000 gallons 40 percent processed on October 1 and 800 gallons 50 percent processed on October 31. Mix-Pack had 600 gallons 50 percent processed on October 1, and 1,000 gallons 30 percent processed on October 31.

Production reports for October show that Cooking started 50,000 gallons into production and completed and transferred 40,200 gallons to Mix-Pack, and Mix-Pack completed and transferred 80,000 one-gallon containers of the finished product to the distribution warehouse.

Required:

a. Prepare in good form quantity reports for the Cooking cost center and for the Mix-Pack cost center.
b. Prepare in good form a Production Cost Report for each of the two cost centers, which computes total cost and cost per unit for each element of cost in inventories and October production. Total cost and cost per unit for transfers should also be computed using the weighted-average cost flow assumption.
c. Prepare journal entries for the month of October.

(AICPA adapted)

45. *Cost Allocation—Various.* A firm produces two products, Product 1 and Product 2, through a joint process. The cost of the joint processing is $100,000. At the split-off point, the products have the following characteristics:

	Units Produced	Product Weight (lbs.)	Product Volume (gals.)	Market Value
Product 1	10,000	20,000	20,000	$250,000
Product 2	20,000	20,000	60,000	150,000

From this information, allocate the common cost between these products, using the following techniques:

a. Units produced
b. Relative weights
c. Relative volumes
d. Market values

Required:

Which technique best allocates the common cost? Why?

46. *Cost Allocation—Various Methods.* A company has four joint products: Keens, Zeena, Deena, and Meena. The total product weight at the split-off point is 10,000 pounds with Keens weighing 4,000 pounds; Deena, 3,000 pounds; Zeena, 2,000 pounds; and Meena, 1,000 pounds. After further processing, Keens weighs 3,000 pounds; Deena, 2,000 pounds; Zeena, 1,500 pounds; and Meena, 500 pounds. The common costs to be allocated total $140,000.

Required:

a. How would the costs be allocated using a physical measure?
b. Assuming an ultimate market value of $50,000 for Keens, $30,000 for Deena, $60,000 for both Zeena and Meena, how would costs be allocated under the market value approach?
c. What assumptions must be made when selecting a physical measure for cost allocation?
d. What assumptions are needed when selecting a market value method for cost allocation?

47. *Cost Accumulation—Common and Separable Costs.* Renegade's manufacturing process results in the production of four products: Beep, Peep, Weep, and Deep. During 20x1, its first year of operations, Renegade incurred $50,000 of production costs, which yielded the following quantity of each product: 4,000 gallons of Beep; 1,000 gallons of Peep; 3,000 gallons of Weep; and 2,000 gallons of Deep. In order to process each product further, the following costs were incurred by Renegade after the split-off point:

Beep	$15,000
Peep	10,000
Weep	25,000
Deep	13,000

Required:

Determine the total costs associated with producing each of these four products. Allocate any common costs to the products based on the relative volume produced.

48. *Cost Allocation and Net Income Determination—Common and Separable Costs.* The Zeta Corporation produces three different products: A, B, and C. Zeta uses market valuation allocation, which requires that separable costs after the split-off point be subtracted from the final market price. In 20x4, the corporation expects A to earn $150,000, B to earn $100,000, and C to earn $70,000 in gross revenues. The separable costs associated with these products are: $50,000 for A, $40,000 for B, and $40,000 for C. Common costs amount to $100,000.

Required:

a. Using Zeta Corporation's method, compute the allocation of common costs. Compute the product income for the three products.
b. Would this analysis be sufficient to make a decision on whether to drop one of the three products? Explain why or why not.

49. *Cost Allocation—Relative Market Value.* Jere, Inc. produces four chemicals in a joint manufacturing process: A, B, C, and D. Each of these products is considered to be a joint product. Assume that common costs of $100,000 were incurred in the production of these chemicals. After joint processing, the quantity of chemicals is as follows:

A	10,000 gallons
B	25,000 gallons
C	5,000 gallons
D	10,000 gallons

Assume that common costs are allocated to all joint products based on the relative market value at the split-off point. Selling prices for each of these products at the split-off point is as follows: (1) A–$4 per gallon, (2) B–$8 per gallon, (3) C–$20 per gallon, and (4) D–$6 per gallon.

Required:

Allocate the common costs incurred by Jere, Inc. to each of the four products manufactured.

50. *Cost Allocation—Relative Market Value With Unknown Value at the Split-Off Point.* Jones, Inc. incurs a total of $100,000 of common costs to produce three products. The quantities of each product produced and the market value of the product at the split-off point are shown below:

Product	Quantity	Market Value
Nixon	1,000 units	$10 per unit
Ford	3,000 units	$ 5 per unit
Carter	2,000 units	?

While the market value of Carter at the split-off point is not known, if Jones completes the production of Carter, it can sell Carter for $15 per unit. Additional processing costs necessary to complete Carter total $5,000.

Required:

Allocate the common costs incurred by Jones to Nixon, Ford, and Carter assuming that relative market values are used to allocate common costs.

51. *Cost Allocation—Physical Measures with Revenue from By-Product.* The joint manufacturing process of Alfie, Inc. results in the production of four products: Aye, Bye, Dye, and Pye. Total joint processing costs of $20,000 were incurred to produce the following quantities of these products.

    Aye ....1,000 units
    Bye ....4,000 units
    Dye ....5,000 units
    Pye ....500 units

    Assume the Pye is a by-product and is sold for $2 per unit. Also assume that separable production costs of $10 per unit, $5 per unit, and $2 per unit were incurred in the further processing of Aye, Bye, and Dye.

    Required:

    a. Allocate the common costs to the three joint products assuming that any revenue earned from the sale of the by-product is used to reduce common costs before allocation.
    b. Determine the total cost of producing Aye, Bye, and Dye.
    c. Repeat (a) and (b) above assuming that revenues from the sale of the by-product are recognized as other income.

52. *Basic Cost Allocation—By-Product.* The Mix-Well Corporation is a large chemical company that treats some of its products as by-products. The net realizable value of the by-product is used to offset the production cost of the joint product. Thus, no profit or loss is attributable to sales of the by-product. One by-product, an oil additive, produces revenue of $61,000. The expected revenue of the joint product is $1,500,000. Common input cost is $1,300,000. The separable cost for the by-product is $40,000.

    Required:

    a. What is the net realizable value of the by-product?
    b. What is the inventory value for the joint product before any sales but after all costs have been considered?
    c. How much of the common costs are assigned to the by-product?
    d. Why is cost allocation considered fundamentally a subjective approach to dividing costs?

53. *Cost Allocation and Income Determination—Various Methods with By-Products.* The LaBreck Company's common cost of producing 1,000 units of Product A, 500 units of Product B, and 500 units of Product C is $100,000. The per-unit sales values of the three products at the split-off point are $20 for Product A, $200 for Product B, and $160 for Product C. Ending inventories include 100 units of Product A, 300 units of Product B, and 200 units of Product C.

    Required:

    a. Compute the amount of common cost that would be included in the ending inventory valuation of the three products: (1) on the basis of their relative sales value and (2) on the basis of physical units.
    b. Discuss the relative merits of each of these two bases of common cost allocation: (1) for financial statement purposes and (2) for decisions about the desirability of selling joint products at the split-off point or processing them further.

c. Assume that Product A is treated as a by-product and common costs are allocated on the basis of physical units. LaBreck chooses to reduce cost of goods sold for by-product revenues. Determine the following dollar amounts: sales revenue, cost of goods sold, and ending inventory valuation of Products A, B, and C.

(AICPA adapted)

54. *Net Income Determination—Cost Allocation and Revenue from By-Products.* 20x1 is the first year of operations for Clipper Company. Clipper Company produces four products: 81, 82, 83, and 84. A total of $60,000 of common costs are incurred prior to the split-off point. These costs are used to manufacture: 500 pounds of 81, 1,000 pounds of 82, 300 pounds of 83, and 200 pounds of 84. Products 81, 82, and 83 are considered to be joint products while Product 84 is a by-product.

Products 81, 82, and 83 are processed beyond the split-off point. The total separable costs of completing these products are $10,000, $30,000, and $21,000, respectively. Product 81 sells for $100 per pound, 82 for $1,310 per pound, and 83 for $200 per pound. In addition, the by-product can be sold for $5 per pound without any further processing. Assume that all inventories are sold.

Required:

a. Determine the total costs associated with producing Products 81, 82, and 83. Allocate common costs based on the pounds of inventory produced and assume that the revenues earned from the sale of the by-product are used to reduce common costs before allocation to joint products.
b. Prepare an income statement for (a) above.
c. Prepare an income statement for Clipper Company assuming that the revenues earned from the sale of the by-product are: (1) used to reduce cost of goods sold and (2) treated as other income. Why are the results using these two approaches identical?

55. *Cost Allocation—Relative Sales Value With By-Product Revenue.* Table Corporation produces three joint products: Salt, Pepper, and Sugar. A total of $30,000 of common costs were incurred to produce 1,000 pounds of Salt, 2,000 pounds of Pepper, and 2,000 pounds of Sugar. At the split-off point, Table can sell Salt for $100 per pound and Pepper for $5 per pound. While Sugar does not have a ready market at the split-off point, this product can be processed further for additional costs of $20,000. When completed, Sugar can be sold for $30 per pound.

In the manufacturing process, an additional product (Sweet'n Low) also results from the production of the three joint products. Sweet'n Low is considered to be a by-product since it has a relatively small contribution to overall revenues. The 100 pounds of Sweet'n Low can be sold for $.30 per pound.

Both Salt and Pepper are sold immediately after the split-off point. Table sells 500 pounds of Salt for $10 per pound and 1,500 pounds of Pepper for $5 per pound. After further processing, the entire inventory of Sugar is sold for $30 per pound.

Required:

a. Allocate the common costs to each product based on the relative market value. Assume that revenue from the sale of the by-product is used to reduce total cost of goods sold at the end of the period.
b. Determine the total production costs associated with each product. Classify these costs as to whether they would be expensed (cost of goods sold) or carried in inventory at the end of the period.
c. Prepare an income statement for Table Corporation.

56. *Cost Allocation and Income Determination—Various Methods with By-Product.* The Alphabet Company produces two joint products and one by-product through a single manufacturing division. The cost associated with operations in this division, Division A, is $30,500. The by-product, Product X, sells on the market for $2 a unit without additional processing. During the current period, 1,000 units of Product X were produced and 500 units were sold. The rest of the units will be sold in the near future. Selling expenses for

Product X were $500, consisting mainly of commissions. The joint products, Product Y and Product Z, are independently processed through separate divisions beyond the split-off point. The relevant information about these products is summarized below (the Alphabet Company has a policy of recognizing neither a profit nor a loss on sales of Product X):

	Cost of Additional Processing	Quantity Produced (units)	Quantity Sold (units)	Selling Costs	Selling Price (per unit)
Product Y	$10,000	25,000	12,500	$5,000	$40
Product Z	20,000	50,000	25,000	10,000	20

Required:

Using this information, answer the following questions and show your calculations.

a. How much cost will be assigned to Product X?
b. Compute the cost to be assigned to Products Y and Z, using the ultimate market value method. Assume that the net by-product revenues are used to reduce common costs prior to allocation.
c. Determine the profitability of Products Y and Z given your answers to parts (a) and (b) above.
d. Compute the cost that will be assigned to Products Y and Z if a physical measure method is used. Assume that Product Y weighs TWO pounds per unit and Product Z weighs FOUR pounds per unit.

57. *Net Income Determination—Various Methods of Allocation.* Mintz Company has a joint manufacturing process. A total of $3,000 of common costs is incurred in the production of three products: J, K, and B. The following information is available with respect to the quantities and market values of these three products at the split-off point.

Product	Quantity	Market Value
J	1,500 pounds	$2 per pound
K	3,000 pounds	$4 per pound
B	4,500 pounds	$2 per pound

The following costs were incurred by Mintz to process these products further after the split-off point: $8,000 for J, $5,000 for K, and $7,500 for B. Assume that 1,000 pounds of J were sold for $10 per pound, 2,000 pounds of K were sold for $15 per pound, and 3,000 pounds of B were sold for $8 per pound.

Required:

a. Determine the total costs of producing each product. Allocate common costs to products using: (1) physical measures and (2) relative market values at the split-off point.
b. Prepare an income statement for each method of allocation in (a) above.

58. *Cost Allocation—Choice Between Alternatives.* A joint process yields two products, named Won and Tu, which can be sold at the split-off point for $2 a unit and $5 a unit, respectively. If these products are processed further, they can be sold for $7 and $8 a unit, respectively. The variable costs of processing Won and Tu through the additional departments are estimated at $4 per unit. Which product or combination of products should the company produce? Support your answer with appropriate calculations.

59. *Cost Allocation and Income Determination—Alternative Processing.* Cope Co. buys 8,000 pounds of input for $40,000. Cope plans to use 6,000 pounds of this input to make 1,000 units of Product Y. The remaining 2,000 pounds will be used to make 4,000 units of Product Z. Product Y will sell for $30 per unit and Z for $5 per unit. If $5,000 of additional processing is performed on Y, it can be sold for $32 per unit. If $15,000 of additional processing is performed on Z, it can be sold for $10 per unit.

Required:

a. By what dollar amount will profits change if additional processing is performed on Product Y or Z?
b. For income determination purposes, common costs are allocated to both products. Determine the profit for Products Y and Z, assuming that Cope Co. will elect to do additional processing only if profits will be increased, and that common costs will be allocated on the basis of input weight.
c. What are the profits on Products Y and Z, assuming that additional processing will be done only if profits will be increased, and that common costs will be allocated on the basis of relative revenue dollars at the split-off point?

60. *Cost Allocation—General Issues.* The Phast Buck Sales Company sells pretzels and potato chips in 5-pound cans to regular customers on established routes. Sales and deliveries are handled by drivers of Phast Buck's two trucks. Pretzels and chips are purchased by the company from a local supplier for $3 a can; in turn, pretzels are sold for $5 a can and potato chips for $4 a can by the driver-salesmen. Until recently, the Phast Buck Company sold a total of 100 cans of pretzels and 100 cans of chips per week. Expenses for operating the trucks amount to $300 a week.

Recently, the owner of the company, Mr. Rob Spindle, asked his bookkeeper, Miss Girtie Track, to allocate the operating expenses among the products sold. Her analysis is presented below.

Phast Buck Sales Company
Operating Expenses

	Product Weight	Allocation Basis	Allocated Cost	Adjusted Market Value	Allocation Basis	Allocated Cost
Pretzels	500	500 ÷ 1,000	$150	$200	200 ÷ 300	$200
Potato Chips	500	500 ÷ 1,000	150	100	100 ÷ 300	100
	1,000			$300		

Product Profitability

	Physical Measure		Profitability Measure	
	Pretzels	Chips	Pretzels	Chips
Sales Revenue	$500	$400	$500	$400
Product Cost	300	300	300	300
Gross Margin	$200	$100	$200	$100
Allocated Cost	150	150	200	100
Net Profit (loss)	$ 50	$ (50)	0	0

Potato chips were clearly a loss for the company, so Mr. Spindle discontinued deliveries of them in an effort to increase profits. Sales of pretzels stayed the same, but during the first week of the new policy instead of making money, the company lost $100.

Required:

a. Did Miss Track make an error in allocating the operating cost?
b. What is the problem with Mr. Spindle's decision?
c. Were the operating costs a common cost? Why or why not?
d. How should the costs have been allocated?
e. What should Mr. Spindle do now?

61. *Cost Allocation—Considering Alternatives.* A process used by Ajak Corp. takes a common material input and produces four joint products: A, B, C, and D. 20,000 pounds of direct material are sufficient to produce 10,000 pounds of A, 5,000 pounds of B, 2,000 pounds of C, and 3,000 pounds of D. Each output has a per-pound market value of $1, $2, $3, and $4, respectively, and direct material costs $1.50 per pound.

    Required:

    a. Using the ultimate market value method of allocating common costs to joint products, determine the gross profit for each product.
    b. Should Ajak Corp. discontinue production of Product A, since its market value is only $1 per pound and the direct material costs $1.50 per pound? Explain.
    c. What is the maximum separable cost Ajak should incur to produce and sell Product B above and beyond its share of the common cost? Does your answer depend upon the particular common cost allocation method used by Ajak?
    d. What is the common cost per pound of Product D, assuming that common costs are allocated according to the relative weight of each coproduct? Should this value be given any consideration when determining a sales price for Product D?

62. *Joint Manufacturing—Cost Allocation and Income Determination.* The Zeta Corporation produces three different products: Product A, Product B, and Product C. Zeta allocates common costs based on market values, which requires that separable costs after the split-off point be subtracted from the final market price. In 20x4, Zeta expects Product A to earn $150,000, Product B to earn $100,000, and Product C to earn $70,000 in gross revenues. The separable costs associated with these products are $50,000, $40,000, and $40,000 for Products A, B, and C, respectively. Common costs totaled $100,000.

    Required:

    a. Using the market value method of allocation, compute the allocation of common costs and the product income for the three products.
    b. Would this analysis be sufficient to decide whether to discontinue one of these three products? Why or why not?

63. *Basic Joint Product Differences.* The product costing procedures used in accounting for joint products seem to be different from those used in single product situations. In many respects, however, they are similar. For each of the activities listed below, indicate whether or not the accounting procedures are different in the joint-product and individual-product situations. If they are different, briefly explain the differences.

    a. Sources of cost information
    b. Recording cost information
    c. Determining product costs
    d. Determining the cost of a manufacturing process
    e. Decision-makers' uses of the product cost information

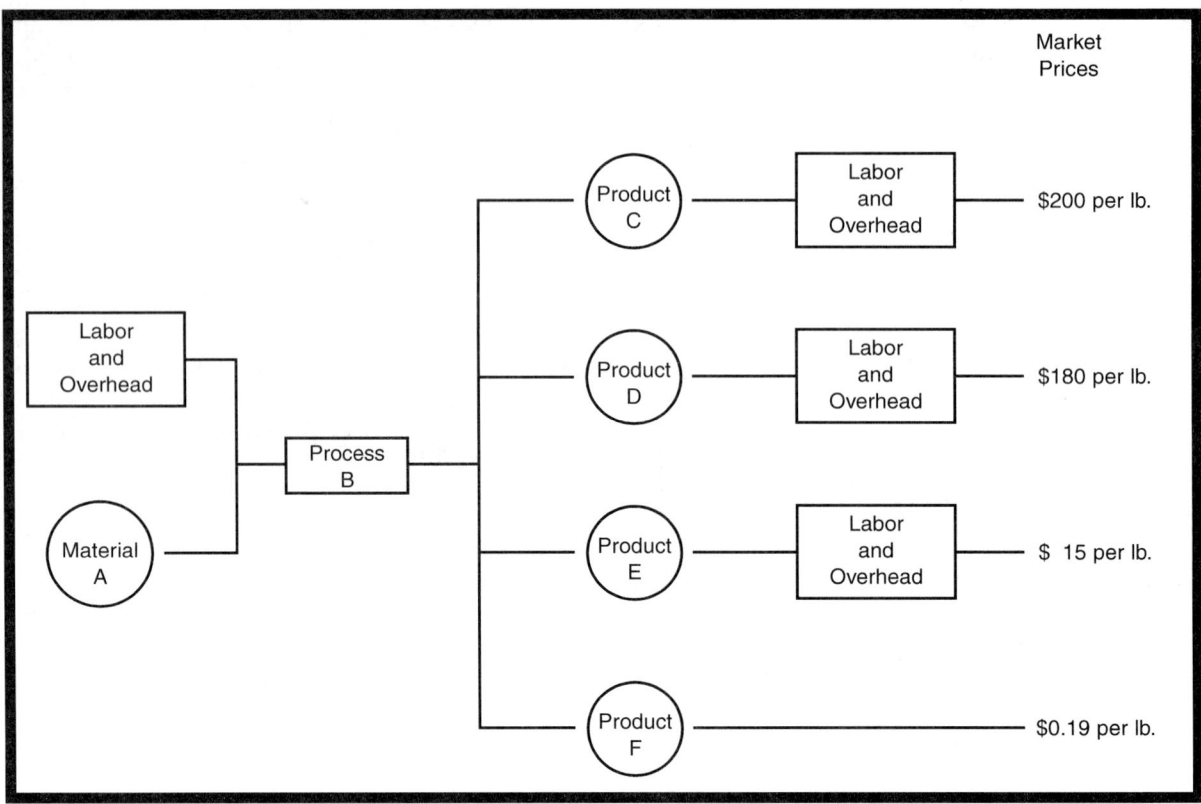

64. *Overview—Joint Production Process.* The diagram below relates to the manufacturing operations of the Bent Joint Company. Use this diagram to answer the following questions about the Bent Joint Company:

   a. What type of process is Process B?
   b. What is Product C?
   c. What can Product C and D be called? Why?
   d. What can Product E be called? Is it different from Products C and D? Why or why not?
   e. What is Product F?
   f. Indicate the split-off point in this operation.

65. *Income Determination—Joint Production.* The MCB Corporation produces one principal product—"Main-Line." Incidental to this production are two additional products—"Co-Line" and "By-Line." Material is started in Process No. 1; the three products come out of this process. "Main-Line" is processed further through Process No. 2. "Co-Line" is processed further through Process No. 3, while "By-Line" is sold without further processing. The following data for February are available:

   1. Material put in Process No. 1, $12,000.
   2. Conversion costs: Process No. 1, $8,000; Process No. 2, $4,000; Process No. 3, $300.
   3. There were no beginning or ending in-process inventories.
   4. Production and sales data:

	Quantity Produced	Quantity Sold	February Average Sales Price	Market Price End of February
Main-Line	5,000	4,000	$6.00	$6.00
Co-Line	3,000	2,000	1.00	.90
By-Line	1,000	900	.50	.55

   5. Selling and administrative expenses are related to the quantity sold. Selling and administrative expenses for the next period are estimated to be the same as actual expenses for February.

Main-Line	$2,000
Co-Line	800
By-Line	36

   6. Standard net profit on Co-Line is 10 percent of sales.
   7. No profit or loss is realized on By-Line sales.

Required:
a. Compute the value of the By-Line inventory and the costs transferred from Process No. 1 to By-Line units during the period.
b. Compute the value of the Co-Line inventory and the costs transferred from Process No. 1 to Co-Line units during the period.
c. Complete the following income statement:

	Main-Line	Co-Line	By-Line	Total
Sales..				
Cost of Goods Sold........................				
Gross Profit....................................				
Selling and Administrative Expenses.............				
Net Profit.......................................				

(AICPA adapted)

66. *Inventory Valuation—Joint Products.* The Town Company manufactures two principal products, X and M, and a by-product known as Bypo. The company has three producing departments: 101, 201, and 301. Direct materials A and B are started in process in Department 101. Upon completion of processing in that department, one-fifth of the material is by-product and is transferred directly to stock. One-third of the remaining output of Department 101 goes to Department 201, where it is made into X, and the other two-thirds goes to Department 301, where it becomes M. The processing of X in Department 201 results in a 50 percent gain in weight of material transferred into the department owing to the addition of water at the start of the processing. There is no gain or loss of weight in the other processes.

The company considers the income from Bypo, after allowing five cents per pound for estimated selling and delivery costs, a reduction of the cost of the two principal products. The company assigns Department 101 costs to the two principal products in proportion to their net sales value at point of separation, computed by deducting costs to be incurred in subsequent processes from the sales value of the products.

The following information concerns the operations during April 20x1:

Inventories

	March 31 Quantity (pounds)	Value	April 30 Quantity (pounds)
Department 101	None		None
Department 201	800	$17,160	1,000
Department 301	200	2,340	360
Finished Stock—X	300	7,260	800
Finished Stock—M	1,200	18,550	700
Finished Stock—Bypo	None		None

Inventories in process are estimated to be one-half complete in Departments 201 and 301, both at the first and last of the month.

Costs

	Material Used	Labor and Overhead
Department 101.................	$134,090	$87,442
Department 201.................	0	31,950
Department 301.................	0	61,880

The material used in Department 101 weighed 18,000 pounds. Sales Prices as of April 30 are:

Sales Prices

X....................	$29.50 per pound
M	17.50 per pound
Bypo	.50 per pound

Prices as of April 30 are unchanged from those in effect during the month.

Required:

You are to prepare the following statements covering the operations of the Town Company. Present all supporting computations in good form.

a. Statement showing costs and production by departments for the month of April. The company uses first-in, first-out to cost out production.
b. A schedule of inventory values for work-in-process and finished goods as of April 30.

67. *Joint Manufacturing Processes—Cost Allocation and Income Determination.* Miller Manufacturing Company buys Zeon for $0.80 per gallon. At the end of processing in Department 1, Zeon splits off into Products A, B, and C. Product A is sold at the split-off point without further processing. Products B and C require further processing before they can be sold. Product B is processed in Department 2 and Product C is processed in Department 3. Following is a summary of costs and other data for the year ended June 30, 20x3.

	Department		
	1	2	3
Cost of Zeon	$96,000	0	0
Direct Labor	14,000	$15,000	$65,000
Manufacturing Overhead	10,000	21,000	25,000

	Products		
	A	B	C
Gallons Sold	20,000	30,000	45,000
Gallons on Hand June 30, 20x3	10,000	0	15,000
Sales (in dollars)	$30,000	$75,000	$135,000

There were no inventories on hand at July 1, 20x2 and there was no Zeon on hand at June 30, 20x3. All gallons on hand at June 30, 20x3 were complete as to processing. Miller uses the relative sales value method of allocating common costs.

Required:

a. Assuming that Product A is a joint product, allocate Department 1 costs to Products A, B, and C.
b. Given your answer to part (a) above, determine the gross profit and inventory balances for the year ended June 30, 20x3.
c. Recalculate (a) and (b) above, assuming that Product A is a by-product and not a joint product.

Appendix A

Process Costing Using the FIFO Method

The process costing system for The American Vegetable Company illustrated in the text used the weighted-average method to allocate manufacturing costs to production. Under the weighted-average method, an "average" manufacturing cost per unit was determined based on production activity and manufacturing costs from (1) one or more prior periods (i.e., beginning work-in-process inventory) and (2) the current period. This average cost per unit is then used to transfer costs as the inventory moves through the various stages of the manufacturing/sales process.

In most manufacturing processes, beginning work-in-process inventory is completed prior to starting (and completing) additional production runs. For example, it is unlikely that American Vegetable would begin producing other batches of vegetables until the items in process at the beginning of January in the Canning Department were completed. In this case, the initial items completed are those included in beginning work-in-process inventory. The total costs of producing items in the beginning work-in-process inventory include costs incurred in one or more prior periods as well as costs incurred in the current period necessary to complete the items.

Once the beginning work-in-process is completed, the production of additional units is begun. Some of these units may be completed during the period while others may remain in process at the end of the period. In either case, the manufacturing costs associated with any units started during the current period would include only that period's costs of direct materials, direct labor, and manufacturing overhead.

The weighted-average method does not distinguish beginning work-in-process inventory and items started during the current period, since an "average" cost per unit is used to accumulate manufacturing costs with both groups of items. If manufacturing costs remain constant from period to period, the weighted-average method provides a fairly accurate depiction of the actual cost of manufacturing these units. However, in cases where the cost of materials, labor, and/or overhead inputs fluctuates from period to period, the use of the weighted-average method may result in large differences in determining manufacturing costs.

In cases where manufacturing costs fluctuate greatly from period to period, costs may be accumulated with inventory using the first-in, first out (FIFO) method. As with the weighted-average method discussed earlier in the chapter, the FIFO method accumulates manufacturing costs with inventory by determining a cost per unit. However, under the FIFO method, the cost per unit reflects only the current period's production activity and manufacturing costs. The flow of production activity and manufacturing costs under the FIFO method is as follows:

1. Items in beginning work-in-process are completed prior to the initiation of any new production. The total costs of producing these items include manufacturing costs from one or more prior periods and manufacturing costs from the current period.
2. The production of other items is begun and some of these items are completed during the current period. The costs accumulated with these items are based on the manufacturing cost per unit during the current period.
3. Production of other items is started and these items are not completed during the current period. The costs of these items are accumulated in work-in-process inventory at the end of the period. Like the items in (2) above, manufacturing costs are accumulated with these items based on the manufacturing cost per unit in the current period.

To accumulate manufacturing costs in the manner described above, the FIFO method calculates a cost per unit for the current period. This cost per unit includes only production activity and the related manufacturing costs during the current period. Thus, unlike the weighted-average method illustrated in the chapter, the FIFO method does not consider either the production activity or manufacturing costs associated with the beginning work-in-process inventory.

To illustrate the accumulation of costs with inventory using the FIFO method, let us revisit the American Vegetable example illustrated in the chapter. Recall that 6,000 cans of vegetables were in process at the beginning of January. Recall that these cans were 100 percent complete as to materials costs and 30 percent complete for conversion costs. An additional 8,000 cans were entered into production during January, of which, 5,000 were completed and 3,000 were in process at the end of January. The 3,000 cans of vegetables in ending work-in-process inventory were 100 percent complete as to materials costs and 40 percent complete for conversion costs.

The information related to the three batches of production in the Canning Department of American Vegetable (the 6,000 cans of beginning work-in-process inventory, the 5,000 cans started and completed during January 20x2, and the 3,000 cans in ending work-in-process at January 31, 20x2) is summarized as follows:

	Beginning Work-in-Process Inventory	Units Started and Completed	Ending Work-in-Process Inventory
Direct Materials	20x1: 6,000 cans (6,000 x 1.00)	20x2: 5,000 cans (5,000 x 1.00)	20x2: 3,000 cans (3,000 x 1.00)
Direct labor And Overhead	20x1: 1,800 cans (6,000 x 0.30) | 20x2: 4,200 cans (6,000 x 0.70)	20x2: 5,000 cans (5,000 x 1.00)	20x2: 1,200 cans (3,000 x 0.40)

The items shaded above represent production that occurred during January 20x2. The equivalent units calculated under the weighted-average method included both the shaded items (representing production activity during January 20x2) and the unshaded items (representing production activity during December 20x1 on the beginning work-in-process inventory). As shown in the Production Cost Report in Illustration 4, equivalent units under the weighted-average method totaled 14,000 and 12,200 cans for materials and conversion costs, respectively. The measure of equivalent units calculated under the FIFO method will include only that production activity during the month of January (the shaded portion of the above schemata).

Total production for January is determined by summing the equivalent units necessary to (1) complete units in beginning work-in-process inventory, (2) complete units started during January 20x2, and (3) begin production of the ending work-in-process inventory. This calculation is shown on page 4-4-43.

	Materials	Labor and Overhead
Complete Beginning Work-in-Process Inventory		
(6,000 cans x 0.00)	0	
(6,000 cans x 0.70)		4,200
Units Started and Completed in January	5,000	5,000
Ending Work-in-Process Inventory		
(3,000 cans x 1.00)	3,000	
(3,000 cans x 0.40)		1,200
Total Equivalent Units	8,000	10,400

The above calculation requires that the number of units started and completed during January be determined; however, this subtotal is not always readily available from production data. A shortcut method that may be used to determine January production is to calculate total production (similar to the equivalent units under the weighted-average method) and subtract the equivalent units associated with the beginning work-in-process inventory. This calculation is as follows:

	Materials	Labor and Overhead
Total Equivalent Units (Weighted-Average Method)	14,000	12,200
Beginning Work-in-Process Inventory:		
(6,000 cans x 1.00)	(6,000)	
(6,000 cans x 0.30)		(1,800)
Total Equivalent Units	8,000	10,400

At this point, a cost per unit can be calculated by dividing January's manufacturing costs by the equivalent units produced during January. It should be noted that this cost per unit reflects only January's production and costs (unlike the weighted-average method, which included both December's production and costs and January's production and costs). From the cost data presented earlier in the chapter (see Illustration 4), the total manufacturing costs incurred in January were $22,200, consisting of $4,000 of direct materials costs, $10,400 of direct labor costs, and $7,800 of overhead costs. The cost per unit under FIFO is calculated as follows:

	Direct Materials	Direct Labor	Manufacturing Overhead
January Manufacturing Costs	$ 4,000	$10,400	$ 7,800
Equivalent Units of Production	÷ 8,000	÷10,400	÷10,400
Total Cost per Unit	$ 0.50	$ 1.00	$ 0.75

Therefore, the manufacturing cost per unit in January under the FIFO method is $2.25 ($0.50 + $1.00 + $0.75 = $2.25).

Illustration 7 shows the Production Cost Report for The American Vegetable Company's Canning Department for the month of January 20x2 assuming a FIFO cost flow. It is apparent that three basic "pools" of costs exist:

1. The total cost of the 6,000 cans of vegetables in beginning work-in-process inventory of $14,470 (see 1 in Illustration 7). Of this, $7,120 was incurred in December 20x1 and $7,350 was incurred in January 20x2 to complete production of these items. Since the beginning work-in-process inventory was only 30 percent complete with respect to labor and overhead costs, 70 percent of the production activity for these costs occurred during January 20x2.
2. The cost of the 5,000 units started and completed in January 20x2 of $11,250. This cost is determined by multiplying the 5,000 cans of vegetables by the cost of producing each can of vegetables (5,000 cans x $2.25 = $11,250) (see 2 in Illustration 7).
3. The cost of the 3,000 cans of vegetables in ending work-in-process inventory of $3,600. This cost is determined by multiplying the equivalent units of production in the ending work-in-process inventory by the applicable cost per can ($0.50 for materials, $1.00 for labor, and $0.75 for overhead) (see 3 in Illustration 7). As shown in Illustration 7, the ending work-in-process is 100 percent complete for materials costs and 40 percent complete for labor and overhead costs.

Illustration 7
The American Vegetable Company
Production Cost Report: Canning Department (FIFO Method)
January 20x2

Cost per Unit (Summarized):

	Direct Materials		Direct Labor		Overhead		Total
January Costs	4,000	+	10,400	+	7,800	=	22,200
	÷		÷		÷		
January Production	8,000		10,400		10,400		
	=		=		=		
Cost per Unit	**$0.50**	+	**$1.00**	+	**$0.75**	=	**$2.25**

Allocation of Manufacturing costs:

Cans Completed:

Beginning WIP (6,000 cans):
    Direct Materials (see Illustration 3) $5,800
    Direct Labor (see Illustration 3) 580
    Overhead (see Illustration 3) 740 $7,120
Costs to Complete:
    Direct Materials .... $ 0
    Direct Labor (6,000 cans x 0.70 x $1.00) 4,200
    Overhead (6,000 cans x 0.70 x $0.75) 3,150   7,350

Total Costs of First 6,000 Units .... **$14,470** ⬅ ①

Cost of 5,000 Units Started and Completed
    in January (5,000 cans x 1.00 x $2.25) .... **11,250** ⬅ ②

Cost of Units Completed and Transferred
    To Packaging **$25,720**

Ending Work-in-Process:
    Direct Materials (3,000 cans x 1.00 x $0.50) $1,500
    Direct Labor (3,000 cans x 0.40 x $1.00) 1,200
    Overhead (3,000 cans x 0.40 x $0.75) 900   **3,600** ⬅ ③

Total Costs Accounted For **$29,320**

Appendix B

Cost Accumulation and Cost Flows in a Just-in-Time Costing Systems

This appendix illustrates the basic methods of cost accumulation and cost flows in a just-in-time (JIT) costing system. JIT costing may be used in conjunction with either a job-order or a process costing system. The distinguishing characteristic of JIT costing is that manufacturing costs are accumulated with inventory at later stages of the manufacturing process. The rationale for this difference is that JIT assumes that small or minimum (if any) quantities of direct materials, work-in-process, and finished goods inventories will be maintained by the organization.

Since JIT assumes that the work-in-process and finished goods inventories maintained by the organization will be minimal, all manufacturing costs associated with production are normally accumulated directly in cost of goods sold in a JIT system. At the end of the period, the manufacturing costs associated with any unsold or uncompleted items are "backed out" and included in either finished goods inventory or work-in-process inventory, respectively, depending upon their status. For this reason, JIT costing is often referred to as "backflush" costing.

To illustrate the use of JIT costing, consider The American Vegetable Company example presented earlier in this chapter. Assume that American Vegetable uses JIT costing for the production of vegetables in its Canning Department during January 20x2. The following transactions summarize the major steps in American Vegetable's production during the month of January (using the weighted-average method):

1. Total manufacturing costs incurred in January 20x2 in the Canning Department were $22,200. These costs consisted of $4,000 of direct materials costs, $10,400 of direct labor costs, and $1,800 of overhead costs. A total of $1,650 of costs were incurred in the Packaging Department, consisting of $330 of direct materials costs, $550 of direct labor costs, and $770 of manufacturing overhead costs.
2. American Vegetable's inventories were as follows:

	January 1, 20x2	January 31, 20x2
Work-in-Process Inventory (Canning)	7,120	4,020
Work-in-Process Inventory (Packaging)	0	0
Finished Goods Inventory	0	12,250

Under a JIT cost accumulation system, costs are accumulated as follows:

- Since JIT systems operate under the assumption that minimal quantities of inventories are maintained, all inventory costs are transferred to cost of goods sold. Thus, at the beginning of January 20x2, the $7,120 of work-in-process inventory costs in the Canning Department are transferred to cost of goods sold.[24]
- Similarly, all manufacturing costs are initially recorded in cost of goods sold instead of work-in-process inventory. Thus, the $22,200 of January manufacturing costs incurred in the Canning Department would be accumulated in cost of goods sold. Similarly, the $1,650 of January manufacturing costs incurred in the Packaging Department would also be directly recorded in cost of goods sold.

At this point, a total of $30,970 (beginning work-in-process costs of $1,120, current manufacturing costs of $22,200 in the Canning Department, and current manufacturing costs of $1,650 in the Packaging Department) has been accumulated in cost of goods sold. If no work-in-process or finished goods inventories existed at January 31, 20x2, this amount would properly reflect the total cost of goods sold to customers during January. However, based on the Production Cost Report shown in Illustration 4, ending work-in-process inventory in the Canning Department is $4,020. In addition, Illustration 5 notes that The American Vegetable Company has ending finished goods inventories of $12,250.

- Once ending inventories have been determined, these costs are then "backed out" of cost of goods sold and transferred to work-in-process and finished goods inventory, respectively. This adjustment is the origin of the term "backflush" costing. Once these costs are transferred, a total of $14,700 ($30,970 – $4,020 – $12,250 = $14,700) remains in cost of goods sold. Recall that this represents the 6,000 cans of vegetables sold to customers at a cost of $2.45 per can (shown earlier in Illustration 5).

The flow of costs in a JIT cost accumulation system is summarized in Illustration 8. It should be apparent that the end results are identical to those illustrated for a conventional cost accumulation system (see Illustration 5). This raises the question of why the JIT cost accumulation system would be utilized in practice. If companies truly maintain minimal quantities of work-in-process and finished goods inventory, the JIT system does not require manufacturing costs to be accumulated with inventory as it is manufactured (work-in-process inventory), transferred upon completion of the units (finished goods inventory), and then transferred as items are sold to customers (cost of goods sold). Instead, costs are initially recorded in cost of goods sold under the assumption that all items will be sold to customers as they are manufactured.

---

[24] Some JIT cost accumulation systems accumulate direct materials costs with inventory in the same manner as a conventional system. That is, these costs are initially accumulated in work-in-process inventory and then transferred to finished goods inventory and cost of goods sold as the inventory is completed and sold, respectively. For simplicity, and to focus on the concept of JIT cost accumulation, the JIT system illustrated in this appendix does not distinguish among product costs in this manner.

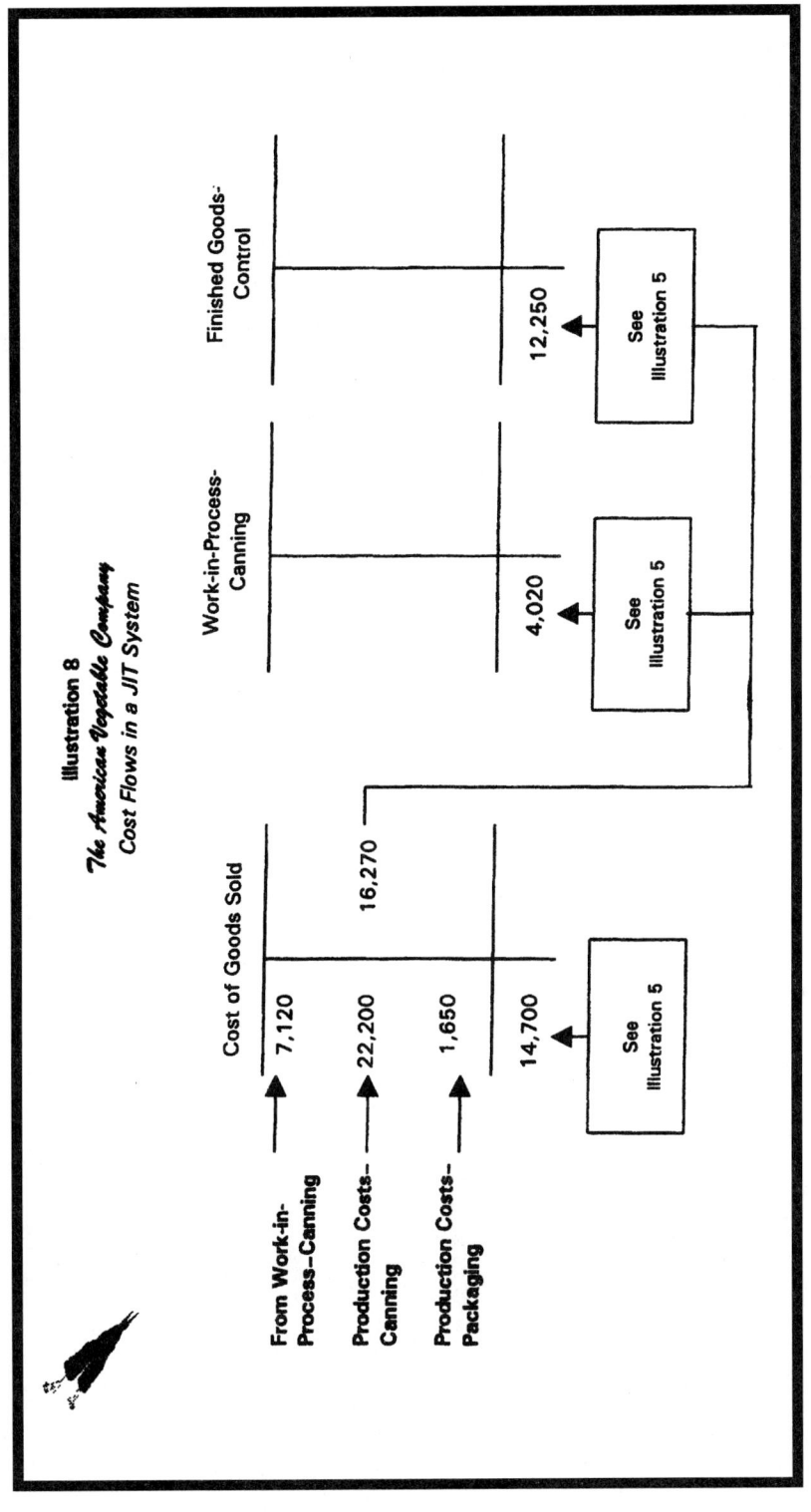

Appendix C

Production Processes Having Multiple Departments

In many process costing systems, inventory must pass through more than one production department prior to completion. The existence of multiple production departments introduces additional issues for the managerial accountant, since materials, labor, and/or overhead costs are incurred in a number of departments for the production of inventory. However, the basic philosophy in these cases is relatively straightforward: *All necessary costs of production should be accumulated with the inventory and transferred with that inventory as it moves through various stages of production.* In these cases, a cost per unit is calculated as in a production process consisting of a single department; the only difference is that the total costs of production include costs incurred by more than one department.

To illustrate cost accumulation in a production process with multiple departments, let us refer to The American Vegetable Company example discussed throughout this chapter. Assume that American Vegetable's production process consists of two departments. First, in the "Canning" Department, vegetables are cleaned, sorted, and canned. The previous chapter focused on the costs incurred and units produced by the Canning Department. Next, once finished products emerge from the Canning Department, they are labeled, weighed (for quality control purposes), and packed for shipping in the "Packaging" Department. The American Vegetable Company's production process is depicted below:

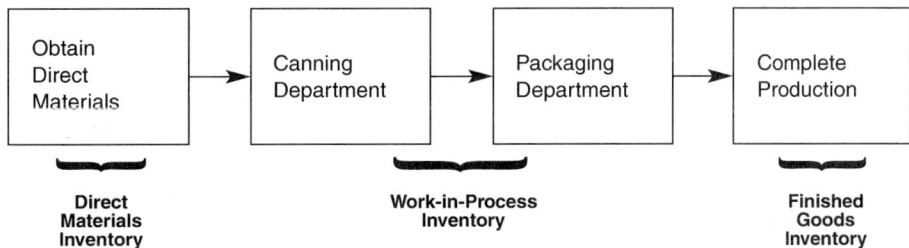

To illustrate the process of cost accumulation and cost allocation in a production process having multiple production departments, we will extend our discussion for The American Vegetable Company to include costs incurred in the Packaging Department. The data for the Canning Department were initially presented in the previous section; assume the use of the weighted-average method in identifying the flow of production costs.

Production Costs—Canning Department

The journal entry to record production costs incurred in the Canning department when multiple production departments exist is shown below. The only difference between this entry and that prepared when a single production department exists is that the costs of work-in-process inventory are identified with a specific production department.

4-49

Work-in-Process—Canning..	22,200	
Direct Materials—Control		4,000
Wages Payable		10,400
Factory Overhead—Control		7,800

Completion of Production—Canning Department

During the month of January, a total of 11,000 cans of vegetables was completed. These cans are then forwarded to the Packaging Department for additional processing. The amount of costs transferred to the Packaging Department is $25,300 (11,000 x $2.30 per can = $25,300).

Work-in-Process—Packaging	25,300	
Work-in-Process—Canning		25,300

Note that this entry is quite similar to that prepared in the original American Vegetable Company example. The only difference is that the costs are transferred to a second work-in-process account instead of finished goods. Since the cans of vegetables are not yet completed at this point, their associated costs are still accumulated in a work-in-process inventory account.

Production Costs—Packaging Department

Once the cans of vegetables are transferred to the Packaging Department, additional production costs are incurred to complete the final inventory. Assume that an additional $2,200 of labor costs were incurred and $1,100 of overhead costs were applied in the Packaging Department. The journal entry required to accumulate these costs is shown below:

Work-in-Process—Packaging	3,300	
Wages Payable		2,200
Factory Overhead—Control		1,100

This entry is quite similar to that used to accumulate production costs incurred by the Canning Department. As before, all production costs are initially accumulated with work-in-process inventory.

Completion of Production

Once the 11,000 cans of vegetables are completed in the Packaging Department, the total costs are then transferred to finished goods inventory. Assuming that no beginning work-in-process inventory existed in the Packaging Department and that all 11,000 cans were completed during January, a total of 11,000 equivalent units were produced by the Packaging Department in that month. The production cost report prepared by American Vegetable Company is shown on the following page in Illustration 9.

The production cost report presented in Illustration 9 accumulates two "groups" of costs: costs incurred in the Canning Department ($25,300) and costs incurred in the Packaging Department ($3,300). Thus, a total of $28,600 of costs were incurred to produce 11,000 finished units (cans of vegetables). Dividing the total costs by the number of cans of vegetables produced results in a cost per can of $2.60.

The following journal entry would be prepared to transfer the costs of the completed cans of vegetables to finished goods inventory. The amount of the transfer can be determined by multiplying the total cost per can ($2.60) by the number of finished cans (11,000).

Finished Goods—Control	28,600	
Work-in-Process—Packaging		28,600

Work-in-Process in Subsequent Production Departments

The above example is somewhat simplified, as no beginning or ending work in-process inventory existed in the Packaging Department. If work-in-process inventory existed in the Packaging Department, American Vegetable would calculate equivalent units of production as in the single-department example introduced previously in the chapter. The production costs would then be divided by these equivalent units to determine a cost per unit. Using this cost per unit, American Vegetable would then allocate production costs between:

(1) ending work-in-process inventory and (2) finished goods inventory in the same manner as before. In this instance, note that The American Vegetable Company would have two types of work-in-process inventory:

1. Inventory that has been partially completed by the Canning Department but has not been entered into the Packaging Department.

2. Inventory that has been completed by the Canning Department and has been partially completed by the Packaging Department.

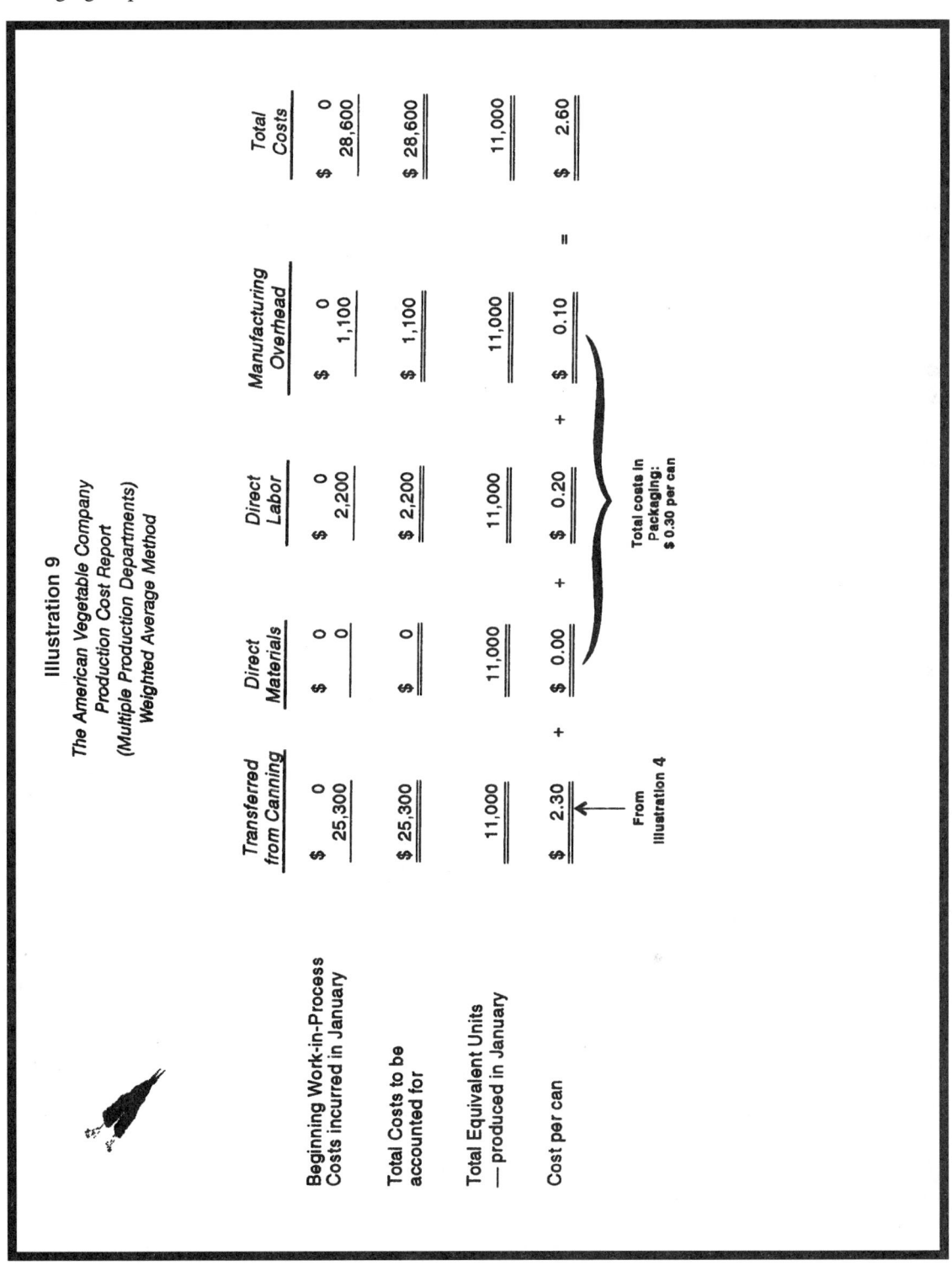

Learning Objectives

Chapter 5 discusses the nature of overhead costs and the process through which these costs are accumulated with the organization's products and services. Studying this chapter should enable you to:

1. Understand the nature of overhead costs and how these costs differ from prime costs (direct materials and direct labor costs).

2. Calculate a predetermined overhead rate for use in applying overhead costs to production.

3. Use a two-stage cost allocation, allocate service department costs to operating departments.

4. Distinguish between the direct method and step-down method of allocating service department costs to operating departments.

5. Discuss activity-based costing and explain how activity-based costing differs from traditional costing.

6. Use activity-based costing to apply overhead costs to production.

Overhead Costs and Activity-Based Costing

INTRODUCTION

Jeffrey Jones and his boss, Jack Evans, continued their discussion regarding the costs incurred by The American Vegetable Company in producing its inventory:

Jeffrey: Jack, you wanted me to determine how much it costs to produce our vegetable products. Our last production run was 10,000 cans. The total materials costs were $1,000 and labor costs were around $2,500. Based on this information, I'd say our costs are about $0.35 a can.

Jack: Is that all? What about the costs of running our machinery? And the cost of ordering and handling the materials we use in production? Aren't these costs we also need to consider?

Jeffrey: Yeah, I guess so. But it's difficult to identify these costs with individual production runs. After all, we really won't know all of the costs of running our machinery until the utilities are paid at the end of each month. Also, how can we determine how the costs of ordering and handling materials relate to a specific batch of products?

Jack: I know it'll be difficult, but we've got to identify all of the costs of manufacturing our inventory. We need this information to set our prices. After all, how can we know what to charge our customers until we know what it costs us to produce the items? We may be losing a ton of money on this product if we don't consider all of these costs.

The above discussion between Jeffrey Jones and Jack Evans recognizes the difficulty of identifying the total costs of manufacturing inventory or providing services. In particular, some costs are not directly identifiable or are difficult to identify with individual units of production. These costs are referred to as manufacturing overhead costs. While we have introduced overhead costs and the basic method of accumulating overhead costs with production in Chapters 3 and 4, this chapter provides an in-depth discussion of these costs and how they are accumulated with products and services.

THE NATURE OF MANUFACTURING OVERHEAD COSTS

As noted in Chapter 3, manufacturing overhead costs include all costs associated with producing the organization's inventory and/or providing the organization's services other than direct materials costs and direct labor costs. Examples of overhead costs include indirect materials and supplies costs, indirect labor costs, and various costs associated with the organization's production equipment and facilities (utilities, depreciation, repairs and maintenance, insurance, and property taxes). The distinguishing characteristic of overhead costs is that these costs are directly related to the production of inventory or services. Therefore, the costs of administrative or sales salaries and costs associated with the organization's administrative or sales facilities (utilities, depreciation, etc.) would not be classified as overhead costs, as these are period costs rather than product costs.

Because overhead costs are a part of the cost of producing inventory or providing services, it is just as important that these costs be accumulated with the organization's products as it is to accumulate direct materials costs and direct labor costs. However, overhead costs present unique problems because it is often quite difficult to accumulate overhead costs with production. For example, consider the production of a gallon of ice cream by Ben & Jerry's. It may be relatively easy to identify the cost of the direct materials (carton and ingredients) and direct labor (wages paid to individuals operating production machinery) associated with producing a gallon of ice cream. However, the cost of producing a gallon of ice cream should also include overhead costs such as the following:

- Wages paid to individuals who handle direct materials and deliver materials to production.
- Wages paid to individuals who prepare production machinery for use.
- Depreciation, utilities, taxes, insurance, and repairs on production machinery and facilities.
- Wages paid to individuals who inspect final products prior to shipment.

Imagine how difficult it would be to associate a portion of any or all of the above costs with a single product. In some cases (utilities, taxes, and repairs), the organization would not know the total costs at the time of production, since these costs are expected to vary throughout the year. In other cases (wages, insurance, and depreciation), the organization may know the total costs but find it much too time-consuming to attempt to associate these costs with a single gallon of product. The need for cost-efficient, timely cost accumulation does not permit the organization to accumulate overhead costs with products or services in the same manner as it accumulates direct materials and direct labor costs.

The significance of overhead costs (and the importance of controlling these costs) is illustrated by the following examples from practice.

> IBM has recently teamed with its biggest distributor (Inacom Corp.) to allow Inacom to assemble and distribute its personal computers. By stocking a wide variety of parts, Inacom has reduced the time from receipt of a customer order to production of the computer from two days to four hours. The overhead costs saved by these efficiencies have reduced the costs of manufacturing an IBM computer by 10 percent.[1]
>
> An important overhead cost facing manufacturers is the cost of quality control, inspection, and rework. In 1993, Boeing identified 3.5 million manufacturing defects across its line of airplanes, an average of 52 defects per seat. The cost of fixing these defects prior to completion was $1 billion, almost as much as that year's net profits ($1.2 billion). In contrast, Toyota generates only 0.75 defects per car, or 0.15 defects per seat.[2]

---

[1] Watch Out, Dell," *Forbes* (March 24, 1997), 84.

[2] "Sleepy in Seattle," *Fortune* (August 7, 1995), 92–97.

> To reduce overhead costs associated with production set-ups, Nokia (a Helsinki, Finland manufacturer of digital mobile phones) has designed its phones to be as similar as possible. This allows different models of phones to be made on the same production line. Nokia can then shift rapidly from one model to another to meet demand. These efficiencies have boosted Nokia's operating margins to 17.7 percent, which exceed those of industry leader Motorola (14.4%).[3]
>
> After studying pit crews at the Indianapolis Motor Speedway, Proctor and Gamble has reduced the time required for changing its plant and equipment from the production of one type of product to another from two days to just two hours. Their overall goal is to reduce overhead costs by a total of $750 million.[4]

Applying Overhead Costs

Because of the above issues, the organization accumulates overhead costs with products using a *predetermined overhead rate*. This predetermined overhead rate is determined by dividing estimated overhead costs by estimated activity (or a *cost driver*). These estimates represent the organization's expectations of the levels of cost and activity that will be incurred for some period of time (a week, month, year) and are normally based on actual levels of cost and activity in prior periods. The resulting predetermined overhead rate provides the organization with a method of accumulating overhead costs with production based on the activity represented by the cost driver. The following diagram summarizes the procedure for accumulating overhead costs with production:

Estimate Levels of Cost and Activity → Calculate the Predetermined Overhead Rate → Apply Overhead Costs to Production

To illustrate the calculation and use of a predetermined overhead rate, let us return to the production of vegetable products by The American Vegetable Company introduced in the preceding chapter. For simplicity, assume that American Vegetable will produce two products during the month of January: canned carrots and mixed vegetables. While American Vegetable produces over 100 different vegetable products, we simplify the analysis by limiting our computations to only two products to focus on how various methods of applying overhead costs affect the total costs of manufacturing these two products. Illustration 1 summarizes the estimated production activity for these two products. (Recall that The American Vegetable Company produces its vegetable products in two manufacturing departments: Canning and Packaging).

Illustration 1

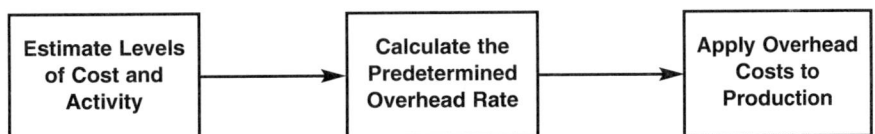

Estimated Production Activity: Carrots and Mixed Vegetables

	Carrots	Mixed Vegetables
Units Produced (cans)	600,000	300,000
Production Runs	45	5
Labor Hours (Canning)	550	1,300
Labor Hours (Packaging)	50	100
Machine Hours (Canning)	2,100	400
Machine Hours (Packaging)	1,000	500

Examining Illustration 1 reveals that the basic nature of the manufacturing processes for these two products differs. In the Canning Department, carrot products are sorted by workers prior to being placed into a mechanized

---
[3] "Grabbing Markets from the Giants," *Business Week Special Issue on 21st Century Capitalism*, 156.
[4] "Procter & Gamble Hits Back," *Business Week* (July 19, 1993), 21.

canning process. Since most of the carrots received are similar in size and weight, relatively little direct labor effort is required for this product. As shown in Illustration 1, a total of 550 labor hours are estimated in the Canning Department to produce 600,000 cans of carrots. In contrast, the production of mixed vegetable products requires a number of different types of vegetables to be sorted, cleaned, and prepared for entry into the mechanized canning process. Compared to carrot products, mixed vegetable products require relatively extensive direct labor effort. As shown in Illustration 1, 1,300 direct labor hours in the Canning Department are estimated for January's production.

Reviewing the estimated machine hours required for each type of product reveals that carrot products are relatively machine-intensive when compared to mixed vegetable products. In manufacturing carrot products, the mechanized canning process cleans, slices, and packs carrots into cans prior to sealing. Conversely, since much of the work involving mixed vegetable products is performed by direct labor, a lower number of machine hours is estimated for this product. As shown in Illustration 1, the total estimated machine hours in the Canning Department for carrot products (2,100 machine hours) far exceeds that of mixed vegetables (400 machine hours).

To calculate a predetermined overhead rate, American Vegetable must identify both the estimated overhead costs and an estimated activity level (or cost driver). In examining its production of carrot and mixed vegetable products, American Vegetable has identified five major types of overhead costs.

1. **Production Machinery Costs.** Depreciation, estimated repairs and maintenance, and estimated utilities costs associated with the production machinery used in the Canning and Packaging Departments.
2. **Production Setup Costs.** The estimated costs of cleaning and rearranging production machinery, calibrating production machinery, and testing production machinery prior to the beginning of a new production run.
3. **Materials Handling Costs.** The estimated costs associated with ordering, storing, and transporting materials inputs necessary for the manufacturing process. These costs include employee wages as well as depreciation and utility costs related to materials storage areas.
4. **Maintenance Costs.** The estimated wages paid to American Vegetable's employees who provide maintenance services.
5. **Other Overhead Costs.** Depreciation and estimated utility costs related to general production facilities (the factory space used for the production of all of American Vegetable's products).

American Vegetable uses estimated direct labor hours to apply overhead costs to production. As shown in Illustration 1, a total of 2,000 direct labor hours (550 + 1,300 + 50 + 100 = 2,000) were anticipated during January. Estimates of overhead costs for January 20x2 (based on levels of cost incurred in prior months as well as expected production during the January) are shown below:

Machinery Costs in Canning	$ 80,000
Machinery Costs in Packaging	120,000
Production Setup Costs	100,000
Materials Handling Costs	40,000
Maintenance Costs	10,000
Other Overhead Costs	20,000
	$370,000

The predetermined overhead rate would then be determined by dividing the total estimated overhead ($370,000) by the estimated level of activity (2,000 direct labor hours). This yields a rate of $185 per direct labor hour, as shown below:

$$\text{Predetermined Overhead Rate} = \frac{\$370,000}{2,000 \text{ hours}} = \$185 \text{ per direct labor hour}$$

This predetermined overhead rate is used to apply overhead costs to production. Assume that total direct materials costs for the carrots and mixed vegetables during January were $27,000 and $13,000, respectively. Recall from Illustration 1 that American Vegetable estimated 600 direct labor hours for carrot products (550 in the Canning Department and 50 in the Packaging Department) and 1,400 direct labor hours for mixed vegetable products (1,300 in the Canning Department and 100 in the Packaging Department). Its direct labor costs averaged $20 per hour (including fringes). Using this information, along with the predetermined overhead rate of $185 per direct labor hour, the expected cost per unit for carrots and mixed vegetables is calculated in Illustration 2. Product costing systems that apply overhead costs based on the volume of activity (such as direct labor hours) are known as *volume-based* (or *throughput-based*) *costing systems*. Once calculated, the cost per unit in Illustration 2 can be used by American Vegetable in setting its prices for sale to customers.

```
                             Illustration 2
                      The American Vegetable Company
                    Cost per Can of Carrots and Mixed Vegetables

                                                                  Mixed
                                                    Carrots      Vegetables

     Direct Materials ..........................  $ 27,000       $ 13,000
     Direct Labor ..............................    12,000ᵃ        28,000ᵇ
     Manufacturing Overhead ...................    111,000ᶜ       259,000ᵈ

     Total Manufacturing Costs .................  $150,000       $300,000
     Estimated Manufacturing Volume (in cans) ...  600,000        300,000

     Manufacturing Cost per Can ................ ÷  $0.25       ÷  $1.00


     ᵃ   600 direct labor hours x  $ 20  =  $ 12,000
     ᵇ 1,400 direct labor hours x  $ 20  =  $ 28,000
     ᶜ   600 direct labor hours x  $185  =  $111,000
     ᵈ 1,400 direct labor hours x  $185  =  $259,000
```

Recording Overhead Costs

In previous chapters, we have illustrated the journal entries used to apply overhead costs to production. As with direct materials and direct labor costs, overhead costs are initially accumulated with inventory in the work-in-process inventory account. Assume that during the month of January, a total of 1,948 direct labor hours were worked. Using the predetermined overhead rate of $185 per direct labor hour, a total of $360,380 of overhead costs would be applied to production (1,948 hours x $185 per hour = $360,380). To record these overhead costs, the following journal entry would be prepared:

Work-in-Process—Control...	360,380	
Factory Overhead—Control		360,380

At the end of January, American Vegetable will determine its actual overhead costs. Assume that actual overhead costs incurred during January 20x2 were $358,200 and include wages paid to various employees (other than direct labor costs), depreciation on production machinery and facilities, and various payables (for utilities, insurance, property taxes, and other overhead costs). The journal entry to record these costs is shown below:

Factory Overhead-Control	358,200	
Wages Payable..		84,500
Accumulated Depreciation—Facilities		23,200
Accumulated Depreciation—Machinery		81,000
Property Taxes Payable		15,500
Prepaid Insurance		20,000
Utilities Payable		128,300
Miscellaneous Accounts		5,700

At this point, both the applied overhead costs (credits to the Factory Overhead—Control account) and actual overhead costs (debits to the Factory Overhead—Control account) have been recorded. It would be very unusual for actual and applied overhead costs to be exactly equal, since applied overhead costs are based on estimated cost and activity levels. In this case, since the amount of overhead applied to production ($360,380) exceeds the actual overhead costs ($358,200), overhead has been *overapplied* to production. In contrast, if the applied overhead costs are less than actual overhead costs, then overhead has been *underapplied* to production. In the example, the amount of overapplied overhead is $2,180, as shown below.

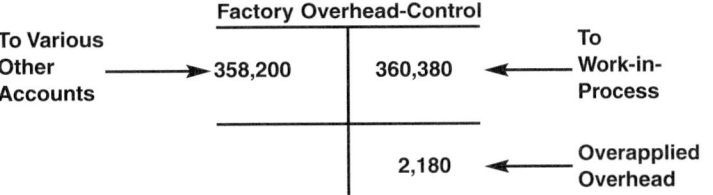

American Vegetable can adjust for the amount of overapplied overhead in one of two ways. If this amount is considered to be immaterial (as it appears to be the case in this instance), overapplied overhead costs may be closed directly to cost of goods sold.

When overhead costs are overapplied, excess overhead costs have been recorded in the inventory accounts and will eventually be expensed as cost of goods sold. To close the Factory Overhead—Control account, the following journal entry would be prepared:

Factory Overhead—Control	2,180	
Cost of Goods Sold		2,180

Another method of treating the overapplied overhead when it is considered to be material in amount is to apportion the overapplied overhead among the work-in-process, finished goods, and cost of goods sold accounts based on the relative balance in each account.[5] The rationale for this method is that the overapplied overhead is reflected in the work-in-process (for inventory not completed), finished goods (for inventory completed but not yet sold), and cost of goods sold (for inventory sold) accounts. This method is more appropriate and should be used if the amount of over- or underapplied overhead is material, since closing this amount directly to cost of goods sold would have a material impact on net income.

To close the overapplied overhead in this fashion, the ending balance in the Work-in-Process—Control, Finished Goods—Control, and Cost of Goods Sold accounts must be determined. The following represent balances taken from the accounting records of The American Vegetable Company for the month of January 20x2.

Work-in-Process	$ 48,000	4% x $2,180 =	$ 87
Finished Goods	336,000	28% x $2,180 =	610
Cost of Goods Sold	816,000	68% x $2,180 =	1,483
	$1,200,000	100%	$2,180

The overapplied overhead would then be closed out with the following journal entry:

Factory Overhead—Control	2,180	
Work-in-Process—Control		87
Finished Goods—Control		610
Cost of Goods Sold		1,483

There are two points that should be emphasized in our discussion of overapplied overhead. First, when overhead is overapplied (applied overhead costs are greater than actual overhead costs), excess costs have been accumulated in the accounting system through the initial entry involving the work-in-process account. Thus, when closing overapplied overhead, cost of goods sold and/or the various inventory accounts are reduced. This reduction is made to compensate for the excessive overhead costs initially recorded in these accounts. The opposite relationship and reasoning is true if overhead is underapplied.

Finally, in this case, the amount of overapplied overhead ($2,180) appears to be immaterial in relation to cost of goods sold for the month ($816,000). Thus, The American Vegtable Company would probably choose to close the overapplied overhead directly to cost of goods sold. As a result, cost of goods sold would be $813,820 ($816,000 – $2,180 = $813,820).

TWO-STAGE ALLOCATIONS OF SERVICE DEPARTMENT COSTS

In both this and the preceding two chapters, we have focused on the process of cost accumulation as the organization manufactures its inventory. In these chapters, the focus was on accumulating manufacturing costs incurred in departments in which the inventory was actually manufactured. These departments are called *production, manufacturing,* or *operating* departments. From The American Vegetable Company example illustrated in the previous section, the Canning Department and Packaging Department are examples of operating departments.

Other departments in an organization may not be directly involved with the manufacturing process but perform activities in support of that process (and the operating departments). These departments are often referred to as *service* or *support departments*. The production setup costs, maintenance costs, materials handling

---

[5] The most theoretically correct method of allocating over- or underapplied overhead among these accounts would be based on the amount of overhead costs applied in each account. However, this information is not ordinarily available from the company's accounting records. In most cases, the use of total balances as opposed to overhead costs to apportion over- or underapplied overhead will not yield markedly different allocations.

costs, and other overhead costs discussed in the previous section are examples of service department costs. Since these costs are incurred to provide assistance to the operating departments, they must also be considered in determining the total cost of manufacturing the organization's inventory. In this chapter, we discuss the methods of accumulating costs incurred by service departments with the inventory manufactured by operating departments.

Determining Departmental Overhead Rates

In the preceding section, overhead was applied to production using a single, predetermined overhead rate (known as a *plantwide rate* or *organizational rate*). In that example, total estimated overhead costs were $370,000 and the total estimated activity rate was 2,000 direct labor hours. Based on this information, a predetermined overhead rate of $185 per direct labor hour ($370,000 ÷ 2,000 direct labor hours) was calculated and used to apply overhead costs to production. As shown earlier in Chapters 3 and 4, these overhead costs are initially accumulated in work-in-process inventory and are later transferred to finished goods inventory (when production is complete) and cost of goods sold (when the products are sold to customers).

In many instances, the use of a plantwide overhead rate may result in inappropriate allocations. For example, referring to the data in Illustration 1, it appears that the Canning Department utilizes a relatively equal mix of direct labor hours and machine hours. As shown therein, total estimated direct labor in Canning was 1,850 hours (550 for carrot products and 1,300 for mixed vegetable products), with total estimated machine hours of 2,500 (2,100 for carrot products and 400 for mixed vegetables). Thus, while some question may exist as to the appropriate cost driver in the Canning Department, the use of direct labor hours at least appears to be reasonable.

In contrast, the Packaging Department requires a greater mix of machine hours compared to direct labor hours. As shown in Illustration 1, total estimated direct labor hours in the Packaging Department was 150 hours (50 for carrot products and 100 for mixed vegetable products) and total estimated machine hours were 1,500 (1,000 for carrot products and 500 for mixed vegetable products). Thus, the number of machine hours estimated in the Packaging Department was ten times greater than the direct labor hours!

Is there a problem with the use of a plantwide overhead rate? While the use of direct labor hours as a cost driver seems reasonable in the Canning Department, it is probably inappropriate for the Packaging Department. As noted above, these departments differ in terms of the nature of their manufacturing processes; however, the use of a plantwide overhead rate does not consider these differences.

A solution to the above dilemma is the use of departmental overhead rates. Departmental overhead rates are similar to plantwide overhead rates except that only the estimated overhead costs and activity *within a single operating department* are considered in establishing the overhead rate. In determining the estimated departmental overhead costs, the company must consider two types of costs. Certain overhead costs are relatively easy to associate with a single operating department, such as depreciation of machinery and rent paid on production facilities. However, the costs incurred by service departments are for services provided to more than a single operating department and must be allocated among these departments. This initial allocation is referred to as the *Stage 1 allocation*.

Once service department costs have been allocated to the operating departments, these costs, along with the costs directly identifiable with each operating department, are then allocated to products manufactured in that operating department. This latter allocation is referred to as the *Stage 2 allocation*. The overall process of determining the overhead costs for use in calculating departmental overhead rates is summarized as follows and is discussed in the following subsection.

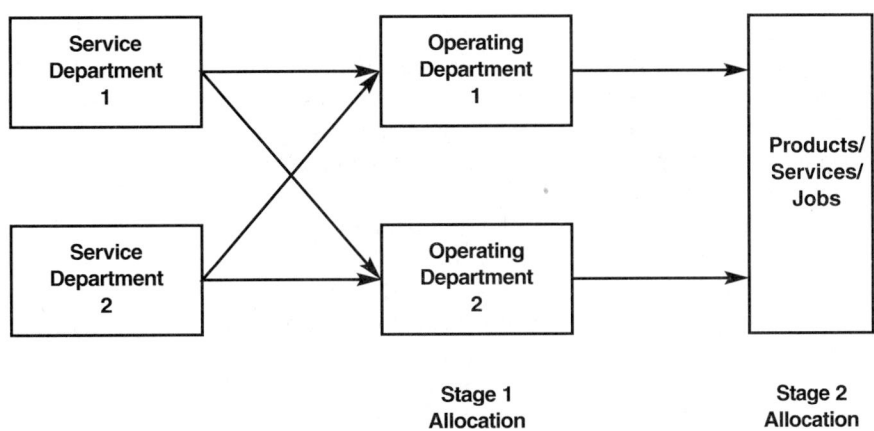

> An interesting allocation of service department costs can be observed in the athletic department at Georgia Tech University. In determining the profitability of its individual sports programs, Georgia Tech considers the costs associated with the university band and cheerleaders. Since the band and cheerleaders perform only at football and basketball games, 50 percent of these costs are allocated to each of these two sports.[6]

Allocating Service Department Costs to Operating Departments (Stage 1 Allocations)

Allocating service department costs to operating departments (the Stage 1 allocation) involves the following four-step procedure:

1. Estimate the costs associated with each service department.
2. Identify an activity base used to allocate service department costs.
3. Estimate the level of activity provided by each service department to other departments.
4. Allocate expected service department costs to other departments.

To illustrate the allocation of service department costs, recall that American Vegetable estimated its total overhead costs for the month of January 20x2 to be $370,000. For purposes of allocation, American Vegetable identifies three categories of service department costs: Production Setup ($100,000), Maintenance ($10,000), and Other Service Departments (other overhead costs of $20,000 and materials handling costs of $40,000). Also recall that estimated machinery costs in the Canning and Packaging Departments were $80,000 and $120,000, respectively. The estimated costs incurred by American Vegetable's operating departments and service departments introduced earlier is summarized as follows:

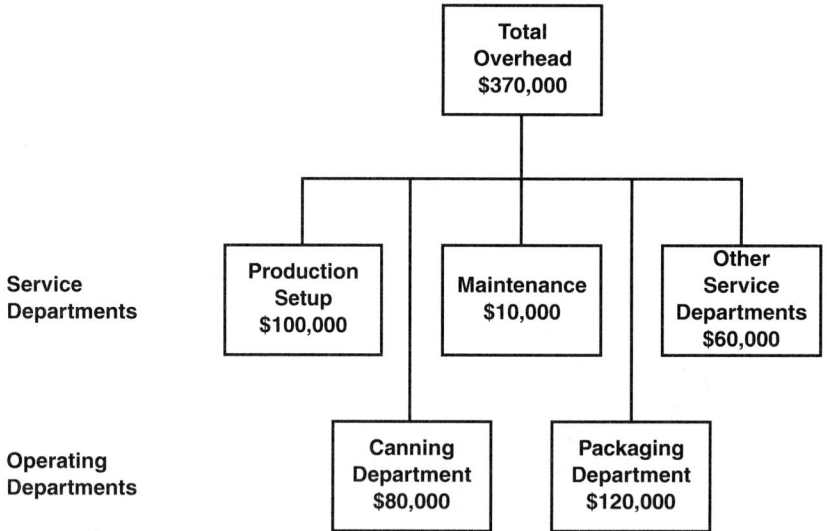

To allocate the service department costs among the operating departments, it is important to identify some measure of the relative utilization of the service departments' activities. Identifying this activity base is the second step in allocating service department costs to operating departments. The American Vegetable Company has decided to allocate production setup costs based on the number of estimated production runs during January; maintenance costs based on the estimated number of hours worked during January; and other service department costs based on estimated direct labor hours worked during January.

Once the appropriate activity base for each service department has been identified, the next step requires the level of activity provided by each service department to the other departments (operating departments and other service departments) to be estimated. American Vegetable has gathered information regarding the number of

---

[6] Strupeck, C.D., K. Milani, and J.E. Murphy. "Financial Management at Georgia Tech," *Management Accounting* (February 1993), 58–63.

production runs (for production setup costs), number of maintenance hours worked (for maintenance costs), and number of direct labor hours worked (for other service department costs) for each of its departments. This information will be used to estimate the activity levels for January. Illustration 3 summarizes the estimated utilization of service department activities by the departments.

Illustration 3
The American Vegetable Company
Utilization of Service Department Activities

	Production Setup	Maintenance	Other Service Departments
Allocation Base	No. Production Runs	No. Hours Worked	Direct Labor Hours
Production Setup	——	100 hours	500 hours
Maintenance	——	——	——
Other Service Departments	——	100 hours	——
Canning Department	40 runs	200 hours	1,850 hours
Packaging Department	10 runs	600 hours	150 hours
Totals	50 runs	1,000 hours	2,500 hours

The columns in Illustration 3 identify the departments that utilize the services provided by American Vegetable's various service departments. For example, reading the column for the Production Setup Department, this department provides services to only the two operating departments (Canning and Packaging); therefore, its costs will be allocated based on the number of estimated production runs in each of those departments in January. In contrast, notice that the Maintenance Department provides services to each of the other two service departments (Production Setup and Other Service) and both of the operating departments (Canning and Packaging).

Once the estimated utilization of service department activities has been identified, their costs can be allocated to the operating department using that activity (the final step in the Stage 1 allocation process). Two methods of allocating service department costs to operating departments are the direct allocation method and the step-down (or step) allocation method. These methods are discussed and illustrated using the above data in the following subsections.

Direct Method. Under the direct method of allocating service department costs to operating departments, only the services provided to operating departments are considered. The estimated manufacturing costs for each service department are allocated to the operating departments based on the relative utilization of services by the operating departments. That is, services provided by one service department to another are not considered in the allocations. For example, recall that Production Setup costs are allocated to the operating departments based on the estimated number of production runs during January. From Illustration 3, American Vegetable estimates that it will begin 40 production runs in Canning and 10 production runs in Packaging. The allocation of the estimated Production Setup costs of $100,000 is shown on the following page.

Department	Estimated Runs	Allocated Percentage	x	Estimated Costs	=	Allocated Costs
Canning	40	(40 ÷ 50)	x	$100,000	=	$ 80,000
Packaging	10	(10 ÷ 50)	x	$100,000	=	20,000
	50	(50 ÷ 50)				$100,000

↑ Total of 50 Runs

↑ Allocate 100% of Production Setup Costs

↑ Entire Production Setup Costs Have Been Allocated

Three points are important in the above allocation. First, the total services provided by Production Setup are based on the 50 production runs that will be initiated in the Canning and Packaging departments during January. Second, as shown in the percentage column, all of Production Setup's estimated costs have been allocated to the two operating departments; i.e., 100 percent (50 runs divided by 50 runs) of the production runs are used to allocate Production Setup's estimated costs. Finally, the total costs allocated to the two operating departments equal $100,000, with $80,000 allocated to Canning and $20,000 to Packaging. These costs will be accumulated with the other manufacturing costs in each of the operating departments in determining the total costs of manufacturing inventory.

The allocation of the costs incurred by the remaining two service departments (Maintenance and Other Service) is similar to that shown above. The difference is that a different basis (estimated maintenance hours worked and estimated direct labor hours) is used to allocate the costs of the Maintenance and Other Service, respectively. These allocations are shown as follows:

Allocation of Maintenance (Based on number of hours worked from Illustration 3).

Department	No. Hours	Allocated Percentage	x	Estimated Costs	=	Allocated Costs
Canning	200	(200 ÷ 800)	x	$10,000	=	$ 2,500
Packaging	600	(600 ÷ 800)	x	$10,000	=	7,500
	800	(800 ÷ 800)				$10,000

Allocation of Other Service Departments (Based on direct labor hours from Illustration 3).

Department	No. Hours	Allocated Percentage	x	Estimated Costs	=	Allocated Costs
Canning	1,850	(1,850 ÷ 2,000)	x	$60,000	=	$55,500
Packaging	150	(150 ÷ 2,000)	x	$60,000	=	4,500
	2,000	(2,000 ÷ 2,000)				$60,000

At this point, the predetermined overhead rates for the two operating departments may be calculated. The estimated overhead costs incurred by Canning and Packaging were $80,000 and $120,000, respectively. Assume that Canning applies overhead costs based on direct labor hours. From Illustration 1, the estimated total direct labor hours worked in Canning during January is 1,850 (550 + 1,300 = 1,850). Also assume that Packaging applies overhead costs to production based on machine hours. From Illustration 1, the estimated machine hours worked in Packaging during January is 1,500 (1,000 + 500 = 1,500). Using this information, the predetermined overhead rate in each department would be calculated as shown in Illustration 4.

Illustration 4
The American Vegetable Company
Summary of Cost Allocations and Calculation
Of Predetermined Overhead Rate
(Direct Method)

	Canning Department	Packaging Department
Estimated Department Overhead Costs	$ 80,000	$120,000
Allocation from Production Setup	80,000	20,000
Allocation from Maintenance	2,500	7,500
Allocation from Other Service Departments	55,500	4,500
Total Overhead Costs	$218,000	$ 152,000
Estimated Activity Base	÷ 1,850	÷ 1,500
Predetermined Overhead Rate	$118 per labor hour[a]	$101 per machine hour[b]

[a] Rounded (actual rate is $117.84).
[b] Rounded (actual rate is $101.33).

The above departmental overhead rates, along with the estimated direct labor hours (for Canning) and estimated machine hours (for Packaging), can be used to apply overhead costs to production. Illustration 1 indicates that the estimated direct labor hours for carrots and mixed vegetables in Canning were 550 and 1,300, respectively. In addition, estimated machine hours for these two products in Packaging were 1,000 and 500 for carrots and mixed vegetables, respectively. Once overhead has been applied to the two products, the total manufacturing costs and manufacturing cost per unit can be determined as shown in Illustration 5.

Illustration 5
The American Vegetable Company
Estimated Cost per Can of Carrots and Mixed Vegetables
(Direct Method)

	Carrots	Mixed Vegetables
Direct Materials (from Illustration 2)	$ 27,000	$ 13,000
Direct Labor (from Illustration 2)	12,000	28,000
Overhead Applied in Canning:		
$118 x 550 labor hours	64,900	
$118 x 1,300 labor hours		153,400
Overhead Applied in Packaging:		
$101 x 1,000 machine hours	101,000	
$101 x 500 machine hours		50,500
Total Manufacturing Costs	$ 204,900	$ 244,900
Estimated Manufacturing Volume (in cans)	÷ 600,000	÷ 300,000
Manufacturing Cost per Can (rounded)	$0.34	$0.82

Step-Down Method. Under the direct method, the costs incurred by the service departments were allocated only to the operating departments. That is, the costs incurred by one or more service departments were not allocated to any other service departments. Thus, for what the direct method of allocation gains in simplicity, it lacks in realism. For example, in addition to Canning and Packaging (both of which are operating departments), Maintenance also provides services for Production Setup and Other Services. In cases where service department costs are significant, a more equitable distribution of estimated service department costs may result if service department costs are allocated among both the operating and service departments.

The *step-down* method of allocation begins by selecting one service department and allocating its expected costs to all of the operating departments and the service departments to which it provides services. Once the costs in a particular service department are allocated, no costs are allocated "back" to this service department. The allocation of costs is identical to that illustrated under the direct allocation method, except that estimated costs in a given service department are allocated to other service departments as well as to the operating departments. The above procedure is repeated until only one service department contains costs. These costs are then allocated to the operating departments, as in the direct allocation method.

To illustrate the step-down method of allocation, consider the allocation of costs for The American Vegetable Company. From Illustration 3, we determine that American Vegetable's service departments provide services to other service departments as follows:

Maintenance:	Production Setup, Other Service Departments
Other Service Departments:	Production Setup
Production Setup:	None

When multiple service departments exist, service department costs are allocated sequentially based on the number of other departments served. Since Maintenance provides services to each of the other service departments, its cost would be allocated first, followed by Other Service Departments, and finally, Production Setup. If the number of departments served is the same, the order of allocation can be made on other bases, for example, based on the relative dollar amounts. The allocation of the $10,000 of maintenance costs is shown below. Note that the basic procedure for allocating these costs is the same as under the direct method. The only difference is that costs are allocated to service departments as well as operating departments.

Department	No. Hours	Allocated Percentage	x	Estimated Costs	=	Allocated Costs
Production Setup	100	(100 ÷ 1,000)	x	$10,000	=	$ 1,000
Other Service	100	(100 ÷ 1,000)	x	$10,000	=	1,000
Canning	200	(200 ÷ 1,000)	x	$10,000	=	2,000
Packaging	600	(600 ÷ 1,000)	x	$10,000	=	6,000
	1,000	(1,000 ÷ 1,000)				$10,000

The next service department costs to be allocated are those of the Other Service Departments. At this point, a total of $61,000 of costs is accumulated in the Other Service Departments ($60,000 of its initial costs plus the $1,000 of costs allocated from Maintenance). Recall that the Other Service Departments provide services to three departments: Production Setup, Canning, and Packaging. The costs of Other Services are allocated based on direct labor hours worked in these three departments as follows:

Department	Direct Labor Hours	Allocated Percentage	x	Estimated Costs	=	Allocated Costs
Production Setup	500	(500 ÷ 2,500)	x	$61,000	=	$12,200
Canning	1,850	(1,850 ÷ 2,500)	x	$61,000	=	45,140
Packaging	150	(150 ÷ 2,500)	x	$61,000	=	3,660
	2,500	(2,500 ÷ 2,500)				$61,000

The final step in the allocation of service department costs using the step-down method of allocation is to allocate the costs accumulated in the final service department (Production Setup) to the two operating departments. Based upon previous allocations, Production Setup has a total of $113,200 of accumulated costs, as follows:

Estimated Production Setup Costs	$100,000
Allocation from Maintenance Department	1,000
Allocation from Other Service Departments	12,200
	$113,200

Using the number of production runs as the activity base, the $113,200 of Production Setup costs would be allocated to the two operating departments as follows:

Department	No. Hours	Allocated Percentage	x	Estimated Costs	=	Allocated Costs
Canning	40	(40 ÷ 50)	x	$113,200	=	$90,560
Packaging	10	(10 ÷ 50)	x	$113,200	=	22,640
	50	(50 ÷ 50)				$113,200

Based on the above allocations, a predetermined overhead rate can be calculated for Canning and Packaging. As under the direct method, overhead costs are applied in Canning and Packaging using direct labor hours and machine hours, respectively; the estimated levels of activity (1,850 direct labor hours and 1,500 machine hours) are shown in Illustration 1. A summary of the calculation of this rate (along with the allocation of service department costs under the step-down method of allocation) is shown in Illustration 6. You may note that these rates ($118 per direct labor hour and $102 per machine hour, respectively) are almost identical to those using the direct method of allocation. This is a result of the fact that the service departments provide a greater amount of service to Canning than to Packaging, with the exception of Maintenance (which had a relatively small amount of costs). In cases such as these, allocating service department costs to other service departments does not markedly influence the final allocations.

Illustration 6

The American Vegetable Company
Allocation of Service Department Costs
(Step-Down Method)

	Maintenance	Other Service	Production Setup	Canning Department	Packaging Department
Estimated Department Costs	$10,000	$60,000	$100,000	$80,000	$120,000
Step 1: Allocate Maintenance	(10,000)	1,000	1,000	2,000	6,000
Totals	0	$61,000	$101,000	$82,000	$126,000
Step 2: Allocate Other Service		(61,000)	12,200	45,140	3,660
Totals		0	$113,200	$127,140	$129,660
Step 3: Allocate Production Setup			(113,200)	90,560	22,640
Total Overhead Costs			0	$217,700	$152,300
Estimated Activity Base				÷ 1,850	÷ 1,500
Predetermined Overhead Rate				$118 per direct labor hour[a]	$102 per machine hour[b]

[a] Rounded (actual rate is $117.68)
[b] Rounded (actual rate is $101.53)

Once the departmental overhead rates are determined, these rates along with the estimated level of activity for each product can be used to determine the cost per unit as under the direct method. The calculation of this cost per unit is shown in Illustration 7.

Illustration 7
The American Vegetable Company
Estimated Cost per Can of Carrots and Mixed Vegetables
(Step-Down Method)

	Carrots	Mixed Vegetables
Direct Materials (from Illustration 2)	$ 27,000	$ 13,000
Direct Labor (from Illustration 2)	12,000	28,000
Overhead Applied in Canning:		
$118 x 550 labor hours	64,900	
$118 x 1,300 labor hours		153,400
Overhead Applied in Packaging:		
$102 x 1,000 machine hours	102,000	
$102 x 500 machine hours		51,000
Total Manufacturing Costs	$ 205,900	$ 245,400
Estimated Manufacturing Volume (in cans)	÷ 600,000	÷ 300,000
Manufacturing Cost per Can (rounded)	**$0.34**	**$0.82**

Other Allocation Methods. An additional allocation method used less frequently in practice is *reciprocal allocation*. Under this procedure, costs from all service departments are simultaneously reallocated to each other, in addition to being allocated to the operating departments. Reciprocal allocation requires the solution of simultaneous equations, which is beyond the scope of this book. Reciprocal allocation is much more complicated than direct or step-down allocation. It may be appropriate, however, where every service department provides services to all other departments, including every other service department. For example, if Other Services also provided services to Maintenance, reciprocal allocation might be appropriate. In every case, however, management must decide whether the benefits obtained from receiving more refined cost estimates outweigh the complications of calculating these allocations.

ACTIVITY-BASED COSTING

The previous section of this chapter illustrated the allocation of service department costs to operating departments and, ultimately, the products or services provided by those operating departments. A weakness of this method of allocation is that it may distort the costs of manufacturing various products. For example, consider the two-stage allocation of production setup costs to products in Canning and Packaging. This basic process is illustrated as follows:

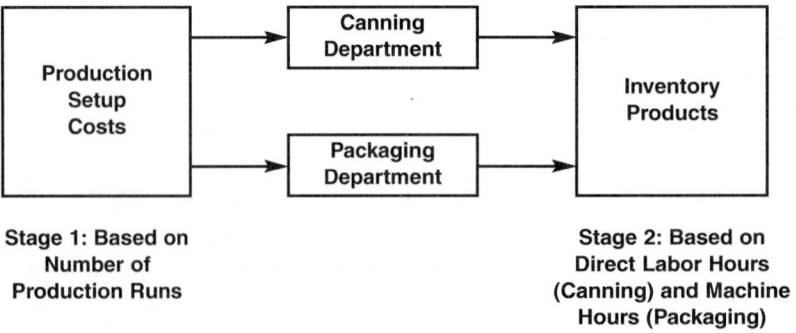

Stage 1: Based on Number of Production Runs

Stage 2: Based on Direct Labor Hours (Canning) and Machine Hours (Packaging)

A cost distortion in the above allocation may result from either of the two cost allocations. It appears that the basis for allocating production setup costs to the operating departments is reasonable (number of production runs), since operating departments with a greater number of production runs would apparently require greater production setup costs. Recall that the expected number of production runs in Canning and Packaging during January were 40 and 10, respectively. Based on the number of production runs, it appears that four times more production setup costs should be allocated to Canning compared to Packaging.

However, what if the production machinery used in Packaging was highly complex and required eight hours of setup time for each production run? Since 10 production runs were expected, the total estimated production setup time in Packaging in January would be 80 hours (10 production runs x 8 hours per run = 80 hours) under these circumstances. In contrast, if the production machinery in Canning is relatively simple and requires only an hour of setup time for each run, the total estimated production setup time in Canning in January would be 40 hours (40 production runs x 1 hour per run = 40 hours). Clearly, differences in the nature of the manufacturing processes in each of the operating departments may result in distortions in the Stage 1 allocation of costs.

Now consider the Stage 2 cost allocation. If the number of production runs is used as the driver in the Stage 1 cost allocation, a relatively large proportion of production setup costs will be allocated to Canning. Because Canning's overhead costs are allocated to inventory products based on the number of direct labor hours, any of the production setup costs allocated to the Canning under the Stage 1 allocation will be allocated to products based on labor hours. From Illustration 1, since mixed vegetable products require more direct labor hours in Canning than carrot products, a relatively large proportion of these production setup costs will be allocated to mixed vegetable products. However, Illustration 1 also reveals that the number of production runs for mixed vegetables and carrots are expected to be 5 and 45, respectively. Thus, under the two-stage allocation shown above, a greater amount of production setup costs will be allocated to mixed vegetable products than to carrot products, despite the fact that the number of production runs for carrot products is nine times greater than that of mixed vegetable products!

Traditionally, the cost driver selected for use by companies in the Stage 2 allocation is based on some measure of production volume (such as direct labor hours or machine hours). However, costs such as production setup costs do not increase with the number of units produced; they increase with the number of production runs. If The American Vegetable Company's cost accumulation system assigns production costs to the carrot products and mixed vegetable products based on the number of production runs of each product, the distortions noted above would be eliminated. Simply stated, the cost accumulation system should assign overhead costs to each product *based on the effort required for that product.*

Activity-based costing (or *ABC*) *systems* attempt to directly link individual costs to products by identifying the appropriate cost driver for that cost and using that cost driver to allocate the costs directly to the individual products. The phrase "activity-based costing" is based on the fact that cost drivers reflect the activity associated with each cost and not some overall level of production volume (such as direct labor hours or machine hours) that cause those costs to occur. ABC systems utilize the following three-step process in assigning overhead costs to products or services. This three-step process is discussed in the remainder of this chapter.

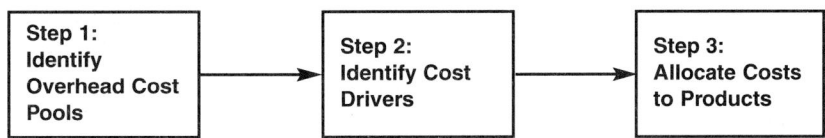

Step 1: Identify Overhead Cost Pools

The initial step in an ABC system is identifying overhead cost pools. ABC systems are unique in that they focus on the specific nature of the activity and the costs associated with that activity. These costs are referred to as *cost pools*. In contrast, traditional cost allocation either makes a general allocation of all overhead costs or allocates these costs by functional unit (or department).

Under ABC, activity cost pools may be classified into four major categories:

1. *Unit-level activities* are those activities performed for individual units of product. Direct materials and direct labor costs are examples of unit-level activities (as the number of cans of vegetables manufactured increases, direct materials and direct labor costs will also increase). With respect to overhead costs, the utilities, maintenance, and depreciation costs associated with production machinery are examples of unit-level activities, since these costs increase with increases in the number of cans of vegetables produced.

2. *Batch-level activities* are performed based on individual production runs (or "batches" of products). The costs associated with production setup are examples of batch-level costs, since products produced in a larger number of production runs (batches) result in greater production setup costs. Other examples of batch-level activities include production order processing costs and inspection costs. Like production setup costs, the costs of processing production orders and inspecting inventory also increases as the number of production runs increases.

3. *Product-level activities* are those activities performed for the development of specific products or product lines. Product-level activities are not incurred at the individual unit level or the production run level. Instead, these costs are related to the overall production of entire products or product lines. An example of a product-level activity for American Vegetable is materials handling costs.
4. *Facility-level activities* differ from the previous types of activities in that they relate to the overall production of all of the organization's products and not a single individual product or product line. Examples of facility-level activities for American Vegetable include maintenance costs and costs related to the general production facilities (such as rent, depreciation, property taxes, insurance, utilities, and maintenance). A unique aspect of facility-level activities is that, while they are necessary to support the overall production process, the level of costs associated with these activities is unaffected by either the quantity or mix of products being manufactured. For example, American Vegetable's depreciation of production facilities would not be affected by the number of units produced (unit-level activities), number of production runs (batch-level activities), or shifts in production from one product to another (product-level activities).

Because facility-level activities cannot be identified with individual products or product lines, these costs must be arbitrarily allocated among the organization's products. Arguments have been made that the relationship between facility-level activities and products is so tenuous that allocating these costs to products does not provide the organization with meaningful product cost information. Proponents of accumulating these costs with products argue that these costs are incurred by the organization and must be recovered through the selling price of the organization's inventory. Failure to accumulate facility-level costs with products may result in the organization's failure to consider these costs in product pricing decisions.

To illustrate the use of ABC, we again return to The American Vegetable Company example discussed throughout this chapter. Recall the initial overhead costs estimated by American Vegetable from our earlier discussion of determining a plantwide overhead rate. These costs are summarized as follows:

Machinery Costs in Canning	$ 80,000	Unit-Level
Machinery Costs in Packaging	120,000	Unit-Level
Production Setup Costs	100,000	Batch-Level
Materials Handling Costs	40,000	Product-Level
Maintenance Costs	10,000	Facility-Level
Other Overhead Costs	20,000	Facility-Level
	$370,000	

Step 2: Identify Cost Drivers

Once overhead cost pools have been identified (as shown above), the organization then identifies cost drivers for each of these pools. A *cost driver* is a measure of activity that has a cause-and-effect relationship with costs. That is, the costs occur because of the activity related to the cost driver. For example, production setup costs occur because organizations initiate new production runs; therefore, the cost driver for production setup costs may be identified as the number of production runs for each product.

As noted earlier, a distortion that may result from traditional cost accumulation systems is that a single cost driver (often, a volume-based cost driver such as direct labor hours or machine hours) may be used to accumulate overhead costs with products. An important characteristic of ABC is that each cost pool is carefully considered to determine the appropriate cost driver for that pool. After identifying the cost drivers, the activity related to that cost driver is then used to accumulate costs with products. Illustration 8 summarizes the cost pools, cost drivers, and expected activity rates for American Vegetable's two product lines discussed throughout this chapter (carrot products and mixed vegetable products). Information on the machine hours, number of production runs, and direct labor hours was presented earlier in Illustration 1. The remaining activities are estimated based on the previous production of carrot products and mixed vegetable products by The American Vegetable Company.

Illustration 8
The American Vegetable Company
Overhead Cost Pools, Cost Drivers, and Expected Activity Rates

		Expected Activity		
Cost Pool	Cost Driver	Carrots	Mixed Vegetables	Total
Machinery Costs (Canning)	Machine Hours	2,100	400	2,500
Machinery Costs (Packaging)	Machine Hours	1,000	500	1,500
Production Setup Costs	No. of Production Runs	45	5	50
Maintenance Costs	Maintenance Hours	800	200	1,000
Materials Handling Costs	No. of Orders Placed	30	10	40
General Overhead Costs	Direct Labor Hours	600	1,400	2,000

Step 3: Allocate Costs to Inventory Items

Once the overhead cost pools and the cost drivers have been identified, the next step in ABC is allocating costs to inventory items based on these cost drivers. This allocation procedure is similar to that using a predetermined overhead rate. The primary difference is that a number of different rates (a separate rate for each cost pool) is used. The predetermined rate is equal to the estimated costs in each cost pool divided by the total estimated activity for that pool.

Unit-Level Activities. To illustrate the application of overhead costs to inventory in an ABC system, let us revisit the two product lines introduced earlier: carrot products and mixed vegetables. With respect to overhead costs, the only unit-level activities for these product lines are the machinery costs in both Canning and Packaging. From Illustration 8, the cost driver for machinery costs in both departments is the number of expected machine hours related to each product. First, let us consider the $80,000 machinery costs in Canning. Since a total of 2,500 machine hours are expected in this department in January, the application rate for machine hours is $32 per machine hour ($80,000 ÷ 2,500 machine hours = $32 per machine hour). As a result, the machine costs in Canning would be allocated among the two products as follows:

Carrots (2,100 machine hours x $32)	$67,200
Mixed Vegetables (400 machine hours x $32)	12,800
	$80,000

The expected machinery costs in Packaging would be allocated in a similar manner. A total of 1,500 machine hours was expected for the month of January in Packaging (Illustration 8). Of these machine hours, 1,000 were for carrot products and 500 for mixed vegetable products. If January's machinery costs in Packaging are expected to be $120,000, the cost per machine hour in Packaging is $80 ($120,000 ÷ 1,500 machine hours = $80 per machine hour). Allocating the $120,000 of machinery costs in Packaging between these two products yields the following:

Carrots (1,000 machine hours x $80)	$80,000
Mixed Vegetables (500 machine hours x $80)	40,000
	$120,000

At this point, both of the unit-level activity costs have been allocated to the products. Note that these costs are allocated using a volume-based measure (machine hours). The rationale for this measure is consistent with the nature of unit level activities; as a greater number of units (cans of vegetables) are manufactured, a greater number of machine hours, and therefore machinery costs, is incurred.

Batch-Level Activities. Our earlier analysis identified one batch-level activity in American Vegetable's manufacturing process: production setup costs. Recall that batch-level activities represent costs that increase with increases in the number of production "batches" or production runs and not the number of units produced. For example, American Vegetable expects to produce 600,000 cans of carrot products in 45 production runs during January 20x2. If production levels for carrot products increase to 800,000 cans without increasing the number of production runs, expected production setup costs would not change. However, if production levels actually decrease to 500,000 cans but the number of production runs increases to 50, production setup costs would increase. Given the nature of these activities, using volume-based cost drivers (such as machine hours or direct labor hours) for batch-level activities may introduce distortion in the cost allocation process.

The total expected production setup costs for January 20x2 are $100,000 and the expected number of production runs is 50 (see Illustration 8). As a result, the production setup cost per production run is $2,000 ($100,000 ÷ 50 production runs = $2,000 per production run). Since the number of expected production runs for carrot products and mixed vegetable products equals 45 and 5 runs, respectively (see Illustration 8), the allocation of production setup costs to these products is summarized below:

Carrots (45 production runs x $2,000)	$90,000
Mixed Vegetables (5 production runs x $2,000)	10,000
	$100,000

Product-Level Activities. Product-level activities are those activities related to individual products or product lines. Because these costs are not incurred at an individual unit level or a batch level, costs associated with product-level activities are ordinarily allocated over the estimated total production for those products. American Vegetable had one type of product-level activity: materials handling costs (estimated at $40,000). Because materials handling costs increase with the number of orders placed by American Vegetable, the number of orders has been selected as the cost driver for this cost pool. A total of 40 orders for materials are estimated during January. As a result, the cost per order is $1,000 ($40,000 ÷ 40 orders = $1,000 per order). Using this rate, materials handling costs can be allocated to the two products as follows:

Carrots (30 orders x $1,000)	$30,000
Mixed Vegetables (10 orders x $1,000)	10,000
	$40,000

As shown above, the allocation of costs associated with product-level activities is based on the extent to which each product line (or type of product) causes these costs to occur. Materials handling costs are not the result of producing individual units (unit-level activities) or production runs (batch-level activites). These costs relate to the overall levels of production of a given product or product line. Under ABC, materials handling costs are allocated based on the number of orders placed for direct materials, which influences the costs required for each product or product line. In the American Vegetable example, because carrot products are expected to require a greater number of orders for direct materials inputs, this product is allocated a greater amount of materials handling costs than mixed vegetable products.

Facility-Level Activities. At this point, the only remaining costs to be allocated to products are facility-level costs. American Vegetable has two types of facility-level costs: maintenance costs and other overhead costs (rent, depreciation, and utility costs associated with its general production facilities). Recall that the distinguishing characteristic of facility-level costs is that they cannot easily be identified with individual units of a product (unit-level cost), production runs of a product (batch-level costs), or overall production of a product (product-level costs). Instead, the costs associated with facility-level activities are related to the Company's overall production effort (the manufacture of both carrot and mixed vegetable products).

To allocate maintenance costs, American Vegetable has identified hours of maintenance as the cost driver (Illustration 8). The Company estimates a total of 1,000 maintenance hours during January 20x2 (800 for carrot products and 200 for mixed vegetable products). Given this information, as well as the estimated total maintenance costs for January ($10,000), maintenance costs will be applied to products at the rate of $10 per maintenance hour ($10,000 ÷ 1,000 hours = $10 per hour). Using this rate, maintenance costs can be applied to The American Vegetable Company's two products as follows:[7]

Carrots (800 hours x $10)	$ 8,000
Mixed Vegetables (200 hours x $10)	2,000
	$10,000

Finally, American Vegetable allocates its other overhead costs. American Vegetable has selected direct labor hours as a cost driver for its general overhead costs (Illustration 8). The Company estimates a total of 2,000 direct labor hours during January 20x2 (600 for carrot products and 1,400 for mixed vegetable products). General overhead costs will be applied to products at the rate of $10 per direct labor hour ($20,000 ÷ 2,000 direct labor hours = $10 per direct labor hour). The allocation of these costs to carrot products and mixed vegetable products is shown below:

Carrots (600 direct labor hours x $10)	$ 6,000
Mixed Vegetables (1,400 direct labor hours x $10)	14,000
	$20,000

Because facility-level costs support the organization's overall production process and are not related to individual products, some questions exist regarding whether they should be considered in determining the overall "cost" of producing the organization's products. To illustrate, consider the nature of the "general overhead" costs of American Vegetable (depreciation, utilities, and maintenance costs associated with the general production facilities). If the Company discontinued the production of both carrot products and mixed vegetable products, it would still incur these general overhead costs, since they are related to the organization's overall manufacturing activities and not to specific products. Thus, some argument exists that American Vegetable's production of carrot and mixed vegetable products did not result in an increase in these costs. The alternative viewpoint is that these are costs incurred by the organization that must be recovered through the sale of the organization's products. As a result, each product or product line should bear a portion of these costs.

At this point, the costs in each of the overhead cost pools have been allocated to individual products. The total costs of producing the two products can be determined as shown in Illustration 9.

Illustration 9

The American Vegetable Company
Estimated Cost per Can of Carrots and Mixed Vegetables
(Activity-Based Costing System)

	Carrots	Mixed Vegetables
Direct Materials (from Illustration 2)	$ 27,000	$ 13,000
Direct Labor (from Illustration 2)	12,000	28,000
Machinery Costs (Canning)	67,200	12,800
Machinery Costs (Packaging)	80,000	40,000
Production Setup Costs	90,000	10,000
Materials Handling Costs	30,000	10,000
Maintenance Costs	8,000	2,000
General Overhead Costs	6,000	14,000
Total Manufacturing Costs	$320,200	$129,800
Estimated Manufacturing Volume (in cans)	÷ 600,000	÷ 300,000
Manufacturing Cost per Can (rounded)	$0.53	$0.43

---

[7] Recall from our discussion of two-stage cost allocations that maintenance services will also be provided to the Production Setup Department and Other Service Departments. However, since the basic philosophy of ABC systems is to allocate costs from cost pools to products, these services provided to other service departments are ignored in establishing an allocation rate.

In the preceding example, costs were allocated to products based on *expected* (and not actual) activity. This provides the management of The American Vegetable Company with information about the estimated cost per can of its carrot and mixed vegetable products. For financial reporting purposes, The American Vegetable Company would apply these overhead costs to production based on the actual level of activities and the application rates for each activity. For example, the total overhead costs applied to a production run requiring 500 machine hours in Canning, 200 machine hours in Packaging, one order of direct materials, 50 hours of maintenance, and 300 direct labor hours would be $38,500, as follows:

Machine Costs (Canning) (500 hours x $32)	$16,000
Machine Costs (Packaging) (200 hours x $80)	16,000
Production Setup Costs (1 setup x $2,000)	2,000
Materials Handling Costs (1 order x $1,000)	1,000
Maintenance costs (50 hours x $10)	500
Other Overhead Costs (300 hours x $10)	3,000
Total Overhead Costs	$38,500

Other Issues Involved with Activity-Based Costing

When Should ABC be Used? The previous section illustrated the basic process through which ABC allocates overhead costs to specific inventory products. An aspect of ABC that should be apparent is that ABC requires information to be gathered and maintained on a number of different activities. As a result, the use of ABC is often quite costly to organizations. This raises the question as to when the benefits to be derived from the use of ABC exceed its costs.

In general, the use of ABC should be considered whenever the organization has relatively large overhead costs and its products require different levels of overhead-related activity (such as production runs and maintenance hours). The following conditions may indicate that the use of a volume-based cost driver (such as direct labor hours or machine hours) is inappropriately assigning overhead costs to products.[8] Each of these conditions is characteristic of situations where the information provided by traditional costing systems may indicate that high volume (yet relatively simple) products are more costly to produce than low volume (yet relatively complex) products.

- Products manufactured in highly-complex manufacturing processes are not priced at a premium yet are reported to be profitable.
- Overall sales are increasing, but profits are decreasing.
- Products that appear to be very profitable are not sold by competitors.
- The prices charged by competitors for high-volume products produced by relatively simple manufacturing processes appear to be low.

Inclusion of Non-Manufacturing Costs. Because of financial reporting requirements, accounting systems have traditionally considered only manufacturing costs (product costs) in determining the total "cost" of producing inventory or providing services. However, with recent emphasis on customer orientation and technological innovation, the total non-manufacturing costs associated with producing inventory and providing services (such as product design costs, data processing costs, and selling and distribution costs) have increased greatly. Organizations have expanded their ABC systems to allocate these costs to their products and services in much the same manner as traditional overhead costs. While not treated as a cost of manufacturing inventory or providing services for financial reporting purposes, allocating these costs to products allows the organization to consider these costs in making internal decisions with respect to the prices to charge for its goods and services.

For example, assume that American Vegetable determines that the cost of processing, filling, and delivering an order to its customers is $1,000 per order. This cost is not traditionally considered to be a manufacturing (product) cost and would not be accumulated with American Vegetable's inventory for financial reporting purposes. However, it should be considered in establishing the selling prices charged to American Vegetable's Customers. If a large grocery store orders 4,000 cans of carrot products per month, the actual "cost" per can would differ depending upon the manner in which this product was ordered (the manufacturing cost per can was determined using ABC in Illustration 9).

---

[8] These were drawn from R. Cooper, "Does Your Company Need a New Cost System?," *Journal of Cost Management* (Volume 1, No. 1), 45–49 and R. Cooper, "You Need a New Costing System When...," *Harvard Business Review* (Volume 67, No. 1), 77–82.

	1 order of 4,000 cans	4 orders of 1,000 cans
Manufacturing Costs (4,000 x $0.53)	$2,120	$2,120
Ordering Costs:		
1 order x $1,000	1,000	
4 orders x $1,000		4,000
Total Costs	$3,120	$6,120
Number of Cans	÷ 4,000	÷ 4,000
Cost per Can	$0.78	$1.53

The above example illustrates the importance of considering the nature of non-manufacturing costs for internal decision-making purposes. In this case, American Vegetable may wish to charge customers a higher price per can when they place a larger number of orders for smaller quantities of product. Viewed from the other perspective, American Vegetable may wish to consider giving a price discount to customers who order carrot products in larger quantities.

Use of ABC in Service Organizations. The American Vegetable Company example utilized throughout this chapter illustrates the use of ABC for a manufacturing organization. However, it is important to note that ABC may provide the same benefits for service organizations. For example, the costs incurred by FedEx in delivering parcels for its customers may be classified in a similar manner as those for the American Vegetable Company, as follows:

- Unit-Level Activities: Costs of processing individual customer requests for parcel deliveries.
- Batch-Level Activities: Costs of jet fuel and wages paid to personnel in transporting parcels to delivery centers.
- Product-Level Activities: Depreciation on airplanes and delivery vehicles.
- Facility-Level Activities: Depreciation on regional delivery centers.

Identification of Cost Drivers. One of the most important aspects of using ABC is the identification of cost drivers. In identifying the appropriate cost driver for each overhead cost pool, the organization should carefully consider the relative costs and benefits of different possible cost drivers. For example, if the time required to rearrange, calibrate, and test production machinery markedly differs for carrot and mixed vegetable products, The American Vegetable Company may wish to consider using the hours of setup time as a cost driver instead of the number of production runs. However, while this proposed cost driver would provide a more accurate allocation of production setup costs to the two products, the additional cost of gathering information on hours of setup time may offset any benefits of more accurate cost allocations.

Consistent with ABC, IBM has begun to "bill" production departments for support costs such as cost accounting and data processing. Prior to this practice, only 25 percent of the total support costs could be directly associated with a product. Now, 75 percent of total support costs can be directly associated with a product without being allocated.[9]

One company that has recently implemented an ABC system is Hewlett-Packard. After implementing this system, they examined the costs assigned to their 57 products under the new (ABC) system and compared these costs to the costs assigned under the traditional costing system. Of the 57 products, the differences in cost under the two systems exceeded five percent for 44 products. Of these, 35 were undercosted (six by more than 50%) and nine were overcosted.[10]

---

[9] R.D. McIlhattan, "How Cost Management Systems Can Support the JIT Philosophy," *Management Accounting* (September 1987), 20–26.

[10] C.M Merz and A Hardy, "ABC Puts Accountants on Design Team at HP," *Management Accounting* (September 1993), 22–27.

USING MANAGERIAL ACCOUNTING DATA: THE AMERICAN VEGETABLE COMPANY

In this chapter, we have illustrated the application of overhead costs to two products produced by The American Vegetable Company: carrot products and mixed vegetable products. Summarized below are the costs per unit determined under the various methods illustrated in this chapter:

	Carrots	Mixed Vegetables
Single, Plantwide Overhead Rate (Illustration 2)	$0.25	$1.00
Two-Step Allocation (Direct Method) (Illustration 5)	0.34	0.82
Two-Step Allocation (Step-Down Method) (Illustration 7)	0.34	0.82
ABC (Illustration 9)	0.53	0.43

The above data reflect differences in the overhead costs applied to the two products. Using a single, plantwide overhead rate, all overhead costs were applied to the products using a single cost driver (direct labor hours). Since mixed vegetable products were relatively labor-intensive, the use of this cost driver resulted in a greater allocation of overhead costs to these products compared to carrot products. Notice that the use of a two-step allocation redistributed the allocation of overhead costs somewhat; however, under this method, the overhead costs associated with Canning were allocated to products based on direct labor hours. Once again, because of the labor-intensive nature of mixed vegetables, a relatively large amount of overhead costs was ultimately assigned to this product.

In contrast, ABC systems apply overhead costs direct to products based on the extent to which these products utilize the activities represented by the overhead cost pool. For example, carrot products require a greater utilization of machine hours, larger number of production runs, larger number of direct materials orders, and greater utilization of maintenance hours compared to mixed vegetable products. As a result, carrot products should have a greater amount of machinery, production setup, materials handling, and maintenance costs allocated to them. This occurs under the use of ABC systems. The greater amount of overhead costs allocated to carrot products (and lower amount of overhead costs allocated to mixed vegetable products) results in the costs of carrot products doubling under ABC (compared to the use of a single overhead rate) and the costs of mixed vegetable products being reduced by almost 60 percent under ABC.

Once the cost of producing its products is determined, The American Vegetable Company can use this information in its product pricing decisions. For example, if the company wishes to earn a 20 percent return on its operating activities, the following prices should be charged to customers for its vegetable products (assuming that the costs were determined using ABC systems):

Carrot Products ($0.53 x 1.20)	$0.64 per can
Mixed Vegetable Products ($0.43 x 1.20)	$0.52 per can

SUMMARY

Chapter 5 discusses overhead costs and illustrates three methods of applying overhead costs to production. These methods include the use of a single, plantwide overhead rate; a two-stage cost allocation; and activity-based costing. The important concepts discussed in Chapter 5 are summarized below.

1. *Manufacturing overhead costs* are all costs that are associated with producing the organization's inventory and/or providing the organization's services and that are not classified as either direct materials costs or direct labor costs. Examples of manufacturing overhead costs include indirect materials and supplies costs, indirect labor costs, and various costs associated with the organization's production equipment and facilities (utilities, depreciation, repairs and maintenance, insurance, and property taxes). Because of the difficulty of associating actual overhead costs with production, these costs are applied to production using a predetermined overhead rate.

2. All manufacturing departments may be classified as either *service departments* or *operating (production) departments*. Operating departments are those departments that are directly involved in the production of an organization's inventory. While not directly responsible for the production of inventory, the main function of service departments is to provide service to other departments (including the operating departments) within the organization.

3. To accumulate service department costs with the organization's products and services, a two-stage cost allocation can be performed. Under this method of allocation, service department costs are initially allocated to operating departments based on some relative measure of service provided to each operating department (Stage 1 allocation). Next, the costs in each operating department are allocated to the products or services of that department (Stage 2 allocation).
4. Under the *direct method* of allocating service department costs, service department costs are allocated only to the operating departments. In contrast, the *step-down method* allocates service department costs to both operating departments and other service departments.
5. *Activity-based costing (ABC) systems* identify overhead cost pools and allocate those costs to inventory using the most appropriate cost driver for that cost pool. Under ABC, activities and costs are classified based on whether they relate to individual units of inventory (unit-level activities), individual production runs of inventory (batch-level activity), the entire production of a specific inventory product or product line (product-level activity), or the organization's overall production efforts (facility-level activity).

KEY DEFINITIONS

Activity-based costing (ABC)—applying overhead to production based on the activity measure most closely related to that particular cost. The unique aspect of ABC is that different types of overhead costs are applied to production using different cost drivers.

Batch-level activities—activities performed on individual production runs (or "batches") of products. Examples of costs of batch-level activities include production setup costs, materials handling costs, production order processing costs, and inspection costs.

Cost driver—that level of activity, or element, that causes costs to change within the relevant range

Direct allocation—method for allocating service department costs in which the costs from a service department are not allocated to other service departments. Thus, under the direct method of allocation, service department costs are allocated only to operating departments.

Facility-level activities—activities that support the organization's overall production activities and not individual products or product lines. Examples of the costs of facility-level activities are the costs associated with the organization's general production facilities (such as depreciation, rent, insurance, maintenance, and utilities).

Operating department (production department)—a department of an organization in which manufacturing activities take place.

Overapplied overhead—the excess of the overhead costs applied to production over the actual overhead costs incurred by the organization. Any overapplied overhead costs at year-end are either closed to cost of goods sold or apportioned among work-in-process inventory, finished goods inventory, and cost of goods sold.

Product-level activities—activities that are performed for the development of specific product or product lines and that do not occur at the individual unit or production run level. Examples of costs of product-level activities include materials handling costs.

Service department—a department of an organization in which services to other departments are provided as requested. Production of inventory does not take place in these departments.

Step-down allocation—method of allocating service department costs in which the services provided by service departments to both operating departments and other service departments are considered.

Underapplied overhead—the excess of actual overhead costs incurred by the organization over the overhead costs applied to production. Any underapplied overhead costs at year-end are either closed to cost of goods sold or apportioned among work-in-process inventory, finished goods inventory, and cost of goods sold.

Unit-level activities—activities related to the production of an individual unit of a product. Examples of overhead costs that relate to unit-level activities include utilities, maintenance, and depreciation costs associated with production machinery.

QUESTIONS

1. What are manufacturing overhead costs? Why is it difficult to accumulate the actual overhead costs incurred by the organization with production?

2. What is the three-step process used to apply manufacturing overhead costs to production?

3. How is the difference between actual overhead costs and applied overhead costs treated by the organization?

4. Define service departments and operating departments. Which departments are necessary in the production of inventory?

5. Describe the basic process used to allocate service department costs to the organization's products.

6. What is the basic procedure used in allocating service department costs under the direct method of allocation? Under the step-down method of allocation?

7. How do the direct and step-down methods of allocation differ?

8. Why might the use of the direct method of allocation be less optimal than the use of the step-down method?

9. What detriment may be faced by companies that do not consider service department costs in product pricing decisions?

10. What is activity-based costing? What are the three basic steps involved with the use of activity-based costing?

11. How does activity-based costing differ from traditional costing?

12. Briefly define each of the four major cost pools used in activity-based costing.

13. What are conditions that suggest the use of activity-based costing may be advantageous for organizations?

EXERCISES AND PROBLEMS

14. *Overhead—Actual and Applied.* ToolCo expected to incur the following costs during 20x4: $2,000,000 of labor costs and $1,000,000 of overhead costs.

    Tool Co uses a job-order cost system and assigns overhead to jobs on the basis of direct labor costs. Job No. 101 required 110 pounds of material at $2 per pound, 560 hours of labor at $10 per hour, and a regular application of overhead. By the end of 20x4, ToolCo had incurred $2,100,000 of labor costs and $700,000 of overhead costs.

    Required:
    a. Determine the total cost of Job No. 101.
    b. Specify the amounts for actual overhead, applied overhead, and over/underapplied overhead.
    c. Will the over/underapplied overhead adjustment to cost of goods sold increase or decrease cost of goods sold?

15. *Overhead—Rates and Applied.* The assignment of overhead to particular jobs involves three separate components: (1) calculating overhead rates, (2) assigning overhead to specific jobs, and (3) reconciling differences between actual and applied overhead. The first two of these components are the subject of each of the following four independent cases. For each case, determine the missing numbers for each of the letters A through H.

	Case 1	Case 2	Case 3	Case 4
Estimated Overhead Cost	$10,000	$20,000	$40,000	G
Estimated Labor Hours	1,000	40,000	E	10,000
Predetermined Overhead Rate	A	C	$2/hr.	$3/hr.
Labor Hours on Job No. 101	50	D	300	50
Overhead Assigned to Job No. 101	B	$ 100	F	H

16. *Overhead—Actual and Applied.* Wilson Mfg. Co. applied (assigned) $100,000 of overhead to departments 1 and 2 during January. Actual overhead for the period amounted to $90,000. All goods produced during January were sold on the last day of the month.

    Required:

    a. Is overhead overapplied or underapplied?
    b. What is to be done with the $10,000 over/underapplied overhead?

17. *Overhead—Rates and Applied.* The Theft Brothers Steel Mill is engaged in specialty steel processing and milling. On Job Order No. 207, the following costs and statistics have been maintained, in addition to comparable data for the entire milling operation.

	Job Order No. 207	Estimated for Total Factory
Machine Hours	80	800
Direct Labor	$500	$3,500
Materials Used	$700	$7,700
Direct Labor Hours	50	400
Overhead		$4,000

    Required:

    a. Using this information, calculate the overhead rates for the following different predetermined bases.
       1. Labor cost
       2. Labor hours
       3. Machine hours

    b. Calculate the total cost of Job No. 207 that results from the use of each of the predetermined overhead rates determined in (a) above.

18. *Overhead—Actual and Applied.* Whenever actual overhead differs from applied overhead, the accountant must reconcile the differences at the end of the period. Below are six independent cases. First, determine the missing numbers for each of the letters A through F. Next, answer the question: "What will happen to the reported income when the over/underapplied overhead is assigned to cost of goods sold?" Use the words "increase" or "decrease" in responding to this question.

	Case 1	Case 2	Case 3	Case 4	Case 5	Case 6
Actual Overhead	$300,000	$300,000	$300,000	$200,000	$ E	$ F
Applied Overhead	290,000	B	C	210,000	300,000	300,000
Over/underapplied overhead	A	(10,000)	10,000	D	(10,000)	10,000
I-Increase/D-Decrease Income	?	?	?	?	?	?

19. *Overhead—Applied.* The Muffin Company assigns overhead to job cost sheets on the basis of $3 per direct labor hour worked. Job No. 101 incurred $1,220 material costs and labor costs of $5 per hour at 200 hours, or $1,000. Job No. 101 sold for $4,000. During the year, total labor hours incurred amounted to 10,000, and total actual overhead amounted to $39,500.

    Required:

    a. How much profit was earned on Job No. 101?
    b. At the end of the year, applied overhead was over/underapplied by what amount?
    c. If all production for the year had been delivered to customers, Muffin should have disposed of the over/underapplied overhead by adjusting which account(s)?

20. *Overhead—Rate and Applied.* The Johnson Company custom-builds boats. When the current budget was prepared, total expected overhead was estimated at $88,000, and expected labor hour volume was estimated at 40,000 hours. These two budgeted numbers were used to determine the applied overhead rate for the current year. During the year, accumulated actual costs for depreciation, gas, oil, rent, indirect labor, and supplies amounted to $83,000. Three boats were under construction during the year, and the actual hours of direct labor incurred on each were 16,000, 12,000, and 14,000. The applied overhead rate is multiplied by the actual hours to determine the applied overhead to be charged to the individual jobs (boats).

All three boats were sold, and the accumulated costs (applied overhead, in addition to direct labor and material) were transferred to the cost of goods sold account. Before preparing an income statement, the accountant for Johnson determines the over/underapplied overhead and adjusts the cost of goods sold account. After the adjustment, the applied overhead component of cost of goods sold equals the actual overhead incurred during the year.

Required:

a. Determine the applied overhead rate.
b. Determine the amount of applied overhead assigned to each of the three boats.
c. Assuming that cost of goods sold was $200,000 before the over/underapplied overhead adjustment, determine its balance after the adjustment.

21. *Overhead—Rate and Applied.* The Phast Buck Sales Company applies overhead to production orders on the basis of direct labor hours in Department 1 and on the basis of machine hours in Department 2. The total budgeted labor hours in Department 1 are 40,000, while total expected overhead is $100,000. Department 2 has 60,000 machine hours available for the year and $90,000 total expected overhead to be applied.

Required:

a. What are the predetermined overhead rates to be used by Phast Buck Sales Company in Departments 1 and 2?
b. Assuming that the company pays a labor rate of $6 per hour, what is the per-unit overhead cost of the following job order?

	Department 1	Department 2	Total
Materials Used	$4,000	$12,000	$16,000
Labor Costs	$2,700	$ 1,200	$ 3,900
Machine Hours	100	900	1,000
Units Produced			1,500

c. Actual overhead costs during the year were $102,500 in Department 1 and $88,000 in Department 2. Actual volume exactly equaled budgeted volume. How much over/underapplied overhead was incurred in each department?
d. How does the managerial accountant typically dispose of the over/underapplied overhead in part (c) above?

22. *Service Department Cost Allocation—Conceptual.* Sam Harvey, the manager of the stamping plant, is very anxious about yearly financial reviews. His plant has been in the red for the past two years. As Harvey explains, the plant would make a profit if only a portion of the corporate costs were not added to his plant costs. Harvey once said, "It's a vicious circle: I'm in the red because of the corporate salaries, and the corporation hires more people to figure out why I'm in the red." Jim Jones' plant is always in the black, and it is seldom visited by anyone from corporate headquarters. Yet Jim's plant is assigned a share of the corporate salaries used to evaluate the Harvey plant.

Required:

a. Is the method of allocating corporate salaries to both plants the best system? Explain your answer.
b. Sam Harvey wants the costs to be allocated to the plants that can pay them. What is wrong with this method, if anything?

c. Jim Jones wants the costs allocated on the basis of use. What is wrong with this method, if anything?
d. Do you think either plant manager will ever be satisfied? Explain why or why not.

23. *Service Department Cost Allocation—Various.* The Sanders Manufacturing Company has two operating departments (Department 1 and 2) and two service departments (Materials Handling and Cafeteria). Materials handling costs are allocated on the basis of the dollar value of items requisitioned by the other departments. The cafeteria costs are allocated to other departments on the basis of the relative number of employees in the departments. Total materials handling costs are $50,000 and cafeteria costs are $20,000. Other data on Sanders' departments are as follows:

	Department 1	Department 2	Materials Handling	Cafeteria
Number of Employees........	50	30	15	5
Cost of Items Requisitioned ...	$300,000	$200,000		$100,000

Required:

a. Using direct allocation, determine the service department costs allocated to Departments 1 and 2.
b. Determine the service department costs allocated to Departments 1 and 2 using step-down allocation (allocate the Materials Handling Department's costs first).

24. *Service Department Cost Allocation—Direct Method.* In manufacturing its inventory, Ace Company's production process requires work in three operating departments (1, 2, and 3). In addition, two departments (X and XX) provide services to the operating departments. Assume the following information for 20x1:

	Service Departments		Operating Departments		
	X	XX	1	2	3
Use of Service Department X (labor hours)		200	400	300	100
Use of Service Department XX (square footage)	1,000		500	250	750
Expected Service Department Costs	$10,000	$20,000			

Required:

Allocate the expected service department costs to each operating department assuming that the direct method of allocation is used.

25. *Service Department Cost Allocation—Step-Down Method.* Redetermine the allocation of the service department costs in 24 if the step-down method is used. Allocate Service Department XX's costs first.

26. *Service Department Cost Allocation—Over/Underapplied Costs.* Estimated service department costs for Jones Construction Company of $600,000 are assigned to the three operating departments on the basis of estimated hours of direct labor. The budget for 20x1 provided the following estimates:

	Operating Department		
	1	2	3
Labor Hours Worked	10,000	20,000	30,000
Allocated Costs	$100,000	$200,000	$300,000

At the end of the year, the following data became available:

Actual Service Department Costs	$800,000
Actual Hours Worked:	
Department 1	5,000
Department 2	20,000
Department 3	45,000

Required:

a. What dollar amounts were allocated to each department in 20x1?
b. What purposes were served by allocating service department costs to the operating departments?
c. Did the allocation process provide useful information?
d. What happened to the over/underapplied service department cost?

27. *Calculation of Overhead Rates with Service Department Costs.* Assume that Page Company has performed the following allocation of its expected service department costs under the direct method:

	Production Department 1	Production Department 2
Cafeteria	$10,000	$20,000
Materials Handling	5,000	5,000

The overhead costs that are expected to be incurred by Production Departments 1 and 2 during 20x2 are $135,000 and $50,000, respectively. Assume that both production departments apply overhead costs to production based on direct labor hours. Expected labor hours in the operating departments during 20x2 are 10,000 for Production Department 1 and 25,000 for Production Department 2.

Required:

a. Calculate the predetermined overhead rates for Production Departments 1 and 2.
b. If Production Department 1 completed production of an inventory item requiring 100 direct labor hours, how much overhead would be applied to that inventory?
c. If Production Department 2 completed production of an inventory item requiring 250 direct labor hours, how much overhead would be applied to that inventory?

28. *Calculation of Overhead Rates with Service Department Costs.* The following allocation of service department costs was performed for Johnson Motors using the step-down method:

	Service Departments			Production Departments	
	1	2	3	1	2
Expected costs	$10,000	$5,000	$8,000	$45,000	$20,000
Allocate 1	(10,000)	1,000	1,000	5,000	3,000
Allocate 2		(6,000)	500	500	5,000
Allocate 3			(9,500)	5,500	4,000
	0	0	0	$56,000	$32,000

Overhead costs for Production Department 1 are applied based on direct labor hours, while Production Department 2 applies its overhead costs based on machine hours. Shown below is the expected activity for 20x2 in these two departments.

	Production Department 1	Production Department 2
Labor hours	8,000	2,000
Machine hours	4,000	16,000

During 20x2, Johnson Motors began and completed Job 501. This job required 200 direct labor hours (150 in Production Department 1 and 50 in Production Department 2) and 100 machine hours (10 in Production Department 1 and 90 in Production Department 2).

Required:

a. Calculate the predetermined overhead rates for Production Department 1 and Production Department 2.
b. What is the total overhead cost applied to Job 501?

29. *Service Department Cost Allocation—Basic.* The Zeus Company has two operating departments (Fabricating and Finishing) and three service departments. The service departments provide services to both operating departments. Service department expenses are allocated to operating departments as follows:

Department	Allocation Base
Building Maintenance	Space Occupied
Timekeeping and Personnel	Number of Employees
Other	One-Half to Fabricating, One-Half to Finishing

Service department expenses for December (not included in departmental overhead above) were:

Building Maintenance	$ 45,000
Timekeeping and Personnel	27,500
Other	39,000
	$111,500

Other information for December 20x1 is presented below:

	Square Feet of Space Occupied	Number of Employees
Fabricating	75,000	180
Finishing	37,500	120
	112,500	300

Required:

a. Allocate service department costs to the two operating departments.
b. Discuss alternate bases for allocating service department costs to the operating departments.

(AICPA adapted)

30. *Service Department Cost Allocation—Direct Method.* The costs of operating the Maintenance Department of Jemco Company are reallocated to three operating departments on the basis of total labor hours. Operating data for 20x3 were:

		Department 1	Department 2	Department 3
Maintenance Department Costs	$300,000			
Total Labor Hours		100,000	200,000	300,000
Allocated Maintenance Costs		$ 50,000	$100,000	$150,000

In 20x4, the activity of Department 1 increased greatly because a sudden temporary surge in demand for its output. The Maintenance Department established and maintained a second production line from surplus equipment. Operations of Department 1 returned to normal by the end of the year, and the second production line was discontinued. Costs of the Maintenance Department in 20x4 were $300,000. The total labor hours worked in the operating departments were 300,000, 200,000, and 300,000, respectively.

Required:

a. Allocate the 20x4 maintenance costs to the operating departments using 20x3 data to determine the overhead rate.
b. As the manager of Department 1, comment about the year-to-year changes in maintenance costs that are allocated to your department in relation to the year-to-year maintenance costs that are allocated to Department 2.
c. As the manager of Department 2, how would you respond to the comments in part (b) above?
d. As the manager of Department 2, would you change your position about the allocation of maintenance costs if Department 1 experienced decreased labor activity rather than the increase actually experienced?

31. *Service Department Cost Allocation—Step-Down Method.* Albo has two service departments (A and B) providing services to three operating departments (M, N, and O). All service department costs are allocated based on the direct labor hours used by the operating departments and service departments. Expected service department costs are $10,000 in A and $20,000 in B. Shown below is the total utilization (in direct labor hours) by department.

Department	A	B	M	N	O
A		100	200	300	400
B	500		250	750	1,000

Required:

Allocate the service department costs to each of the operating departments using the step-down method of allocation. Assume that Department B's costs are allocated first.

32. *Service Department Cost Allocation—Various.* A manufacturer's plant with two service departments (S_1 and S_2) and three operating departments (P_1, P_2, and P_3) wishes to allocate all factory overhead to operating departments. A primary distribution of overhead to all departments has already been made, as indicated below. The company makes the secondary distribution of overhead from service departments to operating departments. Cost data are presented below:

Primary Overhead to be Allocated				
S_1	S_2	P_1	P_2	P_3
$98,000	$117,600	$1,400,000	$2,100,000	$640,000

Required:

a. Distribute service department costs directly to operating departments without interservice department cost allocation, assuming that P_1, P_2, and P_3 have allocation percentages of 60 percent, 30 percent, and 10 percent, respectively.
b. Distribute service department costs to the other departments, starting with S_1, assuming that the allocation percentages for S_1 are 10 percent, 50 percent, 20 percent, and 20 percent assigned to S_2, P_1, P_2, and P_3, respectively, and S_2 are 60 percent, 30 percent, and 10 percent assigned to P_1, P_2, and P_3.

(AICPA adapted)

33. *Service Department Cost Allocation—Various.* The Parker Manufacturing Company has two operating departments (Fabrication and Assembly) and three service departments (General Factory Administration, Factory Maintenance, and Factory Cafeteria). A summary of the cost and other data for each department prior to allocation of service department costs for the year ended June 30 appears below:

	Fabrication	Assembly	General Factory Administration	Factory Maintenance	Factory Cafeteria
Direct Labor Costs	$1,950,000	$2,050,000	$ 90,000	$ 82,100	$ 87,000
Direct Material Costs	3,130,000	950,000		65,000	91,000
Manufacturing Overhead Costs	1,650,000	1,850,000	70,000	56,100	62,000
Total Costs	$6,730,000	$4,850,000	$160,000	$203,200	$240,000
Direct Labor Hours	562,500	437,500	31,000	27,000	42,000
Number of Employees	280	200	12	8	20
Square Footage Occupied	88,000	72,000	1,750	2,000	4,800

The costs of the General Factory Administration Department, Factory Maintenance Department, and Factory Cafeteria are allocated to the operating departments on the basis of direct labor hours, square footage occupied, and number of employees, respectively.

Required:

a. Assuming that Parker elects to distribute service department costs directly to operating departments without interservice department cost allocation, determine the total costs after allocation for the two operating departments.
b. Assuming that Parker elects to distribute service department costs to the other service departments (starting with the service department with the greatest total costs), as well as the operating departments, determine the total costs after allocation for the two operating departments.

(AICPA adapted)

34. *Service Department Cost Allocation—Various.* The production process of the Ballard Company is comprised of three operating departments and two service departments. Ballard's production process begins in Operating Department A, then proceeds to Operating Department B. Once processing in Department B is complete, the units are then completed in Operating Department C. Service department utilization is shown below:

	Service Department 1	Service Department 2
Operating Department A	10,000 hours	250 calls
Operating Department B	2,500 hours	250 calls
Operating Department C	7,500 hours	1,000 calls
Service Department 1	—	500 calls
Service Department 2	5,000 hours	—

The costs incurred by Service Department 1 are allocated based on labor hours; the costs incurred by Service Department 2 are allocated based on the number of service calls. The following costs were expected in each department: Operating Department A, $20,000; Operating Department B, $30,000; Operating Department C, $45,000; Service Department 1, $5,000; and Service Department 2, $6,000. Assume that the costs of Service Department 2 are to be allocated before those of Service Department 1.

Required:

a. Allocate the expected service department costs to the Operating Departments using the direct method of allocation.
b. Allocate the expected service department cost to the operating departments using the step-down method of allocation.
c. For (a) and (b) above, what is the total expected cost that would be transferred from each operating department upon completion of production in that department?

35. *Service Department Cost Allocation and Calculation of Predetermined Overhead Rate—Various.* Wood Products, Inc. produces high quality furniture based on customers' orders. In producing this furniture, products must pass through two separate operating departments: Cutting and Finishing. The expected overhead costs for the first quarter of 20x1 in these departments are $50,000 and $25,000, respectively. Wood Products has two departments that provide services to the operating departments: Personnel and Cafeteria. The expected costs that will be incurred by Personnel and Cafeteria in the first quarter of 20x1 are $6,000 and $12,000, respectively. Because the costs of these departments increase as the number of employees increases, Wood Products allocates expected service department costs to the operating departments based on number of employees. The number of employees in each of the four departments (the two operating departments and two service departments) is summarized as follows:

Cutting	30
Finishing	20
Personnel	5
Cafeteria	10

Both operating departments apply overhead to production based on direct labor hours worked. At the beginning of 20x1, Wood Products estimates that 10,000 labor hours would be worked in Cutting and 2,500 would be worked in Finishing in the first quarter of 20x1.

Required:

a. Using the direct method of allocation, allocate the expected service department costs to the Cutting and Finishing Departments.
b. Using the step-down method of allocation, allocate the expected service department costs to the Cutting and Finishing Departments. The costs of the Personnel Department should be allocated first.
c. For both (a) and (b) above, calculate the predetermined overhead rate used to apply overhead to production.

36. *Service Department Cost Allocation and Calculation of Predetermined Overhead Rate—Various.* Mike's Clothing produces two types of suits: (1) a "fashion" suit that is produced to fit a general customer profile, and (2) a "custom" suit that is made to customer specifications. Expected overhead costs for these two operating departments and expected activity in these departments is summarized below.

Product	Expected Overhead	Direct Labor Hours	Machine Hours
Fashion Suit	$ 50,000	1,000	10,000
Custom Suit	100,000	5,000	1,000

Because custom suits require a great deal of individual attention by tailors, Mike's Clothing applies overhead costs to these suits based on direct labor hours worked. In contrast, since fashion suits are made using machinery and pre-cut patterns, overhead costs are applied to this product based on the number of machine hours required.

In manufacturing suits, two departments provide services to Mike's operating departments: Cafeteria and Inspection. Inspection costs are allocated to operating departments based on the expected number of hours of service provided to these departments. Cafeteria costs are allocated based on the number of persons employed by other departments.

The expected overhead costs and services provided by the service departments are summarized as follows:

	Cafeteria	Inspection
Expected Costs	$10,000	$20,000
Hours of Service:		
To Fashion Suits	—	100
To Custom Suits	—	900
To Cafeteria	—	—
Number of Employees Served:		
Fashion Suits	10	—
Custom Suits	30	—
Inspection	10	—

Required:

a. Allocate the expected costs of the service departments to the operating departments using the direct method and the step-down method. For the step-down method, allocate the expected costs of the Cafeteria first.
b. For each method in (a) above, calculate the predetermined overhead rate.
c. If 100 fashion suits were produced during January and these suits required 200 direct labor hours and 1,000 machine hours, how much overhead would be applied to production (assume the direct method of allocating service department costs)?
d. If ten custom suits were produced during January and these suits required 500 direct labor hours and 50 machine hours, how much overhead would be applied to production (assume the direct method of allocating service department costs)?

37. **Service Department Cost Allocation, Application of Overhead, and Income Determination—Direct Method (Comprehensive).** Alamo Products, Inc. manufactures two primary inventory products through different processes. Two departments (Cafeteria and Packaging) provide services to the operating departments but are not directly involved in the production of inventory. Alamo decides to allocate the expected costs incurred by these service departments to the operating departments based on the number of employees (for Cafeteria) and number of shipments (for Packaging). Expected costs and service department utilization are summarized below:

	Cafeteria	Packaging	Production A	Production B
Costs	$7,000	$30,000	$100,000	$200,000
Number of Employees	10	30	20	50
Number of Shipments	—	—	50	50

Production Department A applies overhead costs to production based on direct labor hours. A total of 10,000 direct labor hours were expected during 20x1. Production Department B applies overhead costs to production based on machine hours. 5,000 machine hours were expected during 20x1. During the first quarter of 20xl, the following production statistics were accumulated by Alamo Products' managerial accountant.

	Production Department A	Production Department B
Direct Materials Costs	$10,000	$25,000
Direct Labor Costs	$10,000	$2,000
Direct Labor Hours	500	100
Machine Hours	50	200
Units Produced	1,000	5,000

Assume that Production Department A sold its production of 1,000 units for $45 per unit and that Department B sold its production of 5,000 units for $30 per unit.

Required:

a. Allocate the service department costs to the two operating departments using the direct method of allocation.
b. Calculate the predetermined overhead rate for Production Departments A and B.
c. Determine the total overhead that would be applied to the inventory produced by Departments A and B.
d. Calculate a total cost per unit for Production Departments A and B. This cost should include materials, labor, and overhead costs.
e. Determine the total net income realized upon sale of the inventory by Production Departments A and B.

38. **Service Department Cost Allocation, Application of Overhead, and Income Determination—Step-Down Method (Comprehensive).** Repeat 37 using the step-down method of allocation. The costs of the Cafeteria should be allocated prior to those of the Packaging Department.

39. **Service Department Cost Allocation—Comprehensive.** Stooge, Inc. began operations in 20x1. Stooge, Inc.'s manufacturing process consists of two service departments and three operating departments. The expected utilization (in direct labor hours) of the service departments by other departments is shown below:

Service Department	Service Departments		Operating Departments			Total
	1	2	A	B	C	
1		500	400	600	500	2,000
2	300		150	150	600	1,200

Assume that expected service department costs are $16,000 for Service Department 1 and $12,000 for Service Department 2. If necessary, Service Department 1's costs should be allocated before Service Department 2's costs.

During 20x1, Stooge began and completed production of 10,000 units of Moe in Operating Department A. Additional production costs incurred in Department A were $20,000. These units were transferred to

Department B for further processing requiring production costs of $30,000. Finally, in Operating Department C, a total of $25,000 of production costs was required to complete the production of the 10,000 units of Moe. A total of 5,000 units was sold to customers for $20 per unit. No work-in-process inventory existed at the end of 20x1.

Required:

a. Allocate the expected service department costs to the production departments using the direct method of allocation.
b. Repeat (a) above using the step-down method of allocation.
c. For (a) and (b) above, determine the cost per unit in each production department.

40. *Activity-Based Costing.* The Ohio Music Company has three service departments (Packaging, Cafeteria, and Maintenance) that serve its operating department. This operating department manufactures two products: compact discs and cassette tapes. The expected costs of these service departments have been allocated to Ohio Music Company's inventory products under traditional costing based on direct labor hours. Shown below is a breakdown of Ohio Music Company's expected overhead costs and activity for each product.

	Expected Costs	Allocation Compact Discs	Allocation Cassette Tapes
Production Department	$100,000	60%	40%
Packaging	10,000	30%	70%
Cafeteria	20,000	50%	50%
Maintenance	15,000	20%	80%

Assume that Ohio Music Company produced 20,000 compact discs and 13,000 cassette tapes during 20x1. Ohio Music Company has decided to use activity-based costing and apply overhead costs to production based on the relative services provided for production of each of their products.

Required:

Calculate the overhead cost per unit for each of Ohio Music's products for 20x1.

41. *Traditional and Activity Based Costing.* Mainware Movers has two operating lines: long-distance moving (trips greater than 500 miles) and local moving (trips within 500 miles). Three departments provide services to these operating lines: Truck Maintenance, Personnel, and Packing. In previous years, Mainware has allocated the costs of these service departments to the operating lines based on miles driven, number of hours worked, and total pounds of items loaded, respectively. These costs were then accumulated with the expected overhead costs in the operating lines and allocated to individual jobs (moving contracts) based on total miles driven. Shown below is the expected level of service provided to each of Mainware Movers' operating lines during 20x1.

	Long Distance	Local
Truck Maintenance	50,000 miles	25,000 miles
Personnel	15,000 hours	15,000 hours
Packing	15,000,000 pounds	10,000,000 pounds

The total expected costs incurred by the service departments during 20x1 are $12,000 for Truck Maintenance, $20,000 for Personnel, and $500,000 for Packing. During June 20x1, Mainware Movers enters into an agreement for a contract to move a family from Washington, D.C. to Houston, TX. The following data were related to that contract (Job 06-01-x1).

Miles Driven	1,200 miles
Personnel Needs	200 hours
Weight Moved	5,000 pounds

Mainware is considering applying service department costs directly to individual jobs using an activity-based costing method. Under this method, Truck Maintenance costs would be applied based on miles driven, Personnel based on number of hours worked, and Packing based on weight moved.

Required:

a. Allocate the expected service department costs to Mainware Movers' two operating lines using the direct method of allocation.
b. Under traditional costing, apply overhead costs to Job 06-01-xl (using miles driven as the application base). *[Hint: Based on the allocation in (a), calculate a predetermined overhead rate for the long-distance line.]*
c. Under activity-based costing, apply overhead costs to Job 06-01-x1.

42. *Activity-Based Costing and Traditional Costing (Comprehensive).* Jerry's Construction operates in two lines of business: building homes to customer specifications and constructing small projects and other types of home improvements. Expected overhead costs for these lines of business during 20x1 were $200,000 for custom homes and $10,000 for small construction projects. Overhead is applied to both types of construction projects using direct labor hours worked. Based on anticipated demand during 20x1, expected direct labor hours were 10,000 hours for custom homes and 1,000 hours for small construction projects.

Several departments provide services to the two construction divisions. The expected costs and services provided by Jerry's service departments are as follows:

Department	Expected Costs	Expected Hours (Custom Homes)	Expected Hours (Other Projects)
Materials Handling	$40,000	1,000	3,000
Inspection	10,000	2,000	500
Cleaning	2,000	250	250
Detailing	5,000	500	125

During January 20x1, Jerry's Construction began work on a custom home for Susan Attaya (Job A-1). This home was completed during February. Shown below are the total hours of labor and services required to complete construction of this home:

Direct Labor	700 hours
Materials Handling	10 hours
Inspection	100 hours
Cleaning	20 hours
Detailing	120 hours

Required:

a. Using traditional costing, allocate the expected service department costs to Jerry's Construction's lines of business (use the direct method of allocation).
b. After considering your allocation in (a) above, calculate the predetermined overhead rate for Jerry's Construction's lines of business.
c. Using the overhead rates calculated in (b) above, apply overhead to Job A-1.
d. Based on the level of activity provided by each service department to Job A-1, apply overhead to this job using activity-based costing.

Part III

Management's Use of Managerial Accounting Information

In the previous section of this text, we focused on the accumulation of production costs with inventory. At this point, the student should realize that the total costs of producing inventory include direct materials costs, direct labor costs, and manufacturing overhead costs. In some cases, total production costs may also include allocations of:

- The costs incurred by departments that provide services to operating departments.
- The costs incurred by operating departments to produce a number of different inventory products (common production costs).

This section of the text discusses how managerial accounting information (primarily, the cost of producing inventory) can be used by the organization's management in fulfilling its various responsibilities. The following chapters discuss the use of managerial accounting information in this fashion.

Chapter 6: Cost Behavior—Cost-Volume-Profit Analysis and Variable and Absorption Costing
Chapter 7: Standard Costing and Variance Analysis
Chapter 8: Budgeting
Chapter 9: Control of the Organization—Responsibility Accounting
Chapter 10: The Use of Managerial Accounting Data in Making Short-Term Decisions
Chapter 11: Capital Budgeting—Search for Long-Run Alternatives

Learning Objectives

This chapter builds on previous discussions of cost behavior and introduces the concept of cost-volume-profit (CVP) analysis. In addition, alternative methods of income determination (absorption costing and variable costing) are discussed. Studying this chapter should enable you to:

1. Define CVP analysis and discuss how CVP analysis may be used by the organization for planning purposes.

2. Define the term contribution margin and indicate the importance of the contribution margin to the organization.

3. Construct and interpret graphs displaying the fundamental elements of CVP analysis.

4. Calculate the levels of sales volume necessary to break even or earn a desired profit using the general equation approach, unit contribution margin approach, and the contribution margin ratio approach.

5. Identify the elements of CVP analysis and indicate how changes in sales price, variable costs, fixed costs, and/or sales volume affect the remaining element(s).

6. Distinguish between the absorption costing and variable costing approaches to income determination and identify the key differences in income statement format for each approach.

6

Cost Behavior—
Cost-Volume-Profit Analysis and
Variable and Absorption Costing

INTRODUCTION

Mike Jones and Susan Lopez are two teenagers considering starting a lawn care business during their summer vacation. Their most important decision is the price that should be charged to customers for mowing and trimming a lawn.

Mike: In setting our price, we need to determine how much it will cost us to cut each lawn. I figure we'll need about $1 in gas for the mower. My little brother said he'd help rake grass clippings for $2 a lawn. That comes to $3. Anything we charge over $3 should be profit.

Susan: Not so fast, Mike. What about the cost of the lawnmower, edger, and weedeater? Those are costs we need to consider. Even though they don't increase when we cut more lawns, we'll lose money unless we charge our customers enough to cover the costs of buying all of this equipment.

Mike: You're right. Let's say we charge $10 a lawn. I'll bet if we cut fifty lawns a month, we could recover all of our costs.

Susan: Who wants to just recover costs? What about making a profit? If we don't make a profit, none of this is worth our time and effort. In addition to covering our costs, we also need to charge enough to earn a profit.

Mike: I guess so. Maybe if we can cut 100 lawns at $10 each, we'll be able to show a profit. That's what we'll do. We'll just cut more lawns.

Susan: One hundred lawns? That's three lawns a day. Instead of cutting more lawns, let's increase the price to $20. If we do that, we can cut fewer lawns and make just as much money.

Mike: Maybe we should just forget about mowing lawns.

An important tool used by organizations in planning and controlling operations is *cost-volume-profit analysis*. Cost-volume-profit (CVP) analysis allows the organization to determine how potential changes in expected sales volumes, selling prices, fixed costs, and/or variable costs affect overall organization profitability. Just as Mike Jones and Susan Lopez must know how the prices they charge to their customers will affect their profits, organizations of all sizes need similar information. CVP analysis allows management to make various types of decisions with respect to establishing selling prices, manufacturing products, and planning overall profitability. Several examples of how different organizations use CVP analysis are as follows:

- How many fans do the Baltimore Orioles need to draw in order to cover their players' salaries if their payroll is $50 million and their average ticket price is $15?
- If it costs General Mills $0.50 to manufacture a box of cereal products, and it can manufacture and sell 2 million boxes of cereal each month, how much does General Mills need to charge grocery distributors to cover its fixed costs and make a desired level of profit?

- What effect will adding flight routes to Long Island, New York have on Southwest Airlines' profitability?
- If Coca-Cola purchases manufacturing equipment that reduces its direct labor costs, how would this affect the level of sales necessary to earn a desired profit?

To illustrate the application of CVP analysis, we will examine the activities of Golden Music Producers, a company that manufactures and sells compact discs and other music products to music and electronic stores throughout the United States. For simplicity, we initially focus on the manufacturing and sales of compact discs. Golden Music currently has the capacity to manufacture 200,000 compact discs each month. After a thorough analysis of its prior costs and manufacturing activity, Golden Music has identified its basic cost and revenue data, these are summarized in Illustration 1.

Illustration 1
Golden Music Producers
Estimated Cost and Revenue Data: Compact Discs

	Dollars	Percent
Selling Price (per compact disc)	$10.00	100.0
Variable Costs (per Compact Disc):		
Direct Materials (Blank Compact Disc)	$1.50	15.0
Direct Labor (including employee benefits)	0.50	5.0
Manufacturing Overhead	3.00	30.0
Artist Royalties	0.75	7.5
Sales Commissions	0.25	2.5
Total Variable Cost (per Compact Disc)	$6.00	60.0
Contribution Margin	$4.00	40.0
Fixed Costs (per Month):		
Depreciation on Plant and Equipment	$250,000	
Supervision and Indirect Labor	50,000	
General and Administrative	200,000	
Total Fixed Costs (per Month)	$500,000	

The data in Illustration 1 classify costs based on their behavior with respect to sales volume. It is important to note that the behavior of these costs may differ if different measures of activity (cost drivers) are selected.

From the above information, you can readily determine that the total variable cost per compact disc is $6 and the selling price is $10. The excess of the selling price over the variable costs is referred to as the *contribution margin*. The amount of the contribution margin is significant for Golden Music's management, since it represents the "profit" made on the sale of each item that is available to cover the organization's fixed costs and, perhaps, earn a profit. Note in Illustration 1 that the contribution margin is expressed both in terms of a contribution margin per unit ($4) and as a percentage of the selling price ($4 ÷ $10 = 40 percent). The contribution margin is an important concept for pricing decisions, since Golden Music should establish its selling prices so that it is able to recover the variable costs associated with its products or services and ultimately earn a profit. In this case, if Golden Music charges less than $6 for its compact discs, it would suffer a loss on each sale!

> Based on analyst estimates, Disney averages a sales price of $14 per tape on "Aladdin" (released in 1993). The variable costs (tape, plastic cartridge, packaging, and transportation) average $2 per tape. Therefore, for each tape it sells, Disney earns $12 to cover its fixed costs (such as advertising) and contribute toward its profits.[1]

---

[1] "Disney's Magic Lamp," *Forbes* (November 22, 1993), 43.

If Golden Music sells all 200,000 of its discs to music and electronics stores, its anticipated monthly income would be $300,000, as shown below:

Sales Revenue (200,000 discs x $10)	$2,000,000
Variable Costs (200,000 discs x $6)	(1,200,000)
Contribution Margin	$ 800,000
Fixed Costs	(500,000)
Net Income	$ 300,000

The income statement above expresses the contribution margin as a dollar total (the difference between the total revenue and total variable costs). In this case, the contribution margin of $800,000 allows Golden Music Producers to recover the fixed costs of manufacturing and selling its compact discs ($500,000) and provides net income of $300,000.

Based on the above information, Golden Music should expect to earn net income of $300,000 per month. However, it is important to emphasize that this calculation is based on estimated cost, volume, and profit data. Actual operating results may (and often do) differ from these expectations. For example, Golden Music may not sell all 200,000 of the compact discs manufactured each month. In addition, the fixed and variable costs actually incurred by Golden Music may differ from the estimated levels shown in Illustration 1. Finally, Golden Music may not be able to realize revenues of $10 per compact disc if it is required to lower selling prices in response to actions of its competitors. CVP analysis allows management to determine how changes in these and other factors affect the relationship between Costs, sales Volume, and Profits (notice that CVP analysis draws its abbreviation from the initial letters of each of these factors).

> When sales of Hillary Rodham Clinton's book, *Living History*, hit 600,000 copies in its first week on the shelves, many in the publishing world concluded that the book was already generating profits for its publisher, Simon & Schuster. However, Simon & Schuster actually had to sell about 754,000 copies just to break even. Total costs associated with the book included an $8 million advance to Ms. Clinton, $2 million for the first printing (1,000,000 copies), $1.2 million in marketing costs, and approximately $1.85 million in overhead cost.[2]

CVP ANALYSIS: GRAPHICAL APPROACH

The income statement prepared in the previous section may be depicted graphically as in Illustration 2. The graph in Illustration 2 summarizes the relationships among revenues, variable costs, fixed costs, and profit and is constructed in the following manner.

1. *Revenues* are graphed by multiplying the estimated selling price by various levels of sales volume. For example, at zero units of sales, sales revenues would obviously be zero. At sales volumes of 200,000 compact discs, sales revenues would equal $2,000,000 (200,000 compact discs x $10 = $2,000,000). As a result, the sales revenue line in Illustration 2 passes through the points (0, $0) and (200, $2,000) (the graph in Illustration 2 is constructed in terms of thousands of units and dollars). The line marked "SR" in Illustration 2 is the line depicting total sales revenue.

2. *Variable costs* are graphed in much the same manner as revenues. In this case, total variable costs are determined by multiplying total sales volume by the variable cost per unit. Recall that the variable cost per compact disc is $6. At zero compact discs, the total variable costs equal $0; at 200,000 compact discs, total variable costs equal $1,200,000 (200,000 compact discs x $6 = $1,200,000). Once again, since the graph in Illustration 2 is stated in terms of thousands of units and dollars, the variable cost line passes through points (0, $0) and (200, $1,200). The variable cost line is marked as "VC" in Illustration 2.

Once the revenues and variable costs have been graphed, the *contribution margin* can be clearly identified. The contribution margin represents the distance between the revenue line and the variable cost line and is marked as "CM" in Illustration 2. Note that at zero units of activity, these two lines intersect, indicating that the total contribution margin equals zero. However, once the first compact disc has been sold, the contribution margin becomes positive and increases as the number of compact discs sold increases.

---

[2] Hardy Green, "Reality Check: Hillary's Hit," *Business Week* (June 30, 2003), 12.

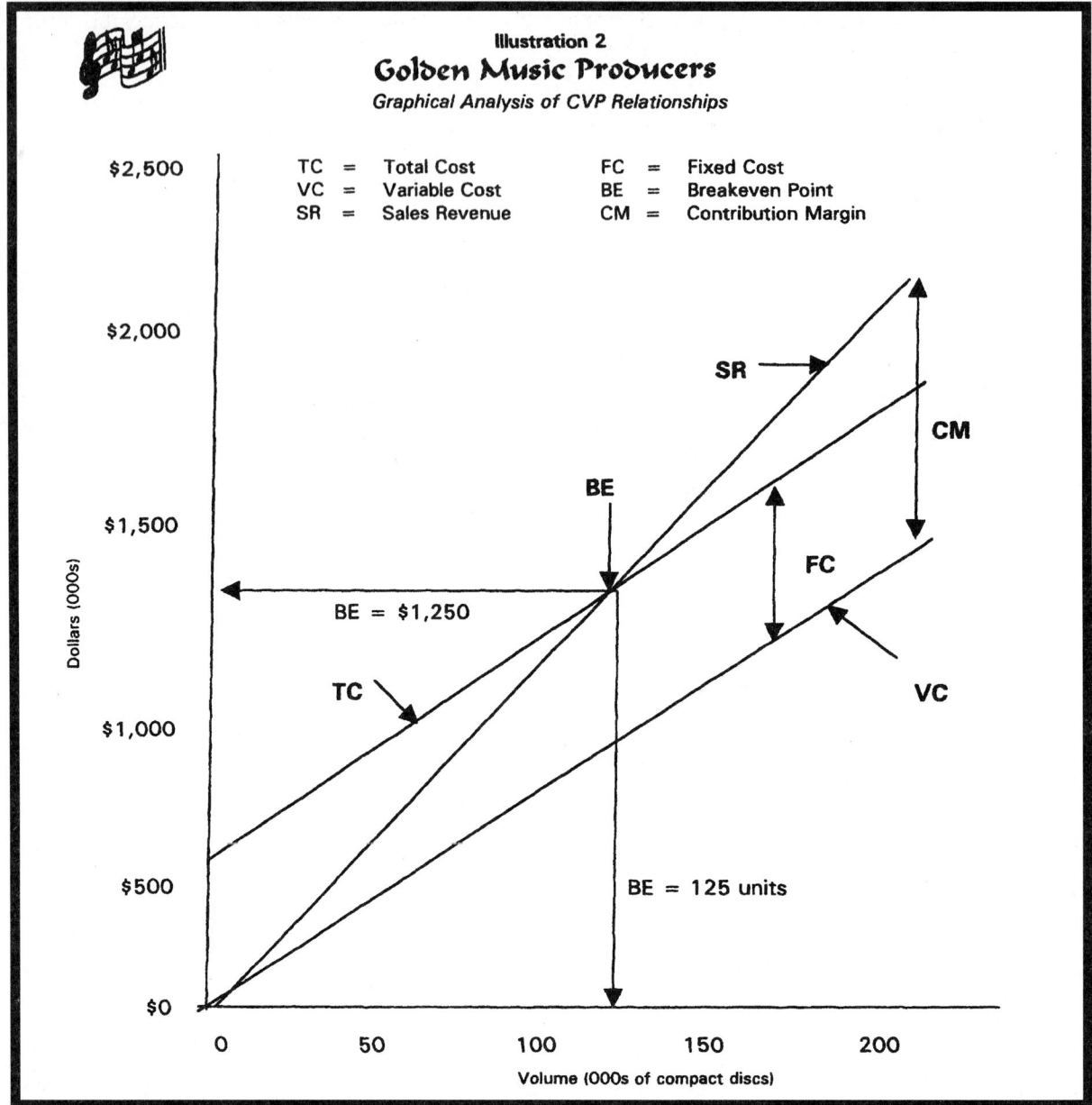

3. *Total costs* include both variable costs [discussed in (2) above] and fixed costs. As shown previously in Illustration 1, estimated fixed costs are $500,000 per month. To determine total costs for a given level of activity, the fixed costs of $500,000 are added to the variable costs at that level of activity. While a total fixed cost line is not presented in Illustration 2, the fixed costs are represented by "shifting" the variable cost line upward (marked as "FC" in Illustration 2) to intersect the vertical axis at the point equal to fixed costs. Total costs at sales volumes of 0 and 200,000 compact discs are shown below (amounts are in thousands). These costs are represented by the "TC" line in Illustration 2.

	Variable Costs	Fixed Costs	Total Costs
0 discs............................	0 × $6 = $ 0	$500	$ 500
200 discs............................	200 × $6 = $1,200	$500	$1,700

4. Profits (or net income) represent the difference between the total sales revenues and total costs at any level of activity. Profits can be expressed as the vertical difference between the sales revenue and total cost lines shown in Illustration 2. For a given level of activity, if the total sales revenues are less than total costs, a net loss would be incurred. In contrast, if total sales revenues exceed total costs, a net profit would be earned.

The intersection of the total sales line and total cost line in Illustration 2 is referred to as the *breakeven point* (marked as "BE" in Illustration 2). The breakeven point is the production point at which total costs are exactly equal to total revenues, and net income equals zero. Note that the breakeven point can be expressed in terms of either units sold or total sales revenues. A cursory examination of the point at which the total sales revenue and total cost lines intersect indicates that the breakeven point is 125,000 compact discs (or $1,250,000 in sales revenue). To verify the breakeven point, the net income earned by Golden Music assuming the sale of 125,000 compact discs during March is shown below:

Sales Revenue (125,000 discs x $10)	$ 1,250,000
Variable Costs (125,000 discs x $6)	(750,000)
Contribution Margin	$ 500,000
Fixed Costs	(500,000)
Net Income	$ 0

Any sales levels above 125,000 compact discs would increase net income by the amount of the contribution margin multiplied by the number of discs sold. This reflects the fact that all fixed costs have been recovered at the breakeven point. As a result, the net income earned on each sale above 125,000 units is the difference between the revenue and the variable costs (in this example, $4 per compact disc).

The following example from the automobile industry illustrates how sales above the breakeven point influence net income:

> **With a surge in demand, Ford could move solidly into the black this year. However, as the The Big Three's lowest-cost producer, Ford breaks even at just 68 percent of capacity, and anything above that increases profits dramatically, says George Peterson, president of Auto-Pacific Group, Inc, a Santa Ana (Calif.) research company. Now running at 91 percent of capacity, Ford is sitting pretty.[3]**

As the previous excerpt suggests, once Ford achieves its breakeven point, each automobile sold increases its net income (before taxes) by the excess of the sales price over its variable costs. This excess was defined earlier as the contribution margin.

Companies can use the breakeven point to evaluate potential risks. One such risk is the likelihood that their sales will decline to such an extent that the organization would not be profitable from the sale of its products or services. As discussed earlier, Golden Music anticipates monthly sales levels of 200,000 compact discs. If the breakeven point is 125,000, Golden Music's safety margin equals 75,000 compact discs (200,000 – 125,000 = 75,000). The *safety margin* provides companies with information about the extent to which sales can decrease before losses will occur. In this case, sales can decline by 75,000 compact discs before Golden Music would not earn profits on the sale of this product. In addition to the number of units, safety margins can also be expressed in terms of sales dollars or in percentage terms. As shown below, these indices suggest that sales could decline by $750,000 (or 37.5%) before Golden Music would not be profitable. Each of these formulae represents the extent to which current sales exceed breakeven sales (in terms of units, dollars, or percentages).

Safety Margin (Dollars)   = $2,000,000 – $1,250,000 = $750,000
Safety Margin (Percentage) = 75,000 ÷ 200,000 = 37.5%

Illustration 3 is another common graph prepared when performing CVP analysis. This graph depicts the relationship between profits and volume. That is, by examining the graph shown in Illustration 3, Golden Music's management is able to answer the question: "what is the total profit at *x* units of sales?" The graph in Illustration 3 shows two main areas: an area of net loss and an area of net profit. Three points on the total profit line in Illustration 3 that describe the relationship between costs and profits are:

1. If no compact discs are sold, Golden Music expects a net loss of $500,000 (the amount of the fixed costs). This loss would occur because, if no units were sold, total variable costs and total sales revenue would equal zero. However, since fixed costs would still be incurred, the net loss equals $500,000.
2. If 125,000 compact discs were sold, Golden Music would break even (that is, earn a net income of $0). In Illustration 3, the point where the profit line equals zero is the breakeven point.
3. At sales levels of 200,000 compact discs, Golden Music would earn net income of $300,000, as illustrated earlier in this chapter.

---

[3] "Red Hot, Red Ink," *Business Week* (January 11, 1993), 26–27.

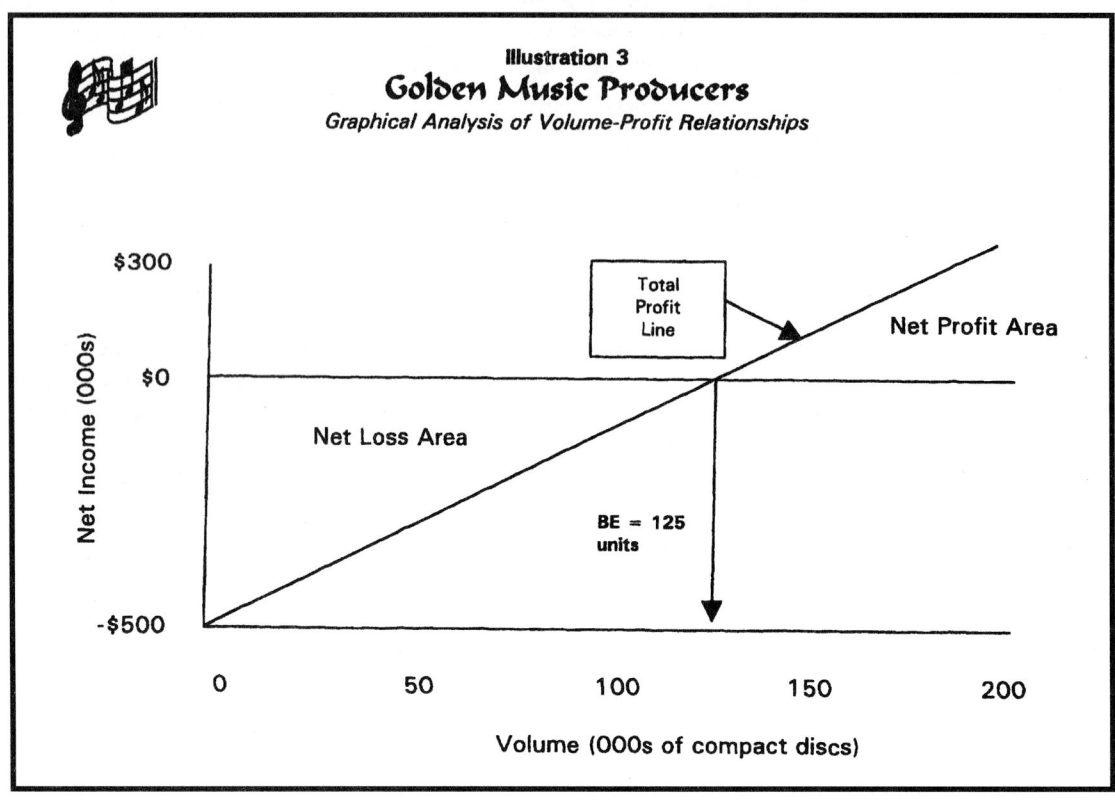

CVP ANALYSIS: EQUATION APPROACHES

A weakness of the graphical analysis is that it may not permit precise measurement of revenues, costs, contribution margins, or profits, Therefore, determining the exact breakeven point (in terms of either sales volume or sales dollars) may be difficult. To overcome these weaknesses, equations based on the construction of the graphs discussed earlier can be used. These equations reflect the mathematical relationships between revenues, variable costs, fixed costs, and desired profits (either before or after taxes).

General Equation Approach

The general form of the equation used in CVP analysis mirrors the income statement and is based on the simple concept that the excess of revenues over costs is profits. If revenues are expressed as the number of units sold multiplied by the selling price, and variable costs are expressed as the number of units sold multiplied by the variable cost per unit, this concept can be algebraically expressed as follows:

$$\text{Sales Price Per Unit}\ (x) - \text{Variable Cost Per Unit}\ (x) - \text{Fixed Costs} = \text{Profit}$$

In the above equation, x represents the number of units sold. To determine the breakeven point for the example illustrated earlier, we solve the above equation for x. Recall that Golden Music estimated the selling price per compact disc at $10, variable cost per compact disc at $6, and fixed costs at $500,000. Since we are determining the breakeven point, profit equals $0.

$$\$10\ (x) - \$6\ (x) - \$500,000 = \$0$$
$$\$4\ (x) - \$500,000 = \$0$$
$$\$4\ (x) = \$500,000$$
$$(x) = 125,000 \text{ compact discs}$$

To express the breakeven point in sales dollars, we merely multiply the number of compact discs needed to break even by the sales price per unit as below:

$$125,000 \text{ compact discs} \times \$10 = \$1,250,000$$

Therefore, as under the graphical approach, Golden Music producers must sell 125,000 compact discs (or generate sales revenues of $1,250,000) to cover its fixed costs and earn a zero profit (i.e., "break even").

Unit Contribution Margin Approach

The unit contribution margin approach for CVP analysis rearranges the general equation presented above to provide a final solution in terms of the number of units. Essentially, the general equation is algebraically manipulated so that x (the number of units that must be sold) is isolated on the left side of the equation. The rearranged form of the equation is shown below:

$$\text{Sales (Units)} = \frac{\text{Fixed Costs + Desired Profit}}{\text{Contribution Margin Per Unit}}$$

The above equation answers the following question: "If we can earn $x on the sale of each unit (contribution margin per unit), how many units must be sold to cover fixed costs and earn a desired level of profit?" The contribution margin per unit is equal to the sales price per compact disc minus the variable cost per unit and is $4 ($10 − $6 = $4). Once the contribution margin per unit has been determined, the breakeven point can be calculated, as shown below:

$$\text{Sales (Units)} = \frac{\$500,000 + \$0}{\$4}$$

$$= 125,000 \text{ compact discs}$$

To translate this breakeven point into dollars, simply multiply the number of compact discs needed to break even by the $10 sales price per unit. Doing so yields a breakeven point in dollars of $1,250,000 (125,000 compact discs x $10 = $1,250,000).

Contribution Margin Ratio Approach

While the organization can determine the level of sales (in terms of dollars) required to break even by calculating the number of units using the contribution margin approach and multiplying this number of units by the sales price, this may not be practical in all cases. For example, grocery stores have a wide variety of products, all having different contribution margins. As a result, these businesses could not identify a single contribution margin for use in the denominator of the equation in the preceding section. However, by considering the contribution margins earned on their various products, as well as the relative sales mix of these products, the contribution margin can be expressed as a percentage of the selling prices of those products. Simply stated, the organization could determine an "average" contribution margin percentage and utilize this information to conduct CVP analysis.

One way to determine the level of sales (in dollars) necessary to achieve a certain level of profit is to express the contribution margin as a percentage of sales prices by dividing the contribution margin per unit by the sales price per unit. As shown in Illustration 1, Golden Music's contribution margin percentage (for compact discs) is 40%. The determination of this percentage is shown below:

$$\text{Contribution Margin \%} = \frac{\text{Contribution Margin}}{\text{Sales Price}} = \frac{\$4}{\$10} = 40\% \text{ (or 0.40)}$$

Once the contribution margin percentage has been determined, the breakeven level of sales (in dollars) can be calculated through the use of the following equation, which states contribution margin as a percentage of sales and not on a per unit basis. This equation restates the equation used in the contribution margin approach in the preceding section by multiplying each side by the sales price per unit.

$$\text{Sales (Dollars)} = \frac{\text{Fixed Costs + Desired Profit}}{\text{Contribution Margin Percentage}}$$

$$= \frac{\$500,000 + \$0}{0.40} = \$1,250,000$$

The above equation is based on the following question: "If each dollar of sales contributes x percent to profit, what level of sales must be generated to cover fixed costs and earn a desired level of profit?" If desired, this breakeven level may be translated into units by dividing by the sales price per unit. Doing so yields a breakeven point of 125,000 units ($1,250,000 ÷ $10 = 125,000). Notice that the breakeven levels (in both units and sales dollars) are identical to those determined under the graphical analysis method, the general equation approach, or the unit contribution margin approach.

OTHER USES OF CVP ANALYSIS

Desired Level of Profit (Before Taxes)

The preceding analysis assumed that Golden Music was interested in knowing the necessary sales levels to cover its costs and break even. However, organizations cannot remain in business unless they ultimately become profitable. This breakeven analysis ordinarily serves as a benchmark for the organization to allow it to evaluate its activities. Assume that the management of Golden Music decides that it must earn $150,000 per month (before taxes) in order to remain in business, what level of sales volume (in units and dollars) must be reached to achieve this level of profitability?

This question can be answered through a simple modification of the preceding CVP analysis. Using either the contribution margin approach or the contribution margin ratio approach, the desired level of profit ($150,000) is substituted into the formula for the breakeven level of profit ($0). Using the contribution margin formula, Golden Music Producers needs to sell 162,500 compact discs to earn a $150,000 profit, as shown below:

$$\text{Sales (Units)} = \frac{\text{Fixed Costs} + \text{Desired Profit}}{\text{Contribution Margin Per Unit}}$$

$$= \frac{\$500,000 + \$150,000}{\$4} = 162,500 \text{ compact discs}$$

Sales (Dollars) = 162,500 compact discs × $10 = $1,625,000

Alternatively, the level of sales necessary to earn the desired profit of $150,000 before taxes can be determined using an *incremental approach*. Under an incremental approach, managers use the original CVP analysis as a baseline and evaluate how changes in the various factors affect the necessary sales volumes. To illustrate, recall that Golden Music originally determined a breakeven point of 125,000 compact discs. If a $150,000 profit before taxes is desired, this is referred to as incremental profit, since the original breakeven analysis assumed a $0 desired profit. To earn an additional or incremental profit of $150,000 before taxes, an additional 37,500 compact discs must be sold, as shown below:

Desired Incremental Profits	$150,000
÷ Contribution Margin per Unit	÷ $4.00
Incremental Sales (Units)	37,500

Adding the incremental sales (in units) to the original breakeven point of 125,000 yields a necessary sales volume of 162,500 compact discs (125,000 + 37,500 = 162,500). Notice that this equals the necessary sales volume determined using the contribution margin approach shown above.

Desired Profit (After Taxes)

Desired profit can also be stated in terms of profit after considering income taxes. In this case, the organization simply needs to convert the profit after taxes to the necessary level of profit before taxes; once this has been done, the analysis proceeds as above. Assume that Golden Music wishes to determine the sales levels necessary to earn a profit of $150,000 per month *after* taxes and its effective tax rate is 25 percent. Profit after taxes is calculated as follows:

Profit After Taxes = Profit Before Taxes × (1 − Tax Rate)

Rearranging the above equation, profit before taxes can be determined as follows:

$$\text{Profit Before Taxes} = \frac{\text{Profit After Taxes}}{(1 - \text{Tax Rate})}$$

$$= \frac{\$150,000}{(1 - 0.25)} = \$200,000$$

Now, substituting the $200,000 for the $0 desired profit (as is customary under breakeven analysis), Golden Music must sell 175,000 compact discs (or generate sales revenue of $1,750,000).

$$\text{Sales (Units)} = \frac{\text{Fixed Costs + Desired Profit}}{\text{Contribution Margin Per Unit}}$$

$$= \frac{\$500,000 + \$200,000}{\$4} = 175,000 \text{ compact discs}$$

$$\text{Sales (Dollars)} = 175,000 \text{ compact discs} \times \$10 = \$1,750,000 \text{ (Dollars)}$$

Notice that the level of sales necessary to earn $150,000 per month after taxes (175,000 compact discs or $1,750,000) exceeds that necessary to earn $150,000 per month before taxes (162,500 compact discs or $1,625,000). This results from the fact that additional revenues must be generated to pay the organization's income taxes. Income taxes are another cost that must be covered by the organization by the sale of its products.

Variable Levels of Profit

In some cases, the desired levels of profit are stated in variable (rather than fixed) dollar terms. For example, instead of stating a goal of earning $150,000 in profit per month (either before or after taxes), the organization may state its desired profits as a percentage (e.g., 8 percent) of its revenues. Stating profits in this manner acknowledges that the organization may earn higher profits if unusual events (such as a significant reduction in costs or a significant increase in production capacity) provide an opportunity to do so. When desired profits are stated in this manner, the organization's overall profitability is assumed to increase at a constant rate as the level of sales increase.

When desired profits are stated as a percentage of revenue, the organization simply adjusts the variable cost per unit in the denominator of the contribution margin equation to include the desired profit (as a percentage of selling prices).

In a sense, the desired profit per item sold is considered as if it were another variable cost that must be recovered by the organization through the sale of its products. If the organization breaks even after considering the desired level of profit per unit or dollar of sales, it has in fact earned that level of profit.

Assume that Golden Music defines its desired level of profit as 8 percent of revenues before income taxes. If defined in this manner, the desired profit on the sale of each item would be $0.80 (0.08 × $10 = $0.80). By subtracting this $0.80 from the original contribution margin of $4, a breakeven level of sales of 156,250 compact discs or $1,562,500, is determined as follows:

$$\text{Sales (Units)} = \frac{\text{Fixed Cost + Desired Profit}}{\text{Contribution Margin Per Unit}}$$

$$= \frac{\$500,000 + \$0}{(\$10 - \$6 - \$0.80)} = 156,250 \text{ compact discs}$$

$$\text{Sales (Dollars)} = 156,250 \text{ compact discs} \times \$10 = \$1,562,500$$

Change in Variable Costs / Contribution Margin

The preceding analysis was based on Golden Music's estimates of variable costs of $6 per compact disc and fixed costs of $500,000. An important use of CVP analysis is determining how potential changes in the levels of these costs would influence the sales necessary to achieve desired profit levels. For example, assume that the cost of materials and renegotiated royalty rates with artists resulted in an increase in variable costs from $6 to $7.50 per disc. Intuitively, this would appear to increase the level of sales required to break even, since the contribution margin per unit would decrease from $4 to $2.50 ($10 − $7.50 = $2.50). The revised breakeven point increases to 200,000 compact discs (or $2,000,000) as shown below:

$$\text{Sales (Units)} = \frac{\text{Fixed Costs + Desired Profit}}{\text{Contribution Margin per Unit}}$$

$$= \frac{\$500,000 + \$0}{(\$10.00 - \$7.50)} = 200,000 \text{ compact discs}$$

$$\text{Sales (Dollars)} = 200,000 \text{ compact discs} \times \$10 = \$2,000,000$$

Change in Fixed Costs

Alternatively, changes in costs may reduce the level of sales necessary to break even. For example, assume that Golden Music has increased the size of its production runs, resulting in a savings of fixed indirect labor costs (manufacturing setup and inspection costs) of $20,000. Because a smaller amount of fixed costs must be covered, this would appear to decrease the level of sales required to break even. Recalling that the breakeven point prior to the increase in costs was 125,000 compact discs (or $1,250,000), the revised breakeven point decreases to 120,000 (or $1,200,000), as shown below:

$$\text{Sales (Units)} = \frac{\text{Fixed Costs} + \text{Desired Profit}}{\text{Contribution Margin per Unit}}$$

$$= \frac{(\$500{,}000 - \$20{,}000) + \$0}{(\$10 - \$6)} = 120{,}000 \text{ compact discs}$$

$$\text{Sales (Dollars)} = 120{,}000 \text{ compact discs} \times \$10 = \$1{,}200{,}000$$

Calculating Necessary Selling Prices

In practice, the most common use of CVP analysis is to determine the sales volumes necessary to earn desired levels of profit. In many cases, market conditions do not provide organizations with much discretion with respect to the selling prices charged for their products. However, CVP analysis can be utilized to allow the organization to determine the selling price it must charge for its products to achieve certain profit levels. This application of CVP is useful in situations where organizations operate in industries where some discretion exists in establishing the prices for the organization's products or services.

To illustrate the use of CVP analysis to determine necessary sales prices, consider the original data for the Golden Music example but now assume that a temporary shortage in the availability of direct materials has reduced its production capacity to 80,000 compact discs. You may recall that the original breakeven point was 125,000 discs. As a result, if Golden Music continues to charge $10 for its compact discs, it will suffer a loss, since its capacity (80,000 compact discs) is less than the level of sales necessary to break even (125,000 compact discs).

The management of Golden Music is attempting to set the selling price of its compact discs so that it can still cover its fixed costs in spite of the reduced level of capacity. To do so, Golden Music can use the contribution margin approach but solve the equation for the necessary selling price. Rather than solving for the necessary sales level (in terms of units), the number of units sold will be set equal to the revised capacity (80,000 compact discs). Doing so yields a selling price of $12.25 per compact disc, as shown below:

$$\text{Sales (Units)} = \frac{\text{Fixed Costs} + \text{Desired Profit}}{\text{Contribution Margin per Unit}}$$

$$80{,}000 = \frac{\$500{,}000 + \$0}{(\text{Selling Price} - \$6)}$$

$$80{,}000 \,(\text{Selling Price}) - \$480{,}000 = \$500{,}000$$

$$80{,}000 \,(\text{Selling Price}) = \$980{,}000$$

$$\text{Selling Price} = \$12.25 \text{ per compact disc}$$

Golden Music Producers can also use this approach to determine the amount of any price increase necessary in response to increases in its manufacturing and other costs. Recall from the previous subsection that Golden Music's breakeven point increased to 200,000 compact discs as a result of an increase in variable costs to $7.50 per compact disc. If Golden Music wished to increase its selling prices in response to these cost increases, it may be interested in knowing the price that must be charged to its customers to continue to break even at sales volumes of 125,000 compact discs. This sales price is $11.50 per compact disc, as shown below:

$$\text{Sales (Units)} = \frac{\text{Fixed Costs} + \text{Desired Profit}}{\text{Contribution Margin per Unit}}$$

$$125{,}000 = \frac{\$500{,}000 + \$0}{(\text{Selling Price} - \$7.50)}$$

$$125{,}000 \,(\text{Selling Price}) - \$937{,}500 = \$500{,}000$$

$$125{,}000 \,(\text{Selling Price}) = \$1{,}437{,}500$$

$$\text{Selling Price} = \$11.50 \text{ per compact disc}$$

In each of these cases, CVP is used to answer the following question: "Given sales of x units, how much should be charged for compact discs if fixed costs are $\$y$ and variable costs are $\$z$ per disc?"

CVP for Multiple Products

To this point, our discussion of CVP analysis has been limited to the relationships among sales, variable costs, fixed costs, and profit for a single product. However, for organizations selling numerous products, it is normally not useful to determine the breakeven point for any one product. Instead, the organization is interested in determining the necessary level of sales on an organization-wide basis. A major assumption necessary for an analysis of this sort is the approximate "mix" (i.e., relative sales volume) of each type of product.

To illustrate CVP analysis for organizations selling multiple products, assume that Golden Music has two other products: cassette tapes and music videos. The expected production capacity, selling prices, variable costs, and fixed costs for the three products are summarized below.

	Production Capacity	Selling Price	Variable Costs	Fixed Costs
Compact Discs	200,000	$10	$6	$500,000
Cassette Tapes	100,000	$5	$3	$150,000
Music Videos	100,000	$15	$5	$250,000

To calculate a breakeven point in the above example, Golden Music can determine its weighted contribution margin ratio for these products. The weighted contribution margin ratio is determined by summing the expected contribution margin for each of the three products and dividing this amount by the expected sales revenue.

	Sales Revenue			Variable Costs		
Compact Discs	200,000 x $10	=	$2,000,000	200,000 x $6	=	$1,200,000
Cassette Tapes	100,000 x $ 5	=	500,000	100,000 x $3	=	300,000
Music Videos	100,000 x $15	=	1,500,000	100,000 x $5	=	500,000
			$4,000,000			$2,000,000

$$\text{Contribution Margin Ratio} = \frac{\text{Contribution Margin}}{\text{Sales Price}}$$

$$= \frac{(\$4,000,000 - \$2,000,000)}{\$4,000,000} = 0.50$$

Once the weighted contribution margin ratio is determined, the breakeven point (in sales dollars) can be calculated by dividing the total fixed costs by this ratio. The total fixed costs for Golden Music equal $900,000 ($500,000 + $250,000 + $150,000 = $900,000). Assuming that the mix of sales made by Golden Music Producers is as expected (200,000 compact discs, 100,000 cassette tapes, and 100,000 music videos per month), the breakeven sales would equal $1,800,000, as shown below:

$$\text{Sales (Dollars)} = \frac{\text{Fixed Costs + Desired Profit}}{\text{Contribution Margin Percentage}}$$

$$= \frac{(\$900,000 + \$0)}{0.50} = \$1,800,000$$

Alternatively, Golden Music Producers can determine the breakeven point in terms of the number of units sold using the contribution margin approach. In a multiple product setting, each "unit" actually represents a "package" of items based on the relative sales mix of the organization's products. In the above example, Golden Music anticipates the sale of 400,000 items, which represents the following sales mix:

Compact Discs	(200,000 ÷ 400,000)	0.50
Cassette Tapes	(100,000 ÷ 400,000)	0.25
Music Videos	(100,000 ÷ 400,000)	0.25
	(400,000 ÷ 400,000)	1.00

Once the sales mix has been identified as above, a weighted contribution margin can be calculated by multiplying the contribution margin for each product by the percentage of total sales represented by that product. Golden Music's weighted contribution margin is calculated as follows:

	Sales Mix		Contribution Margin		Weighted Contribution Margin
Compact Discs	0.50	x	($10 – $6)	=	$2.00
Cassette Tapes	0.25	x	($5 – $3)	=	0.50
Music Videos	0.25	x	($15 – $5)	=	2.50
					$5.00

The weighted contribution margin determined above is then used in the contribution margin approach to determine the breakeven point in terms of number of units. Recalling that total fixed costs are $900,000, the total number of "units" required to break-even is 180,000 as shown below.

$$\text{Sales (Units)} = \frac{\text{Fixed Costs} + \text{Desired Profit}}{\text{Contribution Margin per Unit}}$$

$$= \frac{\$900,000 + \$0}{\$5.00} = 180,000 \text{ units}$$

The 180,000 "units" shown above actually represent three products. Based on the relative sales mix of these three products, the sales of each product required to break even would be 90,000 compact discs (180,000 "units" x 0.50 = 90,000), 45,000 cassette tapes (180,000 "units" x 0.25 = 45,000), and 45,000 music videos (180,000 "units" x 0.25 = 45,000).

The following income statement verifies the calculation of the breakeven points determined above. Note that total breakeven sales are $1,800,000 (as calculated using the contribution margin ratio approach) or 180,000 "units" (as calculated under the contribution margin approach).

Sales:			
Compact Discs (90,000 x $10)	$900,000		
Cassette Tapes (45,000 x $5)	225,000		
Music Videos (45,000 x $15)	675,000	$1,800,000	
Variable Costs:			
Compact Discs (90,000 discs x $6)	$540,000		
Cassette Tapes (45,000 tapes x $3)	135,000		
Music Videos (45,000 videos x $5)	225,000	(900,000)	
Contribution Margin		$900,000	
Fixed Costs		(900,000)	
Net Income		$ 0	

It is important to note that this level of sales will allow Golden Music to break even only if the three products are sold in the anticipated mix. If Golden Music shifts its production and sells a greater mix of music videos (a relatively high margin product), the breakeven sales level would decrease. In contrast, if reduced demand for music videos results in a shift in production to lower margin products (such as compact discs and cassette tapes), the level of sales required to break even would increase. This change reflects the fact that the contribution margin percentage used in the above calculation considers both the contribution margin per unit earned by each of the three products as well as the anticipated sales volume of each of these products.

The importance of a company's sales mix and the resulting effect on profit is illustrated by the following excerpts from practice.

> While growth in new markets is generally viewed as a positive development, investors and analysts expressed some concerns when it became apparent that a significant portion of the Coca-Cola Company's growth was the result of sales of beverages that weren't as profitable as its core brands. Coke increased its sales volume by aggressively expanding into sales of noncarbonated beverages such as bottled water and juice. However, while its core carbonated drinks were contributing a 35% operating margin, sales of some brands of juice and bottled water were generating margins that were much lower and, in some cases, uncomfortably close to zero.[4]

---

[4] Betsy McKay, "Is Less of Coke's Real Thing Wise?" *The Wall Street Journal* (October 29, 2002), C1.

> How did Ford Motor Company increase its net income to $7.2 billion in 1999 while losing market share? A shift in the mix of vehicles it sells. Ford decreased the number of low-margin vehicles (Escorts and Aspires) and increased the level of sales of its high-margin vehicles (Crown Victorias and Explorers). Ford's previous compensation strategy (where salespeople were compensated based on unit sales and not profit margins) contributed to a suboptimal focus on low-margin vehicles.[5]

OPERATING LEVERAGE AND AUTOMATED MANUFACTURING PROCESSES

The automation of manufacturing processes has definite implications for CVP analysis, since automation results in a general shift from variable costs (i.e., direct labor) to fixed costs (i.e., depreciation on manufacturing equipment). This shift results in increased contribution margins per unit sold but a greater amount of fixed costs that must be recovered by the organization. To illustrate, assume that Golden Music has decided to more fully automate its manufacturing processes. This automation was not undertaken to increase its current production capacity (which would remain at 200,000 compact discs per month) but would result in a change in its cost structure. The planned automation will result in additional fixed costs of $400,000 per month, primarily a result of depreciation on additional manufacturing equipment purchased by Golden Music. However, Golden Music estimates that it would realize savings of $2 per compact disc in variable costs as a result of reduced direct and indirect labor costs. Therefore, the new cost structure for Golden Music in the automated manufacturing process is as follows:

Variable Cost (per Compact Disc) ($6 – $2)..	$4
Fixed Costs (per month) ($500,000 + $400,000)	$900,000

Assuming sales were 200,000 compact discs per month, the estimated net income under the existing and automated manufacturing environments is summarized in Illustration 4.

Illustration 4
Golden Music Producers
Analysis of Alternative Manufacturing Processes: Estimated Net Income

	Existing	Automated
Sales (200,000 discs x $10)	$2,000,000	$2,000,000
Variable Costs:		
(200,000 discs x $6)	(1,200,000)	
(200,000 discs x $4)		(800,000)
Contribution Margin.............................	$ 800,000	$1,200,000
Fixed Costs	(500,000)	(900,000)
Net Income	$ 300,000	$ 300,000

Notice from the data in Illustration 4 that net income under these two approaches is identical. However, the cost structure of the two manufacturing systems differs. Specifically, the existing cost structure has a relatively greater proportion of variable costs than fixed costs; conversely, the cost structure under the automated system "shifts" $400,000 of variable costs ($1,200,000 − $800,000 = $400,000) to fixed costs ($500,000 + $400,000 = $900,000). This illustrates the concept of operating leverage. The degree of operating leverage is determined by

---

[5] Peter Coy, "The Power of Smart Pricing," *Business Week* (April 10, 2000), 162.

dividing the contribution margin by the net income at a given sales volume. The degree of *operating leverage* in each of the above manufacturing environments is calculated as follows:

Existing	Automated
Contribution Margin / Net Income	Contribution Margin / Net Income
$800,000 / $300,000	$1,200,000 / $300,000
= 2.67 (rounded)	= 4.00

The degree of operating leverage measures the percentage effect of a change in sales revenue on net income. That is, if sales revenues change by x percent, by what percentage will net income change? To determine how a percentage change in sales revenue affects net income, the organization multiplies the percentage change in sales revenue by the degree of operating leverage.

If Golden Music had the capacity to manufacture and sell an additional 20,000 compact discs, how would its net income be affected in each of the above environments? Assuming that selling prices remain constant at $10 per disc, the additional capacity of 20,000 compact discs represents an increase in sales revenue of 10 percent (20,000 discs ÷ 200,000 discs = 0.10, or 10 percent). The percentage change in net income under each of these two manufacturing processes is shown below:

	Degree of Operating Leverage	x	Change in Sales Revenue	=	Change in Net Income
Existing	2.67	x	10%	=	26.7%
Automated	4.00	x	10%	=	40.0%

Therefore, if sales levels were to increase to 220,000 compact discs, net income would increase to $380,000 in the existing manufacturing process (1.267 x $300,000 = $380,000, after rounding) and $420,000 in the automated manufacturing process (1.40 x $300,000 = $420,000). The following income statements verify these calculations.

	Existing	Automated
Sales (220,000 discs x $10)	$2,200,000	$2,200,000
Variable Costs:		
(220,000 discs x $6)	(1,320,000)	
(220,000 discs x $4)		(880,000)
Contribution Margin	$ 880,000	$1,320,000
Fixed Costs	(500,000)	(900,000)
Net Income	$ 380,000	$ 420,000

Why would net income be higher in the automated manufacturing process? First, it is important to note that Golden Music is operating well above its breakeven point (125,000 compact discs). Since the automated manufacturing process has lower variable costs, it yields a higher contribution margin. Once the fixed costs have been recovered, the manufacturing process with a greater contribution margin will provide higher net income, since the entire amount of contribution margin is profit. As a result, the fact that the automated manufacturing process yields $6 per unit in contribution margin ($10 – $4 = $6) compared to the $4 contribution margin for the existing manufacturing process indicates that this former process results in higher net income.

The relatively high fixed costs associated with capital-intensive (automated) manufacturing processes have the following effect in CVP analysis:

1. Because of the relatively high fixed costs, the breakeven point is ordinarily greater in automated manufacturing processes than in manual manufacturing processes. While not calculated in this subsection, the breakeven point for the automated manufacturing process is 150,000 compact discs ($900,000 ÷ $6.00 per unit = 150,000 compact discs). Recall that the breakeven point in the existing manufacturing process is 125,000 compact discs.

2. Sales beyond the breakeven point result in greater increases in net income for companies with automated manufacturing processes, since each dollar of sales provides a greater overall contribution to profits (because of the lower variable costs and higher contribution margin per unit).

The power of operating leverage is illustrated in the following excerpt from practice.

> **Companies experiencing a financial turnaround can benefit significantly from operating leverage because, once the breakeven point has been reached, small increases in revenue will result in large increases in net income. The Rite Aid drugstore chain is a case in point. After years of being plagued by problems resulting from poor strategic decisions, accounting irregularities and a high debt burden, Rite Aid's margin on sales changed from negative to positive under new management. With sales dollars per share equal to seven times the stock price, owners of Rite Aid shares were able to earn 32 cents in profit with every percentage point increase in net margin.[6]**

ASSUMPTIONS OF CVP ANALYSIS

CVP analysis relies on the following important assumptions:

1. Sales price and variable cost relationships are constant per unit and linear within the relevant range. This assumption also implies that the contribution margin per unit is constant within the relevant range.

2. Fixed costs do not vary with changes in the level of activity within the relevant range.

3. Inventory levels remain relatively constant throughout the period. If inventory levels are relatively constant, the number of units manufactured is approximately equal to the number of units sold. This assumption is necessary to ensure that costs accumulated with inventory during the period are ultimately expensed (through cost of goods sold) during that same period.

4. If CVP is conducted in a multiproduct setting, the sales mix of the products remains constant.

5. The activity used to classify costs as fixed or variable is sales volume. However, it is important to note that certain costs may be fixed with respect to sales volume but variable with respect to other activities. For example, setup labor and inspection costs would ordinarily not be affected by sales volumes, but would vary because of the number of setups and inspections, respectively. As noted in a previous chapter, activity-based-costing systems are characterized by the use of a number of cost drivers. However, CVP analysis focuses on sales volumes as the only cost driver.

PRACTICAL APPLICATION OF CVP ANALYSIS

The following examples illustrate practical applications of CVP analysis:

> **Tri-Star Motion Pictures' film *Hook* (released in 1991) had fixed production costs of $125,000,000 and, based on percentage guarantees to the director (Steven Spielberg) and actors and actresses (Dustin Hoffman, Robin Williams, and Julia Roberts), earned a contribution margin percentage of 62.5 percent. Based on these amounts, a total of 40,000,000 moviegoers would need to attend *Hook* (at an average cost of $5 per ticket) for the film to reach the breakeven point.[7]**

---

[6] Marc Robins, "The Virtue of Leverage," *Forbes* (August 11, 2003), 110.

[7] "Holiday Hits Won't Guarantee Success," *The Wall Street Journal* (November 15, 1991), B1.

> The New York Yankees baseball team signed Japanese pitcher Hideki Irabu to a contract that paid him $3 million for 1997. In his first appearance, the attendance was over 51,000 (greater by 30,000 than the previous average). The increased attendance resulted in additional revenues of $830,000 for tickets, food, and souvenirs. At this pace, the Yankees will break even after Irabu pitches his fourth game.[8]
>
> Eye clinics charge $1,500 to $2,200 per eye for photorefractive keratectomy, a form of laser surgery used to correct myopia. Despite these high charges, the new laser procedure needs to be heavily marketed, because laser machines cost $500,000 plus up to $50,000 a year for maintenance. Using these estimates, a typical machine must treat roughly 700 eyes a year to break even.[9]

INCOME DETERMINATION: ABSORPTION AND VARIABLE COSTING

A basic assumption underlying CVP analysis is that the organization maintains constant levels of inventory; thus, during the current period, the level of its production approximates the level of sales. To illustrate why this assumption is necessary, assume that Golden Music manufactured 200,000 compact discs during the month of March 20x1; however, because of unanticipated lack of demand from customers, the company sold only 100,000 discs during that month. Relevant cost data introduced in Illustration 1 is summarized below:

Direct Materials (Blank Compact Disc)	$1.50
Direct Labor (including employee benefits)	0.50
Manufacturing Overhead	3.00
Artist Royalties	0.75
Sales Commissions	0.25
Total Variable Cost (per Compact Disc)	$6.00
Depreciation on Plant and Equipment	$250,000
Supervision and Indirect Labor	50,000
General and Administrative	200,000
Total Fixed Costs (per Month)	$500,000

Absorption (Full) Costing

Under generally accepted accounting principles (GAAP), companies classify the above costs as either product costs or period costs. Recall that product costs are those costs directly related to manufacturing the organization's inventory or providing the organization's services. Product costs are initially accumulated with the organization's inventory until the items are sold to customers, when they are recognized as an expense (through cost of goods sold). Three variable costs incurred by Golden Music are classified as product costs: direct materials, direct labor, and manufacturing overhead. For Golden Music, the depreciation on plant and equipment and supervision and indirect labor are examples of fixed costs that would be classified as product costs (both costs are considered manufacturing overhead costs).

In contrast, period costs are those costs that are not directly associated with manufacturing the organization's inventory or providing the organization's services. Under GAAP, period costs are expensed when incurred. In the Golden Music example, the royalties paid to artists, sales commissions, and general and administrative costs of $200,000 are classified as period costs.

The method of income determination required under GAAP (and discussed above) is referred to as *absorption* (or *full*) *costing*. This title reflects the fact that the inventory includes the "full" cost (both variable product costs and fixed product costs) of manufacturing the items. The term absorption costing reflects the fact

---

[8] "Great Pitcher? Maybe. Great Marketing? For Sure," *Business Week* (July 28, 1997), 38.

[9] "Seeing-eye Ads," *Forbes* (June 17, 1996), 96.

that the inventory items "absorb" the fixed overhead costs associated with their production. Under GAAP, Golden Music would determine the following cost per unit for financial reporting purposes:

Direct Materials (200,000 discs x $1.50)	$ 300,000
Direct Labor (200,000 discs x $0.50)	100,000
Variable Manufacturing Overhead (200,000 discs x $3)	600,000
Fixed Manufacturing Overhead ($250,000 + $50,000)	300,000
Total Manufacturing Costs	1,300,000
Compact Discs Manufactured	÷ 200,000
Cost per Compact Disc	$ 6.50

Recall that Golden Music sold compact discs for $10 per disc. Assume that it had no beginning inventory of compact discs on March 1, 20x1. If Golden Music manufactured 200,000 compact discs during March 20x1 and sold 100,000 of these discs, the income statement and partial balance sheet prepared by Golden Music for March 20x1 are shown in Illustration 5.

Illustration 5
Golden Music Producers
Income Statement for the month ended March 31, 20x1
Full (Absorption) Costing

Sales Revenue (100,000 discs x $10)	$1,000,000
Cost of Goods Sold:	
Direct Materials (100,000 discs x $1.50)	(150,000)
Direct Labor (100,000 discs x $0.50)	(50,000)
Variable Overhead (100,000 discs x $3)	(300,000)
Fixed Overhead (100,000 discs x $1.50[a])	(150,000)
Gross Margin	$ 350,000
Artist Royalties (100,000 discs x $0.75)	(75,000)
Sales Commissions (100,000 discs x $0.25)	(25,000)
General and Administrative	(200,000)
Net Income	$ 50,000

Golden Music Producers
Balance Sheet (Partial) at March 31, 20x1
Full (Absorption) Costing

Current Assets:

Inventory (100,000 discs x $6.50)	$ 650,000

[a] $300,000 ÷ 200,000 disks = $1.50 per disc

Notice that the income statement in Illustration 5 reports net income of $50,000. However, from our previous analysis, we know that Golden Music determined its breakeven point to be 125,000 compact discs. Since the current sales volume (100,000 compact discs) is less than the breakeven level (125,000 compact discs), we would expect Golden Music to suffer a net loss at sales volumes of 100,000. Why didn't this happen?

The answer to this question lies in the treatment of fixed overhead costs. Recall that CVP analysis treats all fixed overhead costs as an "expense" in the period incurred. That is, in order to break even, the organization must earn a sufficient contribution margin to offset its entire fixed costs. However, under GAAP, the fixed overhead costs of $300,000 are not all expensed during the current period. As shown in Golden Music's Income Statement in Illustration 5, a total of $150,000 of the fixed overhead costs are expensed during March 20x1, since these costs relate to the 100,000 compact discs sold to customers (100,000 discs x $1.50 = $150,000).

This raises a question as to the disposition of the remaining $150,000 of fixed overhead costs ($300,000 − $150,000 = $150,000). Under GAAP requirements, the fixed overhead costs related to the unsold units are included in inventory (100,000 discs x $1.50 = $150,000). Note that, if all of the fixed overhead costs were expensed (as suggested in the CVP analysis), Golden Music would report a net loss of $100,000 during March 20x1 consistent with the breakeven analysis presented earlier in this chapter.

Net Income (Absorption Costing)	$ 50,000
Additional Fixed Overhead Costs	(150,000)
Net Income	($100,000)

Variable (Direct) Costing

As discussed in the preceding section, absorption costing is required for external financial reporting purposes; however, its use for internal decision-making purposes may not always result in optimal decisions. For example, if Golden Music were using CVP analysis to establish its selling prices, the use of absorption costing may understate the selling price needed to recover the organization's fixed costs (including fixed overhead costs). The selling price yielded by CVP would only allow Golden Music to recover the fixed costs associated with the items sold to customers (and not the total fixed costs incurred during March).

Additionally, the nature of absorption costing results in net income being influenced by levels of production. To illustrate, assume that Golden Music could increase its production levels to 300,000 compact discs without incurring any additional fixed overhead costs. Continuing with the scenario shown in Illustration 5, if 100,000 compact discs were sold to customers and no other changes in costs occurred, the net income recognized under absorption costing would increase by $50,000 to $100,000, as shown below:

Original Net Income (see Illustration 5)	$ 50,000
Original Fixed Overhead Costs Expensed	150,000
Revised Fixed Overhead Expensed [($300,000 ÷ 300,000 discs) x 100,000 discs]	(100,000)
Revised Net Income	$100,000

Why did net income increase without the sale of any additional compact discs or changes in costs or selling prices? The $300,000 of fixed overhead costs is simply allocated over a greater number of compact discs, resulting in lower expenses being recognized on the 100,000 compact discs sold to customers. If evaluated strictly based on absorption costing net income, managers apparently have incentives to increase production in order to increase net income. Of course, increased production may not always be desirable because of the high costs of carrying inventories. In this example, the increase in net income resulting from increased levels of production is referred to as *phantom profits*. Golden Music has not performed more effectively during March 20x1; the increased profits are strictly a result of how income is recognized under absorption costing.

Under *variable* (or *direct*) *costing*, only the variable manufacturing costs are accumulated with inventory. As under absorption costing, all period costs (both fixed and variable) are expensed as incurred. The primary difference relates to the treatment of fixed overhead costs: under variable costing, fixed overhead costs are treated in a manner similar to period costs and are expensed as they are incurred. Variable costing draws its title from the fact that only the *variable* manufacturing costs (that is, the costs that are most *directly* related to manufacturing inventory) are accumulated with inventory. Variable costing proponents argue that fixed overhead costs will be incurred regardless of whether inventory is produced; accordingly, these costs should be expensed as incurred.

Illustration 6 presents the Income Statement and partial Balance Sheet for Golden Music for March 20x1. Note that the format of the Income Statement differs from that prepared under absorption costing. In variable costing, variable costs (both product and period costs) are deducted from sales revenue to determine the contribution margin. Fixed costs are then deducted from the contribution margin to determine net income. Of particular importance is the fact that all fixed overhead costs incurred (not just the fixed overhead costs related to the units sold during the period) are expensed in determining net income under variable costing.

As shown in Illustration 6, under variable costing, all of the $300,000 in fixed overhead costs incurred during March 20x1 are expensed in that month. In addition, the partial balance sheet shown in Illustration 6 reveals that only variable product costs are accumulated with the inventory manufactured. Notice that, consistent with the earlier CVP analysis conducted for Golden Music, a net loss is anticipated at a sales volume of 100,000 compact discs. This loss is anticipated, since Golden Music determined that it needed to sell 125,000 compact discs in order to break even.

Comparing Absorption and Variable Costing

Comparing the net income recognized under absorption and variable costing reveals a difference of $150,000. As shown in Illustration 5, the net income under absorption costing is $50,000; however, Illustration 6 reveals a net loss under variable costing of $100,000. What causes this $150,000 difference? Examining the partial balance sheets in Illustrations 5 and 6 reveals an offsetting difference of $150,000. The inventories reported under absorption costing are $150,000 higher than those reported under variable costing ($650,000 − $500,000 = $150,000). These differences are summarized below:

	Inventory	Net Income
Absorption Costing	$650,000	$ 50,000
Variable Costing	500,000	(100,000)
Difference	$150,000	($150,000)

$150,000 of Fixed Overhead Included in Inventory ↑ $150,000 of Fixed Overhead Included as Expense ↑

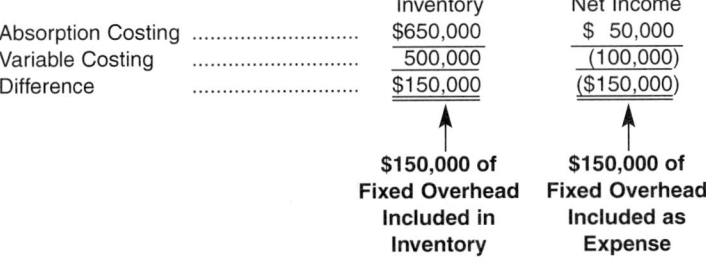

Illustration 6
Golden Music Producers
Income Statement for the month ended March 31, 20x1
Variable (Direct) Costing

Sales Revenue (100,000 discs × $10)	$1,000,000
Variable Costs:	
Direct Materials (100,000 discs × $1.50)	(150,000)
Direct Labor (100,000 discs × $0.50)	(50,000)
Variable Overhead (100,000 discs × $3)	(300,000)
Artist Royalties (100,000 discs × $0.75)	(75,000)
Sales Commissions (100,000 discs × $0.25)	(25,000)
Contribution Margin	$ 400,000
Fixed Costs:	
Fixed Overhead ($250,000 + $50,000)	(300,000)
General and Administrative	(200,000)
Net Income	$ (100,000)

Golden Music Producers
Balance Sheet (Partial) at March 31, 20x1
Variable (Direct) Costing

Current Assets:

Inventory (100,000 discs × $5ª) .... $ 500,000

ª $1.50 + $0.50 + $3.00 = $5.00

Notice that the differences in the net income and inventory under the two methods relate solely to the treatment of fixed overhead costs. Under absorption costing, these costs are included in inventory until the items are sold to customers, when they are expensed through cost of goods sold. In contrast, variable costing expenses fixed overhead costs as they are incurred and, as such, treats them as period costs.

In this example, why was net income greater under absorption costing than under variable costing? Recall that 200,000 compact discs were manufactured during March 20x1 and 100,000 compact discs were sold. Under absorption costing, only the fixed overhead costs relating to the 100,000 compact discs that were sold were expensed; however, the entire $300,000 of fixed overhead costs were expensed under variable costing. Therefore, assuming that costs remain constant from period to period, net income under absorption costing will exceed net income under variable costing if production exceeds sales. The effect of changing inventory costs on this relationship is beyond the scope of this text.

What would happen if the level of sales exceeded production? Assume in April that an additional 200,000 compact discs were manufactured and that total sales were 250,000 compact discs (recall that 100,000 compact discs were in inventory at March 31, 20x1). If the revenue and cost structure for Golden Music in April was identical to that in March, the fixed overhead costs expensed during April under absorption and variable costing would be as follows:

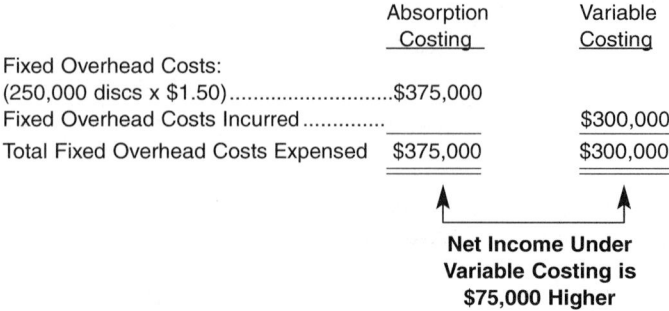

	Absorption Costing	Variable Costing
Fixed Overhead Costs:		
(250,000 discs x $1.50)............................$375,000		
Fixed Overhead Costs Incurred..............		$300,000
Total Fixed Overhead Costs Expensed	$375,000	$300,000

Net Income Under Variable Costing is $75,000 Higher

In this instance, net income under variable costing would be $75,000 higher than the income under absorption costing ($375,000 − $300,000 = $75,000). Again, the difference is strictly related to the treatment of fixed overhead costs. While not illustrated, it should be evident at this point that as long as sales equal production, either approach would yield the same net income (assuming no change in the cost structure from month to month).

The difference in income recognized under absorption and variable costing can be determined by multiplying the net change in inventory by the fixed overhead rate per unit. Recalling that Golden Music did not have any inventory of compact discs on March 1, 20x1, the differences in absorption and variable costing income illustrated under the two scenarios discussed above are as follows:

	Increase (Decrease) in Inventory (Units)	x	Fixed Overhead Rate per Unit	=	Absorption Income − Variable Income
Sales = 100,000 Production = 200,000	100,000	x	$1.50	=	$150,000
Sales = 250,000 Production = 200,000	(50,000)	x	$1.50	=	($75,000)

The relationship between production and sales levels and the effect of this relationship on the net income recognized under absorption and variable costing is summarized as follows:

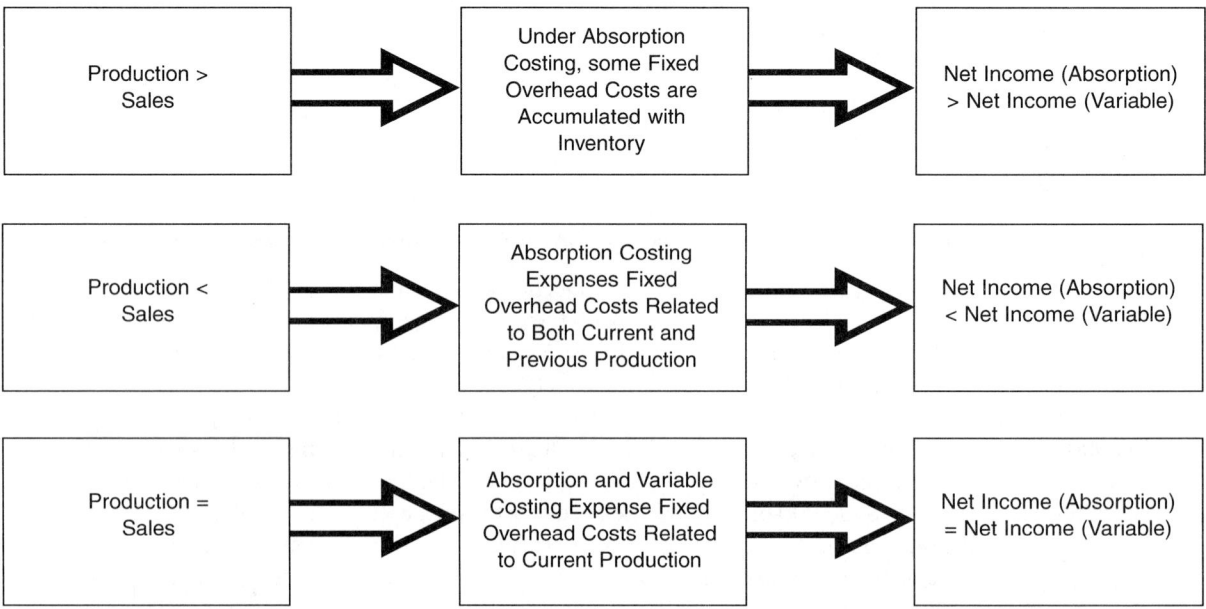

As shown above, absorption and variable costing yield the same results when the level of production equals the level of sales. As more organizations utilize just-in-time (JIT) manufacturing processes that manufacture inventory based on customer demand, differences between production and sales are minimized. As a result, for companies utilitizing JIT manufacturing, the use of absorption and variable costing do not result in markedly different levels of net income.

In addition to differences in the amount of net income recognized under the two costing methods, some differences in the format of the income statements are apparent from a review of Illustrations 5 and 6. These differences are:

- Absorption costing classifies costs by functional area (production versus non-production). In contrast, variable costing classifies costs by their behavior in response to changes in activity (variable versus fixed).

- An important subtotal in the absorption costing income statement is the gross margin, which is the difference between sales revenue and the product costs associated with the items sold (cost of goods sold). The variable costing income statement highlights the contribution margin, which represents the difference between sales revenue and variable costs (both product and period costs).

USING MANAGERIAL ACCOUNTING INFORMATION: GOLDEN MUSIC PRODUCERS

Throughout this chapter, we have illustrated how Golden Music uses CVP analysis to determine the level of sales necessary to break even or earn a desired level of profit. However, understanding the basic relationships between costs, volumes, and profits can also assist management in determining how various courses of action will affect the organization's overall profitability. For example, assume that Golden Music is attempting to decide whether it should purchase additional equipment to further automate its manufacturing process. The purchase of this equipment would result in an increase in depreciation expense of $20,000 per month; thus, if acquired, fixed costs would total $520,000 ($500,000 + $20,000 = $520,000). However, the use of this new equipment in the manufacturing process would increase Golden Music's production capacity by 10,000 compact discs as well as reduce its variable costs by $0.30 per disc; therefore, the variable cost per compact disc would be reduced to $5.70 ($6.00 − $0.30 = $5.70). Golden Music is attempting to decide whether this purchase is feasible (from a profitability standpoint), assuming it can sell the additional 10,000 compact discs. Summarized below are relevant cost data based on two alternatives: existing equipment (and manufacturing capacity of 200,000 compact discs) and the acquisition of the additional equipment.

	Existing Equipment	Additional Equipment
Capacity (compact discs)	200,000	210,000
Fixed Costs	$500,000	$520,000
Variable Cost per Compact Disk	$6.00	$5.70

Two different approaches can be used to evaluate the above decision. First, income statements can be prepared using these alternative assumptions to determine whether the proposed equipment acquisition would result in increased profitability. Recalling that Golden Music sells its compact discs for $10 each, the net income under each alternative is shown below:

	Existing Equipment	Additional Equipment
Sales:		
200,000 discs x $10	$2,000,000	
210,000 discs x $10		$2,100,000
Variable Costs:		
200,000 discs x $6	(1,200,000)	
210,000 discs x $5.70		(1,197,000)
Contribution Margin	$ 800,000	$ 903,000
Fixed Costs	(500,000)	(520,000)
Net Income	$ 300,000	$ 383,000

Alternatively, Golden Music can use an incremental approach and consider only those factors that differ between the two alternatives. This incremental approach is shown below:

Incremental Revenues (10,000 discs x $10)	$100,000
Variable Costs of Additional Production	
(10,000 discs x $5.70)	(57,000)
Savings in Variable Costs on Current Production	
(200,000 discs x $0.30)	60,000
Incremental Fixed Costs	(20,000)
Incremental Net Income	$ 83,000

Notice that the incremental income is the difference between the net income calculated based on the purchase of the additional manufacturing equipment ($383,000) and current manufacturing capacity ($300,000) ($383,000 − $300,000 = $83,000). One advantage associated with the incremental approach is that only factors that differ between the two alternatives are considered. Thus, management can focus on characteristics that would be affected by the decision to purchase additional manufacturing equipment. The incremental approach only considers the following factors:

- The revenue and variable costs associated with the additional capacity (and sale) of 10,000 compact discs.
- The increased fixed costs of $20,000 per month.
- The decreased variable costs of $0.30 per compact disc.

Note that the incremental approach did not consider (1) the $500,000 of fixed costs relating to existing manufacturing capacity, (2) the sale of 200,000 compact discs at $10 per disc, or (3) the $5.70 variable cost per compact disc. These factors are not affected by the decision to purchase the additional manufacturing equipment.

In either case, the use of CVP analysis would indicate that Golden Music should purchase the additional manufacturing equipment. Doing so will increase its profits by $83,000 (before taxes).

SUMMARY

This chapter introduces cost-volume-profit analysis (CVP) and illustrates how information on costs, sales volumes, and profits can be used in the managerial decision-making process. Some of the more important concepts discussed in this chapter are:

1. *Cost-volume-profit analysis* (CVP) is a planning tool that considers the inherent relationships among selling prices, costs, sales volumes, and profits. CVP analysis can be used to identify the level of sales necessary to earn a desired level of profit, how changes in the organization's cost structure influence its overall profitability, and the sales price that should be charged by the organization for its products or services to earn a desired profit.

2. An important element of CVP analysis is the *contribution margin*. The contribution margin is defined as the difference between revenue and variable costs. This is an important subtotal to management, since the sales of a company's products or services should at least cover the variable costs associated with that product or service.

3. The *breakeven point* is the level of sales volume (or sales dollars) needed to recover the organization's fixed costs. At the breakeven point, net income is equal to $0. Using CVP analysis, the breakeven point can be determined through both graphical and equation approaches. These approaches modify the following general equation for expressing the relationship between revenues, costs, and profits, where x equals the sales volume:

$$\text{Sales Price Per Unit} \,(x) - \text{Variable Cost Per Unit} \,(x) - \text{Fixed Costs} = \text{Desired Net Profit Before Taxes}$$

4. If CVP analysis is undertaken on an organization-wide basis and the organization sells multiple products with different levels of contribution margin, the relative sales "mix" (i.e., volume of sales of each product) needs to be estimated. Once estimated, the CVP analysis proceeds in a similar fashion to that conducted in a single-product setting.

5. Two approaches to income determination are *absorption* (or *full*) *costing* and *variable* (or *direct*) *costing*. The primary difference in these two methods is their treatment of fixed overhead costs. Absorption costing accumulates fixed overhead costs with inventory and expenses these costs as the items are sold to customers. In contrast, variable costing treats fixed overhead costs in a manner similar to period costs and expenses these costs as they are incurred. As a result of this difference, net income will differ under these two approaches when the level of sales differs from the level of production.

KEY DEFINITIONS

Absorption costing—also referred to as full costing. This method of income determination accumulates fixed manufacturing overhead costs with inventory and only expenses these costs as the items are sold to customers. Under absorption costing, both variable and fixed product costs are accumulated with inventory and expensed when inventory is sold to the organization's customers.

Breakeven point—the level of volume (or dollars) of sales where total costs equal total revenues.

Contribution margin—the difference between revenues and variable costs.

Contribution margin approach—an approach used in CVP analysis which expresses the level of sales needed to earn a stated profit (or to break even) in units. Under the contribution margin approach, total fixed costs plus desired profits are divided by the contribution margin per unit.

Contribution margin ratio—the contribution margin divided by sales.

Contribution margin ratio approach—a method of CVP analysis which expresses the level of sales needed to earn a stated profit (or to break even) in sales dollars. Under the contribution margin ratio approach, total fixed costs plus desired profits are divided by the contribution margin ratio.

Cost-volume-profit analysis (CVP)—a tool which allows the organization to determine how potential changes in sales volume, selling prices, fixed costs, and/or variable costs affect overall organization profitability.

Operating leverage—determined by dividing the contribution margin by the net income at a given level of sales. The degree of operating leverage measures the percentage effect of a change in sales revenue on the organization's net income.

Safety margin—the excess of budgeted or expected sales over breakeven sales.

Variable costing—also referred to as direct costing. This method of income determination treats fixed overhead costs in a manner similar to period costs and expenses these costs as they are incurred. Under variable costing, only the variable product costs are accumulated with inventory.

QUESTIONS

1. What types of information can be provided to the organization by cost-volume-profit analysis?

2. Define contribution margin. Why is the contribution margin an important amount for the organization?

3. What is the breakeven point? Why is this point of interest to an organization's management?

4. What information is presented in a CVP graph? How is the breakeven point determined in a CVP graph?

5. What is the safety margin? Why is this an important concept for the organization?

6. Holding other factors constant, how would each of the following factors influence the organization's breakeven point? (increase, decrease, or no effect)

    a. An increase in the organization's selling prices.
    b. A decrease in the variable cost per unit.
    c. An increase in fixed costs.
    d. An increase in the organization's production capacity.

7. How does CVP analysis differ if, instead of merely breaking even, the organization wishes to earn a desired level of profit?

8. How is CVP analysis conducted in a multiple-product setting when different products have different contribution margins?

9. What are the basic assumptions underlying CVP analysis?

10. What is the degree of operating leverage? How does the degree of operating leverage influence the organization's breakeven point? How does the degree of operating leverage influence the effect of sales beyond the breakeven point on net income?

11. How do cost accumulation and income determination differ under absorption costing and variable costing?

12. Contrast the format of an absorption costing income statement with the format of a variable costing income statement.

13. A cost-volume-profit chart, as illustrated below, is a useful technique for showing relationships between costs, volume, and profits.

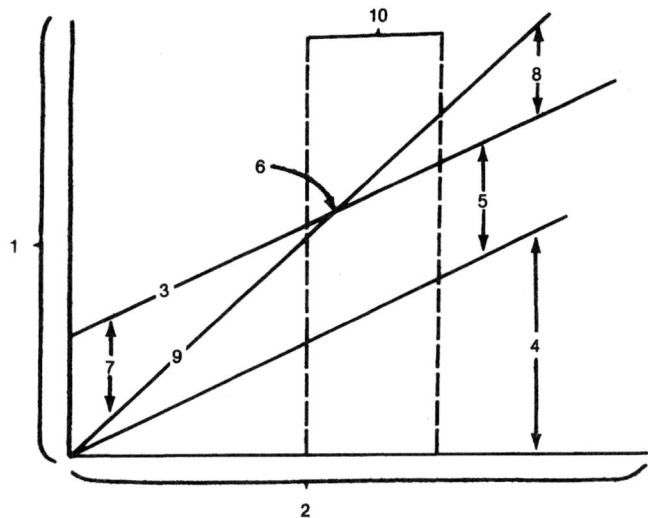

a. Identify the numbered components of the breakeven chart.
b. Discuss the significance of the concept of the "relevant range" to breakeven analyses.

(AICPA adapted)

EXERCISES AND PROBLEMS

14. *Graphical CVP Analysis.* Shown below are examples of cost-volume-profit graphs for three separate companies. Analyze each graph and answer the following questions about them. All measurements are in hundreds of thousands.

Required:

a. Are the fixed costs for Company X greater than for Company Y? Explain.
b. Does Company Y or Company Z have a higher breakeven point?
c. If volume is 400,000, will Company X have higher net income than Company Z? Explain.

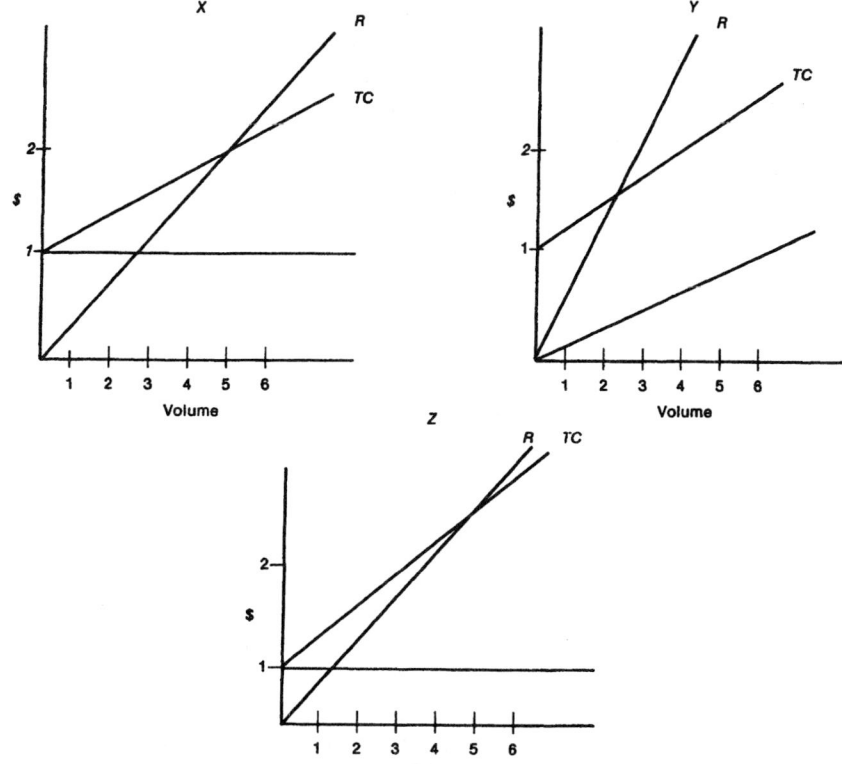

15. *Graphical CVP Analysis.* The illustration shows the cost-volume-profit graph of a company contemplating two separate pricing policies. Analyze the graph and answer the following questions.

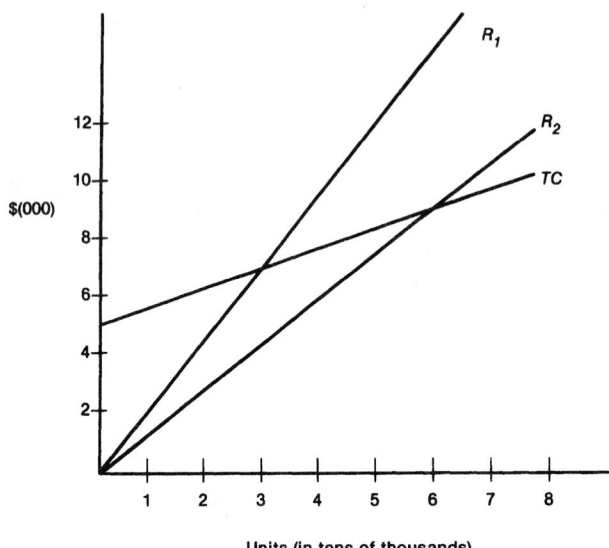

Required:

a. Which pricing policy, R_1 or R_2, represents the lower price? Which will have the lower breakeven point?
b. Which pricing policy, R_1 or R_2, will produce the most profit at 50,000 units of production? Why?
c. What considerations other than breakeven must be considered in selecting a unit price? If breakeven were the only consideration, what price would produce the smaller (lower) point?

16. *Graphical CVP Analysis.* The following graph represents one company that has two different total cost lines (TC_1 and TC_2).

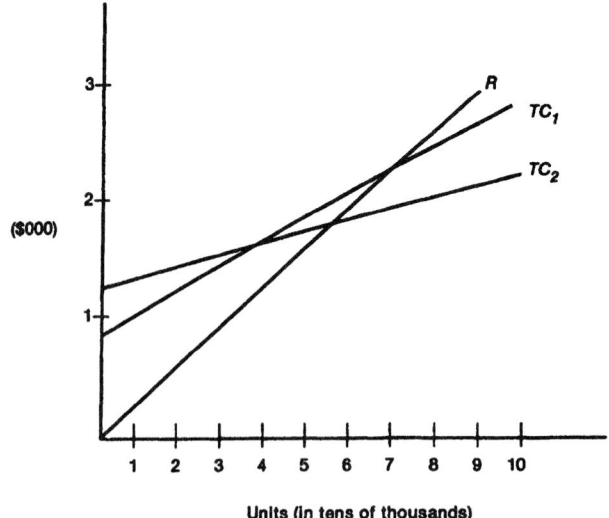

Analyze the graph and answer the following questions.

a. Which of the two cost lines has the higher fixed cost? Which has the greater variable cost per unit?
b. At the production level of 20,000, which cost profile will result in greater losses? Why?
c. What is the breakeven point advantage (approximately) to total cost TC_1 over total cost TC_2?
d. Would businesses operating near the breakeven point prefer TC_1 or TC_2? Explain. Would businesses operating well above the breakeven point prefer TC_1 or TC_2? Which total cost line would be preferred by businesses operating below the breakeven point?

17. *Graphical CVP Analysis.* The graph below represents one company that has two different total cost lines.

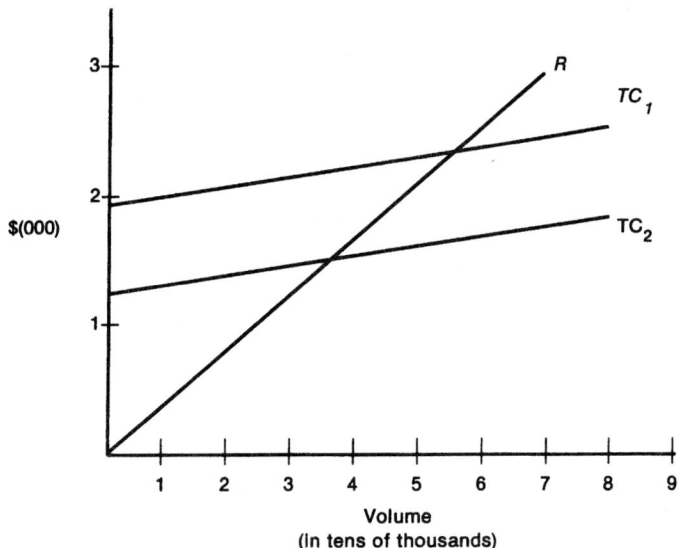

Analyze the graph and answer the following questions.
a. What is the approximate breakeven point in units for total cost TC_1 and total cost TC_2?
b. Which of the two cost profiles has the greater variable costs per unit?
c. Which of the two cost profiles has the greater fixed costs?
d. At the 500,000-unit volume level, which cost profile will produce the greater profit? At the 900,000-unit volume level?

18. *Graphical CVP Analysis.* The Peters Company converts steel from ingots to sheets. Most of its expenses are fixed and only a fraction are variable. Those costs that do fit the mixed category have been broken into their fixed and variable segments. The estimates for next year include sales of $2,000,000, fixed costs of $800,000, and variable costs of 40 percent of every sales dollar. The tax bracket for the Peters Company is 50 percent.

Required:

a. Graph the breakeven point before taxes from the information given.
b. Add the tax computation to the breakeven chart.
c. What does the area between the costs after tax and the sales line represent?
d. Can cost-volume-profit analysis be calculated for firms selling more than one product? If so, what type of measuring unit is shown on the volume (horizontal axis) scale?
e. Since costs and revenues do not behave strictly in a linear fashion, do techniques exist that make it possible to calculate a breakeven point for situations in which the mathematical description of cost and revenue functions is known? In such situations, will it be possible to calculate the volume at which profits will be maximized?

19. *Basic CVP Analysis.* Bilo Co. has a budget that reports the following:

Revenue	$2,000,000
Variable Costs	(1,500,000)
Fixed Costs	(300,000)
Expected Profit	$ 200,000

At what volume of revenue does Bilo just break even? How much revenue must Bilo generate to earn profits of $400,000?

20. *Basic CVP Analysis.* Shown below are two independent sets of facts:

   a. Dice Co. has drawn a budget that calls for the following: expected profits, $250,000; fixed cost, $300,000; and a contribution margin ratio of 20 percent (i.e., variable costs are 80% of revenue). How much revenue must Dice generate to reach its goal?
   b. The Emac Co. sells a single product for $300 per unit. The company's cost structure is composed of $540,000 fixed costs and variable costs equal to 90 percent of revenue. How many units must Emac sell to earn a profit of $10,000?

21. *Basic CVP Analysis.* Shown below are two independent sets of facts:

   a. The Filup Co. sells a single product for $90 per unit. Fixed costs are $160,000, variable costs equal 80 percent of revenue. If fixed costs increase by $80,000, Filup will have to increase sales by how many dollars just to earn profits equal to those it earned before the cost increase?
   b. Gala Co. has drawn a budget that calls for the following: expected profits, $150,000; fixed cost, $200,000; and a contribution margin ratio of 40 percent (i.e., variable costs are 60% of revenue). How much revenue must Gala generate to reach its goal?

22. *Basic CVP Analysis.* The president of the Midway Company has estimated that he will need profits of $50,000 this year to satisfy the stockholders and asks you for a volume that will attain his goal. He intends to use this information to motivate and direct the sales manager. He gives you the following information:

Unit Selling Price	$50
Variable Cost per Unit	$35
Fixed Costs per Unit (based on 9,000 Units)	$ 1
Plant Capacity	12,000 units

   a. Compute the volume needed to achieve the $50,000 profit goal.
   b. Graph the cost-volume-profit relationship.
   c. Which cost seems higher than normal? Would a sales or a manufacturing company be more likely to have this type of cost structure?
   d. If the 9,000-unit production last year was the highest that sales had ever been, is it likely that the stockholders will be satisfied?
   e. Do variable costs always vary directly with volume? Give an example of a variable cost that may increase at an increasing rate as volume increases. Give an example of a variable cost that may increase at a decreasing rate as volume increases.

23. *Basic CVP Analysis.* In a recent period Zero Company had the following experience:

	Fixed	Variable	
Sales (10,000 units @ $200)			$2,000,000
Costs:			
Labor	$ 0	$ 200,000	
Materials	0	400,000	
Factory Overhead	160,000	600,000	
Administrative Expenses	180,000	80,000	
Other Expenses	200,000	120,000	
Total Costs	$ 540,000	$1,400,000	1,940,000
Net Income			$ 60,000

Required:

Each item below is independent.

   a. Calculate the breakeven point for Zero in terms of units and sales dollars. Show your calculations.
   b. What sales volume would be required to generate a net income of $96,000? Show your calculations.
   c. What is the breakeven point if management makes a decision that increases fixed costs by $18,000? Show your calculations.

(AICPA adapted)

24. *Basic CVP Analysis.* Your employer leased manufacturing facilities for production of a new product. Estimated annual sales are 24,000 units. The following cost data have been made available to you:

	Amount	Per Unit
Estimated Costs:		
Material	$96,000	$4.00
Labor	14,400	0.60
Overhead	24,000	1.00
Administrative Expense	28,800	1.20
Total	$163,200	$6.80

Selling expenses are expected to be 15 percent of sales, and desired profit is $1.02 per unit.

Required:

a. Compute the selling price per unit.
b. Given the selling price calculated in part (a), prepare an income statement for the year.
c. Compute a breakeven point expressed in dollars and in units assuming that overhead and administrative expenses are fixed but that other costs are fully variable.

25. *Basic CVP Analysis.* Mr. Calderone started a pizza restaurant in 20x0. For this purpose, he rented a building for $400 per month. Two employees were hired to work full time at the restaurant, and six college students were hired to work thirty hours per week delivering pizza. An outside accountant was hired for tax and bookkeeping purposes. For this service, Mr. Calderone pays $300 per month. The necessary restaurant equipment and delivery cars were purchased with cash. Mr. Calderone has noticed that expenses for utilities and supplies have been fairly constant.

Mr. Calderone increased his level of sales between 20x0 and 20x3. Profits have more than doubled since 20x0. Mr. Calderone does not understand why his profits have increased faster than his volume.

A projected income statement for 20x4 prepared by the accountant is shown below:

Calderone Company
Projected Income Statement
For the Year Ended December 31, 20x4

Sales (38,000 pizzas x $2.50)		$95,000
Cost of Food Sold	$28,500	
Wages and Fringe Benefits of Restaurant Help	8,150	
Wages and Fringe Benefits of Delivery Workers	17,300	
Rent	4,800	
Accounting Services	3,600	
Depreciation of Delivery Equipment	5,000	
Depreciation of Restaurant Equipment	3,000	
Utilities	2,325	
Supplies (soap, floor wax, etc.)	1,200	73,875
Net Income before Taxes		$21,125
Income Taxes (30% of net income)		6,338
Net Income		$14,787

Required:

a. What is the breakeven point in number of pizzas that must be sold?
b. What is the breakeven point in sales dollars?
c. Mr. Calderone would like an after-tax net income of $20,000. What volume must be reached in number of pizzas in order to obtain the desired income?
d. Briefly explain to Mr. Calderone why his profits have increased at a faster rate than his sales.

(CMA adapted)

26. **Basic CVP Analysis—Multiple Settings.** Use the contribution margin ratio approach to cost-volume-profit analysis and calculate: (a) the contribution margin ratio, (b) the breakeven revenue, and (c) the revenue necessary to earn the desired level of profit in each of the following independent cases:

	Case A	Case B	Case C	Case D
Price	$10	$20	$30	$40
Variable Cost	9	14	18	32
Fixed Cost	30,000	90,000	60,000	40,000
Desired Profit	10,000	10,000	20,000	30,000

27. **Basic CVP Analysis—Multiple Settings.** Breakeven analysis is just a special case of cost-volume-profit analysis in which desired profit is set equal to zero. Determine the missing data in each of the following independent cases:

	Case A	Case B	Case C	Case D	Case E
Price	$10	$9	$8	$7	?
Variable Cost	$8	$6	$6	?	$7
Fixed Cost	$20,000	$30,000	$?	$20,000	$20,000
Desired Profit	$10,000	?	$10,000	$10,000	$10,000
Sales Volume	?	40,000	20,000	15,000	30,000

28. **Basic CVP Analysis—Multiple Facts.** The Blanks Company can select from several alternative sales volumes and prices to achieve set goals. The president estimated various costs for each sales price and volume, thus producing a contribution-margin figure. However, some of the figures were lost (designated by an "x").

    Required:

    Using the remaining figures, reconstruct the lost figures.

Sales Volume	Sales Price	Variable Expenses	Fixed Expenses	Before-Tax Income	Contribution Margin
10,000	$5	x	$15,000	x	50%
9,000	6	x	x	6,400	40
8,000	7	$29,700	x	9,300	x
6,000	10	30,000	20,000	x	x

29. **Basic CVP Analysis with Safety Margin.** Royal Beverages manufactures bottled sports drinks sold through health clubs and specialty stores. Its basic cost and profit information is summarized below:

Selling price (per bottle)	$1.10
Variable cost (per bottle)	$0.60
Fixed cost (total per month)	$20,000

Royal Beverage has the capacity to manufacture up to 100,000 bottles of its sports drinks per month.

Required:

a. What is the breakeven point in terms of number of bottles? In terms of dollars of sales?
b. If Royal Beverage could sell all 100,000 bottles of its production, what is its safety margin (expressed in number of bottles, sales dollars, and as a percentage of sales)?
c. What is the necessary sales volume (in number of bottles and in sales dollars) for Royal Beverage to earn $10,000 in net income (before taxes)?
d. What is the necessary sales volume (in number of bottles and in sales dollars) for Royal Beverage to earn $14,300 in net income (after taxes)? Assume that Royal Beverage's tax rate is 35 percent.
e. What is the necessary sales volume (in number of bottles and in sales dollars) for Royal Beverage to earn a profit equal to 20 percent of its revenues?
f. If a shortage in direct materials resulted in Royal Beverage being able to manufacture only 20,000 bottles of its sports drink in the month of January, at what price would it need to sell its sports drinks in order to break even?

30. CVP Analysis with Analysis of Operating Leverage. The Authors' Choice publishes brief "how to" books for using computer software. While the prices of its books vary slightly, the average book retails for approximately $5.25. The Authors' Choice's current cost structure is as follows:

Variable cost (per book)	$4.25
Fixed costs (total per month)	$15,000

The Authors' Choice is considering a change in its manufacturing technology. Specifically, it is contemplating the purchase of additional binding machinery that would reduce some of the variable costs associated with publishing its books. The new technology would reduce the variable cost per book by $0.25 but increase the total monthly fixed costs by $5,000.

Required:

a. Calculate the breakeven point (in books and in sales dollars) under the current and proposed cost structures. Would you recommend the purchase of the binding machinery to The Authors' Choice?
b. If The Authors' Choice has the capacity to manufacture 20,000 books per month, what is the safety margin (expressed in units, sales dollars, and percentage of sales) under each cost structure?
c. What is the degree of operating leverage at 20,000 books per month under the current and proposed cost structures?
d. If The Authors' Choice experienced an increase in sales volumes of 20 percent, how would net income be influenced under the current and proposed cost structures?
e. Based on your answer to (d) above, would you recommend the purchase of the binding machinery to The Authors' Choice if they could increase sales volumes by 20 percent?

31. CVP Analysis—Multiple Products. The Dooley Co. manufactures two products: Baubles and Trinkets. The following are projections for the coming year.

	Baubles		Trinkets		Totals
	Units	Amount	Units	Amount	
Sales	10,000	$10,000	7,500	$10,000	$20,000
Costs:					
Fixed		$ 2,000		$ 5,600	$ 7,600
Variable		6,000		3,000	9,000
		$ 8,000		$ 8,600	$16,600
Income before Taxes		$ 2,000		$ 1,400	$ 3,400

Required:

a. Assuming that the facilities are not jointly used, determine the breakeven volume in units for Baubles.
b. Determine the breakeven volume in dollars for Trinkets.
c. If Baubles and Trinkets become one-to-one complements and there are no changes in Dooley Co.'s cost functions, determine the breakeven volume in units.
d. Given the assumption in part (c) above, determine the weighted contribution margin ratio.

32. CVP Analysis—Multiple Products. Energy, Inc. manufactures three products: Ino, Eno, and Uno. Relevant data concerning these products are shown below:

	Selling Price (per unit)	Variable Cost (per unit)	Fixed Cost (total)
Ino	$10	$ 6	$1,000
Eno	20	15	500
Uno	5	4	100

In addition to the above fixed costs, a total of $400 in additional fixed production costs is incurred by Energy. Assume that Energy sells an equal "mix" of each product (i.e., unit sales of Ino, Eno, and Uno are expected to be equal).

Required:

Determine the number of "packages" of inventory that must be sold by Energy to: (a) break even, (b) earn a profit of $2,000 before taxes, and (c) earn a profit of $2,000 after taxes, assuming a tax rate of 40 percent.

33. *CVP Analysis—Multiple Products.* Jones Company manufactures three products: A, B, and C. Relevant data pertaining to these products are shown below:

	Selling Price (per unit)	Variable Cost (per unit)
A	$15	$10
B	10	8
C	10	5

In addition, fixed production costs are expected to equal $1,500. Assume that Jones expects to sell its products in the following mix: one unit of C, 3 units of A, and 5 units of B.

Required:

Determine the sales volume (in units) needed to earn the following level of profits: (a) $0 (break even), (b) $3,000 before taxes, and (c) $6,000 after taxes, assuming a 40 percent tax rate. Express your answer both in terms of "packages" of inventory as well as quantities of each specific product.

34. *CVP with Multiple Products.* Plastidine manufactures three grades of PVC pipe for sale to home improvement and hardware stores. These grades are labeled as Grade A, Grade B, and Grade C and are distinguished by their durability and thickness. The variable cost per grade and selling price are summarized below:

Grade	Selling Price	Variable Cost
A	$0.60 per foot	$0.10 per foot
B	$0.35 per foot	$0.07 per foot
C	$0.30 per foot	$0.05 per foot

Plastidine incurs monthly fixed costs of $14,350. Based on prior years' sales, Plastidine anticipates that its sales mix will be 50 percent Grade C pipe, 40 percent Grade B pipe, and 10 percent Grade A pipe. Plastidine's anticipated monthly sales volume equals 100,000 feet of pipe.

Required:

a. Calculate the weighted-contribution margin ratio for Plastidine.
b. Calculate the weighted-contribution margin per unit for Plastidine.
c. Determine the level of sales (in dollars) that would be required for Plastidine to break even.
d. Determine the level of sales (in units) that would be required for Plastidine to break even. Translate this breakeven point into units of each of the individual grades of pipe.

35. *CVP with Multiple Products.* The Office Store is a discount retail outlet that sells office supplies to individuals and other businesses. For purposes of its CVP analysis, it classifies products into one of three categories: (1) computers and related equipment, (2) office products, and (3) office furniture. The Office Store earns relatively large contribution margins on the sales of its office furniture and relatively low contribution margins on the sales of its office products. Summarized below are the company's average contribution margin ratios for these product classifications:

Office products	0.10
Computers and related equipment	0.20
Office furniture	0.60

Office products, computers and related equipment, and office furniture typically account for 60, 25, and 15 percent, respectively, of The Office Store's total sales. The Office Store's fixed costs average $15,000 per month.

Required:

a. Calculate the weighted contribution margin ratio for The Office Store.
b. Determine the monthly level of sales (in dollars) that would be required for The Office Store to (1) break even and (2) earn a monthly profit of $10,000 (before taxes).
c. Verify the calculations in (b) above by preparing an income statement for The Office Store at each level of volume.
d. If The Office Store were only able to generate $60,000 in monthly sales (while keeping the sales mix among the three classifications of products at current levels), what weighted contribution margin ratio would be required to earn in order to break even? Earn a monthly profit of $10,000 before taxes?
e. Assume that the mix of sales shifted to 30, 20 and 50 percent for office products, computers and related equipment, and office furniture, respectively. Determine the monthly level of sales (in dollars) that would be required for The Office Store to (1) break even and (2) earn a monthly profit of $10,000.

*36. *Probabilistic CVP Analysis.* Determine the expected profits for the following assumed facts:

	Probabilities		
	.3	.5	.2
Revenue..........................	$1,000,000	$900,000	$800,000
Variable Cost...................	800,000	600,000	500,000
Fixed Cost.......................	100,000	100,000	50,000

*37. *Probabilistic CVP Analysis.* Consider the following two independent sets of facts:

a. Hyup Co. produces a unit with a variable cost of $6 each and sells it at a price of $8 each. Hyup breaks-even when it sells $800,000 worth of units. What are Hyup's fixed costs? When Hyup sells $900,000, how much profit will it earn?
b. Inco's budget calls for the following: expected profits, $40,000; fixed cost, $50,000; and variable cost, $3 per unit. The price Inco charges will depend upon the price set by its competition. There is a 60 percent chance that competitors will set a price of $4 and a 40 percent chance that the price will be $9. If Inco had to aim for one amount, how many units should Inco expect to sell in order to reach its goal?

*38. *Probabilistic CVP Analysis.* Consider the following two independent sets of facts:

a. Smith thought he would be able to sell his product at $10 per unit with a 0.8 probability or at $9 per unit with a 0.2 probability. Variable costs are $7 per unit, and fixed costs are $20,000. What is Smith's expected breakeven volume in terms of units?
b. Jones thought he could sell his product for $100,000 with a 0.7 probability or for $110,000 with a 0.3 probability. Variable costs are 60 percent of revenues. Fixed cost will be $30,000 with a 0.8 probability or $40,000 with a 0.2 probability. What is Jones' expected breakeven volume in terms of sales dollars (before taxes)?

*39. *Probabilistic CVP Analysis.* The Robert R. Baker Company has a product that sells for a price ranging between $15 and $20. The sales manager thinks the price should be $15 but expects that the president, Robert R. Baker, Sr., will overrule him and make the price $20. He assigns a 60 to 40 chance to the adoption of the $20 price. The variable rate could be $12 or $10 per unit, and the cost department thinks the $12 figure more likely by 75 to 25. They also estimate fixed costs at $100,000 with a probability of 60 percent; $120,000, with a 30 percent probability; and $150,000 at 10 percent probability.

Required:

a. Calculate the total expected breakeven volume for this situation. Remember, $20 has a 60 percent chance of being the established price this year.
b. If you are 100 percent sure that fixed costs will be $120.00, what is the total expected breakeven point?
c. If you know with certainty that the variable cost will be $12 and the price $20, how many units would have to be sold to produce a profit of $10,000?
d. How would an employee of Baker Company derive estimates for the likelihood that an event will occur?

40. **CVP Analysis—Changing Relationships.**

   a. The Acme Co. sells a single product for $20 per unit. The company's cost structure is composed of $100,000 fixed costs and variable costs of $15 per unit. Acme will have to generate how much revenue in order to earn a desired profit of $20,000?
   b. If fixed costs are reduced by $10,000, by how much will profits increase (losses decrease)?
   c. If variable costs decrease, what will happen to the level of profits at any level of production?

41. **CVP Analysis—Changing Relationships.** Carey Company sold 100,000 units of its product at $20 per unit. Variable costs are $14 per unit (manufacturing costs of $11 and selling costs of $3). Fixed costs, which are incurred uniformly throughout the year, total $792,000 (manufacturing costs of $500,000 and selling costs of $292,000). There are no beginning or ending inventories.

   Required:

   a. Determine the breakeven point in terms of dollars and units.
   b. How many units must be sold to earn before-tax income of $60,000?
   c. How many units must be sold to earn $90,000 income after taxes, assuming that the tax rate is 40 percent?
   d. If labor costs are 50 percent of variable costs and 20 percent of fixed costs, a 10 percent increase in wages and salaries would increase the number of units required to break even by how many units?

   (AICPA adapted)

42. **CVP Analysis—Changing Relationships.** The following data relate to a year's budgeted activity for Patsy Corporation, a single-product company:

	Units
Beginning Inventory	30,000
Production	120,000
Available for Sale	150,000
Sales	(120,000)
Ending Inventory	30,000

	Per Unit
Selling Price	$5
Variable Manufacturing Costs	1
Variable Selling Costs	2
Fixed Manufacturing Costs	$25,000
Fixed Selling Costs	65,000

    Total fixed costs remain unchanged within the relevant range of 25,000 units to total capacity of 160,000 units.

    Required:

    a. Determine the projected annual breakeven sales in units for Patsy Corporation.
    b. Determine the net income for Patsy Corporation assuming that volume reaches the budgeted level.

c. Assuming that volume reaches the budgeted level, consider the following changes: selling price increases by 20 percent, variable manufacturing costs increase by 10 percent, variable selling costs remain the same, and total fixed costs increase to $104,400. How many units must now be sold to generate a profit equal to 10 percent of the contribution margin?

d. A special order is received to purchase 10,000 units to be used in an unrelated market. Given the original data, what price per unit should be charged on this order to increase Patsy Corporation's net income by $5,000?

43. *CVP Analysis—Changing Relationships.* The president of Beth Corporation, which manufactures tape decks and sells them to producers of sound reproduction systems, anticipates a 10 percent wage increase for the manufacturing employees on January 1 of next year (variable labor). He expects no other changes in costs. Overhead will not change as a result of the wage increase. The president has asked you to assist him in developing the information he needs to formulate a reasonable product strategy for next year.

    You are satisfied by regression analysis that volume is the primary factor affecting costs. You have separated the semivariable costs into their fixed and variable components by means of the least-squares criterion. You also observe that the beginning and ending inventories are never materially different.

    Below are the current-year data assembled for your analysis:

Current Selling Price per Unit	$80
Variable Cost per Unit:	
Material	$30
Labor	12
Overhead	6
Total	$48
Annual Volume of Sales	5,000 units
Fixed Costs	$51,000

    Required:

    Provide the following information for the president using cost-volume-profit analysis:

    a. What increase in the selling price is necessary to cover the 10 percent wage increase and still maintain the current breakeven point (in terms of units)?
    b. How many tape decks must be sold to maintain the current net income if the sales price remains at $80 and the 10 percent wage increase goes into effect?
    c. The president believes that an additional $190,000 of machinery (to be depreciated at 10% annually) will increase present capacity (5,300 units) by 30 percent. If all tape decks produced can be sold at the present price and the wage increase goes into effect, how would the estimated net income before capacity is increased compare with the estimated net income after capacity is increased? Prepare computations of estimated net income before and after the expansion.

    (AICPA adapted)

44. *CVP Analysis—Changing Relationships.* The Green Company, a producer of small parts, has each of its plants compute a breakeven point. The West Penn Plant produces a part that sells for $5. At maximum capacity the plant can produce 1,000,000 of these parts. The cost manager estimates that the total variable costs are $4 per unit and the fixed costs are $200,000.

    Required:

    a. What is the breakeven point for the West Penn Plant?
    b. Graph the breakeven point.
    c. If variable costs go up by $0.50, what is the breakeven point? Will the plant be able to continue production?
    d. If the president of Green requests a profit of $50,000, how many units must be produced? Will the West Penn Plant be able to produce this many units? What would be the total revenue needed to provide the $50,000 profit?
    e. We usually assume that the price, variable costs per unit, fixed costs, and/or level of production are known with certainty. If these amounts are not known with certainty, but you do know probabilities expressing the likelihood that certain amounts will occur, can a probabilistic breakeven point be calculated? If so, describe the process.

45. *CVP Analysis—Changing Relationships.* R.A. Ro and Company, makers of high-quality handmade pipes, has experienced a steady growth in sales for the past five years. Increased competition, however, has led Mr. Ro, the president, to believe that an aggressive advertising campaign will be necessary next year to maintain the company's present growth.

To get ready for next year's advertising campaign, the company's accountant has prepared the following data for the current year (20x4) for Mr. Ro:

Variable Costs:		
Labor	$ 8.00/pipe	
Materials	3.25/pipe	
Variable Overhead	2.50/pipe	
	$13.75/pipe	
Fixed Costs:		
Manufacturing	$ 25,000	
Selling	40,000	
Administrative	70,000	
	$ 135,000	
Selling Price per Pipe	$ 25.00	
Expected Sales, 20x4 (20,000 units)	$ 500,000	
Tax Rate	40%	

Mr. Ro has set the sales target for 20x5 at a level of $550,000 (or 22,000 pipes).

Required:

a. What is the projected after-tax net income for 20x4?
b. What is the breakeven point in units for 20x4?
c. Mr. Ro believes that, all other costs remaining constant, an additional selling expense of $11,250 for advertising in 20x5 will be necessary to attain the sales target. What will be the after-tax net income for 20x5 if the additional $11,250 is spent?
d. What will be the breakeven point in dollar sales for 20x5 if the additional $11,250 is spent for advertising?

46. *CVP Analysis—Contribution Margin Ratio.* Calculate the missing data in each of the following independent cases:

	Case A	Case B	Case C	Case D
Revenue	$100,000	$200,000	$300,000	?
Variable Cost	80,000	120,000	?	$210,000
Fixed Cost	15,000	?	25,000	35,000
Original Desired Profit	?	30,000	35,000	55,000
Contribution Margin Ratio	?	?	?	?
Breakeven Revenue	?	?	?	?
CVP Revenue at $20,000 Profit	?	?	?	?

47. *Comprehensive CVP Analysis—Basic and Changing Relationships.* Summarized below is relevant cost information for The Chocolate Factory's production of its candy products (averaged across all products).

Variable Costs (per candy product):	
Direct materials	$0.01
Direct labor	0.02
Manufacturing overhead	0.05
Other variable costs	0.02
Total variable cost	$0.10
Fixed Costs (per week):	
Depreciation on manufacturing equipment	$5,000
Indirect labor	2,000
General and administrative	2,000
Other	1,000
Total fixed costs	$10,000

The Chocolate Factory sells its candy products for an average of $0.42 per candy product and has the capacity to manufacture up to 100,000 candy products per week.

The Chocolate Factory is considering automating its manufacturing processes. Doing so would result in additional fixed costs of $1,500 per week for depreciation on manufacturing equipment and $500 per week for indirect labor. However, by automating these processes, the variable cost per candy product could be reduced from $0.10 to $0.08 per candy product. In addition, The Chocolate Factory's manufacturing capacity would increase from 100,000 products per week to 130,000 candy products per week.

Required:

a. Determine the level of sales (in both units and sales dollars) necessary to (1) break even, (2) earn a desired profit of $18,000 per week (before taxes), and (3) earn a desired profit of $18,000 per week (after taxes) under both the existing and proposed manufacturing processes. Assume a tax rate of 40 percent for the Chocolate Factory.
b. Based on your answer to (a) above, determine the safety margin (in units, sales dollars, and percentage of sales) under both the existing and proposed manufacturing processes.
c. Assume that a shortage in direct materials resulted in the The Chocolate Factory having maximum manufacturing capacity of 40,000 candy products per week. What sales price must be charged to customers to (1) break even, (2) earn a desired profit of $18,000 per week (before taxes), and (3) earn a desired profit of $18,000 per week (after taxes) under both the existing and proposed manufacturing processes.
d. What is the degree of operating leverage at 100,000 candy products under both the existing and proposed manufacturing processes?
e. Using an incremental analysis, evaluate the profitability of the two manufacturing processes assuming that the maximum sales volume per week is (1) 100,000 candy products and (2) 130,000 candy products.

48. *Income Statement Preparation—Variable Costing.* The Omega Company manufactures a single product it sells to its customers: X. Omega manufactures 8,000 units of product X during 20x1 (its first year of operations); the company was able to sell 5,000 of these units for $40 per unit. Cost data for 20x1 was as follows:

Variable Manufacturing Costs (per unit)	$ 25
Fixed Manufacturing Costs (total)	12,000
Variable Nonmanufacturing Costs (per unit sold)	5
Fixed Nonmanufacturing Costs (total)	5,000

Given the above information, prepare an income statement for Omega Company using variable costing.

49. *Income Statement Preparation—Absorption Costing.* Given the data in 48 above, prepare an income statement for Omega Company assuming the use of absorption costing.

50. *Income Statement Preparation—Absorption Costing and Variable Costing.* 20x1 is the first year of operations for College Corporation. You are able to obtain the following information from the records of College Corporation related to its production and sale of MBA, its primary product:

Variable Product Costs (per unit)	$ 5
Variable Selling Costs (per unit sold)	2
Fixed Product Costs (total)	10,000
Fixed Selling Costs (total)	5,000
Units Produced	5,000
Units Sold	3,000

Assume that College Corporation sold each unit for $20 per unit.

Required:

Prepare an income statement for 20x1 for College Corporation assuming the use of absorption costing and variable costing.

51. *Income Statement Preparation—Absorption and Variable Costing.* Jackie Company had the following data related to 20x1 (its first year of operations):

Direct Materials Cost (per unit)	$ 2.00
Direct Labor Cost (per unit)	5.00
Variable Overhead Cost (per unit)	2.50
Fixed Overhead Cost (total)	1,000

In addition to the above product costs, Jackie incurred variable selling expenses of $2 per unit sold. Other fixed nonmanufacturing expenses (mostly administrative) totalled $4,000 during 20x1. Jackie produced 5,000 units during 20x1; 2,000 were sold for $20 per unit.

Required:

Prepare income statements for 20x1 for Jackie Company under both absorption costing and variable costing.

52. *Income Statement Preparation—Absorption and Variable Costing.* Flear Company has a maximum manufacturing capacity of 210,000 units per year. Variable manufacturing costs are $11 per unit. Fixed factory overhead is $360,000 per year. Variable selling expenses are $5 per unit sold and fixed selling expenses are $252,000 per year. The unit sales price is $20.

During 20x1, 180,000 units were manufactured; 150,000 were sold. Flear had no beginning inventory.

Required:

a. Prepare formal income statements for 20x1 under both absorption and variable costing.
b. Briefly account for the difference in net income between the two costing alternatives.

53. *Income Statement Preparation—Absorption and Variable Costing.* The S. T. Shire Company uses variable costing for internal management and absorption costing for external reporting. Thus, at the end of each year, financial information must be converted from variable costing to absorption costing to satisfy external requirements.

At the end of 20x1, sales were anticipated to rise 20 percent for the next year. Therefore, production was increased from 20,000 units to 24,000 units to meet this expected demand. However, economic conditions kept the sales level at 20,000 units for both years.

The following data pertain to 20x1 and 20x2:

	20x1	20x2
Selling Price per Unit	$ 30	$ 30
Sales (units)	20,000	20,000
Beginning Inventory (units)	2,000	2,000
Production (units)	20,000	24,000
Ending inventory (units)	2,000	6,000
Under-Absorbed Overhead	$ 5,000	$ 4,000

Variable costs per unit for 20x1 and 20x2:

Labor	$ 7.50
Materials	4.50
Variable Overhead	3.00
	$ 15.00

Annual fixed costs for 20x1 and 20x2 (budgeted and actual):

Production	$ 90,000
Selling and Administrative	100,000
	$190,000

The overhead rate under absorption costing is based on practical plant capacity, which is 30,000 units per year. All accompanying under/overabsorbed overhead is taken to cost of goods sold. All taxes should be ignored.

Required:

a. Present the income statement based on variable costing for 20x2.
b. Present the income statement based on absorption costing for 20x2.

(CMA adapted)

54. *Inventory Valuation—Absorption and Variable Costing.* Shawn, Inc. had the following information related to the production of its inventory during 20x1 and 20x2. Assume that Shawn began its operations in 20x1.

	20x1	20x2
Variable Cost per Unit	$ 3	$ 3
Fixed Production Costs	$ 5,000	$10,000
Production	2,500 units	5,000 units
Sales	2,000 units	5,200 units

    Required:

    Determine the valuation of Shawn's inventory at the end of 20x1 and 20x2 using absorption costing and variable costing.

55. *Inventory Valuation—Absorption and Variable Costing.* 20x1 was the first year of operations for Archer Company. Archer manufactured 2,000 units of inventory during this year and sold a total of 1,000 units. Cost data for 20x1 is shown below:

Direct Materials (per unit)	$ 2.00
Direct Labor (per unit)	1.50
Variable Overhead (per unit)	1.00
Variable Selling (per unit sold)	3.00
Fixed Overhead (total)	10,000
Fixed Administration (total)	15,000

    Required:

    Determine the valuation of the ending inventory for Archer Company at December 31, 20x1 using the absorption costing method and variable costing method.

56. *Inventory Valuation—Absorption and Variable Costing.* Product costs for the ABC Company include the following elements:

Direct Labor	$400,000
Direct Material	300,000
Variable Overhead	200,000
Fixed Overhead	600,000

    During the year, 10,000 units were produced and 7,000 were sold. Ending inventory consists of 3,000 units, since no inventory was on hand at the beginning of the year.

    Required:

    a. Calculate the cost of ending inventory under absorption costing.
    b. Calculate the cost of ending inventory under variable costing.

57. *Inventory Valuation—Absorption and Variable Costing.* Shown below are five independent cases. Assume that each case represents the sales and production data for a company in its first year of operations. For each case, determine the valuation of the ending inventory under both absorption costing and variable costing.

	A	B	C	D	E
Variable Production Costs (per unit)	$ 4.00	$ 5.00	$ 4.00	$ 2.50	$ 3.00
Variable Selling Costs (per unit sold)	$ 1.00	$ 2.00	$ 1.50	$ 2.00	$ 2.50
Fixed Production Costs (total)	$ 10,000	$ 15,000	$ 5,000	$ 8,000	$ 10,000
Fixed Selling Costs (total)	$ 1,500	$ 6,000	$ 5,000	$ 7,000	$ 4,000
Units Produced	20,000	30,000	2,500	12,000	15,000
Units Sold	15,000	10,000	1,250	12,000	9,000

58. *Income Statement Preparation and Inventory Valuation—Absorption and Variable Costing.* The following cost data has been gathered for January and February for Axis Corporation. Assume that these two months are the first months of Axis' operation:

	January 20x1	February 20x1
Direct Materials (per unit)	$ 2.00	$ 3.00
Direct Labor (per unit)	5.00	5.00
Variable Overhead (per unit)	2.50	2.50
Variable Selling (per unit sold)	1.50	2.00
Fixed Overhead (total)	15,000	20,000
Fixed Selling (total)	5,000	8,000

In January, Axis produced 7,500 units and sold 5,000 units. In February, 9,000 units were produced; 10,000 units were sold. Assume a FIFO inventory flow and a $20 per unit selling price in both months.

Required:
a. Prepare an income statement for January 20x1 and February 20x1 assuming the use of absorption costing.
b. Repeat (a) above assuming the use of variable costing.
c. For both absorption and variable costing, use your answers in (a) and (b) above to determine the total variable and fixed expenses recognized each month.
d. Determine the valuation of Axis' inventory at the end of January and February using both absorption and variable costing.

59. *Income Determination—Absorption and Variable Costing.* The ABC Company (described in Problem 56 in this chapter) sells products at an established price of $200 per unit. Selling and administrative costs amount to $100,000.

Required:
a. Calculate net income under absorption costing.
b. Calculate net income under variable costing.

60. *Income Determination—Absorption and Variable Costing.* During 20x1 (its first year of operations), Mayes Company produced a total of 20,000 units of inventory. Variable costs of production were $10 per unit; fixed production costs totalled $15,000. Variable selling and administrative expenses were $5 per unit sold. Mayes sold a total of 15,000 units for $25 per unit during 20x1.

Required:

What is the net income for Mayes Company during 20x1 assuming the use of absorption costing and variable costing?

61. *Income Determination and Inventory Valuation—Absorption and Variable Costing.* Goldilocks Company had the following cost and sales data related to 20x1, its first year of operations:

   1. Sales of 10,000 units at $25 per unit.
   2. Variable costs of production during 20x1 were $8 per unit. These costs included direct materials costs, direct labor costs, and overhead costs. In addition to variable production costs, variable selling and administrative costs were $2 per unit sold.
   3. Fixed production costs during 20x1 were $30,000. In addition, fixed selling and administrative expenses were $5,000.
   4. A total of 15,000 units were produced during 20x1.

   Required:

   a. Determine the net income recognized by Goldilocks Company during 20x1 using absorption costing and variable costing.
   b. Determine the valuation of the Goldilocks Company inventory at the end of 20x1 using absorption costing and variable costing.

62. *Income Determination and Inventory Valuation—Absorption and Variable Costing.* The Wilson Supply Company began its manufacturing operations on January 1, 20x4. At the end of the first year of production and sales activity, the following information was available:

Units Manufactured	25,000 units
Direct Material Costs	$ 56,250
Direct Labor Costs	$ 77,500
Variable Manufacturing Overhead Costs	$ 37,500
Fixed Manufacturing Overhead Costs	$ 75,000
Units Sold	15,000 units
Ending inventory	10,000 units
Sales Revenue	$ 270,000
Fixed Selling Costs	$ 17,000
Fixed Administrative Costs	$ 13,000

   Required

   a. Prepare an income statement for 20x4 using an absorption costing approach.
   b. Assuming that Wilson Supply Company uses an absorption costing approach, what value will be assigned to the ending inventory?
   c. Construct an income statement that uses the variable costing approach.
   d. If variable costing is used by Wilson Supply Company, what value will be assigned to the ending inventory?

63. *Income Determination and Inventory Valuation—Absorption and Variable Costing.* The New Process Company was formed in 20x4 with an original capital investment of $100,000 by its owner, Roger Buck. To house the manufacturing operation, a building with an expected useful life of ten years was purchased for $50,000. Equipment was leased under a five-year agreement for $10,000 a year. Mr. Buck hired Rod Ram as manager of manufacturing. To attract Mr. Ram from his former employer, Mr. Buck gave him a three-year contract calling for a salary of $15,000 per year. During 20x4, the company produced 14,500 units. Production costs included $33,350 of materials and $73,950 for labor (paid on a piece-work basis). Mr. Buck managed to sell 10,000 units in 20x4 at $12 each. In 20x5, the company produced 10,000 units using $20,000 of material and $28,000 of direct labor. Mr. Buck lowered the price per unit to $11 and was able to sell 12,000 units. The company uses a FIFO (first-in, first-out) method of inventory valuation.

   Required:

   Prepare comparative income statements for the New Process Company for the years 20x4 and 20x5, one using an absorption costing approach and one using a variable costing approach. Also, calculate the value of the ending inventory for both years, using both valuation approaches.

64. *Income Determination and Inventory Valuation—Absorption Costing.* The following information is made available by the Conversion Corporation, which produces a single product. The data relate to the last two years of the firm's operations.

	Year 1	Year 2
Sales Revenue	$ 76,500	$ 153,000
Cost of Goods Sold	(49,500)	(95,000)
Gross Margin	$ 27,000	$ 58,000
Selling Expenses	(9,200)	(14,800)
Administrative Expenses	(13,400)	(15,200)
Net Income before Taxes	$ 4,400	$ 28,000
Selling Price per Unit	$8.50	$9.00
Units Produced	12,000	14,000
Variable Costs per Unit	$4.50	$4.75
Units Sold	9,000	17,000
Beginning Inventory	0	3,000
Fixed Costs	$12,000	$12,000

The firm uses a FIFO (first-in, first-out) method for determining cost flows. All selling and administrative expenses are fixed.

Required:

a. Does the company use absorbtion or variable costing in preparing its financial statements?
b. Calculate the cost of the ending inventory included in the company's balance sheet at the end of year 1.
c. Prepare income statements for years 1 and 2 using variable costing.
d. Calculate the cost of the ending inventories for year 1 and 2 using variable costing.

65. *Expense Recognition and Inventory Valuation—Absorption and Variable Costing.* The following information is available for Keller Corporation's new product line:

Selling Price per Unit	$ 15
Variable Manufacturing Costs Per Unit of Production	8
Total Annual Fixed Manufacturing Costs	25,000
Variable Administrative Costs Per Unit of Production	3
Total Annual Fixed Selling and Administrative Expenses	15,000

There was no inventory at the beginning of the year. During the year 12,500 units were produced and 10,000 units were sold.

Required:

a. Determine the ending inventory balance under variable costing.
b. Determine the ending inventory balance under absorption costing.
c. Determine the total variable costs charged to expense for the year, assuming that Keller uses variable costing.
d. Determine the total fixed costs charged to expense for the year, assuming that Keller uses absorption costing.

(AICPA adapted)

66. *Expense Recognition and Inventory Valuation—Absorption Costing.* Walter, Inc. uses the absorption costing method of cost accumulation. During 20x1 (Walter's first year of operations), Walter produced 10,000 units of its primary inventory product, Payton. Variable production costs of Payton (including materials, labor, and overhead costs) were $2 per unit. During 20x1, a total of $8,000 of fixed overhead costs were incurred. Of the 10,000 units of Payton produced, Walter sold 6,000.

In 20x2, Walter produced another 5,000 units of Payton. Total variable production costs were $2 per unit. A total of $4,000 of fixed overhead costs were incurred during 20x2. During 20x2, 7,000 units of Payton were sold to Walter's customers.

For both years, variable selling costs were $2 per unit sold. There were no fixed selling costs incurred in either year.

Required:

a. What is the total variable expense recognized each year by Walter, Inc.?
b. What is the total fixed expense recognized each year by Walter, Inc.?
c. What is the value of the ending inventory at the end of 20x1 and 20x2 for Walter, Inc.?

67. *Expense Recognition and Inventory Valuation—Variable Costing.* Repeat Problem 66 assuming that Walter, Inc. uses variable costing instead of absorption costing.

68. *Expense Recognition and Inventory Valuation—Absorption and Variable Costing.* During its first year of operations, Stone Corporation manufactured 10,000 units of inventory. Of these units, 6,000 were sold to customers. The costs incurred by Stone during 20x1 are shown below:

Direct Materials (per unit)	$ 3.00
Direct Labor (per unit)	1.50
Variable Overhead (per unit)	2.00
Variable Selling (per unit sold)	0.50
Fixed Overhead (total)	15,000
Fixed Selling (total)	6,000

Required:

a. Determine the total amount of variable cost recognized as expense during 20x1 under absorption costing and variable costing.
b. Determine the total amount of fixed costs recognized as expense during 20x1 under absorption costing and variable costing.
c. Determine the valuation of Stone's ending inventory at the end of 20x1 under absorption costing and variable costing.

69. *Expense Determination—Absorption and Variable Costing.* Baltimore, Inc. utilizes a continuous production process which results in the manufacture of two main products. Relevant data concerning these products for the first month of operations (January 20x1) for Baltimore, Inc. are shown below:

	Product A	Product B
Direct Materials (per unit)	$ 3.00	$ 5.00
Direct Labor (per unit)	2.00	4.00
Variable Overhead (per unit)	1.75	3.00
Variable Selling (per unit sold)	3.00	1.00
Fixed Overhead (total)	10,000	25,000

No fixed selling or other period costs were incurred by Baltimore, Inc. during January of 20x1. A total of 20,000 units of Product A were produced; 15,000 of these units were sold for $30 per unit. Also, Baltimore produced 25,000 units of Product B; 15,000 of these were sold for $25 per unit.

During February, the following cost data are available for Baltimore, Inc:

	Product A	Product B
Direct Materials (per unit)	$ 4.50	$ 5.00
Direct Labor (per unit)	2.50	5.00
Variable Overhead (per unit)	2.75	2.70
Variable Selling (per unit sold)	3.50	3.00
Fixed Overhead (total)	20,000	30,000

During February, Baltimore, Inc. produced an additional 5,000 units of Product A and 5,000 units of Product B. Total February sales are shown below:

Product A:	10,000 units x $35 per unit =	$350,000
Product B:	12,000 units x $40 per unit =	480,000
		$830,000

Assume that Baltimore, Inc. uses a FIFO cost-flow assumption.

Required:

a. Determine the amount of expense recognized by Baltimore, Inc. during January and February of 20x1. Classify the expenses based on the type (direct materials, direct labor, etc.). Assume that Baltimore, Inc. uses absorption costing.
b. Repeat (a) above, assuming the use of variable costing.
c. For both January and February, determine the valuation of Baltimore's ending inventory using absorption costing and variable costing.

70. *Effect of Costing on Net Income.* A firm began its manufacturing operations in 20x4. Its production process is characterized by large annual amounts of fixed cost. Over the years, the following amounts were produced and sold:

Year	Units Produced	Units Sold
20x4	10,000	8,000
20x5	5,000	7,000
20x6	5,000	5,000
20x7	10,000	4,000
20x8	10,000	4,000
20x9	0	12,000

Throughout the years the production costs were stable, although in 20x6 the sales price per unit increased from $10 to $15 where it stayed until 20x9. Using this information, complete the following table concerning the characteristics of the firm.

	Ending Inventory Level (as compared to the beginning Inventory)		
Year	Number of Units	Dollar Value	Profits (as compared to absorption costing)
20x4	increased	?	?
20x5	?	decreased	?
20x6	same	?	?
20x7	?	?	lower
20x8	?	increased	?
20x9	?	?	higher

71. *Effect of Costing on Income and Inventory.* The Jack Palmer Company produces Better Flite golf balls which are sold in pro shops throughout the country. The company uses an absorption costing approach to valuing its inventory. At the beginning of the current year, the inventory was 2,000 boxes of golf balls (each box contains 3 balls). The inventory was valued at $3 a box ($6,000 in total). This valuation included a proportionate share of the fixed manufacturing costs, which are $18,000 per year. During the year, 10,000 boxes of golf balls were produced. Direct material, direct labor, and fixed costs were the same as they were the previous year.

The owner of the Jack Palmer Company, Mr. Arnold Nicklaus, is considering changing from absorption costing to direct costing for income reporting and inventory valuation. He wants to know which method will produce the higher inventory valuation for each of the possible sales situations listed below. Use the terms "absorption costing higher," "direct costing higher," or "no difference" as your answer. Also, briefly explain the reasons for your answers.

a. Sales for the period were 8,000 units.
b. Sales for the period were 10,000 units.
c. Sales for the period were 11,000 units.
d. Sales for the period were 12,000 units.
e. There were no sales during the period.

Appendix

Probabilistic Estimates for CVP Analysis

One method for considering cost-volume-profit relationships caused by uncertainty regarding future activity is to introduce probabilistic estimates that explicitly consider the likelihood that a future event will occur. Probability is represented by a decimal ranging between 0 and 1. A zero probability indicates that an event will not occur, whereas a probability of 0.9 indicates that the event will occur nine out of ten times. If reasonable probabilities for sales prices, variable costs, and fixed costs can be estimated, an expected breakeven point can be determined which incorporates various possible outcomes.

To illustrate a simple use of probabilistic CVP analysis, the expected cost and sales data for Bob's Burger Barn is shown below:

Sales Price..................................	$ 2.50 per cheeseburger
Variable Cost..............................	1.50 per cheeseburger
Fixed Costs	25,000

It was assumed that Bob knew the selling price of $2.50 per cheeseburger with certainty. Obviously, this "perfect" level of information may not exist in practice. Suppose that Bob thought his selling price had a 50 percent chance of being $2.50 and a 50 percent chance of being $2.00. The breakeven point at each of these levels is summarized below:

$$\text{Units} = \frac{\$25{,}000 + \$0}{(\$2.50 - \$1.50)} = 25{,}000 \text{ Units}$$

$$\text{Units} = \frac{\$25{,}000 + \$0}{(\$2.00 - \$1.50)} = 50{,}000 \text{ Units}$$

The question at this point is "what is the breakeven point?" Since the probability of the two selling prices is equal (50 percent), it is equally likely that breakeven would be 25,000 or 50,000. A "weighted-average" breakeven can be calculated through the following formula:

Breakeven at Condition x	x	Probability of Condition x	=	Weighted-Average Breakeven Point

Using the above example, the breakeven for Bob's Burger Barn in this case would be 37,500 cheeseburgers, as calculated below:

Breakeven	x	Probability	=	Breakeven
25,000	x	0.50	=	12,500
50,000	x	0.50	=	25,000
				37,500

The term "condition" merely refers to a set of assumptions regarding expected selling prices, variable costs, and fixed costs. While the above example illustrates how different assumptions for sales prices affect the breakeven point, it is important to note that variable costs and fixed costs may also not be known with certainty. For example, in addition to the sales prices, assume that Bob Adams forms the following estimates (along with probabilities) for the variable costs and fixed costs of Bob's Burger Barn:

Variable Costs:	$1.50	(60%)
	$1.80	(40%)
Fixed Costs:	$25,000	(80%)
	$30,000	(20%)

For these types of situations, a "probability tree" can be formed to determine the probability of various conditions. Illustration 7 shows the probability tree for Bob's Burger Barn's probabilistic CVP analysis and summarizes the probability of each condition. As shown in Illustration 7, the sum of the joint probabilities for all of the conditions is 1.00 (or 100 percent). The probability of a given condition is calculated as follows:

$$\text{Probability of Sales Price} \times \text{Probability of Variable Cost} \times \text{Probability of Fixed Cost}$$

For example, the probability of the first condition (sales price of $2.50, variable cost of $1.50, and fixed costs of $25,000) is 0.24 (or 24 percent), as calculated below:

$$0.50 \times 0.60 \times 0.80 = 0.24$$

Once the probabilities have been calculated (through Illustration 7), the accountant would determine the breakeven point for each condition. The weighted-average breakeven point is then determined by:

1. Multiplying the breakeven point at a condition by the probability of that condition.

2. Summing the products in (1) above.

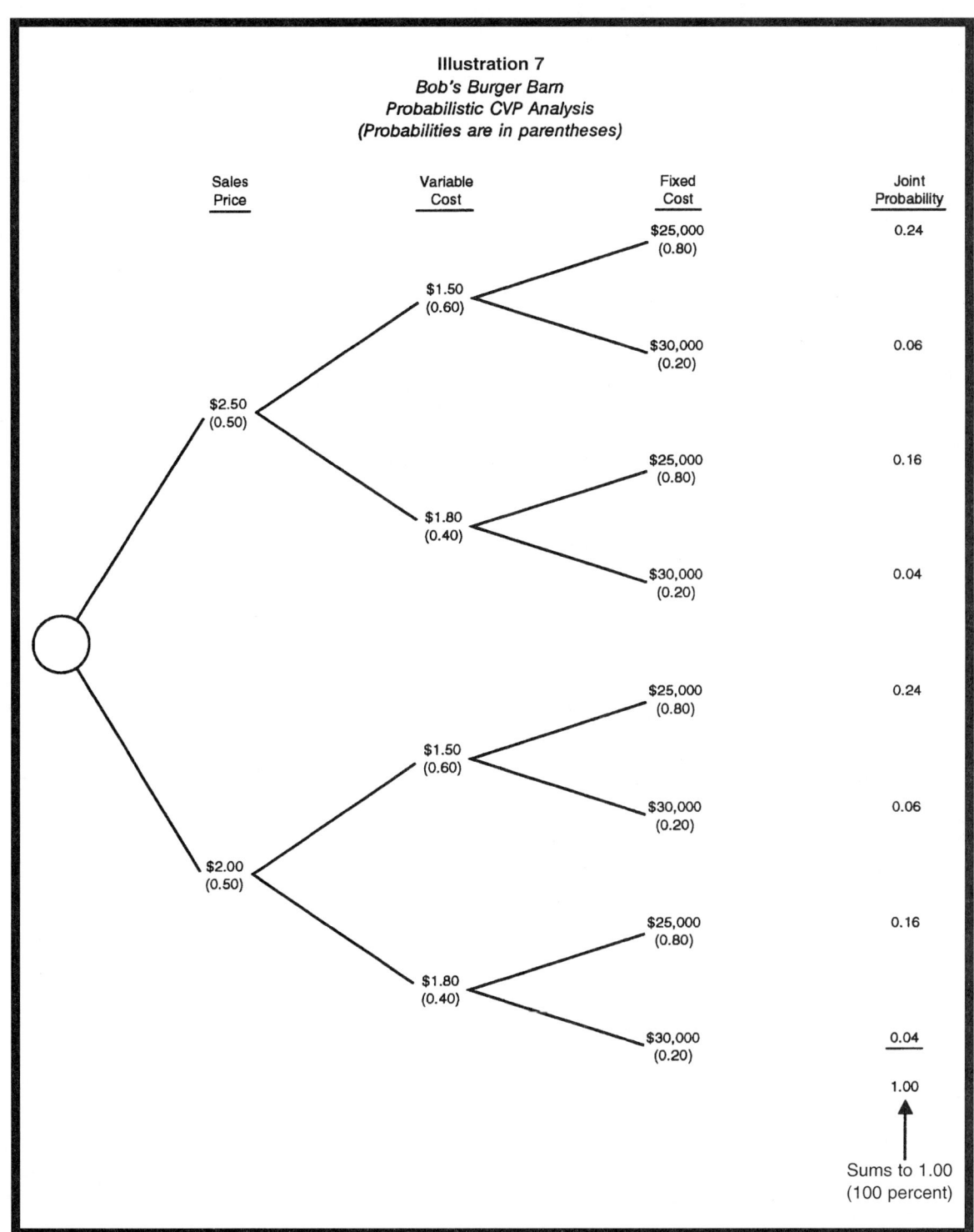

Learning Objectives

This chapter introduces the development of performance standards and the subsequent use of these standards for cost accumulation and organizational control. Also discussed is the calculation and interpretation of variances from anticipated (or standard) costs of actual direct materials and direct labor. The variances for manufacturing overhead costs are discussed in the appendix to the chapter. Studying these materials should enable you to:

1. Define performance standards and standard costs.

2. Understand how performance standards are established for an organization's manufacturing costs.

3. Calculate direct material and direct labor variances and identify the causes of these variances.

4. Discuss how performance standards and variance analysis are used for organizational control and cost accumulation.

5. Prepare flexible budgets for manufacturing overhead costs assuming different levels of activity.

6. Perform a two- and three-way analysis of overhead variances to identify differences between actual overhead costs and overhead costs applied to production.

7

Standard Costing and Variance Analysis

INTRODUCTION

Jeff Harwell, the production manager of SportsWorld (a manufacturer of sporting good products), was overheard discussing his division's performance with the corporate vice-president, Laura Martin:

Laura: I simply don't understand why your costs were so high last year. Your department produced fewer items than in the past, yet costs were much higher. Why did this happen?

Jeff: I wish I knew. We bought our materials from the same suppliers, so I doubt it was because of higher material costs. Also, we didn't produce many new products or hire additional employees, so our workers should have been familiar with the manufacturing process. It just doesn't seem to make sense.

Laura: Wait a minute. Didn't we decide to use higher quality materials so that our products will last longer? That would account for some of the problem, since materials costs would be higher. Also, didn't it take your workers longer to process the products than before?

Jeff: You know, you're right. We tried to reduce material waste, so it took longer to prepare materials for production. I was also told that the new grade of materials we used this year was harder to work with.

Laura: I wonder what else could have caused your costs to be so high. Maybe we should take a closer look at our manufacturing data.

How much rubber should Goodyear use in manufacturing tires? How long should it take Dell Computer to assemble a personal computer for a customer? What level of utility costs should DaimlerChrysler incur in producing automobiles? In our discussion of cost accumulation to this point, we have focused on the actual amount (and cost) of materials, labor, and overhead inputs incurred by organizations in manufacturing inventory or providing services. An issue that was not addressed was how the organization evaluates the reasonableness of the costs incurred in manufacturing its inventory. The organization is obviously interested in controlling its manufacturing costs to the extent possible. Doing so would allow any inefficiencies in its manufacturing process to be identified (and, hopefully, corrected).

A method of identifying inefficiencies in the manufacturing process is through the use of performance standards. This chapter discusses the use of performance standards and variance analysis for the organization's manufacturing costs.

PERFORMANCE STANDARDS

Performance standards represent expectations for the activities of the organization. From a manufacturing standpoint, performance standards specify the number and cost of inputs (direct materials, direct labor, and overhead) necessary to manufacture a specified level of output. Simply stated, if Compaq manufactures 1,000 personal computers, what is the total cost of materials that should be incurred? What is the total wages that should be paid to assemble the computers? What other costs should be incurred? Notice that performance standards focus on the costs that *should* be incurred by the organization in manufacturing its inventory or providing its services.

Although several methods may be used to develop performance standards, the results of alternative methods can vary in their "tightness," or degree of attainability. At one extreme is the *ideal standard*. Ideal standards provide no allowances for waste or spoilage of direct materials (for direct materials costs) or equipment breakdowns or employee fatigue (for direct labor and manufacturing overhead costs). Because ideal standards are unattainable (or, at the very least, very difficult to attain), they do not provide the organization with a clear indication of where production inefficiencies exist since it is highly unlikely that they will ever be achieved. In addition, the use of ideal standards will reduce morale as employees continually fail to achieve these difficult and usually unattainable standards.

Alternatively, performance standards may be based on levels of past performance and are referred to as *past performance* (or *performance-based*) standards. Unlike ideal standards, past performance standards are attainable, since they are based on the production activity of prior periods. However, the use of past performance standards assumes that performance in prior periods represented desirable levels of performance. If this is not the case, the use of past performance standards will be ineffective in allowing the organization to identify manufacturing inefficiencies, since current performance may be superior to the standard although opportunities for improvement may still exist. In addition, if manufacturing conditions have changed so that past performance is no longer considered to be desirable, the less rigorous performance standards would result in employees exerting less than full effort to meet these standards. This would result in reduced levels of employee motivation and performance.

Perhaps the most reasonable and effective approach to setting performance standards is the use of attainable performance standards. *Attainable performance standards* reflect efficient levels of performance but include allowances for reasonable spoilage, waste, machine downtime, and employee fatigue. Attainable standards are attractive from the organization's standpoint, since these reflect efficient levels of performance against which actual performance can be measured. In addition, from the employee's standpoint, these standards provide a challenging goal that is attainable and allows for "normal" inefficiencies. Thus, employees will be highly motivated to meet attainable standards and must perform efficiently to do so.

The importance of selecting appropriate performance standards is illustrated by the following excerpt from practice.

> In legal proceedings related to several fatal accidents resulting from Firestone tire failures during the summer of 2000, retired Bridgestone/Firestone employees testified that they were pressed to examine more than 100 tires per hour. Because this hourly inspection rate was believed to compromise the quality of the employees' work, this "performance standard" may have resulted in the manufacture and distribution of substandard tires. As a result, over 6.5 million tires manufactured at the Decatur, Illinois plant at which these retirees worked were recalled.[1]

Direct Materials and Direct Labor Costs

To illustrate the nature of performance standards, consider the manufacturing process of SportsWorld, a medium-sized producer of sporting goods operating in the midwestern United States. While SportsWorld manufactures a wide variety of products, our focus is on the production of SportsWorld's most popular product: footballs. The manufacturing cost of one football for SportsWorld has been estimated through the use of attainable performance standards. The resulting *standard cost* represents the cost that should be incurred by SportsWorld in producing its products, assuming efficient operations.

Standard costing should be clearly distinguished from two other costing strategies. *Target costing* refers to the process through which both a product and its manufacturing process are designed to allow that product to be manufactured at a desired (target) cost. Thus, target costing efforts occur prior to the beginning of the manufacturing process. If a product can be manufactured at its target cost and sold at a desired selling price (target price), it will provide the organization with a desired profit margin (target margin). *Kaizen costing* refers to the reduction of costs during (and not prior to) the manufacturing process. The term kaizen is drawn from the Japanese philosophy of realizing continual and gradual improvements through relatively small betterment activities.

The following business press excerpts describe the approaches that two companies use to implement a kaizen philosophy in their production efforts.

---

[1] Timothy Aeppel, "Ex-Firestone Workers to Testify in Suit," *The Wall Street Journal* (August 23, 2000), A3.

> Unlike workers at traditional factories who are assigned to operate only a single machine or perform a single function, workers at Westinghouse Air Brake Company's Chicago plant are expected to perform multiple tasks at peak performance levels. Applying the Japanese principle of kaizen, or "continuous improvement," Westinghouse strives to derive from every moment of an employee's day the most productive effort. A typical worker at the plant is responsible for operating three different machines simultaneously, while also checking regularly for defects in finished items.[2]
>
> Pella Corporation, a well-known maker of windows and doors, practices kaizen in a practical way, striving to make immediate changes for the better without becoming obsessed with trying to attain perfection. Pella's standard kaizen session lasts for five days. The kaizen team meets on Monday to discuss the problem at hand. Tuesday is dedicated to brainstorming possible solutions, with Tuesday evenings saved for any trial rearrangements of machinery or facilities. Changes are actually put into effect on Wednesday, with necessary adjustments made as production occurs. On Thursday, the arrangement is finalized so that results, rather than plans, may be presented and reviewed on Friday.[3]

The standard direct material and direct labor cost of manufacturing one football is shown in Illustration 1.

Notice that the above performance standards are expressed in both *quantities* and *dollars*. For example, based on these standards, SportsWorld should require 0.5 yard of leather to manufacture one football; also, each yard of leather should cost SportsWorld $2. As a result, SportsWorld *should* incur $1 of leather costs for each football (0.50 yards x $2 = $1), assuming that its personnel are operating in accordance with the production standard. Similarly, SportsWorld should require 0.15 hours of direct labor to manufacture one football. The average wage rate paid to its workers should be $20 per hour. Therefore, SportsWorld *should* incur $3 in direct labor costs for each football manufactured (0.15 hours x $20 = $3). It is important to point out that both standards appear to be examples of currently attainable standards, since they include allowances for inefficiencies, such as reasonable amounts of both material waste and machine downtime.

Illustration 1
SportsWorld
Standard Direct Materials and Direct Labor Costs: Footballs

Direct Materials (Leather):

Leather for Footballs.............................	0.45 yards x $2	....	$0.90
Allowance for Waste in Trimming Leather	0.05 yards x $2	....	0.10
Total Standard Materials Cost..................	0.50 yards x $2	....	$1.00

Direct Labor:

Direct Labor...	0.14 hours x $20	....	$2.80
Allowance for Machine Downtime	0.01 hours x $20	....	0.20
Total Standard Labor Cost.......................	0.15 hours x $20	....	$3.00

How does SportsWorld establish performance standards for direct materials and direct labor? For quantities, management must obtain information about the manufacturing process by observation of the manufacturing department, discussions and interviews with key manufacturing personnel, and inspection of previous records. These previous records may include Materials Requisitions (which provide information as to the quantity of direct materials used) and Work Tickets (which provide information as to the quantity of direct labor hours worked). In addition, for direct labor standards, time and motion studies may be conducted to determine the time required to perform various tasks. However, simply basing performance standards on this evidence may result in previous inefficiencies being incorporated into the current performance standard. To attempt to improve the

---

[2] Timothy Aeppel, "Rust-Belt Factory Lifts Productivity, and Staff Finds It's No Picnic," *The Wall Street Journal* (May 18, 1999), A1, A10.

[3] Philip Siekman, "Glass Act: How a Window Maker Rebuilt Itself," *Fortune* (November 13, 2000), 384[F].

efficiency of the manufacturing process, management may "adjust" the data based on past performance to make the standard more stringent (i.e., allow smaller quantities of direct materials and fewer direct labor hours).

A unique approach to establishing time standards for production line changeovers is described in the following excerpt from the business press.

> When General Mills CEO Steve Sanger sought to make production-line changes more efficient, he looked to the experts. He sent General Mills technicians to the NASCAR races in North Carolina to observe the pit crews in action. When the technicians applied the techniques they had learned from the pit crews to General Mills' lines, they were able to drive down the line changeover time from five hours to 20 minutes.[4]

In establishing a price standard for direct materials and direct labor, management evaluates current market conditions that influence the price (or cost) of these inputs.[5] This may include reviewing recent purchases of leather made by SportsWorld (for direct material prices) and contracts or union agreements (for direct labor prices). It is critical that management specify the quality of materials and labor inputs required prior to establishing the price standard, since higher desired qualities will ordinarily result in higher standard prices. In addition, factors such as additional charges for rush orders of direct materials and overtime premiums paid for direct labor should be considered in establishing direct materials and direct labor price standards.

Examples of performance standards used in greatly different time periods are illustrated below.

> The records of Thomas Jefferson (the third president of the United States) provide an early example of the use of performance standards. For example, the following are some performance standards related to direct labor established by Thomas Jefferson for producing nails.
>
> | | |
> |---|---|
> | A worker with six months of experience | 500 nails per day |
> | A worker with one year of experience | 600 nails per day |
> | The "best" worker | 884 nails per day[6] |
>
> An unusual example of a "direct materials" standard is that used by an unnamed Las Vegas casino in preparing drinks. This casino has developed a performance standard of 1.5 ounces of alcohol per drink. Therefore, bartenders are expected to serve 21.3 drinks from a 32 ounce bottle of alcohol (32 ÷ 1.5 ounces = 21.3 drinks).[7]
>
> United Parcel Service tells drivers how fast to walk (three feet per second), how many packages to deliver daily (approximately 400), how to hold their keys (in their third finger with the teeth of their keys facing upward), and to knock on customer's doors to reduce the time spent searching for doorbells. Each of these standards attempts to reduce the time necessary to deliver parcels to UPS customers.[8]

Manufacturing Overhead Costs

When establishing performance standards for manufacturing overhead costs, the fact that overhead costs include both fixed and variable components must be considered. As with direct materials and direct labor standards, SportsWorld would conduct a review of previous overhead costs and activity. However, because overhead costs include both fixed and variable components, each of these costs must be classified in terms of its behavior (i.e., fixed or variable) with respect to the appropriate activity (cost driver). As with direct materials and direct labor standards, SportsWorld may wish to establish its performance standards for overhead costs at a more demanding level than historical activity in order to improve the efficiency of the manufacturing process.

---

[4] Julie Forster, "The Lucky Charm of Steve Sanger," *Business Week* (March 26, 2001), 76.

[5] The terms "price" and "cost" are often used interchangeably when discussing performance standards for direct materials and direct labor. We use the term *"price"* to refer to the consideration paid for direct materials or direct labor on a per unit basis (quantity of direct material or hour of direct labor). The term *"cost"* is used to refer to the product of input prices and input quantities.

[6] E.M. Betts (editor), *Thomas Jefferson's Farm Book* (Princeton University Press 1953), 110.

[7] J.H. Bullock, "How Las Vegas Casinos Budget," *Management Accounting* (July 1980), 35–39.

[8] "As UPS Tries to Deliver More to Its Customers, Labor Problems Grow," *The Wall Street Journal* (May 23, 1994), A1.

Assume that SportsWorld has completed a comprehensive analysis of its overhead costs and identified the behavior of those costs with respect to changes in the cost driver. Because SportsWorld's manufacturing process is machine intensive, it has selected machine hours as the appropriate cost driver. Recall from our earlier discussion of activity-based costing that, in practice, a large number of different cost drivers can be used to apply overhead costs to production. To focus on the development and use of performance standards, this chapter assumes that SportsWorld uses machine hours as its sole cost driver. The nature of SportsWorld's manufacturing overhead costs is summarized in Illustration 2.

Illustration 2

SportsWorld
Behavior of Overhead Costs

Variable Costs (per Machine Hour):

Indirect Labor (Maintenance and Repairs)	$14
Utilities	15
Indirect Materials and Supplies	1
Total Variable Cost (per Machine Hour)	$30

Fixed Costs (January 20x1):

Depreciation on Plant and Equipment	$10,000
Indirect Labor (Setup, Supervision, and Inspection)	8,000
Insurance and Taxes	2,000
Total Fixed Cost	$20,000

The overhead cost data in Illustration 2 reflect two basic relationships between cost and activity. First, variable overhead costs increase directly and proportionately with increases in activity. SportsWorld's variable overhead cost per machine hour is $30; thus, for each additional machine hour worked by SportsWorld, overhead costs are expected to increase by $30. Second, SportsWorld anticipated total fixed overhead costs of $20,000 in January 20x1, which are not expected to vary with changes in the cost driver (machine hours).

Once the behavior of overhead costs has been identified, a performance standard (in the form of a predetermined overhead rate) can be established by SportsWorld. To illustrate, assume that the normal production capacity for SportsWorld is 8,000 footballs per month and that SportsWorld has developed a standard of 0.25 machine hours per football. Thus, SportsWorld's normal production activity (capacity) can be expressed as either 8,000 footballs or 2,000 machine hours (8,000 footballs x 0.25 machine hours = 2,000 machine hours).

Based on the above manufacturing capacity, as well as the fixed and variable cost information shown in Illustration 2, the standard predetermined overhead rate used by SportsWorld is $40 per machine hour, as calculated below:

Variable Overhead	$30
Fixed Overhead ($20,000 ÷ 2,000 Machine Hours)	10
Predetermined Overhead Rate	$40

Alternatively, the predetermined overhead rate could be expressed in terms of the overhead cost per football. Recalling that SportsWorld's capacity is 8,000 footballs and that each football should require 0.25 machine hours, the standard predetermined overhead rate per football would be $10, as follows:

Variable Overhead ($30.00 x 0.25 Machine Hours)	$ 7.50
Fixed Overhead ($20,000 ÷ 8,000 Footballs)	2.50
Predetermined Overhead Rate	$10.00

The relationship between these two performance standards reflects the fact that the standard activity per football is 0.25 machine hours. This relationship is depicted below:

| Standard Overhead Rate Per Machine Hour | x | Standard Machine Hours per Football | = | Standard Overhead Rate per Football |

The standard overhead rate per machine hour can be converted to a standard overhead rate per football by multiplying the standard overhead rate per machine hour by the standard number of machine hours per football ($40 per machine hour x 0.25 machine hours per football = $10 per football). Alternatively, the standard overhead rate per football can be converted to a standard overhead rate per machine hour by dividing the standard overhead rate per football by the standard machine hours per football ($10 per football ÷ 0.25 machine hours per football = $40 per machine hour).

VARIANCE ANALYSIS: DIRECT MATERIALS AND DIRECT LABOR COSTS

In a standard costing system, the difference between the actual costs of manufacturing inventory or providing services and the costs that should be incurred based on performance standards (standard costs) is referred to as a *variance*. Variances are important, because management can use them to identify potential inefficiencies in the manufacturing process. Using variances in this fashion is an example of *management by exception*. Under management by exception, an organization's managers focus on those areas of the organization's operations that are not functioning as intended.

In general, a total variance can be decomposed into two components for further analysis as shown below:

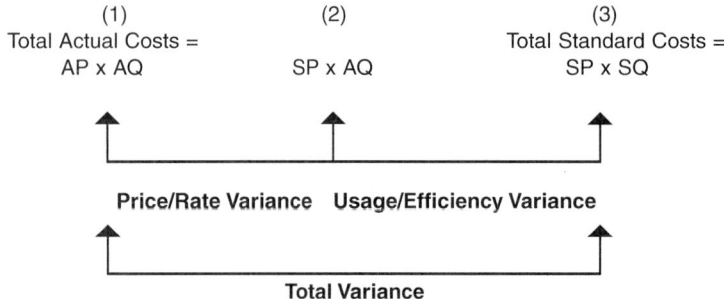

The total variance is the difference between the actual costs and standard costs. Actual costs can be viewed as the actual quantity of an input used (AQ) multiplied by the average actual price (cost) of that input (AP). Similarly, standard costs can be viewed as the standard quantity of an input allowed (SQ) multiplied by the standard price (cost) of that input (SP). Therefore, the difference between points (1) and (3) above represents the total variance.

From the above discussion, it is apparent that variances arise because of two factors. First, the actual price (cost) of the input may differ from the standard price (cost). While the terms are used somewhat interchangeably in practice, this difference is normally referred to as a *price variance* (for direct materials costs) or a *rate variance* (for direct labor costs). To illustrate, recall that SportsWorld has established a standard cost of its leather of $2 per yard. If excess demand for leather results in shortages in supply, the actual cost paid by SportsWorld would likely exceed this standard. In contrast, if SportsWorld purchased leather from vendors in large quantities, they would likely receive a bulk purchase discount, which may result in the actual cost being less than the $2 standard cost. Similarly, if SportsWorld utilized the services of either more- or less-skilled laborers in the production of footballs, the actual labor cost may differ from the standard labor cost of $20 per hour.

Comparing points (1) and (2) in the above diagram reveals that both amounts are based on the actual quantity of inputs (AQ). In contrast, point (1) is based on the actual cost or price of the input (AP), while point (2) is based on the standard cost or price of the input (SP). This difference represents the price/rate variance, which is calculated using the following formula:

| Price or Rate Variance | = | (AP x AQ) – (SP x AQ) |
| | = | AQ x (AP – SP) |

A second explanation of the difference between actual and standard costs is based on differences in the quantity of the inputs used. That is, the actual quantity of direct materials used or direct labor hours worked may differ from the standard quantity of direct materials or direct labor hours allowed. To illustrate, SportsWorld's use of skilled workers may result in more efficient use of leather and, therefore, less materials waste. If so, the actual quantity of leather used may be less than the standard of 0.50 yard per football. Similarly, skilled workers would presumably be more efficient in manufacturing footballs, resulting in fewer direct labor hours worked than the standard 0.15 hours per football.

Variances arising from differences in the quantity of inputs used are referred to as *usage variances* (for direct materials costs) or *efficiency variances* (for direct labor costs). Comparing the costs represented by points (2) and (3) in the preceding diagram reveals that both are based on standard costs or prices (SP). However, the cost represented by point (2) is based on actual quantities (AQ), while the cost represented by point (3) is based on standard quantities allowed (SQ). Based on the preceding diagram, the usage/efficiency variance can be determined by using the following formula:

$$\text{Usage or Efficiency Variance} = (SP \times AQ) - (SP \times SQ)$$
$$= SP \times (AQ - SQ)$$

To illustrate the calculation of direct materials and direct labor variances for SportsWorld, assume that it manufactured a total of 10,000 footballs during January 20x1. The following information was determined by reference to SportsWorld's accounting records for that month:

Direct Materials (Leather) Purchased (6,000 yards x $2.10 per yard).........................	$12,600
Direct Materials (Leather) Used in Production	4,800 yards
Direct Labor Costs (1,400 hours x $22.50 per hour)	$31,500

Direct Material Variances

Given the actual manufacturing data, as well as the performance standards for direct materials, SportsWorld can calculate its total direct materials variance. Recall that the material standards for each football have been established at the following level (see Illustration 1):

	Quantity		Cost		Total Cost
Leather........................	0.50 yd	x	$2	=	$1

Since 10,000 footballs were produced during January 20x1 and the standard materials quantity per football was 0.50 yard of leather, the standard quantity of leather allowed is 5,000 yards (10,000 footballs x 0.50 yard per football = 5,000 yards). The total direct materials variance can be decomposed into its price and usage variance as shown in Illustration 3.

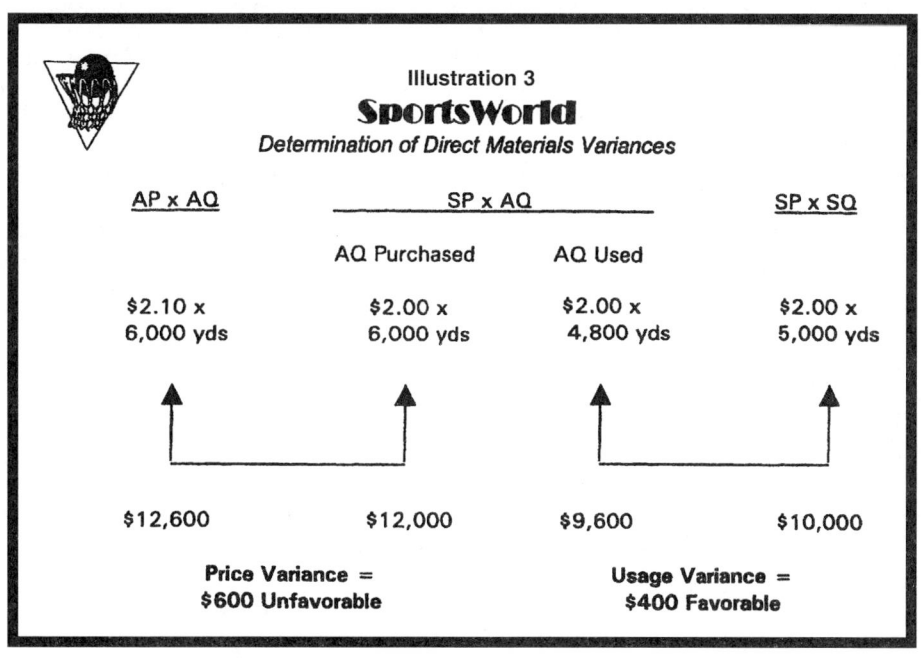

Alternatively, these variances can be calculated using the formulas as follows:

Direct Materials Price Variance	=	AQ x (AP – SP)
	=	6,000 yds. x ($2.10 – $2.00)
	=	$600 Unfavorable
Direct Materials Usage Variance	=	SP x (AQ – SQ)
	=	$2 x (4,800 yds. – 5,000 yds.)
	=	$400 Favorable

Examining the direct materials price variance, the actual price paid by SportsWorld for its leather ($2.10) exceeds the standard price ($2). As a result, this variance is *unfavorable*, because it reflects the fact that actual direct materials costs are higher than standard costs. With respect to the direct materials usage variance, the actual yards of leather used in the production of the 10,000 footballs (4,800 yards) was less than the standard quantity allowed (10,000 footballs x 0.50 yards per football = 5,000 yards). Therefore, the direct materials usage variance is considered to be *favorable*, since the seemingly efficient use of direct materials has resulted in lower direct materials costs than expected.

Who is responsible for these variances? Normally, SportsWorld's purchasing agent (or purchasing department) should be held responsible for the direct materials price variance. Presumably, these individuals should be in a position to select vendors, negotiate prices with vendors, and anticipate events in the marketplace to secure favorable prices for the direct materials inputs. Initially, the $600 unfavorable direct materials price variance suggests that the purchasing agent (or department) has performed in a substandard manner. However, conditions should be carefully evaluated prior to charging these individual(s) with the above variance. For example, assume that SportsWorld decided to significantly increase its January production of footballs late in December because of unexpectedly high levels of sales during the holiday season. In response to this late increase in production, SportsWorld's purchasing agent may have been required to pay a premium price in order to ensure prompt shipment of sufficient leather for use in manufacturing the footballs. Similarly, an unexpectedly low supply of leather that is totally beyond these individual(s)' control may result in higher costs that could not have been foreseen. In any case, the underlying reason(s) behind this variance should be carefully investigated.

The following excerpt, which describes the potential effects of a proposal to increase the regulation of international cargo, illustrates the type of uncontrollable cost increase that might lead to an unfavorable price variance for material purchases.

> **U.S. freight carriers and manufacturers have expressed concern over recent proposals to increase regulation of international cargo. The new rules, which are intended to help thwart terrorist activities, require that transportation companies alert the Bureau of Customs and Border Protection by computer or fax about the contents and recipients of international cargo in advance of its delivery to the U.S., with specific advance notification requirements that vary by mode of transport. The American Electronics Association, a trade group which includes Intel Corporation and Motorola Corporation, estimates that the changes will add from $4 to $6 to the cost of a typical international parcel delivery.[9]**

The direct materials usage variance is ordinarily the responsibility of the production supervisor (or foreman), since this individual is in a position to observe the efficient (or inefficient) use of direct materials. In the above SportsWorld example, the favorable variance of $400 suggests that the production department has performed efficiently in terms of using direct materials to manufacture footballs. However, when interpreting the direct materials usage variance, the following factors should also be considered.

- Quality of the direct materials purchased. In general, higher quality materials should result in lower levels of waste and a favorable direct materials usage variance.

- Skill level of the direct labor. As the organization utilizes more skilled direct laborers, the level of waste of direct materials should be reduced, resulting in a favorable direct materials usage variance.

---

[9] Rick Brooks, "Shippers Say New Border Rules Could Delay Just-in-Time Cargo," *The Wall Street Journal* (August 29, 2003), A1, A10.

- Overall quality of the product. Higher quality products ordinarily require the use of greater quantities of direct materials, resulting in an unfavorable direct materials usage variance.

Another point that should be emphasized in the above calculations is the actual quantities used in calculating the direct materials price and usage variances. Notice that the direct materials price variance uses the *actual quantity of direct materials purchased.* This is because when the purchasing agent or purchasing department pays a higher or lower price for direct materials than the performance standard, that higher or lower price is paid for material purchased and not just the material used in production. In the SportsWorld example shown above, the $0.10 additional cost per yard of leather ($2.10 − $2.00 = $0.10) has been incurred for all 6,000 yards of leather that were purchased in January, not just the 4,800 yards used in production. Basing the direct materials price variance on the quantity of direct materials purchased isolates that variance at the point at which it occurs.

In contrast, the direct materials usage variance is based on the *actual quantity of direct materials used in production.* Recall that this variance attempts to measure the efficiency of the production supervisor (and production department) in using direct materials. Thus, this variance should be based on the direct materials used in production and not the amount of direct materials purchased from vendors. In the above example, the direct materials usage variance reflects the difference of the actual materials used in production (4,800 yards) and not the materials purchased from vendors (6,000 yards).

Direct Labor Variances

The total direct labor variance can be decomposed into price/rate and usage/efficiency variances in a manner similar to the total direct materials variance. Recall that SportsWorld's actual direct labor costs for January 20x1 totaled $31,500, based on 1,400 actual direct labor hours worked during the month and an average wage rate of $22.50 per direct labor hour (1,400 hours x $22.50 = $31,500). Recall that 10,000 footballs were manufactured during January 20x1 and the direct labor standards for each football have been established as follows (see Illustration 1):

	Quantity		Cost		Total Cost
Direct Labor...	0.15 hrs	x	$20	=	$3

Thus, the standard quantity of direct labor hours allowed for the production of 10,000 footballs is 1,500 (0.15 hours x 10,000 footballs = 1,500 hours). The total direct labor variance can be calculated by taking the difference between the actual direct labor costs and standard direct labor costs and would be $1,500, as shown below.[10] Since actual direct labor costs incurred exceed standard direct labor costs allowed, this variance would be considered to be unfavorable.

Standard Direct Labor Costs ($20 per hr. x 1,500 hrs.)..	$30,000
Actual Direct Labor Costs..	(31,500)
Direct Labor Variance	$ 1,500 Unfavorable

The total direct labor variance can be decomposed into its rate and efficiency components, as shown in Illustration 4. Note that this decomposition is similar to that used for the direct materials variance (Illustration 3), with the exception that only one actual quantity (actual quantity of direct labor hours worked) is utilized in the calculations:

Alternatively, these variances may be calculated using the following formulas:

Direct Labor Rate Variance	=	AQ x (AP − SP)
	=	1,400 hrs. x ($22.50 − $20.00)
	=	$3,500 Unfavorable
Direct Labor Efficiency Variance	=	SP x (AQ − SQ)
	=	$20 x (1,400 hrs. − 1,500 hrs.)
	=	$2,000 Favorable

---

[10] Because the direct materials price variance is based on actual quantities purchased and the direct materials usage variance is based on actual quantities used, a similar calculation is not made to determine the overall direct materials variance. Since different individuals or departments are responsible for the two direct materials variances, these variances are ordinarily not combined to form an overall direct materials variance having any significant meaning.

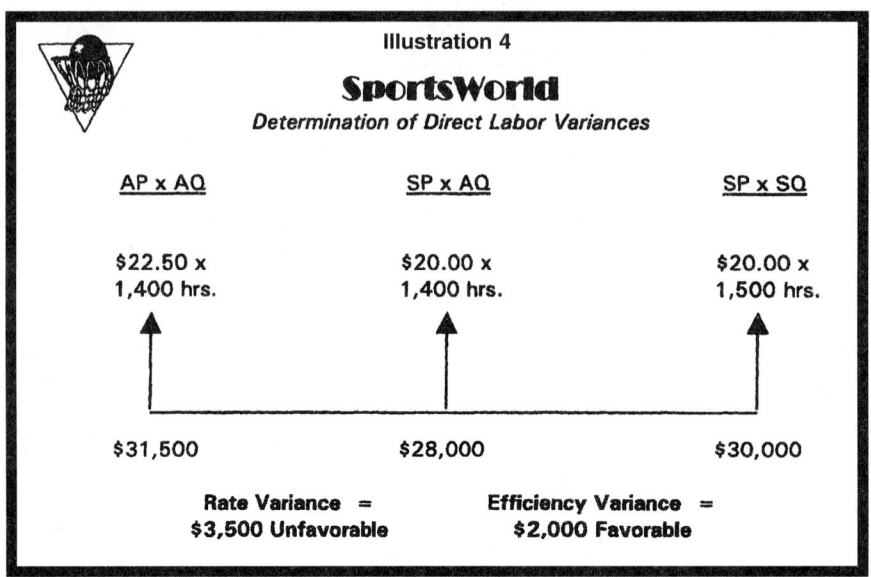

The interpretation of the above variances is similar to that for the direct materials variances. For the direct labor rate variance, the actual wage rate paid to SportsWorld's production workers ($22.50) is higher than the standard wage rate ($20). As a result, this variance is unfavorable because it reflects the fact that actual direct labor costs exceed standard direct labor costs. Conversely, the actual direct labor hours worked (1,400 hours) are less than the standard direct labor hours allowed (1,500 hours); therefore, the direct labor efficiency variance is favorable. This variance is favorable since working fewer direct labor hours than the standard allowed results in lower actual direct labor costs than standard direct labor costs. Note that the net of these two variances accounts for the total direct labor variance calculated earlier in this section ($3,500 unfavorable − $2,000 favorable = $1,500 unfavorable).

Who is responsible for the above variances? Since direct labor variances are related to the manufacturing process, these variances are the responsibility of the production supervisor. The production supervisor is ordinarily responsible for decisions regarding the mix of production workers utilized in the manufacturing process. As more skilled (and highly paid) workers are utilized, unfavorable direct labor rate variances should result. However, the trade-off is that these employees should perform more efficiently, resulting in a favorable direct labor efficiency variance (and vice versa). Note that this possibility is reflected in the above direct labor variances for SportsWorld. The unfavorable direct labor rate variance results from the use of employees earning higher wages than the performance standard. However, these employees worked fewer direct labor hours than the performance standard. In addition to influencing the mix of direct labor utilized in the manufacturing process, the production supervisor may be able to influence the efficient use of direct labor through work scheduling and motivating employees to achieve manufacturing goals.

Despite the production supervisor's influence in the manufacturing process, care should be taken in interpreting favorable and unfavorable direct labor variances. Some examples of extenuating circumstances that may affect the direct labor rate and direct labor efficiency variances include:

- The decision to accept "rush orders" or use a just-in-time manufacturing philosophy may result in the need to pay overtime premiums to manufacturing employees. These overtime premiums would typically result in unfavorable direct labor rate variances.

- Unusual equipment failures, machine setup delays, and material shortages may result in excessive idle time for manufacturing employees, which would typically result in an unfavorable direct labor efficiency variance.

- Decisions to purchase lower quality materials in order to receive a more favorable price may require more highly skilled manufacturing employees and may require additional time in the manufacturing process. In this case, the organization would likely incur unfavorable direct labor rate and direct labor efficiency variances.

COST ACCUMULATION IN A STANDARD COSTING SYSTEM

In a standard costing system, manufacturing costs are accumulated with production based on *standard* (not actual) manufacturing costs. This feature of a standard costing system simplifies the cost accumulation process since an organization can use a single (standard) cost to accumulate its direct materials, direct labor, and overhead costs with production. Assume that SportsWorld began January 20x1 with 500 yards of leather that were purchased for $1.80 per yard during December 20x0. As previously noted, SportsWorld purchased 6,000 additional yards of leather during January at a price of $2.10 per yard. Since 4,800 yards of leather were used to manufacture footballs during January 20x1, SportsWorld had 1,700 yards of leather in inventory at the end of January (500 yards + 6,000 yards – 4,800 yards =1,700 yards).

While the quantity of direct materials inventory can be determined by a physical count, determining the cost of this inventory is somewhat more problematic. Under an actual costing system, SportsWorld would make certain assumptions regarding the cost of materials issued into production. For example, does the ending materials inventory represent materials purchased during January or some combination of materials on hand at the beginning of January and materials purchased during January? In determining the ending balance in direct materials inventory and the cost of materials issued into production, organizations must keep numerous records when the cost of materials inputs changes. Similar issues arise for the work-in-process and finished goods inventory accounts when the costs of direct labor inputs and manufacturing overhead inputs change during the period. Under a standard costing system, this issue does not arise since all materials are maintained in the accounts at the standard cost per unit ($2 per yard). Therefore, one advantage involved with the use of a standard costing system is simplified recordkeeping.

Purchase of Direct Materials. Standard costing systems are similar to actual costing systems. The sole difference is that the standard (and not actual) manufacturing costs are accumulated with inventory. However, the flow of costs through the inventory and cost of goods sold accounts is identical. To illustrate the use of a standard costing system, recall the manufacturing activity of SportsWorld during January 20x1—the cost data and amounts of variances were determined in previous sections of this chapter. Recall that SportsWorld purchased 6,000 yards of leather during January 20x1 at a price of $2.10 per yard. Also, recall that the standard price per yard of leather is $2. The following journal entry would be used to record the purchase of direct materials in January 20x1:

```
Direct Materials—Control (6,000 yds. x $2) .................................................. 12,000
Direct Materials Price Variance................................................................         600
    Accounts Payable (6,000 yds. x $2.10) ..............................................                12,600
```

As in an actual costing system, purchases of direct materials inventory are initially recorded in the Direct Materials-Control account. Note that the Direct Materials-Control account is maintained at the standard cost of the materials purchased ($12,000) and that the accounts payable is recorded at the actual amount of the purchase ($12,600), since this is the amount that will eventually be paid by SportsWorld. The difference between these two amounts represents the unfavorable direct materials price variance of $600. Notice that unfavorable variances are recorded with a debit to the variance account. In a sense, unfavorable variances can be considered as being similar to expenses (which also have a debit balance).

Issuance of Direct Materials to Production. Following the purchase of direct materials, SportsWorld issued 4,800 yards of materials to production. The standard material allowed for the production of the 10,000 footballs was 5,000 yards (10,000 footballs x 0.50 yards = 5,000 yards). The following journal entry records the issuance of direct materials to production:

```
Work-in-Process—Control (5,000 yds. x $2) ............................................. 10,000
    Direct Materials Usage Variance......................................................            400
    Direct Materials—Control (4,800 yds. x $2) .....................................          9,600
```

As in an actual costing system, the issuance of direct materials to production is recorded by increasing (debiting) work-in-process inventory and decreasing (crediting) direct materials inventory. Notice that this journal entry accumulates direct materials costs with work-in-process inventory at the standard material costs (both price and quantity of materials) for the units produced. In addition, the direct materials inventory is reduced for the actual quantity of materials issued to production at the standard price of those materials. Thus, both the direct materials and work-in-process inventory accounts are maintained at standard costs. Finally, notice that the favorable material usage variance has a credit balance. In a sense, favorable variances can be considered as being similar to revenues (which also have a credit balance).

Accumulation of Direct Labor Costs with Production. Similar to direct materials costs, direct labor costs are also accumulated with work-in-process inventory. In a standard costing system, these costs are accumulated at standard (and not actual) costs. Recall that the standard direct labor costs required for SportsWorld to manufacture 10,000 footballs were $30,000 (10,000 footballs x 0.15 hours per football x $20 per hour = $30,000) and that actual direct labor costs incurred were $31,500. In addition, the previous variance analysis revealed an unfavorable direct labor rate variance of $3,500 and a favorable direct labor efficiency variance of $2,000. The following journal entry records the accumulation of direct labor costs with work-in-process inventory in a standard costing system:

Work-in-Process—Control	30,000	
Direct Labor Rate Variance	3,500	
Direct Labor Efficiency Variance		2,000
Wages Payable		31,500

Completion of Production. At this point, the 10,000 footballs are completed and ready for sale to the organization's customers. As in an actual costing system, the costs of these 10,000 footballs are transferred from work-in-process inventory to finished goods inventory; however, a standard costing system records this transfer at the standard (and not actual) manufacturing costs. SportsWorld's standard cost per football is $14, as follows:

Direct Materials (see Illustration 1)	$ 1
Direct Labor (see Illustration 1)	3
Manufacturing Overhead ($40 per machine hour x 0.25 machine hrs. per football)	10
Total Standard Cost per Football	$14

The journal entry to record the completion of the 10,000 footballs and transfer the associated cost from work-in-process inventory to finished goods inventory is as follows:

Finished Goods—Control (10,000 footballs x $14)	140,000	
Work-in-Process—Control		140,000

Sale of Inventory. Finally, assume that 8,000 of these footballs were sold to customers at a price of $25 per football. In addition to recognizing revenue on the sale of the footballs, SportsWorld would also transfer the cost of these footballs from finished goods inventory to cost of goods sold. In a standard costing system, this transfer would be made using the standard manufacturing cost per football ($14).

Accounts Receivable (8,000 footballs x $25)	200,000	
Sales Revenue		200,000
Cost of Goods Sold (8,000 footballs x $14)	112,000	
Finished Goods—Control		112,000

Closing Variance Accounts and Adjusting for Differences Between Standard and Actual Costs. At this point, SportsWorld's direct materials inventory, work-in-process inventory, finished goods inventory, and cost of goods sold accounts are maintained at standard manufacturing costs. In addition, several variances have been recorded within the standard costing system used by SportsWorld. These variances are summarized below ("F" denotes favorable variances and "U" denotes unfavorable variances):

Direct Materials Price Variance	$ 600 U
Direct Materials Usage Variance	400 F
Direct Labor Rate Variance	3,500 U
Direct Labor Efficiency Variance	2,000 F

While SportsWorld has simplified its recordkeeping process by using a standard costing system, the end result is that its inventory (direct materials, work-in-process, and finished goods) and cost of goods sold accounts are recorded using standard, not actual, costs. If differences between actual and standard costs are material in amount, the use of standard costs is not acceptable under GAAP for external reporting purposes. To approximate the use of an actual costing system, SportsWorld can close the variances (which represent the difference between actual and standard costs) to either:

- Cost of goods sold
- Direct materials inventory, work-in-process inventory, finished goods inventory, and cost of goods sold, based on the relative balances in these accounts.

Closing the variances in either of the above ways basically "adjusts" the accounts for differences between standard and actual costs. In most cases, if variances are not material in amount, they will be closed directly to cost of goods sold. Assuming that the variances are closed directly to cost of goods sold, the following entry would be prepared:

Cost of Goods Sold	1,700	
Direct Materials Usage Variance	400	
Direct Labor Efficiency Variance	2,000	
Direct Materials Price Variance		600
Direct Labor Rate Variance		3,500

In this example, notice that closing the materials and labor variances to cost of goods sold increases cost of goods sold by $1,700. Because the overall net effect of these variances was unfavorable, actual manufacturing costs were higher than standard manufacturing costs. When standard manufacturing costs are less than actual manufacturing costs (as in this example), the organization recognizes lower cost of goods sold than if actual manufacturing costs were accumulated with inventory. In essence, the journal entry to close the variance accounts increases cost of goods sold to reflect the fact that a lesser amount of materials and labor costs have been accumulated in inventory (and will eventually be recognized as cost of goods sold when the inventory is sold to customers).

An example of the use of a standard cost system from practice is summarized below:

> Dutch Pantry, Inc. is a chain of full-service restaurants operating in the eastern United States. Dutch Pantry uses a standard costing system to record the flow of costs as food is prepared. For example, the costs of direct materials, packaging, and ingredients are calculated by the use of a recipe sheet that accumulates the amount of materials that should be used in preparing various dishes.[11]

RECENT DEVELOPMENTS IN THE MANUFACTURING ENVIRONMENT

Several recent developments in the manufacturing environment have important implications for establishing and evaluating performance standards. These developments are briefly discussed below. It is important to note that these developments influence both the interpretation of variances of actual manufacturing costs from standard manufacturing costs as well as the level of the performance standards established by the organization.

Highly Automated Manufacturing Processes. As manufacturing processes become highly automated, the composition of the organization's cost structure shifts from relatively high direct labor costs (in a manual manufacturing environment) to relatively high overhead costs (in an automated manufacturing environment). As a result, the significance of direct labor costs (and the accompanying variances) declines as the organization's manufacturing process becomes more highly automated. In such cases, the analysis of direct labor variances is either ignored or combined with the analysis of overhead variances. When combined with overhead, many organizations determine standard "conversion costs" and compare these to the combined actual direct labor and manufacturing overhead costs incurred.

Just-in-Time (JIT) Manufacturing. In JIT manufacturing environments, production is initiated based on customer demand, and inventories of both direct materials and finished goods are maintained at relatively low levels. As a result, when operating in this type of environment, organizations frequently need to manufacture inventory with relatively short lead times. These short lead times often result in the need to incur additional direct materials costs (in the form of additional charges for "rush" orders) and direct labor costs (in the form of overtime premiums paid to workers), ultimately resulting in unfavorable direct materials price and direct labor rate variances, respectively. In addition, manufacturing based on customer demand will not allow the production supervisor to influence the efficient use of manufacturing capacity, rendering the fixed overhead volume variance meaningless. The fixed overhead volume variance is discussed in the appendix to this chapter.

---

[11] D.M. Boll, "How Dutch Pantry Accounts for Standard Costs," *Management Accounting* (December 1982), 32-35.

> Companies using lean manufacturing practices and just-in-time inventory methods have discovered that it can be very difficult to handle unanticipated surges in product demand. Because lean manufacturing systems leave little margin for error, responding to unexpected levels of customer demand often results in excessive overtime costs, expensive overnight shipments, neglect of machinery maintenance and repair and high worker-turnover rates.[12]

Value- and Non-Value-Added Activities. The focus on reducing (or, in some cases, eliminating) non-value-added activities influences the overhead costs incurred by the organization. Efficient scheduling of manufacturing activities, along with implementation of a JIT manufacturing philosophy, often reduces the overhead costs associated with materials storage and transfer, machine setup, and product inspection. These cost reductions result in favorable variable and fixed overhead spending variances and may require adjustment of the performance standards for manufacturing overhead costs. In addition, more efficient scheduling of manufacturing activities may result in the ability to manufacture inventory using fewer machine hours, resulting in a favorable variable overhead efficiency variance. (The variable overhead spending variance, fixed overhead spending variance, and variable overhead efficiency variance are discussed in the appendix to this chapter).

The following examples from practice describe actions that companies have taken to eliminate non-value-added activities and associated costs.

> Delta Consolidated, a maker of plastic toolboxes for pickup trucks owned by Danaher Corporation, formerly allowed finished boxes to "cure" for 48 hours on the assembly floor. When the company learned that it actually took only 20 minutes for these boxes to cure, its manufacturing process was greatly shortened. Reducing the curing process allowed production to be moved to a space one-eighth of the size of the previous area and eliminated work-in process inventory.[13]
>
> By changing the construction of the overhead bin frames on its 747, Boeing was able to reduce the weight of the plane by 175 pounds. According to the supervisor responsible for the change, if that reduction in weight allows an airline to sell one more seat, "there's $200,000 a year [per plane] in extra revenue for them." The same supervisor cut the assembly time for landing gear supports, and the associated parts supply, from an average of 40 days to 12 days, significantly reducing its inventory carrying costs.[14]

Total Quality Management (TQM). To this point, the focus in evaluating SportsWorld's manufacturing efforts has been based exclusively on financial considerations, such as the level of direct materials, direct labor, and manufacturing overhead costs incurred relative to the performance standard. Obviously, if manufacturing costs are minimized to the detriment of product quality, the organization will suffer rather than benefit in the long run. Total quality management (TQM) reflects an organization-wide philosophy that attempts to enhance the quality of products or services provided to the organization's customers. TQM attempts to minimize the overall costs of providing the organization's products or services while enhancing the quality of these products or services by explicitly considering the costs associated with substandard products (referred to as *failure costs*). Under TQM, the organization views costs incurred to ensure high quality products or services (such as inspection and testing costs) as worthwhile if these costs are less than the costs associated with inferior products (such as the costs of reworking products, the costs of honoring product warranties, and the costs of processing customer returns).

The following excerpt illustrates the devastating consequences that can result from a failure to consider the costs of a substandard production system.

---

[12] Peter Galuszka and Stephanie Forest-Anderson, "Just-In-Time Manufacturing is Working Overtime," *Business Week* (November 8, 1999), 36–37.

[13] Brandon Copple, "The Forbes Platinum List: Capital Goods," *Forbes* (January 10, 2000), 100.

[14] Stephane Fitch, "Reengineering 101," *Forbes* (May 13, 2002), 88.

> In October of 1997, massive production problems led Boeing to announce a $2.6 billion charge to earnings—the biggest write-off in the company's history. Boeing was not adequately prepared for the huge influx of orders that accompanied the economic recovery in the early 1990s, and its antiquated parts-tracking system couldn't keep up with the increased production volume. Negative production performance indicators, such as overtime, parts shortages, rework, defective parts, and out-of-sequence work, increased to the point where orders could not be delivered on time, and enormous late fees were incurred.[15]

How does TQM affect the development of performance standards and interpretation of the resulting variances? While unfavorable direct materials, direct labor, and manufacturing overhead variances seem to imply substandard performance, these variances may actually be beneficial to the organization as a whole if they result in higher-quality products or services. Similarly, favorable variances may actually be detrimental to the organization if the cost savings results in lower quality products or services. For example, the favorable direct materials usage variance of $400 (see Illustration 3) would be viewed negatively by SportsWorld's management if they incurred $750 of costs in replacing defective footballs and processing customer returns.

Activity-Based Costing (ABC). Throughout this chapter, SportsWorld's performance standards and overhead variances were determined using a single cost driver (machine hours). While this assumption was used to focus on the determination of variances in a standard costing system, many organizations use multiple cost drivers to apply overhead to production under activity-based costing (ABC) systems. The classification of overhead costs as fixed or variable is clearly dependent upon the cost driver selected by the organization. For example, while SportsWorld's costs of indirect labor relating to machine setups are classified as fixed using machine hours as a cost driver (see Illustration 2), this cost would be classified as variable using the number of setups as a cost driver.

If organizations use ABC systems, the analysis of overhead variances discussed in the appendix to this chapter is modified to (1) reclassify overhead costs based on the cost driver(s) used by the organization and (2) accommodate a number of different cost drivers. To illustrate, if SportsWorld added a second cost driver (the number of machine setups), the estimated machine setup costs would be reclassified as a variable overhead cost and would be applied to production based on the standard number of machine setups. Similar to other variable overhead costs, the level of setup costs that should be incurred based on the actual number of machine setups would be determined to identify the spending and efficiency variances related to machine setup costs. This would result in a separate analysis of variable overhead costs for each cost driver identified by the organization. Further analysis and discussion of this issue is beyond the scope of this text.

BENEFITS OF PERFORMANCE STANDARDS AND STANDARD COSTING

The use of performance standards and standard costing systems provides several benefits to the organization, including the following:

1. **Recordkeeping.** Because standard costing systems accumulate the costs of manufacturing inventory or providing services at standard (and not actual) costs, organizations are not required to recalculate the costs of their products or services for recordkeeping purposes each time the costs of direct materials, direct labor, or manufacturing overhead inputs change. This feature of standard costing systems results in a direct savings to the organization (in the form of decreased recordkeeping costs).

2. **Employee Performance Evaluation.** While certain limitations should be considered, the use of performance standards provides employees with an indication of the organization's expectations against which their subsequent performance can be evaluated. In addition, performance standards may be used in a motivational sense to encourage the organization's employees to perform their duties in an efficient manner.

3. **Planning.** The organization can use direct materials and direct labor quantity standards to ensure that sufficient direct materials inventory and direct labor workers are available to meet future production needs. For example, given SportsWorld's planned activity of 8,000 footballs in January, it needs to ensure that 4,000 yards of leather (0.50 yard per football x 8,000 footballs = 4,000 yards) and 1,200 hours of direct labor (0.15 hours per football x 8,000 footballs = 1,200 hours) are available for use in the manufacturing process.

---

[15] Stanley Holmes and Mike France, "Boeing's Secret," *Business Week* (May 20, 2002), 110–120.

4. Improved Short-Term Decisions. An advantage of using performance standards and standard costing systems is that short-term decisions are not unduly influenced by temporary changes in the organization's cost structure. For example, assume that extraordinary circumstances resulted in shortages in the supply of leather and that SportsWorld was required to pay $3.50 per yard for leather during January. If an actual costing system was used to determine a cost per unit manufactured, SportsWorld may unnecessarily raise the price of its footballs in order to ensure that it recovers its (temporarily) higher costs. However, the use of a standard costing system would not trigger an immediate price increase of this nature. Obviously, if this shortage became more permanent in nature, SportsWorld should consider revising its standard materials cost to reflect this higher cost.

USING MANAGERIAL ACCOUNTING INFORMATION: SPORTSWORLD

Throughout this chapter, we have discussed the determination of variances of actual manufacturing costs from standard manufacturing costs and the use of a standard costing system. Information generated from the standard costing system is primarily used in the control function of management. This function involves the following major activities:

1. Establish desired measure(s) of performance.
2. Identify actual measure(s) of performance.
3. Compare actual measure(s) of performance to desired measure(s) of performance and take corrective action, if necessary.

Standard costing systems assist management in the control function by comparing actual performance (in terms of quantities or costs of manufacturing inputs) to desired performance (as measured by performance standards). This comparison results in the determination of a variance, which can be evaluated in greater detail to identify its cause.

To illustrate the use of standard cost information in the control function of management, consider the variances incurred by SportsWorld during January 20x1. The variances that would ordinarily be considered as the responsibility of the production supervisor are summarized in a variance exception report shown in Illustration 5.

Illustration 5

SportsWorld
Variance Exception Report: Production Foreman

	Amount of Variance ($)	Standard Costs	Percentage Deviation
Direct Materials:			
Usage Variance	400 F	10,000	4.0%
Direct Labor:			
Rate Variance	3,500 U	30,000	11.7%
Efficiency Variance	2,000 F	30,000	6.7%
Overhead:[a]			
Volume Variance	5,000 F	100,000	5.0%
Efficiency Variance	7,500 F	100,000	7.5%

[a] See the appendix for the calculation of the overhead variances
F = Favorable Variance
U = Unfavorable Variance

Illustration 5 expresses the variances that are the responsibility of SportsWorld's production supervisor both in terms of dollar amounts and as a percentage of the standard manufacturing costs for the input related to the variance. It is important to note that actual manufacturing costs would rarely equal standard manufacturing costs; thus, SportsWorld's management would utilize the variance exception report shown in Illustration 5 to focus their attention on the more significant variances. Initially, the dollar magnitude of the fixed overhead volume variance ($5,000) and variable overhead efficiency variance ($7,500) suggests that these receive prompt attention from SportsWorld's management since these variances are the two largest. (The fixed overhead volume variance and variable overhead efficiency variance are discussed in the appendix to this chapter.)

A limitation of using the absolute dollar amount of the variance is that, holding other factors constant, as the standard cost of a manufacturing input increases, the variance associated with that input also increases. To overcome this limitation, organizations often express variances as a percentage of the standard cost. Referring to Illustration 5, it appears that the unfavorable direct labor rate variance of $3,500 (or 11.7 percent of standard direct labor costs) is the most significant. If SportsWorld identifies variances exceeding ten percent of standard costs as representing significant areas of exception, only the direct labor rate variance would be investigated in more detail. An explanation for this variance is the use of highly skilled laborers (who command a wage premium) in the manufacturing process. Based exclusively on this variance, SportsWorld's management would conclude that the production supervisor's performance was unsatisfactory.

While none of the remaining variances shown in Illustration 5 meet SportsWorld's criteria for investigation (ten percent of standard costs), it is important that management consider the overall effect of the production supervisor's decision to utilize highly skilled direct labor. For example, it could be argued that the use of more highly skilled labor had the following overall effect(s) on SportsWorld's manufacturing process:

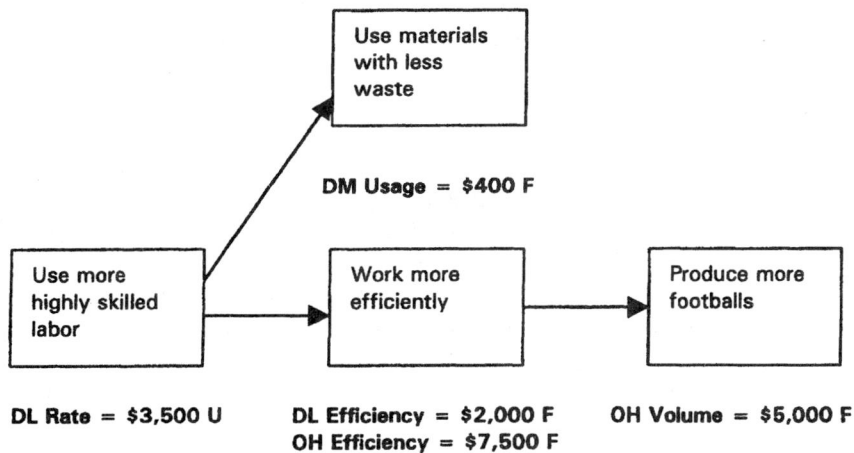

In short, the above analysis suggests that using the abilities of highly skilled laborers may (1) reduce the waste of direct materials inventory in the manufacturing process (direct materials usage variance) and (2) result in more efficient manufacture of inventory and utilization of production machinery (direct labor and overhead efficiency variance). These factors may then enable SportsWorld to increase its production of footballs beyond planned levels, since direct labor and machine hours "saved" on the expected production can then be freed up for use in additional production (overhead volume variance). Thus, the net effect of using more highly skilled labor may be viewed in the following manner:

		DM Usage	$ 400 F
		DL Efficiency	2,000 F
DL Rate = $3,500 U	vs.	OH Efficiency	7,500 F
		OH Volume	5,000 F
			$ 14,900 F

Based on the above, it appears that the production supervisor has performed effectively during January 20x1. The production supervisor has incurred an unfavorable direct labor rate variance to realize favorable direct materials usage, direct labor efficiency, overhead efficiency, and overhead volume variances. The net effect is a favorable variance of $11,400 ($14,900 favorable - $3,500 unfavorable = $11,400 favorable).

While the above analysis appears straightforward, the use of performance standards in the control function is a highly complex matter. Some additional factors that should be considered by SportsWorld's management are summarized below.

1. **Controllability.** Variances may arise because of factors beyond an individual's control. For example, the use of highly skilled labor by the production supervisor may be necessitated by management's decision to increase production levels beyond current capacity. Alternatively, the higher wage rates implied by the unfavorable direct labor rate variance may be a result of overtime premiums paid to employees that are necessitated by management's decision to increase production levels. If so, the production supervisor should not be penalized for these variances.

2. **Trade-offs Among Variances.** The above evaluation of SportsWorld's production supervisor illustrates the importance of considering the overall effect of various decisions. If the production supervisor used highly skilled labor in an effort to reduce direct materials and overhead costs, these variances should be considered collectively. Clearly, if the use of highly skilled labor resulted in all of the variances shown in Illustration 5, this appears to be a highly favorable decision on the part of the production supervisor. The unfavorable direct labor rate variance should not be considered in isolation.

3. **Alternative Explanations.** It is highly unlikely that any single factor accounts for the entire amount of any one variance. For example, the overhead volume variance may be influenced by SportsWorld's decision to decrease the production levels of certain other products, as opposed to being strictly related to the efficiency of a highly skilled labor force. Similarly, the favorable direct materials usage variance may be affected by the purchase of higher quality direct materials (consistent with the unfavorable direct materials price variance of $600, noted previously in this chapter). When evaluating SportsWorld's production supervisor, these and other alternative explanations should be considered.

4. **Historical Considerations.** Variances that regularly occur in a consistent fashion deserve additional attention. For example, if SportsWorld consistently has a highly favorable direct labor efficiency variance, its production supervisor may be performing exceptionally well in scheduling its workforce, minimizing downtimes, and/or motivating employees. An alternative explanation is that changes in the manufacturing technology (such as more advanced manufacturing equipment) or manufacturing processes (such as scheduling larger production runs of individual products) have made the performance standard used by SportsWorld (0.15 direct labor hours per football) obsolete. All performance standards should be periodically evaluated to ensure their applicability under current manufacturing conditions.

In addition to regularly recurring variances, management may wish to consider the trend of the variances over time. For example, referring to Illustration 5, SportsWorld has a favorable direct materials usage variance of 4.0% during January 20x1. While this variance does not currently meet the ten percent threshold for investigation, contrast the decision facing management if the direct materials usage variances in the preceding three months were as follows (unfavorable variances are in parentheses):

	Case A	Case B
October 20x0	6.0%	1.5%
November 20x0	(1.5%)	2.4%
December 20x0	3.1%	3.6%

The direct materials usage variance identified in January 20x1 would be viewed quite differently in the above contexts. In Case A, no real pattern exists with respect to the direct materials price variance. The January 20x1 variance does not appear to be unreasonable based on variances noted in previous months. The consistently-increasing trend of this variance reflected in Case B suggests one of two possibilities: (1) employees are increasingly becoming more efficient in utilizing direct materials in the manufacturing process or (2) the direct material standard is outdated and needs to be revised. While the January 20x1 direct materials usage variance would not be investigated based on SportsWorld's ten percent threshold, the consistently increasing trend reflected in Case B would clearly draw management's attention to this variance.

SUMMARY

This chapter discusses the process through which performance standards are developed and variances are calculated to identify differences between actual and standard manufacturing costs. Some of the more important concepts discussed in this chapter are:

1. Performance standards are expectations for the activities of the organization. As they relate to the organization's manufacturing activities, performance standards specify the quantity and cost of inputs (direct materials, direct labor, and manufacturing overhead) necessary to manufacture a given level of output (inventory).

2. The difference between actual manufacturing costs and the manufacturing costs expected based on performance standards is a *variance*. Variances are classified as *favorable* when the actual costs are less than the costs based on the performance standard. When actual costs exceed the costs based on the performance standard, the variance is classified as *unfavorable*.

3. Direct materials and direct labor variances can result from one of two causes. First, the price actually paid for the direct materials or direct labor input may differ from the standard price of the input. The resulting variance is the *direct materials price variance* (for direct materials costs) or the *direct labor rate variance* (for direct labor costs).

4. A second cause of direct materials and direct labor variances reflects the fact that the quantity of direct materials or direct labor inputs required for production may differ from the standard quantity allowed. The resulting variance is the *direct materials usage variance* (for direct materials costs) or the direct *labor efficiency variance* (for direct labor costs).

5. The *total overhead variance* is the difference between the total applied overhead costs (standard overhead costs) and the total actual overhead costs incurred by the organization. If the actual overhead costs incurred are less than the total overhead costs applied to production, a favorable overhead variance results. In contrast, if the actual overhead costs exceed the applied overhead costs, an unfavorable overhead variance is incurred.

6. Fixed overhead variances can result from different levels of production than anticipated *(fixed overhead volume variance)* and differences in the cost of items comprising fixed overhead *(fixed overhead spending variance)*. Variable overhead variances may result from different levels of activity than the standard activity allowed *(variable overhead efficiency variance)* and differences in the cost of items comprising variable overhead *(variable overhead spending variance)*.

7. In a *two-way analysis* of overhead variances, the total overhead variance is decomposed into two components: the fixed overhead volume variance and the overhead budget variance. The overhead budget variance is the sum of the variable overhead efficiency variance, the fixed overhead spending variance, and the variable overhead spending variance.

8. The *three-way analysis* of overhead variance decomposes the total overhead variance into the fixed overhead volume variance, variable overhead efficiency variance, and overhead spending variance (which includes both the variable overhead spending variance and fixed overhead spending variance).

KEY DEFINITIONS

Direct labor efficiency variance—this variance arises when actual direct labor hours worked differ from standard direct labor hours allowed. The direct labor efficiency variance is calculated by multiplying the standard direct labor rate by the difference between actual direct labor hours worked and standard direct labor hours allowed.

Direct labor rate variance—this variance arises when the actual direct labor rate differs from the standard direct labor rate. The direct labor rate variance is calculated by multiplying the actual direct labor hours worked by the difference between the actual direct labor rate and the standard direct labor rate.

Direct materials price variance—this variance arises when the actual price (cost) of direct materials differs from the standard price (cost). The direct materials price variance is calculated by multiplying the actual quantity of direct materials purchased by the difference between the actual price per unit of direct materials and the standard price per unit.

Direct materials usage variance—this variance arises when the actual quantity of direct materials required for production differs from the standard quantity allowed. The direct material usage variance is calculated by multiplying the standard price (cost) of direct materials by the difference between the actual quantity of direct materials used and the standard quantity of direct materials allowed.

Favorable variance—a variance that occurs when actual costs or utilization are less than standard costs or utilization.

Fixed overhead volume variance—this variance occurs when actual activity differs from expected activity. The fixed overhead volume variance can be calculated by multiplying the standard fixed overhead rate by the difference between actual activity and expected activity.

Fixed overhead spending variance—the difference between the actual fixed overhead costs incurred by the organization and the budgeted fixed overhead costs.

Flexible budget—an estimate of costs prepared assuming multiple levels of activity.

Kaizen costing—the reduction of costs during the manufacturing process from realizing continual and gradual improvements through relatively small betterment activities.

Overhead budget variance—this variance is calculated under a two-way analysis of overhead variances. The overhead budget variance is the difference between: (1) the expected overhead costs at actual activity (standard direct labor hours allowed) and (2) actual overhead costs. This variance includes the variable overhead efficiency variance, variable overhead spending variance, and fixed overhead spending variance.

Overhead variance (total)—the difference between actual overhead costs incurred by the organization and the overhead costs applied to production (based on standard measures of activity).

Performance standards—expectations for the activities of the organization which specify the number and costs of inputs necessary to achieve a specified level of output.

Standard costs—the costs which should be incurred (based on performance standards developed by the organization) in manufacturing the organization's inventory or providing the organization's services.

Static budget—an estimate of costs prepared for a single level of activity.

Target costing—designing products and manufacturing processes in such a manner that that the product can be manufactured at a cost necessary to provide a desired level of profit.

Three-way analysis of overhead variances—an analysis of overhead variances that separates the total overhead variance into three components: the overhead spending variance, the variable overhead efficiency variance, and the fixed overhead volume variance.

Two-way analysis of overhead variances—an analysis of overhead variances that separates the total overhead variance into two components: the overhead budget variance and the fixed overhead volume variance.

Unfavorable variance—a variance that occurs when actual costs or utilization are greater than standard costs or utilization.

Variable overhead efficiency variance—this variance arises when the standard activity used to apply overhead costs to production differs from actual activity. The variable overhead efficiency variance is calculated by multiplying the variable overhead rate by the difference between standard activity and actual activity.

Variable overhead spending variance—the variable overhead spending variance is the difference between the actual variable overhead costs incurred by the organization and the expected level of variable overhead costs at the actual level of activity.

Variance—the difference between the actual costs of manufacturing inventory or providing services and the costs that should be incurred based on performance standards (standard costs).

QUESTIONS

1. What are performance standards and variances? How can performance standards and variances be used to evaluate the efficiency of the manufacturing process?

2. What is a standard cost? Contrast standard costing with target costing and kaizen costing.

3. What are the two primary causes of direct materials and direct labor variances?

4. What is the relationship between actual prices and standard prices when a price variance is favorable? Unfavorable?

5. What is the relationship between actual quantities used and standard quantities allowed when a usage variance is favorable? Unfavorable?

6. What is the primary difference between cost accumulation in an actual costing system and a standard costing system?

7. In addition to the amount and nature of the variance, what factors should be considered in evaluating an individual's performance based on variances?

8. How is the total overhead variance calculated?

*9. What variances explain differences between actual fixed overhead costs and fixed overhead costs applied to production (based on standard activity)? What variances explain differences between actual variable overhead costs and variable overhead costs applied to production (based on standard activity)?

*10. What causes the fixed overhead volume variance to occur? When will this variance be favorable? Unfavorable?

*11. What causes the variable overhead efficiency variance to occur? When will this variance be favorable? Unfavorable?

*12. Which overhead variances are calculated in a two-way analysis of overhead? A three-way analysis?

EXERCISES AND PROBLEMS

13. *Labor Variances—Conceptual.* A company established $4 an hour as the standard labor rate for factory craftsmen. Recently, the personnel manager hired several more experienced craftsmen at $6 an hour, and the experienced workers were able to produce twice as much as their $4-an-hour colleagues. Obviously, an unfavorable rate variance of $2 an hour will result. To whom should this unfavorable variance be charged? Does this seem to be a reasonable action? How will the person charged react to the variance?

14. *Performance Standards—Conceptual.* Standard costing procedures are widely used in manufacturing operations and, more recently, have become common in many nonmanufacturing operations.

    a. Define standard costs. Distinguish between ideal and attainable standards.
    b. What are the advantages of a standard cost system?

15. *Variance Analysis—Conceptual.* Variances can sometimes indicate the existence of performance tradeoffs within the firm. For example, more expensive material (unfavorable direct materials price variance) may result in less scrap (favorable direct materials usage variance). For each of the variances described below, indicate what possible tradeoffs could have taken place:

    a. Unfavorable direct labor rate variance; favorable direct labor efficiency variance.
    b. Unfavorable direct material price variance; favorable direct labor efficiency variance.
    c. Favorable direct material usage variance; unfavorable direct labor efficiency variance.
    d. Favorable direct labor rate variance; unfavorable direct labor efficiency variance.
    e. Favorable direct material price variance; unfavorable direct material usage variance.

16. *Standard Costs and Variance Analysis—Conceptual.* The Acme Corporation prepares weekly performance reports for each of its operating divisions. Reproduced below is a performance report for the Finishing Department for the week ended June 7, 20x6.

---

* Questions, Exercises, and Problems related to the appendix are marked with an asterisk (*).

Acme Corporation
Performance Report
Finishing Department
Week Ended June 7, 20x6

Actual Costs		Variances	
Materials............	$10,000	Material Price...........	$2,000
		Material Usage...........	(3,000)*
Labor............	20,000	Labor Rate............	4,000
		Labor Efficiency...........	(2,000)*
Overhead...........	30,000	Overhead Spending............	(1,000)*
		Overhead Efficiency............	1,000
Total Cost...........	$60,000	Total Variance...........	$1,000

* Denotes an unfavorable variance.

After examining this report, answer the following questions about it.

a. What is the purpose of this report? Who would receive a copy of it?
b. What was the standard cost of direct materials? What was the standard cost of direct labor?
c. What are some possible bases that Acme Corporation could have used to assign overhead to the Finishing Department?
d. Present a possible explanation for the direct labor efficiency variance and the direct material usage variance.
e. Who, besides the Finishing Department, should receive a report of the direct material price variance? The direct labor efficiency variance?
f. What reaction to this report would probably come from the supervisor of the Finishing Department?

17. *Standard Costs—Conceptual.* Last year Crowley Corporation adopted a standard cost system. Labor standards were set on the basis of time studies and prevailing wage rates. Material standards were determined from material specifications and prices then in effect. In determining its standard for overhead, Crowley estimated that a total of 6,000,000 finished units would be produced during the next five years to satisfy demand for its product. The five-year period was selected to average out seasonal and cyclical fluctuations and allow for sales trends. By dividing the total annual budgeted overhead by the annual average of 1,200,000 units, a standard cost was developed for manufacturing overhead.

At June 30, 20x9, the end of the current fiscal year, analysis of accounting records determined the following variances:

Materials Price	$25,000	favorable
Materials Usage............	9,000	unfavorable
Labor Rate............	30,000	unfavorable
Labor Efficiency............	7,500	unfavorable

Standards were set at the beginning of the year and have remained unchanged. All inventories are priced at standard cost.

Required:

a. What conclusions can be drawn from each of the four variances shown in Crowley's trial balance?
b. Justify each of the following methods of accounting for the net amount of all standard cost variances: (1) presenting the net variance as an income or expense on the income statement, (2) allocating the net variance among inventories and cost of goods sold, and (3) presenting the net variance as an adjustment to cost of goods sold.

(AICPA adapted)

18. *Labor Standards—Conceptual.* Harden Company has experienced increased production costs. The primary area of concern identified by management is direct labor. The company is considering adopting a standard cost system to help control labor and other costs. Useful historical data are not available because detailed production records have not been maintained.

Harden Company has retained Finch & Associates, an engineering consulting firm, to establish labor standards. After a complete study of the work process, the engineers recommended a labor standard of one unit of production every thirty minutes or sixteen units per day for each worker. Finch further advised that Harden's wage rates were below the prevailing rate of $3 per hour.

Harden's production vice-president thought this labor standard was too tight and the employees would be unable to attain it. From his experience with the labor force, he believed a labor standard of forty minutes per unit or twelve units per day for each worker would be more reasonable.

The president of Harden Company believed the standard should be set at a high level to motivate the workers, but he also recognized that it should be set at a level that would provide adequate information for control and reasonable cost comparisons. After much discussion, management decided to use a dual standard. The labor standard recommended by the engineering firm of one unit every thirty minutes would be employed in the plant as a motivation device, and a cost standard of forty minutes per unit would be used in reporting. Management also concluded that the workers would not be informed of the cost standard used for reporting purposes. The production vice-president conducted several sessions prior to implementation in the plant, informing the workers of the new standard cost system and answering questions. The new standards were not related to incentive pay but were introduced at the time wages were increased to $3 per hour.

The new standard cost system was implemented on January 1, 20x4. At the end of six months of operation, the following statistics on labor performance were presented to top management:

	January	February	March	April	May	June
Production (units)	5,100	5,000	4,700	4,500	4,300	4,400
Direct Labor Hours	3,000	2,900	2,900	3,000	3,000	3,100
Variance from Labor Standard	$1,350U	$1,200U	$1,650U	$2,250U	$2,550U	$2,700U
Variance from Cost Standard	$1,200F	$1,300F	$ 700F	$ 0	$ 400U	$ 500U

Direct material quality, labor mix, and plant facilities and conditions have not changed to any great extent during the six-month period.

Required:

a. Discuss the impact of different types of standards on motivation, including the effect on motivation in Harden Company's plant of adopting the labor standard recommended by the engineering firm.
b. Evaluate Harden Company's decision to employ dual standards in its standard cost system.

(CMA adapted)

19. *Basic Standard Costing and Variance Analysis.* Shown below are the performance standards related to the production of Product X:

Direct Materials	1 unit	x	$5	=	$ 5
Direct Labor	3 hours	x	$6	=	$ 18

There were no inventories on hand at the beginning of 20x1. During 20x1, 500 units of Product X were manufactured. A total of 600 units of direct materials were purchased for $2,400 and used to produce these units. In addition, a total of 1,400 hours of direct labor were required in production. The labor rate per hour was $6.30.

Required:

a. Determine the standard production costs and actual production costs incurred during 20x1.
b. Calculate the total direct materials variance and the total direct labor variance.
c. For each variance calculated in (b), separate the total variance into its price and usage components.

20. *Determining Actual Cost Data.* The following information summarizes the standard costs of producing one hoop for Lori Company. All inventory balances are zero at the beginning of January.

Materials	1 pound	x	$2	=	$2
Labor	2 hours	x	$5	=	$10

Assume that Lori Company produced 4,000 hoops during 20x1. In addition, Lori had no ending inventory of direct materials. The variances for production during 20x1 are summarized below:

Direct Materials Price	$2,400 unfavorable
Direct Materials Usage	900 favorable
Direct Labor Rate	3,280 favorable
Direct Labor Efficiency	500 unfavorable

Required:

Determine the following actual cost data for Lori Company:
a. Actual direct labor hours worked.
b. Actual direct labor rate.
c. Actual direct materials used.
d. Actual price per unit for materials.

21. *Direct Materials Variances and Responsibility.* El Tronics Company purchased 100,000 pounds of material for $46,000 and used 90,000 pounds to produce 20,000 finished units. The standard price for material was $0.45 per pound, and the standard quantity was five pounds per unit.

Required:

a. Determine the material variances.
b. Identify possible causes for material variances. Identify the job title of persons who might bear responsibility for these variances.
c. Define the meaning of the words "favorable" and "unfavorable."

22. *Direct Materials Variances and Responsibility.* The Cal Lender Company is a manufacturing firm that incurred a considerable amount of material costs during the month of June. The actual price paid for material was $4 a pound. The firm purchased 7,000 pounds of material during the month and actually used 5,000 pounds to produce 1,000 units. The standard price per pound is $4.50, and the quantity standard is 4.7 pounds per unit.

Required:

a. What is the direct material price variance for the month of June? Who within the firm is generally held responsible for this variance?
b. What is the direct material usage variance for the month of June? Who would be held responsible for it?
c. How much was the total direct materials variance for the month of June? What does this variance mean? Who would be held responsible for it?

23. *Direct Materials.* The A. C. Counting Company uses a standard cost system as a basis for evaluating operational performance. The following information concerning operations during the month of March, when 200 units of product were produced, is made available.

	Standard	Actual
Material Cost	$2.00 per lb.	$2.20 per lb.
Material Used	1-1/2 lbs. per unit	280 lbs.
Labor Cost	$5.00 per hr.	$2,400
Labor Used	2-1/2 man hrs. per unit	600 hrs.

Required:

Calculate the following variances for the A. C. Counting Company. Also, indicate whether or not the variance is favorable by using the words "favorable" or "unfavorable."

a. Material price and usage variances; total material variance.
b. Direct labor rate and efficiency variances; total direct labor variance.

24. *Direct Labor Variances and Explanations.* The H. G. Company uses a standard cost system in accounting for the cost of one of its products. The standard is based on budgeted monthly production of 100 units per day for the usual twenty-two work days per month. Standard cost per unit for direct labor is sixteen hours at $1.50 per hour. During the month of September, the plant operated only twenty days. Actual direct labor cost for the 2,080 units produced was:

$$32,860 \text{ hours } @ \$1.52 = \$49,947.20$$

Required:

Determine the direct labor variances and suggest factors that might explain the reasons for these variances.

(*AICPA adapted*)

25. *Direct Labor Variances and Explanations.* A production foreman was forced to use master craftsmen who were paid $7 an hour for a job normally performed by apprentices. The craftsmen were able to complete the job in 150 hours, which was forty hours less than the standard time. Apprentices are normally paid $4 an hour.

    Required:

    a. What was the direct labor rate variance for this job?
    b. What was the direct labor efficiency variance for this job?
    c. What was the total direct labor variance for this job?
    d. Was the foreman's action wise? Who within the firm should be held responsible for these variances?

26. *Direct Material and Direct Labor Variances and Explanations.* During January, Megleno Tool Company completed 2,000 units by combining 2,010 pounds of direct material inputs with 5,980 hours of labor. To meet these production needs, Megleno acquired 4,000 pounds of material for $14,800 and incurred total payroll costs of $30,463. The following standards have been established for material and labor:

Material...	1 pound	x	$4 per pound
Labor	3 hours	x	$5 per hour

    Required:

    Calculate material and labor variances and determine possible causes for these variances.

27. *Direct Materials and Direct Labor Variances.* ToolCo purchased 800 pounds of material for $1,600. Exactly 600 pounds were placed into production, and from them 100 equivalent units were produced. The standard price paid for material is $2.05 per pound, and the standard quantity used is 6.5 pounds per unit.

    Labor standards were set at $3.75 per hour and four hours per unit. Actual labor costs were $3.50 per hour; 420 hours were required to produce the 100 equivalent units.

    Required:

    a. Determine price and usage variances for labor and material.
    b. The foreman argues that his labor quantity variance was the direct result of poor quality material. Do you accept his explanation?
    c. The foreman explains his material quantity variance as follows: "Untrained, inexperienced, low-priced, new employees wasted too much material by creating too much scrap." Would you accept or reject his explanation? Why?

28. *Direct Material and Direct Labor Variances—Schedule.* The Jones Furniture Company uses a standard cost system in accounting for its production costs. The standard cost of a unit of furniture follows:

Lumber (100 ft. @ $150 per 1,000 ft.)	$ 15
Direct Labor (4 hrs. @ $2.50 per hr.)	10

The actual unit costs for the month of December were as follows:

Lumber Used (110 ft. @ $120 per 1,000 ft.)	$13.20
Direct Labor (4.25 @ $2.60 per hr.)	11.05

Required:

Prepare a schedule that shows an analysis of each element of the total variance from standard cost for the month of December.

(AICPA adapted)

29. *Direct Material and Direct Labor Variances—Schedule.* The Dearborn Company manufactures Product X in standard batches of 100 units. A standard cost system is in use. The standard costs for a batch are as follows:

Direct Materials (60 lbs. @ $.45 per lb.)	$ 27.00
Direct Labor (36 hrs. @ $2.15 per hr.)	77.40
Overhead (36 hrs. @ $2.75 per hr.)	99.00
	$203.40

Production for April 20x0 amounted to 210 batches. The relevant statistics follow:

Standard Output per Month	24,000 units
Direct Materials Used	13,000 lbs.
Cost of Direct Materials Used	$ 6,110.00
Direct Labor Cost	16,790.40
Overhead Cost	20,592.00
Average Overhead Rate per Hour	2.60

Management has noted that actual costs per batch deviate somewhat from standard costs per batch.

Required:

Prepare a statement containing a detailed explanation of the difference between actual costs and standard costs (ignore overhead variances).

(AICPA adapted)

30. *Direct Materials and Direct Labor Variances.* You are provided with the following standard cost information for the production of one unit of Alpha, Inc.'s Inventory:

```
2 lbs. of steel  x  $2  =  $4
1 hr. of labor   x  $5  =  $5
```

In addition to the above materials and labor costs, Alpha applies overhead at a rate equal to one-half of the standard direct labor cost per unit. At the beginning of 20x1 (its first year of operations), Alpha purchased 2,000 units of steel for $2.50 per pound to begin production.

During 20x1, Alpha produced 1,000 units of inventory. These units required 1,800 pounds of steel and 1,150 hours of direct labor. In addition. Alpha purchased an additional 2,000 units of steel for $2.50 per pound during 20x1. The total payroll for direct labor during 20x1 was $6,000.

Required:

Calculate the following variances:
a. Direct materials price variance.
b. Direct materials usage variance.
c. Direct labor rate variance.
d. Direct labor efficiency variance.

31. *Direct Materials and Direct Labor Variances with Journal Entries.* Joseph utilizes a standard cost system. Assume that you have obtained the following information concerning actual cost data during 20x1, Joseph's first year of operations:

Direct Material Purchases (15,000 lbs.)	$16,500
Direct Labor Costs (500 hrs.)	$ 5,500
Direct Materials Used	5,000 pounds
Units of Inventory Produced	600 units

The standard material and labor cost per unit is $20 as shown below:

Direct Materials	10 lbs.	x	$ 1	=	$10
Direct Labor	1 hr.	x	$10	=	10
Total					$20

Required:

a. Calculate all direct materials and direct labor variances.
b. Prepare the journal entries required to record: (1) the purchase of the direct materials, (2) the use of direct materials in production, or (3) the use of direct labor in production.

32. *Direct Materials and Direct Labor Variances with Closing Entry.* You have been given the following actual cost information for Lane, Inc.:

Actual Labor Hours Worked	1,000 hours
Actual Labor Rate per Hour	$6.00 per hour
Actual Materials Used in Production	1,200 pounds
Actual Materials Purchased	1,500 pounds
Cost of Materials Purchased	$3.50 per pound
Actual Production	600 units

Standard direct material and direct labor cost for one unit of Lane, Inc.'s inventory is $17.50. The calculation of this cost per unit is shown below:

Materials	1.5 lbs.	x $3.00	=	$ 4.50
Labor	2 hrs.	x $6.50	=	13.00
Total				$17.50

Required:

a. Calculate the following variances for Lane, Inc.:
   1. Direct materials price variance.
   2. Direct materials usage variance.
   3. Direct labor rate variance.
   4. Direct labor efficiency variance.
b. Prepare the journal entry necessary to close the above variances, assuming they are closed directly to cost of goods sold.

33. *Direct Material and Direct Labor Variances.* The Groomer Company manufactures two products, Florimene and Glyoxide, both used in the plastics industry. The company uses a flexible budget in its standard cost system to develop variances. Selected data follow:

	Florimene	Glyoxide
Data on Standard Costs:		
Direct Material per Unit	3 lbs. @ $1 per lb.	4 lbs. @ $1.10 per lb.
Direct Labor per Unit	5 hrs. @ $2 per hr.	6 hrs. @ $2.50 per hr.
Units Produced in September	1,000	1,200
Costs Incurred for September:		
Direct Material	3,100 lbs. @ $.90 per lb.	4,700 lbs. @ $1.15 per lb.
Direct Labor	4,900 hrs. @ $1.95 per hr.	7,400 hrs. @ $2.55 per hr.

Assume that purchases of direct materials were equal to direct materials used.

Required:

Using this information, calculate the following variances. Indicate whether or not the variances were favorable by using the terms "favorable" and "unfavorable" in your answer.

a. The total variance for both products for September.
b. The labor efficiency variance for both products for September.
c. The labor rate variances for both products for September.
d. The direct material price variances for both products for September.
e. The direct material usage variances for both products for September.

34. *Direct Materials and Direct Labor Variances.* During January, the Copen Tool Company completed 1,000 units of Product X, which required as inputs 3,110 pounds of direct material and 5,840 hours of labor. To meet these needs, Copen acquired 4,000 pounds of material for $15,200 and incurred total payroll costs of $18,104. Copen has established the following standards for material and labor (per one standard output of Product X):

Material	3 lbs. @ $4 per lb.
Labor	6 hrs. @ $3 per hr.

Required:

a. What were the material price and quantity variances for the Copen Tool Company?
b. What were the labor rate and efficiency variances for the company?
c. Does an unfavorable variance necessarily mean that performance was unfavorable? Explain why or why not.

35. *Direct Materials and Direct Labor Variances.* The Carberg Corporation manufactures and sells a single product. The cost system used by the company is a standard cost system. The standard cost per unit of product is shown below:

Material (1 lb. plastic @ $2)	$2.00
Direct Labor (1.6 hrs. @ $4)	6.40

Carberg produced 5,000 units during November. These units required 5,300 pounds of material and 8,200 hours of direct labor. Total payroll expense for direct labor was $33,620.

The purchasing department normally buys about the same quantity as is used in production during a month. In November 5,200 pounds were purchased at a price of $2.10 per pound.

Required:

a. For the data given above, calculate the following variances from standard costs:
   1. Materials price
   2. Materials quantity
   3. Direct labor rate
   4. Direct labor efficiency

b. The company has divided its responsibilities so that the purchasing department is responsible for the price at which materials and supplies are purchased, while the manufacturing department is responsible for the quantities of materials used. Does this division of responsibilities solve the conflict between price and quantity variances? Explain your answer.

(CMA adapted)

36. *Direct Materials and Direct Labor* Variances. Almonzo, Inc. has developed the following performance standards with respect to the direct materials and direct labor costs required to manufacture one unit of Product A, the primary inventory sold by Almonzo. Assume that Almonzo is beginning its first year of operations.

Direct Material B	1 lb. x $0.45 = $ 0.45
Direct Material C	3 yds. x $2.00 = $ 6.00
Direct Labor	2 hrs. x $5.50 = $11.00

During 20x1, Almonzo purchased 500 pounds of Direct Material B for a total price of $260. In addition, 1,800 yards of Direct Material C were purchased for $4,500. In order to produce 400 units of Product A (the actual production for Almonzo during 20x1), a total of $5,100 of direct labor costs were incurred. These costs represented the cost of the 850 direct labor hours actually used by Almonzo during 20x1.

In addition to the direct labor hours, Almonzo also utilized 380 pounds of Direct Material B and 1,235 yards of Direct Material C in production. Ignore overhead costs for purposes of this problem.

Required:

a. What is the total standard cost of direct materials needed to manufacture the 400 units of Product A during 20x1?
b. What is the total standard cost of direct labor needed to manufacture the 400 units of Product A during 20x1?
c. Determine the following variances for Almonzo, Inc. during 20x1: (1) direct materials price, (2) direct materials usage, (3) direct labor rate, and (4) direct labor efficiency.

37. *Direct Materials and Direct Labor Variances—Multiple Products.* Giant, Inc. produces three main inventory products: 1, 2, and 3. Each of these products requires the use of two direct materials (A and B) as well as direct labor. The standard cost of these inputs is as follows: Direct Material A, $2 per pound; Direct Material B, $1.50 per pound; and direct labor, $6 per hour. Shown below are the standard materials and labor quantities required to manufacture one unit of each product.

Inventory Product	Standard Quantity of Direct Materials Required		Standard Quantity of Direct Labor Hours
	Material A	Material B	
1	1 lb.	1.5 lbs.	3 hrs.
2	1 lb.	2 lbs.	1 hr.
3	2 lbs.	1 lb.	2 hrs.

Purchases of direct materials during 20x1 are shown below:

Material A	9,000 lbs. for $22,500
Material B	10,000 lbs. for $17,500

Total production during 20x1 was as follows:

Product 1	1,000 units
Product 2	400 units
Product 3	500 units

The amount of inputs used to produce these units is shown below:

Material A	8,000 lbs.
Material B	8,200 lbs.
Direct Labor	13,000 hrs. (cost = $65,000)

Assume that Giant did not have any inventory at the beginning of 20x1.

Required:

a. Determine the total standard costs (both materials and labor) of manufacturing each of Giant's three inventory products during 20x1.
b. Calculate all direct materials and direct labor variances associated with Giant's production during 20x1 (Note: you will not be able to calculate these separately for each product).

38. *Direct Materials and Direct Labor Variances with Journal Entries.* Marie, Inc. required two direct materials (M and N) to manufacture its inventory. During January, Marie manufactured 1,000 units of inventory. Marie purchased 5,000 feet of Material M and 6,000 gallons of Material N at the beginning of January for $5,250 and $5,800, respectively. During January, 1,500 feet of Material M and 3,250 gallons of Material N were used by Marie in its production of the 1,000 units. Assume that Marie had no inventories on hand at the beginning of January.

In order to manufacture its inventory, Marie incurred direct labor costs of $5,000. A total of 1,000 actual direct labor hours were worked during January. Marie established the following standard cost for producing one unit of its inventory:

Material M	1 ft.	x	$1.00	=	$1.00
Material N	1 gal.	x	$1.20	=	$1.20
Direct Labor	1.5 hrs.	x	$4.00	=	$6.00

Required:

a. Calculate all necessary direct material and direct labor variances.
b. Prepare journal entries to record the following transactions: (1) purchase of the direct materials, (2) use of the direct materials in production, and (3) use of direct labor in production.
c. Prepare the journal entry needed to close the variance accounts at the end of January, assuming that Marie closes its variances to cost of goods sold.

39. *Closing Entries—Variances.* Stephens, Inc. utilizes a standard cost system. At the end of 20x1, Stephens had the following balances related to direct materials and direct labor variances:

	Debit	Credit
Direct Materials Price	$1,500	
Direct Materials Usage		$1,200
Direct Labor Rate		2,000
Direct Labor Efficiency	400	

Required:

Prepare the closing entry needed at the end of 20x1 for Stephens, Inc. Assume that Stephens closes all variances to cost of goods sold.

40. *Standard Cost Journal Entries.* Wilsonian Supply Company uses a standard cost system and records all variances from the standards in its accounting records. The following events occurred in Wilsonian Supply during the month of July:

1. One thousand two hundred pounds of direct material, which cost $2,040, were used in producing 5,000 units of product. The standard price of direct material is $1.50 a pound and the standard quantity is one-fourth pound of material per unit.
2. A total of 10,000 direct labor hours were worked during the month. The direct labor payroll was $42,000. The standard labor cost per unit is $9, based on a standard rate of $4 an hour.
3. Variable factory overhead is applied at the rate of $0.20 per direct labor hour.

Required:

Using this information, make summary journal entries to record the basic information and the component variances for the Wilsonian Company for the month of July. Also, make summary closing entries to reflect this information.

41. *Standard Cost Accumulation with Journal Entries.* Jake Company began operations on January 1, 20x1. During 20x1, Jake Company produces 5,000 knives that required 10,000 ounces of plastic and 5,000 ounces of steel. A total of 15,000 ounces of plastic were purchased for $5,000, and 6,000 ounces of steel were purchased for $1,250. Jake's employees worked a total of 13,000 direct labor hours; the total payroll for 20x1 was $65,000. Jake Company established the following performance standards related to its production of one knife:

Material:
Plastic .... 2.5 ounces x $0.60 = $ 1.50
Steel .... 1.5 ounces x $0.20 = $ 0.30
Labor.. 3 hours x $6.00 = $18.00

Required

a. Calculate all direct material and direct labor variances incurred by Jake Company during 20x1.
b. Assuming that Jake Company utilizes a standard cost system, prepare the journal entries needed to record the following transactions. Ignore overhead costs for purposes of this problem.
 1. Purchase of direct materials
 2. Transfer of direct materials costs to work-in-process inventory
 3. Direct labor costs incurred by Jake Company
 4. Transfer of the cost of 5,000 knives to finished goods inventory
 5. Sale of 3,000 knives to Jake's customers for $30 per knife

*42. *Calculation of Predetermined Overhead Rate.* During 20x1, Saints Company expects a total of $500,000 of overhead costs (both fixed and variable) to be incurred. Based on its previous experience, Saints Company expects overhead costs to vary closely with direct labor hours worked and utilizes direct labor hours as the activity base. Assume that Saints Company expects to work a total of 50,000 direct labor hours during 20x1.

Required:

Calculate the predetermined overhead rate for Saints Company during 20x1.

*43. *Application of Overhead Costs to Production.* Redskin Corporation utilizes a standard cost system to account for its production costs. Based on an analysis of its expected overhead costs, Redskin expects variable overhead costs per direct labor hour to be $3. In addition, Redskin expects a total of $50,000 of fixed overhead costs. Based on previous experience, Redskin has established performance standards of five direct labor hours per unit of inventory manufactured. Assume that Redskin planned to produce a total of 1,000 units of inventory during the coming year.

Required:

a. Calculate the predetermined overhead rate for Redskin Corporation (express this rate in terms of cost per direct labor hour).
b. If 1,200 units were actually produced during the year, how much overhead would be applied to production?

*44. *Application of Overhead Costs to Production.* Riggs, Inc. utilizes a standard cost system to account for its production of footballs. Riggs expects to incur a total of $100,000 of overhead costs during the coming year (20x2). This total includes both fixed overhead costs and variable overhead costs. Based on past experience, Riggs expects to work a total of 25,000 standard direct labor hours. This measure has been selected as an activity base by Riggs because overhead costs tend to fluctuate with changes in direct labor hours. The 25,000 direct labor hours reflects the standard number of hours allowed to produce 10,000 footballs, Riggs' expected level of production. Assume that Riggs actually manufactured 15,000 footballs during 20x2.

Required:

a. Calculate Riggs' predetermined overhead rate.
b. How much overhead would be applied to production by Riggs during 20x2?

*45. Overhead Variances—General. Assume that as a result of its standard cost system, Reed, Inc. calculates the following overhead variances (under a three-way analysis of overhead):

Overhead Volume Variance	$5,000 favorable
Overhead Efficiency Variance	3,000 unfavorable
Overhead Spending Variance	1,500 favorable

Required:

a. Prepare the journal entry necessary to close these variances to cost of goods sold.
b. For each of the above variances, provide a possible explanation for the cause of the variance.

*46. Overhead Variances—General. You were asked to analyze the incomplete records of Road, Inc. While Road's managerial accountant has calculated the following variances, he was not sure whether the variances were unfavorable or favorable.

Overhead Volume Variance	$ 500
Overhead Budget Variance	2,000

Other information:

1. Expected production was 10,000 units; actual production was 11,000 units.
2. The standard direct labor hours required by Road during 20x1 were 5,500.
3. At the beginning of 20x1, Road expected total overhead costs of $15,000 ($10,000 variable and $5,000 fixed). Road's expected activity was 5,000 direct labor hours.
4. Road actually incurred a total of $18,000 of overhead costs.

Required:

a. Illustrate the calculation of Road, Inc.'s overhead variances given the above information.
b. Determine whether Road's overhead variances were favorable or unfavorable.

*47. Overhead Variances and Journal Entries. The following data are available from the records of Micro, Inc. Any variances in parentheses represent unfavorable variances.

Standard Applied Overhead	$45,000
Actual Overhead Costs	41,000
Overhead Volume Variance	(2,000)
Overhead Budget Variance	6,000

Required:

Prepare summary journal entries for the following four events: (1) applying standard overhead costs to production, (2) recording actual overhead costs, (3) recognizing the overhead variances incurred, and (4) closing the overhead variances to cost of goods sold.

*48. Overhead Variances and Journal Entries. Shown below is information extracted from the accounting records of Dale, Inc. Any variances in parentheses represent unfavorable variances.

Actual Overhead Costs	$11,000
Overhead Volume Variance	(1,000)
Overhead Spending Variance	2,000
Overhead Efficiency Variance	3,000
Applied Overhead Costs	?

Required:

a. Determine the amount of applied overhead costs for Dale, Inc.
b. Prepare the journal entries necessary to: (1) apply overhead costs to production, (2) record actual overhead costs, (3) recognize all necessary overhead variances, and (4) close the overhead variances to cost of goods sold.

***49.** *Calculation of Predetermined Overhead Rate and Application of Overhead.* Byner Corporation utilized a standard cost system to account for its production of Frank, the primary inventory produced by Byner. In establishing its predetermined overhead rate for 20x1, Byner estimated that $600,000 of overhead costs (both fixed and variable) would be incurred during that year. This total reflected $450,000 of variable overhead costs and $150,000 of fixed overhead costs.

Byner expected to manufacture 100,000 units of Frank during 20x1. Its performance standards indicated that each unit of Frank required three standard direct labor hours. During 20x1, assume that Byner actually manufactured 90,000 units of Frank. Assume that overhead was applied to production based on standard direct labor hours allowed.

Required:

a. Calculate the predetermined rate used by Byner to apply overhead to production.
b. How much overhead was actually applied to production by Byner during 20x1?
c. Calculate the total expected overhead costs for Byner, Inc. given its actual level of production during 20x1.
d. Determine Byner's overhead volume variance for 20x1.

***50.** *Two-Way Analysis of Overhead Variances.* Jerry, Inc. manufactured 5,000 units of Product X during 20x1 (its first year of operations). Jerry utilizes a standard cost system to record the costs associated with manufacturing its inventory. The standard overhead cost per direct labor hour is shown below (assume that each unit of Product X required a standard of two direct labor hours):

Variable Overhead	$2
Fixed Overhead	$3

The above overhead rates were calculated based on an expected activity of 12,000 direct labor hours. During 20x1, a total of 9,000 direct labor hours were actually worked by Jerry at a total cost of $46,000. Actual overhead costs incurred during 20x1 totaled $62,500.

Required:

Calucate the fixed overhead variance and overhead budget variance for Jerry, Inc., during 20x1.

***51.** *Three-Way Analysis of Overhead Variances.* Repeat Problem 50 using a three-way analysis of overhead variances.

***52.** *Two-Way Analysis of Overhead Variances.* The Fast Company manufactures shipping cartons. The standard overhead costs relating to the production of one shipping carton are shown below:

Variable Overhead	$4
Fixed Overhead	2
Overhead Cost per Unit	$6

The expected production of shipping cartons during January 20x1 is 1,000 units. A total of 950 cartons were actually manufactured during the month of January. Actual overhead costs incurred by Fast Company during January 20x1 were $5,800.

Required:

Determine the overhead volume variance and overhead budget variance for January 20x1.

***53.** *Two-Way Analysis of Overhead Variances.* Brought, Inc. manufactures one basic type of inventory: Product Z. In order to establish the predetermined overhead rate for its production, Brought developed the following estimates of its overhead costs and activity:

Fixed Overhead	$50,000
Variable Overhead	$25,000
Standard Direct Labor Hours	12,500

The performance standards developed by Brought, Inc. indicate that each unit of Product Z requires two standard direct labors. A total of 7,000 units of Product Z were manufactured during 20x1. Assume that actual overhead costs were $50,000 during 20x1.

Required:

Determine the overhead volume variance and the overhead budget variance for Brought, Inc.

***54.** *Three-Way Analysis of Overhead Variances.* Assuming that actual direct labor hours worked during 20x1 were 16,500, perform a three-way analysis of overhead costs for Brought, Inc. based on the data in Problem 53.

***55.** *Two-Way Analysis of Overhead Variances.* Eon, Inc. produces electronic parts. The standard costs of manufacturing one part is as follows:

Direct Materials (2 lbs. x $1)	$ 2.00
Direct Labor (2 hrs. x $5)	10.00
Variable Overhead	1.50
Fixed Overhead	2.00
	$15.50

The level of activity used to calculate the predetermined overhead rate was 4,000 units. Last month, 4,200 units were produced. The total actual manufacturing overhead costs during the month were $18,000.

Required:

a. Calculate the total overhead variance.
b. Calculate the overhead volume variance and overhead budget variance:

***56.** *Two-Way Analysis of Overhead Variances with Journal Entries.* Sam's Company had the following information related to its production during 20x1.

Fixed Overhead per Standard Direct Labor Hour	$2.00	
Variable Overhead per Standard Direct Labor Hour	$2.50	
Standard Labor Requirements (per unit)	2	hours
Expected Activity (standard direct labor hours)	5,000	hours
Actual Production	2,200	units
Actual Direct Labor Hours Worked	4,000	hours
Actual Overhead Costs	$19,800	

Required:

a. Calculate the fixed overhead volume variance and the overhead budget variance.
b. Prepare journal entries to record the following transactions:
   1. Application of overhead to production.
   2. Recording actual overhead costs.
   3. Recording overhead variances.
   4. Closing overhead variances to cost of goods sold.

***57.** *Three-Way Analysis of Overhead Variances.* Doc Company manufactures screws in standard batches of 1,000 screws. The standard costs for a batch of screws is as follows:

Direct Materials (100 lbs. x $.08)	$ 8
Direct Labor (3 hrs. x $5)	15
Overhead (3 hrs. x $3)	9
	$32

The following data is available for the month of June:

Planned Production	200 batches
Actual Production	220 batches
Actual Direct Labor Costs	$3,500
Actual Direct Labor Hours	650 hours
Actual Overhead Costs	$2,300
Expected Fixed Overhead Costs	$ 600

Required:

Prepare a three-way analysis of overhead variances by calculating the overhead volume variance, overhead efficiency variance, and overhead spending variance. (Hint: Use the relationship between the expected fixed overhead costs and planned production to decompose the standard overhead cost per batch into fixed and variable components.)

*58. *Three-Way Analysis of Overhead Variances.* Janet Company determined the following overhead costs per standard direct labor hour worked for 20x1.

Variable Overhead	$2.00
Fixed Overhead	3.50
	$5.50

In calculating this standard overhead rate, Janet assumed an expected activity of 1,000 standard direct labor hours. Other performance standards developed by Janet indicated that four direct labor hours were required to manufacture one unit of inventory. During 20x1, Janet produced a total of 400 units of inventory. In order to produce these units, Janet incurred total direct labor costs of $10,000 (1,500 actual direct labor hours worked) and total overhead costs of $11,100.

Required:

Calculate the overhead volume variance, the overhead efficiency variance, and the overhead spending variance.

*59. *Three-Way Analysis of Overhead Variances with Journal Entries.* The following production data was available from the records of CPA, Inc.:

Actual Production (in units)	500
Actual Overhead Costs	$2,350
Actual Labor Costs	$6,700
Actual Direct Labor Hours	870

Shown below is the calculation of the standard cost of producing one unit of CPA, Inc.'s inventory. The standard overhead costs per unit was calculated assuming an expected activity of 400 units (or 800 standard direct labor hours).

Direct Materials (4 lbs. x $1)	$ 4
Direct Labor (2 hrs. x $7.50)	15
Variable Overhead	1
Fixed Overhead	2
	$22

Required:

a. Calculate the (1) fixed overhead volume variance, (2) variable overhead efficiency variance, and (3) overhead spending variance (combined fixed and variable).
b. Prepare the journal entries necessary to (1) apply overhead costs to production, (2) record actual overhead costs, (3) record the overhead variances, and (4) close the overhead variances to cost of goods sold.

*60. Two-Way Analysis of Overhead Variances. Whitney Company uses a standard cost system to record costs related to the production of its inventory. Whitney applies manufacturing overhead costs to production based on the standard direct labor hours allowed to manufacture its inventory. Assume that Whitney has developed the following performance standards related to the production of one unit of its inventory for direct labor and overhead costs:

Direct Labor	2 hours x	$10 =	$20
Variable Overhead	2 hours x	2 =	4
Fixed Overhead	2 hours x	1 =	2

When calculating the predetermined overhead rate, assume that Whitney expected to produce 10,000 units of inventory. During 20x1, 11,000 units of inventory were actually manufactured by Whitney. These units required a total of 23,500 actual direct labor hours. From an analysis of Whitney's accounting records, you determined that Whitney actually incurred $21,000 of fixed overhead costs and $43,100 of variable overhead costs during 20x1.

Required:

a. Determine (1) the overhead applied to production by Whitney during 20x1 and (2) the expected overhead costs at 11,000 units of production.
b. Determine the overhead volume variance and the overhead budget variance.
c. For the variances calculated in (b) above, identify the fixed and variable components of each variance.

*61. Three-Way Analysis of Overhead Variances. Repeat Problem 60, assuming that Whitney's management desires a three-way analysis of overhead variances. In addition to the requirements for part (a), also determine the expected overhead costs at the actual direct labor hours worked (23,500 direct labor hours).

*62. Two-Way Analysis of Overhead Variances. Kingman Corporation has established the following expected overhead costs and activity levels to calculate its predetermined overhead rate:

Expected Fixed Overhead Costs	$10,000
Expected Variable Overhead Costs	$ 5,000
Expected Standard Direct Labor Hours	2,500 hours

During 20x1, Kingman actually manufactured 1,500 units of inventory. Based on its performance standards, Kingman expects to work two direct labor hours for each unit of inventory produced. Since Kingman utilizes a standard cost system, overhead costs are applied based on standard direct labor hours allowed.

An analysis of Kingman's payroll information indicates that the total payroll during 20x1 was $12,500. This payroll represents 3,200 direct labor hours, the number actually worked during 20x1. Actual overhead costs during 20x1 were $9,000 and $6,250 for fixed and variable components, respectively.

Required:

a. Calculate the predetermined overhead rate used by Kingman Corporation to apply overhead to production.
b. Calculate the fixed overhead volume variance and overhead budget variance for Kingman Corporation during 20x1.
c. For each of the variances calculated in (b) above, determine the fixed and variable cost components of that variance.

*63. Three-Way Analysis of Overhead Variances. For the information provided in Problem 62, calculate the fixed overhead volume variance, the variable overhead efficiency variance, and the overhead spending variance. Separate each of these variances into their fixed and variable cost components.

*64. Two-Way and Three-Way Analysis of Overhead Variances. McGraw has determined the following standard cost data necessary to manufacture one unit of Duece, its primary inventory.

Direct Materials (2 lbs. x $2)	$ 4
Direct Labor (3 hrs. x $5)	15
Overhead	10
	$29

The predetermined overhead rate was calculated based on expected variable overhead costs of $30,000 and expected fixed overhead costs of $20,000. The expected level of activity used by McGraw was 5,000 units.

During 20x1, McGraw produced a total of 5,500 units. These units required 10,000 pounds of direct materials (which were purchased for $2.20 per pound). In addition, total payroll for direct labor was $86,000; a total of 15,100 direct labor hours were actually worked during 20x1. Actual variable overhead costs incurred in production during 20x1 were $35,500; actual fixed overhead costs were $22,000.

Required:

a. Perform a two-way analysis of the overhead variance by calculating the overhead volume variance and the overhead budget variance.
b. For each of the variances calculated in (a) above, determine the fixed and variable components.
c. Perform a three-way analysis of the overhead variance by calculating the overhead volume variance, overhead efficiency variance, and overhead spending variance.
d. For each of the variances calculated in (c) above, determine the fixed and variable components.

***65.** *Two-Way Analysis of Overhead Variances with Journal Entries.* Kellog, Inc. has developed the following performance standards for its production of one unit of Alco, its primary inventory product.

Direct Materials (3 oz. x $.50)	$ 1.50
Direct Labor (2 hrs. x $6)	12.00
Variable Overhead (2 hrs. x $3)	6.00
Fixed Overhead (2 hrs. x $2)	4.00
	$23.50

The following production data were available for 20x1:

Expected Production	1,000 units
Actual Production	900 units
Actual Direct Labor Hours Worked	2,100 hours
Actual Overhead Costs (including fixed overhead costs of $4,000)	$8,700

Required:

a. Determine the total overhead costs applied to production during 20x1.
b. Determine the total expected overhead costs for the production of 900 units.
c. Calculate the overhead volume variance and the overhead budget variance. For each variance, determine the fixed and variable components.
d. Prepare the necessary journal entries to record: (1) the application of overhead costs to production, (2) the actual overhead costs incurred during 20x1, (3) the overhead budget variance and the overhead volume variance, and (4) the entry to close the overhead variances to cost of goods sold.

***66.** *Three-Way Analysis of Overhead Variances with Journal Entries.* For the information presented in 65, calculate the overhead volume variance, overhead spending variance, and overhead efficiency variance. In addition, determine the variable and fixed components of each variance and prepare the journal entries requested in part (d) of Problem 65.

***67.** *Comprehensive Problem: Direct Materials, Direct Labor, and Overhead Variances with Journal Entries.* Delta, Inc. has developed the following direct materials and direct labor performance standards for the production of one unit of its inventory.

Direct Materials (1 lb. x $5)	$ 5.00
Direct Labor (3 hrs. x $4.50)	13.50

Expected overhead costs during 20x1 were $60,000. These costs included $40,000 of variable overhead costs and $20,000 of fixed overhead costs. Expected activity during 20x1 was 20,000 standard direct labor hours. During 20x1, actual production was 6,000 units. The following costs and inputs were used to manufacture these units:

Direct Materials Used	6,500 pounds
Direct Materials Purchased	7,000 pounds
Cost of Direct Materials	$4 per pound
Direct Labor Hours Worked	16,700 hours
Direct Labor Costs	$83,500
Actual Overhead Costs	$51,200

Required:

a. Calculate the direct materials price variance and the direct materials usage variance.
b. Calculate the direct labor rate variance and the direct labor efficiency variance.
c. Calculate the fixed overhead volume variance, the fixed and variable overhead spending variances, and the variable overhead efficiency variance.
d. Prepare the journal entries necessary to record:
   1. the purchase of direct materials.
   2. the transfer of direct materials to work-in-process inventory.
   3. the use of direct labor in production.
   4. the application of overhead costs to production.
   5. the actual overhead costs incurred during 20x1.
   6. the entry to recognize the overhead variances.
   7. the entry to close all variances directly to cost of goods sold.

*68. Comprehensive Problem: Direct Materials, Direct Labor, and Overhead Variances. The Groomer Company manufactures two products, Florimene and Glyoxide, both used in the plastics industry. The company uses a flexible budget in its standard cost system to develop variances. Selected data follow:

	Florimene	Glyoxide
Data on Standard Costs:		
Direct Material per unit	3 lbs. @ $1 per lb.	4 lbs. @ $1.10 per lb.
Direct Labor per unit	5 hrs. @ $2 per hr.	6 hrs. @ $2.50 per hr.
Variable Factory Overhead per Unit	$3.20 per direct labor hr.	$3.50 per direct labor hr.
Fixed Factory Overhead per Month	$20,700	$26,520
Normal Activity Per Month	5,750 direct labor hrs.	7,800 direct labor hrs.
Units Produced In September	1,000	1,200
Costs Incurred For September:		
Direct Material	3,100 lbs. @ $0.90 per lb.	4,700 lbs. @ $1.15 per lb.
Direct Labor	4,900 hrs. @ $1.95 per hr.	7,400 hrs. @ $2.55 per hr.
Variable Factory Overhead	$16,170	$25,234
Fixed Factory Overhead	$20,930	$26,400

Required:

a. Calculate the direct material price and usage variances.
b. Calculate the direct labor rate and efficiency variances.
c. Perform a two-way analysis of overhead variances by calculating the fixed overhead volume variance and the overhead budget variance.
d. Perform a three-way analysis of overhead variances by calculating the fixed overhead volume variance, overhead spending variance, and variable overhead efficiency variance.

Appendix

Variance Analysis: Manufacturing Overhead Costs

The total overhead variance is the difference between actual overhead costs and the overhead costs applied to production. Recall that in a standard costing system, overhead costs are applied to production using the standard level of activity (cost driver) necessary for actual production. From our earlier discussion, SportsWorld has calculated the following predetermined overhead rate (see Illustration 2):

Variable Overhead (per Machine Hour)..	$30
Fixed Overhead ($20,000 ÷ 2,000 Machine Hours)	10
Predetermined Overhead Rate (per Machine Hour)	$40

Other relevant information related to the production of footballs and the application of overhead costs to production is summarized below:

Actual Production in January 20x1 (Footballs)	10,000
Standard Machine Hours per Football	0.25

Earlier in this chapter, the overhead standard was expressed in terms of both (1) standard levels of activity (measured in machine hours at $40 per hour) and (2) actual units of production ($40 per machine hour x 0.25 machine hours per football = $10 per football). The overhead costs applied to production based on actual units manufactured and standard machine hours allowed for actual production are shown below. Note that either method results in $100,000 of overhead costs being applied to production.

Based on actual units of production (10,000 footballs):	Based on standard activity allowed for actual production (2,500 standard machine hours):
10,000 footballs x $10 per football	2,500 machine hours x $40 per machine hour
= $100,000	= $100,000

The fact that the overhead applied to production under either of the above bases is identical raises the question as to which base should be used to apply overhead costs to production. If companies produce only one type of product, either measure will allow overhead costs to be reasonably applied to production. However, assume that SportsWorld is attempting to apply overhead costs to all of its products (not just footballs, as illustrated in this chapter). In calculating a predetermined overhead rate, SportsWorld expects the following activity during January 20x1:

	Units		Machine Hours per Unit		Total Machine Hours
Footballs	10,000	x	0.25	=	2,500
Baseballs	5,000	x	0.10	=	500
Basketballs	7,500	x	0.20	=	1,500
	22,500				4,500

The above example illustrates a major limitation of using actual units produced to apply overhead costs to production when an organization manufactures multiple products. It is simply not logical to sum footballs, basketballs, and baseballs to arrive at a meaningful quantity, since each product requires different levels of activity (machine hours). However, if standard activity is used to apply overhead costs, a meaningful total can be determined. In this example, the predetermined overhead rate would be determined using 4,500 machine hours as the cost driver. Therefore, in most cases, measures of standard input allowed for actual production (such as direct labor hours or machine hours) are more appropriate for applying overhead costs to production than actual measures of output (production).

In conducting its analysis of overhead variances for the month of January 20x1, assume that SportsWorld has assembled the following data:

Actual Production of Footballs in January	10,000
Actual Machine Hours Worked in January	2,250
Actual Variable Overhead Costs in January	$65,200
Actual Fixed Overhead Costs in January	$19,500

At this point, the total overhead variance can be calculated. The total overhead variance is the difference between actual overhead costs and standard overhead costs applied to production. In this example, the overhead variance would be $15,300. Since actual overhead costs are less than applied overhead costs, this variance would be classified as favorable.

Applied overhead costs (2,500 machine hours x $40)	$100,000
Actual overhead costs in January ($65,200 + $19,500)	(84,700)
Overhead variance	$ 15,300

The remainder of this section will discuss the decomposition of this variance in further detail.

VARIABLE OVERHEAD COSTS

The total variance associated with variable overhead costs for SportsWorld is $9,800, as shown below. This variance is considered to be favorable, since the *actual overhead* costs ($65,200) are less than the overhead costs applied to production ($75,000). In our earlier discussion of overhead, this situation was referred to as *overapplied overhead* costs.

Applied Variable Overhead Costs (2,500 machine hours x $30)	$ 75,000
Actual Overhead Costs in January	(65,200)
Variable Overhead Variance	$ 9,800

Illustration 6 identifies the variance associated with variable overhead costs as well as the cause(s) of that variance. Four levels of variable overhead costs are determined: (1) actual variable overhead costs, (2) budgeted variable overhead costs at actual machine hours, (3) budgeted variable overhead costs at standard machine hours, and (4) variable overhead costs applied to production. Points (2) and (3) are sometimes referred to as *flexible budgets,* since they represent budgeted variable overhead costs at different levels of activity. In contrast, a *static budget* only presents estimated costs at a single level of activity. Note from Illustration 6 that points (3) and (4) (the budgeted overhead at standard machine hours and variable overhead applied to production) reflect the same level of variable overhead costs. This relationship is observed because standard machine hours are used to apply overhead costs to production.

Variable Overhead Efficiency Variance

The *variable overhead efficiency variance* arises when the actual level of activity (as represented by the cost driver) differs from the standard level of that activity allowed for actual production levels. This variance recognizes that actual variable overhead costs will differ from expected overhead costs if the actual level of the cost driver differs from the expected level. For SportsWorld, the variable overhead efficiency variance occurs because the machine hours actually worked (2,250 machine hours) are less than the standard machine hours allowed to manufacture 10,000 footballs (2,500 machine hours). In this case, since 250 fewer machine hours are worked than the standard level (2,500 machine hours − 2,250 machine hours = 250 machine hours), actual variable overhead costs are less than expected, resulting in a favorable variable overhead efficiency variance. As shown later, working fewer machine hours than expected would not influence the level of fixed overhead costs, since fixed overhead costs do not vary in response to changes in the level of activity represented by the cost driver. Based on Illustration 6, the variable overhead efficiency variance can be calculated as follows:

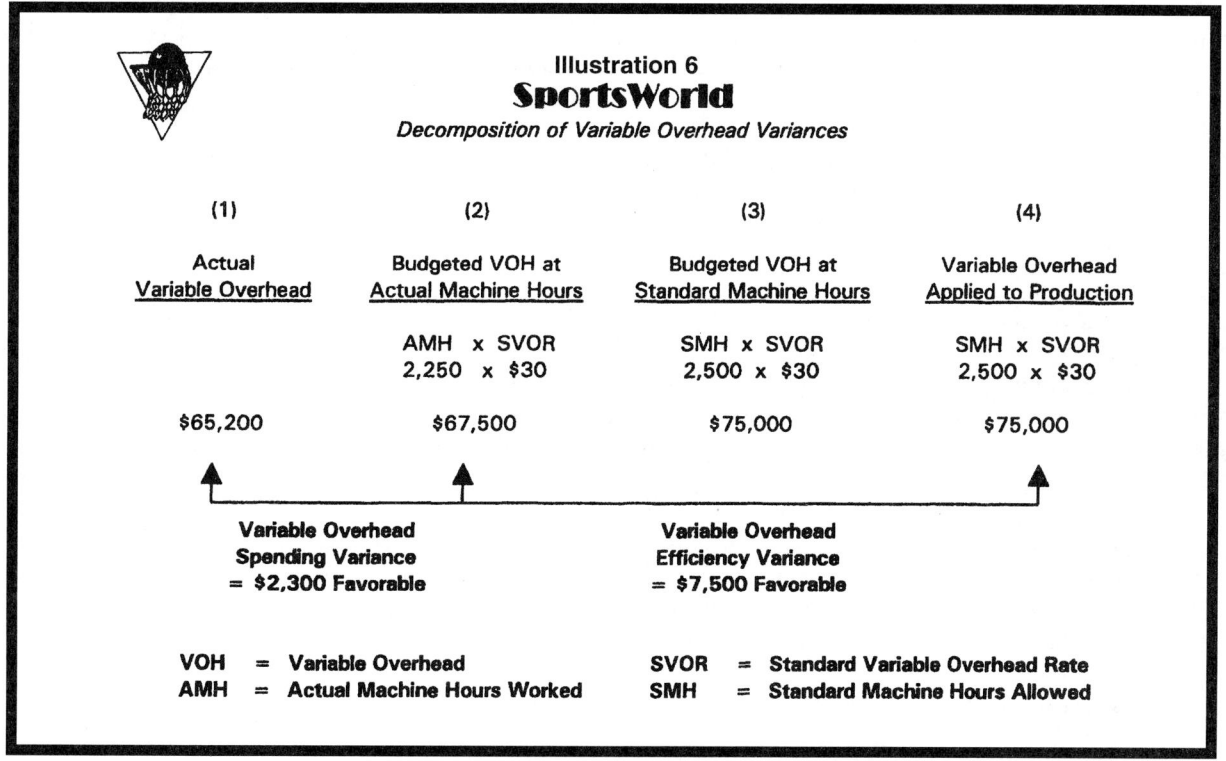

Variable Overhead Efficiency Variance	=	(AMH × SVOR) − (SMH × SVOR)
	=	(AMH − SMH) × SVOR
	=	(2,250 hours − 2,500 hours) × $30
	=	$7,500 Favorable

Variable Overhead Spending Variance

The second variable overhead variance shown in Illustration 6 is the variable overhead spending variance. The *variable overhead spending variance* is the difference between the actual variable overhead costs incurred by the organization and the expected variable overhead costs at actual levels of activity—points (1) and (2) in Illustration 6, respectively. Since both points reflect variable overhead costs incurred (or variable overhead costs that should be incurred) at the actual machine hours worked (2,250 machine hours), the spending variance does not result from unexpected differences in activity. Instead, this variance is caused strictly by the difference in costs incurred and expected (i.e., the organization "spent" more or less for its variable overhead than anticipated). As shown in Illustration 6, this variance can be calculated using the following formula:

Variable Overhead Spending Variance	= Actual Variable Overhead − (AMH × SVOR)
	= $65,200 − (2,250 machine hours × $30)
	= $2,300 Favorable

SportsWorld's variable overhead spending variance is favorable, since the actual variable overhead costs are less than the expected variable overhead costs at 2,250 machine hours (the actual level of activity). How could this occur? Considering the nature of the variable overhead costs shown earlier in the chapter in Illustration 2, this variance may reflect differences in either the price or quantity of those inputs used in the manufacturing process. For example, the favorable variable overhead spending variance may result from SportsWorld's maintenance employees working fewer hours than anticipated, SportsWorld paying maintenance workers a lower wage than anticipated, or a combination of these factors.

Summary: Variable Overhead Variances

In this section, we began by identifying the difference between the total actual variable overhead costs ($65,200) and the total variable overhead costs applied to production ($75,000) during January 20xl. This difference is the total variable overhead variance, and was $9,800 ($75,000 - $65,200 = $9,800) during January 20x1. Since actual variable overhead costs were less than the variable overhead costs applied to production, this variance was favorable. Two separate causes of this variance were then identified:

1. The actual machine hours worked by SportsWorld (2,250 machine hours) were less than the standard machine hours allowed for actual production (2,500 machine hours). This component of the variable overhead variance is the *variable overhead efficiency variance.*

2. The actual cost or quantity of variable overhead inputs was less than expected. This component of the variable overhead variance is the *variable overhead spending variance.*

Who is ordinarily held responsible for the above variances? Similar to the direct labor efficiency variance, the production supervisor can generally influence the number of machine hours worked by effectively scheduling production runs and motivating employees to perform in a more efficient manner. With respect to the variable overhead spending variance, the individual component of variable overhead costs that caused this variance should be investigated in detail prior to assessing responsibility for this variance. For example, increases or decreases in the utilities cost per kilowatt hour would not ordinarily be controllable by company personnel. As a result, the production supervisor would not be held responsible for a variable overhead spending variance resulting from this phenomenon. In contrast, if the variable overhead spending variance resulted from higher indirect labor costs than expected, this variance would typically be the responsibility of the production supervisor.

FIXED OVERHEAD COSTS

As with variable overhead costs, the total variance associated with fixed overhead costs is the difference between actual fixed overhead costs incurred and the fixed overhead costs applied to production (based on standard levels of activity necessary for actual production). Recall that SportsWorld determined its fixed overhead rate to be $10 per standard machine hour and the standard machine hours necessary to manufacture 10,000 footballs to be 2,500 (0.25 machine hours per football x 10,000 footballs = 2,500 machine hours). Also recall that the actual fixed overhead costs incurred by SportsWorld in January 20x1 were $19,500. Based on this information, SportsWorld had a favorable fixed overhead variance of $5,500 in January 20x1, as follows:

Applied Fixed Overhead Costs (2,500 machine hours x $10)	$ 25,000
Actual Fixed Overhead Costs in January	(19,500)
Fixed Overhead Variance	$ 5,500

Similar to the analysis of the variable overhead variance in the preceding section, Illustration 7 decomposes the total fixed overhead variance ($5,500 favorable) based on identifying four levels of fixed overhead costs: (1) actual fixed overhead costs, (2) budgeted fixed overhead costs at actual machine hours, (3) budgeted fixed overhead costs at standard machine hours, and (4) fixed overhead costs applied to production.

Note from Illustration 7 that the budgeted level of fixed overhead costs at actual machine hours (point 2) and budgeted fixed overhead costs at standard machine hours (point 3) are identical ($20,000). These costs represent the expected level of fixed overhead costs during January 20x1 (see Illustration 2). The lack of differences for these two levels reflects the nature of fixed overhead costs, since fixed costs are expected to remain constant (in total) across different levels of activity within the relevant range.

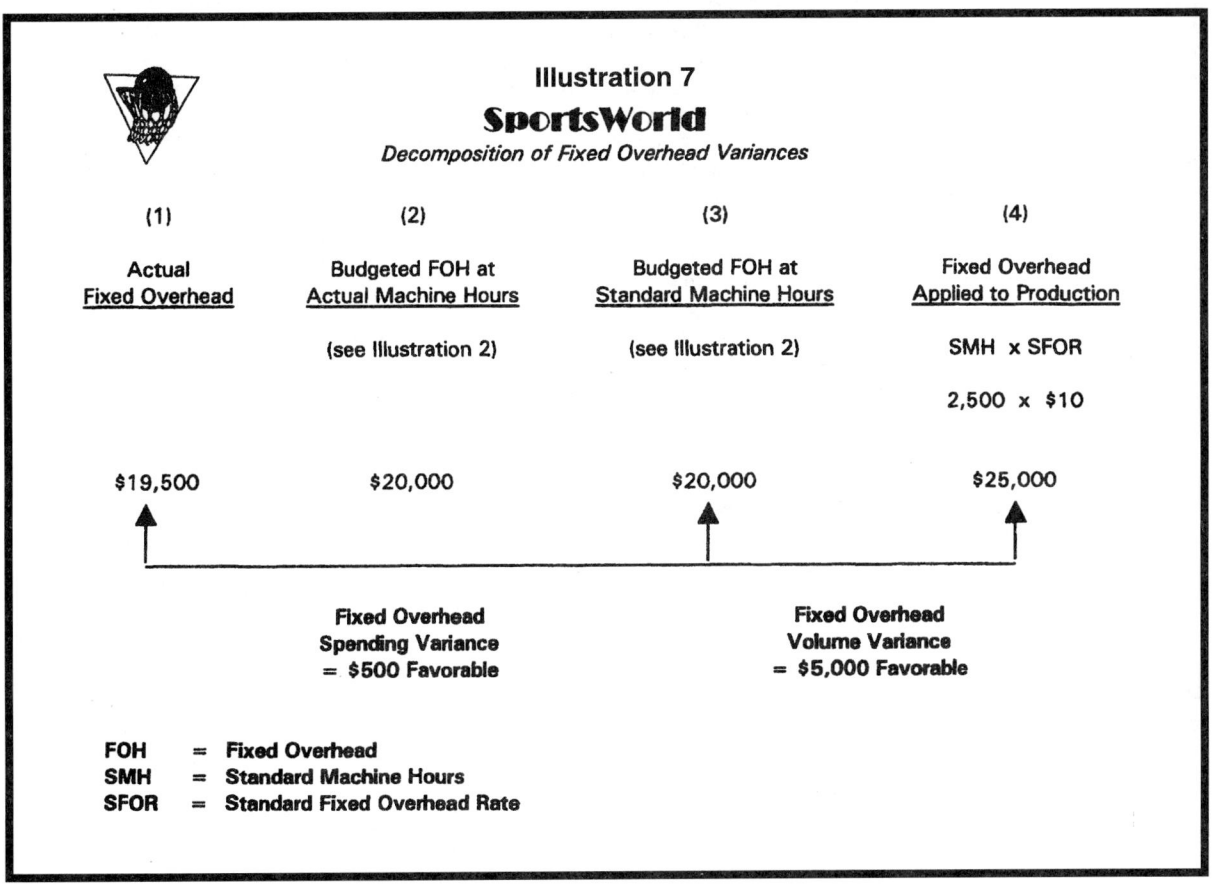

Fixed Overhead Volume Variance

One source of the total fixed overhead variance can be identified by comparing the budgeted fixed overhead costs (based on the standard machine hours for expected levels of activity) with the fixed overhead costs applied to production (based on the standard machine hours for actual levels of activity). As shown in Illustration 7, this results in a $5,000 difference. This difference is referred to as the *fixed overhead volume variance.*

The fixed overhead volume variance arises because fixed overhead costs are applied to production based on 2,500 standard machine hours; however, the predetermined fixed overhead rate of $10 per machine hour is based on a capacity of 2,000 standard machine hours. Viewed another way, the predetermined overhead fixed overhead rate assumed the production of 8,000 footballs and use of 2,000 machine hours (8,000 footballs x 0.25 machine hours per football = 2,000 machine hours). However, during January 20x1, 10,000 footballs were actually manufactured, which should have required 2,500 standard machine hours (10,000 footballs x 0.25 machine hours = 2,500 machine hours). The fixed overhead volume variance can be calculated using the following formula:

$$\text{Fixed Overhead Volume Variance} = \text{SFOR} \times \left(\text{SMH for Expected Production} - \text{SMH for Actual Production} \right)$$

$$= \$10 \times (2{,}000 \text{ machine hours} - 2{,}500 \text{ machine hours})$$

$$= \$5{,}000 \text{ Favorable}$$

A final issue that must be addressed is why the above variance is considered to be favorable. Since the number of footballs actually manufactured by SportsWorld is greater than expected, a greater amount of fixed overhead costs are applied to production. As a result, standard costs exceed actual costs, resulting in a favorable fixed overhead volume variance. A second line of reasoning is that by producing a larger number of units (or accumulating costs for a larger number of standard machine hours), the organization maximizes the use of its fixed overhead costs. Recall that fixed overhead costs remain constant over all levels of activity within the relevant range. In this case, SportsWorld produced 2,000 more footballs than anticipated without incurring any additional fixed overhead costs. In essence, these footballs were free (in terms of fixed overhead costs).

> An example from practice of the interpretation of the fixed overhead volume variance is illustrated by the major automobile manufactures' practice of producing automobiles on an around-the-clock schedule. For example, by adding a third production shift, General Motors can expect to increase its production of trucks by 200,000 per year. Also, Ford Motor Company has increased its production to 110 percent of nonovertime capacity. In doing so, these auto manufacturers are producing automobiles beyond what had been considered full capacity without spending any additional costs for manufacturing equipment (fixed overhead). By producing large quantities of automobiles, Chrysler Chairman Lee Iaccoca stated: "You get 50,000 more minivans for nothing."[16]
>
> Hewlett-Packard (HP) has implemented a unique method of reducing the consequences of the overhead volume variance. HP has developed a system that provides its customers with a discount or premium based on their demand. For example, if a customer's orders exceed HP's forecasted demand, that customer receives a discount approximately equal to the favorable fixed overhead volume variance generated by that sale; conversely, a premium is charged when sales to a customer are for fewer units than their anticipated demand.[17]

In spite of the above rationale, it is important to note that producing additional inventory is not always advantageous to the organization. If the additional items cannot be sold to customers, the organization has incurred additional variable costs (direct materials, direct labor, and variable overhead costs) without benefit. As a result, many organizations do not classify a volume variance as being either favorable or unfavorable. Instead, they use the volume variance as a method of identifying whether (and how) actual production levels differ from anticipated levels. However, since producing a greater number of items than expected results in applied fixed overhead costs exceeding actual fixed overhead costs by a greater amount, we classify SportsWorld's fixed overhead volume variance as favorable.

Fixed Overhead Spending Variance

Similar to variable overhead costs, another possible explanation for actual fixed overhead costs differing from fixed overhead costs applied to production relates to differences in either the actual costs or quantities of fixed overhead components from expected costs or quantities of these components. This difference between the budgeted fixed overhead costs and actual fixed overhead costs is referred to as the *fixed overhead spending variance*. As shown in Illustration 7, the fixed overhead spending variance for SportsWorld is $500. Furthermore, since the actual fixed overhead costs incurred by SportsWorld ($19,500) are less than the budgeted fixed overhead costs ($20,000), this variance is considered to be favorable.

Illustration 2 in the chapter indicates that SportsWorld's fixed overhead costs may be classified into three major categories: depreciation on plant and equipment, indirect labor, and insurance and taxes. The favorable fixed overhead spending variance indicates that these costs were $500 less than anticipated. This difference may reflect the retirement of plant and equipment (and reduced levels of depreciation expense), lower property tax and insurance costs than anticipated, or unpaid vacation or other reductions in the wages paid to indirect labor.

Summary: Fixed Overhead Variances

Illustration 7 revealed a total fixed overhead variance of $5,500. Since actual fixed overhead costs ($19,500) are less than fixed overhead costs applied to production ($25,000), this variance is considered to be favorable. Subsequent analysis revealed two causes of this variance.

1. The actual level of production (10,000 footballs) exceeded the expected level of production (8,000 footballs), resulting in the fixed overhead costs applied to production exceeding budgeted fixed overhead costs. The component of the fixed overhead variance resulting from this cause is referred to as the *fixed overhead volume variance*.

2. The actual cost or quantity of fixed overhead inputs was less than expected. This component of the fixed overhead variance is the *fixed overhead spending variance*.

---

[16] General Motors: Open All Night," *Business Week* (June 1, 1992), 82-83; "Day of the Night Shift," *Business Week* (May 30, 1994), 37; "Detroit: Hiballing It into Trucks," *Business Week* (March 7, 1994), 46.

[17] C.M. Merz and A. Hardy, "ABC Puts Accountants on Design Team at HP," *Management Accounting* (September 1993), 22–27.

Currently, some debate exists regarding the responsibility for the fixed overhead variances. For the fixed overhead volume variance, some argue that efficient utilization of capacity is the responsibility of the production supervisor, making this individual responsible for the fixed overhead volume variance. Conversely, others note that decisions regarding manufacturing volumes should be based on near-term demand for the organization's products. Under this line of reasoning, the production supervisor does not influence production decisions and, therefore, would not be held responsible for the fixed overhead volume variance.

A similar debate exists regarding fixed overhead spending variances. If these costs are truly fixed (and, therefore, cannot be "saved" in the short run), it seems inappropriate to charge (or credit) any variances of actual fixed overhead costs from standard fixed overhead costs to individual(s) in the organization. Clearly, depreciation, insurance, and taxes on equipment that has been acquired through past decisions cannot be influenced in the short term by the production supervisor or any of SportsWorld's employees without significantly altering its manufacturing capacity. Alternatively, if SportsWorld's management is willing to reduce the number of employees whose activities fall into the "fixed indirect labor" category (product inspectors, production supervisors, and machine setup personnel), SportsWorld's production supervisor could influence the levels of these costs by efficiently scheduling its manufacturing activities. For example, manufacturing footballs in larger production runs would presumably reduce setup costs and may reduce inspection and supervision costs to some extent.

OVERALL ANALYSIS OF OVERHEAD VARIANCES

In the preceding sections, we separately analyzed differences between actual fixed and variable overhead costs and the amount of fixed and variable overhead costs applied to production for SportsWorld. In so doing, four levels of overhead costs were determined: (1) actual overhead costs, (2) budgeted overhead costs at actual machine hours, (3) budgeted overhead costs at standard machine hours, and (4) overhead costs applied to production. The previous calculations from Illustrations 6 (for variable overhead costs) and 7 (for fixed overhead costs) are summarized in Illustration 8:

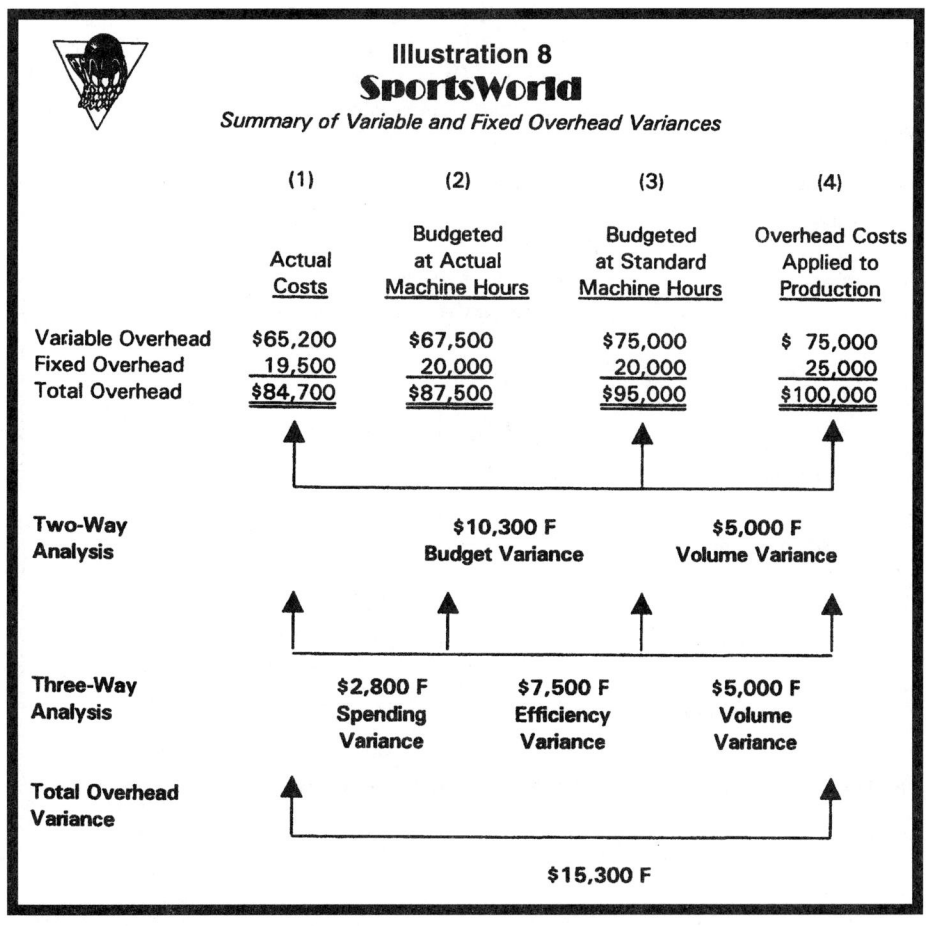

Illustration 8 shows that the difference between actual overhead costs and overhead costs applied to production can be decomposed into components by calculating budgeted overhead costs at two levels of activity: actual machine hours and standard machine hours allowed for actual production. Budgets prepared by the organization that reflect different levels of activity are referred to as *flexible budgets*. Note that the budgeted fixed overhead costs at either level of activity are expected to be $20,000. This reflects the nature of fixed costs, since these costs do not differ across different levels of activity within the relevant range. Also notice that the budgeted variable overhead costs differ between the two budgeted levels of activity, since variable costs vary directly and proportionally with changes in activity. Under the concept of flexible budgeting, budgeted overhead costs for any desired level of activity can be determined using the following general formula:

$$\text{Budgeted Overhead Costs} = \left(\text{Level of Activity} \times \text{Variable Overhead Rate} \right) + \text{Budgeted Fixed Overhead}$$

The two- and three-way analyses of overhead variances provide management with information regarding the reason(s) for differences in the overhead costs applied to production and the actual overhead costs incurred. A *three-way analysis* of overhead variances subdivides the total overhead variance into three components: (1) the fixed overhead volume variance (which relates entirely to fixed overhead costs), (2) the variable overhead efficiency variance (which relates entirely to variable overhead costs), and (3) the overhead spending variance (which includes variances related to both fixed and variable overhead costs). Note from the above analysis that the variable overhead costs in points (3) and (4) are identical ($75,000); therefore, the volume variance associated with variable overhead costs is zero. Similarly, the fixed overhead costs in points (2) and (3) above are identical ($20,000). As a result, the efficiency variance related to fixed overhead costs is also zero.

In a *two-way analysis* of overhead variances, the total overhead variance is decomposed into two components: (1) the fixed overhead volume variance (which is identical to that calculated in the three-way analysis of overhead variances) and (2) the overhead budget variance. The *overhead budget variance* represents the difference between actual overhead costs (point 1 in Illustration 8) and budgeted overhead costs at standard levels of activity (point 3 in Illustration 8). This variance essentially combines the overhead spending variance and the variable overhead efficiency variance from the three-way analysis of overhead variances.

The total overhead variance, decomposition of this variance, and fixed and variable components of this variance are summarized in Illustration 9. Note that neither the total amount of the overhead variance nor the nature of the overhead variance (fixed overhead costs versus variable overhead costs) is affected by the use of a two- or three-way analysis of overhead variances.

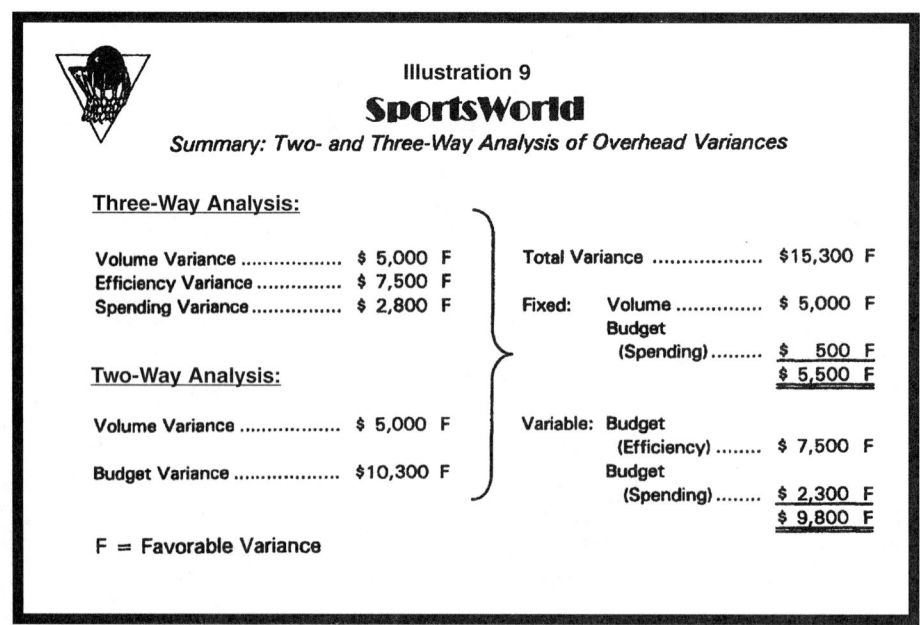

ACCUMULATION OF MANUFACTURING OVERHEAD COSTS WITH PRODUCTION

Recall that SportsWorld applied $100,000 of standard overhead costs to production and that actual overhead costs incurred by SportsWorld during January 20x1 were $84,700. As in an actual costing system, applied overhead costs are accumulated with work-in-process inventory while actual overhead costs are accumulated in the Manufacturing Overhead—Control account. The two journal entries prepared by SportsWorld to record its actual and applied overhead costs are shown below.

```
Work-in-Process—Control ..................................................................  100,000
    Manufacturing Overhead—Control..................................................            100,000

Manufacturing Overhead—Control ......................................................   84,700
    (Various Credits) ...........................................................................             84,700
```

In an actual costing system, the difference between actual and applied overhead costs is referred to as under- or over-applied overhead. In a standard costing system, this difference reflects manufacturing overhead variances. The following journal entry recognizes the overhead variances calculated in a previous section of this chapter (assuming a three-way analysis of overhead variances) and closes the manufacturing overhead account.

```
Manufacturing Overhead—Control...........................................................  15,300
    Overhead Volume Variance ..............................................................            5,000
    Overhead Efficiency Variance ..........................................................            7,500
    Overhead Spending Variance ..........................................................            2,800
```

As with direct materials and direct labor variances, manufacturing overhead variances can be closed to either cost of goods sold or apportioned among direct materials, inventory, work-in-process inventory, and finished goods inventory. Assuming that the variances are closed directly to cost of goods sold, the following entry would be prepared.

```
Overhead Volume Variance.......................................................................   5,000
Overhead Efficiency Variance...................................................................   7,500
Overhead Spending Variance ..................................................................   2,800
    Cost of Goods Sold..........................................................................           15,300
```

Learning Objectives

Chapter 8 provides an overview of budgeting and the process through which budgets are prepared. The preparation and use of the major types of budgets prepared by organizations (operating budgets, financial and resource budgets, and special decision budgets) are illustrated. Studying this chapter should enable you to:

1. Define budgeting and describe the budgeting process.

2. Define strategic planning and tactical planning and discuss how each of these processes relate to budgeting.

3. Discuss how budgets are used by organizations in conducting their activities.

4. Distinguish between operating budgets, financial and resource budgets, and special decision budgets.

5. Understand the hierarchy of preparation of the organization's operating budgets.

6. Identify the information required to prepare operating budgets and the financial statements related to operations.

7. Identify the information required to prepare financial and resource budgets and the budgeted Balance Sheet.

8. Prepare a comprehensive set of budgets (or Master Budget) from a set of case data.

8

Budgeting

INTRODUCTION

Meghan Scott, the co-owner of a small clothing store, was discussing the store's finances with Alice Burton, her partner. The store had just completed one of its busiest months, yet Meghan and Alice were perplexed by the cash balance shown on their most recent bank statement.

Meghan: How are we doing so far this month?

Alice: Pretty well, I think. Last week, our sales were much higher than we expected. It must be the season—people just love to buy new clothes at the end of the spring. In fact, we've had our best spring ever. I don't think our sales have ever been so high!

Meghan: That's odd—I just received our bank statement. Our cash balance is really low. If our sales are so high, why don't we have more cash?

Alice: Ever since we've offered store credit, cash sales have decreased. In fact, almost no one pays with cash anymore. Why should they? We offer them interest-free credit for ninety days.

Meghan: I know we began offering credit to increase our sales, but I didn't think it would have this much of an effect on our cash balance. I'm not sure we can continue much longer with the cash we have available now.

Alice: It's really a double-edged sword. When sales increase, we purchase more inventory. When we purchase inventory, we pay cash to our vendors. And vendors require us to pay for our purchases within ten days of delivery.

Meghan: There's the problem! We allow our customers ninety days to pay their accounts, but our vendors give us only ten days. We need to sit down and draw up a budget to see what our cash position will be in the future.

The above scenario illustrates a simple yet critical problem: how to ensure that an organization has sufficient cash with which to conduct its operating activities. In this scenario, Meghan and Alice can prepare various budgets to determine their anticipated cash position and identify any potential future cash shortages. These shortages may indicate a need to obtain financing to ensure that their store can continue to operate.

While the above discussion illustrates the importance of budgeting for a small business, budgets are essential for companies of all sizes. A *budget* is a formal plan that expresses a course of action in quantitative terms. Some questions that organizations answer by preparing budgets include:

- If Walt Disney World expects an average of 1.2 million visitors per day during the summer months, how many employees should be scheduled to work each day?

- If a Starbucks location serves 400 customers each morning, how many cups of coffee will be sold? How many pounds of coffee should Starbucks have on hand to serve these customers?

- If the CBS network charges $400,000 per minute for advertising during a prime-time television show, how much advertising revenue will it earn each month?

- If Delta Airlines schedules 10,000 additional flights during the year, how will its net income be affected?

- If DuPont increases the amount of paint products manufactured for sale to its customers, how much direct materials must it purchase?

This chapter focuses on the budgeting process and the use of budget information by the organization.

PURPOSES OF BUDGETING

The process of budgeting assists the management of an organization in conducting three major types of activities: planning, communicating, and evaluating. Budgets allow managers to effectively plan the organization's activities by forcing managers to go beyond a focus on day-to-day activities and explicitly consider future events. For example, considering future sales demand for vehicles will require the Production Manager of General Motors to determine the levels of production necessary to satisfy this anticipated future demand. These levels of production will be summarized in General Motors' Production Budget. Preparing this budget requires the Production Manager to plan future activities so that sufficient direct materials and direct labor resources are available to meet desired levels of production. Doing so allows potential production shortages to be identified early on and provides management with an opportunity to take appropriate action to overcome this potential problem. Establishing production goals is one of the basic purposes of planning.

A second activity affected by budgeting is communicating information and coordinating the operations of the organization. To operate effectively, it is important that the plans of individual departments are known by other departments. Continuing with the preceding example, once General Motors has estimated the demand for its automobiles, this information is communicated to the Production Department to ensure that the level of production is sufficient to meet this demand. Once the Production Department has determined the necessary level of production, it must communicate this information to the Purchasing Department so that sufficient direct materials inputs can be obtained to produce the desired number of automobiles. Only by communicating information throughout its various departments can the activities of these departments (Production and Purchasing) be properly coordinated.

Finally, budgets are also used in evaluating the performance of individuals and units within the organization. In this sense, budgets act as "targets" or standards that individuals or departments attempt to achieve. For example, a Toyota dealer normally establishes Sales Budgets (or "quotas") for its salespeople to encourage them to increase their sales. By comparing the actual number and types of vehicles sold to these quotas, a measure of the performance of the salespeople can be obtained. Production Departments will prepare budgets for the costs of direct materials, direct labor, and manufacturing overhead against which actual costs can be compared. Similar to the use of performance standards, differences between actual and budgeted costs may reveal effective or ineffective levels of performance. For budgeting to be successful in improving performance, employees and managers should be rewarded in a manner consistent with the goals expressed in the organization's budgets.

> Prior to its dramatic turnaround in the mid-1990s, Continental Airlines had little communication between employees who set the flight schedules and those overseeing airport and flight operations. This lack of communication resulted in operating departments having mechanics, aircraft parts, and flight crews in the wrong locations. As a result, the operating departments were saddled with a flight schedule they had no hope of achieving.[1]
>
> DaimlerChrysler has recently reorganized its organizational structure to enhance the degree of communication between functional areas. In the past, DaimlerChrysler's engineers were organized into a single function (for example, designing engines for automobiles). Now, DaimlerChrysler assigns its engineers to report to the manager of that design team. The enhanced communication among engineers and other individuals involved in the production process has saved $475 million a year through fewer design changes.[2]

---

[1] G. Brenneman, "How We Saved Continental," *Harvard Business Review* (September-October 1998), 9.

[2] "Chrysler May Actually be Turning the Corner," *Business Week* (February 10, 1992), 32.

THE BUDGETING PROCESS

The budgeting process typically begins with *strategic planning* by the organization's top-level management. A strategic plan communicates the goals and objectives of the organization for a relatively long-term period of time (5-10 years). For example, PepsiCo's strategic plan may indicate the desired relative contributions of snack foods and beverage products to overall revenues over the next five to ten years. Wal-Mart's strategic plan may describe whether it intends to pursue domestic or international expansion of its stores. Once developed, the strategic plan acts as a blueprint for the organization that ultimately drives the organization's day-to-day activities.

Based on the goals and objectives established by the strategic plan, organizations plan their activities accordingly. *Tactical planning* allows the organization to achieve its strategic plan and provides important benchmarks against which progress toward achieving the strategic plan can be measured. For example, if PepsiCo's goal is to have 40 percent of its revenues from snack foods at the end of five years, a tactical plan might establish targets of 20 percent at the end of year 1, 25 percent at the end of year 2, 33 percent at the end of year 3, and 38 percent at the end of year 4. Tactical planning is shorter-range in nature than strategic planning and provides an indication as to the progress toward meeting the goals and objectives included in the strategic plan. The end result of tactical planning may be the preparation of a set of forecasted financial statements for each year of the strategic plan.

Budgets serve as the most basic element of the strategic planning process. Budgets typically cover a period of a year or less and can be prepared monthly, quarterly, or at whatever interval management desires. Budgets provide an effective (yet near-term) basis for evaluating the organization's progress toward its goals and objectives as identified in the strategic plan. For example, consider PepsiCo's goal of 40 percent of revenues from the sale of snack foods in five years. If a tactical plan has identified a target of 25 percent at the end of year 2, budgets can be prepared for each quarter of year 2 to monitor PepsiCo's progress toward this goal. The relationships among strategic planning, tactical planning, and budgeting are shown below:

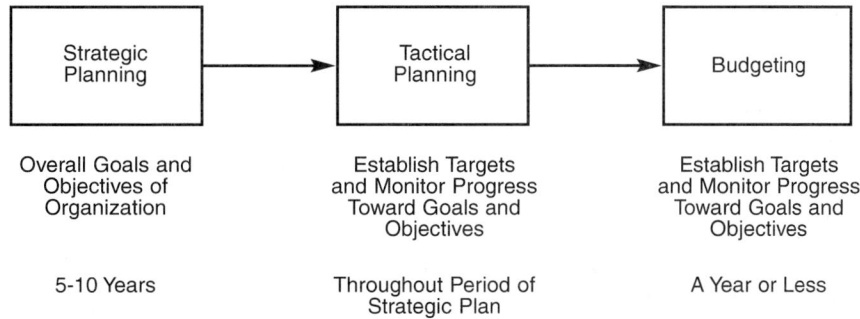

Preparing budgets requires the joint efforts of employees throughout the organization. In some instances, the responsibility for preparing and distributing the budget is delegated to a budget committee, which includes managers representing various functions of the organization (such as sales, production and finance). In some organizations, the budgeting process includes participation of employees and administrators at all levels of operations. This type of budgeting is called *participative budgeting*. Many believe that participative budgeting fosters cohesiveness and strengthens motivation among employees. Nonetheless, in many organizations, for a variety of reasons, managers establish goals and determine the means of accomplishing these goals without consulting lower-level employees.

Budgeting practices vary widely. A comprehensive system of budgets (or *master budget*) includes at least three types of budgets: operating budgets, financial and resource budgets, and special decision budgets. *Operating budgets* reflect the primary activities of the organization, such as producing inventory, using direct materials and direct labor, and incurring overhead and other nonmanufacturing expenses. Examples of operating budgets include the Sales Budget, Production Budget, Direct Materials Purchases Budget, and Direct Labor Budget. Once operating budgets are prepared, the organization can prepare a budgeted (or *pro forma*) Income Statement that indicates the net income anticipated from operating activities for the period covered by the budget.

Financial and resource budgets focus on the expected levels of the organization's assets and liabilities based on the level of activity assumed in preparing the operating budgets. Examples of financial and resource budgets are the Cash Receipts Budget, Cash Disbursements Budget, and Accounts Receivable Budget. Once the financial and resource budgets have been prepared, the organization can prepare a budgeted (or *pro forma*) Balance Sheet that indicates the assets, liabilities, and equity of the organization at various dates throughout the budget period.

The final budget prepared in a comprehensive budgeting system is a *special decision budget*. Unlike both operating budgets and financial and resource budgets, a special decision budget is not prepared at fixed points in time. These budgets are prepared as requested by management for a variety of decisions related to issues other than the organization's ordinary ongoing operations and activities. For example, assume that Coca-Cola has incurred losses on the sale of one of its recently introduced products. The management of Coca-Cola may request a budget (or analysis) that summarizes the effects on net income of discontinuing the sale of this product. A common type of special decision budget, the *capital budget*, analyzes the feasibility of long-term investments in productive resources, such as operating machinery.

COMPREHENSIVE EXAMPLE: OPERATING BUDGETS

To illustrate the budgeting process and the preparation of budgets, we will consider the operations of Toy Concepts, Inc. Toy Concepts is a manufacturer of battery-powered vehicles that seat up to two children and are targeted for operation by children from four to six years of age. Toy Concepts' products are sold in specialty toy shops and general-purpose retailers throughout the United States. As is common for most toy manufacturers, Toy Concepts' business is highly seasonal, with approximately 30 percent of its annual sales in the months of November and December.

Toy Concepts currently manufactures ten different types of battery-powered vehicles, including construction vehicles (dump trucks and cement mixers) and service vehicles (police vehicles and fire engines). For the purposes of our discussion, we will consider one of their most popular models: the Jeep Sports Utility Vehicle.[3] Based on its organizational policy, Toy Concepts prepares short-term operating budgets at the beginning of each quarter; we illustrate the preparation of these budgets for the first quarter of 20x2. As a starting point, Toy Concepts' balance sheet at December 31, 20x1 is presented in Illustration 1.[4]

Illustration 1

Toy Concepts, Inc.
Balance Sheet: December 31, 20x1

Assets:		
Cash		$ 4,000
Accounts Receivable		20,000
Inventories:		
Direct Materials (692 lbs. x $.50)	346	
Work-in-Process	100	
Finished Goods (160 units x $24)	3,840	4,286
Property, Plant and Equipment (net of		
accumulated depreciation of $24,000)		46,000
Total Assets		$ 74,286
Liabilities and Shareholders' Equity:		
Accounts Payable (from December purchases)		$ 300
Notes Payable		40,000
Shareholders' Equity		33,986
Total Liabilities and Shareholders' Equity		$ 74,286

Toy Concepts uses a standard costing system that accumulates production costs with inventory based on its variable manufacturing costs (direct materials, direct labor, and variable manufacturing overhead). Recall that this type of costing system is referred to as *variable* (or *direct*) *costing*. While variable costing may be used for internal budgeting purposes, it is not allowed for external reporting purposes. The primary direct material used by Toy Concepts in manufacturing its vehicles is plastic. The cost of the remaining materials is included in

---

[3] Limiting the consideration to a single product allows us to focus on the preparation of budgets and interrelationships between and among different types of budgets for a reasonable amount of data. It is important to note that all of Toy Concepts' budgets prepared in this chapter would consider planned activities related to all of their products.

[4] In practice, the budgeting process for the following year (period) typically begins prior to the end of the preceding year (period). Because actual balance sheet data are not available, estimated data serve as the starting point for the budgeting process. These estimated data can subsequently be revised to the extent that actual balance sheet data differ from the estimated data.

overhead as indirect materials. The standard variable cost of manufacturing a Jeep is $24; this cost is based on the following performance standards established by Scott Andrews, the manager of the Manufacturing Division:

Direct Materials (Plastic) (4 lbs. x $0.50)	$ 2.00
Direct Labor (0.60 hrs. x $15.00)	9.00
Variable Overhead	13.00
Total Standard Cost	$ 24.00

Sales Budget

The Sales Budget is the cornerstone of the budgeting process. The remaining operating budgets are dependent on the forecasted level of sales. For example, Toy Concepts cannot determine how many vehicles it must manufacture without estimating its sales. Further, if the level of production is not known, the materials, labor, and manufacturing overhead requirements cannot be determined. Therefore, the budgeting process must begin with the preparation of the Sales Budget.

Basic information required to prepare the Sales Budget includes:

1. The expected level of Toy Concepts' sales (in units).
2. The estimated selling prices of Toy Concepts' products.

Normally, selling prices are established by management based on a number of factors such as the costs of manufacturing the products, the desired profit levels, and the level of competition and existence of alternative products in the marketplace. After considering these and other factors, assume that the management of Toy Concepts has established a selling price of $80 for its Jeep; this selling price is the same as that charged in 20x1.

In determining the estimated level of sales, management considers a number of factors including:

1. Past sales levels and trends.
2. The market for the company's products and changes in that market, such as products introduced by competitors or pricing strategies of competitors.
3. General economic conditions and changes in these conditions, such as favorable conditions that would result in customers having increased levels of disposable income.
4. Strategic actions by the company, such as increases or decreases in the selling price of other products.

Once the selling price and the sales levels have been estimated, the organization can prepare its Sales Budget. Toy Concepts estimated that sales will drop noticeably in January (following the holiday season) but would steadily increase by approximately 10 percent per month for the first five months of 20x2. Based on estimated January sales of 200 units, as well as the 10 percent increase in sales for the first five months of 20x2, Toy Concepts' Sales Budget is presented in Illustration 2. While the budgeting focus is on the first quarter of 20x2, estimated sales for the months of April and May are included because these estimates are required to prepare other budgets for the first quarter of 20x2.[5]

Illustration 2
Toy Concepts, Inc.
Sales Budget
January - May 20x2

	January	February	March	April	May
Estimated Unit Sales	200	220	242	267	294
x Estimated Selling Price	x $80	x $80	x $80	x $80	x $80
Estimated Sales	$16,000	$17,600	$19,360	$21,360	$23,520

Note that the Sales Budget in Illustration 2 includes both units and dollars of sales. The sales dollars will ultimately be included in Toy Concepts' budgeted Income Statement. The estimated unit sales are considered in preparing Toy Concepts' Production Budget, which is discussed in the following subsection.

---

[5] Throughout this example, all nondollar items are expressed in whole units (units of sales, hours of direct labor, pounds of direct materials, etc.) rounded to the highest whole number. Dollar amounts are rounded to the nearest dollar.

Production Budget

The second step in the budgeting process is the preparation of the Production Budget. The Production Budget is used to determine the number of units that must be manufactured during the period to satisfy the estimated sales demand for the period, considering both beginning and ending inventory levels. The estimated level of necessary production is determined as follows:

Desired Ending Inventory	+	Estimated Unit Sales	−	Beginning Inventory
↑		↑		↑
Based on Company Policy		**From Sales Budget (Illustration 2)**		**From Previous Balance Sheet (Illustration 1)**

As shown in the preceding equation, the estimated unit sales are available from the Sales Budget. Desired inventory levels (both beginning inventory and ending inventory) are typically based on management policies. In deciding to maintain inventory balances, the organization's management must weigh both the advantages (reducing the likelihood of lost sales because of unanticipated demand) and disadvantages (requiring funds to be invested in inventory) of doing so. To avoid potential inventory shortages resulting from unexpected production downtime and to satisfy unanticipated demand, Toy Concepts has established a policy of maintaining its finished goods inventory at 80 percent of the following month's estimated sales. For example, referring to Toy Concepts' December 31, 20x1 balance sheet (see Illustration 1), ending finished goods inventory consists of 160 Jeeps, which represents 80 percent of January's estimated unit sales from the Sales Budget (Illustration 2) (0.80 x 200 units = 160 units). Alternative policies could include maintaining constant levels of inventory or, using a just-in-time manufacturing philosophy, maintaining either minimal or no inventory.

Toy Concepts' Production Budget is presented in Illustration 3. Like the Sales Budget (Illustration 2), information relating to periods other than the first quarter of 20x2 is presented because this information will be required to prepare subsequent budgets. The Production Budget highlights two common relationships. First, notice that the desired ending inventory balance for one period is the beginning inventory balance for the following period. Also, the desired balance of ending inventory for one period is based on the estimated sales for the following period. That is, the beginning inventory balance is related to the current period's sales activity. For example, referring to Illustration 3, the 176 units estimated to be in inventory at the end of January (beginning of February) represent 80 percent of estimated sales during February (0.80 x 220 units = 176 units).

Illustration 3

Toy Concepts, Inc.
Production Budget
January - April, 20x2

	January	February	March	April
Estimated Sales (from Illustration 2)	200	220	242	267
Add: Desired Ending Inventory[a]	176	194	214	236
Total Production Needs	376	414	456	503
Less: Beginning Inventory[b]	(160)	(176)	(194)	(214)
Units to be Produced	216	238	262	289

[a] 0.80 multiplied by the following month's sales (see Illustration 2), as follows:
  January: 220 Jeeps x 0.80 = 176
  February: 242 Jeeps x 0.80 = 194
  March: 267 Jeeps x 0.80 = 214
  April: 294 Jeeps x 0.80 = 236
[b] Equal to ending inventory from the preceding month. The January balance is from Toy Concepts' December 31, 20x1 Balance Sheet (see Illustration 1)

The important effect of sales estimates on production is illustrated in the following examples.

> Since most sales for toy manufacturers occur in the last three months of the year and toys are greatly subject to "fad buying," it is critical that accurate sales estimates be developed by toy manufacturers when planning their production for the busy holiday season. On average, it takes three months to make, ship, and stock a particular toy product on the shelves of a retailer; thus, timely and accurate sales estimates are critical.[6]
>
> Nike requires retailers to order up to 80 percent of their purchases six to eight months in advance in return for guaranteed delivery times and large discounts. This procedure takes much of the uncertainty out of estimating sales for the upcoming period. Through the use of this approach, Nike has enough information about its sales so that production can be planned relatively early.[7]
>
> The costs of poor sales estimates can be seen by examining the experience of Fruit of the Loom, Inc. With sales of underwear and apparel slowing, Fruit of the Loom cut its production. The shortage of inventory resulting from unanticipated demand cost Fruit of the Loom over $200 million of lost sales.[8]

The result of preparing the Production Budget is that Toy Concepts must manufacture 216, 238, and 262 units in January, February, and March of 20x2, respectively, in order to meet its anticipated demand and maintain the levels of ending inventory desired by management. It is important to note that the Production Budget shown in Illustration 3 (and the budgets shown in the following sections) are based on this anticipated level of activity. These budgets are referred to as *static budgets*. Some organizations prepare budgets assuming more than a single level of activity, referred to as *flexible budgets*. For example, Toy Concepts could prepare Production Budgets (and subsequent budgets) assuming that sales differed from expectations by 10 percent (either greater or less than the level of sales assumed in Illustration 2). An advantage of flexible budgets is that they provide the organization with an indication of how fluctuations in sales estimates influence budgeted operating results.

Once the estimated manufacturing volumes are known, the organization can then determine the estimated quantity and cost of its manufacturing inputs (direct materials, direct labor, and overhead). Budgets for these inputs are illustrated in the following subsections.

Direct Materials Purchases And Usage Budgets

Once the budgeted production levels have been determined, Direct Material Purchases and Usage budgets are prepared. These budgets summarize the quantity and cost of direct materials that must be purchased and used in manufacturing inventories. The quantity of direct materials purchased depends on both the level of production (as determined in the Production Budget in Illustration 3) as well as the desired ending levels of direct materials inventory. Similar to finished goods inventory, the desired ending level of direct materials inventory is normally based on management policy. Because it has occasionally experienced some delay from suppliers in obtaining direct materials, Toy Concepts has implemented a policy of maintaining a desired ending balance of direct materials inventory at 80 percent of *the following month's* production requirements. That is, the desired direct materials quantities on hand at the end of January 20x2 should be 80 percent of the materials required for February's production. These additional quantities of direct materials inventory should enable Toy Concepts to continue production even when delivery of direct materials from suppliers is delayed. The budgeted quantity of direct materials purchased is determined as follows:

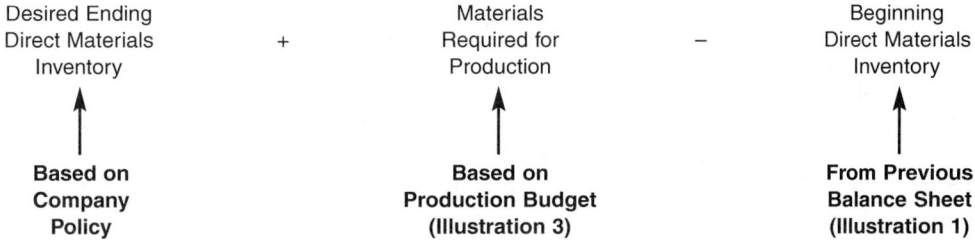

In addition to identifying the level of production and desired levels of direct materials inventory, Toy Concepts also must determine the quantities and prices of direct materials required for production when preparing the Direct Materials Purchases Budget. This information would normally be obtained from the

---

[6] "Toy Industry Finds It's Harder and Harder to Pick the Winners," *The Wall Street Journal* (December 21, 1993), A1, A5.

[7] "Can Nike Just Do It?," *Business Week* (April 18, 1994), 89.

[8] "Too Much Pruning Stunts Fruit of the Loom," *Business Week* (June 6, 1994), 38.

manager of the Manufacturing Division. As indicated earlier, the performance standards specify that 4 pounds of plastic are required per vehicle at a cost of $0.50 per pound. The Direct Materials Purchases and Usage Budgets are summarized in Illustration 4.

Illustration 4

Toy Concepts, Inc.
Direct Materials Purchases Budget
January - March, 20x2

	January	February	March
Units Produced in Following Month (from Illustration 3)	238	262	289
Standard Materials per Unit (pounds)	x 4	x 4	x 4
Total Production Requirements in Following Month (pounds)	952	1,048	1,156
x 80%	x 0.80	x 0.80	x 0.80
Desired Ending Inventory (pounds)	762	839	925
Units Produced in Current Month (from Illustration 3)	216	238	262
Standard Materials per Unit (pounds)	x 4	x 4	x 4
Total Production Requirements (pounds)	864	952	1,048
Desired Ending Inventory (pounds)	762	839	925
Total Material Needs (pounds)	1,626	1,791	1,973
Less: Beginning Inventory (pounds)	(692)	(762)	(839)
Purchase Requirements (pounds)	934	1,029	1,134
x Cost per pound	x $0.50	x $0.50	x $0.50
Total Direct Materials Purchases	$ 467	$ 515	$ 567

Toy Concepts, Inc.
Direct Materials Usage Budget
January - March, 20x2

	January	February	March
Total Production Requirements (pounds)	864	952	1,048
x Cost per pound	x $0.50	x $0.50	x $0.50
Total Cost of Direct Materials Used in Production	$ 432	$ 476	$ 524

It is important to distinguish between the two direct materials budgets. The Direct Materials Purchases Budget provides the purchasing agent with information concerning the quantity of direct materials that should be purchased during the budget period. These purchases are made for two purposes: to produce the necessary number of units (from the Production Budget) and to maintain the desired level of direct materials inventory on hand. In contrast, the Direct Materials Usage Budget shows the production manager the quantities and cost of direct materials needed for the budgeted level of production.

Direct Labor and Manufacturing Overhead Budgets

Similar to the Direct Materials Usage Budget, once the expected levels of production have been determined (by preparation of the Production Budget), Toy Concepts can prepare budgets for its remaining manufacturing costs. These budgets utilize two types of information: (1) the level of production (from the Production Budget in Illustration 3) and (2) performance standards for direct labor and manufacturing overhead costs. Recall that the standard direct labor cost was $9 per unit (0.6 hours x $15 = $9) and the standard variable overhead cost was $13 per unit. In addition, assume that your discussions with Scott Andrews (the manager of the Manufacturing Division) revealed that fixed overhead costs were approximately $2,000 per month. Toy Concepts' Direct Labor and Manufacturing Overhead Budgets for the first quarter of 20x2 are shown in Illustration 5.[9]

---

[9] In practice, the Manufacturing Overhead Budget may be prepared in greater detail than shown in Illustration 5. For example, the Manufacturing Overhead Budget may be expanded to include budgeted amounts for the various types of variable and fixed overhead costs incurred by the organization. We have prepared summary budgets for simplicity and to focus on the budgeting process and the information required to prepare various types of operating budgets.

Illustration 5

Toy Concepts, Inc.
Direct Labor Budget
January - March 20x2

	January	February	March
Units to be Produced (from Illustration 3)....................	216	238	262
x Standard Hours per Unit......................................	x 0.60	x 0.60	x 0.60
Direct Labor Hours Required.....................................	130	143	158
x Direct Labor Cost per Hour................................	x $15	x $15	x $15
Total Direct Labor Costs	$1,950	$2,145	$2,370

Toy Concepts, Inc.
Manufacturing Overhead Budget
January - March 20x2

	January	February	March
Units to be Produced (from Illustration 3)....................	216	238	262
x Standard Variable Overhead Rate......................	x $13	x $13	x $13
Total Variable Overhead Costs	$2,808	$3,094	$3,406
Total Fixed Overhead Costs	2,000	2,000	2,000
Total Manufacturing Overhead Costs	$4,808	$5,094	$5,406

Nonmanufacturing Expense Budget

The final budget necessary before the preparation of the budgeted financial statements related to operations is the Nonmanufacturing Expense Budget. Toy Concepts has two major types of nonmanufacturing expenses. First, it pays its salespersons a five percent commission on all sales. To determine the budgeted sales commissions, Toy Concepts must identify the expected level of sales for a given month from the Sales Budget (Illustration 2). In addition, fixed nonmanufacturing expenses are incurred for rent on the administrative facilities ($1,600) and interest on the note payable ($40,000 x 12% x 1/12 = $400 per month). The Nonmanufacturing Expense Budget for Toy Concepts for the first quarter of 20x2 is shown in Illustration 6.

Illustration 6

Toy Concepts, Inc.
Nonmanufacturing Expense Budget
January - March 20x2

	January	February	March
Estimated Sales (from Illustration 2)....................	$16,000	$17,600	$19,360
x Commission Rate	x 0.05	x 0.05	x 0.05
Variable Selling Expenses	$ 800	$ 880	$ 968
Rent on Administrative Facilities........................	1,600	1,600	1,600
Interest Expense	400	400	400
Total Nonmanufacturing Expenses.....................	$ 2,800	$ 2,880	$ 2,968

BUDGETED FINANCIAL STATEMENTS—OPERATIONS

At this stage, Toy Concepts has prepared all of the necessary operating budgets. These budgets will provide information concerning: (1) the number of units which should be produced each month to meet anticipated demand; (2) the amounts and costs of direct materials, direct labor, and manufacturing overhead used in production; and (3) the amount of nonmanufacturing expenses incurred. Companies typically prepare three major operating financial statement budgets: the Cost of Goods Manufactured Statement, the Cost of Goods Sold Statement, and the Income Statement.

The cost of goods manufactured represents the transfers from work-in-process inventory to finished goods inventory for units completed during a period. Most of the information required to determine budgeted cost of goods manufactured has already been identified in previous operating budgets. For example, the direct materials costs, direct labor costs, and manufacturing overhead costs are included in the Direct Materials Usage Budget (Illustration 4), Direct Labor Budget (Illustration 5), and Manufacturing Overhead Budget (Illustration 5), respectively. Because Toy Concepts uses variable costing in its budgeting process, only the expected *variable* overhead costs are accumulated with inventory. As shown later in the budgeted Income Statement, fixed overhead costs are expensed as they are incurred under variable costing.

The only remaining information needed to prepare the Cost of Goods Manufactured Budget is the desired level of work-in-process inventories maintained. Like finished goods and direct materials inventories, the desired levels of work-in-process inventories are normally maintained based on management policy. Because of the continuous nature of Toy Concepts' production process, work-in-process inventory is expected to exist throughout the budget period at a relatively constant (but low) amount ($100 per month).

Given the above information, Toy Concepts' Cost of Goods Manufactured Budget is presented in Illustration 7.

Illustration 7
Toy Concepts, Inc.
Budgeted Cost of Goods Manufactured
Variable Costing Format
January - March 20x2

	January	February	March
Beginning Work-in-Process...	$ 100	$ 100	$ 100
Add: Manufacturing Costs			
Direct Materials Used (Illustration 4).............................	432	476	524
Direct Labor (Illustration 5)...	1,950	2,145	2,370
Variable Manufacturing Overhead			
(Illustration 5)...	2,808	3,094	3,406
Goods Available for Completion......................................	$ 5,290	$ 5,815	$ 6,400
Less: Ending Work-in-Process...	(100)	(100)	(100)
Cost of Goods Manufactured	$ 5,190	$ 5,715	$ 6,300

The budgeted cost of goods manufactured, along with the beginning and ending balances of finished goods inventory, are used to determine budgeted Cost of Goods Sold. Recall that Toy Concepts' policy is to maintain levels of finished goods inventory equal to 80 percent of the following month's sales. From Illustration 3 (the Production Budget), the desired ending levels of finished goods inventory in January, February, and March are 176 units, 194 units, and 214 units, respectively. In addition, Toy Concepts' December 31, 20x1 balance sheet (see Illustration 1) revealed that 160 units were on hand at the beginning of January 20x2. Using this information, along with the standard variable manufacturing cost per unit ($24), the budgeted ending finished goods inventory balances are calculated as follows:

December 20x1:	160 units	x	$24	=	$3,840
January 20x2:	176 units	x	$24	=	$4,224
February 20x2:	194 units	x	$24	=	$4,656
March 20x2:	214 units	x	$24	=	$5,136

These balances, along with the budgeted cost of goods manufactured (from Illustration 7) are then used to prepare the budgeted Cost of Goods Sold Statement shown in Illustration 8.

At this point, a *budgeted* (or *pro forma*) *Income Statement* may be prepared. The budgeted Income Statement incorporates information from four other budgets: the Sales Budget (Illustration 2), the budgeted Cost of Goods Sold (Illustration 8), the Manufacturing Overhead Budget (Illustration 5), and the Nonmanufacturing Expense

Illustration 8

Toy Concepts, Inc.
Budgeted Cost of Goods Sold
Variable Costing Format
January - March 20x2

	January	February	March
Beginning Finished Goods Inventory	$ 3,840	$ 4,224	$ 4,656
Add: Cost of Goods Manufactured (from Illustration 7)	5,190	5,715	6,300
Goods Available for Sale	$ 9,030	$ 9,939	$10,956
Less: Ending Finished Goods Inventory	(4,224)	(4,656)	(5,136)
Cost of Goods Sold	$ 4,806	$ 5,283	$ 5,820

Budget (Illustration 6). Toy Concepts' budgeted income statement is shown in Illustration 9. It should be noted that Toy Concepts uses variable costing in preparing its internal budgets. As a result, fixed overhead costs are not accumulated with inventory but are expensed as incurred. Also, recall that a variable costing income statement classifies expenses by behavior (fixed or variable) and not activity (manufacturing or nonmanufacturing).

Illustration 9

Toy Concepts, Inc.
Budgeted Income Statement
Variable Costing Format
January - March 20x2

	January	February	March
Sales (from Illustration 2)	$ 16,000	$ 17,600	$ 19,360
Less: Cost of Goods Sold (from Illustration 8)	(4,806)	(5,283)	(5,820)
Variable Nonmanufacturing Costs (from Illustration 6)	(800)	(880)	(968)
Contribution Margin	$ 10,394	$11,437	$12,572
Less: Fixed Overhead Costs (from Illustration 5)	(2,000)	(2,000)	(2,000)
Fixed Nonmanufacturing Costs (from Illustration 6)	(2,000)	(2,000)	(2,000)
Net Income	$ 6,394	$ 7,437	$ 8,572

FINANCIAL AND RESOURCE BUDGETS

The operating budgets illustrated provide an indication of the organization's profitability (as shown in the preparation of the budgeted Income Statement). However, these budgets do not provide information concerning the anticipated level of its assets and obligations. *Financial and resource budgets* are concerned with budgeting the expected level of the organization's assets and liabilities. The culmination of the financial and resource budgeting process is the preparation of a budgeted (or *pro forma*) Balance Sheet.

Cash Budget

Because most of an organization's transactions will ultimately result in the receipt or payment of cash, the preparation of a Cash Budget is a critical step in the budgeting process. Since shortages of cash may prevent the organization from conducting its day-to-day operations in the usual manner, it is essential that effective cash budgeting procedures are utilized. To reduce the likelihood of cash shortages, Toy Concepts has established a policy that a minimum of $4,000 of cash must be maintained at all times. This balance serves as a "cushion" in the event that cash receipts and disbursements differ from expected collections and payments. While usually not as costly as a cash shortage, maintaining excess cash often results in incurring an opportunity cost, since the cash could be earning a return if invested elsewhere.

In preparing the Cash Budget, companies must consider expected *cash receipts* and *cash disbursements*. The only source of cash receipts for Toy Concepts is from the collection of sales made to its customers on account. Because of its strict credit policy, Toy Concepts has experienced only small losses from uncollectible accounts. All of Toy Concepts' sales are made on account. The normal collection of these sales is as follows:

- 50 percent is collected in the month of the sale.
- 40 percent is collected in the month following the sale.
- 10 percent is collected in the second month following the sale.

Thus, the budgeted collection of January's sales of $16,000 would be as follows:

	January	February	March
($16,000 x 0.50)	$8,000		
($16,000 x 0.40)		$6,400	
($16,000 x 0.10)			$1,600

Toy Concepts' Cash Receipts Budget is presented in Illustration 10. Note that the $20,000 of accounts receivable at year-end represents sales made on account in December and November. For the purposes of our example, assume that $16,000 of these accounts receivable were related to December sales and $4,000 were related to November sales. Since the accounts receivable related to December sales represented half of that month's sales, December sales were $32,000 ($32,000 x 0.50 = $16,000).

Illustration 10
Toy Concepts, Inc.
Cash Receipts Budget
January - March 20x2

	January	February	March
November Sales	$ 4,000		
December Sales:			
$32,000 x 0.40	12,800		
$32,000 x 0.10		$ 3,200	
January Sales (from Illustration 2):			
$16,000 x 0.50	8,000		
$16,000 x 0.40		6,400	
$16,000 x 0.10			$ 1,600
February Sales (from Illustration 2):			
$17,600 x 0.50		8,800	
$17,600 x 0.40			7,040
March Sales (from Illustration 2):			
$19,360 x 0.50			9,680
Total Cash Receipts	**$ 24,800**	**$ 18,400**	**$ 18,320**

Like the Cash Receipts Budget, Toy Concepts' *Cash Disbursements Budget* considers information from operating budgets as well as information concerning the timing of cash flows. Toy Concepts considers when disbursements will be made for the various costs it incurs. Cash disbursements are made for four primary purposes: direct materials purchases (from the Direct Materials Purchases Budget in Illustration 4), direct labor (from the Direct Labor Budget in Illustration 5), manufacturing overhead (from the Manufacturing Overhead

Budget in Illustration 5), and nonmanufacturing expenses (from the Nonmanufacturing Expense Budget in Illustration 6).

In addition to these costs, Toy Concepts also must consider the timing of the actual disbursements. Toy Concepts has made arrangements with its suppliers to pay 25 percent of its purchases of direct materials in the month of the purchase and the remainder in the next month. All other costs (direct labor, manufacturing overhead, and nonmanufacturing expenses) are paid for in the month incurred. For example, the total cash disbursements for Toy Concepts in January 20x2 would be the sum of the following:

1. 75 percent of direct materials purchases in December 20x1
2. 25 percent of direct materials purchases in January 20x2
3. Expected direct labor costs incurred in January 20x2
4. Expected manufacturing overhead costs incurred in January 20x2
5. Expected nonmanufacturing expenses incurred in January 20x2

Another point should be considered in preparing the Cash Disbursements Budget. Certain overhead and nonmanufacturing costs (such as depreciation) do not require cash outlays. These costs should be excluded from the Cash Disbursements Budget. As shown in Illustration 5, fixed overhead costs are expected to be $2,000 per month, of which $500 is depreciation on manufacturing equipment and facilities. As a result, the cash required for manufacturing overhead costs should not include the $500 in depreciation costs. Toy Concepts' Cash Disbursements Budget is shown in Illustration 11.

Illustration 11
Toy Concepts, Inc.
Cash Disbursements Budget
January - March 20x2

	January	February	March
December Purchases of Direct Materials....................	$ 300[a]		
January Purchases of Direct Materials (Illustration 4):			
$467 x 0.25	117		
$467 x 0.75		$ 350	
February Purchases of Direct Materials (Illustration 4):			
$515 x 0.25		129	
$515 x 0.75			386
March Purchases of Direct Materials (Illustration 4):			
$567 x 0.25			142
Payments for Direct Materials Purchases..................	$ 417	$ 479	$ 528
Payment of Direct Labor Costs (Illustration 5)	1,950	2,145	2,370
Payment of Manufacturing Overhead Costs, less Depreciation of $500 (Illustration 5)..............	4,308	4,594	4,906
Payment of Nonmanufacturing Costs (Illustration 6)..	2,800	2,880	2,968
Total Cash Disbursements	$ 9,475	$10,098	$10,772

[a] Represents the balance in accounts payable from Toy Concepts' December 31, 20x1 Balance Sheet (see Illustration 1)

Once the Cash Receipts and Cash Disbursements Budgets have been prepared, the Cash Budget can be prepared. The Cash Budget provides information regarding the amount of cash on hand at the end of each month. This budget can be used to identify potential shortages of cash that may require short-term borrowings to allow Toy Concepts to continue its day-to-day operating activities. Conversely, overages of cash may provide Toy Concepts with an opportunity to utilize excess cash to retire debt or invest in securities.

Toy Concepts' Cash Budget is shown in Illustration 12. This Cash Budget adds budgeted cash receipts (from the Cash Receipts Budget in Illustration 10) and subtracts cash disbursements (from the Cash Disbursements Budget in Illustration 11) from the beginning cash balance. Recall that Toy Concepts has established a policy of maintaining a minimum of $4,000 in cash at the end of each month. From the Cash Budget in Illustration 12, cash shortages do not appear likely during the first quarter of 20x2. In fact, since the Cash Budget indicates that it will have over $30,000 in cash available at the end of March 20x2, Toy Concepts may wish to consider alternative methods of investing this excess cash to earn an increased return on its capital.

Illustration 12
Toy Concepts, Inc.
Cash Budget
January - March 20x2

	January	February	March
Beginning Cash Balance	$ 4,000[a]	$ 19,325	$ 27,627
Add: Cash Receipts (from Illustration 10)	24,800	18,400	18,320
Less: Cash Disbursements (from Illustration 11)	(9,475)	(10,098)	(10,772)
Ending Cash Balance	$ 19,325	$ 27,627	$ 35,175

[a] Represents the balance in cash from Toy Concepts' December 31, 20x1 Balance Sheet (Illustration 1)

Accounts Receivable Budget

Two types of transactions affect Toy Concepts' accounts receivable: sales made to customers on account (from the Sales Budget in Illustration 2) and cash receipts from sales made on account (from the Cash Receipts Budget in Illustration 10). Using this information, along with the accounts receivable balance from Toy Concepts' December 31, 20x1 balance sheet, the Accounts Receivable Budget can be prepared. Ending accounts receivable would be determined as follows:

The accounts receivable budget is shown in Illustration 13. It should be noted that the ending accounts receivable balance could also be directly estimated based on sales. Recall that Toy Concepts collects 50, 40, and 10 percent of its sales in the month of the sale, the month following the sale, and the second month following the sale, respectively. As a result, accounts receivable at the end of January would represent 10 percent of December's sales and 50 percent of January's sales, as follows:

December:	$ 32,000	x	0.10	=	$ 3,200
January:	$ 16,000	x	0.50	=	8,000
					$ 11,200

Inventory Budgets

Inventory budgets typically reflect the desired levels of ending inventories (direct materials, work-in-process, and finished goods) maintained by the organization. As noted earlier, organizations carefully budget the level of inventory they maintain to balance the costs of inventory shortages (lost sales to customers and delays in manufacturing) with those of inventory overages (excess funds invested in inventories).

Illustration 13

Toy Concepts, Inc.
Accounts Receivable Budget
January - March 20x2

	January	February	March
Beginning Accounts Receivable Balance	$ 20,000[a]	$ 11,200	$ 10,400
Add: Sales (from Illustration 2)	16,000	17,600	19,360
Less: Cash Receipts (from Illustration 10)	(24,800)	(18,400)	(18,320)
Ending Accounts Receivable Balance	$ 11,200	$ 10,400	$ 11,440

[a] Represents the balance in accounts receivable from Toy Concepts' December 31, 20x1 Balance Sheet (Illustration 1)

In determining its budgeted direct materials inventories, recall that Toy Concepts maintains a level of direct materials inventory sufficient to meet 80 percent of the following month's production. This information has been presented in the Direct Material Purchases Budget (Illustration 4). Referring to this budget, the desired levels of ending direct materials inventory are 762, 839, and 925 pounds of plastic in January, February, and March, respectively. To determine the dollar amount of direct materials inventory, these quantities are multiplied by the standard cost of plastic per pound ($0.50). The resulting budgeted dollar amounts of direct materials are:

January:	762 pounds	x	$0.50	=	$381	
February:	839 pounds	x	$0.50	=	$420	(rounded)
March:	925 pounds	x	$0.50	=	$463	(rounded)

As noted previously, Toy Concepts assumes that $100 of work-in-process inventory exists at the end of each month. Thus, the balance in work-in-process inventory shown on its budgeted Balance Sheet would be $100 for each of the first three months of 20x2.

In budgeting the desired levels of finished goods inventory, Toy Concepts' policy is to maintain a sufficient level of ending inventory to meet 80 percent of the sales expected in the following month. For example, since sales in February were budgeted at 220 units (see the Sales Budget in Illustration 2), Toy Concepts should maintain 176 units of finished goods inventory on hand at the end of January (220 x 0.80 = 176). Once the number of units of finished goods inventory has been determined, the organization multiplies that figure by the standard manufacturing cost per unit (in this example, $24). The resulting budgeted dollar amounts of finished goods inventory are:

January:	176 units	x	$24	=	$4,224
February:	194 units	x	$24	=	$4,656
March:	214 units	x	$24	=	$5,136

↑
From Illustration 3
(Production Budget)

Property, Plant, and Equipment Budget

Since neither purchases nor disposals of property, plant and equipment are anticipated during the first quarter of 20x2, the only change in this account arises from the depreciation expense of $500 incurred each month. Thus the net amount of plant and equipment will decrease by $500 for each month in the first quarter of 20x2 as the accumulated depreciation increases. The Property, Plant and Equipment Budget prepared by Toy Concepts is shown in Illustration 14.

Illustration 14

Toy Concepts, Inc.
Property, Plant and Equipment Budget
January - March 20x2

	January	February	March
Property, Plant and Equipment Balance (Gross)	$ 70,000[a]	$ 70,000	$ 70,000
Beginning Accumulated Depreciation Balance	$ 24,000[a]	$ 24,500	$ 25,000
Add: Depreciation Expense	500	500	500
Ending Accumulated Depreciation Balance	$ 24,500	$ 25,000	$ 25,500
Ending Property, Plant and Equipment Balance (Net)	$ 45,500	$ 45,000	$ 44,500

[a] Represents the balance in Property, Plant, and Equipment and Accumulated Depreciation from Toy Concepts' December 31, 20x1 Balance Sheet (Illustration 1)

Accounts Payable Budget

As noted in the discussion of the Cash Disbursements Budget (see Illustration 11), Toy Concepts pays most of its expenses (e.g., labor costs, manufacturing overhead costs, and nonmanufacturing costs) as incurred. However, Toy Concepts' purchases of direct materials from suppliers are made on account and are paid for as follows: 25 percent in the month of the purchase and 75 percent in the month following the purchase. Thus, in budgeting accounts payable, both purchases and payments for direct materials must be considered.

The ending balance in accounts payable can be determined as:

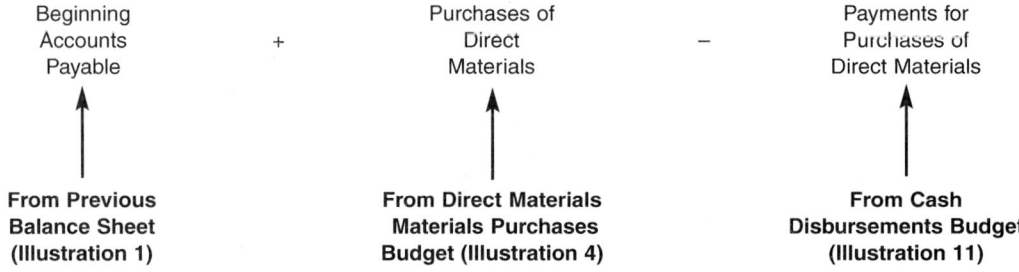

Beginning Accounts Payable (From Previous Balance Sheet (Illustration 1)) + Purchases of Direct Materials (From Direct Materials Purchases Budget (Illustration 4)) − Payments for Purchases of Direct Materials (From Cash Disbursements Budget (Illustration 11))

Both the purchases of direct materials on account (see Illustration 4) and the payments made for these purchases (Illustration 11) have already been determined in the preparation of previous budgets. Given this information, the Accounts Payable Budget can be prepared and is shown in Illustration 15.

Illustration 15

Toy Concepts, Inc.
Accounts Payable Budget
January - March 20x2

	January	February	March
Beginning Accounts Payable Balance	$ 300[a]	$ 350	$ 386
Add: Purchases (from Illustration 4)	467	515	567
Less: Cash Disbursements (from Illustration 11)	(417)	(479)	(528)
Ending Accounts Payable Balance	$ 350	$ 386	$ 425

[a] Represents the balance in accounts payable from Toy Concepts' December 31, 20x1 Balance Sheet (Illustration 1)

Alternatively, accounts payable could be directly estimated as 75 percent of the purchases made in a given month. For example, January's ending accounts payable would be determined by multiplying January purchases by 75 percent, resulting in a balance of $350 ($467 x 0.75 = $350).

Notes Payable Budget

Budgeted notes payable would include any repayments or additional borrowings. Toy Concepts' notes payable are due annually in $10,000 increments beginning in 20x4, with interest to be paid monthly at the coupon rate (12 percent). Since no repayments or additional borrowings are anticipated during the first quarter of 20x2, the balance in notes payable each month is $40,000.

Budgeted Shareholders' Equity

The final step in the financial and resource budgeting process is determining budgeted shareholders' equity. Shareholders' equity is affected by three transactions: the issuance or retirement of stock, the payment of dividends to shareholders, and the net income or loss of the period. Since no issuances or retirements of stock occurred during the first quarter of 20x2 and no dividends were declared or paid to shareholders during this quarter, the only change in budgeted shareholders' equity results from the expected net income earned. This income has been determined in the preparation of the budgeted Income Statement (see Illustration 9). At this time, the budgeted shareholders' equity can be determined and is presented in Illustration 16.

Illustration 16
Toy Concepts, Inc.
Shareholders' Equity Budget
January - March 20x2

	January	February	March
Beginning Shareholders' Equity Balance	$ 33,986[a]	$ 40,380	$ 47,817
Add: Net Income (from Illustration 9)	6,394	7,437	8,572
Ending Shareholders' Equity Balance	$ 40,380	$ 47,817	$ 56,389

[a] Represents the balance in Shareholders' Equity from Toy Concepts' December 31, 20x1 Balance Sheet (Illustration 1)

Now that the expected balance of each account has been determined, Toy Concepts can prepare a *budgeted* (or *pro forma*) *Balance Sheet*. This balance sheet presents the expected financial position given the expected level of activity assumed in preparing the operating budgets and is shown in Illustration 17. Note that the information presented in the budgeted balance sheet has been determined throughout the company's entire budgeting process.

Illustration 18 shows the flow of budgetary information for Toy Concepts discussed throughout this chapter. The process begins with the preparation of the Sales Budget (leftmost budget in Illustration 18) and concludes with the preparation of the financial and resource budgets (rightmost budgets in Illustration 18). As an example of this flow of information, budgeted accounts receivable are based on the Sales Budget and the Cash Receipts Budget (which is also influenced by the Sales Budget). Of particular interest in Illustration 18 is the fact that most of the financial and resource budgets are affected by at least one operating budget.

Illustration 17
Toy Concepts, Inc.
Budgeted Balance Sheet
January - March 20x2

	January	February	March
Assets:			
Cash (Illustration 12)	$ 19,325	$ 27,627	$ 35,175
Accounts Receivable (Illustration 13)	11,200	10,400	11,440
Inventories:			
Direct Materials Inventory	381	420	463
Work-in-Process Inventory	100	100	100
Finished Goods Inventory	4,224	4,656	5,136
Property, Plant and Equipment (Net) (Illustration 14)	45,500	45,000	44,500
Total Assets	$ 80,730	$ 88,203	$ 96,814
Liabilities and Shareholders' Equity:			
Accounts Payable (Illustration 15)	$ 350	$ 386	$ 425
Notes Payable	40,000	40,000	40,000
Shareholders' Equity (Illustration 16)	40,380	47,817	56,389
Total Liabilities and Shareholders' Equity	$ 80,730	$ 88,203	$ 96,814

NONQUANTITATIVE ASPECTS OF BUDGETING

The quantitative nature of budgets often overshadows the fact that individuals in the organization are affected by budgets. It is important that the budget be viewed as *one* (and not the only) barometer of performance. Important nonquantitative aspects of budgeting (the difficulty of budgets and permitting subordinate participation in the budgeting process) are discussed below.

The Difficulty Of Budget Standards

Similar to performance standards, budgets may be established to provide various levels of attainability. When establishing budgets, management (or the budget committee) should consider how different types of budgets motivate employee behavior. For example, assume that the demand for Toy Concepts' products is increasing at approximately five percent per year. Consider three possible Sales Budgets that may be established by Toy Concepts' budget committee:

1. Budgeted sales equal to sales of previous years.
2. Budgeted sales reflecting a 10 percent increase in sales.
3. Budgeted sales reflecting a 50 percent increase in sales.

These three budgets reflect different levels of difficulty, ranging from relatively easy (budget 1) to relatively difficult (budget 3). The budget established in budget 1 above would be relatively easy for Toy Concepts' salespeople to achieve. As a result, it would not normally motivate them to make additional sales calls or solicit additional customers. Also, since salespeople should be able to meet their budgeted level of sales, Toy Concepts would not be able to identify superior performance by comparing actual sales to budgeted sales. Thus, from an overall organizational standpoint, this budget would not be useful from either a motivational or evaluative tool.

In contrast, the budget in (3) may initially motivate salespeople to perform more effectively and increase sales. However, once salespeople felt that the budget was unattainable, they may "give up" and fail to increase sales beyond those made in previous years. In addition, from an evaluative standpoint, most (if not all) of the organization's salespeople would be judged as performing inadequately in terms of this budget. Therefore, similar to the less difficult budget depicted in (1), this budget target would not be useful from either a motivational or evaluative perspective.

Budget (2) (budgeted level of sales representing a 10 percent increase from the previous year) is one that should be considered by the budget committee. It presents a challenging, yet attainable goal to Toy Concepts'

8 / Budgeting 8-19

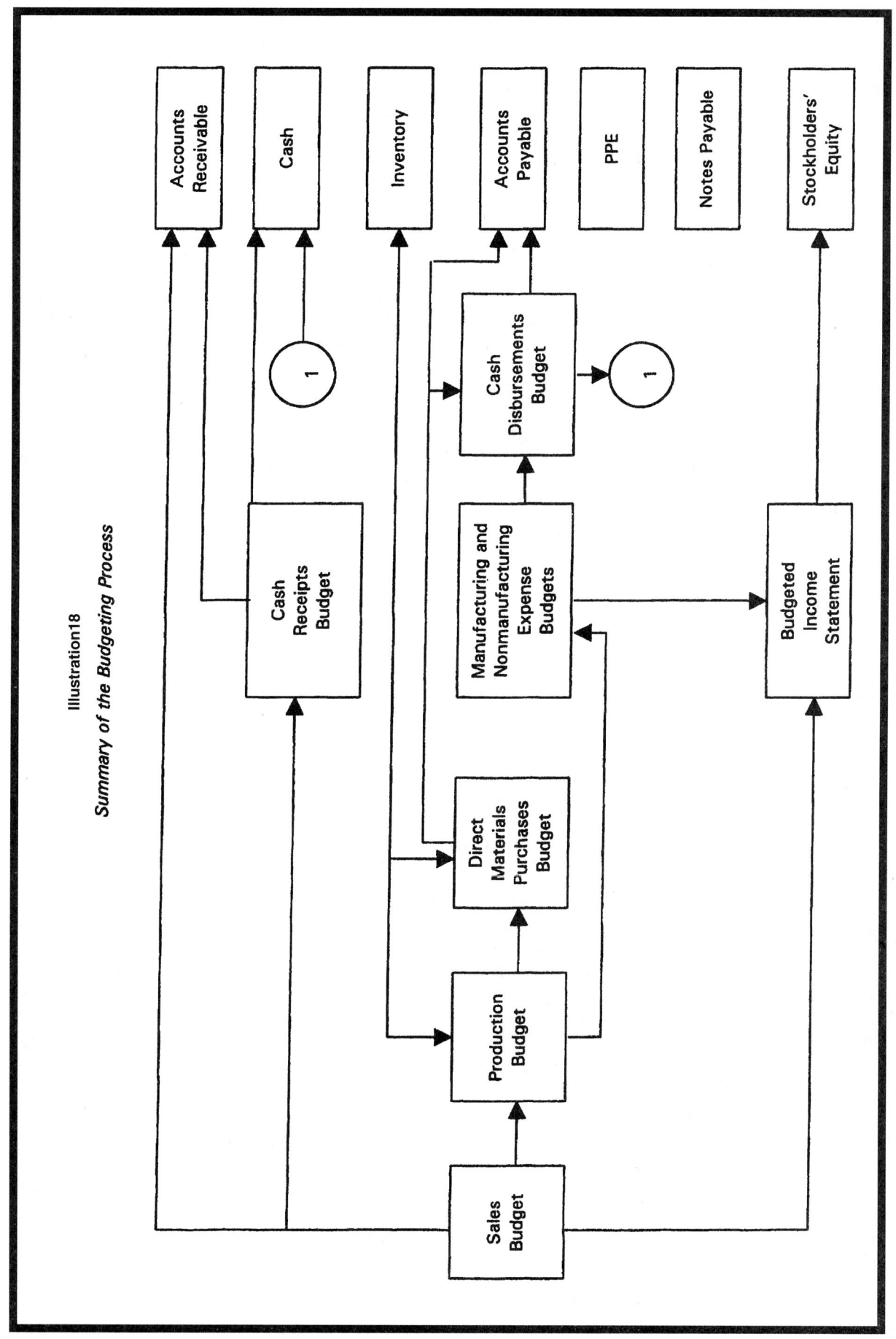

Illustration 18
Summary of the Budgeting Process

salespeople. It seems reasonable that with additional effort salespeople could at least approach the goal of increasing sales by 10 percent, since a five percent increase in demand is anticipated. An attainable budget provides employees with motivation, since the goal is reasonable but not impossible to achieve. In addition, while this budget is attainable, it can only be met by above average performance on the part of salespeople. Thus, this budget can be used to effectively motivate employees and evaluate their performance.

Participative Budgeting and Slack

While most budgeting processes require information provided by both individuals and departments, participative budgeting allows subordinates to directly assist the budget committee in establishing the final budget goals. In a sense, subordinates interact with the budget committee and negotiate their budgets in the final stages of the budget process. An advantage of participative budgeting is that employees normally feel that the resulting budgets are realistic and fair and may be more motivated to achieve these budgets. Simply stated, the feeling that "management gave us this unrealistic budget" does not exist. Instead, subordinates are aware that the budget was developed only after their opinions were at least considered by management and the budget committee. Evidence suggests that participatively-determined budgets result in individuals being more likely to be committed to a budget's success than if the budgets were simply imposed by management.

A major weakness of participative budgets is the tendency for employees to underestimate their level of performance. For example, if salespeople knew that the demand for products has increased by ten percent, they may not be willing to communicate this fact to the budget committee. Instead, salespeople may provide a more conservative (lower) estimate of sales levels. This action is referred to as creating "slack" in budgets (or "padding" the budget). Slack is created when expected revenues (or sales quotas) are understated and expected expenditures are overstated. The creation of slack introduces two primary disadvantages for the organization:

- Budgets containing slack are not useful in evaluating employee performance, since employees are not evaluated against a "true" budget target.

- Budgets containing an underestimate of sales may result in insufficient levels of production and purchases of direct materials to meet the demand for the organization's products or services.

Why is slack created? Clearly, if employees provide conservative information to management, they are more likely to achieve the budget goals and receive a favorable performance evaluation. While creating slack is not a favorable outcome, it is an inevitable disadvantage of allowing subordinate participation. However, the advantages of participative budgeting often outweigh a small amount of slack. The budget committee should recognize that subordinates will tend to submit budget estimates containing slack and consider this factor in preparing the final budgets.

BUDGETS FOR MERCHANDISING AND SERVICE ORGANIZATIONS

The focus of this chapter is on the preparation of budgets for a manufacturing organization (Toy Concepts, Inc.). However, it is important to note that budgeting is equally important for merchandising and service organizations as well as for other entities, both profit and nonprofit. For example, AutoZone (an automobile parts and supplies retailer) needs information concerning the expected demand for its products to ensure that sufficient quantities of these products are available for customers. Similarly, Continental Airlines needs information about the number of flights originating from its various departure cities to ensure that sufficient personnel, aircraft fuel, and aircraft are available to serve those cities. While the type of information and manner in which this information is presented may differ slightly from the examples shown in this chapter, these needs are addressed by the preparation of budgets.

USING MANAGERIAL ACCOUNTING INFORMATION: TOY CONCEPTS, INC.

The previous sections of this chapter illustrate the preparation of operating budgets for Toy Concepts, Inc. for the first quarter of 20x2. Recall that Toy Concepts had a policy of maintaining a minimum of $4,000 in cash each month. Based on its Cash Budget (Illustration 12), its estimated cash balances at the end of January, February, and March were $19,325, $27,627, and $35,175, respectively.

After preparing its budgets, assume that Toy Concepts' management is considering the following:

- Because of a shift in demand in its market, Toy Concepts is considering expanding its product lines to include vehicles targeted toward female children. This would require a $10,000 investment in equipment and facilities during the month of February. In addition, operating expenses for this product line would be approximately $2,000 in February and March. Toy Concepts does not anticipate introducing these products to the market until May.

- Toy Concepts' current property, plant and equipment is in need of repair. The estimated cost of these repairs is $2,000 in January and $1,000 in February.

- Toy Concepts' plans to declare (and pay) a $2,000 dividend to its shareholders on March 15, 20x2.

- Toy Concepts' plans to make a quarterly income tax payment of $7,500 at the end of March.

In addition, Toy Concepts' management is considering the possibility of retiring some of the notes payable prior to their maturity, since these notes were obtained during a period of relatively high interest rates. Toy Concepts is able to issue and retire notes in $2,000 increments. Because of lower current interest rates and low transaction costs, Toy Concepts feels that it would be cost-effective to use temporary cash overages to retire currently outstanding notes even if additional notes would be issued to cover a cash shortage at the end of a subsequent month.

Illustration 19 provides an analysis of Toy Concepts' cash balances after considering the above payments. As shown therein, Toy Concepts could use excess cash at the end of January to retire $12,000 of notes payable (recall that notes can only be issued and retired in $2,000 increments). However, this will deplete its cash balance to such an extent that an additional $4,000 of notes would need to be issued in both February and March. The net effect of these transactions is that Toy Concepts' balance in notes payable would be $36,000 at the end of March 20x2 ($40,000 − $12,000 + $4,000 + $4,000 = $36,000). In this case, cash budgeting provides the management of Toy Concepts, Inc. with information concerning the influence of potential transactions on the need to obtain additional financing.

Illustration 19
Toy Concepts, Inc.
Revised Cash Budget and Analysis
January - March 20x2

	January	February	March
Beginning Cash Balance	$ 4,000 [a]	$ 5,325	$ 4,627
Original Cash Receipts (Illustration 10)	24,800	18,400	18,320
Original Cash Disbursements (Illustration 11)	(9,475)	(10,098)	(10,772)
Investment in Equipment and Facilities		(10,000)	
Increased Operating Costs		(2,000)	(2,000)
Repairs on Current Property, Plant and Equipment	(2,000)	(1,000)	
Dividends Paid to Shareholders			(2,000)
Tax Payments			(7,500)
Ending Cash Balance (Before Borrowing/Repayment)	$ 17,325	$ 627	$ 675
Retirement of Notes	(12,000)		
Issuance of Notes		4,000	4,000
Ending Cash Balance	$ 5,325	$ 4,627	$ 4,675

[a] From Illustration 12

SUMMARY

This chapter introduces the concept of budgeting as well as the basic budgeting process. In addition, a comprehensive budgeting example has been discussed and the process of preparing operating and financial and resource budgets has been illustrated. The important points in this chapter are summarized below.

1. A *budget* is a formal plan expressing a course of action in quantitative terms. Budgets are used in planning, communicating information coordinating the efforts of personnel in the organization, and evaluating the performance of individuals and departments.
2. Three primary types of budgets are operating budgets, financial and resource budgets, and special decision budgets. *Operating budgets* summarize the primary activities of the organization, such as manufacturing inventory, using direct materials and direct labor, and incurring manufacturing overhead and nonmanufacturing expenses. *Financial and resource budgets* summarize the expected level of the organization's assets and liabilities given the level of activity assumed in the preparation of the operating budgets. *Special decision budgets* are prepared as requested by management for a variety of decisions related to issues other than the organization's ordinary and ongoing operations and activities.
3. *The Sales Budget* is the starting point in the budgeting process. This budget summarizes the estimated sales dollars and volume for the budgeted period. Once the expected sales volume has been determined, the *Production Budget* can be prepared. This budget indicates the level of production necessary to meet expected sales demand and allow the desired levels of inventories to be maintained.
4. Following the preparation of the Production Budget, the Direct Materials Purchases Budget, Direct Materials Usage Budget, Direct Labor Budget, and Manufacturing Overhead Budget may be prepared. These budgets determine the expected amount of manufacturing costs, given the level of production established in the Production Budget as well as the cost of material, labor, and overhead inputs. The final result of the operating budget process is the preparation of a *budgeted* (or *pro forma*) *Income Statement*.
5. Following the preparation of the operating budgets, the organization can prepare its *financial and resource budgets*. These budgets summarize the estimated account balances for the organization's assets and liabilities. The culmination of the process of preparing financial and resource budgets is the preparation of the *budgeted* (or *pro forma*) *Balance Sheet*.
6. In preparing budgets, the organization should consider both the attainability of the budget as well as the possibility that "slack" is introduced in the budget. Regarding attainability, maximum performance ordinarily results from providing challenging (yet attainable) budget goals for subunits and employees. When considering employee input in the budgeting process, the organization should consider the tendency of employees to underestimate their performance (and create "slack" in the budget) to enhance their likelihood of achieving the budget.

KEY DEFINITIONS

Budget—a formal plan expressing a course of action in quantitative terms. Budgets are used to plan the organization's activities, communicate information and coordinate the efforts of personnel in the organization, and assist management in evaluating the performance of individuals and subunits in the organization.

Budget committee—the committee charged with preparing the organization's budgets. This committee is frequently composed of members representing the sales, production, and finance functions.

Financial and resource budgets—these budgets are concerned with the expected levels of the organization's assets and liabilities based on the activity assumed when preparing its operating budgets. After all financial and resource budgets are prepared, a budgeted (or *pro forma*) Balance Sheet can be prepared.

Master budget—a comprehensive system of budgeting which includes operating budgets, financial and resource budgets, and special decision budgets.

Operating budgets—these budgets are concerned with the primary activities of the organization, such as producing inventory, using direct materials and direct labor, and incurring manufacturing overhead and nonmanufacturing expenses. The end result of the preparation of operating budgets is the budgeted (or *pro forma*) Income Statement.

Participative budgeting—a form or budgeting where input from employees and administrators at all levels of the organization is received prior to the preparation of the organization's budgets.

Slack—the process through which employees intentionally underestimate the expected revenues or overestimate expected costs to create a more easily attainable budget.
Special decision budgets—these budgets are prepared as requested by management for a variety of decisions related to issues other than the organization's ordinary operations and activities.
Strategic planning—process of identifying the goals and objectives of the organization for a relatively long-term period of time (5–10 years).
Tactical planning—process through which the organization attempts to achieve the goals and objectives identified in the strategic plan.

QUESTIONS

1. What is a budget? List three uses of budgets by organizations.

2. Define strategic planning and tactical planning. How do these processes relate to the preparation of budgets?

3. List and define each of the three major types of budgets prepared in a comprehensive budgeting system.

4. What information is provided in an organization's Sales Budget? What is the source of this information?

5. What information is provided in an organization's Production Budget? What is the source of this information?

6. What budget(s) are ordinarily prepared immediately following the Production Budget? What information is contained in each of these budgets?

7. What information is provided in an organization's Direct Materials Purchases Budget? What is the source of this information?

8. List the order in which an organization's operating budgets are prepared. For each budget, indicate which other budget(s) provide information necessary for that budget.

9. What information is required for preparing the organization's Cash Receipts and Cash Disbursements Budgets?

10. Why is the amount of budgeted cash so important to the organization?

11. What information affects the budgeted balances in the following accounts?

    a. Accounts receivable.
    b. Inventory.
    c. Property, plant and equipment.
    d. Accounts payable.
    e. Notes payable.
    f. Stockholders' equity.

12. How does the attainability of the budget influence employee motivation?

13. What is participative budgeting? What is a disadvantage of permitting participative budgeting?

14. How can the introduction of slack in the budgeting process be disadvantageous to the organization?

EXERCISES AND PROBLEMS

15. *Production Budget Relationships.* Below are data on three independent cases. Complete the Production Budget by substituting a number for each letter.

	Case 1	Case 2	Case 3
Beginning Finished Goods Inventory	7	4	6
Ending Finished Goods Inventory	5	b	4
Units to be Produced	14	15	c
Units to be Sold	a	9	13

16. *Labor Usage Requirements.* The supervisor of the material handling department had to develop a labor schedule for the month of June. Each handler can move 2,000 pounds (or 1 ton) of direct material per hour, forty hours per week, four weeks per month. One finished unit requires one-half ton of direct material (1 ton per 2 finished units), and the company expects to sell 75,000 finished units during June. Beginning and desired ending balances of finished goods and direct materials are as follows:

	Beginning Balance	Ending Balance
Finished Goods (units)	15,000	10,000
Direct Materials (tons)	1,000	1,200

Required:

How many material handlers must be scheduled to transport the direct materials purchased during June?

17. *Production and Material Requirements.* Copen Company expects to sell 2,000 units in June and 4,000 in July. At the end of May, Copen has 500 units on hand, since its policy is to maintain ending finished goods inventories at one-fourth expected next-month activity. Direct materials on May 30 amount to 5,000 pounds, while the desired level on June 30, is 3,000 pounds. Eight pounds are required to make one finished unit. How many pounds of direct materials should Copen buy in June? How many finished units does Copen expect to make in June?

18. *Inventory Purchase Requirements.* The Acme Company started the month of June with 10,000 units in its inventory. Each unit costs $3. During the month of June, Acme expects to sell 50,000 units at $5 each. Acme would like to have 8,000 units in inventory at the end of June, both to ensure adequate stock on hand and to facilitate sales in July. Inventory costs are expected to be constant during June, and all purchases made in June will be paid for during July. What dollar amount will Acme have to pay during July for June's purchases?

19. *Production, Materials, and Labor Requirements.* Shown below is relevant data for the Onion Corporation.

	January	February
Expected Sales (in units)	1,000	2,000
Beginning Finished Goods Inventory (in units)	500	
Beginning Direct Materials Inventory (in pounds)	4,000	

Other information related to Onion Corporation is as follows:

1. Each unit requires four pounds of direct materials and three hours of labor.
2. Onion's policy is to maintain a sufficient level of finished goods inventory to meet 50 percent of the following month's sales.
3. Onion desires a sufficient level of direct materials inventory at the end of each month to meet the following month's entire level of sales.

Required:

Answer the following questions concerning the operations for Onion Corporation for the month of January. In each case, also indicate the budget on which this information would usually be shown.

    a. How many units will be produced?
    b. How many pounds of direct materials will be purchased?
    c. How many pounds of direct materials will be used?
    d. How many hours of direct labor are needed in January?

20. *Budgets Production and Material Purchases.* Shown below are the expected sales for Jerry Company (in units) for the first quarter of 20x2:

	January	February	March
Sales (in units)	1,500	2,000	3,000

In addition, expected sales in April are 4,000 units and expected sales in May are 5,000 units. On January 1, 20x2, Jerry Company had 1,350 units in its inventory. Jerry has a policy of maintaining a level of ending inventory sufficient to meet 90 percent of its demand for the following month.

To produce each unit, Jerry requires four pounds of direct materials. At the beginning of 20x2, Jerry had 6,000 pounds of direct materials on hand. Jerry desires ending direct materials inventory levels sufficient to meet the following month's production demands. Each pound of direct materials costs $1.

Required:

    a. Prepare the Production Budget for Jerry Company for the first quarter of 20x2.
    b. Prepare the Direct Materials Purchases Budget for the first quarter of 20x2.

21. *Budgets—Materials, Labor and Overhead.* The Production Budget for Susan Cities, Inc. indicated the following levels of production for the first quarter of 20x2:

January	2,000 units
Feburary	5,000 units
March	8,000 units

Shown below are the standard costs for each unit:

Direct Materials (2 lbs. x $2)	$4
Direct Labor (1 hr. x $6)	6
Variable Overhead (1 hr. x $6)	6
	$16

In addition to the above costs, Susan Cities expects fixed overhead costs of $2,000 per month during 20x2.

Required:

Prepare the Direct Materials Usage Budget, Direct Labor Budget, and Manufacturing Overhead Budget for the first quarter of 20x2.

22. *Budgets—Materials, Labor and Overhead.* Tyson expects to produce 10,000 units of inventory in January, 12,000 in February, and 9,000 in March. The standard variable production cost of this inventory is shown below:

Direct Materials (10 lbs. x $0.60)	$6
Direct Labor (2 hrs. x $5.00)	10
Variable Overhead	5
	$21

In addition, Tyson incurs $10,000 of fixed overhead costs each month.

Required:

Prepare the Direct Materials Usage Budget, Direct Labor Budget, and Manufacturing Overhead Budget for Tyson for the first quarter.

23. *Budget Relationships—General.* Tone Company's production facilities are shared by multiple production departments. Tone produces celllular phones for sale to its customers. The variable costs of producing one cellular phone are shown below:

Direct Materials (3 units x $5)	$15
Direct Labor (1 hour. x $6)	6
Variable Overhead	3
	$24

In January, Tone expects to sell 10,000 phones. Tone expects sales to increase by 5 percent in the month of Feburary and an additional 10 percent in March. April sales are expected to be 12,000 phones. Tone has 5,000 phones on hand at the beginning of the period. This is consistent with its policy to maintain finished goods inventory equal to one-half of the following month's sales.

Tone currently has no direct materials on hand; however, beginning with the end of January, Tone wishes to have 6,000 units of direct materials on hand at the end of each month.

Required:

Answer the following questions with respect to Tone. For each question, indicate the budget on which the information would usually appear.

a. What is the expected production for each month in the first quarter of the year?
b. How many pounds of direct materials will be purchased in each month? What is the cost of these purchases?
c. How many pounds of direct materials will be used each month? What is the cost of direct materials used?
d. How many hours of direct labor are needed each month? What is the cost of those hours?
e. What is the variable overhead cost for each month?

24. *Budgets—Purchasing.* The usual planning period in many organizations is one year, broken down by quarters or months. *Continuous budgets* maintain a twelve-month forecast by continually adding another time period as one period has ended. The Cope Corporation has a three-month planning horizon and maintains a continuous Purchasing Budget. Cope wishes to have an ending inventory balance equal to 150 percent of the current month's production needs. The current inventory of ten tons of materials is just sufficient to produce the current month's production of 100,000 units. Production is expected to grow at a rate of 10 percent per month for the next two months and shrink by 20 percent per month thereafter.

Required:

a. Prepare a Purchasing Budget for the first three months.
b. At the end of the first month, the actual ending inventory equaled seventeen tons, rather than the amount originally planned. The deviation was caused by a one-time efficiency spurt that is not expected to continue. Prepare a revised three-month budget for periods 2, 3, and 4.

25. *Budgets–Various.* Tableware, Inc, sells two products: Salt and Pepper. Tableware forecasts sales of 1,000 units of Salt and 2,000 units of Pepper in January 20x2. Tableware expects sales of both units to increase by 10 percent each month for the remainder of 20x2. Assume that Salt will sell for $100 per unit and Pepper for $150 per unit. Tableware has 500 units of Salt and 1,000 units of Pepper in its beginning inventory. These levels are consistent with its policy of maintaining a level of beginning inventory sufficient to satisfy one-half of the following month's sales.

Salt and Pepper required one common direct material. The production of one unit of Salt uses 10 pounds of this material; 15 pounds are needed to produce one unit of Pepper. The direct material costs $5 per pound. Tableware has 8,000 pounds of direct materials on hand at the beginning of 20x2; however, because of previous shortages, it wishes to maintain enough direct materials on hand to meet 60 percent of the following month's production.

Required:

Prepare the following budgets for the first quarter of 20x2 and show all supporting computations in good form:

a. Sales Budget.
b. Production Budget.
c. Direct Materials Purchases Budget (in pounds and dollars).
d. Direct Materials Usage Budget (in dollars).

26. *Budgeted Cost of Goods Manufactured and Supporting Budgets.* Aikman Manufacturing prepares two products: Johnson and Jones. It takes two hours of labor to produce one unit of Johnson and three hours of labor to produce one unit of Jones. Direct labor costs are $10 per hour. Variable overhead is applied at the rate of $5 per unit for both Johnson and Jones. A total of $10,000 in fixed overhead is expected.

    In the first quarter of 20x1, Aikman wishes to manufacture 1,000 units of Johnson and 2,500 units of Jones. The direct materials required to produce one unit of Johnson and one unit of Jones are as follows:

	Cost/lb.	Johnson	Jones
Direct Material A	$1	5 lbs.	10 lbs.
Direct Material B	6	7 lbs.	5 lbs.

    Assume no beginning or ending work-in-process inventories.

    Required:

    Determine the budgeted Cost of Goods Manufactured for Aikman Manufacturing. Prepare all necessary supporting budgets used to determine budgeted cost of goods manufactured.

27. *Budgeted Cost of Goods Manufactured and Cost of Goods Sold.* Spike has asked you to prepare a budgeted Cost of Goods Sold Statement covering the first quarter of 20x1. Work-in-process inventory on January 1, 20x1 was $10,000. It is expected that this inventory will be increased by 5 percent for each month of 20x1.

    Spike wishes to produce 5,000 units in January, 6,000 in February, and 7,500 in March. Each unit requires three pounds of direct materials, which cost $5 per pound. In addition, each unit requires one-half hour of labor at $10 per hour. Variable overhead costs are applied at $4 per hour. Fixed overhead is expected to be $5,000 per month.

    Assume the following budgeted balances in Spike's finished goods inventory account:

January 1, 20x1	$13,500
February 1, 20x1	20,000
March 1, 20x1	15,500
April 1, 20x1	17,000

    Required:

    a. Prepare the Cost of Goods Manufactured Budget for Spike Company.
    b. Prepare the budgeted Cost of Goods Sold Statement for Spike Company.

28. *Operating Budgets—Comprehensive.* The Ajax Company has a planning horizon of three months: January through March. Ajax manufactures and sells three products in two sales territories. The following is a forecast of monthly unit sales.

    Territory 1 and 2, respectively, account for 20 percent and 80 percent of Product X, 60 percent and 40 percent of Product Y, and 70 percent and 30 percent of Product Z. Products X, Y, and Z sell for $6, $7, and $8, respectively. All three products are made with one common material that costs $1 per pound. Products X, Y, and Z, respectively, require 1, 2, and 2 pounds of material per unit. Labor costing $4 per hour produces output at the following rates: 2 units of X per hour, 4 units of Y per hour, and 6 units of Z per hour. At the end of any month, Ajax wishes to maintain a basic finished goods inventory equal to 70 percent of next month's sales and a direct materials inventory equal to 120 percent of the current month's production needs. Salaries, wages, rent, and research and development costs are paid as incurred. Sales commissions are 5 percent of sales, and research and development costs are 2 percent of sales. Salaries amount to $600 per month, and rent is $400 per month. Monthly depreciation is $1,000.

Presented below are two schedules, the first a sales forecast and the second a balance sheet for the year just ended, 20x0.

Ajax Company
Sales Forecast—20x1
(in units)

Products	January	February	March	April
X	500	500	500	500
Y	600	700	800	900
Z	900	500	300	100

Ajax Company
Balance Sheet—20x0

Cash		$ 5,100
Accounts Receivable (from December sales)		8,600
Inventories (direct materials and finished goods):		
Direct Materials (4,320 lbs. @ $1)	$ 4,320	
Product X (350 @ $3)	1,050	
Product Y (420 @ $3)	1,260	
Product Z (630 @ $2.67)	1,680	8,310
Plant and Equipment	$150,000	
Accumulated Depreciation	(30,000)	120,000
Total		$142,010
Accounts Payable (December purchases)		$ 2,700
Loan Payable		5,000
Interest Payable		100
Owners' Equity		134,210
Total		$142,010

Required:

Prepare a master budget consisting of a Sales Budget, Production Budget, Purchases Budget, Labor Schedule, and a Nonmanufacturing Expense Budget.

29. *Operating Budgets—Comprehensive.* Jordan Company produces basketballs. Jordan predicts total sales of 100,000 basketballs during the first quarter of 20x2 at $80 per basketball. Jordan has developed the following standard cost data for use in determining the cost of producing a basketball:

Materials:	
Leather (1 unit x $10)	$10.00
Rubber (2 units x $2)	4.00
Direct Labor (1 hour x $15)	15.00
Variable Overhead	7.50
	$36.50

During the first quarter of 20x2, Jordan expects fixed overhead costs of $50,000 and nonmanufacturing costs of $120,000. Jordan's beginning inventories consisted of 500 units of leather, 1,500 units of rubber, and 10,000 basketballs. Jordan wishes to increase all of these inventories by 10 percent during the first quarter of 20x2. There is no beginning or desired ending work-in-process. For budgeting purposes, assume that Jordan costs its finished goods inventory based on the variable cost of production.

Required:

Prepare the following budgets in good form. Use variable costing for income determination.

   a. Production Budget (in units).
   b. Direct Materials Purchases Budget (in units and dollars).
   c. Direct Materials Usage Budget.
   d. Direct Labor Budget.
   e. Manufacturing Overhead Budget.
   f. Cost of Goods Manufactured Statement.
   g. Cost of Goods Sold Statement.
   h. Income Statement.

30. *General—Financial and Resource Budgets.* Below are the 20x3 cash budget and budgeted income statement, the 20x2 actual balance sheet, and the 20x3 budgeted balance sheet for Hylo Corp. Determine the dollar value of each of the missing (lettered) accounts. (Hint: Do them in alphabetical order.)

Budgeted Income Statement	Revenues	$600			
	Expenditures	A			
	Depreciation	200			
	Net profit......................	$100			

Cash Budgets	*Cash Receipts*			*Cash Payments*	
	Revenues	$ B		Pay Dividends	$150
	Issue Stock	C		Repay Notes	700
	Sell Bonds	600		Expenditures	D
	Sell Land	1,000			
	Total.......................	$2,200		Total.......................	$ E

		20x2	20x3		20x2	20x3
Budgeted Balance Sheet	Cash	$1,000	G	Current Liabilities	$3,000	$3,000
	Land	5,000	H	Bonds Payable	I	1,600
	Other Assets (net)........	800	600	Notes Payable	900	K
	Investments..................	F	1,000	Stock	2,200	2,200
				Retained Earnings	J	L
		$7,800	$7,650		$7,800	$7,650

31. *Financial and Resource Budgets—Various.* Flybi Company plans to sell 11,000 widgets in January at an average price of $10 per unit. In recent months, 80 percent of sales have been collected during the month of sale, and the remaining 20 percent have been collected the following month. The company writes off estimated uncollectible accounts in the month of the sale for budgeting purposes. Labor and other operating expenses, which are expected to be $40,000 for the month, are paid as incurred. Depreciation amounts to $6,000 per month. Direct materials purchases during January are expected to cost $60,000; half of them will be paid for in February. Flybi's balance sheet for the year just ended reflects the following balances: cash, $13,000; accounts receivable, $15,000; and accounts payable, $25,000.

Required:

If Flybi doesn't borrow or lend during January, what will be the balances in the cash account, the accounts receivable account, and the accounts payable account at the end of the month?

32. *Cash Receipts Budget.* Sloane, Inc. is to begin operations in January of 20x2. Sloane expects the following sales during the first quarter of 20x2: $100,000 in January, $125,000 in February, and $130,000 in March. Based on the experience of similar companies, assume that Sloane's cash collections will be as follows:

> 40 percent in the month of sale.
> 30 percent in the month following the sale.
> 25 percent two months following the sale.
> 5 percent uncollectible.

Required:

Prepare the Cash Receipts Budget for Sloane, Inc. for the first quarter of 20x2.

33. *Budgets—Cash Receipts and Accounts Receivable.* Turner Company sells rental movies to subscribers. During 20x1, Turner sold each movie for $4; however, because of increased costs, it plans to sell the movies for $5 in 20x2. Turner's sales for 20x1 (actual sales) and 20x2 (budgeted sales) are shown below:

> November 20x1 .... 10,000 movies
> December 20x1 .... 15,000 movies
> January 20x2 .... 17,000 movies
> February 20x2 .... 16,000 movies
> March 20x2 .... 20,000 movies

Based on past experience, Turner expects to collect 50 percent of the sales in the month of the sale, 40 percent in the month after the sale, and 10 percent in the second month following the sale.

Required:

Prepare the Cash Receipts Budget and the Budgeted Accounts Receivable for Turner Company for the first quarter of 20x2.

34. *Budgets—Sales, Cash Receipts, Accounts Receivable.* Forbes Company is beginning its operations in January 20x2. Forbes will manufacture and sell two products: J and S. In the month of January, Forbes believes that it will sell 5,000 units of J and 8,000 units of S. Forbes believes that sales of each product will increase by 10 percent each month during 20x2 as the company and its products become known in the marketplace. Forbes plans to charge $10 per unit for J and $25 per unit for S.

In estimating its cash receipts for each month, Forbes believes that it can collect 50 percent of the sales in the month of the sale, 40 percent in the month following the sale, and 5 percent in the second month following the sale. Forbes believes that 5 percent of its sales will ultimately prove to be uncollectible.

Required:

Prepare the following budgets for Forbes Company for the first quarter of 20x2: Sales Budget, Cash Receipts Budget, and Accounts Receivable Budget.

35. *Cash Disbursements Budget.* Tettleton Corporation is a medium-sized furniture manufacturer. In order to manufacture its product, Tettleton purchases lumber and other supplies it needs in production from selected vendors. These vendors require Tettleton to pay for one-third of the supplies in the month of purchase; the remaining payment is due the following month. Tettleton pays according to this policy, since late payments are assessed additional interest charges. Assume that based on the direct materials purchases budget, Tettleton expects to make purchases in the following amounts during the first quarter of 20x2:

January	$24,000
February	36,000
March	21,000

In addition to these purchases, Tettleton expects to incur a total of $30,000 of other expenses each month. These expenses are paid as they are incurred.

Assuming that actual purchases of materials and supplies were $42,000 in December of 20x1, prepare Tettleton's Cash Disbursements Budget for the first quarter of 20x2.

36. *Budgets—Cash Disbursements and Accounts Payable.* Attaya manufactures two products: Mary and Kim. Attaya can sell Mary for $10 per unit and Kim for $8 per unit. Attaya's expected production schedule for the first quarter of 20x1 is shown below:

	Mary	Kim
January	1,000	2,000
February	3,000	5,000
March	4,000	6,000

To produce Mary and Kim, Attaya needs two direct materials. The cost per pound of these materials, as well as the pounds of direct materials needed to produce one unit of Mary and Kim, are shown below:

	Cost/lb.	Mary	Kim
Direct Material (A)	$1	3 lbs.	4 lbs.
Direct Material (B)	2	2 lbs.	1 lbs.

Attaya has 100 pounds of A and 200 pounds of B in its beginning direct materials inventory. Attaya wishes to increase these inventories by twenty pounds at the end of each month.

Attaya's beginning accounts payable are $20,000. Assume that Attaya pays 75 percent of each month's purchases in the month of the purchase; the remaining 25 percent is paid in the following month. In conducting its operations, Attaya expects to incur $10,000, $20,000, and $30,000 of other expenses in January, February, and March, respectively. These expenses are paid as they are incurred.

Required:

Prepare a Direct Materials Purchases Budget, a Cash Disbursements Budget, and an Accounts Payable Budget for the first quarter of 20x1.

37. *Cash Budget.* On December 31, 20x3, the Orion Co. had a cash balance of $7,000, accounts receivable of $30,000, and accounts payable of $40,000. The company expects to sell $50,000 worth of goods for $70,000 in January. One-half of all sales are collected during the month of sale and the other half the following month. All purchases are made on account and paid for during the following month. Inventory levels are to remain constant during January. Other expenses and dividends are expected to equal $60,000 during January.

Required:

If Orion desires to maintain a cash balance of $5,000, what amount must it borrow?

38. *Comprehensive—Cash Budget.* Shown below is data taken from the operating budgets prepared by the Nasus Corporation for the first quarter of 20x2:

	Sales	Direct Materials Purchases
January	10,000 units	5,000 lbs.
February	5,000 units	2,000 lbs.
March	8,500 units	4,000 lbs.

Nasus expected to receive $20 per unit from sales of its inventory; direct materials costs were expected to be $10 per pound.

Based on its past experience, Nasus collects half of its sales in the month of the sale; the remaining half is collected in the month following the sale. Nasus' accounts receivable at December 31, 20x1 was $60,000; this represented one-half of Nasus' December sales.

Nasus pays for 60 percent of its direct materials purchases in the month of the purchase; the remaining 40 percent is paid in the following month. Nasus' account payable at December 31, 20x1 was $23,000. This amount represented 40 percent of the previous month's purchases of direct material.

In addition to purchases of direct materials, Nasus also expects to incur the following expenses each month. These expenses will be paid as they are incurred:

Labor Costs	$10,000
Overhead Costs	20,000 (including depreciation of $5,000)
Other Costs	3,000

The balance in Nasus' cash account at December 31, 20x1 was $25,000.

Required:

Prepare the Cash Receipts Budget, Cash Disbursements Budget, and Cash Budget for Nasus Corporation for the first quarter of 20x2.

39. *Budgets—Purchases, Cash Receipts, Cash Disbursements.* Tomlinson Retail seeks your assistance in developing cash and other budget information for May, June, and July, 20x3. At April 30, 20x3, the company had cash of $5,500, accounts receivable of $437,000, inventories of $309,400, and accounts payable of $133,055. The budget is to be based on the following assumptions:

Sales:
1. Each month's sales are billed on the last day of the month.

2. Customers are allowed a 3 percent discount if payment is made within ten days after the billing date. Receivables are booked at gross amounts.
3. Sixty percent of the billings are collected within the discount period, 25 percent are collected by the end of the month, 9 percent are collected by the end of the second month, and 6 percent prove uncollectible.

Purchases:

1. Fifty-four percent of all purchases of material and selling, general, and administrative expenses are paid in the month purchased and the remainder in the following month.
2. Each month's units of ending inventory are equal to 130 percent of the next month's units of sales.
3. The cost of each unit of inventory is $20.
4. Selling, general, and administrative expenses, of which $2,000 is depreciation, are equal to 15 percent of the current month's sales.

Actual and projected sales are as follows:

20x3	Dollars	Units
March	$354,000	11,800
April	363,000	12,100
May	357,000	11,900
June	342,000	11,400
July	360,000	12,000
August	366,000	12,200

Required:

a. How much are budgeted cash disbursements during the month of June 20x3?
b. How much are budgeted cash collections during the month of May 20x3?
c. What is the budgeted number of units of inventory to be purchased during July 20x3?

(AICPA adapted)

40. *Budgeted Income Statement and Balance Sheet.* Acme Co. is a merchandising concern which buys inventory in large quantities for $20 per unit and resells it to its customers for $30 per unit. Acme buys its inventory on account (terms 30 days) and sells it for cash. Acme's inventory policy requires that the end of the month inventory balance equal 50 percent of anticipated sales for the next month. Operating expenses typically equal 10 percent of sales revenues.

Acme ends the month of May with the following balances: cash, $50,000; inventory, $180,000; accounts payable, $100,000. Acme expects to sell 18,000 units in June and 20,000 in July.

Required:

Prepare a budgeted Income Statement and a budgeted Balance Sheet to reflect expected activity for June.

41. *Budgets—Income Statement and Balance Sheet.* A June 1 balance sheet for the Mobley Corporation reflects the following balances:

Cash	$ 15,000	Accounts Payable	$ 30,000
Accounts Receivable	45,000	Loans Payable	10,000
Inventory	35,000		
Investments	60,000	Owners' Equity	115,000
Total	$155,000	Total	$155,000

Expected sales for June are 11,000 units at $8 each. Credit sales terms allow customers thirty days in which to pay. Typically 30 percent of the current sales are for cash and the remaining 70 percent is collected during the following month. The desired ending inventory balance is established at 5,000 units. Inventory can be purchased for $4 per unit, payable within forty-five days. Typically, 40 percent of the purchases are for cash, and the remaining 60 percent is paid during the following month. Mobley's cash policy specifies a desired minimum ending balance of $10,000. Deficiencies will be borrowed under existing lines of credit and any excess will be used to reduce outstanding loans payable. Rental payments of $12,000 for the building and fixtures are made on the last day of the month. Additional investments are to be purchased for $16,000 during June.

Required:

Prepare a budgeted Income Statement for June and a June 30 budgeted Balance Sheet.

42. *Accounts Payable Budget.* Oriole, Inc. wishes to determine its budgeted accounts payable for the last quarter of 20x2. In order to allow you to prepare this budget, Oriole has prepared the following Direct Materials Purchases Budget for the last quarter of 20x2:

October	$50,000
November	60,000
December	70,000

The balance in accounts payable as of September 30, 20x2 is $26,000.

In budgeting accounts payable, Oriole assumes that one-half of each month's direct materials purchases are paid for in the month of the purchase with the remaining one-half paid in the following month. The beginning balance in accounts payable represents one-half of September's purchases of $52,000.

Required:

Prepare Oriole Inc.'s Accounts Payable Budget for the last quarter of 20x2. Also prepare any other budgets which are necessary to prepare the Accounts Payable Budget (with the exception of the Direct Materials Purchases Budget).

43. *Flexible Budgets.* Holman Company requests that you assist in preparing its flexible budget for the first quarter of 20x2. Holman chooses sales volume as its desired measure of activity. Holman manufactures one product, which it sells for $100 per unit. The following relationships between costs and volume are determined by Holman:

	Variable Cost Per Unit	Fixed Cost
Materials	$ 5	
Direct Labor	10	
Manufacturing Overhead	3	$10,000
Nonmanufacturing	1	20,000
Other		10,000

Included in the "other costs" are $5,000 of training costs. These costs remain fixed at $5,000 for levels of sales volume up to 5,000; for any levels above 5,000, these costs increase to $8,000.

Required:

Prepare a flexible budget for both revenues and costs for Holman Company for the first quarter of 20x2 assuming the following levels of activity: 3,000 units sold, 6,000 units sold, and 10,000 units sold.

44. *Flexible Budgets.* Jackson Company requests that you assist in preparing its flexible budget for the first quarter of 20x2. Based on the historical relationship between costs and volume, Jackson selects direct labor hours as the appropriate measure of activity. The following relationships between costs and volume have been developed by Jackson:

	Variable Cost Per Hour	Fixed Cost
Materials	$10	
Direct Labor	8	
Manufacturing Overhead	5	$16,000
Nonmanufacturing	4	5,000
Other		22,000

Required:

Prepare a flexible budget for the costs of Jackson Company for the first quarter of 20x2 assuming the following levels of activity: 10,000 direct labor hours, 20,000 direct labor hours, and 30,000 direct labor hours.

45. *Flexible Budgets.* The Jones Company has a flexible budget for which the sales manager supplies sales figures. His most conservative figure is 500,000 units, and his most likely figure is 550,000, but it is possible that Jones will sell 625,000 units. The president of Jones says, "If you are going to generate three different budgets, why not produce two more? Give me one for 575,000 units and one for 600,000 units." The product sells for $0.50 per unit and has fixed costs of $60,000. Variable costs are 17 percent of sales dollars, and mixed costs are $30,000 plus 10 percent of sales. Assume an income tax of 40 percent.

   a. What is the flexible budget for each of these volumes?
   b. Is it reasonable to assume that the fixed costs will remain fixed in the volume range of 500,000 units to 625,000 units?
   c. Why would the president request that volumes other than the most likely volume be used?

46. *Flexible Budgets.* Department A, one of fifteen departments in the plant, is involved in the production of all of the six products manufactured. The department is highly mechanized, and, as a result, its output is measured in direct machine hours. Flexible budgets are utilized throughout the factory in planning and controlling costs, but this problem is concerned only with flexible budgets in Department A. The following data covering a time span of approximately six months were taken from the various budgets, accounting records, and performance reports (only representative items and amounts are utilized here).

    On March 15, 20x1, the following flexible budget was approved for the department; it will be used throughout the 20x2 fiscal year which begins July 1, 20x1. This flexible budget was developed through the cooperative efforts of the department manager, his supervisor, and certain staff members from the Budget Department.

Department A
20x2 Flexible Budget

Controllable Costs	Fixed Amount Per Month	Variable Rate Per Direct Machine Hour
Employee Salaries	$ 9,000	
Wages	18,000	$.07
Materials		.09
Other Costs	6,000	.03
	$33,000	$.19

On May 5, 20x1, the annual sales plan and the Production Budget were completed. In order to continue preparation of the annual profit plan (which was detailed by month), the Production Budget was translated to planned activity for each of the factory departments. The planned activity for Department A was:

	For the Twelve Months Ending June 30, 20x2				
	Year	July	August	September	Etc.
Planned Ouput in Direct Machine Hours	325,000	22,000	25,000	29,000	249,000

On August 31, 20x1, the manager of Department A was informed that his planned output for September had been increased to 34,000 direct machine hours. He expressed some doubt as to whether this volume could be attained.

At the end of September 20x1, the accounting records provided the following actual data for the month for the department.

Actual Output in Direct Machine Hours.. 33,000

    Actual Controllable Costs Incurred:
        Employee Salaries .... $ 9,300
        Wages 20,500
        Materials... 2,850
        Other Costs 7,510
                                                                                                                                                   $40,160

Required:

a. What activity is utilized as a measure of volume in the budget for this department? How should one determine the range of the activity base to which the variable rates per machine hour are relevant? Explain.

b. Explain and illustrate how the flexible budget should be utilized:
  1. In budgeting costs when the annual sales plan and production budget are completed (about May 5, 20x1 or shortly thereafter).
  2. In budgeting a cost revision based upon a revised production budget (about August 31, 20x1 or shortly thereafter).
  3. In preparing a cost performance report for September 20x1.

(AICPA adapted)

47. *Flexible Budgets.* Jones Corporation is preparing a flexible budget for the costs it expects to incur during the first quarter of 20x2. Jones selects direct labor hours as the appropriate volume base. Jones has two variable costs: materials, which are approximately $2 per direct labor hour, and labor, which is $5 per direct labor hour. These variables have been established based on the relationships experienced by Jones in the past.

In addition to the variable costs noted above, Jones has budgeted the two following fixed costs for the first quarter of 20x2: depreciation of $4,000 and training costs of $6,000. The depreciation expense of $4,000 will remain constant for levels of activity up to 25,000 direct labor hours. For levels higher than that, additional plant and equipment will need to be purchased, resulting in additional depreciation expense of $2,000 for the quarter. The training costs of $6,000 will remain constant for up to 15,000 direct labor hours. For each additional increment of 5,000 direct labor hours, an additional $2,000 of training costs are expected.

Required:

Prepare a flexible budget for Jones assuming the following levels of activity: 10,000 direct labor hours, 20,000 direct labor hours, and 30,000 direct labor hours.

48. *Budgeting—Comprehensive.* Modern Products Corporation, a manufacturer of molded plastic containers, determined in October 20x8 that it needed cash to continue operations. The corporation began negotiating for a one-month bank loan of $100,000, which would be discounted at 6 percent per annum on November 1. In considering the loan, the bank requested a Cash Budget for the month of November. The following information is available:

1. Sales were budgeted at 120,000 units per month in October 20x8, December 20x8, and January 20x9 and at 90,000 units in November 20x8.

    The selling price is $2 per unit. Sales are billed on the 15th and last day of each month on terms of 2/10, net/30. Past experience indicates that sales occur evenly throughout the month, and that 50 percent of the customers pay within the discount period. Remaining balances are paid at the end of thirty days, except for bad debts, which average one-half percent of gross sales. On its income statement, the corporation deductsfrom sales the estimated amounts for cash discounts on sales and losses on bad debts.

2. The finished goods inventory on October 1 was 24,000 units. The finished goods inventory at the end of each month is to be maintained at 20 percent of anticipated sales for the following month. Modern Products Corporation does not maintain any work-in-process inventory.

3. The inventory of direct materials on October 1 was 22,800 pounds. At the end of each month, the direct materials inventory is to be maintained at no less than 40 percent of production requirements for the following month. Materials are purchased as needed in minimum quantities of 25,000 pounds per

shipment. Direct material purchases for each month are paid in the following month on terms of net thirty days.

4. All salaries and wages are paid on the 15th and the last day of each month for the period ending on the date of payment.
5. All manufacturing overhead and selling and administrative expenses are paid on the 10th of the month following the month in which they were incurred. Selling expenses are 10 percent of gross sales. Administrative expenses, which include depreciation of $500 per month on office furniture and fixtures, total $33,000 per month.
6. The cost of a molded plastic container, based on "normal" production of 100,000 units per month, is as follows:

Materials (0.5 lb.)	$0.50
Labor	0.40
Variable Overhead	0.20
Fixed Overhead	0.10
Total	$1.20

Fixed overhead includes depreciation on factory equipment of $4,000 per month.

7. The cash balance on November 1 is expected to be $10,000.

Required:

Assuming that the bank loan is granted, prepare the following for Modern Products Corporation (do not consider income taxes):

a. Schedules computing inventory budgets by month for:
   1. Finished goods production (in units) for October, November, and December.
   2. Direct material purchases (in pounds) for October and November.
b. A cash budget for the month of November showing the beginning balance, cash receipts (itemized by dates of collection), cash disbursements, and ending balance.

(AICPA adapted)

Learning Objectives

A major function performed by managerial accountants is controlling the activities of the organization. This chapter discusses control and introduces the concept of responsibility accounting. In addition, the definition and evaluation of various types of responsibility centers is illustrated. Studying this chapter should enable you to:

1. Define control and identify three major elements of an effective management control system.
2. Define responsibility accounting and discuss how responsibility accounting is related to the concept of control.
3. Define and distinguish cost centers, profit centers, and investment centers.
4. Identify how cost centers, profit centers, and investment centers should be evaluated.
5. Calculate and interpret variances that result from differences between the actual and standard net income earned by profit centers.
6. Understand the issues involved in using return on investment and residual income in evaluating the performance of investment centers.
7. Define transfer pricing and discuss the methods of establishing transfer prices between an organization's responsibility centers.
8. Discuss total quality management and the balanced scorecard concept and how these tools influence the performance of responsibility centers.

9

Control of the Organization— Responsibility Accounting

INTRODUCTION

John and Jane Alexander, a happily married young couple, have just received their bank statements in the mail (they maintain separate checking accounts). The Alexanders normally pay bills from John's account and allow themselves to spend $500 each per month for their own personal needs. After reviewing their bank statements and the checks written over the past month, they both agree that they were spending too much money. In discussing their finances, Jane began:

Jane: John, I can't believe you spent over $3,000 last month. Even counting our monthly bills, you should only have spent about $2,000. Where did the extra money go?

John: Gosh, you're right. It didn't seem like I spent any more than usual. Let's take a look at the checks. Wait a minute. Here's a check for $1,400 for our property taxes. Here's another one for $200—remember that time we had to call the plumber? These expenses aren't really my fault; it's not like I went out and spent a lot of additional money on myself.

Jane: I see your point. These expenses aren't the same as buying yourself a set of golf clubs or new clothes. You really didn't have any choice; we had to make these payments.

John: I don't feel so bad anymore. You know, it's really important that we consider the nature of the expenditures we made when we evaluate our cash payments.

Jane: You're right. There's no sense in our blaming each other for things that are beyond our control.

The above vignette illustrates the concept of *control*. In evaluating John Alexander's spending patterns, it is clearly not reasonable to hold him accountable for the property taxes and plumbing repairs since these are beyond his control. Similarly, organizations must carefully identify those factors for which they hold their managers accountable. This process is referred to as *responsibility accounting* and is the focus of this chapter.

MANAGEMENT CONTROL SYSTEMS

A *management control system* is the process through which an organization's management makes planning and control decisions, motivates employee behavior, and evaluates employee performance. The primary objective of a management control system is to achieve *goal congruence* between the objectives of the organization and the actions of its employees. Goal congruence is achieved when employees make decisions that are consistent with the overall objectives of the organization as a result of maximizing their own perceived best interests. For example, if one of Dell Computer's objectives is to minimize the time required to manufacture its personal computers, it may implement a system to reward its employees for achieving this level of efficiency. The rewards established by management would be designed to encourage Dell Computer's employees to achieve these levels of efficiency, which results in congruence between management's goals and the actions of Dell's employees.

A management control system includes the following interrelated components:

1. **Communicating Plans and Objectives.** Any control system begins with a statement of the plans or objectives of the organization. These plans or objectives are ordinarily established by the top-level management of the organization. Since the purpose of control is to ensure that the actions of individuals are consistent with the organization's overall objectives, it is important that these objectives are clearly both specified and communicated throughout the organization.

2. **Measuring Activities.** As the organization conducts its activities, the level of activity related to the plans and objectives must be measured and recorded to permit the organization to monitor the progress made toward achieving the goals and objectives identified.

3. **Providing Feedback to Appropriate Individuals.** Once the organization has established plans and objectives and recorded the level of activity related to these plans and objectives, the final stage of the control process is to provide feedback to individuals. This feedback includes a comparison of actual performance to the plans and objectives of management. Once this feedback has been received, individuals can modify their activities to achieve the organization's objectives.

In a sense, a management control system is similar to a thermostat operating to maintain a desired temperature in a room. The major steps are as follows:

1. Set the thermostat for the desired temperature (goals and objectives).
2. The thermostat measures the current room temperature and identifies differences between that temperature and the desired temperature. When a deviation between the actual and the desired temperature is noted, the thermostat starts the heater or air conditioner.
3. The thermostat continues to monitor the room temperature and the process is repeated.

> **The benefits of control can be illustrated by the experiences of Martin Industries, a manufacturer of heating products operating in Florence, Alabama. In the mid-1980s, Martin industries began to distribute reports to its employees on the travel costs they incurred in an attempt to increase their awareness of these costs. No formal restrictions or other policy on travel were implemented during this time. In 1989, total miles traveled increased by 37 percent; however, the total costs of this travel decreased by 55 percent![1]**

Management control systems are particularly important in *decentralized organizations*. A decentralized organization is one that provides a relatively large amount of authority and autonomy to managers of various subunits in operating the activities of those subunits. Decentralization has a number of benefits:

- Permitting decisions regarding the subunit to be made by managers of that subunit who often have superior information and knowledge regarding the relevant issues facing that subunit.
- Improving the decision-making skills of managers and providing them with higher levels of prestige and job satisfaction.
- Allowing managers to be evaluated on a basis comparable with other managers.

However, decentralization also introduces certain disadvantages. A primary disadvantage of decentralization is that the managers may act in their own best interests rather than the overall interests of the organization. For example, if managers are provided with substantial bonuses based on the profitability of their subunits, they may make decisions that provide short-run benefits (in terms of profitability) but are harmful to the organization over the long run. As noted earlier, the use of management control systems attempts to ensure congruence between the goals of the organization and the actions of the manager and employees of a decentralized subunit.

RESPONSIBILITY CENTERS

At the heart of a management control system and the concept of decentralization is the identification of an organization's *responsibility centers*. A responsibility center is a division, segment, individual, or other subunit

---

[1] R.F. Briner, J.D. Akers, J.W. Truitt, and J.D. Wilson, "Coping with Change at Martin Industries," *Management Accounting* (July 1989), 45–49.

of an organization that is accountable for the results of that subunit's activities. For example, ExxonMobil's Exploration Division is responsible for identifying sources of oil and gas products. The Service Department of a Chevrolet dealership is responsible for providing customers with effective service. The Research Division of Abbott Laboratories focuses on identifying and developing new pharmaceutical products. These three subunits are examples of responsibility centers. Their common characteristic is that they are accountable (or responsible) for the results of their activities (identifying sources of oil and gas products, providing effective service to customers, or developing new pharmaceutical products).

It is important to note that a particular subunit (or set of activities) typically operates under a number of different individuals or departments throughout the organization. For example, the machines used to manufacture Nike's apparel products (such as T-shirts and other sportswear) at a specific manufacturing location may be the responsibility of an individual production supervisor at that location. The entire production of apparel products (which includes production at a number of locations) would be the responsibility of the head of the apparel product line. Finally, the production of Nike's entire product lines (including both apparel and shoes) is a responsibility center for the President of Nike.

The methods used to measure and evaluate the performance of responsibility centers (and their managers) are referred to as *responsibility accounting*. Under ideal conditions, responsibility centers within an organization are evaluated based solely on those costs, revenues, and capital investment (or assets) subject to their control. Costs, revenues, and assets are considered to be controllable when they can be identified with the responsibility center on a nonarbitrary basis and can be influenced by the responsibility center or the manager of that responsibility center.

It is important that both of these criteria be met in classifying a particular item as controllable. Certain items can be identified with a responsibility center but cannot be influenced by the manager of that center. For example, while the depreciation expense on manufacturing equipment may be directly identified with the Production Department, the manager of that department has little influence on the amount of depreciation expense incurred, since depreciation relates to a previous expenditure for manufacturing equipment and choice of depreciation method. Therefore, he or she should not be held responsible for the level of depreciation expense incurred by the department. In contrast, the manager of the Production Department would ordinarily be in a position to influence the cost and quantities of direct materials and direct labor used in manufacturing the organization's products; accordingly, he or she should be held responsible for these costs.

> At Borg-Warner Automotive, production managers initiate requests to order production tools; however, the quantity of production tools ordered is determined by the purchasing department. Originally, production managers were charged with the cost of production tools ordered. Borg-Warner's responsibility accounting system was modified to charge production managers with the cost of tools used (and not ordered).[2]

RESPONSIBILITY ACCOUNTING AT BLAST! SNACK FOODS

To illustrate the concept of responsibility accounting and the evaluation of responsibility centers, we will examine the activities of BLAST! Snack Foods. BLAST! produces two major types of products: (1) soda, iced tea, and juice drinks (the Beverage Division) and (2) snack foods such as pretzels, potato chips, and cookies (the Snack Food Division). These products are sold to grocery stores, convenience stores, vending machine operators, and restaurants throughout the United States. The manager of the Beverage Division (Susan Meghan) has considerable latitude in operating the activities of her division. Susan receives a capital allocation from corporate headquarters and is free to manufacture and market different types of products. In addition, the Beverage Division can expand its production and product lines beyond current levels, if estimated demand warrants such an expansion. Susan can also establish the selling prices for her division's products.

In contrast, the manager of the Snack Food Division (Margaret Knight) has less autonomy in conducting her division's activities. Because the upper management of BLAST! feels that the snack food market has less potential for future growth than the beverage market, Margaret is provided with specified production levels for her division's products. She is charged with increasing the sales of BLAST!'s current snack food products and minimizing the overall costs of producing these products. Margaret is not allowed to introduce additional product lines or expand production without the prior approval of corporate management.

Within the Beverage and Snack Food Divisions are subunits organized around that division's product lines. For example, the Beverage Division is organized around two primary product lines (soda products and flavored

---

[2] G.F. Hanks, M.A. Fried, and J. Huber, "Shifting Gears at Borg-Warner Automotive," *Management Accounting* (February 1994), 25–29.

juice and tea products). Within each product line are other subunits that focus on the production and sale of those products.

Illustration 1 summarizes the organizational structure of BLAST! Snack Foods. In this organizational structure, only detail regarding the Beverage Division and Soda Products Line is shown. However, it is important to note that similar responsibility centers would exist for each of the remaining divisions and product lines of BLAST!

Three primary types of responsibility centers are reflected in the organizational structure shown in Illustration 1.

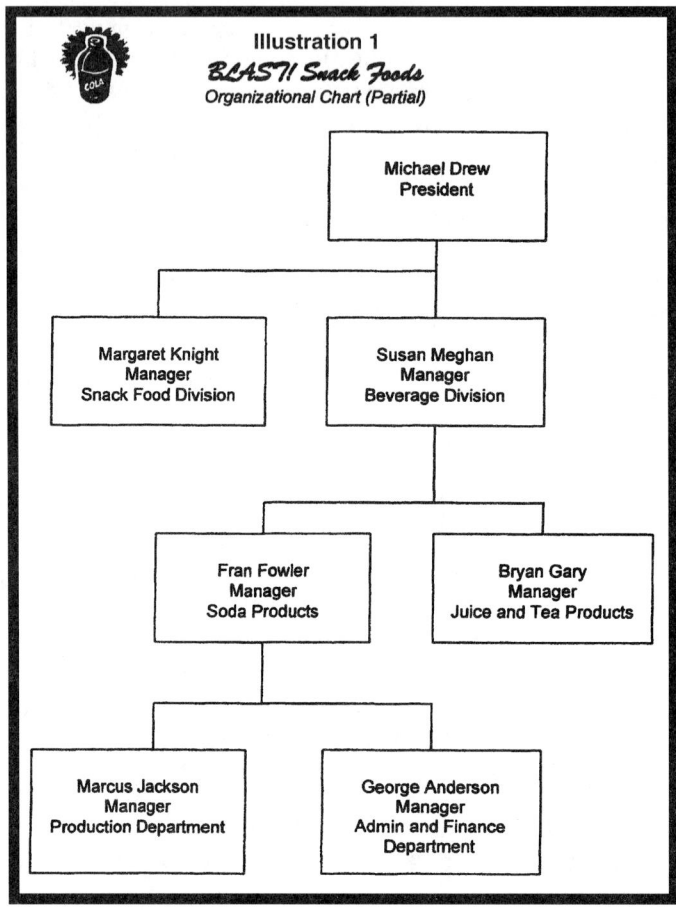

1. A *cost center* is a responsibility center that can control only its costs. Cost centers are unable to influence either the revenues they earn or the use of capital to conduct their activities. The Production Department for the Soda Products Line of BLAST! and its manager (Marcus Jackson) is an example of a cost center. The Production Department is responsible for manufacturing high-quality soda products at the lowest possible cost.

2. A *profit center* is a responsibility center that can influence both its costs and the revenue it earns. However, a profit center cannot control the use of the capital invested in that center. In the above example, the Soda Products Line (and its manager, Fran Fowler) is a profit center. Fran is responsible for increasing the level of profit generated by her responsibility center; however, she does not have the authority to make decisions regarding the use of capital within her responsibility center.

3. An *investment center* is a responsibility center that is able to influence costs, revenues, and the use of capital invested in that center. Recall that Susan Meghan (manager of the Beverage Division of BLAST!) has been delegated the authority to explore additional types of products and expand the level of production of beverage products. Therefore, this responsibility center is classified as an investment center, and Susan Meghan is recognized as its manager.[3]

---

[3] The terms "profit center" and "investment center" are often used interchangeably in practice to refer to responsibility centers that influence revenues, costs, and the investment of capital within that center. However, we distinguish between profit and investment centers based upon their ability to make decisions involving the use of invested capital.

COST CENTERS

As noted above, cost centers are responsibility centers that can only influence the level of costs that they incur and have little (if any) influence over the revenues they earn or the use of capital invested in their operations. The most common method of evaluating cost centers is comparing the level of costs actually incurred in these centers to the standard (or expected) costs that should be incurred based on the actual level of activity for that responsibility center.

> Georgia Tech University's Athletic department has developed a responsibility center approach that is organized around individual sports. Because sports other than football and basketball cannot generate large amounts of their own revenues from ticket sales, television and radio rights, and advertising fees, these sports are evaluated by comparing their actual costs to expected costs. That is, non-revenue-producing sports are evaluated as cost centers.[4]

Illustration 2 is a performance report for Marcus Jackson, manager of the Production Department of the Soda Products Line for BLAST! Snack Foods. Data are presented for both the month of April 20x1 and for the year to date. Note from Illustration 2 that certain costs are related to the Production Department but are not considered

Illustration 2
BLAST! Snack Foods
Performance Report ·
Marcus Jackson, Manager: Production Department
Beverage Division: Soda Products Line
(all amounts are in thousands)

	Actual Costs		Standard Costs[a]		Variance[b]	
	April 20x1	Year to Date	April 20x1	Year to Date	April 20x1	Year to Date
Controllable Variable Expenses:						
Direct Materials	$ 376	$2,022	$ 414	$2,100	$38	$78
Direct Labor	154	720	120	700	(34)	(20)
Indirect Materials and Supplies	56	200	66	200	10	0
Utilities	54	202	70	192	16	(10)
Other Variable Costs	20	85	12	80	(8)	(5)
Total Variable Expenses	$ 660	$3,229	$ 682	$3,272	$22	$43
Controllable Fixed Expenses:						
Supervisor's Salaries	$ 45	$ 180	$ 40	$ 160	($ 5)	($20)
Other Fixed Expenses	99	291	107	320	8	29
Total Fixed Expenses	$ 144	$ 471	$ 147	$ 480	$ 3	$ 9
Total Controllable Expenses	$ 804	$3,700	$ 829	$3,752	$25	$52
Noncontrollable Expenses:						
Depreciation on Equipment	$ 40	$ 160	$ 40	$ 180	$ 0	$20
Rent on Manufacturing Facilities	10	40	12	48	2	8
Salary of Production Manager	4	16	4	16	0	0
Total Noncontrollable Expenses	$ 54	$ 216	$ 56	$ 244	$ 2	$28
Total Expenses	$ 858	$3,916	$ 885	$3,996	$27	$80

[a] Based on the actual level of production for April 20x1 and the year to date.
[b] Unfavorable Variances are shown in parentheses.

---

[4] C.D. Strupeck, K.Milani, and J.E. Murphy, "Financial Management at Georgia Tech," *Management Accounting* (February 1993), 58–63.

to be controllable by Marcus, such as the depreciation on equipment, rent on manufacturing facilities, and Jackson's own salary. Therefore, while the total costs incurred by the Production Department in April 20x1 were $858, Jackson is evaluated only on the portion of these costs that are controllable by him ($804). It is important that management evaluate the individual variances presented in the performance report and not merely the total difference between actual and standard costs. If Jackson's superiors considered only the overall variance, they might conclude that Marcus did an adequate job of controlling costs since the overall variance is favorable. However, an examination of individual variances reveals that both favorable and unfavorable variances occurred during April 20x1 and these offset one another.

In evaluating the variances included in the performance report shown in Illustration 2, the management of BLAST! Snack Foods may calculate component variances for direct materials, direct labor, and manufacturing overhead costs (as discussed in a previous chapter). The following additional factors should be considered:

- The controllability of variances (for example, shortages of direct materials may necessitate that the Production Department pay additional costs for its direct materials inputs).

- Trade-offs among variances (for example, utilizing higher quality materials may result in lower direct labor costs).

- Alternative explanations of variances (are unfavorable overhead variances the result of decisions to increase production levels or, instead, the consequence of production inefficiencies?).

- The historical nature of variances (are variances consistently favorable or unfavorable? Is the magnitude of the variance increasing or decreasing over time?)

Illustration 3 provides an example of the hierarchical nature of performance reports for the responsibility centers of BLAST! (for brevity, only the actual and standard items for April 20x1 are shown). As shown therein, the Production Department of the Soda Products Line incurred costs of $858 during April 20x1; recall from Illustration 2 that $804 of these costs were controllable by Marcus Jackson (the manager). The entire $858 of costs incurred by the Production Department also appears on the performance report of Fran Fowler, the manager of the Soda Products Line. This illustrates a basic tenet of responsibility accounting: if a manager of a responsibility center (in this case, Marcus Jackson) is responsible for certain items, his or her superior (in this case, Fran Fowler) is also held responsible for these items. In addition, the hierarchical performance reports shown in Illustration 3 indicate that Fran Fowler is responsible for the $54 of costs incurred by the Production Department that were not controllable by Marcus Jackson ($858 − $804 = $54).

Because the Soda Products Line is a profit center, its manager is responsible for both the revenues earned and costs incurred by that product line. These costs include the costs incurred by the Production Department ($858, see Illustration 2), the Administration and Finance Department ($146), and other product line expenses that cannot be traced to either department ($100). Thus, Fran Fowler is evaluated based on the net profit earned by her responsibility center ($106). Also, note that the $106 profit earned by Soda Products is included in the responsibility report of Susan Meghan (manager of the Beverage Division). The Beverage Division's responsibility report would also include the profit from the Juice and Tea Products Line as well as any other costs incurred by the Beverage Division that could not be traced to either Soda Products or Juice and Tea Products. Finally, note that the responsibility report for the overall company includes the profit of the Beverage Division and Snack Food Division as well as expenses that cannot reasonably be traced to specific divisions/departments of BLAST!

Illustration 3
BLAST! Snack Foods
Hierarchical Performance Reports
April 20x1
(all amounts are in thousands)

	Actual	Standard	Variance
Overall Company			
Michael Drew (President)			
Snack Food	$160	$200	($ 40)
Beverage	366	164	202
Corporate Expenses	(200)	(180)	(20)
Income Tax Expense	(135)	(150)	15
Total Net Income	$191	$ 34	$157
Beverage Division			
Susan Meghan (Manager)			
Soda Products	$106	($ 76)	$182
Juice and Tea Products	310	300	10
Divisional Expenses	(50)	(60)	10
Total Profit	$366	$164	$202
Soda Products Line			
Fran Fowler (Manager)			
Revenues	$1,210	$1,040	$170
Production Department	(858)	(885)	27
Admin & Finance	(146)	(136)	(10)
Other Expenses	(100)	(95)	(5)
Total Profit	$ 106	($ 76)	$182
Production Department			
Marcus Jackson (Manager)			
Variable Expenses	$660	$682	$22
Fixed Expenses	144	147	3
Noncontrollable Expenses	54	56	2
Total Expenses	$858	$885	$ 27

PROFIT CENTERS

Profit centers are responsibility centers that control both the costs they incur and the revenues they earn. However, profit centers are unable to control the investment of assets within their responsibility centers. Recall that the Soda Products Line of the Beverage Division of BLAST! is an example of a profit center. The manager of this center (Fran Fowler) oversees operations, establishes selling prices, and makes decisions regarding the marketing and distribution of soda products. However, Fran does not have authority to make major investment decisions. As a result, her performance should be based on the profits earned by this product line and should not consider the level of assets available to conduct its activities.

> General Motors (GM) has recently assigned responsibility for each truck and car platform to a single executive who oversees a model's development from the early stages of design until its completion. These executives have profit and loss responsibility for their vehicles, which would classify them as profit centers.[5]

---

[5] "Reviving GM," *Business Week* (February 1, 1999),119.

Similar to cost centers, profit centers are evaluated by comparing the actual operating results to standard results. The total actual and standard profit of Soda Products was $106 and $86, respectively, resulting in a favorable variance of $20, as indicated below (all amounts are in thousands):[6]

	Actual	Standard	Variance
Revenues	$1,210	$1,040	$170
Expenses:			
Production Department	(858)	(723)	(135)
Administration and Finance	(146)	(136)	(10)
Nontraceable Product Line Expenses	(100)	(95)	(5)
Total Profit	$ 106	$ 86	$ 20

Because variable expenses are highly influenced by the level of sales, the evaluation of profit centers is ordinarily conducted in two stages. First, differences between the actual and standard contribution margins are determined and variance analysis is undertaken to isolate the cause(s) of the overall variance. This analysis provides potential explanations for differences between expected and actual levels of sales and variable costs. Then differences between actual and standard fixed costs are evaluated to identify potential explanations for these differences.

To illustrate the analysis of profit centers, assume that the Soda Products Line produces and sells its beverages in three types of containers: two-liter plastic bottles (sold in grocery stores), six-packs of cans (sold in grocery stores and vending machines), and six-packs of 20-ounce plastic bottles (sold in grocery stores and vending machines). The following summary represents actual and forecasted sales of these products in April 20x1 (in thousands).

		Per Unit		Total		
	Quantity	Sales Price	Variable Expenses	Sales Revenue	Variable Expenses	Contribution Margin
Actual:						
Two-liter bottles	600	$0.50	$0.40	$ 300	$240	$ 60
Six-pack cans	400	$0.90	$0.50	360	200	160
Six-pack bottles	500	$1.10	$0.44	550	220	330
	1,500			$1,210	$660	$550
Forecasted:						
Two-liter bottles	650	$0.70	$0.40	$ 455	$260	$195
Six-pack cans	325	$0.80	$0.40	260	130	130
Six-pack bottles	325	$1.00	$0.40	325	130	195
	1,300			$1,040	$520	$520

Using the above data, Illustration 4 presents income statements for BLAST! based on: forecasted sales volumes, mixes, and prices (the "Forecast" columns in Illustration 4); actual sales volumes and mixes with forecasted prices (the "Control" columns in Illustration 4); and actual sales volumes, mixes, and prices (the "Actual" columns in Illustration 4). Data are presented in both dollars and as a percentage of sales.

In terms of contribution margin, the net variance for BLAST! is $30. This amount is determined by comparing the forecasted contribution margin from the first set of columns in Illustration 4 ($520) to the actual contribution margin from the final set of columns in Illustration 4 ($550). Since the actual contribution margin exceeds the forecasted contribution margin, this variance is favorable. The middle set of columns is referred to as the control budget, which represents the budgeted sales, variable costs, and contribution margin based on the actual quantity and mix of sales at standard prices and costs. In other words, if the Soda Products Line sold 600 two-liter bottles, 400 six-packs of cans, and 500 six-packs of bottles (actual quantity and mix), what contribution margin would be expected?

Four variances can be calculated to identify why the actual contribution margin of $550 differs from the forecasted contribution margin of $520. The first variance arises when the overall volume of sales differs from that anticipated. Recall that Soda Products forecasted sales of its three products at 650 two-liter bottles, 325

---

[6] The standard expenses for the Production Department ($723) differ from those reflected in Marcus Jackson's performance report (see Illustration 2) and the hierarchical performance reports shown in Illustration 3. The reason for this difference is that the performance reports shown in Illustrations 2 and 3 are based on actual levels of activity (sales), while the $723 reflects budgeted levels of sales.

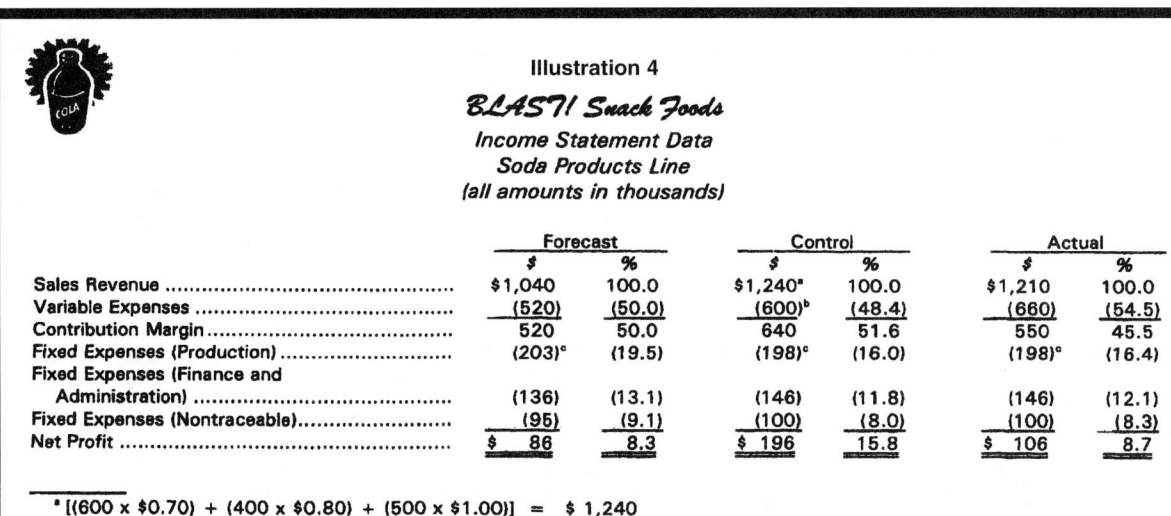

Illustration 4

BLAST! Snack Foods
Income Statement Data
Soda Products Line
(all amounts in thousands)

	Forecast $	Forecast %	Control $	Control %	Actual $	Actual %
Sales Revenue	$1,040	100.0	$1,240[a]	100.0	$1,210	100.0
Variable Expenses	(520)	(50.0)	(600)[b]	(48.4)	(660)	(54.5)
Contribution Margin	520	50.0	640	51.6	550	45.5
Fixed Expenses (Production)	(203)[c]	(19.5)	(198)[c]	(16.0)	(198)[c]	(16.4)
Fixed Expenses (Finance and Administration)	(136)	(13.1)	(146)	(11.8)	(146)	(12.1)
Fixed Expenses (Nontraceable)	(95)	(9.1)	(100)	(8.0)	(100)	(8.3)
Net Profit	$ 86	8.3	$ 196	15.8	$ 106	8.7

[a] [(600 × $0.70) + (400 × $0.80) + (500 × $1.00)] = $ 1,240
[b] [(600 × $0.40) + (400 × $0.40) + (500 × $0.40)] = $ 600
[c] Includes the controllable fixed expenses and the noncontrollable fixed expenses from the Production Department Manager's performance report in Illustration 3.

six-packs of cans, and 325 six-pack of bottles; however, actual sales quantities of these three products were 600, 400, and 500, respectively. The sales volume variance for BLAST! is calculated as follows:

Sales Volume Variance = (Forecast Budget Sales − Control Budget Sales) × Forecast Contribution Margin %

= ($1,040 − $1,240) × 0.50

= $100 Favorable

The interpretation of this variance is that the contribution margin earned by the Soda Products Line of BLAST! is $100 higher than expected because sales volumes were greater than anticipated. Both the forecast and control budget sales are based on standard selling prices; therefore, since the control budget sales exceed the forecast budget sales, actual sales volumes must have exceeded forecasted sales volumes. This can be verified by reference to the detailed sales data, which reveals that total actual sales volumes were 1,500 units, while forecasted sales volumes were 1,300 units.

In addition to sales volumes, the mix of products sold also influences the contribution margin earned by the Soda Products Line. In other words, while total sales volumes were higher than forecasted, contribution margins may actually be lower than expected if these additional sales provided lower contribution margins. The sales mix variance identifies how the mix of products sold influences the total contribution margin earned:

Sales Mix Variance = (Forecast Budget Contribution Margin % − Control Budget Contribution Margin %) × Control Budget Sales

= (0.50 − 0.5161) × $1,240

= $20 Favorable (rounded)

The interpretation of the sales mix variance is that the Soda Products Line's contribution margin was higher than anticipated because it sold a more profitable mix of products than forecasted. Note that a contribution margin percentage of 50% was forecasted; however, based on actual product sales, the contribution margin percentage from the control budget was 51.6%.

The following recent excerpts from the business press illustrate the effect of sales mixes on profitability.

> General Motors' (GM's) lower profit margins compared to those of Ford and DaimlerChrysler are primarily related to the mix of products sold. High margin sports utility vehicles accounted for only 47% of GM's sales in 1998, compared to 71% and 61% for DaimlerChrysler and Ford, respectively.[7]
>
> As Coca-Cola and PepsiCo plan their entry into the bottled water market, one concern is that customers may substitute purchases of less profitable water products for those of more profitable soda products. Coca-Cola CEO M. Douglas Ivester noted that "...we don't want to replace high-margin soft drinks with low-margin water."[8]
>
> Best Buy Co. (the largest retailer of consumer-electronics goods in the United States) has redesigned its store formats to place higher-margin digital items in the center aisles and relegate less profitable products (such as cables and headphones) to self-serve sections. Placing higher-margin products in more visible locations will allow Best Buy to better use its sales staff to sell more lucrative items.[9]
>
> Intel Corp. (the largest manufacturer of computer microprocessors) prices its chips along three product lines: Celeron chips used in low cost machines, Pentium III chips for power users, and Xeon chips for corporate servers. With prices ranging from $63 for the Celeron chip to $3,692 for the Xeon, Intel's challenge is to sell enough Xeons to maintain an average chip price of $250.[10]

The final two variances that may be used to identify why the actual contribution margin differed from the forecasted contribution margin evaluate the effect of differences in sales prices and variable costs, holding both sales volumes and sales mixes constant. Since both the control budget and actual budget are based on actual sales volumes and mixes, comparing the sales revenues and variable costs from these budgets will isolate the effect of differences in sales prices and variable costs, respectively. The sales price variance and variable expense variance are calculated as follows:

Sales Price Variance = Control Budget Sales − Actual Budget Sales
  = $1,240 − $1,210
  = $30 Unfavorable

Variable Expense Variance = Control Variable Expenses − Actual Variable Expenses
  = $600 − $660
  = $60 Unfavorable

Interpreting these two variances indicates that the actual contribution margin earned by Soda Products is lower than forecasted by $30 and $60 because of lower sales prices and higher variable costs, respectively. It is important to reiterate that comparing control budget sales and variable expenses with actual sales and variable expenses allows the effect of different sales prices and variable costs to be isolated, since both budgets are based on actual sales volumes and sales mixes.

In summary, the higher contribution margin earned by Soda Products ($550) compared to the forecasted (standard) contribution margin ($520) is based on the following four factors ("F" denotes a favorable variance, "U" an unfavorable variance):

Higher sales volumes than anticipated (Sales Volume Variance)	$100 F
A more profitable sales mix than anticipated (Sales Mix Variance)	20 F
Lower sales prices than expected (Sales Price Variance)	30 U
Higher variable expenses than expected (Variable Expense Variance)	60 U
Overall Variance ($550 − $520)	$ 30 F

---

[7] "Reviving GM," *Business Week* (February 1, 1999), 120.

[8] "Guess Who Wants to Make a Splash in Water," *Business Week* (March 1, 1999), 36.

[9] "Best Buy Co. is Stacking the Shelves to Add to Profits," *The Wall Street Journal* (April 28, 1999), B4.

[10] "Reinventing Intel," *Forbes* (May 3, 1999), 157.

> Dell Computer provides a great example of how a focus on cost containment can lead to reduced variable expenses and increased profit. While Dell is competitive on price, the company is even more competitive on cost. At Dell, the cost of labor-related overhead is approximately 11.5 percent of sales, compared to 16 percent at Gateway, 21 percent at Compaq and 22.5 percent at Hewlett-Packard. Dell also stays lean by maintaining only five days' of inventory (rivals generally maintain 30-day or 45-day parts inventories), a major advantage in an industry in which the cost of component parts drops by an average of 1 percent each week.[11]

In addition to the contribution margin, the differences in budgeted and actual fixed expenses would also be evaluated further. Where applicable, these differences would be evaluated at the cost center level (for fixed costs incurred by and the responsibility of the Production Department and Administration and Finance Department). To illustrate, referring to Illustration 4, the Production Department anticipated fixed costs of $203; actual fixed costs were $198, resulting in a $5 favorable fixed expense variance. It is important to note that additional fixed costs are incurred at the Product Line level. If they are controllable by Fran Fowler (the manager of Soda Products), the reason(s) for differences in these fixed costs should be investigated and charged to her responsibility center.

INVESTMENT CENTERS

An *investment center* is a responsibility center in which the manager has the ability to make decisions that affect both profitability (costs and revenues, similar to profit centers) and utilization of invested assets (capital). Managers of investment centers are typically in a position to add new product lines, acquire additional plant and equipment, and make significant decisions with respect to the mix of products and services provided by their center. An investment center is analogous to placing the manager in a position of running his or her own business. This should be contrasted with profit centers, which do not have the authority to make major investment and operational decisions.

> The distinction between a profit center and investment center can be illustrated by Borg-Warner Chemical's method of evaluating its plastic distribution centers. Using the classical definition, these responsibility centers would be classified as investment centers, since the managers are responsible for revenues, expenses, and the investment used in generating them. However, since most of the assets available to these centers could not only be used in a discretionary fashion, Borg-Warner classified these responsibility centers as profit centers.[12]

Referring to our earlier discussion of BLAST! and the organizational chart shown in Illustration 1, both Susan Meghan (manager of the Beverage Division) and Michael Drew (president of BLAST!) are classified as managers of investment centers. Susan Meghan has been provided with the authority to explore additional types of products and/or expand the production levels of existing products. In addition, Susan also has authority to establish the selling prices of the Beverage Division's products. Michael Drew's position as president of BLAST! provides him with similar responsibilities for all of the organization's product lines.

Management control systems attempt to achieve congruence between the goals of managers of decentralized responsibility centers and those of the organization. From a profitability standpoint, the organization's goal is to utilize assets in the most effective manner to earn maximum levels of profit. As a result, the managers of investment centers are typically evaluated based on the profit they generate in relation to the assets that are available for use. Two methods of evaluating investment centers (return on investment and residual income) are discussed below.

Return on Investment (ROI)

Return on investment (ROI) measures the profitability of an investment center in relation to its investment base. ROI is a measure which answers the following question: how much net income has the investment center

---

[11] Richard Miniter, *The Myth of Market Share: Why Market Share is the Fool's Gold of Business* (New York: Crown Publishing Group), 2002.

[12] J.F. Mosberg, "Managing for Profit," *Management Accounting* (August 1991), 51–53.

earned given the level of assets (investment) available to that center? ROI acknowledges that investment centers with more assets (investment) at their disposal should generate higher levels of net income. While several variations of ROI exist in practice, one common formula used to calculate ROI is:[13]

$$\text{Return on Investment (ROI)} = \frac{\text{Net Income}}{\text{Assets}}$$

Consider the performance of the following investment centers:

	Center A	Center B
Net income	$ 50,000	$ 3,000
Assets	$312,500	$15,000
ROI	16%	20%

If judged based strictly on net income, the performance of Center A would be evaluated as higher than that of Center B, since Center A earned over sixteen times more net income than Center B. However, compared to Center B, Center A had over twenty times more assets available to it. ROI attempts to place investment centers on an equal footing by relating the net income earned by the investment center to the assets available to that center to generate that income.

Illustration 5 presents an income statement for the Beverage Division of BLAST! for April 20x1. Using this income statement information, as well as the average total assets available for use of $3,100,000, the ROI for Susan Meghan is calculated.

Illustration 5
BLAST! Snack Foods
Income Statement: Beverage Division (in thousands)
(for the month ended April 30, 20x1)

Sales			
Soda Products		$1,210	
Juice and Tea Products		1,500	$2,710
Less: Variable Expenses			
Soda Products		(660)	
Juice and Tea Products		(890)	(1,550)
Contribution Margin			$1,160
Less: Fixed Expenses			
Soda Products		(444)	
Juice and Tea Products		(300)	
Other Divisional Expenses		(50)	(794)
Net Income			$ 366

$$\text{Return on Investment (ROI)} = \frac{\text{Net Income}}{\text{Assets}}$$

$$= \frac{\$366}{\$3,100}$$

$$= 11.81\% \text{ (rounded)}$$

Once calculated, ROI would be compared to either historical levels of ROI or a standard measure established by the organization. For example, if BLAST! desires a minimum return on investment of 10 percent (based on average total assets available for use), the Beverage Division would be considered to have performed adequately, since it has earned a return that exceeds the standard established by the organization. In addition, because the ROI measure controls for the level of assets available for use by the responsibility center, ROIs can be compared

---

[13] ROI is also referred to as "return on capital," "return on assets," and "return on invested capital." While the numerator and denominator of this ratio may differ based on the variation employed, these alternative measures divide some measure of profitability by some measure of available assets.

among the organization's various responsibility centers to evaluate the managers of these centers on a relative basis.

Decomposing ROI. A weakness of ROI in evaluating divisional performance is that it may obscure factors that provide additional insight into why a responsibility center's performance was either favorable or unfavorable. This occurs because net income is used in calculating ROI. For example, the fact that the ROI earned by the Beverage Division of BLAST! (11.81%) exceeded the targeted amount (10%) may result from either (or both) the ability to effectively:

1. Generate revenues using divisional assets.

2. Control expenses and maximize net income.

Clearly, information concerning these factors is important in allowing an investment center to improve its ROI (and overall performance). To further analyze ROI, this measure can be expressed in two separate components. One component (*asset turnover*) measures the ability of the investment center to generate revenues, while the other (*profit margin*) reflects the ability of an investment center to control its costs. These components of ROI are summarized below:

$$\text{Return on Investment (ROI)} = \text{Asset Turnover} \times \text{Profit Margin}$$

$$= \frac{\text{Sales}}{\text{Assets}} \times \frac{\text{Net Income}}{\text{Sales}}$$

From an algebraic standpoint, multiplying these two components together eliminates the "sales" in the numerator of the asset turnover and denominator of the profit margin, resulting in net income divided by assets or ROI.

Referring to Illustration 5, the ROI of the Beverage Division of BLAST! can be decomposed as follows:

$$\text{Return on Investment (ROI)} = \frac{\text{Sales}}{\text{Assets}} \times \frac{\text{Net Income}}{\text{Sales}}$$

$$= \frac{\$2{,}710}{\$3{,}100} \times \frac{\$366}{\$2{,}710}$$

$$= 0.87 \text{ (rounded)} \times 13.56\% \text{ (rounded)}$$

$$= 11.81\% \text{ (rounded)}$$

The interpretation of the asset turnover of 0.87 is that the Beverage Division generated $0.87 in revenues for each $1.00 of assets available to the investment center. The profit margin of 13.56% indicates that for each $1.00 of sales the Beverage Division realized approximately $0.14 in net income. Both measures can be compared to those for prior years, other investment centers, or organization standards to identify potential areas for improvement. For example, consider the ROI, asset turnover, and profit margin earned by the Beverage Division in the first quarter of 20x1 (along with the data for April 20x1):

Month	ROI	Asset Turnover	Profit Margin
January 20x1	12.25%	1.10	11.14%
February 20x1	12.10%	0.95	12.74%
March 20x1	11.90%	0.92	12.93%
April 20x1	11.81%	0.87	13.56%

Clearly, the gradual decline in ROI over the first quarter of 20x1 is the result of a decreasing asset turnover over this period. This may be the result of one of two factors: a large investment in property, plant and equipment that has not yet begun generating sufficient revenues or a general decline in the Beverage Division's ability to generate revenues using existing assets. Susan Meghan (the manager of the Beverage Division) will investigate the nature of this decrease further to determine its cause. Examining the profit margins over this same period of time reveals a gradual increase, indicating that the Beverage Division has effectively controlled its costs over this period and, in fact, is improving in its ability to do so.

When using the components of ROI to evaluate investment centers, it is important that management consider the profit structures of different investment centers. To illustrate, because of lower ingredient costs and less competitive market conditions, the Beverage Division may be in a position to earn higher profits on the sale of its products than other divisions of BLAST! (such as the Snack Food Division). These higher profits result in a higher profit margin and ROI. Conversely, if the nature of the production process for beverage products is such that large investments in property, plant and equipment are necessary, this division may not have the ability to generate large revenues in relation to its assets, resulting in a lower asset turnover and ROI. Factors such as these should be considered if intra-division comparisons are made using ROI and its components.

Examining the components of ROI reveals several ways that managers can improve their responsibility centers' ROIs. Improvements in profit margin would require managers to increase the net income resulting from each sale. This can be accomplished by increasing the selling price of the organization's products, decreasing the expenses incurred by the responsibility center, or both. In order to improve asset turnover, managers must either generate greater revenues using existing asset bases or reduce their asset bases without a corresponding reduction in revenues. While it may be difficult to significantly increase the revenues generated by the responsibility center, managers may take actions to dispose of nonproductive assets or otherwise reduce the denominator of the ROI measure. An example of an action of this type is shown in the following excerpt.

> **The extensive use of return on assets (ROA) as a performance measure has resulted in Compaq Computer Corp. using outsourcing and partnership deals with other manufacturers. These arrangements reduce Compaq's investment in assets such as plant and inventory. Doing so allows the home personal computer division to deliver a 20 percent ROA despite the fact that operating margins for this product are only 2 percent.**[14]

Weaknesses of ROI. A weakness of ROI as a performance evaluation tool is that it may not provide the manager of an investment center with incentives to act in a manner consistent with the organization's objectives. Recall that a goal of management control systems is goal congruence between the organization's goals and those of its subunits. Instances where subunits take actions that are not beneficial to the organization are classified as *suboptimal*. The use of ROI may result in suboptimization if managers forego investment opportunities that are beneficial to the organization but reduce ROIs.

To illustrate, recall that BLAST! established a target ROI for its Beverage Division of 10 percent. During April 20x1, Susan Meghan is presented with an opportunity to acquire additional production machinery with a cost of $2,000,000. Based on an analysis of expected production costs, this machinery would reduce current operating costs by $120,000 per year (after taxes). The ROI for this particular investment would be 6 percent ($120,000 ÷ $2,000,000 = 0.06 or 6 percent).

If Susan Meghan could obtain the capital for this purchase at a cost of 5 percent, it seems clear that she should make this investment, since it would return 6 percent. As a result, the optimal decision from the organization's standpoint is to purchase the production machinery. However, what decision would she make based on her division's ROI? The impact of this purchase on the Beverage Division's ROI is shown below (dollar amounts are in thousands):

$$\text{Return on Investment (ROI)} = \frac{\$366 + \$120}{\$3{,}100 + \$2{,}000} = 9.53\% \text{ (rounded)}$$

- $366 / $3,100: Original Income and Investment
- $120 / $2,000: Income and Investment from Purchase of Machinery

Since Susan Meghan's target ROI is 10 percent, she may be reluctant to purchase the machinery, since this purchase would lower her ROI from an acceptable level (11.81%) to an unacceptable level (9.53%). This occurs because, while the return on the investment exceeds the cost of capital, it is less than the Beverage Division's ROI prior to making the investment. The ultimate result is that Susan Meghan would not act in a manner beneficial to the overall organization, inconsistent with the implementation of management control systems and decentralization.

What is the problem with the use of ROI in the above example? It ignores an important piece of information: the cost of obtaining capital. As long as an investment center can earn a return greater than the cost of its capital,

---

[14] "Big Blue Has a Clone of Its Own," *Business Week* (November 2, 1992),152.

the organization as a whole benefits from this investment. An alternative method of evaluating investment centers that attempts to reduce this suboptimal behavior by considering the cost of capital to the responsibility center is residual income. This method is discussed in the following section.

Residual Income

Residual income represents the level of the investment center's net income that remains after deducting an implied or imputed charge for the assets (capital) it uses. The imputed charge for capital represents the organization's cost of obtaining capital through either debt or equity financing and is typically specified by management. This charge does not represent an actual payment that must be made by the investment center; rather, it reflects the fact that the overall organization would like its investment centers to earn some stated level of return on the assets used by those centers. The basic formula used to calculate residual income is:

$$\text{Residual Income} = \text{Investment Center Net Income} - \left(\text{Investment Center Assets} \times \text{Imputed Charge for Capital}\right)$$

Recall Susan Meghan's decision regarding the purchase of new machinery. Using ROI, Susan would forgo this opportunity, despite the fact that its "return" (6 percent) exceeded the cost of obtaining capital (5 percent). Shown below are the residual incomes that would be earned by the Beverage Division of BLAST! with and without the purchase of this new machinery (assuming a cost of capital of 5 percent). Recall that the new machinery would cost $2,000,000 and result in cost savings of $120,000 (all amounts below are in thousands of dollars).

Without Purchase of Machinery		With Purchase of Machinery	
Net Income............................	$366	Net Income ($366 + $120)	$486
Assets $3,100		Assets ($3,100 + $2,000) $5,100	
Cost of Capital .... x 0.05	(155)	Cost of Capital .... x 0.05	(255)
Residual Income	$211	Residual Income	$231

The above example indicates how the use of residual income enhances the goal congruence between the managers of the organization's subunits and the organization as a whole. If evaluated strictly based on residual income, Susan Meghan would clearly decide to invest in the additional machinery since it would increase the Beverage Division's residual income from $211,000 to $231,000 (recall that the above amounts are in thousands).

Using residual income to evaluate managers of investment centers, the organization can compare the residual income earned by the responsibility center to that earned in prior years or to some targeted level of residual income established by the organization's management. Clearly, higher levels of residual income represent superior levels of performance, and vice versa. Negative residual income indicates that the responsibility center's net income was insufficient to offset the cost of providing assets for use by that center and is a signal that management action may be necessary.

Residual income is similar to *economic value added (or EVA)*, a measure developed by Stern Stewart & Co. to evaluate corporate performance. Economic value added is calculated as follows:

$$\text{EVA} = \text{Net Operating Income} - \left\{\left(\text{Long-Term Liabilities} + \text{Shareholders' Equity}\right) \times \text{Cost of Capital}\right\}$$

The measures used to calculate EVA are modified to reflect the use of consistent GAAP accounting methods (for example, the cost flow assumption used for inventories) as well as to account for certain items in a non-GAAP manner (for example, capitalizing both research and development costs and operating leases).

Corporations such as Quaker Oats, Coca-Cola, and AT&T have adopted EVA as financial performance measures.[15]

---

[15] For example, see "A Star to Sail By?" *The Economist* (August 2, 1997), 61, 63; G.A. Achstatter, "EVA: Performance Gauge for the 1990s?" *Investor's Business Daily* (June 1995), 1–2.

Disadvantage of Residual Income. A major disadvantage of residual income in evaluating investment centers is that it has a bias toward larger investment centers. To illustrate, assume that the Snack Food Division of BLAST! earned net income of $1,181,000 using assets of $10,000,000. As a result, its ROI is identical to that of the Beverage Division ($1,181,000 ÷ $10,000,000 = 11.81%). However, the residual income of this investment center is over three times as high as the Beverage Division, as shown below (all amounts are in thousands of dollars):

Net Income..		$ 1,181
Assets	$ 10,000	
Cost of Capital	x 0.05	(500)
Residual Income		$ 681

Once an investment center earns income in excess of its imputed cost of capital, its residual income will increase disproportionately as the assets available to that responsibility center size increase. To earn $681,000 in residual income on an asset base of $3,100,000, the Beverage Division would have to earn a net income of $836,000 ($836,000 - [0.05 x $3,100,000] = $681,000). This net income of $836,000 would equate to an ROI of almost 27 percent ($836,000 ÷ $3,100,000 = 26.97%)!

ISSUES IN EVALUATING INVESTMENT CENTERS

The use of ROI and residual income is highly dependent upon the definition of "assets" employed by the organization. From a behavioral standpoint, a method used by managers of investment centers to increase ROIs and residual incomes is to minimize the amount of assets on which these measures are based. Common definitions of assets that may be used by organizations in calculating ROI and residual income include:

- Total assets.

- Total "productive" assets (total assets minus assets that not available for use, such as plant under construction, assets held for sale, or goodwill resulting from an acquisition).

- Total assets minus current liabilities.

- Net assets (shareholders' equity).

It is important to note that each of these measures may include assets, liabilities, and shareholders' equity solely related to the investment center as well as an allocated percentage of corporate items. While allocations are necessary to reflect the fact that assets may not be solely related to a single responsibility center, the methods of allocation are often arbitrary and may dilute the meaning of ROI and residual income.

There are advantages and disadvantages for each of these definitions. The use of total assets encourages managers to evaluate all assets under their control and dispose of those assets that are not being utilized in the operations of their responsibility center. In addition, it reflects the philosophy that the role of the responsibility center manager is to put the center's assets to their best possible use in generating profits. Finally, the use of total assets is easily obtained from, and consistent with, amounts reported in the organization's financial statements.

Using total productive assets does not charge managers with assets (such as plant under construction) that cannot be used currently in the center's operations. However, this measure does not provide managers with an incentive to dispose of nonproductive assets and reinvest any proceeds received from the disposal of these assets in more productive assets. In addition, from a theoretical standpoint, if managers decide to construct additional property, plant and equipment for the investment center's use in generating future profits, they should be "charged" for that decision by including these items in the denominator of the ROI formula.

Remaining definitions of "assets" are total assets minus current liabilities and net assets (shareholders' equity). Using the difference between total assets and current liabilities provides managers with incentives to use short-term (and normally interest-free) financing to conduct operations, since the use of such financing reduces the asset base on which their ROI and residual income is calculated. Therefore, if managers have control over obtaining this type of financing, this measure encourages them to act in the overall interests of the organization. Finally, while using net assets focuses on how well the manager is using funds provided by shareholders in generating net income, this approach requires that long-term debt be allocated to the organization's responsibility centers. In many cases, these allocations may be arbitrary. As a result, the use of net assets in the denominator of the ROI formula is not frequently employed in practice.

In addition to the items included in the measure of "assets," other considerations are the valuation method used and the time period over which assets are measured. Assets can be valued at gross book value (acquisition costs), net book value (acquisition costs minus accumulated depreciation), or current market value. An advantage of net book value is that this valuation corresponds to the manner in which assets are reported on the organization's balance sheet. However, the use of net book value has the following disadvantages:

- The use of net book value artificially inflates both ROI and residual income over time as the accumulated depreciation increases (and net book value decreases).

- If net book values are used, managers of responsibility centers may be reluctant to replace aging property, plant and equipment (lower net book values) with new property, plant and equipment (higher net book values).

- Net book values are highly influenced by the depreciation method selected and the useful life assigned to assets, both of which are estimates.

The difficulty of obtaining objective measures of the current market value of some assets makes the use of this basis difficult. Given this characteristic, as well as the disadvantages associated with net book value discussed above, most organizations use gross book values in determining ROI and residual income.

In addition to the valuation basis for assets, organizations must consider the time period over which assets are measured. Two alternatives are year-end asset values and average asset values. Average assets values (which are calculated by dividing the sum of beginning assets and ending assets by 2) are ordinarily preferred. First, the use of average values is consistent with the measurement of net income, which has been earned throughout the period over which the investment center is being evaluated. Also, the use of average values limits the effect of year-end acquisitions or disposals of assets on the investment center's ROI or residual income.

Net Income

The measure of net income used to evaluate investment centers should consider only those revenues and costs that can be directly influenced by the investment center or its manager. This approach excludes expenses incurred at the corporate level (such as interest expense, income tax expense, and depreciation expense related to corporate assets) that are allocated to the organization's various responsibility centers. Some organizations deduct allocated corporate expenses in determining the responsibility center's net income under the premise that the organization's responsibility centers must generate sufficient revenues to offset these expenses.

Another controversial expense is depreciation. Including depreciation expense holds the manager of the responsibility center accountable for his or her past decisions to purchase property, plant and equipment. Conversely, once property, plant and equipment have been purchased, this cost cannot be influenced by the manager and should be excluded from the measure of responsibility center net income. Those espousing this latter viewpoint include revenues, variable costs, and discretionary fixed costs (fixed costs that can be modified by the manager of the responsibility center on a short-term basis) in determining responsibility center net income.

Life of Investment

A final factor that must be considered in evaluating investment centers using ROI and residual income is the timing of the investment and the related effects of this investment on responsibility center income. For example, assume that Susan Meghan is considering the purchase of machinery to increase production capacity for the Beverage Division. This machinery would cost $2,000,000 and is expected to have a useful life of three years. Assuming that the Beverage Division's net income (given current production levels) would remain constant over the three-year period and that the increase in net income from this investment is greater in the later years of the machinery's life, the ROIs over the three-year period are as follows (all amounts are in thousands of dollars):

	Current	Year 1	Year 2	Year 3
Net Income Before Investment	$ 366	$ 366	$ 366	$ 366
Increase in Net Income From Investment	0	100	200	400
Total Net Income	$ 366	$ 466	$ 566	$ 766
Assets	$3,100	$5,100	$5,100	$5,100
ROI	11.8%	9.1%	11.1%	15.0%

Susan Meghan may decide to forgo this investment because of its negative impact on ROI in Years 1 and 2. However, the increased production capacity provides a benefit to the organization in the long run as evidenced by the higher ROI in year 3. While ROI and residual income are frequently used in practice, it is important to note that these are short-run measures of performance and do not consider the operations of the responsibility center beyond the year being evaluated.

Transfer Pricing

When evaluating the performance of either profit or investment centers, it is important to provide special consideration when one responsibility center in an organization provides goods or services to another responsibility center in the same organization. These situations introduce additional issues for the evaluation of responsibility centers, since the transfer of goods or services represents revenues for one responsibility center and costs for another responsibility center. The internal price charged by a responsibility center for goods and services provided to another responsibility center in the organization is known as a *transfer price*.

To illustrate the issues involved in establishing transfer prices, assume that the Beverage Division of BLAST! has experienced difficulty in obtaining reliable delivery for its products. This problem has resulted in vendor dissatisfaction and threats to discontinue purchasing the Beverage Division's products. To ensure prompt delivery to vendors, Susan Meghan has purchased a small number of delivery trucks to transport the Beverage Division's products to nearby vendors. To reduce the cost of underutilized delivery capabilities, as well as provide additional sources of revenue, the Beverage Division also provides delivery services to other companies. The upper management of BLAST! has approved the use of the delivery vehicles for this purpose, under the condition that the products sold by the other companies are not competitive with any of BLAST!'s own products. Illustration 6 summarizes the standard costs and prices of delivery services charged to external customers.

Illustration 6

BLAST! Snack Foods

Standard Costs and Revenues for Delivery Services
Beverage Division

Standard Cost (per mile):		
Gasoline..	$0.10	
Driver's Salary...................................	0.70	
Variable Overhead..............................	5.00	
Variable General and Administrative.....	0.50	$ 6.30
Fixed Overhead..................................		3.00
Fixed General and Administrative........		0.70
Total Standard Cost (per mile).............		$10.00
Markup on Total Cost (20%).................		2.00
Delivery Charge (per mile)...................		$12.00

Margaret Knight, the manager of the Snack Food Division of BLAST!, has inquired about the possibility of using the Beverage Division's delivery trucks to ship some of its inventory. Currently, the Snack Food Division is paying $12 per mile for delivery services. Margaret feels that using the Beverage Division's vehicles would result in an overall benefit to the organization, since the cost to the Beverage Division ($10 per mile) is less than the price paid by the Snack Food Division to external providers ($12 per mile). However, Susan Meghan correctly notes that the Beverage Division would lose revenues earned by providing delivery services to external customers.

Assuming that the Beverage Division was to provide this service to the Snack Food Division, what would represent a "fair" transfer price? Viewed from each division's standpoint, the following possibilities exist:

> **Snack Food Division:** Since the Snack Food Division is currently paying $12 per mile for external delivery services, this represents the maximum amount that it would be willing to pay to the Beverage Division for delivery services.
>
> **Beverage Division:** The minimum acceptable transfer price for the Beverage Division would be the sum of the additional costs of providing delivery services to the Snack Food Division plus any revenues forgone from the sale of delivery services to external customers.

These two amounts represent the range over which acceptable transfer prices can be established. If the transfer price exceeds the external market price ($12 per mile), the organization as a whole is better off by allowing the Snack Food Division to obtain these services externally. If the transfer price is below the sum of the additional costs of providing services internally and the revenues forgone from providing services to external customers, it is beneficial to the organization to allow the Beverage Division to continue to provide delivery services to external customers only and have the Snack Food Division purchase these services from external suppliers.

From the organization's standpoint, the first question that must be answered is whether it is logical for a transfer to be made in this situation. The answer to this question depends upon whether the Beverage Division would need to reduce sales to its external customers to provide services to the Snack Food Division. As shown below, if no excess capacity exists, the organization is indifferent as to whether the transfer should occur, since the sum of the costs of providing delivery services ($6.30) and contribution margin forgone on external sales ($5.70) exactly equals the cost paid by the Snack Food Division for delivery services ($12). Alternatively, if excess capacity exists, the organization can incur $6.30 per mile of delivery costs (in the Beverage Division) to save $12 per mile that the Snack Food Division pays to external delivery services. Note that fixed costs would be incurred regardless of whether the delivery services are provided to the Snack Food Division, so they are not considered.

	No Excess Capacity	Excess Capacity
Savings of Snack Food Division on external delivery services	$12.00	$12.00
Variable cost of providing delivery services	(6.30)	(6.30)
Contribution margin lost by Beverage Division on sale of external services ($12.00 – $6.30)	(5.70)	
Net benefit (detriment) to organization	$ 0.00	$ 5.70

This analysis suggests that the organization benefits by the Beverage Division providing delivery services to the Snack Food Division, assuming that excess capacity exists. But what transfer price should be charged by the Beverage Division for these services? It is important to note that the overall organization is unaffected by the transfer price, since it represents the price charged by one division to another. However, the transfer price does serve to divide the net savings of $5.70 per mile (assuming that excess capacity exists) between the Snack Food and Beverage Divisions. To achieve goal congruence, it is critical that the transfer price provides the managers of both divisions with incentives to enter into the transaction. Common methods of establishing transfer prices are briefly discussed below.

Cost. Transfer prices can be established based on either the actual or standard costs of the supplying responsibility center (the Beverage Division) in providing goods or services to the receiving responsibility center (the Snack Food Division). A limitation of actual costs is that they provide no incentives for the supplying responsibility center to control its costs, since these costs can be passed on to the receiving responsibility center in the form of higher transfer prices. As a result, using standard costs (as opposed to actual costs) in cost-based transfer pricing schemes aligns the incentives of the managers of responsibility centers with those of the organization.

Referring to Illustration 6, BLAST! could define the "cost" of the delivery services in the following ways:

- Total variable costs of providing delivery services ($6.30). This amount represents the additional costs that are incurred by the Beverage Division in providing delivery services to the Snack Food Division. Using the total variable costs does not provide the Beverage Division with incentive to provide delivery services for the Snack Food Division, since it will not recover any of its fixed costs or earn a profit by doing so.

- Total costs (both fixed and variable) of providing delivery services ($10.00). This amount offsets the variable costs incurred by the Beverage Division as well as allowing it to recover some of its fixed costs. However, like transfer prices based on total variable costs, the Beverage Division will not recognize a profit by providing delivery services to the Snack Food Division,

- Total costs plus a mark-up. This amount would allow the Beverage Division to recover its costs as well as providing it with some measure of profit. However, if the amount of the mark-up were lower than that charged to external customers, the Beverage Division would not be favorably disposed to the transfer if excess capacity does not exist.

Any of the above cost-based transfer prices should be reduced for savings that are realized by providing the delivery services internally as opposed to externally. For example, assume that the variable costs of $6.30 per mile included $0.20 of general and administrative costs incurred with processing orders that would be saved if the delivery services were provided to the Snack Food Division. In this case, the additional variable cost of providing delivery services is $6.10 ($6.30 − $0.20 = $6.10) and each of the above transfer prices should be reduced to reflect this cost savings.

Market Price. The primary limitation of cost-based transfer prices is that they fail to recognize the revenues that are forgone by the supplying responsibility center to provide goods or services to the receiving responsibility center. The use of market prices overcomes this limitation and allows a more equitable recognition of income (from the standpoint of the supplying responsibility center). In addition, the market price would presumably equal the cost paid to external suppliers by the receiving responsibility center. As shown in Illustration 6, transfers made at market prices would result in the Snack Food Division paying $12 per mile for delivery services to the Beverage Division.

If excess capacity exists, organizations benefit from internal transfers, assuming that the costs of providing the services are less than the market price of the services. If excess capacity does not exist and no cost savings are realized by providing goods or services internally, the organization will be indifferent as to the desirability of market-based transfers. This indifference reflects the fact that market prices represent the amounts received by the Beverage Division from existing services and the amounts paid by the Snack Food Division for external services. However, if internal cost savings exist, the organization would benefit from the use of market prices. To illustrate, if the Beverage Division can save $0.20 of variable general and administrative costs by providing services to the Snack Food Division as opposed to an external customer, BLAST! would benefit from this transfer as follows:

	No Excess Capacity	Excess Capacity
Savings of Snack Food Division on external delivery services	$12.00	$12.00
Variable cost of providing delivery services	(6.10)	(6.10)
Contribution margin lost by Beverage Division on sale of external services ($12.00 − $6.30)	(5.70)	
Net benefit (detriment) to organization	$ 0.20	$ 5.90

While market-based transfer prices are based on an objective, arm's-length measure, problems with the use of these measures may exist if consistent market prices do not exist (for example, delivery costs range from $10 per mile to $16 per mile). In addition, a reliable external market may not exist for all products and services. Finally, if differences exist in the quality of products and services provided within and outside the organization, market prices should be adjusted to reflect those differences.

Negotiated Transfer Prices. In some instances, organizations allow managers of responsibility centers to negotiate with one another to establish transfer prices. When transfer prices are established in this manner, both the supplying and receiving responsibility centers evaluate current market conditions and cost information in arriving at a price that is acceptable to both centers. Negotiated transfer prices are most frequently used when an external market does not exist for the supplying division's product or service. A limitation of negotiated transfer prices is that divisions may be evaluated based on their ability to negotiate and not based on efficiencies in providing goods and services. For example, if Susan Meghan (the manager of the Beverage Division) is able to consistently prevail over Margaret Knight (the manager of the Snack Food Division) in negotiations, Susan's responsibility center will continually show higher levels of profit.

Dual Pricing. Dual-pricing arrangements establish two "transfer" prices. The supplying responsibility center records the transfer at the market price of the goods or services, while the receiving responsibility center records the transfer at the cost (ordinarily, variable cost) of the goods or services. Dual-pricing arrangements provide both responsibility centers with a clear advantage for making the transfer. The supplying responsibility center receives the same price for its good or service as it would in the marketplace and thus is indifferent between internal and external sales. The receiving responsibility center pays less for the goods or services than it would to an external supplier. To illustrate, if the market price of delivery services is $12 per mile, the variable cost of providing the delivery services is $6.30 per mile, and a $0.20 per mile cost savings would be realized if delivery services were provided internally, the use of a dual-pricing arrangement would provide the following benefits to the Beverage and Snack Food Divisions:

	Before Transfer	After Transfer	Net Benefit
Beverage Division:			
Selling price of services (per mile)	$12.00	$12.00	$ 0.00
Costs of providing services (per mile)	(10.00)	(9.80)	0.20
Net profit (per mile)	$ 2.00	$ 2.20	$ 0.20
Snack Food Division:			
Costs of delivery services (per mile)	$12.00	$ 6.10	$5.90

It is important to note that the sum of the net benefits to the two divisions ($6.10) exceeds the net revenues recognized by the organization of $5.90 ($12.00 − $6.10 = $5.90). Essentially, the $0.20 of cost savings has been included in the performance of both divisions. From an external reporting standpoint, this will be reconciled when preparing organization-wide financial statements.

Other Transfer Pricing Incentives. Multinational organizations may operate in parts of the world with vastly different income tax rates and import/export tariffs. In these settings, transfer prices are often established in such a manner as to minimize the total taxes and/or tariffs paid by the organization. Doing so allows the organization to "shift" income from countries with higher income tax rates/tariffs to those with lower income tax rates/tariffs. While laws vary from country to country, the Internal Revenue Service's guidelines suggest that transfer prices should meet a reasonableness test of reflecting an arm's-length transaction between independent parties.

Summary: Transfer Pricing. The above discussion illustrates the wide diversity of prices that could result from various transfer pricing schemes. While no specific rules exist in practice, two authors recommend the following method of calculating transfer prices to provide a starting point for establishing these prices.[16]

$$\text{Transfer Price} = \text{Variable Costs of Good or Service to Supplying Responsibility Center} + \text{Contribution Margin Forgone by Supplying Responsibility Center on Sales to Customers}$$

In our example, the transfer price resulting from this formula would be $11.80 per mile, as shown below:

$$\text{Transfer Price} = \text{Variable Costs of Good or Service to Supplying Responsibility Center} + \text{Contribution Margin Forgone by Supplying Responsibility Center on Sales to Customers}$$

$$= (\$6.30 - \$0.20) + (\$12.00 - \$6.30)$$

$$= \$11.80$$

A survey of large companies revealed that 31 percent used market prices, 47 percent used cost or some variation of cost, and 22 percent used negotiations in establishing transfer prices.[17] Clearly, a great deal of diversity exists in the methods used to establish transfer prices in practice.

TOTAL QUALITY MANAGEMENT

Thus far our discussion of responsibility centers and management control systems has focused on financial aspects of performance, such as variances of actual costs/profits from standard costs/profits, return on investment, and residual income. However, focusing only on financial aspects may result in organizations experiencing short-term success at the expense of long-term failure. Unless the organization maintains the quality of its products and services, the long-run survival of that organization is questionable. However, quality has traditionally been thought of as requiring additional costs to be incurred without commensurate increases in revenues.

Total quality management (or *TQM*) refers to the processes used by organizations to ensure that the products and services provided to customers are of the highest level of quality. Total quality management requires the organization to monitor and evaluate four major types of quality costs:

1. *Prevention costs* are the costs of preventing substandard products or services and include costs associated with quality training, systems development, and reliability engineering.

---

[16] R.L. Benke and J.D. Edwards, "Transfer Prices: Techniques and Uses," *Management Accounting* (June 1980), 44–46.

[17] R. Vancil, *Decentralization: Managerial Ambiguity by Design* (New York: Financial Executives Foundation, 1979).

2. *Appraisal costs* are costs incurred by the organization for the purpose of evaluating the overall quality of its products and services and determining whether substandard products or services have been provided. Examples of appraisal costs include inspection and testing costs.

3. *Internal failure costs* are incurred by the organization to remedy substandard products or services prior to their sale to customers. Examples of internal failure costs include the costs of scrap, repair and rework, and downtime for production employees.

4. *External failure costs* are costs of remedying substandard products or services following their sale to customers. These costs include costs actually incurred by the organization (such as warranty costs, costs of processing customer complaints, and costs of repairs and replacements) as well as costs that are not directly incurred (such as the loss of reputation and customer dissatisfaction).

Providing high quality products and services requires that prevention and appraisal costs be incurred by the organization to both prevent and identify product or service failures; this reduces the extent of internal and external failure costs incurred. Establishing low levels of quality (high percentage of substandard products) results in lower prevention and appraisal costs but may eventually result in the failure of the organization. In contrast, high levels of quality (low percentage of substandard products) require higher prevention and appraisal costs that may harm the organization's profitability. In evaluating the above costs, the organization attempts to minimize the sum of these costs (referred to as total quality costs).

Traditionally, the optimal level of product quality was thought to be the level of substandard products or services where the sum of prevention and appraisal costs equaled the sum of internal and external failure costs. At this point, the total costs of quality were assumed to be minimized. However, this traditional viewpoint largely ignored the failure costs that are not directly incurred by organizations (such as the loss of reputation and customer dissatisfaction).

Japanese control expert Genichi Taguchi concluded that, after considering failure costs such as the loss of reputation and customer dissatisfaction, organizations minimize their total quality costs at a level of zero product or service failures. This relationship is shown below (Q = quality costs, F = internal and external failure costs, PA = prevention and appraisal costs). Note that total quality costs would equal total prevention and appraisal costs at zero percent defects since internal and external failure costs are presumed to be zero. Also note that at 100 percent defects, total quality costs would equal internal and external failure costs, since the organization would not need to incur any prevention and appraisal costs. This conceptualization is based on the premise that the failure costs associated with substandard products and services is quite costly to organizations and should be minimized (if not eliminated).

The importance of product and service quality is further evidenced by the issuance of International Standards Organization (ISO) 9000 standards, which require companies to develop well-defined quality control systems and document all aspects of that system. Originally targeted for companies selling products in Europe, the ISO standards are now being implemented in the United States.

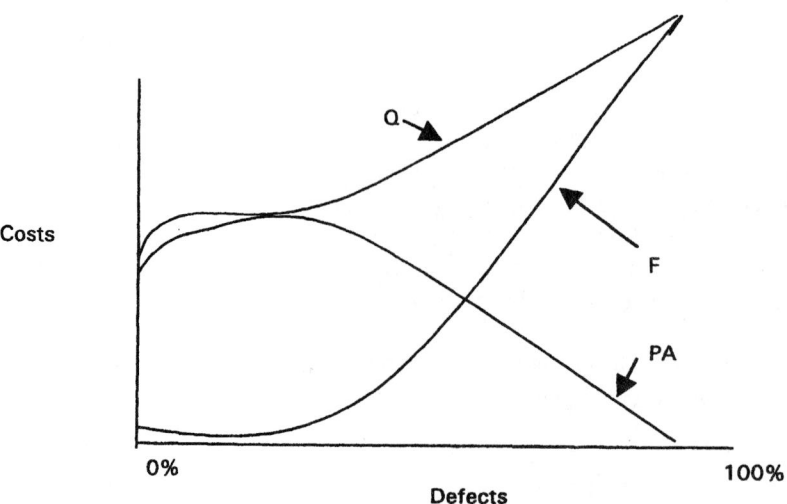

> Dell Computer identified reducing the number of times that each hard drive (the most sensitive part of a personal computer) was handled during assembly as the most important determinant of product quality. Changes in production lines reduced the number of "touches" from 30 to 15; these changes reduced the rate of rejected hard drives by 40% and the overall failure rate for Dell's personal computers by 20%.[18]

NONFINANCIAL PERFORMANCE AND THE BALANCED SCORECARD

In addition to TQM's focus on improving product and service quality, organizations are increasingly providing their managers with goals and incentives to improve all aspects (both financial and nonfinancial) of the organization's performance. These organizations often utilize *balanced scorecards* in an attempt to identify, monitor, and evaluate the organization's progress toward meeting important goals and objectives (often referred to as *critical success factors*). The balanced scorecard derives its name from the fact that financial performance (and the shareholders' viewpoint of the organization) is but one element in measuring the performance of the organization. Balanced scorecards measure organizational performance using the following four perspectives:[19]

1. **Financial Perspective** (profitability, sales growth, cash flows, return on investment)
2. **Customer Perspective** (ability to provide customers with on-time delivery, customer satisfaction)
3. **Internal Business Perspective** (introduction of new products or services, manufacturing cycle times, costs of providing products or services)
4. **Innovation and Learning Perspective** (extent of focus on key products or services, time required to bring new products or services to the marketplace)

It is important to note that these perspectives interact with one another and ultimately influence the organization's financial performance. For example, if Wal-Mart reduces customer waiting times by opening additional register stations during peak shopping hours (an element of the internal business perspective), it will increase customer satisfaction (an element of the customer perspective). This increase in customer satisfaction will, in all likelihood, result in increased profitability as Wal-Mart's customers increase their patronage. If Motorola focuses more extensively on its key products and services (an element of the innovation and learning perspective), it should improve its manufacturing cycle time (an element of the internal business perspective) and have the ability to be more responsive to customer demands (an element of the customer perspective). As with Wal-Mart, the increase in customer satisfaction resulting from changes in these factors is likely to result in increased profitability.

An illustration of the benefits of a focus on the customer perspective is provided by the following excerpt from practice.

> Managers frequently find that the best measures of productivity result when performance is viewed from the perspective of the customer. For example, when the performance of call-center representatives is measured simply by the length of an average phone call, a suboptimal result may occur. That is, the company may get a lot of repeat calls from its customers because their problems are not adequately addressed the first time. A better measure might be the percentage of customers whose problems are solved in a single call.[20]

USE OF MANAGERIAL ACCOUNTING INFORMATION: BLAST! SNACK FOODS

In this chapter, we have illustrated the evaluation of three types of responsibility centers: cost centers, profit centers, and investment centers. The following summarizes the performance of selected responsibility centers for BLAST! Snack Foods discussed throughout this chapter.

---

[18] "Michael Dell Turns the PC World Inside Out," *Fortune* (September 8, 1997), 79.

[19] These perspectives are drawn from R.S. Kaplan and D.P. Norton, "The Balanced Scorecard—Measures that Drive Performance," *Harvard Business Review* (January-February 1992), 72.

[20] Cynthia Karen Swank, "The Lean Service Machine," *Harvard Business Review* (October 2003), 123–129.

Type of Center	Example for BLAST!	Method of Evaluation
Cost Center	Marcus Jackson Production Department	Actual Costs of $858 versus Standard Costs of $885
Profit Center	Fran Fowler Soda Products Line	Actual Profit of $106 versus Standard Profit of $86
Investment Center	Susan Meghan Beverage Division	ROI of 11.81% versus organization standard of 10%

In each of these instances, BLAST!'s management would evaluate the managers' performance as favorable, since the actual costs were lower than standard (Production Department), actual profits were greater than standard (Soda Products Line), and the return on investment exceeded the organization's guidelines (Beverage Division). Management would also undertake the analysis described in the chapter to provide further insights into the reasons for the favorable performance. To illustrate, recall that individual variance calculations revealed that the favorable performance of the Soda Products Line (and its manager, Fran Fowler) resulted from higher sales volumes and more profitable sales mixes than anticipated (favorable sales volume and sales mix variances of $100 and $20, respectively). Also recall that the favorable ROI earned by the Beverage Division (and its manager, Susan Meghan) resulted from improvements in the profit margin despite reduced levels of asset turnover.

SUMMARY

1. A *management control system* consists of the processes by which an organization's management makes planning and control decisions, motivates employee behavior, and evaluates employee performance. Management control systems consist of the following components: (1) communicating plans and objectives, (2) measuring activities, and (3) providing feedback to appropriate individuals. The purpose of management control systems is to achieve congruence between the objectives of the organization and the actions of its employees.

2. A *responsibility center* is a division, segment, individual, or other subunit of an organization that is held accountable for the results of its activities. The methods used to measure and evaluate the performance of a responsibility center (and its manager) are referred to as *responsibility accounting*. Under responsibility accounting, a responsibility center is evaluated based only on those costs, revenues, and capital investment (or assets) subject to its control.

3. A responsibility center is classified based on the factors under its control. A *cost center* controls only the costs it incurs. A *profit center* controls both the costs it incurs and the revenues it earns. An *investment center* controls the costs it incurs, the revenues it earns, and the use of capital (assets) invested in that center. Investment centers are able to make major operating decisions with respect to the activities of that center.

4. Cost and profit centers are evaluated by comparing actual costs (cost centers) and net income (profit centers) to standard amounts. For profit centers, variance analysis allows factors that result in differences between actual net income and standard net income to be identified. These factors include different sales volumes than anticipated (sales volume variance), different sales mixes than anticipated (sales mix variance), different sales prices than anticipated (sales price variance), and different expenses than anticipated (variable and fixed expense variances).

5. Two methods used to evaluate investment centers are *return on investment (ROI)* and *residual income*. Both of these methods evaluate the profitability of an investment center while considering the amount of capital (assets) available for that center's operations.

6. The price charged by one division in an organization for goods or services provided to another responsibility center in the same organization is referred to as a *transfer price*. Common methods of establishing transfer prices are cost-based transfer prices, market transfer prices, negotiated transfer prices, and dual transfer prices.

KEY DEFINITIONS

Balanced scorecard—a tool used by organizations to identify, monitor, and evaluate the organization's progress toward meeting important goals and objectives. Balanced scorecards measure organizational performance using financial, customer, internal business, innovation, and learning perspectives.

Cost center—a responsibility center that can control only the costs it incurs.

Decentralized organization—an organization that provides a relatively large amount of authority to managers of various subunits in operating the activities of those subunits.

Goal congruence—situation in which employees make decisions consistent with the overall objectives of the organization as a result of maximizing their own perceived best interests.

Investment center—a responsibility center that is able to influence the costs, revenues, and use of capital (assets) invested in that center.

Management control system—the processes through which an organization's management makes planning and control decisions, motivates employee behavior, and evaluates employee performance. Management control systems consist of the following components: communicating plans and objectives, measuring activities, and providing feedback to appropriate individuals.

Profit center—a responsibility center that can influence both the costs it incurs and the revenue it generates.

Residual income—the level of the investment center's net income that remains after deducting an implied or imputed charge for the assets (capital) used by the investment center.

Responsibility accounting—the methods used to measure and evaluate the performance of responsibility centers and their managers.

Responsibility center—a division, segment, individual, or other subunit of an organization that is held accountable for the results of that subunit's activities.

Return on investment (ROI)—ROI measures the profitability of an investment center in relation to its investment base. ROI can be decomposed into two components: asset turnover (sales divided by assets) and profit margin (net income divided by sales).

Total quality management (TQM)—the processes used by organizations to ensure that the products and services provided to their customers are of the highest level of quality. TQM requires organizations to evaluate and monitor prevention costs, appraisal costs, internal failure costs, and external failure costs.

Transfer price—the internal price charged by one responsibility center (the supplying responsibility center) for goods or services provided to another responsibility center (the receiving responsibility center) in the organization.

QUESTIONS

1. Define management control systems. What are the major components of a management control system?

2. Define goal congruence and decentralized organizations. Why is goal congruence particularly important in a decentralized organization?

3. What are some of the benefits of decentralization? What are some of the disadvantages of decentralization?

4. Define responsibility centers and responsibility accounting.

5. What are the criteria for classifying an item as controllable by a responsibility center?

6. Define cost centers, profit centers, and investment centers. What factors can be influenced by each of these types of responsibility centers?

7. What is the primary method of evaluating cost centers?

8. What is the primary method of evaluating profit centers? Describe how the sales mix variance, the sales volume variance, the sales price variance, and the variable and fixed expense variances identify how the actual income earned by profit centers differs from standard income.

9. What is return on investment (ROI)? What are the components of ROI? How do each of these components influence the responsibility center's profitability?

10. How can the use of ROI in evaluating the performance of investment centers introduce suboptimization?

11. What is residual income? How does the use of residual income overcome a limitation associated with the use of ROI in evaluating the performance of investment centers?

12. Define transfer pricing. List methods used by organizations to establish transfer prices.

13. What is the general formula used as a starting point for determining transfer prices? How does the existence of excess capacity influence the transfer prices established by the organization?

14. Define total quality management (TQM) and the costs associated with TQM.

15. How does the level of quality established by the organization influence the costs associated with TQM?

16. What is a balanced scorecard? What different perspectives are included in the balanced scorecard?

EXERCISES AND PROBLEMS

17. *Responsibility Accounting—General.* The managers of Harris Tool Company strongly believe in responsibility accounting. Each supervisor is responsible for the actions of the employees under his or her control. The amount of labor scheduled by each supervisor each day is based on the number of units to be produced. When the union refused to agree to short-run layoffs in one department if additional hiring were taking place anywhere in the plant, management was forced to maintain employment of skilled labor at peak levels, even when there was no skilled work to be done. The excess skilled labor provides a pool available for any nonskilled production job. The production supervisors claim that skilled labor cannot be made to produce efficiently, because they know that assignments from the pool are temporary and they cannot be fired by the production supervisors.

    Required:

    a. If a production supervisor cannot fire skilled workers, should he or she be held responsible for their output?
    b. What morale problem might occur with skilled laborers moving into production jobs?
    c. If the production supervisors are not held responsible for the skilled labor working for them, who is? If no one is held responsible, what will be the consequences to production?
    d. Since skilled workers will be paid a higher rate than unskilled workers, what should be done with the wage differential when a skilled worker is performing an unskilled task on a temporary assignment?

18. *Responsibility Accounting—General.* The administrator of the Parkville Community Hospital was concerned about a recent action taken by the hospital's board of trustees. Relying on the advice of a professional consulting firm, the board decided that responsibility accounting techniques should be used in the hospital to control expenditures.

    "The situation is absurd," complained the administrator. "Theoretically, I have responsibility for all expenditures, but I have no control over them. When a patient is admitted, a staff physician provides the necessary care and treatment. We cannot look at costs when matters of life and death are at stake. I see no benefit from responsibility accounting in this situation."

Required:

a. Is the administrator's point valid? Comment and explain why or why not.
b. Can responsibility accounting techniques be used in any nonprofit organization, such as a hospital? Would there be any benefit to the organization in using them?
c. What advantages could the Parkville Community Hospital derive from using responsibility accounting? What disadvantages would also be present?

19. *Responsibility Accounting—General.* Responsibility accounting techniques trace costs to the individual responsible for the costs, or to whoever exercises control over them. What happens in situations in which one cost is controllable by two or more managers at the same time? Which type of accounting procedure should be used in these situations?

20. *Cost Classification.* Each of the following cases describes an independent situation. For each case, determine whether or not the manager should be held responsible for the cost. Use the terms "responsible" or "not responsible" as your answers. If the manager should not be held responsible for the cost, explain why.

   a. A production supervisor is responsible for scheduling production workers on an assembly line. The wage rate is fixed by a contract negotiated between the company and the union.
   b. A maintenance supervisor hires and assigns workers in response to requests from the production supervisor.
   c. Production supervisors are assigned a portion of the company's research and development costs.
   d. A personnel manager hires production employees and sets their wage rates in accordance with her perceptions of the existing job market.
   e. An advertising manager is given a fixed budget at the beginning of the year. She makes all decisions about how the budgeted funds will be spent.

21. *Cost Classification.* For each of the following costs, indicate whether the cost is generally controllable (C) or noncontrollable (NC) by the production foreman and directly (D) or indirectly (I) traceable with respect to the production department.

   a. Direct materials
   b. Direct labor
   c. Salary of production manager
   d. Salary of production foreman
   e. Depreciation on production building (purchased ten years ago)
   f. Depreciation on production equipment (purchased ten years ago)
   g. Interest expense (for the overall organization)
   h. Advertising expense (for the overall organization)
   i. Indirect materials and labor

22. *Cost Classification.* The manager of Department 1 has responsibility for the purchase of supplies, maintenance and repair costs, and labor costs. Shown below are the costs that are directly traceable to his department:

Departmental Supplies	$ 5,000
Salary of Manager	40,000
Direct Labor	3,500
Repairs and Maintenance	4,000
Rent on Building	8,500
Depreciation on Equipment	10,000

Required:

Identify the costs that are controllable by the manager of Department 1.

23. *Cost Classification.* With respect to a production supervisor and a production department, indicate whether the following costs are: controllable (C) or noncontrollable (NC), and direct (D) or indirect (I).

   a. Direct materials
   b. Direct labor
   c. Salary of production manager
   d. Salary of production supervisor
   e. Depreciation on production building (purchased eight years ago)
   f. Depreciation on production equipment (purchased eight years ago)
   g. Interest expense (organization-wide)
   h. Advertising expense (organization-wide)
   i. Indirect materials and labor
   j. Heat, power, and light

24. *Cost Classification.* The following data are excerpted from the records of a cost center controlled by Vince Mota, the manager of that cost center. Vince Mota is supervised by a vice president. These cost records represent the actual costs incurred by Vince Mota's cost center during the month of January.

Direct Materials	$20,000
Depreciation on Equipment (purchased by the vice president)	15,000
Repairs and Maintenance	5,000
Vince Mota's Salary	30,000
Vice President's Salary	45,000
Rental for Floor Space (negotiated by the vice president)	10,000
Heat, Light, and Power	6,000

    Required:

    Indicate which of the above costs are controllable by: (1) Vince Mota and (2) the vice president who supervises Vince Mota.

25. *Cost Classification.* Shown below is a very simplified organizational chart showing the lines of responsibility for Jackson Brewing Company.

    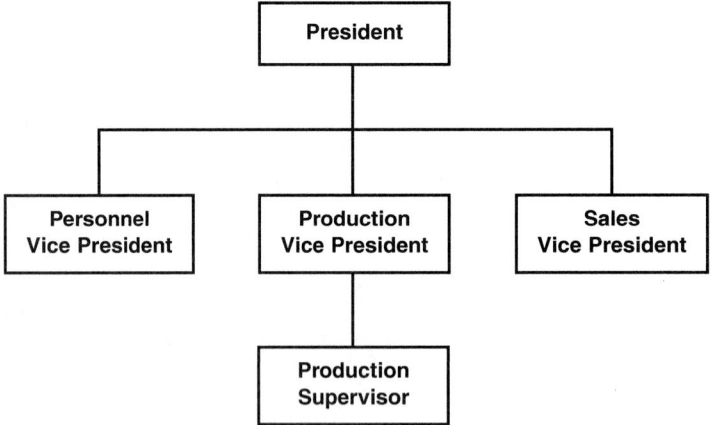

    For each of the following costs, indicate which of the above individuals could normally control that cost.

    a. Direct material used in production
    b. Repairs and maintenance in production
    c. Salary of production vice president
    d. Salary of sales vice president
    e. Salary of production supervisor
    f. Salesman's salaries
    g. Direct labor used in production
    h. Depreciation on machinery used in production (purchased by the foreman)
    i. Salary of personnel manager

26. *Historical Comparison.* Shown below are cost data related to the Production Department of Sole, Inc. for the previous four years.

	20x4	20x3	20x2	20x1
Direct Materials	$1,500	$1,200	$1,800	$1,400
Direct Labor	2,000	1,800	1,800	1,600
Indirect Labor	900	1,000	1,100	1,000
Heat, Power, and Light	500	600	600	800
Supervision	1,100	800	400	400
Indirect Materials	800	1,000	1,100	1,200

Required:

For each of the above costs, express the current year's cost (20x4) in terms of 20x1 costs (as a percentage). Based on this historical analysis, which costs would be of the most concern to the manager of Sole's Production Department?

27. *Historical Comparison.* Data for the costs incurred by Hasty's production department over the last three years are shown below.

	20x3	20x2	20x1
Direct Labor	$15,000	$12,000	$10,000
Direct Materials	11,000	8,000	3,500
Variable Overhead	12,000	10,000	12,000
Fixed Overhead	15,000	15,000	15,000

During 20x4, Hasty incurred the following production costs: direct labor, $16,000; direct materials, $15,000; variable overhead, $14,000; and fixed overhead, $15,000.

Required:

Prepare a performance report for the production foreman of Hasty Company for the above costs using a historical analysis. This performance report should include the years 20x1–20x4. Assume that all of the above costs are controllable by the production foreman.

28. *Historical and Standard Cost Comparison.* Foremen of each production department of Toolco receive comparative production reports at the end of each month. These reports contain data on the number of units produced, the total cost incurred, and the cost per unit of production for the current month and two preceding months. John Jackson, foreman of Department 1, received the following report at the end of June 20x7, and he requests that you assist him in interpreting the statement.

Toolco
Comparative Production Report
Department 1
Month of June 20x7

	4/x7	5/x7	6/x7
Number of Units	10,000	9,000	8,000
Total Cost	$20,000	$18,900	$17,600
Cost per Unit	$ 2.00	$ 2.10	$ 2.20

Required:

a. From a historical perspective, is Jackson's performance improving or deteriorating? Was his performance for June satisfactory?
b. The per-unit cost for Department 1 is increasing at about a 5 percent per month rate. Assume that all departments of Toolco experienced increased costs per unit of 5 percent during these three months. In the context of cost increases for the whole company, would you evaluate Jackson's performance as improving, deteriorating, or remaining consistent?

c. Assume that the budgeted production for Department 1 for June called for the assembly of 7,900 units at a total cost of $17,700. Was Jackson's performance for June satisfactory in relation to managerial expectations?
d. Can the decrease in production each month be used as a measure of effectiveness even when costs are disregarded? If so, in what context? Disregarding the number of units produced, can the total cost per month be used as a measure of effectiveness? Will managers who use units of production as measures of effectiveness generally reach the same conclusions or make the same decisions as other managers who use total cost as a measure of effectiveness?
e. Can either number of production or total cost be used alone as a measure of efficiency?

29. *Similar Activity Comparison.* Dallas, Inc. has three independent production departments which manufacture different types of inventory products. During the second quarter of 20x1, the following cost data (for controllable costs) was accumulated in those departments.

	Department 1	Department 2	Department 3
Direct Materials	$9,000	$9,500	$6,000
Direct Labor	7,000	9,000	4,000
Repairs and Maintenance	1,000	3,000	4,500
Supplies	800	1,400	300
Indirect Labor	1,100	1,500	2,000

Based on the quantity and type of inventory produced in each department, assume that the total production costs should have been approximately $20,000 for each department.

Required:

Using a similar activity comparison, evaluate the performance of each of the three production departments of Dallas, Inc.

30. *Similar Activity and Standard Cost Comparison.* Each production foreman at Amco receives a comparative production report at the end of each week. These reports contain data on the number of units produced, the total cost incurred, and the cost per unit of production for each of the three production departments. All departments produce the same type of units. Norman Ives, foreman of Department 1, received the following report covering production activity for the last week in July, and he requests that you assist him in interpreting the statement.

Amco
Comparative Production Report
Last Week of July

	Department 1	Department 2	Department 3
Number of Units	1,000	1,200	1,300
Total Cost	$ 500	$ 612	$ 637
Cost per Unit	$0.50	$0.51	$0.49

Required:

a. How does the performance of Department 1 compare with that of the other two departments? Should performance be measured in terms of number of units, total cost, or cost per unit?
b. Assume that Department 1 had the oldest machines and the least experienced workers and that it was budgeted to produce 900 units at a total cost of $459 (whereas Department 2 was budgeted for 1,300 units at a total cost of $650, and Department 3 was budgeted for 1,400 at a total cost of $686). How would you evaluate Ives' performance?
c. Assume that all three departments have met their production quotas for each of the past four weeks and that the per-unit costs for the first, second, and third weeks of July for each department were as follows:

Department 1	$0.54	$0.52	$0.51
Department 2	0.48	0.49	0.50
Department 3	0.45	0.52	0.50

Should Ives be congratulated or reprimanded for the relative performance of his department?

d. Assume that the performance of each department relative to budget was as described in (b) above, but the historical trend was as in (c) above. Evaluations based on historical trends may conflict with those based on expectations. How are such conflicts to be resolved?

31. *Standard Cost Comparison.* Shown below are data related to the actual and expected (standard) production costs for Hinckley Company. Assume that all of these costs are directly traceable to Hinckley Company's production department.

	Actual	Standard
Direct Materials	$25,000	$32,500
Direct Labor	10,000	12,200

Required:

While you do not know the actual cause of the above variances, how would you evaluate the production foreman if the above variances were caused exclusively by higher materials and labor costs than anticipated? Higher utilization of materials and labor than anticipated?

32. *Standard Cost Comparison.* Michael, Inc. established materials and labor performance standards related to the production of its inventory. Shown below are the standard materials and labor costs necessary to produce one item of Product A, Michael's primary inventory.

Direct Materials	2 lbs. x $2 = $4
Direct Labor	3 hrs. x $7 = $21

During January 20x1, a total of 3,000 units of Product A were produced by Michael's Production Department. In order to manufacture these units, 5,000 pounds of direct materials and 10,000 hours of direct labor were required. The actual cost per pound of materials was $2.50; the actual cost per hour of labor was $8.

Assume that the production foreman was responsible for the amount of materials and labor required to produce Product A; however, he had no control over the cost of the inputs used in production (materials and labor). The purchasing agent was responsible for the purchase price of direct materials; the personnel department negotiated the labor wage rates and, therefore, was accountable for the labor cost per hour.

Required:

a. Evaluate the performance of the above cost center by calculating the materials variances and labor variances (see Chapter 7, if necessary, for a review).
b Which variances are the responsibility of the production foreman? the purchasing agent? the personnel department?

33. *Standard Cost Comparison—Multiple Departments.* Eastco has four operating departments that produce identical units of output, although each has slightly different production facilities. Foremen of each department receive comparative production reports at the end of each month. These reports contain data on the number of units produced, the total actual costs, and the actual cost per unit. In addition to the amounts budgeted for these items for the current period, Bill Novak, foreman of Department 1, received the following report on the activity for September 20x4. He requests that you assist him in interpreting the statement.

Eastco
Comparative Production Report
September 30, 20x4

	Actual	Budgeted	Variance
Number of Units	1,000	900	100
Total Cost	$ 5,500	$ 4,800	$ 700
Cost per Unit	$ 5.50	$ 5.33	$ 0.17

Required:

a. Is it better to produce more or fewer units than called for by the budget? Is it better to incur more or less cost than called for by the budget? Which of the three measures—number of units, total cost, or cost per unit—is a more meaningful guide in evaluating whether Novak has been relatively effective in complying with expectations?

b. Assume that the variance column of the reports for Departments 2, 3, and 4 were as follows (parentheses and asterisks indicate that "actual" is smaller than "budget"):

	Department 2	Department 3	Department 4
Number of Units	200	(100)*	150
Total Cost	$ 900	$ (150)*	$ (150)*
Cost per Unit	$0.12	$(0.05)*	$(0.10)

How effective was Novak's performance in relation to that of the other foremen?

c. Assume that the cost per unit in Department 1 was $6, $5.25, $5.75, and $5.50 for the months May, June, July, and August, respectively. How could this information be used to help evaluate Novak's September performance?

34. *Performance Report—Standard Cost Comparison.* Shown below are the standard costs of producing one unit of Product F, the primary inventory manufactured by Grace Company.

Direct Materials	$2.50
Direct Labor	3.00
Indirect Materials	1.00
Indirect Labor	2.00
Repairs, Heat, and Light	0.50

During 20x1, Grace Company manufactured a total of 10,000 units of Product F. The actual costs incurred in the production of these units were as follows:

Direct Materials	$30,000
Direct Labor	28,200
Indirect Materials	8,200
Indirect Labor	16,700
Repairs, Heat, and Light	7,200

Required:

Assuming that all of the above costs were controllable by the production supervisor, prepare a performance report for the production supervisor of Grace Company that illustrates how the actual costs incurred in the production of Product F differ from the standard costs.

35. *Performance Report—Standard Cost Comparison.* Shown below are cost data for the Production Department of Simms Company for the month of October. Assume that all of these costs are controllable by Simms' production supervisor.

Standards for Controllable Costs:
Direct Materials	$ 2.00	per unit
Direct Labor	5.00	per unit
Repairs and Maintenance	1.00	per unit
Indirect Supplies and Labor	2.00	per unit
Actual Production	5,000	units

Actual Costs:
Direct Materials	$ 9,700
Direct Labor	29,800
Repairs and Maintenance	6,200
Indirect Supplies and Labor	12,100

Required:

Based on the relationship between actual costs and standard costs, prepare a performance report for the production supervisor of Simms Company for the month of October.

36. *Performance Report—Standard Cost Comparison.* Shown below are the controllable costs for the Assembly Division of the Walsh Manufacturing Company for March of 20x1:

Standard Costs (per unit):	
Direct Materials	$5.50
Direct Labor	2.00
Indirect Materials	2.50
Other	1.00
Actual Production	1,000 units
Actual Costs:	
Direct Materials	$6,250
Direct Labor	3,400
Indirect Materials	2,120
Other	970

Required:

Prepare a responsibility accounting report using a standard cost comparison for the Assembly Division of Walsh Manufacturing Company for March of 20x1.

37. *Performance Report—Standard Cost Comparison.* Clarence Weatherby is the manager of the Production Department of Alpha, Inc. Shown below are costs which are directly traceable to his department:

	Standard	Actual
Direct Materials	$12,000	$14,000
Direct Labor	28,000	26,000
Heat, Light, and Power	15,000	12,500
Repairs and Maintenance	5,500	4,800
Weatherby's Salary	22,000	25,000
Depreciation on Equipment	6,000	6,000

Assume that Weatherby is responsible for all costs incurred by the Production Department, except for his salary and the depreciation on manufacturing equipment.

Required:

Prepare a performance report for Clarence Weatherby for May 20x1. Include only those costs controllable by Weatherby and show all variances.

38. *Performance Report—Standard Cost Comparison.* Lester Hayes is the production supervisor of Raider, Inc.'s Production Department. Raider utilizes a responsibility accounting system that charges individuals/departments in the organization with only the costs they can control. An examination of the cost records and performance standards for Raider, Inc.'s Production Department indicated the following actual and standard costs for 20x1 that are directly traceable to the Production Department.

	Actual	Standard
Direct Materials	$15,000	$12,000
Direct Labor	10,000	13,000
Indirect Material	5,000	4,000
Heat, Light, and Power	2,000	2,100
Depreciation on Equipment	10,000	11,000
Rent on Building	16,000	22,500
Salary of Supervisor	25,000	26,000
Salary of Manager of Department	36,000	32,000

Of the above costs, Lester can control the materials, labor, heat, light, and power costs. Lester's manager (Ted Watts) is responsible for negotiating Lester's salary and the annual rent on the manufacturing facilities.

Required:

a. Prepare a performance report for Lester Hayes for 20x1. Only the costs that can be controlled by Lester should be included on this report.
b. Assuming that Ted Watts is the manager of the Production Department, prepare a performance report for him for 20x1. Only the costs that can be controlled by Ted should be included on this report.

39. *Performance Report—Standard Cost Comparison.* Janet Jackson is the manager of the Production Department of Safeco. Safeco uses responsibility reporting for its various departments. Janet is held responsible for various costs incurred by her department, such as the purchase and use of direct materials, the use of direct labor, repairs and maintenance expense, and indirect materials and supplies. Shown below are data from the month of January for the production department of Safeco.

	Budget	Actual
Direct Materials	$25,000	$30,000
Direct Labor	15,000	12,000
Repairs and Maintenance	3,000	2,000
Indirect Materials and Supplies	2,500	3,400
Depreciation on Equipment	5,000	6,000
Salary of Supervisor	20,000	20,000
Salary of Manager	15,000	15,000

Required:

Prepare a performance report for Janet Jackson. Show only the costs that are controllable by Janet.

40. *Performance Report—Standard Cost Comparison.* Using the information presented in Problem 39, prepare the performance report for Janet Jackson's supervisor. Assume that her supervisor can influence Janet Jackson's salary as well as any costs controllable by Janet Jackson. This performance report should only show costs controllable by Janet's supervisor.

41. *Performance Report—Standard Cost Comparison.* Washington Company has three primary departments: a Staff Department (including personnel and other services), a Production Department, and a Sales Department. Each department incurs the following costs that are controllable by the manager of that department. Shown below are the expected controllable costs for each department in the month of June.

	Staff	Production	Sales
Direct Materials		$15,000	
Direct Labor		25,000	
Salaries	$30,000		$45,000
Supplies	2,500	5,000	1,000
Other	1,200	1,000	3,000
Total	$33,700	$46,000	$49,000

The actual costs incurred during June are as follows:

	Staff	Production	Sales
Direct Materials		$22,400	
Direct Labor		21,200	
Salaries	$33,000		$43,400
Supplies	2,260	4,890	1,500
Other	1,270	1,800	4,000
Total	$36,530	$50,290	$48,900

Required:

a. Prepare a performance report for the manager of the Production Department. Include only those costs controllable by that manager and illustrate all variances.

b. Assuming that a supervisor is respsonsible for the operations of all three departments, prepare a performance report for the supervisor. In preparing this report, use only the "total costs" for each department; it is not necessary to itemize each cost. Also assume that the "other costs" controllable by the supervisor during the month of June were budgeted at $48,200. The actual level of these costs was $50,100.

42. *Profit Center—Sales Mix Variance.* From the information listed below, calculate the sales mix variance for the Reagan Company. Assume that all data relate to the year 20x2.

	Forecast Budget	Control Budget
Sales Revenue	$420,000	$450,000
Variable Costs:		
Costs of Goods Sold	316,000	335,000
Salesmen's Commissions	21,000	25,000
Selling Expenses	11,500	14,300
Fixed Costs:		
Salaries	23,000	23,000
Rent	10,300	10,300

43. *Profit Center—Variance Analysis.* Division A of the Delta Company has the following forecast budget for the first quarter of 20x1.

Sales @ $15 per Unit*	$60,000
Variable Costs @ $10 per Unit*	40,000
Contribution Margin	$20,000
Fixed Costs	15,000
Net Income before Taxes	$ 5,000

*Weighted average based on forecast sales mix

The contribution margin from the control budget is $15,000, which represents a 40 percent contribution margin on sales. Actual data obtained from Delta Company's records during the first quarter of 20x1 indicated that sales were $54,000, variable costs were $39,600, and fixed costs were $13,000. Total assets for Division A were budgeted at $45,000 but were actually $42,000.

Required:

Prepare a variance worksheet in good form assuming that Division A is a profit center. This worksheet should illustrate the calculation of all relevant variances.

44. *Profit Center—Variance Analysis.* Assume that the management of Phoenix Company has prepared the following forecast budget for Department B. Department B is classified as a profit center.

Sales	$20,000
Variable Costs	10,000
Contribution Margin	$10,000
Fixed Costs	5,000
Net Income before Taxes	$ 5,000

The above forecast budget was prepared based upon a weighted average selling price of $5 per unit and a weighted average variable cost of $2.50 per unit. These amounts were based upon a forecasted sales mix. The contribution margin on the control budget is $5,000, which is a 45 percent contribution margin. Total assets for Department B were forecasted at $30,000.

At the end of the period, the following actual data were available from the accounting records of Phoenix Company.

Sales	$24,000
Variable Costs	13,200
Fixed Costs	7,500
Total Assets	25,000

Required:

Prepare a variance worksheet for Department B. This worksheet should include the forecast budget, control budget, and actual results as well as any variances incurred by Department B.

45. *Profit Centers—Variance Analysis and Performance Report Preparation.* The Fabricating Division of the Kayne Corporation produces two products: A and B. The following data refer to the selling price and cost per unit for these two products:

	A	B
Selling Price	$7.00	$12.00
Variable Costs:		
Cost of Goods Sold	3.00	5.00
Sales Commissions	0.50	1.10

Total fixed costs were budgeted at $70,000 for the year. Sales revenue was budgeted (forecast) as follows:

	Amount	Units
Product A	$84,000	12,000
Product B	96,000	8,000

Given below is the actual income statement for the year 20x1.

Sales Revenue		$250,000
Less: Variable Costs		
Cost of Goods Sold	$125,000	
Sales Commissions	20,000	145,000
Contribution Margin		$105,000
Less: Fixed Costs		80,000
Income before Taxes		$ 25,000
Income Taxes		12,500
Net Income		$ 12,500

The above actual data reflect sales of 19,000 units of Product A and 11,500 units of Product B.

Required:

a. Prepare a variance worksheet for the Fabricating Division. Determine the income before taxes for the forecast budget and the control budget. Determine the volume/mix and the price/expense variance.
b. Prepare a performance report for the manager of the Fabricating Division in which the forecast budget income is reconciled with the actual income before taxes.

46. *Profit Center—Variance Analysis.* Mr. Andrews is the manager of the Finishing and Processing Division of the Ross Company. The Finishing and Processing Division is a profit center. The following data illustrates a partial variance worksheet for the division for 20x3, its first year of operations:

Ross Company
Finishing and Processing Division
Variance Worksheet

	Forecast Budget	Control Budget	Actual
Sales	$1,500,000	$1,250,000	$1,400,000
Less: Variable Costs	(1,050,000)	(750,000)	(1,150,000)
Contribution Margin	$ 450,000	$ 500,000	$ 250,000
Less: Fixed Costs	(150,000)	(150,000)	(100,000)
Income before Taxes	$ 300,000	$ 350,000	$ 150,000

Required:

Compute the following variances.
1. Sales Volume
2. Sales Mix
3. Sales Price
4. Variable and Fixed Expense

47. *Profit Center—Variance Analysis and Performance Report Preparation.* Mr. Johnson is the manager of the Machining and Polishing Division of the Phillips Company. The Machining and Polishing Division is a profit center. A partial variance worksheet for the division is illustrated by the following data.

Phillips Company
Machining and Polishing Division
Variance Worksheet

	Forecast Budget	Control Budget	Actual
Sales	$700,000	$600,000	$900,000
Less: Variable Costs	(280,000)	(230,000)	(270,000)
Contribution Margin	$420,000	$370,000	$630,000
Less: Fixed Costs	(150,000)	(150,000)	(175,000)
Income before Taxes	$270,000	$220,000	$455,000

Required:

Compute the following variances:
1. Sales Volume
2. Sales Mix
3. Sales Price
4. Variable and Fixed Expense

48. *Profit Centers—Variance Analysis.* The following data illustrate a partial variance worksheet for the Finishing and Processing Division of the Oliver Company. The Finishing and Processing Division is a profit center.

Oliver Company
Finishing and Processing Division
Variance Worksheet

	Forecast Budget	Control Budget	Actual
Sales	$2,000,000	$1,900,000	$2,100,000
Less: Variable Costs	(900,000)	(900,000)	(955,000)
Contribution Margin	$1,100,000	$1,000,000	$1,145,000
Less: Fixed Costs	(400,000)	(400,000)	(475,000)
Less: Income Taxes	(350,000)	(300,000)	(345,000)
Net Income	$ 350,000	$ 300,000	$ 325,000

Required:

Compute the following variances:
1. Sales Volume
2. Sales Mix
3. Sales Price
4. Variable and Fixed Expense

49. *Profit Centers—Income Statement Preparation and Variance Analysis.* The Royal Paper Company manufactures three types of envelopes: standard envelopes, window envelopes, and clasp envelopes. The forecasted and actual sales volumes, sales prices, and variable costs for a box of 100 of each type of envelope are summarized below (volumes are weekly quantities):

	Sales Volume	Sales Price	Variable Costs
Forecasted:			
Standard	1,000 boxes	$1.50	$0.50
Window	1,000 boxes	$2.00	$0.75
Clasp	2,000 boxes	$3.50	$1.00
Actual:			
Standard	3,000 boxes	$1.75	$0.45
Window	1,000 boxes	$1.90	$0.70
Clasp	1,000 boxes	$3.60	$1.50

Total fixed manufacturing costs were forecasted to be $1,500 per week, while actual fixed costs were $1,600 per week.

Required:

a. Prepare a forecasted income statement, control income statement, and actual income statement for Royal Paper Company.
b. Calculate the following variances for Royal Paper Company:
   1. Sales Volume Variance
   2. Sales Mix Variance
   3. Sales Price Variance
   4. Variable and Fixed Expense Variances
c. Using the variances calculated in (b) above, reconcile forecasted net income to actual net income. What are some explanations for the differences in these two amounts?

50. *Profit Centers—Income Statement Preparation and Variance Analysis.* QuickJet operates a limited number of flights between major United States cities. QuickJet prices its tickets at four levels: first class passengers, business passengers, leisure passengers, and frequent flier passengers. The following data represent forecasted and actual operating data for weekly flights from Houston, Texas to Denver, Colorado.

	Ticket Price	Variable Cost	Sales Mix (%)
Forecasted:			
First Class	$1,200	$250	0.05
Business	650	130	0.20
Leisure	150	130	0.65
Frequent Flier	0	130	0.10
Actual:			
First Class	$1,100	$280	0.07
Business	720	90	0.30
Leisure	140	90	0.60
Frequent Flier	0	90	0.03

During the week, a total of 1,000 passengers were served; the forecast volume was 1,330 passengers. QuickJet forecasted weekly fixed costs of $100,000; its actual weekly fixed costs were $120,000.

Required:

a. Prepare a forecasted income statement, control income statement, and actual income statement for QuickJet
b. Calculate the following variances for QuickJet:
   1. Sales Volume Variance.
   2. Sales Mix Variance.
   3. Sales Price Variance.
   4. Variable and Fixed Expense Variance.
c. Using the variances calculated in (b) above, reconcile forecasted net income to actual net income. What are some explanations for the differences in these two amounts?

51. *Return on Investment—Conceptual.* The following information relates to the Machining Division of the Chi Corporation for the year 20x1. The budgeted ROI on total assets was set as 25 percent and the budgeted ROI on corporate investment was set at 30 percent.

Net Income before Taxes	$150,000
Sales	900,000
Total Assets	650,000
Corporate Investment	425,000

Required:

a. Compute the actual ROI on total assets and actual ROI on corporate investments.
b. Name two ways that the ROI on total assets may be improved and two ways the ROI on corporate investment may be improved if necessary for this situation.

52. *Return on Investment—Conceptual.* A company is decentralized into two divisions: A and B. At the end of the year, Division A had a return on investment of 12 percent, and Division B had a return on investment of 10 percent.

Required:

a. On the basis of this performance measure is Division A superior to Division B?
b. What does return on investment mean in this case?
c. Should the company consider closing Division B because of its performance? List reasons both for and against this action,
d. Would your answer to part (a) be different if it were known that Division A was a grocery store and Division B a jewelry store? Explain why or why not.

53. *Return on Investment—Conceptual.* Bill Smith, the new president of Sanders Corporation, was recently promoted from his old position as vice-president for sales. One of Bill's first acts was to evaluate his divisional managers. Examining the residual income statements, he extracted the following information:

	Division 1	Division 2	Division 3
Segment Margin	$ 600,000	$ 400,000	$ 300,000
Investment Charge	500,000	200,000	200,000
Residual Income	$ 100,000	$ 200,000	$ 100,000
Book Value of Assets	$1,000,000	$1,000,000	$ 600,000

Bill then divided the residual income by the book value of assets to determine a return on investment. ROI figures produced by Bill are 10 percent, 20 percent, and 16 percent for Divisions 1, 2, and 3, respectively. When he saw that the manager for Division 1 had an ROI much smaller than those produced by other managers, Bill decided to fire him. But first he consults with you, the corporate controller.

Required:

a. Do you agree with Mr. Smith's calculations of ROI? If not, recompute a more appropriate set.
b. Should terminal action such as firing a divisional manager be based solely upon examination of ROI data for one period? If not, how should ROI figures be used?
c. If the evaluation criterion was residual income instead of ROI, which manager would be evaluated as "best?" Can ROI and residual income measures rank-order divisional managers in different order for comparative evaluation purposes? Explain the causes of such differences.

54. *Investment Centers—Return on Investment.* Below are three independent cases (with missing data) that concern performance measures to evaluate decentralized organizational efficiency. Determine the value associated with each letter.

	Case 1	Case 2	Case 3
Assets	$ a	$200,000	$ g
Return on Investment	20%	d%	h%
Sales	$ b	$600,000	$900,000
Asset Turnover	8	e	3
Net Income	$40,000	$ f	$ i
Profit Margin	c%	5%	3.3%

55. *Investment Centers—Return on Investment.* Selected data for three divisions of a decentralized company are presented below:

	Division 1	Division 2	Division 3
Assets	$1,000,000	$2,000,000	$3,000,000
Segment Margin	550,000	660,000	770,000

Required:

a. Rank the divisions from "best" to "worst" in terms of their return on investment.
b. Rank the divisions from "best" to "worst" in terms of their residual income, assuming that the strategic plan requires a 10 percent return on investment.
c. Rank the divisions from "best" to "worst" in terms of their residual income, assuming that the strategic plan requires a 20 percent return on investment.

56. *Investment Centers—Return on Investment.* You have been recently hired by Ellington Inc. to work in its cost accounting department. Your initial task is to calculate the ROI for the recent year. Unfortunately, the sales figures for that year have been lost. Determined to show your technical skills, you state that you can still calculate ROI with only the income of $75,000 and the investment of $800,000 being known.

Required:

Calculate ROI and show how the volume of sales has no effect.

57. *Investment Centers—Return on Investment.* The Wilson Products Corporation is decentralized into several operating divisions. The company management is interested in evaluating the performance of the Home-Care Products Division. The following information about this division is made available. It is not arranged in any particular order.

Gross Sales	$4,700,000
Sales Returns and Allowances	200,000
Accounts and Notes Receivable	120,000
Accounts and Notes Payable	230,000
Inventory	470,000
Net Fixed Assets	910,000
Average Fixed Overhead Cost	50,000
Net Income before Interest and Taxes	189,000
Interest	9,000
Taxes	80,000
Contribution Margin per Unit	4

Required:

a. What is the asset turnover for this division? What does this measure indicate about the division's performance?
b. What is the margin on sales for this division? What does this measure indicate about the division's performance?
c. What is the return on investment for this division? What does this measure indicate about the division's performance?
d. How many units must the division sell in order to have a return on investment of 10 percent if all factors remain at the present levels?
e. If sales of 40,000 units are expected and all factors remain at their present levels, what must the sales price per unit be in order to have an asset turnover of 4?

58. *Investment Centers—Return on Investment.* The Multiple Parts Corporation makes components and also assembles electronic calculators in its several operating divisions. One of these divisions, the Dot Company, makes the component that controls the positioning of decimal points in the calculators. The manager of Dot Company, Mr. Pres Key, has tentatively placed a selling price of $5 a unit on his product for both internal transfers and external sales. His division's asset and cost structure is as follows:

Total Assets	$500,000
Annual Fixed Overhead Cost	280,000
Variable Cost per Unit	2.50

The corporation treats each of its divisions as an investment center and uses return on investment as a performance measure. The corporation has set 15 percent as the desired rate of return on investment for the Dot Company.

Required:

a. How many units must Dot sell to reach the desired return on investment?
b. If sales do reach the level required in part (a), what would be the asset turnover?
c. If sales reach the desired level, what would be the margin on sales?

59. *Investment Centers—Return on Investment.* The following data pertain to an investment center of Kappa Enterprises for the years 20x1, 20x2, and 20x3.

	20x1	20x2	20x3
Net Income before Taxes	$200,000	$120,000	$ 70,000
Sales Revenue	950,000	750,000	600,000
Total Assets	800,000	650,000	500,000

Required:

a. Calculate the profit margin, asset turnover, and the ROI (based on total assets) for the three years 20x1–20x3.
b. Rank the performance of the investment center for the three years based on ROI.

60. *Investment Centers—Return on Investment.* The following data pertain to three investment centers of Papa Enterprises.

	A	B	C
Net Income before Taxes	$150,000	$175,000	$225,000
Income Taxes	100,000	175,000	150,000
Sales Revenue	700,000	800,000	950,000
Current Assets	200,000	250,000	325,000
Long-term Assets	400,000	425,000	500,000

Required:

a. Calculate the profit margin, asset turnover, and the ROI (based on total assets) for the three investment centers.
b. Rank the performance of the three investment centers using ROI.

61. *Investment Centers—Residual Income.* Below are presented the balances for the major classifications needed to construct a residual income statement. Data are presented in alphabetical order. Construct a residual income statement in good form.

Assignable Central Administration Cost	$ 100,000
Discretionary Fixed Costs	450,000
Investment Charges	150,000
Revenue	1,800,000
Traceable Committed Fixed Cost	200,000
Variable Cost	630,000

62. *Investment Centers—Residual Income.* Below are three independent cases that explore the relationship between elements associated with the computations of residual income. In each case, two elements are missing. Determine the number that corresponds to each missing element, A through F.

	Case 1	Case 2	Case 3
Segment Margin	$200,000	C	$ 500,000
Investment Charge	$ 50,000	D	E
Residual Income	A	$100,000	$ 300,000
Divisional assets	$250,000	$800,000	$1,000,000
Minimum Desired ROI	B	10%	F

63. *Investment Centers—Residual Income.* The Washington Company reported sales of $1,000,000, an asset turnover of 4, and a return on investment of 30 percent. Strategic policy of Washington calls for a minimum desired return on investment for all assets of 10 percent. Determine the residual income for Washington Company.

64. *Investment Centers—Return on Investment and Residual Income.* The divisions of Conglomerate Company are all independent subsidiaries that operate in separate markets. Central management plans to establish a single performance criterion for its divisions and is currently considering either return on investment or residual income. Management wishes to select the criterion that promotes goal congruity; that is, management wants the goals of the subsidiaries to be in conformity with the goals of central management.

To help demonstrate the relationship between goal congruity and performance criteria, the controller of Conglomerate asked you to prepare a demonstration based upon the assumed information:

Corporate Goal:	Maximize income, given a 20 percent minimum required return on investment
Proposed Project A:	$12,000 income on $50,000 investment
Proposed Project B:	$15,000 income on $80,000 investment
Existing Divisional Income:	$120,000
Existing Divisional Investment:	$400,000

Required:

a. Will Project A be accepted if residual income is the performance criterion? Explain.
b. Will Project B be accepted if residual income is the performance criterion? Explain.
c. Will Project A be accepted if ROI is the performance criterion? Explain.

65. *Investment Centers—Return on Investment and Residual Income.* Selected data for three divisions of a decentralized company are presented below:

	Division 1	Division 2	Division 3
Assets	$1,000,000	$2,000,000	$3,000,000
Segment Margin	550,000	660,000	770,000

Required:

a. Rank the divisions from "best" to "worst" in terms of their return on investment.
b. Rank the divisions from "best" to "worst" in terms of their residual income, assuming that the strategic plan requires a 10 percent return on investment.
c. Rank the divisions from "best" to "worst" in terms of their residual income, assuming that the strategic plan requires a 20 percent return on investment.

66. *Investment Centers—ROI, Residual Income, and Investment Opportunity.* Comparative income statement data for the Communication Division of Romey Corporation for the years ended December 31, 20x1 and 20x2 are presented below:

	20x1	20x2
Sales	$200,000	$250,000
Variable Costs	(100,000)	(150,000)
Contribution Margin	$100,000	$100,000
Fixed Costs	(80,000)	(50,000)
Net Income	$ 20,000	$ 50,000

The total assets available to the Communication Division at December 31, 20x0, 20x1, and 20x2 are $100,000, $150,000, and $250,000, respectively.

Required:

a. Calculate the ROI for the Communication Division of Romey Corporation for 20x1 and 20x2 based on year-end assets and average assets.
b. Calculate the asset turnover and profit margin for the Communication Division of Romey Corporation for 20x1 and 20x2 based on year-end assets and average assets.
c. Based on (a) and (b) above, evaluate the performance of the Communication Division of Romey Corporation in 20x1 and 20x2.
d. If the cost of capital to the Communication Division is set at 10 percent of average assets, determine the residual income earned by the Communication Division in 20x1 and 20x2.
e. Assume that during 20x2 the Communication Division has an opportunity to obtain funds to purchase additional broadcast equipment costing $20,000. This equipment would provide additional net income of $3,000 (after considering depreciation). Using average total assets, what is the ROI and residual income that would be earned by the Communication Division if this investment were undertaken?
f. Would the manager of the Communication Division favor making this acquisition if evaluated under ROI? Residual income?

67. *Transfer Pricing.* The Appliance Division of General Industries manufactures a wide variety of kitchen appliances for sale to specialty retailers and department stores. One of General Industries' most popular products is dishwashers. The Appliance Division currently purchases the motors for its dishwashers from external vendors for $100.

General Industries' Mechanical Division manufactures and sells similar types of motors to other appliance manufacturers. The Mechanical Division's cost of manufacturing these motors is summarized below:

Variable Cost (per Motor)	$ 65
Fixed Costs (per week)	$2,000
Allocated Corporate Costs (per week)	$1,500

The Mechanical Division currently has the capacity to manufacture 100 motors per week. In discussions among the management of General Industries, some questions were raised about the possibility of having the Appliance Division purchase motors from the Mechanical Division in order to realize potential cost savings.

Required:

a. Including fixed costs and allocated corporate costs, what is the total cost per motor manufactured by the Mechanical Division?
b. Assume that the Mechanical Division prices its motors to earn a 10% profit on full costs (including fixed costs and allocated corporate costs). What is the selling price charged by the Mechanical Division to its external customers?
c. Given the selling price determined in (b) above, what is the net advantage or disadvantage (per week) of having the Mechanical Division sell motors to the Appliance Division if the Mechanical Division has sufficient excess capacity to meet the Appliance Division's needs?
d. Given the selling price determined in (b) above, what is the net advantage or disadvantage (per week) of having the Mechanical Division sell motors to the Appliance Division if the Mechanical Division does not have sufficient capacity and would need to reduce its sales to external customers by 50 motors per week?
e. Given the selling price determined in (b) above, what is the minimum transfer price that should be charged by the Mechanical Division if excess capacity exists? What is the minimum transfer price that should be charged by the Mechanical Division if no excess capacity exists and the Mechanical Division is able to sell its entire output to external customers?

68. *Transfer Pricing.* Collins Computer purchases integrated circuit boards for its personal computers from external suppliers at a cost of approximately $75 per board. However, some delays in supply have resulted in Collins considering purchasing circuit boards from one of its internal divisions (the Circuitry Division). Traditionally, Collins Computer's management felt that purchasing circuit boards from external suppliers resulted in cost savings without a marked loss in quality.

Tom Squyres (manager of the Computer and Peripheral Division) requested that management obtain a price quote from Mike Smith (manager of the Circuitry Division). Mike provided the following quote based on sales of circuit boards to its external customers:

Variable Cost (per Circuit Board)	$45
Fixed Cost (per Circuit Board)	10
Allocated Corporate Cost (per Circuit Board)	20
Markup (20% of Total Cost)	15
Total Price	$90

Mike indicates that he is currently able to sell 800 circuit boards per week to external customers at this price. He also feels that his division has capacity to manufacture a total of 1,000 circuit boards per week.

Required:

a. What are some possible transfer prices that could be utilized in this situation?
b. What is the maximum transfer price that Tom Squyres would be willing to pay for circuit boards?
c. What is the minimum transfer price that Mike Smith would be willing to charge for circuit board sales to the Computer and Peripheral Division if its demand is 200 circuit boards per week, 600 circuit boards per week, and 1,000 circuit boards per week.

d. If the transfer price is set at $45 (the variable cost of manufacturing circuit boards), what is the net advantage or disadvantage to Collins Computer if the number of circuit boards sold by the Circuitry Division to the Computer and Peripheral Division per week is 200? 600? 1,000?
e. Would your answer in (d) above be affected if the transfer price was set at $55 (the variable and fixed costs of manufacturing circuit boards)? What if the transfer price was $66 (the variable and fixed costs of manufacturing circuit boards plus a 20% markup)?

Learning Objectives

We now begin our discussion of the final major function of the managerial accountant: providing information used by the organization in making decisions. This chapter illustrates the use of managerial accounting data in the short-term decision-making process. The next chapter illustrates how managerial accounting data are used in making longer-term decisions related to capital investments. Studying the current chapter should enable you to:

1. Define the term "decision" and identify attributes that make data relevant to a particular decision.
2. Define relevant costs, incremental costs, avoidable costs, sunk costs, and opportunity costs.
3. Identify the factors considered by management in making pricing decisions for the organization's inventories and services.
4. Evaluate the process through which management decides whether to accept or reject special orders.
5. Determine whether a given segment, product line or service should be continued or discontinued and specify the costs and benefits of the decision with regard to this segment, product line or service.
6. Identify the factors relevant to management's decision as to whether or not to process a product further after a split-off point.
7. Determine the financial consequences of make-or-buy decisions.

10

The Use of Managerial Accounting Data in Making Short-Term Decisions

INTRODUCTION

Thomas Gamble owns a small hardware store. While his business has earned steady profits over the last few years, Thomas noticed that sales of lawn care products (such as fertilizer, weed killers, and insecticides) were rather low. After a careful analysis, he has concluded that his store actually loses money on the sale of these products. Thomas met with his supplier, Rebecca Jackson, and notified her that he was no longer interested in carrying these lawn care products in his store. The following discussion ensued:

Thomas: I've analyzed these products over and over and I'm losing money on every sale. It just doesn't make sense for me to carry them. If I add other products, I'll earn higher profits.

Rebecca: Are you certain? I know your selling prices for these products; it's much more than your cost. You pay only $5 for a bag of fertilizer and charge your customers $12. How can you be losing money?

Thomas: The purchase price of these products is only a small part of my total cost. There are other costs as well. I must allocate some of the rent and utilities costs that I incur in running my store. There's also the cost of the wages and benefits I pay to my employees. All of these overhead costs are important. If I don't consider these costs, I won't know how much I really earn.

Rebecca: I know you need to consider all of your costs in your overall strategy, but how are these costs affected by lawn care products? Will you really save money on rent, utilities, and wages if you discontinue the sale of your lawn products?

Thomas: That's a good point. Some of those costs aren't really related to lawn care products as they're a general cost of doing business. Maybe you're right. I'll reevaluate all of these costs and revenues and call you in the morning.

To this point in the text, we have focused on how management uses managerial accounting information in fulfilling its major functions. Previous chapters have examined the use of managerial accounting information in planning, directing operations, and controlling the activities of the organization. We now examine the final major function of management: decision-making. This chapter examines how managerial accounting information is used in making short-term decisions. Long-term investment decisions, also known as capital budgeting decisions, are considered in the next chapter.

Short-term decisions are important, as they have a impact on the day-to-day operations of the organization as well as on the pricing and availability of its products and services. The process of analyzing these questions and issues (and short-term decisions) is illustrated in this chapter.

TERMINOLOGY FOR SHORT-TERM DECISIONS

In order to illustrate the role of the managerial accountant and the use of managerial accounting data in the short-term decision process, it is necessary at the outset to define and provide examples of the relevant terminology used in this process. The following sections will clarify and illustrate some of the terminology which will be used throughout the remainder of this chapter. It is critical that you have a thorough understanding of this terminology as you undertake the study of the short-term decision process.

Decisions

A *decision* is the act of selecting a course of action from among various alternative choices. To decide, one must review alternatives, exercise judgment, reach conclusions, and finally select a particular alternative. Decisions are action-oriented in that the decision-maker is planning to buy, to make, to hire, or to do. Think of all the decisions you have already made today: you have decided what to wear, what to eat, and whether or not to attend class. At this point, you have even decided to read this chapter! In any of the above decisions, you considered various alternatives about what to wear, eat, and how to spend your time.

An important aspect of a decision is that it is contemporaneous; that is, decisions can only be made in the present or in the future. For example, you obviously cannot decide now what to wear yesterday or what to eat for yesterday's breakfast. Choices among past alternatives are evaluations—"I should never have gotten out of bed yesterday." Evaluations play an important role in the decision-making process, since they are basic elements in the judgment exercised in making a choice among alternative courses of action.

To illustrate the nature of the decision-making process, consider the decision that confronts many students over the spring semester: should I take a vacation during my spring break or should I remain on campus and study? In making such a decision, each student has a vast array of alternatives (he or she could go skiing, go to the beach, visit his or her parents, or stay on campus and study). Notice that the decision must, by definition, consider a present or a future choice, since the student obviously cannot change his or her decision on how the spring break was spent during the previous year. At this point, we will consider the various factors that may be evaluated in the decision-making process (that is, in selecting from among various alternatives).

Relevant Costs

In making a decision, it is critical that the decision-maker focus only on those factors which are relevant to the particular decision under consideration. For many types of managerial decisions, it is important to focus on the relevant costs and revenues associated with each alternative. Relevant costs and revenues possess the following characteristics:

1. They pertain to the future and are related to a specific alternative.
2. They differ among the various decision alternatives under consideration.

Relevant costs are critical in the decision-making process. These costs represent expected differences between alternative courses of action (decisions). Thus, relevant costs allow management to focus on the expected benefits or detriments associated with a particular alternative.

To illustrate the concept of relevance, assume that you have the following alternatives as to how to spend your spring break: (1) vacation at the beach, by flying, at a cost of $220 (round trip); (2) vacation at the beach, by driving for one day (each way); and (3) remaining on campus. The length of your spring break is seven days. If you decide to vacation at the beach, you will require six days of lodging at a cost of $35 per day. Regardless of whether you vacation or remain on campus, your estimated meal costs will be $12 per day. Finally, assume that the estimated costs of driving to the beach (gasoline, oil, repairs, etc.) total $150.[1]

Illustration 1 shows the total cost you would expect to incur for each of the three alternatives. Notice that the least expensive of the three alternatives is remaining on campus. The only cost of remaining on campus is the cost of meals (7 days x $12 per day = $84). If you decide to vacation at the beach, the total cost is either $514 (flying) or $444 (driving).

---

[1] In this example, all items under consideration are costs (there are no revenues associated with any of the alternatives under consideration). It is important to note that many decisions involve revenues and that these revenues must be considered in a similar fashion.

Illustration 1
Cost Incurred Under Vacation Alternatives

	Vacation by Flying	Vacation by Driving	No Vacation
Travel Cost	$220	$150	$ 0
Cost of Lodging[a]	210	210	0
Cost of Meals[b]	84	84	84
Total Cost	$514	$444	$84

[a] 6 days x $35 per day = $210
[b] 7 days x $12 per day = $ 84

Which of these costs are relevant in this decision? Remember that relevant costs possess two characteristics: the cost is anticipated in the future under at least one of the alternatives and the costs differ under the alternatives considered. Assume that you are choosing between staying on campus and driving to the beach. The difference in costs between these two alternatives is $360 ($444 – $84). As shown above, the costs associated with lodging ($210) and travel ($150) are relevant, since they differ between the two alternatives. Conversely, since the cost of meals is $84 under either alternative under consideration, this cost is not relevant to the decision; that is, the student would not consider the cost of meals in deciding whether or not to take the vacation. The calculation of this difference is shown below:

Vacation by Driving

Lodging		
(6 nights x $35)	$210	} Relevant Costs
Costs of Driving	150	
Cost of Meals	84	} Not a Relevant Cost
Total Cost	$444	

No Vacation

Cost of Meals	$84	Not a Relevant Cost
Total Cost	$84	

Difference in Relevant Costs = $360

The costs of meals clearly is not a relevant cost. While this cost meets the initial criterion of a relevant cost (expected to be incurred under one or more of the alternatives under consideration), it fails to meet the second criterion (differs between alternatives). Thus, in deciding between a vacation at the beach by driving or remaining on campus, the only costs which should be considered in making this decision are the costs of lodging and driving.

Next, consider the two vacation alternatives. Remember that the cost of a vacation at the beach if you fly will be $514; the cost of the vacation if you drive will be $444. Thus, the difference in these costs is $70 ($514 – $444). Once again, this difference only results from differences in the relevant costs. The difference in the cost of the two alternatives is the cost of transportation, as shown below:

Vacation by Driving

Cost of Driving		
(6 nights x $35)	$150	Relevant Cost
Cost of Lodging	210	} Not Relevant Costs
Cost of Meals	84	
Total Cost	$444	

Vacation by Flying

Cost of Airfare	$220	Relevant Cost
Cost of Lodging	210	} Not Relevant Costs
Cost of Meals	84	
Total Cost	$514	

Difference in Relevant Costs = $70

Notice that neither the cost of meals (7 days x $12 per day = $84) nor the cost of lodging (6 days x $35 per day = $210) is relevant in making this decision. While expected to be incurred in the future if either of these choices is made, these costs do not differ between the two alternatives under consideration. Therefore, these costs are not relevant in selecting between the two vacation alternatives. Considering only relevant costs, if you wished to take a vacation and your goal was to minimize your costs, you would drive to the beach. Similarly, when an organization must make a choice between two alternative courses of action, the only costs (and revenues) that should be considered are those that differ between the alternatives under consideration.

Two terms that are often used interchangeably with relevant costs are incremental costs and avoidable (or escapable) costs. *Incremental costs* are the difference in total costs incurred by selecting one alternative rather than another. *Avoidable* (or *escapable*) *costs* are costs that can be saved (or avoided) by selecting a particular alternative. In our spring break example, when deciding between taking a vacation or remaining on campus, the cost of lodging is an incremental cost because it is incurred only when you decide to take a vacation during spring break. Similarly, the cost of lodging can be saved (and, therefore, is avoidable) if you decide to remain on campus. Notice that if two options exist, costs that are incremental based on one alternative are also avoidable under the other alternative, as shown below.

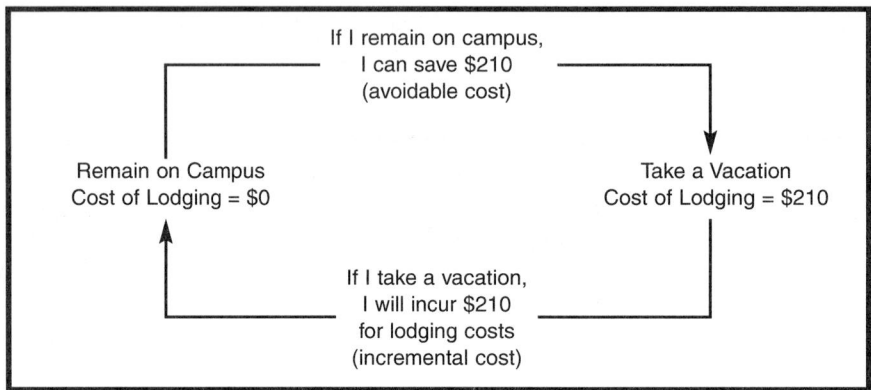

1. The *incremental cost* of lodging associated with taking either type of vacation is $210.

2. The cost of lodging of $210 is *avoidable* if the student decides to remain on campus.

The example above illustrates a situation in which only costs are involved. However, the concept of relevance also applies to scenarios involving both costs and revenues. *Relevant revenues* are conceptually similar to relevant costs. A relevant revenue is a revenue that pertains to the future and is expected to be earned under a given alternative and differs among the various decision alternatives under consideration. When organizations are making decisions such as whether to continue or discontinue a segment, product line, or service, they consider both the relevant revenues and relevant costs of the various decisions. Decisions such as this are discussed later in this chapter.

Qualitative Considerations. In the above example, we assume that the costs of the various alternatives can be expressed numerically or quantified. We express the cost of meals, lodging, and travel in dollars. In making our decision, we considered only the quantitative factors—the total costs related to each alternative. If minimizing the total cost incurred is the goal of the student, he or she would select the alternative with the lowest total cost. The student would remain on campus during spring break. This decision is reached since the cost of remaining on campus ($84) is lower than that of either driving ($444) or flying ($514) to the beach.

A limitation of the approach described above is that there are many factors which simply cannot be quantified (or expressed in dollars). These factors often play an important role in a decision. For example, in deciding whether to stay on campus or vacation at the beach, the student should also consider the amount of studying he or she could (or would) do and the anticipated enjoyment he or she could have at the beach. In deciding whether to fly or drive to the beach, the inconvenience of driving and the safety of flying or driving should be considered. These are referred to as *qualitative factors*. While qualitative factors must be considered, the difficulty of expressing these factors in terms of dollars makes their incorporation into the decision-making process difficult.

In many decisions, the qualitative considerations may actually outweigh quantitative (or dollar) factors. Food processors willingly incur large inspection costs to ensure that their products are free from contaminants. From a strict "dollars and cents" standpoint, it is difficult to argue that spending $100,000 on inspection will provide a return of at least an equal amount in revenues. The food processor must give greater consideration to the qualitative (and unmeasurable) "costs" of selling contaminated products than to the quantitative (measurable) costs of inspection. Qualitative factors may involve such concerns as a loss of the consumer's goodwill or potential costs resulting from lawsuits. Although the accountant strives to simplify decisions by reducing as many factors as possible to quantitative terms, qualitative factors are often impossible to express in terms of dollars.

> For many companies, the key to success is customer relationship management—identifying and satisfying their most important customers. For example, sales of Lexus automobiles represent only 2% of Toyota's total sales, but provide one-third of the company's profit. Business travelers comprise less than 10% of airline passengers while providing more than 40% of airline ticket sales revenues, and the top 0.2% of car-rental customers account for 25% of the vehicles rented. These relationships demonstrate how critical it is for companies to understand and capitalize on the special needs of their best customers.[2]

Opportunity Costs

Opportunity costs are benefits forgone by selecting one alternative rather than another. Continuing with the spring break illustration, assume that you have an offer to work part-time during that week and could earn $250. If you decide to vacation, the opportunity cost of the vacation would include this $250. Notice that this is not an "out-of-pocket" cost, like lodging and travel. Rather, it represents the benefits that you gave up by selecting one alternative over another. Since opportunity costs relate to the future and differ between alternatives, they are relevant and should be considered in making a decision.

To illustrate the impact of opportunity costs on decisions, assume that you consider the potential employment offer of $250 in your decision as to how to spend your spring break. Illustration 2 shows the total costs of the three alternatives after including the opportunity cost of what you could earn by remaining on campus. From a cost basis, the decision to remain on campus becomes more advantageous: the total costs of the three alternatives are now $764, $694, and $84 for flying to the beach, driving to the beach, and remaining on campus, respectively. Once again, if your decision is solely to minimize your total costs (including opportunity costs), clearly you would remain on campus during spring break.

Illustration 2
Total Costs Incurred Under Vacation Alternatives
(including Opportunity Costs)

	Vacation by Flying	Vacation by Driving	No Vacation
Travel Cost...........................	$220	$150	$ 0
Cost of Lodging	210	210	0
Cost of Meals	84	84	84
Income Forgone by Taking a Vacation......	250	250	0
Total Cost	$764	$694	$84

(Opportunity Cost Which Differs Between Alternatives)

It should be emphasized that opportunity costs exist whenever choices are made. In some cases, these costs are quantifiable. For example, assume that you had two employment opportunities during spring break: one for $250 and another for $200. The opportunity cost of selecting the $250 offer would be $200 (the benefits forgone by not selecting the second alternative). Thus, even in situations where the "optimal" (in terms of dollars) decision is made, opportunity costs still exist.

In other cases, opportunity costs simply are not quantifiable. The above analysis suggests that you do not "lose" any benefits by remaining on campus. Clearly, that is not the case. If you remain on campus and accept the $250 employment offer, the opportunity cost of not taking a vacation is the enjoyment and relaxation that you would have realized. From a strictly quantitative standpoint, these costs are difficult to incorporate into an analysis, however.

Sunk Costs

Sunk costs refer to costs which have already been incurred (or are currently being incurred) and cannot be changed regardless of the alternative selected. Sunk costs do not meet the criteria for classification as a relevant cost, since these costs are not expected to be incurred in the future. Rather, they were incurred in the past. In the

---

[2] Jim Harris, Blindsided: *How to Spot the Next Breakthrough That Will Change Your Business Forever,* (Hoboken, NJ: John Wiley & Sons, Inc., 2002).

spring break example, any apartment rent or dormitory fees you are paying cannot be avoided if you vacation. Since these costs have been incurred because of a past decision, they cannot be changed and do not differ under any of the decision alternatives. Therefore, in making your decision, you would not include the costs of dormitory fees or apartment rent. Because sunk costs cannot be saved, they are often referred to as *unavoidable costs*.

> While "no proposition in economics is more firmly established than the supreme irrelevance of sunk costs," it appears to be very difficult for individuals to ignore past costs in their decision-making processes. The decision the New York Yankees made to start Kenny Rogers in the fourth game of the 1996 World Series provides a good illustration of how decision-makers can feel compelled to justify past costs. Despite the fact that Rogers was off his regular game in the weeks leading up to the Series, the Yankees started him anyway, mainly, it seems, because Yankees owner George Steinbrenner had previously paid $20 million to sign him.[3]

To illustrate the role of sunk costs in the decision-making process, assume that your dormitory fees are $200 per month. Allocating this cost equally over the month, your cost per week is $50 ($200 ÷ 4 weeks). Your total costs for dormitory fees during spring break week will be $50 regardless of your decision, since this cost must be paid if you remain on campus or if you take a vacation. Thus, this cost is not relevant and would not be considered in your decision.

Summary: Terminology for Short-Term Decisions

While this section has examined a non-business decision, it is important to note that the identical conceptual process is used by organizations in making a wide variety of decisions. For example, when deciding whether to continue or discontinue a segment or product line, organizations evaluate the relevant costs and revenues associated with that segment or product line. In addition, if the production facilities that would become available if a segment or product line is eliminated could be used to generate revenues in another use, the alternative use of these production facilities is an opportunity cost that must also be considered. Finally, the depreciation expense related to production equipment is a sunk cost and should not be considered. While the vacation example was quite different, it also consisted of various types of incremental costs, opportunity costs, and sunk costs.

Illustration 3 summarizes the terminology discussed to this point and indicates how the related costs and revenues should be evaluated in making decisions.

Illustration 3
Decision Terminology and Effect on Managerial Decisions

Term	Definition	How Decisions are Affected
Relevant Costs (or incremental costs or avoidable costs) and Revenues	Costs and revenues that will be incurred in the future and will differ between alternatives	Should be considered in deciding between alternatives
Opportunity Costs	The benefits forgone by selecting one alternative over another	Should be considered in deciding between alternatives
Sunk Costs	Costs that have been incurred (or are being incurred) and cannot be modified in the future	Should not be considered in deciding between alternatives

THE USE OF MANAGERIAL ACCOUNTING DATA IN MAKING SHORT-TERM DECISIONS

The previous section discussed important terminology related to costs and revenues that influence management's decision-making process. At this point, the use of managerial accounting data in making

---

[3] Dan Seligman, "Of Mice and Economics," *Forbes* (August 24, 1998), 62.

short-term decisions is explored further. The basic process through which these decisions are made is summarized below:

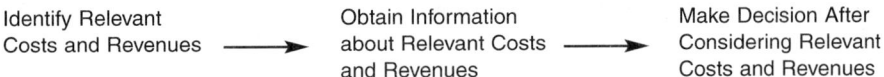

Five major types of decisions will be examined in the remainder of this chapter: (1) product pricing decisions, (2) special orders, (3) continuation of a segment or product line, (4) additional processing, and (5) make-or-buy decisions. To examine these decisions in an organizational setting, we will consider various decisions faced by LawnMasters, a company providing commercial and residential landscaping and irrigation services. LawnMasters provides three major types of services to its customers: (1) lawn maintenance (mowing, fertilization, and pesticide and weed control); (2) landscaping (trees, flower beds, shrubbery, and lawn planting); and (3) irrigation (installation of sprinkler and drainage systems).

PRODUCT PRICING DECISIONS

Establishing selling prices for products and services is a critical decision that must be made in every business. Pricing decisions have a direct impact on the inflow of funds and the profitability of the company. If the prices charged by an organization are too high, customer demand and overall revenues will decrease. On the other hand, if the prices charged are too low, the organization will suffer losses because it could have earned more revenue from sales of the same quantity of products. Once an organization establishes its pricing policy, it is often difficult and costly to change.

As shown below, large corporations are beginning to evaluate the profitability of serving their customers.

A bank's investment of the funds provided by a fictitious depositor with an average checking account balance of $1,500 will provide $90 of revenue. However, the cost of maintaining records ($89.04), processing checks ($26.04), teller transactions ($22.50), and withdrawals from automated teller machines ($4.50) means that the bank is spending $142.08 to earn $90.00. Bank consultant James Moore indicates that 20 percent of a bank's customers account for all consumer-banking profits while three out of five customers are money losers for banks.[4]

American Telephone & Telegraph (AT&T) loses $500 a year servicing 15 to 20 million "occasional communicators," who generate less revenue in long-distance billing than the expenses of billing and servicing their accounts. CEO C. Michael Armstrong noted that "we've gotten a lot smarter about separating the customers we do want from the customers we don't." Also, Citibank Corp. increased its minimum balance requirements for free checking accounts to $6,000, hoping that customers who maintain small balances but write a large number of checks and make a large number of teller visits will take their banking business elsewhere.[5]

Turning its back on "a century of industry doctrine," Ford Motor Company is cutting capacity, discontinuing slow-moving models, and slashing its low-margin sales to rental car companies in an attempt to improve profits. The decision to abandon a traditional high-volume strategy is one that is particularly difficult in the auto industry, where manufacturers face enormous structural costs and labor costs are effectively fixed, due to the anti-layoff provisions of United Auto Workers contracts. While Ford's new focus on profitability has required that it sacrifice market share, it enabled the company to post first-quarter 2004 earnings that were double investors' expectations.[6]

By necessity, an organization's pricing policy should consider the costs associated with its products and services. Organizations should set their prices to allow them to recover their costs and, hopefully, earn a profit! Two approaches for determining the "cost" of manufacturing a product or providing a service are the contribution margin (variable) approach and the full-cost (absorption) approach. These approaches are discussed in detail below.

---

[4] "Get Out of Here!" *Newsweek* (June 3, 1996), 54.

[5] "Get Lost, Buster," *Forbes* (February 23, 1998), 90.

[6] Joseph B. White and Norihiko Shirouzu, "At Ford Motor, High Volume Takes Backseat to Profits," *The Wall Street Journal* (May 7, 2004), A1.

Contribution Margin (Variable) Approach

One approach to product pricing assumes that the price charged for a given product or service should at least be sufficient to recover the variable costs of producing that product or providing that service. This approach is the *variable (or contribution margin) approach* to pricing. Since fixed costs do not increase with increases in activity within the relevant range, establishing the selling price of a product or service at an amount equal to the variable costs of producing each product or providing that service will allow the organization to at least "break even." In almost every instance, the variable cost should be the minimum selling price. If products or services are sold for less than variable cost, a loss will be incurred. This loss results from the fact that the incremental cost to the organization of providing goods and services is (at a minimum) the variable cost.

> An episode of the sitcom "I Love Lucy" illustrates the problems that can occur if selling prices are lower than variable costs. In this episode, Lucy and Ethel have decided to go into business selling salad dressing prepared based on a family recipe. As the orders pile in, Lucy and Ethel are daydreaming about how they will spend all of the money they will earn. When Ricky asks them about the costs, they determine that they are *losing* 10 cents on every jar that they sell! They decide to fill all existing orders and immediately get out of the salad dressing business.

To illustrate the contribution margin approach to pricing, assume that LawnMasters is attempting to determine the price it will charge to customers for its lawn mowing services. For planning purposes, LawnMasters uses an average lawn size of 1/4 acre and has identified three primary costs associated with these services:

1. Direct labor costs of wages paid to employees providing lawn mowing services. For expediency, three workers typically service each lawn (one for mowing, one for edging and weedeating, and one for cleanup). On average, each worker earns $6 per hour and each yard requires 20 minutes (or 0.33 hours) to complete.

2. Variable overhead costs associated with gasoline, oil, and repairs to equipment. LawnMasters incurs approximately $100 of these costs per month, while the average number of lawns serviced per month is 250.

3. Fixed overhead costs of supervision, depreciation on equipment and vehicles. These costs average approximately $3,000 per month.

Under the contribution margin approach to product pricing, LawnMasters would consider only the variable costs identified below. In this case, the price charged for lawn services would be $6.40, as follows:

Direct Labor (3 workers x 0.33 hours x $6 per hour)..................	$6.00
Gasoline, oil, and repairs to equipment ($100 per month ÷ 250 lawns per month)	0.40
Total variable cost per lawn...	$6.40

Stated another way, the *incremental costs* to LawnMasters of providing lawn services is $6.40 per lawn. If lawn services are priced at $6.40, the incremental revenue to LawnMasters would be $6.40. Under the contribution margin approach to pricing, incremental costs equal incremental revenues. This allows the organization to "breakeven."

Full-Cost (Absorption) Approach

Alternatively, management's decision to produce a particular product (or provide a particular service) may result in incurring additional fixed costs. If so, these costs become relevant and are considered in the decision-making process. However, in these instances, only the *incremental fixed costs* should be considered. Recall that incremental fixed costs are the fixed costs that differ between alternatives; thus, these costs are relevant to the particular decision.

In certain cases, a decision to provide products or services to customers may result in incurring additional fixed costs. For example, if LawnMasters operates its equipment at full capacity, it would need to purchase additional equipment to service additional yards. If so, the price charged to customers should at least reflect the additional fixed costs necessary to service those customers. While these costs are fixed in nature, the rationale for considering them in establishing the price charged to customers is that these costs are increased by the decision to provide goods or services to additional customers.

LawnMasters has received a bid from commercial clients for lawn maintenance services. However, because of its limited capacity, accepting these jobs would require the purchase of additional lawn equipment at a cost of $2,400. Using a two-year useful life, depreciation expense for this equipment is $100 per month ($2,400 ÷ 24 months). However, purchasing the equipment would also provide LawnMasters with the capacity to service an additional 50 lawns per month. If 50 additional lawns were serviced each month, the price set by LawnMasters to recover its variable costs and incremental fixed costs would be $8.40, as shown below:

Variable costs	$6.40
Incremental fixed costs ($100 ÷ 50 lawns)	2.00
Total incremental cost	$8.40

Note from the above example that the existing fixed overhead costs of supervision, depreciation on mowing equipment, and depreciation on transportation vehicles of $3,000 per month are not considered under the full-cost approach. These costs are sunk costs, since they have already been incurred and are not affected by a decision to provide additional lawn services.

Considering both the incremental variable and fixed production costs in establishing selling prices is referred to as *full-cost* (or *absorption*) *pricing*. An example follows:

> One approach to considering fixed costs in product pricing is to base the price on the level of capacity, not on the level of production. For example, based on actual activity, the total cost of services provided by the telephone service center of a regional bank was $0.766 per minute. Using capacity instead of actual production, the cost per minute was $0.533. Since additional services could be provided without increasing total fixed costs, this latter amount can be used as the basis for product pricing decisions to allow the organization to adequately cover its costs of providing services.[7]

Setting Prices to Earn a Profit

Each of the examples above illustrates minimum pricing decisions. These calculations provided LawnMasters with an indication of the price it could charge to customers for lawn services that would allow it to offset: (1) the variable costs of providing lawn services (contribution approach) or (2) the incremental costs (both fixed and variable) of providing lawn services (full-cost approach). The calculations provided management the answer to the following question: What is the lowest price at which we can service customers without losing money?

Obviously, simply covering its costs (whether variable costs or total costs) will not allow an organization to remain in business for long. Pricing decisions must also consider some desired level of profit. For example, assume that LawnMasters wished to earn $5,000 per month from its lawn services. Also recall that the incremental costs per lawn are $8.40, monthly fixed costs associated with existing machinery and equipment are $3,000, and the typical number of yards serviced per month is 300 (250 prior to the purchase of the new equipment + 50 additional lawns following the purchase). Using this information, LawnMasters would establish a price of $28.40 per lawn, as follows:

$$\text{Revenues} - \text{Costs} = \text{Profit}$$
$$(300 \text{ lawns} \times \text{price}) - [(\$8.40 \times 300 \text{ lawns}) + \$3,000] = \$5,000$$
$$\text{Price} = \$28.40$$

For these cases, the above examples could be modified to allow a specified profit to be earned. If management desires a specified level of profit, the total variable cost (under contribution margin pricing) or total incremental cost (under full-cost pricing) of production is increased by a desired profit margin, or markup. The important point in the above examples is that, when establishing the selling price of a particular product or service, a minimum price should be established to allow the organization to recover any incremental costs associated with the production of that product or service.

---

[7] G. Y. Yang and R. C. Wu, "Strategic Costing & ABC," *Management Accounting* (May 1993), 33–37.

A survey of Fortune 1,000 companies indicated that 83 percent of these firms typically consider both variable and fixed costs in pricing their products; the remaining 17 percent consider only variable costs in their pricing decisions.[8]

The following excerpt describes the flexible pricing system that contributes to Dell Computer's market dominance.

> **Dell Computer employs a cost-forecasting system that allows its sales force to price fluidly and, consequently, win customers from its rivals. Cost information collected from Dell's factories and suppliers is accumulated in a spreadsheet that sales managers use to both calculate what each product costs Dell now and project what it will cost six months into the future. Dell managers, who are authorized to set profit goals for all their accounts, can use this open access to cost information to adjust PC prices based on quantity, profit targets, and proposed delivery dates. Sales representatives can sell at any price that provides a margin consistent with the objectives of the regional sales manager. Sales representatives can also call a "special pricing" team to request an evaluation of a price below the target margin; the team will give a decision on the price within an hour.[9]**

Elasticity of Demand

An additional factor which should be considered by the organization in establishing its prices is the impact of its prices on demand for the product or service. While a complete discussion of supply and demand is beyond the scope of an introductory managerial accounting course, it is obvious that pricing policy must consider the interrelationships among prices, costs, and volume. The price-volume relationship is frequently described as *elasticity of demand*. Elasticity of demand represents the relative change in quantity demanded caused by a change in price.

For example, assume that LawnMasters established the price for its lawn mowing services at $28.40 and, at this price, was able to service 300 yards per month. In response to higher prices charged by competitors, LawnMasters is considering increasing its price to $32.00 (an increase of 12.67%). While this action may result in some customer dissatisfaction and, ultimately, reduced demand, LawnMasters should ask the following question: "If we increase prices by 12.67 percent, how will it affect the demand for our services?" To illustrate various possibilities, consider the total revenues earned by LawnMasters if demand is reduced from 300 lawns to 270 lawns (a 10% reduction) or to 240 lawns (a 20% reduction).

Current revenues (300 lawns x $28.40)....................................	$8,520
Reduction to 270 lawns (270 lawns x $32.00)...........................	8,640
Reduction to 240 lawns (240 lawns x $32.00)...........................	7,680

Elasticity of demand is usually measured as the percentage change in volume divided by the percentage change in price. Demand is said to be elastic if a given percentage change in price produces a larger percentage change in volume (and revenues). A price increase for products that have a relatively inelastic demand will increase total revenues while a price decrease will decrease total revenues. For instance, if the price increase from $28.40 to $32.00 (12.67%) reduces demand by 10 percent (from 300 lawns to 270 lawns), the demand is inelastic—note that a volume of 270 lawns yields an increase in total revenues from $8,520 to $8,640. The elasticity of demand in this instance is 0.79 (0.10 ÷ 0.1267 = 0.79).

In contrast, demand is said to be elastic if a given percentage change in price produces a larger percentage change in volume (and revenues). To illustrate, if increasing prices by 12.67 percent would result in a demand of 240 lawns (a reduction of 20%), the overall revenues would decrease from $8,520 to $7,680. In this situation, the 12.67 percent increase in prices resulted in a 20 percent decrease in volume. The elasticity of demand equals 1.58 (0.20 ÷ 0.1267 = 1.58).

---

[8] V. Govindarajan and R.N. Anthony, "How Firms Use Cost Data in Price Decisions," *Management Accounting* (July 1983), 30–36.

[9] Gary McWilliams, "Lean Machine: How Dell Fine-Tunes Its PC Pricing to Gain Edge in a Slow Market," *The Wall Street Journal* (June 8, 2001), A1, A8.

Product pricing decisions should consider factors other than the incremental costs and revenues associated with the product. An example of a product pricing strategy that has met mixed success in the restaurant industry is shown below:

> If a restaurant offers half-price coupons, early-bird, or pre-theater dinners for $7, the incremental cost of $4 per meal would be relevant if new customers could be enticed to eat at an early hour when regular customers would not be displaced. However, if customers who would normally pay $14 per meal decided to alter their plans (by taking advantage of the special or eating elsewhere because of crowded conditions), the restaurant's total contribution margin could actually be reduced.[10]

Other strategies are appropriate for companies that offer "perishable" products or services.

> The pricing strategies of airlines and hotel rooms are slightly different because these products are "perishable." That is, if they are not sold, the revenue opportunity is lost forever. For these companies, it makes sense to reduce prices to increase capacity if doing so doesn't reduce the prices paid by other customers. While airlines and hotels have effectively used differential pricing for a number of years, the increasing availability of price information on the Internet may make it difficult for these companies to continue the practice.[11]

SPECIAL ORDERS

A decision similar to the pricing decision discussed above is management's decision to accept or reject a special order. Special orders arise when an individual customer or buyer wishes to purchase goods or services at a price different than that ordinarily charged to the organization's regular customers. This opportunity can be attractive to the organization, since it can provide goods or service without a great deal of effort and, in some cases, possibly identify potential new customers. In addition, special orders can often be filled without incurring costs associated with sales to the organization's existing customers.

A major difference between a special order decision and a product pricing decision is that, for a special order, the customer offers a given price. When considering whether or not to accept a special order, the focus should be on the incremental costs and revenues associated with the order. What is the amount of revenue which will be earned by making the sale? What are the additional costs incurred in filling the special order? In most cases, as long as the incremental revenues exceed the incremental costs, the organization will accept the customer's special order.

From a strict financial standpoint, the organization should accept a special order if the total incremental revenues from the special order exceed the total incremental costs. To illustrate, recall that LawnMasters has identified the full cost of providing lawn services to its existing customers at $18.40 per lawn as follows:

Direct labor (3 workers x 0.33 hours x $6 per hour)..................	$ 6.00
Gasoline, oil, and repairs to equipment ($100 per month ÷ 250 lawns per month).............................	0.40
Fixed overhead costs ($3,000 per month ÷ 250 lawns per month)..........................	12.00
Total cost per lawn	$18.40

LawnMasters' price of $28.40 per yard is established to consider all of the above costs. Now assume that while providing lawn services for a commercial customer, the owners of nearby properties have offered LawnMasters $120 to provide them with weekly lawn services. These properties represent the equivalent of eight yards; thus, the average price per property is $15 ($120 ÷ 8 yards).

LawnMasters' initial instinct may be to decline this offer. After all, it would receive "only" $15 per yard for a service that "costs" it $18.40 per yard. However, the decision to provide lawn services to these customers does not result in an additional $18.40 in costs. If LawnMasters would not be required to reduce its services to its existing customers, the effect of accepting this special order on total income is an additional $68.80 per week.

---

[10] R. W. Koehler, "Triple-Threat Strategy," *Management Accounting* (October 1991), 30–34.

[11] Peter Coy, "The Power of Smart Pricing," *Business Week* (April 10, 2000), 160.

Since the incremental revenues exceed the incremental costs, this order should be accepted if the decision is based solely on financial considerations:

Incremental revenues (8 properties x $15.00)	$120.00
Incremental costs:	
Direct labor (8 properties x $6.00)	(48.00)
Variable overhead (8 properties x $0.40)	(3.20)
Net incremental revenues	$68.80

An example of idle capacity from recent practice follows.

> FMI Forms Manufacturers is a medium-sized printing company that produces various types of business forms, such as invoices and purchase orders. When bidding on special orders (or "rush" jobs), FMI Forms does not ignore fixed manufacturing costs when idle capacity exists. FMI assigns a higher markup on rush jobs than normal because these types of jobs are considered to be constraints on capacity and not a way to use idle capacity.[12]

No Excess Capacity

In the above example, LawnMasters had the additional capacity to accept the special orders. In cases where such excess capacity does not exist, however, the decision to accept a special order may impose additional costs on the organization. These costs may take one of two forms: (1) the need to obtain additional equipment or other resources to provide products or services related to the special order, or (2) the need to forgo current sales to existing customers. The analysis must be expanded to consider these costs in cases where excess capacity is not available.

Assume that LawnMasters received an offer to provide lawn services to eight properties for a fee of $15 per property. How would it react if it did not have the current capacity to provide these services? LawnMasters has identified two possible means of providing the services related to the special order:

1. Rent additional equipment at a cost of $50 per day. Since all eight properties could be serviced in a single day, the total cost to LawnMasters is $50 per week.

2. Discontinue providing services to some of LawnMasters' current customers. This would result in forgone revenues of $28.40 per property, per week.

The net incremental revenues associated with the decision to fill the special order by renting additional equipment are $22. The total incremental costs associated with the special order include the direct labor costs and the costs of renting the equipment. Note that the variable overhead costs are not considered, since the equipment is not owned by LawnMasters.

Incremental revenues (8 properties x $15.00)	$120.00
Incremental costs:	
Direct labor (8 properties x $6.00)	(48.00)
Rental of equipment	(50.00)
Net incremental revenues	$22.00

Alternatively, LawnMasters could fill the special order by discontinuing services provided to some of its current customers. While this choice would not result in additional costs, it would result in the loss of revenue. This loss of revenue represents an opportunity cost. Recall that opportunity costs are the benefits forgone by selecting one alternative rather than another. Essentially, if LawnMasters decided to accept the special order by discontinuing services to its existing customers, it would sacrifice servicing eight properties at $28.40 to service properties for $15.

A cost savings that LawnMasters would realize by accepting this special order relates to direct labor. Since these properties are adjacent to that of a customer already served by LawnMasters, it estimates that the total time required per property would decrease from 20 minutes (0.33 hours) to 15 minutes (0.25 hours) because of reduced travel times to the job site. As a result, the variable direct labor cost per property would be $4.50

---

[12] J. L. Rogers, S. M. Comstock and K. Pritz, "Customize your Costing System," *Management Accounting* (May 1993), 31–32.

(3 workers x 0.25 hours x $6.00 per hour). Assuming a total capacity of 250 properties, the net incremental revenue earned by accepting the special order is summarized below:

Incremental revenues (8 properties x $15.00)	$120.00
Costs savings [8 properties x ($6.00 – $4.50)]	12.00
Incremental costs:	
Revenues forgone (8 properties x $28.40)	(227.20)
Net incremental revenues	($ 95.20)

Notice that only two relevant costs exist in the above scenario: the cost savings because of reduced travel time and the revenues forgone by accepting the special order. The variable overhead costs are not considered, since these resources would be transferred from existing customers to the special order. An alternative approach to this decision which more clearly highlights the relevant costs and revenues is to construct income statements for the two alternatives (accept or reject special order).

	Reject Order	Accept Order	Difference
Revenues from Existing Customers:			
250 x $28.40	$7,100.00		
242 x $28.40		$6,872.80	($227.20)
Revenues from Special Order:			
8 x $15.00		120.00	120.00
Direct Labor Costs			
250 x $6.00	(1,500.00)		
242 x $6.00		(1,452.00)	
8 x $4.50		(36.00)	12.00
Variable Overhead Costs			
250 x $0.40	(100.00)	(100.00)	0.00
Net Income	$5,500.00	$5,404.80	($ 95.20)

The following observations may be made from the above analyses:

1. The opportunity cost of accepting the special order is $227.20 (the difference in sales to existing customers if the special order is accepted or rejected).
2. The incremental revenues of accepting the special order are $120 (the sales from the special order).
3. A cost savings of $12 would result from accepting the special order (reduced direct labor costs because of less travel time for workers).
4. LawnMasters would suffer a loss of $95.20 if the special order is accepted.

Qualitative Considerations

While the quantitative factors involved with analyzing management's decision to accept or reject a special order are relatively straightforward, other factors may also play a role in management's decision. For example, additional consideration would be given to the following:

1. What effect would a special price offered to one customer have on other customers? Would these customers demand similar price concessions? Would LawnMasters current customers continue to purchase lawn services for $28.40 once they learn that other customers are charged only $15?
2. What effect will a special order have on current and future capacity? Will this special order eventually lead to an expansion of other resources? For example, rather than renting equipment for $50 per week, LawnMasters could purchase additional equipment for $3,000 in order to increase its overall capacity from 250 to 300 properties. While this purchase would permit LawnMasters to both fill the special order and expand its operations, it should carefully consider whether the demand for lawn services is sufficient to warrant the additional expenditure. In addition, LawnMasters should determine whether it will need to hire additional workers and incur other expenditures to allow it to serve the additional properties.

3. Is the special order a "one-time" event or could it result in an ongoing relationship? For example, LawnMaster's decision to accept the special order for lawn services may result in providing irrigation, fertilization, and weed control services as well. If so, LawnMasters should consider the potential revenues that may be earned from the sales of its other products and services.

Summary: Special Orders

The following guidelines are normally used in deciding whether to accept or reject a special order:

- If incremental revenues exceed the incremental costs of production (including any lost sales to existing customers), accept the order.

- If incremental revenues are less than the incremental costs of production (including any lost sales to existing customers), do not accept the order.

CONTINUATION OF A SEGMENT OR PRODUCT LINE

Decisions to continue or discontinue a segment or product line are ordinarily based upon data supplied by incremental analysis. This analysis should focus exclusively on the incremental revenues and costs associated with the segment or product or service line under consideration. Recall that LawnMasters engages in three major areas of business: lawn maintenance, landscaping, and irrigation. For some time, Peter Casey, the owner of LawnMasters, has suspected that the lawn maintenance business has not been profitable because of the limited revenue it generates. Peter requested a breakdown of the revenues and cost by area of service. Patricia Todd, his chief accountant, submitted the following monthly information (in highly summarized form) for his review:

	Lawn Maintenance	Landscaping	Irrigation
Revenues	$12,000	$28,000	$35,000
Variable costs:			
Direct materials	($1,000)	($5,000)	($8,000)
Direct labor	(1,500)	(6,000)	(5,000)
Overhead	(1,000)	(1,500)	(2,000)
General and administrative	(500)	(1,500)	(1,000)
Contribution margin	8,000	14,000	19,000
Fixed costs:			
Overhead	(4,000)	(5,600)	(6,200)
General and administrative	(5,000)	(5,000)	(5,000)
Net income	($1,000)	$3,400	$7,800

At first glance, Peter's suspicions appear to be correct. It appears that the LawnMasters is losing money on its lawn maintenance services. Then, Peter began considering the various costs incurred:

- All variable costs (direct materials, direct labor, overhead, and general and administrative costs) are related exclusively to providing services in each of the divisions. For example, the cost of fertilizer and weed control are only incurred for lawn maintenance services. In addition, employees providing lawn maintenance services do not provide services in either of the other areas of LawnMasters' operations (landscaping and irrigation).

- Two types of costs are included in the fixed overhead costs: (1) the costs associated with service vehicles and equipment (these costs are allocated among the three service lines based on expected utilization), and (2) the salaries paid to supervisors in each of the major service lines. Of these, only the salary paid to supervisors would be saved if the service line was discontinued.

- Fixed general and administrative costs are allocated equally to the three services lines (for lack of a more meaningful method of allocation). LawnMasters has a relatively "lean" office support staff and, as a result, it is unlikely that discontinuing one service line would result in a reduction of office staff or these costs.

In considering this issue, Peter began to distinguish between two categories of costs. Since the variable costs could be saved if LawnMasters decided to discontinue its lawn maintenance services, these costs are *avoidable* costs. As noted earlier, avoidable costs are costs that can be saved (or avoided) by selecting a particular alternative. Avoidable costs are also relevant, since they differ between the two alternatives (providing lawn maintenance services versus not providing lawn maintenance services). As a result, avoidable costs should be considered in Peter's evaluation of the desirability of providing lawn maintenance services.

A portion of fixed overhead costs could also be saved if LawnMasters discontinued its lawn maintenance services. Since each service line has a supervisor working only with that line, the salary paid to the supervisor in the lawn maintenance service line could be avoided if LawnMasters decided to discontinue that service line. Thus, despite the fact that these costs are "fixed" with respect to their pattern of behavior, they are also relevant to LawnMasters' decision to continue providing lawn maintenance services, since they could potentially be saved. Of the $4,000 of fixed overhead costs included in the lawn maintenance division, $2,500 represents the supervisor's salary.

Alternatively, the overhead costs associated with service equipment and the fixed general and administrative costs would not be avoided if LawnMasters discontinued providing lawn maintenance services. These costs are not relevant to this decision. As Peter began thinking about the cost of service equipment, this made sense: "We bought this equipment ten years ago. The costs are allocations; it's not like dollars are being spent on a current basis." Depreciation on service equipment represents a *sunk cost*, since it relates to an expenditure that has been made in the past and cannot be altered in the future. As noted earlier, sunk costs are not relevant for decision-making purposes.

After analyzing and classifying costs in the above manner, Patricia Todd modified the initial analysis somewhat and scheduled a meeting with Peter. This time, Patricia began the meeting: "Mr. Casey, I've looked into some of these costs further. If we discontinue landscaping services, it will cost us $40,000 a year. Let me show you why." With this, she presented Peter the analysis shown below:

	Continue Lawn Maintenance	Discontinue Lawn Maintenance
Contribution margin	$41,000 [a]	$33,000 [b]
Fixed overhead costs	(15,800) [c]	(13,300) [d]
Fixed general and administrative costs	(15,000) [e]	(15,000) [e]
Net income	$10,200	$4,700

[a] $8,000 + $14,000 + $19,000
[b] $14,000 + $19,000
[c] $4,000 + $5,600 + $6,200
[d] ($4,000 − $2,500) + $5,600 + $6,200
[e] $5,000 + $5,000 + $5,000

The net loss of discontinuing lawn maintenance service is $5,500 ($10,200 − $4,700 = $5,500). How did this occur? If we consider the incremental revenues earned by LawnMasters from this service and the incremental costs incurred in generating these revenues, lawn maintenance is actually profitable, as shown below:

Incremental revenues	$12,000
Direct materials	(1,000)
Direct labor	(1,500)
Variable overhead	(1,000)
Variable general and administrative	(500)
Fixed overhead (supervisor's salary)	(2,500)
Incremental net income	$ 5,500

Ford Motor Company made what was viewed at the time as a revolutionary move when it eliminated seven of its weaker-selling models including the Thunderbird, a sentimental favorite. Ford found that the cost of marketing and distributing these models outweighed the benefits of keeping them in its lineup. While this may seem like an obvious decision, it is actually quite unusual for the automotive industry. Automakers rarely terminate models because their dealers and suppliers complain and their market share generally suffers.[13]

---

[13] Alex Taylor III, "The Gentlemen at Ford are Kicking Butt," *Fortune* (June 22, 1998), 73.

Other Considerations—Resource Constraints

In addition to the incremental costs and revenues associated with a particular segment or product/service line, other factors also should be considered in a decision to continue or discontinue a segment or product/service line. For example, management may face a constraint on its resources such that it needs to allocate those resources among a limited number of products or services. Constraints on capacity may result in management being forced to discontinue one or more products or services that are profitable.

The preceding discussion reveals that all of LawnMasters' service lines are profitable. Assume that LawnMasters direct labor availability (hourly-wage workers) is 1,600 hours per month. Because of a shortage of part-time labor, LawnMasters does not feel that it can increase this capacity in the short term. In this instance, direct labor hours are a constrained resource; regardless of the types of services provided, LawnMasters is limited to 1,600 direct labor hours per month. Therefore, the decision facing LawnMasters is how to best utilize the available 1,600 direct labor hours.

The following information is available for the three service lines provided by LawnMasters:

	Lawn Maintenance	Landscaping	Irrigation
Average revenue per job	$30.00	$750.00	$2,100.00
Variable cost	(10.00)	(225.00)	(966.00)
Incremental fixed cost	(1.00)	(3.00)	(5.00)
Total incremental profit	$19.00	$522.00	$1,129.00
Direct labor hours per job	0.25	4.00	25.00

After examining the above analysis, Peter Casey said "That's amazing! We're providing the wrong services. We should shift all of our labor into irrigation! We would earn over a thousand dollars a job!" While this line of thinking seems to be logical, LawnMasters must also consider the *volume* of services that can be provided. For example, since lawn maintenance jobs require ¼ of an hour per job, LawnMasters could service 6,400 lawns (1,600 direct labor hours ÷ 0.25 hours per job = 6,400 jobs). In contrast, LawnMasters could only provide 64 irrigation services per month if its labor force were dedicated to this area (1,600 direct labor hours ÷ 25 hours per job = 64 jobs). The illustration below summarizes the total profit that LawnMasters could earn assuming that its entire capacity was dedicated to that service.

Total Profit Earned on the Sale of Services*

	Lawn Maintenance	Landscaping	Irrigation
Total Capacity (direct labor hours)	1,600	1,600	1,600
÷ Direct labor hours per job	÷ 0.25	÷ 4	÷ 25
Total jobs	6,400	400	64
x Profit per unit	x $19.00	x $522.00	x $1,129.00
Total Profit	$121,600	$208,800	$ 72,256

*Total profit earned if only that service is provided.

Based on the analysis above, it appears that LawnMasters would benefit by discontinuing its lawn maintenance and irrigation services and providing only landscaping services, since the total incremental profit for landscaping services ($208,800) exceeds that for either of the other services ($121,600 and $72,256 for lawn maintenance and irrigation services, respectively). Notice that organization-wide fixed costs are not considered in this decision, since they do not differ among the alternatives and, therefore, are not relevant. However, since all three services are profitable (that is, the incremental revenues exceed the incremental costs), the following factors should be considered prior to making this decision:

- Does sufficient demand exist to provide 400 landscaping services per month? If this level of demand does not exist, it would not be wise for LawnMasters to dedicate its entire capacity to this service. Doing so would result in lost profits that could be earned from providing lawn maintenance and irrigation services.

- Would the decision to discontinue providing lawn maintenance and irrigation services reduce the demand for LawnMasters' landscaping services? It is possible that providing lawn maintenance and irrigation services may introduce LawnMasters to customers that eventually decide to purchase landscaping services.

Summary: Continuation of a Segment or Product Line

In deciding whether to discontinue a segment or product line, the following guidelines apply:

- If incremental revenues exceed incremental costs, continue the product line.
- If incremental revenues are less than incremental costs, discontinue the product line.

> Based on an internal report indicating an operating deficit of $800,000, Utah State University considered eliminating its football program. Upon closer scrutiny, Utah State's evaluation committee discovered that a large portion of the football program's expenditures were either related to financial aid given to athletes (representing dollars allocated from the Athletic Department to other departments on campus) or expenses that were allocated to the football program on an arbitrary basis (e.g., costs of maintaining the ticket office, sports information office, etc.). Since these costs would not be eliminated if the football program were eliminated, they should not be considered in deciding whether to discontinue the football program. The bottom line indicated that eliminating the football program would result in a net loss of $187,000 per year to Utah State University![14]

ADDITIONAL PROCESSING

To this point, we have assumed that organizations produce their inventory in a completed form for sale to their customers without an intermediate market for partially completed products. The manufacturing process for some products involves numerous steps where products exist in various stages of completion. In some industries, external markets exist where products can be sold at different stages of the production process. For example, in the process of manufacturing steel products, markets exist for iron ore, pellet concentrates, pig iron, rolled steel, sheets, and other intermediate forms closer to the finished product. Whenever intermediate products can be sold, a producer must decide if products should be sold in an intermediate form or processed further and sold at completion.

It is important to note that the decision to process a particular product further should consider only the incremental costs and revenues resulting from the additional processing. Any processing costs incurred prior to the additional processing are sunk costs and, therefore, are not a relevant consideration. While joint production processes were discussed previously, this section focuses on management's decision about further processing.

To illustrate the additional processing decision, assume that LawnMasters occasionally removes trees as part of its landscaping services at an average price of $200 per tree removal. LawnMasters estimates that the cost to remove each tree (including labor, equipment, and disposal costs) is approximately $50. These trees are then sold to non-competitors for use in manufacturing mulch and other compost products at an average price of $50 per tree. LawnMasters is currently considering the alternative of processing these trees itself to produce its own mulch products. This would provide a savings of $5 per bag of mulch that it currently pays to external suppliers. In order to process these trees, LawnMasters would need to lease equipment at a cost of $1,000 per month. If LawnMasters removes 20 trees per month, and each tree yields 50 bags of mulch, the relevant costs and revenues associated with each of these alternatives are shown below:

	Sell Trees	Process Trees into Mulch
Incremental Revenues:		
$50 x 20 trees	$1,000	
$5 x 20 trees x 50 bags		$5,000
Incremental Costs:		
Cost of equipment	0	(1,000)
	$1,000	$4,000

---

[14] C.R. Skousen and F.A. Condie, "Eliminating a Sports Program: Goalposts vs. Test Tubes," *Management Accounting* (November 1988), 43–49.

The above analysis reveals three relevant costs and revenues: (1) the $1,000 that would be received upon the sale of removed trees, (2) the $5,000 that could be saved by LawnMasters if it produced its own mulch,[15] and (3) the rental of equipment for $1,000. It is clear that the most profitable course of action would be for LawnMasters to process removed trees, since doing so provides an incremental contribution to net income of $3,000 ($4,000 of income if trees are processed – $1,000 of income if trees are sold = $3,000).

Notice that the analysis does not consider the revenue earned from the removal of trees of $4,000 (20 trees x $200 per tree = $4,000) or the costs associated with the removal of these trees of $1,000 (20 trees x $50 per tree = $1,000). These costs do not differ between alternatives and, therefore, are not relevant to this particular decision.

MAKE-OR-BUY DECISIONS

Many products are comprised of a wide variety and nature of component parts. To illustrate, the parts of an automobile include the frame, engine, seats and upholstery, windows and windshields, radio/cassette deck/compact disc player, tires, and many, many more. Many of these components involve specialized assembly or technology and are normally purchased from external suppliers. For example, General Motors normally purchases its radios/cassette decks/compact disc players from companies that specialize in the production of these products. Other component parts (such as the shaped glass for windows and windshields) could be purchased externally or manufactured internally. Assuming that management has the capability and the capacity to produce component parts, an important decision must be made about whether to produce the component part internally or purchase it from an external supplier. The choice between internally-produced parts and purchased parts is often referred to as a "make-or-buy decision." The costs of the various alternatives is summarized below.

Costs to "Make"	*Costs to "Buy"*
Incremental Production Costs (normally variable production costs and incremental fixed costs)	Invoice price along with other costs incurred (such as freight, insurance, and ordering costs)

Notice that the costs of the "make" alternative include only the incremental costs needed to manufacture the component part. Allocated fixed costs that remain unchanged in total when components are produced are not relevant to make-or-buy decisions, as these costs do not differ between the two alternatives (make the component part or buy the component part).

An important decision faced by all types of organizations is the *outsourcing decision* (also referred to as a *make-or-buy decision* when the decision relates to manufacturing versus purchasing a component part). These decisions consider the alternatives of the organization in manufacturing components or providing services itself versus contracting with external providers or suppliers for the components or services. In general, the outsourcing decision should be based on the total costs of manufacturing/providing products or services versus the total costs of purchasing these products or services externally. Assuming that quality or opportunity costs are not a consideration (discussed later), the organization should choose the least expensive alternative.

To illustrate, assume that LawnMasters is considering the possibility of outsourcing a part of its lawn irrigation services. Specifically, Peter Casey has noticed that it requires his crews four hours per lawn (at an average cost of $15 per labor hour) to wire the irrigation systems to allow the use of a programmed timer. He has received an offer from a non-competitor to wire irrigation systems at a cost of $180 per lawn. To evaluate this offer, Peter requested that his accountant provide him with an analysis of the actual costs of wiring an irrigation system. This cost is summarized below:

Direct materials (timer and wire)	$ 5
Direct labor (4 hours x $15 per hour)	60
Variable overhead	5
Supervision and checking	100
Fixed overhead	18
Total cost per lawn	$ 188

---

[15] An alternative way of classifying the $5,000 would be as a cost savings. However, the classification of this item does not alter the decision that would be made by LawnMasters or the process used to make this decision.

Initially, it appears that LawnMasters should outsource the wiring services, since the total cost of LawnMasters doing it ($188 per system) exceeds the cost charged by the electrician ($180 per system). However, Peter began to consider the nature of the wiring costs. The direct materials, direct labor, and variable overhead costs are all costs that could be totally eliminated if LawnMasters did not wire the irrigation systems itself. On the other hand, the fixed overhead costs are different. These costs ($118 per lawn) include two major types of costs that have been allocated based on the anticipated number of lawn irrigation systems typically installed by LawnMasters in a given year:

- The salary paid to employees who supervise and check the wiring process and demonstrate the use of the automated timer to the customer. LawnMasters pays $50,000 to the employees who supervise the wiring of approximately 500 irrigation systems. Thus, the fixed labor cost per system is $100 ($50,000 ÷ 500 systems). Because the work of these employees is related to checking the wiring and demonstrating the use of the timer, this cost could not be eliminated if the wiring services were outsourced.

- Depreciation of equipment and supplies used to install irrigation systems. These costs are allocated to various activities based on the relative time spent in each of the major activities in installing irrigation systems (planning and blueprinting, trenching, cutting and laying pipe, and wiring the irrigation system). Because depreciation relates to equipment and supplies already purchased, none of these costs ($18 per irrigation system) would be saved if the wiring services were outsourced.

After giving this further consideration, Peter produced the analysis shown below:

	"Make"	"Buy"
Cost to wire systems:		
Direct materials	$ 5	
Direct labor	60	
Variable overhead	5	
Supervision and checking	100	
Cost to outsource		$180
Total cost	$170	$180

From the above, it is apparent that LawnMasters should continue to wire the irrigation systems itself, since the incremental cost ($170 per irrigation system) is less than the cost of outsourcing this function ($180 per irrigation system). Notice that the allocated fixed costs of $18 per lawn for depreciation on equipment and supplies is not considered in this analysis, since it would not be "saved" if the services were outsourced. Accordingly, the relevant costs in this scenario are the costs of materials, labor, variable overhead, and avoidable fixed overhead (salaries paid to individuals directly involved in the wiring process).

Alternative Use of Capacity

Decisions to manufacture or purchase component parts hinge upon the availability of capacity. If other uses for the resources currently used to produce the component parts exist, these uses should be considered before reaching a final decision.

Qualitative Considerations

To this point, the quantitative factors involved with make-or-buy decisions have been emphasized. However, it is important to note that make-or-buy decisions often hinge upon qualitative considerations as well. The decision to manufacture one or more component parts reduces an organization's dependence upon suppliers and insures a smoother flow of component parts for its production schedule.

Alternatively, manufacturing component parts may place the organization at a disadvantage in situations where an emergency situation dictates that the parts be obtained externally. This disadvantage results from the failure of the organization to develop strong relationships with its suppliers.

General Motors (GM) is a recent example of a company facing important make-or-buy decisions.

> In the early 1990s, the mass production techniques used to assemble steering columns in its Saginaw, Michigan plant resulted in high costs, and GM considered the use of outside suppliers. Recent improvements have at least temporarily resulted in GM continuing to use the Saginaw plant to supply its assembly plants with steering columns. However, GM says it must continue to retain the right to subcontract work to cheaper outside suppliers in order to remain competitive with Ford Motor Co. and Chrysler Corp., both of which rely almost exclusively on outside suppliers.
>
> GM is faced with an interesting dilemma in the form of a make-or-buy decision. While GM could purchase certain parts used to assemble seatbelts from a lower-cost external supplier, contracts with the United Automobile Workers guarantee that GM's assembly workers are paid regardless of whether these component parts are being produced. Thus, GM cannot "save" the wages paid to assembly workers if these parts are purchased externally. As Joseph Paul (an analyst for Sanford C. Bernstein) notes, "(GM) actually can reduce cost by not buying from the low-cost producer."[16]
>
> GM's use of internal parts-making operations results in a higher cost per automobile compared to Ford Motor Co. and Chrysler Corp. For each one million vehicles, GM employs 34,200 parts-plant workers compared to 18,800 for Ford and 18,200 for Chrysler. The lower cost paid by Ford and Chrysler to outside labor (less than half of the $43 per hour paid to United Auto Workers laborers) allows these manufacturers to produce an automobile for $443 and $598 less than GM, respectively.[17]
>
> Saturn, a division of General Motors (GM), is increasing its reliance on external suppliers for parts used in manufacturing its automobiles. Forty-five of the 152 parts on the 1996 SL 2 sedan were manufactured by GM parts plants. In contrast, GM plans to obtain only five of the 164 major parts for the 1997 model from GM plants.[18]

Other recent examples of outsourcing decisions follow:

> During the 1999 Christmas season, eToys, the online retailer specializing in children's toys, outsourced its packing and shipping to Federated Department Store's Fingerhut Companies. While this arrangement reduced eToys's costs (referred to as fulfillment costs), poor performance by Fingerhut resulted in a number of orders not being delivered on time. The dissatisfaction related to these late deliveries was at least partially responsible for continued poor results for eToys during 2000.[19]
>
> Cisco Systems, a leading manufacturer of routers and other computer equipment, purchases most of its inventory from Jabil Circuit, Inc. Jabil saves Cisco 30% from what it would cost Cisco to assemble the product itself. Carl Redfield, Cisco's senior vice-president for manufacturing, notes that "we've cleaned up the supply chain. You don't add value by having multiple people touch a product."[20]

---

[16] "The Saginaw Solution," *Business Week* (July 15, 1996), 78.

[17] "GM's Per-Vehicle Costs Exceed Rival's Due to In-House Parts Work, Study Says," *The Wall Street Journal* (June 25, 1996), A2.

[18] "New Saturn Is Heavy on Outsourcing," *USA Today*, (July 5, 1996), B1.

[19] "The eToys Saga: Costs Kept Rising While Sales Slowed," *The Wall Street Journal* (January 22, 2001), B1, B10.

[20] "Bill Morean's $1.2 Billion Haircut," *Forbes* (June 14, 1999), 142.

Recently, U.S. automakers have adopted a new outsourcing strategy—they have begun to pressure their suppliers to do the outsourcing for them.

> In an effort to reduce their own production costs, the Big Three automakers are pressuring their suppliers to take advantage of the lower labor costs that can be realized by shifting jobs overseas. Constrained by the job-protection restrictions included in their United Auto Workers labor agreements, U.S. automakers are not free to take advantage of the opportunity to outsource their own production. They can, however, pressure their suppliers to take advantage of the lower costs that exist in foreign markets. Both General Motors and Ford Motor Company now use Chinese auto-parts suppliers' prices—prices that reflect China's average wage cost of 90 cents an hour—as global benchmark prices for component parts ranging from electric-wire cables to aluminum wheels. U.S. suppliers to the Big Three are beginning to realize that the only way they can offer competitive prices is to move some of their own jobs or subcomponent purchases to low-cost countries like China.[21]

Other Considerations

In addition to the incremental costs associated with providing services or manufacturing products, it is important to consider the alternative uses of any resources "freed up" if a service is outsourced. For example, as Peter Casey began thinking even further about the costs of wiring its irrigation systems, he realized that some of the employees' efforts could be reallocated to other jobs and LawnMasters would have the capacity to install an additional 40 irrigation systems over the year. These additional 40 irrigation systems would provide incremental net profits (beyond the variable costs associated with these jobs) of $16,000 (or $400 per system). Thus, the opportunity cost of wiring the irrigation systems can be expressed as $32 per current system ($16,000 ÷ 500 systems).

Assuming that outsourcing the wiring services would allow LawnMasters to install an additional 40 irrigation systems, the analysis should be modified to include the opportunity costs (in the form of incremental profits) associated with the use of direct labor. That is, one "cost" to LawnMasters of wiring irrigation systems is that it reduces the number of irrigation systems that could be installed. Revising the analysis, the total cost of wiring irrigation systems is now $202 (the costs incurred by LawnMasters of $170 plus the incremental profit of $32 that could be earned by installing additional systems). Since this cost exceeds the cost of outsourcing wiring services, LawnMasters should outsource the wiring function and use the employees formerly involved in wiring the irrigation systems to install additional systems.

To this point, the financial (quantitative) factors involved with outsourcing decisions have been emphasized. However, it is important to note that outsourcing decisions often hinge upon qualitative considerations as well. An advantage (irrespective of the relative costs) of LawnMasters wiring its own systems is that it is not dependent upon other parties for this service and has a better opportunity to control the quality of those services. Alternatively, to the extent that wiring irrigation systems requires specialized skills, LawnMasters may find itself too highly dependent upon a small number of employees and may experience problems if these employees depart the organization. In addition, LawnMasters may find itself unable to increase its capacity because of the lack of a critical mass of employees with these specialized skills.

The following excerpt from practice provides an example of a company that is electing not to outsource, despite the dramatic cost reductions that might result from sending work overseas.

> To Allen-Edmonds, maintaining high quality is more important than realizing the cost savings that would result from overseas manufacturing. The company, which makes small batches of men's dress shoes that sell for upwards of $200 per pair, has a loyal customer following that includes both U.S. Presidents named Bush. As an alternative to outsourcing, Allen-Edmonds is investing $1 million in factory layout redesign and computerized machinery in order to increase manufacturing efficiency. The company's president, John Stollenwerk, hopes that these improvements will enable the company to save 5 percent on each shoe—not a very impressive achievement when compared with the 60 percent that could be saved if he moved manufacturing operations to China. Allen-Edmonds remains one of the very few hold-outs in the industry. In fact, according to the American Apparel and Footwear Association, about 98.5 percent of shoes sold in the United States are now made abroad.[22]

---

[21] Norihiko Shirouzu, "Chain Reaction: Big Three's Outsourcing Plan: Make Parts Suppliers Do It," *The Wall Street Journal* (June 10, 2004), A1, A6.

[22] Aaron Nathans, "Allen-Edmonds Keeps Its Shoes on an American Factory Floor," *The New York Times* (May 29, 2004), C1.

SUMMARY

This chapter has introduced the role of the managerial accountant and managerial accounting data in the short-term decision-making process. The major points discussed in this chapter are summarized below:

1. In making decisions, management must focus on relevant information. Relevant costs (and revenues) are those costs and revenues that: pertain to the future and are expected to be incurred or earned under a given alternative and differ among the various decision alternatives under consideration. Other terms used to describe relevant costs are incremental costs and escapable (avoidable) costs.

2. Opportunity costs are defined as the benefits forgone by the organization by selecting one alternative over another. Since opportunity costs relate to the future and differ between alternatives, these costs are relevant and should be considered in the decision-making process.

3. Sunk costs are costs which have already been incurred and cannot be modified in the future. Since these costs do not represent future costs pertaining to alternative decisions, they are not relevant and should not be considered by management in the decision-making process.

4. Five types of short-term, nonrecurring decisions discussed are: (a) pricing decisions, (b) accepting or rejecting special orders, (c) continuing or discontinuing a product line, (d) selling an intermediate product or processing it further, and (e) manufacturing a component part or purchasing the component from an external supplier. Each type of decision should be evaluated based on expected cost and revenue information.

KEY DEFINITIONS

Avoidable (escapable) costs—costs which are saved or eliminated by making a particular decision or selecting a given alternative.
Contribution approach to pricing—price should be sufficient to recover variable costs.
Decision—the act of selecting a course of action from among alternatives.
Elasticity of demand—the relative change in quantity demanded caused by a change in price.
Excess capacity—the ability to accept additional orders with existing resources.
Full-cost (absorption) approach to pricing—considers both the incremental variable and fixed costs.
Incremental costs and revenues—the difference in the total costs incurred and revenues earned by the organization that results from selecting one alternative over another alternative.
Limiting factor—the resource which is in shortest supply. The limiting factor is important, since it may influence management's choice among decision alternatives.
Make or buy—the decision to produce a good (or service) internally or buy it from external sources.
Opportunity costs—the benefits forgone by rejecting one alternative in favor of the alternative selected.
Qualitative factors—non-monetary costs or benefits of alternatives.
Quantitative factors—total dollar costs and revenues associated with alternatives.
Relevant costs and revenues—costs and revenues which pertain to the future and are expected to be incurred or earned under a given alternative and differ among alternatives.
Special order—a sale at a price different than that ordinarily charged to regular customers.
Sunk costs—costs which have been incurred and cannot be changed regardless of the alternative selected. As a result, sunk costs are not considered to be relevant for decision-making purposes.

QUESTIONS

1. Define the word "decision" and identify what is necessary to make data relevant to a decision.

2. Identify the role of the accountant in the decision-making process.

3. Can decisions ever be associated with activity that has already occurred? Contrast the word "evaluation" with what this chapter defines as a "decision."

4. Identify some qualitative factors that would be associated with a decision to discontinue a product line.

5. List some historical costs and some opportunity costs associated with a decision to make component parts rather than purchase them. In what ways do opportunity costs differ from historical costs?

6. Process A can produce 65,000 units for $32,500, while Process B can produce 100,000 units for $40,000. Determine the average cost per unit for A and B, as well as the incremental cost for the extra production available from B.

7. Why are sunk costs irrelevant to all decisions?

8. Product A has a total variable cost of $20 and sells for $30, while Product B has a total variable cost of $50 and sells for $80. For which of these two products should demand first be satisfied? Why? If Product A requires two hours of labor, and Product B requires six hours of labor and only 10,000 hours of labor are available, which of these two products should be given first consideration? Why?

9. Product X is composed of $4 of variable cost and $6 of fixed cost. What price is required to recover full cost plus a profit equal to 20 percent of cost? What percentage mark-up on variable cost is required to produce the same price? What are the advantages of variable cost pricing over full cost pricing?

10. The Hardrock Salt Company currently sells 1,000,000 cases of salt per year for $2.40 per case. A 20 percent decrease in price is expected to boost volume to 1,100,000 cases per year. Should Hardrock decrease prices? Why? What one term technically describes the relationship between price and volume for Hardrock?

11. If the Hardrock Salt Company described above determined that a $0.24 per unit increase in price would reduce volume by only 50,000 units, should it increase prices? Why?

EXERCISES AND PROBLEMS

12. *Pricing Decisions—Effect of Changes in Price on Profit.* The Tassel Corporation, a manufacturer of men's shoes, is currently averaging sales of 200,000 pairs of shoes per year. The average selling price per pair of shoes is $85, while the average cost of manufacturing these shoes is $55 per pair. The sales department of Tassel Corporation estimates that unit sales could be increased by 75,000 pairs if the selling price was lowered to $60 per pair. From estimates received from the manufacturing department, Tassel believes that the production costs would decrease to $50 per pair at a production level of 275,000 units (the level of production anticipated if the price per pair of shoes was lowered to $60).

    Required:

    If Tassel lowered the selling price of its shoes to $60 per pair, how would this decision affect overall profitability?

13. *Pricing Decisions—Effect of Changes in Price on Profit.* Cramp, Inc. manufactures running shoes as its primary inventory product. Cramp's current sales are at 125,000 pairs per year at an average selling price of $70 per pair. The production cost of these running shoes is approximately $50 per pair. Recent market surveys indicate that if the average selling price was lowered to $60 per pair, total unit sales could be increased to 150,000 pairs per year. The increased production would lower the average production cost to $45 per pair, due mostly to the allocation of fixed production costs.

    Required:

    a. How would lowering the selling price of the running shoes affect Cramp, Inc.'s profitability?
    b. Should Cramp, Inc. decide to lower its selling prices?

14. *Pricing Decisions.* The Reduction Gear Company produces and sells its standard product to machinery manufacturers in the Southeastern United States. Each gear sells for $30, and total sales approximate 600,000 units each year. During the current budget year, variable production and distribution costs are expected to reach $18 per unit, while expected fixed production and distribution costs will amount to

$6,000,000 (or $10 per unit for 600,000 units). Reduction received an offer from a foreign manufacturer to purchase 50,000 units. Domestic sales would not be affected by this transaction. If the offer is accepted, variable distribution costs will increase $2 per unit for insurance, shipping, and import duties. Fixed costs will be unaffected since Reduction has excess capacity.

Required:

If Reduction desires a minimum contribution of $3 per unit on foreign sales, what is the lowest price that it would consider for this special order?

15. *Pricing Decisions.* Gyro Gear Company produces a special gear used in automatic transmissions. Each gear sells for $28, and the company sells approximately 500,000 gears each year. Unit cost data for 20x3 are presented below:

Direct Material	$6	
Direct Labor	5	

Other Costs:	Variable	Fixed
Manufacturing	$2	$7
Distribution	4	3

Gyro has received an offer from a foreign manufacturer to purchase 25,000 gears. Domestic sales would be unaffected by this transaction. If the offer is accepted, variable distribution costs will increase $1.50 per gear for insurance, shipping, and import duties. What is the dollar amount of the unit cost that is relevant to a pricing decision on this offer?

16. *Pricing Decisions.* Berg and Sons builds custom-made pleasure boats, which range in price from $10,000 to $250,000. For the past thirty years, Mr. Berg, Sr. has determined the selling price of each boat by estimating the costs of material, labor, and a prorated portion of overhead and adding 20 percent to these estimated costs.

For example, a recent price quotation was determined as follows:

Direct Materials	$ 5,000
Direct Labor	8,000
Overhead	2,000
	$15,000
Plus 20%	3,000
Selling Price	$18,000

    The overhead figure was determined by estimating total overhead costs for the year and allocating them at 25 percent of direct labor.
    If a customer rejected the price and business was slack, Mr. Berg, Sr. would often be willing to reduce his markup to as little as 5 percent over estimated costs. Thus, average markup for the year is estimated at 15 percent.
    Mr. Berg, Jr. believes that the contribution margin approach to pricing would be helpful in determining the selling prices of their custom-made pleasure boats.
    Total overhead, which includes selling and administrative expenses for the year has been estimated at $150,000, of which $90,000 is fixed and the remainder is variable in direct proportion to direct labor.

Required:

a. Assume that the customer in the example rejected the $18,000 quotation and also rejected a $15,750 quotation (5% markup) during a slack period. The customer countered with a $15,000 offer.

1. What is the difference in net income for the year between accepting or rejecting the customer's offer?
2. What is the minimum selling price Mr. Berg, Jr. could have quoted without reducing or increasing net income?

b. What advantages does the contribution margin approach to pricing have over the approach used by Mr. Berg, Sr.?

c. What pitfalls are there, if any, to contribution margin pricing?

17. *Pricing Decisions.* Costello and Costello Company paves driveways for residential homes. The average driveway costs about $5,000 to pave as determined below:

Direct materials	$2,500
Direct labor	1,500
Overhead	1,000
	$5,000

The overhead cost includes both fixed and variable costs and it is always allocated to each job by multiplying two-thirds times direct labor. Total overhead for the year is $50,000, of which $40,000 is fixed. The remainder is variable and is directly proportional to direct labor.

Mr. Costello has always used a direct markup of 25% on full costs in the past, but his wife believes he should change his pricing strategy to the contribution margin approach. He has extra time and capacity to do more jobs than he gets orders for, so he decides to listen to what his wife has to say.

Currently, a customer has offered to pay $4,800 to have his driveway paved. This driveway is what Mr. Costello defines as an "average" driveway and, therefore, he usually charges $6,250 for the job (25% x $5,000) + $5,000.

Required:

a. Taking his wife's advice, what is the minimum selling price which could be charged if Mr. Costello used the contribution margin approach to pricing
b. Should Mr. Costello pave this customer's driveway for $4,800?

(CMA adapted)

18. *Pricing Decisions.* The Feel Better While You Live Company produces a high protein drink and vitamins A, C, and E. With changing market conditions, the company has hired you to evaluate the current pricing strategy for these products. The following information is available:

	High Protein Drink	Vitamins A	Vitamins C	Vitamins E
Demand (in packages)	1,000,000	1,250,000	2,500,000	750,000
Current Sales Price (per package)	$7.98	$2.95	$1.95	$3.95
Variable Costs (per package)	$2.45	$0.51	$0.65	$0.74

Fixed Costs	
Plant and Equipment Depreciation	$ 2,450,000
Manufacturing Overhead	3,950,000
Selling and Administrative	3,780,000
Total	$10,180,000

Note—Fixed costs are distributed as follows: 56 percent to the high-protein drink, 12 percent to Vitamin A, 15 percent to Vitamin C, and 17 percent to Vitamin E. (Assume that these fixed costs are directly related to the products as indicated. Thus, if a product is dropped, so are its fixed costs.)

Required:

a. What would be the minimum price for short-run and long-run operations?
b. Which product, if any, should be dropped if demand increases 30 percent for the high protein drink and 12 percent for each of the vitamins (assuming there is no loss in disposing of fixed assets)?
c. What is your evaluation of the current pricing strategy, given the available information?
d. Given the current pricing policy, how much profit will this company make?

19. *Incremental Costs and Revenues—Additional Production.* The Majic Corporation is currently producing 90,000 units of inventory per year. Shown below are relevant cost and selling price data for the most recent period (20x1):

Selling Price	$25.00 per unit
Variable Manufacturing Costs	9.00 per unit
Fixed Manufacturing Costs	800,000
Variable Selling Expense	0.50 per unit
Fixed Selling Expense	200,000

Majic's marketing department estimates that an additional 15,000 units could be sold per year if production was increased. The additional production requirements would be within the plant's present capacity.

Required:

Determine the incremental revenue and costs that would result from the additional production and state whether Majic should produce the additional units.

20. *Incremental Costs and Revenues—Additional Production.* James Company has been producing 10,000 units of its product per year and has the capacity to produce an additional 2,000 units per year. The marketing department believes that the additional units could be sold at current prices if they were produced. James Company has the following cost structure:

Selling Price	$9.00 per unit
Variable Manufacturing Costs	1.20 per unit
Fixed manufacturing Costs	50,000
Variable Selling Expense	0.30 per unit
Fixed Selling Expense	20,000

Required:

a. What are the incremental revenues associated with the additional production?
b. What are the incremental costs associated with the additional production?
c. Based on the answers to (a) and (b) above, should the James Company decide to manufacture the additional units?

21. *Incremental Costs and Revenues.* Allen Tool Company is making plans for the coming year. Management feels that a target profit of $425,000 before income taxes would represent a satisfactory continuation of their growth pattern of earnings, which has been a steady 7 percent over the last six years. Marketing management has studied the market for the coming year and predicted the following sales possibilities.

	Selling Price	Advertising	Unit Sales
Alternative A	$5.00	No change	1,000,000
Alternative B	5.00	Up $60,000	1,120,000
Alternative C	5.50	No change	700,000
Alternative D	5.50	Up $60,000	810,000

Estimated fixed expenses for next year are $825,000, and estimated variable expenses are $3.75 per unit of product. These expense estimates do not include any changes in advertising.

Required:

a. What should the marketing strategy be?
b. Suppose that management decided to change the selling price to $5.25 and raise advertising by $45,000. If this will give unit sales of 775,000, will the target profit be achieved?

22. *Incremental Analysis—Buy New Machine or Keep Old Machine.* The Hugger Belt Company has an old machine with a book value of $12,000 and a current salvage value of $5,000. This machine is expected to operate for an additional four years, at which time it will have a salvage value of $1,000. Hugger can now purchase a new machine for $20,000; the new machine is expected to reduce operating costs by $8,000 per year for the next four years.

Required:

Prepare an incremental analysis of the alternative to "buy new machine" and the alternative to "keep old machine."

23. *Incremental Analysis.* The Davis Company has been producing 20,000 units per month but wants to begin producing 25,000 units per month (capacity is 28,000 units per month) because of an increase in demand for its product. Davis has the following cost structure:

Selling price	$1.60 per unit
Variable manufacturing costs	$.35 per unit
Fixed manufacturing costs	$15,400
Variable selling expense	5% of selling price
Fixed selling expense	$ 2,000

Required:

a. Determine the incremental revenues and costs of producing the additional units.
b. Should Davis produce the additional units?

24. *Limiting Factors of Production.* The Big Boyd Kyte Company can produce either of two models of luxurious kites. Selected information on each product is as follows:

	Model A	Model B
Sales Price per Dozen	$40	$30
Variable Manufacturing and Distribution Costs	20	10
Contribution Margin	$20	$20
Contribution Margin Ratio	50%	67%
Labor Hours per Dozen	1.5	2.5

Required:

a. If prices for kites are "elastic," which model will be most financially renumerative, assuming that prices are lowered and that there are not production constraints?
b. If only 30,000 hours are available for production, which model is preferable? Determine the incremental financial consequences of the best alternative.

25. *Special Orders.* The Johnson Manufacturing Company receives an order for 10,000 units at $15 each from a new customer. The product will be slightly modified and will bear the trade name of the purchaser so as to differentiate it from the same products sold to regular customers. These modifications will not affect the direct production costs of the product. Management expects to incur its regular $12 unit variable cost for each unit produced under this special order. In addition, the customer demands that management absorb the $5,000 cost of freight to deliver the finished product. Since Johnson currently is working at 100 percent of

capacity, regular production will be reduced by 10,000 units if the special order is accepted. The contribution margin on existing production is $3 per unit.

Required:

Should Johnson accept the order? Why or why not?

26. *Special Orders.* The Hubbard Corporation receives an order for 10,000 units, conditional upon receiving a 50 percent discount from the regular price. Hubbard normally sells its product at $40 per unit. Production and distribution costs normally amount to $10 variable cost and $25 fixed cost per unit, and normal volume is 30,000 units. Excess capacity for additional production is available.

Required:

What are the financial consequences of accepting this order? What additional factors should be considered before a final decision is made?

27. *Special Orders.* A valued custom parts customer has asked Mr. Jackson if he would manufacture 5,000 special units for him. Mr. Jackson is working at capacity and would have to give up some other business in order to accept the special order. He can't renege on custom orders already accepted, but he could reduce the output of his standard product by about one-half for one year while producing the specially requested custom part. The customer is willing to pay $7 for each part. The material cost will be about $2 per unit, and the labor will be $3.60 per unit. Mr. Jackson will have to spend $2,000 for a special device which will be discarded when the job is done. Variable production costs for existing customers is $4 per unit, and the current price is $6.50. Fixed cost per unit at capacity is $.42 per unit.

Required:

a. Calculate the following costs related to the 5,000-unit custom order:
   1. The incremental cost of the order.
   2. The full cost of the order.
   3. The opportunity cost of rejecting the order.
b. Should Mr. Jackson take the order? Explain your answer.

28. *Special Orders.* The Divot Corp. has annual sales of 1,000 sets of golf clubs. The production cost of these clubs includes fixed costs of $110,000 and variable costs of $150 per set. Divot manufactures only one model of golf clubs, and its selling price is $300 per set. Divot has the production capacity to produce an additional 200 sets of clubs without purchasing any additional production equipment. Therefore, total fixed production costs will remain at the current level unless more than 200 additional sets of clubs are manufactured. Divot has just received an offer from a regional distributor to buy an additional 100 sets of clubs for $225 per set.

Required:

a. Should Divot accept this order?
b. If Divot does not have the excess capacity, should it accept the order?

29. *Special Orders.* The Bowhead Company sells 200,000 bows annually. They have fixed production costs of $500,000 and variable production costs of $2 per bow. Bowhead could produce an additional 50,000 bows with its current production facility if the demand were present. The company recently received an offer from a large national department store to buy 40,000 bows at a selling price of $1.75 per bow, which is below its normal selling price of $5 per bow.

Required:

a. Should Bowhead accept this order?
b. If Bowhead does not have the excess capacity, should it accept the order?

30. *Special Orders.* The Memphis Company produces and sells 75,000 units of its inventory each year. Shown below is the income statement for the Memphis Company:

Sales		$750,000
Variable Costs:		
Direct Material	$200,000	
Direct Labor..	90,000	
Overhead..	300,000	
Selling...	15,000	
Shipping..	20,000	(625,000)
Contribution Margin.....................................		$125,000
Fixed Overhead		(70,000)
Fixed Selling and		
Administrative Expenses.....................		(30,000)
Net Income before Taxes...........................		$25,000

A company that is not within Memphis's normal selling region has offered to purchase 15,000 units of Memphis's inventory for $9.50 per unit. While this price is below the price normally charged by Memphis to its customers, the purchaser will supply its own shipping and Memphis will not have to pay sales commissions.

Required:

Should Memphis accept this offer? Provide calculations to support your answer.

31. *Special Order.* The Squeak-E Tennis Shoe Company sells 20,000 pairs of tennis shoes annually. The company has fixed costs of $38,000 and direct costs of $6.00 per pair. The shoes sell for $9.00 per pair. Squeak-E has a capacity of 5,000 in excess of the 20,000 pairs of shoes it sells annually. The company has just received an offer from a company outside its present sales territory to buy 4,500 pairs of tennis shoes for $6.25 per pair.

Required:

a. Should Squeak-E accept this order?
b. If Squeak-E did not have the excess capacity, should it accept the order?

Sales		$450,000
Variable Costs:		
Material	$100,000	
Labor	140,000	
Overhead	70,000	
Selling	13,500	
Shipping	25,000	(348,500)
Contribution Margin		$101,500
Fixed Overhead		(30,000)
Fixed Selling and Administrative Expenses..		(42,000)
Net Income before Taxes............................		$ 29,500

32. *Special Order.* The Shelby Company normally produces and sells 50,000 units per year but has the capacity to produce 75,000 units per year. Last year the company had the following income:
    Shelby Company does not expect these relationships to change this year. Another company that is not within Shelby's selling area has offered to buy 20,000 units at $6.90 per unit. Since there will be no salesmen involved, Shelby will not have to pay the sales commissions.

Required:

Determine whether Shelby should sell these units at $6.90. Give the incremental profit or loss if the extra units are sold.

33. *Special Orders.* George Jackson operates a small machine shop. He manufactures one standard product available from many other similar businesses, and he also manufactures products to customer order. His accountant prepared the annual income statement shown below:

	Custom Sales	Standard Sales	Total
Sales	$50,000	$25,000	$75,000
Material	$10,000	$ 8,000	$18,000
Labor	20,000	9,000	29,000
Depreciation	6,300	3,600	9,900
Power	700	400	1,100
Rent	6,000	1,000	7,000
Heat and Light	600	100	700
Other	400	900	1,300
	$44,000	$23,000	$67,000
	$ 6,000	$ 2,000	$ 8,000

The depreciation charges are for machines used in the respective product lines. The power charge is apportioned on the estimate of power consumed. The rent is for the building space which has been leased for ten years at $7,000 per year. The rent and heat and light are apportioned to the product lines based on amount of floor space occupied. All other costs are current expenses identified with the product line causing them.

A valued custom parts customer has asked Mr. Jackson if he would manufacture 5,000 units for him. Mr. Jackson is working at capacity and would have to give up some other business in order to take this special order. He can't renege on custom orders already agreed to, but he could reduce the output of his standard product by about one-half for one year while producing the specially requested custom part. The customer is willing to pay $7 for each part. The material cost will be about $2 per unit and the labor will be $3.60 per unit. Mr. Jackson will have to spend $2,000 for a special device which will be discarded when the job is done.

Required:

a. Calculate and present the following costs related to the 5,000-unit custom order:
   1. The incremental cost of the order.
   2. The full cost of the order.
   3. The opportunity cost of taking the order.
   4. The sunk costs related to the order.
b. Should Mr. Jackson take the order? Explain your answer.

(CMA adapted)

34. *Special Orders.* Anchor Company manufactures several different styles of jewelry cases. Management estimates that during the third quarter of 20x1 the company will be operating at 80 percent of normal capacity. Because the company desires a higher utilization of plant capacity, the company will consider a special order.

Anchor has received special order inquiries from two companies. The first order is from JCP Inc., which would like to market a jewelry case similar to one of Anchor's cases. The JCP jewelry case would be marketed under JCP's own label. JCP Inc. has offered Anchor $5.75 per jewelry case for 20,000 cases to be shipped by October 1, 20x1. The cost data for the Anchor jewelry case that is similar to the specifications of the JCP special order are as follows:

Regular Selling Price per Unit	$9.00
Cost per Unit:	
Raw Materials	$2.50
Direct Labor (.5 hrs. @ $6)	3.00
Overhead (.25 machine hrs. @ $4)	1.00
Total Costs	$6.50

According to the specifications provided by JCP Inc., the special-order case requires less expensive raw materials. Consequently, the raw materials will only cost $2.25 per case. Management has estimated that the remaining costs, labor time, and machine time will be the same as for the Anchor jewelry case.

The second special order was submitted by the Krage Co for 7,500 jewelry cases at $7.50 per case. These jewelry cases, as with the JCP cases, would be marketed under the Krage label and have to be shipped by October 1, 20x1. However, the Krage jewelry case is different from any jewelry case in the Anchor line. The estimated per unit costs of this case are as follows:

Raw Materials	$3.25
Direct Labor (.5 hrs. @ $6)	3.00
Overhead (.5 machine hrs. @ $4)	2.00
Total Costs	$8.25

In addition, Anchor will incur $1,500 in additional set-up costs and will have to purchase a $2,500 special device to manufacture these cases. This device will be discarded once the special order is completed.

The Anchor manufacturing capabilities are limited to the total machine hours available. The plant capacity under normal operations is 90,000 machine hours per year or 7,500 machine hours per month. The budgeted fixed overhead for 20x1 amounts to $216,000. All manufacturing overhead costs are applied to production on the basis of machine hours at $4 per hour.

Anchor will have the entire third quarter to work on the special orders. Management does not expect any repeat sales to be generated from either special order. Company practice precludes Anchor from subcontracting any portion of an order when special orders are not expected to generate repeat sales.

Required:

Should Anchor Company accept either special order? Justify your answer and show your calculations.

(CMA adapted)

35. *Decision to Process Further.* The Tinka Toy Company has a large inventory of a specific type of toy that is deemed to be obsolete and, thus, unsaleable at its current price. The recorded value of this inventory is $50,000. Tinka may either modify the toys at an additional cost of $15,000 or sell them to a competitor in their current state for $5,000. The costs of modification include the cost of purchasing new equipment for $10,000; the new equipment could be sold after the toy modification for $5,000. If Tinka modifies the toys, the total expected net sales revenue would be $40,000.

Required:

a. Should Tinka sell the toys in their present state or modify them?
b. Identify any incremental costs, incremental revenues, and sunk costs that exist in this example.

36. *Decision to Process Further.* The Dale Corporation recently experienced uninsured losses caused by Hurricane Jody. After conducting a physical count of its inventory, management was faced with the decision to either remachine inventory with a book value of $80,000 for an additional $35,000 or sell the inventory as scrap for $8,000. If remachined, Dale could sell the items for a total of $50,000.

Required:

What should the management of Dale do?

37. *Decision to Process Further.* Dude Company recently uncovered a scheme perpetrated by one of its disgruntled employees that destroyed $100,000 of its inventory. Management has the option of either selling the inventory as scrap for $10,000 or reworking it for an additional $40,000, which would yield sales proceeds of $60,000.

Required:

How would you advise Dude Company to proceed?

38. *Decision to Process Further.* The Softwood Coffin Company has been unable to sell 8,000 coffins made of knotty pine. These coffins have an average cost of $69 each and were priced at a mere $247. Management is considering the following alternatives:

   1. Place legs on the coffins after removing lids and rails, and sell them as flower troughs. The cost of additional work and advertising will amount to $80,000, and the expected sales price is $100 per unit.
   2. Continue selling coffins at a reduced price of $150 even though the opportunity costs associated with the space amounts to $50 per unit.
   3. Sell them for firewood for an immediate return of $480,000.
   4. Keep them and do nothing new.

   Required:

   Determine the financial consequences of the best alternative.

39. *Decision to Process Further.* From a particular joint process, Watkins Company produces three products: X, Y, and Z. Each product may be sold at the point of split-off or processed further. Additional processing requires no special facilities, and production costs of further processing are entirely variable and traceable to the products involved. In 20x3, all three products were processed beyond split-off. Joint product costs for the year were $60,000. Sales values and costs needed to evaluate Watkins' 20x3 production policy follow: Joint costs are allocated to the products in proportion to the relative physical volume of output.

   Required:

Product	Units Produced	Sales Values at Split-Off	Additional Costs and Sales Values If Processed Further	
			Sales Values	Added Costs
X	6,000	$25,000	$42,000	$9,000
Y	4,000	41,000	45,000	7,000
Z	2,000	24,000	32,000	8,000

   a. For units of Z, what dollar amount of cost is most relevant to a sell-or-process-further decision?
   b. To maximize profits, Watkins should subject which products to additional processing? Determine the total profits from this product mix.

40. *Decision to Process Further.* The Easy Sleep Company is a large manufacturer of waterbeds. Unfortunately, due to the current water shortage, waterbeds have been forbidden by law. Easy Sleep has a $60,000 inventory of waterbeds at the present time. Easy Sleep must make a decision to either sell the waterbeds as scrap for a total of $5,000 or modify the beds to be sold as life rafts. The modification will cost a total of $12,000, which includes the purchase of a special machine. (This machine will be sold after the modifications are finished for $3,000.) The total sales expected from the life rafts are $16,000 less 10% sales commissions.

   Required:

   Should Easy Sleep modify the beds or sell them as scrap?

41. Decision to Continue Product. The Trypod Company reported the following data for the most recent period:

	Products			
	A	B	C	Total
Revenue	$400,000	$300,000	$800,000	$1,500,000
Variable Cost	$200,000	$100,000	$300,000	$ 600,000
Discretionary Fixed Cost	100,000	100,000	200,000	400,000
Committed Fixed Cost	150,000	110,000	100,000	360,000
Total Cost	$450,000	$310,000	$600,000	$1,360,000
Profit (loss)	$ (50,000)	$ (10,000)	$200,000	$ 140,000

Required:

a. Determine the financial consequences of discontinuing Product A, Product B, and both Products A and B.
b. The space currently occupied by Products A and B can be rented for $120,000 and $60,000, respectively. Which products, if any, should be discontinued?
c. List some qualitative factors that should be considered in the decision to discontinue a product line.

42. Decision to Continue Department. The Hermanson Company has three operating divisions: X, Y, and Z. Monthly division income statements are prepared and serve as the basis for evaluating division performance. The current month's figures, shown below in thousands of dollars, continue to indicate a trend in operations. For the past several periods, Division Y has performed at a loss. Management is considering the discontinuance of Division Y. Determine the financial consequences of discontinuing operations of Division Y.

	Departments			
	X	Y	Z	Total
Revenue	$200	$300	$400	$900
Variable Costs	120	230	250	600
Contribution Margin	$ 80	$ 70	$150	$300
Fixed Costs:				
Separable	$ 30	$ 40	$ 60	$130
Allocated	40	40	40	120
Total Fixed Costs	$ 70	$ 80	$100	$250
Net Income	$ 10	$ (10)	$ 50	$ 50

43. Decision to Continue Department. Presented below is the 20x1 income statement for Buster, Inc. that has been prepared by its accountants. All fixed expenses are allocated in an arbitrary manner to each department.

	Department A	Department B	Department C
Sales	$200,000	$125,000	$145,000
Variable Cost of Goods Sold	(125,000)	(90,000)	(80,000)
Variable Selling	(15,000)	(10,000)	(15,000)
Contribution Margin	$ 60,000	$ 25,000	$ 50,000
Fixed Manufacturing Expenses	(30,000)	(20,000)	(25,000)
Fixed Selling Expenses	(15,000)	(15,000)	(10,000)
Net Income	$ 15,000	$(10,000)	$ 15,000

Required:

Advise executive management on the future of Department B.

44. *Decision to Continue Department.* The following information was made available concerning the four departments of the Roast Company.

	Dept. A	Dept. B	Dept. C	Dept. D
Sales	$100,000	$20,000	$50,000	$70,000
Variable Cost of Goods Sold	70,000	10,000	30,000	45,000
Contribution Margin from Manufacturing	$ 30,000	$10,000	$20,000	$25,000
Operating Expenses:				
Fixed Expenses	20,000	4,000	10,000	15,000
Variable Selling Expenses	10,000	3,000	6,000	12,000
Net Income (Loss)	$ 0	$ 3,000	$4,000	($2,000)

Chuck Roast, the president of the company, has decided that one department must be dropped. Fixed expenses have been arbitrarily assigned according to the sales of each department. No matter which department is dropped, the company's fixed expenses will be reduced by one-fourth.

Required:

Which department should be dropped so as to give the greatest benefit to the company? What will be the company's income?

45. *Decision to Continue Product Line.* The 20x1 income statement for the King Company is shown below. This income statement separately presents revenues and expenses for each of King's three main inventory products: X, XX, and XXX. Fixed production costs are allocated arbitrarily to each of these products. Fixed costs cannot be reduced unless all three products are not manufactured.

	X	XX	XXX
Sales	$100,000	$62,500	$72,500
Variable Cost of Goods Sold	(60,000)	(30,000)	(35,000)
Variable Selling Expenses	(15,000)	(10,000)	(15,000)
Contribution Margin	$ 25,000	$22,500	$22,500
Fixed Expenses	(30,000)	(5,000)	(10,000)
Net Income	$ (5,000)	$17,500	$12,500

Required:

Because of the loss incurred on Product X, management is considering discontinuing this product line. Is this decision correct? Why or why not?

46. *Decision to Continue Department.* Stonewall Corp. operates four departments within its organization with fixed expenses being arbitrarily allocated between these departments. The management of Stonewall has decided that one of the departments must be dropped to reduce the fixed costs that the company incurs. It is estimated that fixed expenses will be reduced by 20 percent if any of the four departments is discontinued, regardless of the specific department that is eliminated. The following information represents the net income data for these departments:

	Department A	Department B	Department C	Department D
Sales	$100,000	$200,000	$310,000	$90,000
Variable Cost of Goods Sold	(60,000)	(90,000)	(220,000)	(50,000)
Contribution Margin	$ 40,000	$110,000	$ 90,000	$40,000
Fixed Expenses	(30,000)	(110,000)	(95,000)	(25,000)
Net Income	$ 10,000	0	($ 5,000)	$15,000

Required:

Determine which department should be dropped based upon the information given above.

47. *Decision to Continue Product.* Ralph Company sells three products. Product B has yielded a net loss of $10,000 for the past three years, and there is no reason to expect a change in the future. Company officials also feel that the sales of the three products are not interrelated. Fixed expenses are allocated equally among the products in determining product profitability. Total annual fixed expenses are $42,000. Company records show:

	Product A	Product B	Product C
Contribution margin per unit	$6.50	$4.00	$7.00
Net income (loss)	$13,000	($10,000)	$16,000

Required:

Based on the information given, should Product B be dropped?

(AICPA adapted)

48. *Decision to Continue Product.* The officers of Bradshaw Company are reviewing the profitability of the company's four products and the potential effect of several proposals for varying the product mix. An excerpt from the income statement and other data follow:

	Totals	Product P	Product Q	Product R	Product S
Sales	$62,000	$10,000	$18,000	$12,000	$22,000
Cost of Goods Sold	44,274	4,750	7,056	13,968	18,500
Gross Profit	$18,326	$ 5,250	$10,944	$ (1,368)	$ 3,500
Operating Expenses	12,012	1,990	2,976	2,826	4,220
Income before Income Taxes	$ 6,314	$ 3,260	$ 7,968	$ (4,194)	$ (720)
Units Sold		1,000	1,200	1,800	2,000
Sales Price per Unit		$ 10.00	$ 15.00	$ 7.00	$ 11.00
Variable Cost of Goods Sold per Unit		$ 2.50	$ 3.00	$ 6.50	$ 6.00
Variable Operating Expenses per Unit		$ 1.17	$ 1.25	$ 1.00	$ 1.20

Required:

Each of the following proposals is to be considered independently of the other proposals. Consider only the product changes stated in each proposal, as the activity of other products will remain stable. Ignore income taxes.

a. If Product R is discontinued, how will income be affected?
b. If Product R is discontinued, and a consequent loss of customers causes a decrease of 200 units in sales of Q, what will be the total effect on income?
c. If the sales price of R is increased to $8 and the number of units sold decreased to 1,500, what will be the total effect on income?
d. The plant in which R is produced can be utilized to produce a new product T. The total variable costs and expenses per unit of T are $8.05, and 1,600 units can be sold at $9.50 each. If T is introduced and R is discontinued, what will be the total effect on income?
e. Part of the plant in which P is produced can easily be adapted to the production of S, but changes in quantities may make changes in sales prices advisable. If production of P is reduced to 500 units (to be sold at $12 each), and production of S is increased to 2,500 units (to be sold at $10.50 each), what will be the amount of the total effect on income?
f. Production of P can be doubled by adding a second shift, but higher wages must be paid, which would increase variable cost of goods sold to $3.50 for each of the additional units. If the 1,000 additional units of P can be sold at $10 each, what will be the total effect on income?

(AICPA adapted)

49. **Make-or-Buy Decision.** Anders Manufacturing Company traditionally purchases its component part A-104, but the availability of excess capacity during the current period makes management wonder whether Anders should produce the part itself.

   Total costs and costs per unit are presented for five different cost classes. Anders can acquire these same parts from an external vendor for $30 per unit. Should Anders Company make or buy these parts?

	Cost Per Unit	Cost for 10,000 Units
Direct Material	$16	$160,000
Direct Labor	6	60,000
Variable Overhead	3	30,000
Fixed Overhead—Discretionary	3	30,000
Fixed Overhead—Committed (allocated)	4	40,000
	$32	$320,000

50. **Make-or-Buy Decision.** Costs and other data for two component parts used by Griffon Electronics are presented below:

	Part A	Part B
Direct Material	$ .40	$ 8.00
Direct Labor	1.00	4.70
Factory Overhead	4.00	2.00
Unit Cost	$5.40	$14.70
Units Needed per Year	6,000	8,000
Machine Hours per Unit	4	2
Unit Cost if Purchased	$5.00	$15.00

   In past years, Griffon has manufactured all of its required components; however, in 20x4 only 30,000 hours of otherwise idle machine time can be devoted to the production of components. Accordingly, some of the parts must be purchased from outside suppliers. In producing parts, factory overhead is applied at $1 per standard machine hour. Fixed capacity costs, which will not be affected by any make-or-buy decision, represent 60 percent of the applied overhead.

   Required:

   a. The 30,000 hours of available machine time are to be scheduled in such a way that Griffon realizes maximum potential cost savings. What is the dollar amount of the relevant unit production costs which should be considered in the decision to schedule machine time?

   b. If the allocation of machine time is based upon potential cost savings per machine hour, then how many units of each part should Griffon produce?

   (AICPA adapted)

51. **Make-or-Buy Decision.** The management of the Norway Company is currently deciding whether to continue the in-house production of one of the component parts of its product or to purchase the component from another company. The production costs of this component are as follows:

Direct Labor	$1.20 per unit
Direct Materials	2.50 per unit
Variable Overhead	2.25 per unit
Avoidable Fixed Overhead (if component is purchased)	$25,000

   Norway requires 25,000 units of this component annually. The lowest price quote for the purchase of this component is $7 per unit.

Required:

Should Norway purchase the component part or continue to produce it?

52. *Make-or-Buy Decision.* The Floyd Corporation has been buying 20,000 units of one of its component parts for $10.50 per unit. Management is currently trying to decide whether to continue this practice or begin manufacturing the component part in-house. The manufacturing department estimates the following expenses associated with manufacturing this component:

>| | |
>|---|---|
>| Direct Material | $5.00 per unit |
>| Direct Labor | 1.50 per unit |
>| Variable Overhead | 2.00 per unit |

The manufacturing department also estimates that an additional $16,000 of fixed costs would be incurred annually if the component is produced in-house.

Required:

Should Floyd continue to purchase this component or should it manufacture the component?

53. *Make-or-Buy Decision.* Woodville, Inc. has been buying one of its component parts for $6.47 per unit. The management of Woodville feels that the company could make this part with an increase in fixed costs of $27,000. They expect to need about 18,000 units per year. Variable costs per unit will be:

>| | |
>|---|---|
>| Direct materials | $2.00 |
>| Direct labor | 1.80 |
>| Variable overhead | 1.28 |

Required:

Determine whether the company should make the part or continue to purchase the part.

54. *Make-or-Buy Decision.* The Vernom Corporation, which produces and sells to wholesalers a highly successful line of summer lotions and insect repellents, has decided to diversify in order to stabilize sales throughout the year. A natural area for the company to consider is the production of winter lotions and creams to prevent dry and chapped skin.

After considerable research, a winter products line has been developed. Because of the conservative nature of the company management, Vernom's president has decided to introduce only one of the new products for this coming winter. If the product is a success, the product line will be expanded in future years.

The product selected (called Chap-off) is a lip balm that will be sold in a lipstick-type tube. The product will be sold to wholesalers in boxes of twenty-four tubes for $8 per box. Because of available capacity, no additional fixed charges will be incurred to produce the product. However, a $100,000 fixed charge will be absorbed by the product to allocate a fair share of the company's present fixed costs to the new product.

Using the estimated sales and production of 100,000 boxes of Chap-off as the standard volume, the accounting department has developed the following costs:

>| | |
>|---|---|
>| Direct Labor | $2.00 per box |
>| Direct Materials | 3.00 per box |
>| Total Overhead | 1.50 per box |
>| Total | $6.50 per box |

Vernom has approached a cosmetics manufacturer to discuss the possibility of purchasing the tubes for Chap-off. The price of the empty tubes from the cosmetics manufacturer would be $0.90 per twenty-four tubes. If the Vernom Corporation accepts the purchase proposal, it is estimated that direct labor and variable overhead costs would be reduced by 10 percent and direct material costs would be reduced by 20 percent.

Required:

a. Should the Vernom Corporation make or buy the tubes? Show calculations to support your answer.
b. What would be the maximum purchase price acceptable to the Vernom Corporation for the tubes? Support your answer.
c. Instead of sales of 100,000 boxes, revised estimates show sales volume at 125,000 boxes. At this new volume, additional equipment, at an annual rental of $10,000, must be acquired to manufacture the tubes. This incremental cost would be the only additional fixed cost required, even if sales increased to 300,000 boxes. (The 300,000 level is the goal for the third year of production.) Under these circumstances, should the Vernom Corporation make or buy the tubes? Show calculations to support your answer.
d. The company has the option of making and buying at the same time. What would be your answer to part (c) if this alternative was considered. Explain.

(CMA adapted)

Learning Objectives

Chapter 11 introduces the concept of capital budgeting and illustrates how the organization evaluates various capital projects based on different capital budgeting techniques. Studying this chapter should enable you to:

1. Define an investment decision and contrast capital budgeting with other forms of budgeting.
2. Identify how the time value of money may impact management's preferences for capital investment projects.
3. Evaluate capital investment projects using the payback method and the average (accounting) rate of return method.
4. Use two techniques that consider the time value of money (net present value method and internal time-adjusted rate of return) in evaluating alternative capital projects.
5. Identify limitations of using the net present value model to evaluate capital projects.

11

Capital Budgeting—
Search for Long-Run Alternatives

INTRODUCTION

Tim McGee and John Andrews are two college students who operate a moving service on a part-time basis. Their service specializes in moving small loads of furniture and packages over short distances. Tim and John each own small pick-up trucks that they use in their business. These trucks are now over ten years old and Tim and John are considering purchasing new trucks. Tim began their most recent conversation as follows:

Tim: You know, we should really consider buying new trucks for our business. I spent over $2,000 last year on repairs and maintenance for my truck. $2,000! I could almost make payments on a new truck with that kind of money. Plus, it would be nice to drive a new truck for a change.

John: From a business standpoint, we should only buy new trucks if the savings are greater than the cost of the trucks. Besides repairs, what other savings would we have?

Tim: Well, my truck only gets about fifteen miles per gallon of gas. These new trucks can get almost twenty miles per gallon. That seems like a big savings.

John: Let's see—we drove about 5,000 miles last year in moving furniture and packages. If we can get an extra five miles per gallon on gasoline, that would be less gas we would need to buy. We could probably save at least $200 on gasoline.

Tim: Two thousand dollars for maintenance and $200 for gas. This is really starting to add up! You know, if we buy a new truck, couldn't we also depreciate it and save money on our income taxes? There's some more savings we should consider.

John: Maybe you're right. Buying new trucks might make sense. Let's go out and price them and see what it will cost.

Previously, we discussed how managerial accounting data are used in making short-term, nonroutine decisions. These decisions included: (1) pricing the organization's inventory, (2) accepting special orders, (3) making component parts or purchasing them externally, (4) incurring costs for additional processing, and (5) discontinuing a segment or product line. While important to the organization, the short-term decisions we discussed usually involve relatively small dollar amounts to be received and paid over a fairly short time frame. In this chapter, we discuss investment decisions. Investment decisions are extremely critical to the organization, since they involve relatively large amounts of money and affect the organization over relatively long periods of time. These investment decisions are usually referred to as capital budgeting decisions.

Because of the long-term nature of capital budgeting decisions, it is important for management to carefully evaluate capital budgeting alternatives (investments). As with the short-term decisions discussed in the previous chapter, managerial accounting data play a major role in the analysis of these alternatives. Thus, an understanding of managerial accounting and the role of the managerial accountant in the decision-making process is not complete without considering how managerial accounting data are used in the capital budgeting process.

AN INTRODUCTION TO CAPITAL BUDGETING

This chapter is concerned with planning for investment decisions. Usually, investment decisions involve the acquisition of capital assets (such as plant, machinery, or equipment) in exchange for cash or some combination of cash and other considerations. When making investment decisions, companies must estimate the expected future benefits of purchasing capital assets (normally cash inflows in the form of operating cost savings)[1] and evaluate the inflows resulting from these benefits against the cost of the assets. A typical investment decision may evaluate a question such as:

> "Purchasing this machine would cost $100,000 but would save us $30,000 per year in operating costs. Should we make this purchase?"

Planning for investment decisions is commonly called *capital budgeting*. Capital budgeting differs from other forms of budgeting discussed earlier in this text (operating and financial budgeting) in three important ways. First, capital budgeting situations may occur randomly and are nonroutine. Capital budgeting decisions may arise when current capital assets become obsolete or technologically inferior, which rarely occurs at fixed intervals. In contrast, operating and financial budgets are prepared routinely. These budgets may be prepared annually, quarterly, or even monthly. Second, capital budgeting projects typically have longer lives than operating and financial budgets. Decisions to purchase capital assets may affect the company's operations for five, ten, or even more years. In contrast, operating and financial budgets rarely attempt to predict future events beyond one year. Third, the primary purpose of capital budgeting is to help managers make decisions about investment opportunities, whereas operating and financial budgets are concerned with enabling managers to plan, communicate information, coordinate operations, and evaluate performance.

Despite these differences, capital budgets share an important characteristic with operating and financial budgets. Both types of budgets deal with uncertain events that may or may not occur in the future. By its very nature, the term "budgeting" implies future events and activities. As will be seen in this chapter, capital budgeting is no different in this regard.

The capital budgeting process normally proceeds as follows:

1. The organization identifies investment opportunities. These opportunities can be decisions to: (1) invest in a particular capital project or not invest in a capital project (i.e., make no investment), or (2) invest in capital project A or invest in alternative capital projects B, C, or D.

2. The organization identifies the criteria used to evaluate the capital project(s). Common criteria include the time period over which the project(s) return the initial investment, the total return of the project(s) over their life, or the present value of the net cash inflows associated with the project(s).

3. Once the criteria used to evaluate the capital project(s) have been identified, the organization selects one or more project(s) based on those criteria.

4. After an investment decision has been reached, the organization should continue to monitor and evaluate that decision throughout the remainder of its life. This evaluation is referred to as a *postaudit*.

To illustrate, assume that the organization needs to replace production equipment and has identified two alternatives: Machine A and Machine B. The primary criterion used by the organization to evaluate alternative capital projects is the time period over which the cost savings associated with the two machines allow the organization to recover its initial investment. If Machine A allows the organization to recover its investment in three years while Machine B requires four years, the organization's decision process may be summarized as follows:

---

[1] Throughout this chapter, we use the terms "cash inflows" and "cost savings" interchangeably. While cost savings do not technically result in inflows of cash, these savings do reduce the outflows of cash. Thus, they have the same net effect of increasing cash as do cash inflows.

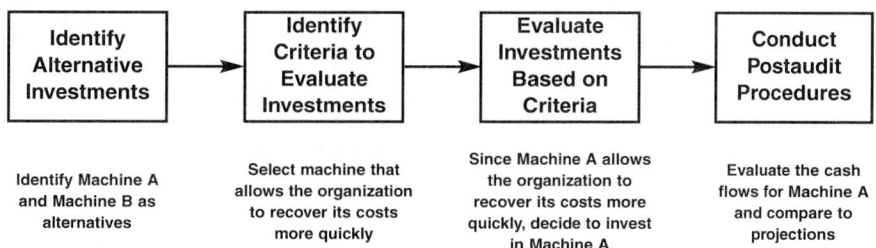

Types of Capital Budgeting Decisions

As discussed above, capital budgeting decisions involve a current expenditure of funds (to purchase capital assets) to earn a return (either an increase in revenues or a reduction in costs) in the future. These decisions may take many different forms, such as:

- **Decisions to Replace Capital Assets.** The company currently has capital assets that it uses in its operations and is deciding whether or not to replace these assets. Normally, the replacement assets being considered will provide benefits, either in the form of increased productivity or reduced operating costs. An example of a replacement decision would be an airline's decision to replace older aircraft with more fuel-efficient, newer aircraft.

- **Expansion Decisions.** The company does not own a certain type of capital asset and is deciding whether or not to purchase this asset to expand its operations. The acquisition would allow companies to earn revenues from an additional source. For example, a manufacturing company may decide to purchase special manufacturing equipment to produce a new product line.

- **Lease-or-Buy Decisions.** In this type of decision, a company may currently be leasing capital assets or contracting services involving capital assets from external parties. If capital assets are purchased, savings in costs would be analyzed to determine if this savings offsets the cost of the capital assets. For example, companies may decide to purchase rather than lease automobiles.

The above decisions may be classified into two categories. An *acceptance decision* results when managers decide whether a particular capital investment decision is feasible. Generally, in an acceptance decision, a single investment is considered alone without comparison to other capital investments. In this type of decision, the organization has sufficient funds to undertake a project. The primary concern is whether or not this project is worthwhile. An example of an acceptance decision would be comparing the estimated cost savings that would be realized by purchasing a particular capital asset to the cost of that asset to determine whether that investment is feasible and desirable.

A second type of capital budgeting decision is a *capital rationing decision*. In this type of decision, managers select from among alternative capital investments—the organization has limited resources and is considering alternative capital investments. For example, assume that an organization has determined that it must replace its production equipment and delivery trucks sometime in the near future. A total of $600,000 is available for capital projects in the current year. If new production equipment would cost $500,000 and new delivery trucks $350,000, only one of these projects can be selected. The organization would evaluate the feasibility of the purchase of production equipment and delivery trucks and select the one that is most beneficial to it.

Capital Budgeting—Quantitative Factors

In making capital budgeting decisions, the primary considerations are quantitative factors. To illustrate, suppose that you have received an inheritance of $1,000 and are deciding how to invest this money. You have identified two alternatives. First, you could invest the $1,000 in the stock of a corporation that pays regular annual dividends. You estimate that you will receive $100 per year in dividends for three years and will sell the stock in the fourth year for $1,400. Alternatively, a friend has asked to borrow the $1,000 and promises to repay a total of $1,500 over the four-year period as follows: $700 at the end of year 1, $500 at the end of year 2, $200 at the end of year 3, and $100 at the end of year 4. The initial investment and the cash inflows expected from each of these investments are summarized in Illustration 1.

Which alternative would you choose? A useful rule in reaching a decision is to compare the total returns from the two investments and select the alternative with the higher return over the four-year period. Using this

> **Illustration 1**
> **Cash Flows From Two Investment Opportunities**
>
> | Alternative | Flow | End of Period | Amount | |
> |---|---|---|---|---|
> | Invest in Stock | Outflow | 0* | $ (1,000) | |
> | | Inflow | 1 | $ 100 | ⎫ |
> | | Inflow | 2 | 100 | ⎬ Dividends |
> | | Inflow | 3 | 100 | ⎭ |
> | | Inflow | 4 | 1,400 | ← Proceeds from sale of stock |
> | | Total Inflows | | $ 1,700 | |
> | | Net | | $ 700 | |
> | Lend to Friend | Outflow | 0* | $(1,000) | |
> | | Inflow | 1 | $ 700 | ⎫ |
> | | Inflow | 2 | 500 | ⎬ Repayments |
> | | Inflow | 3 | 200 | ⎭ |
> | | Inflow | 4 | 100 | |
> | | Total Inflows | | $ 1,500 | |
> | | Net | | $ 500 | |
>
> *The initial outflow occurs at the inception of this investment proposal when no time has passed, hence, the "0" time.

criterion, you would invest in the stock because it would return an additional $700. In contrast, lending the money to your friend would only return an additional $500. This conclusion implies that you are interested only in the $200 greater return that investing in stock provides over the total four-year period.

Would everyone accept the decision to invest in stock? Probably not. Some investors may be concerned that the stock does not provide large returns early in the life of the investment. That is, while investing in stock returns a total of $1,700 over the life of the investment (versus $1,500 for making the loan), a large percentage of this return ($1,400) is received in the fourth year. In contrast, lending money would provide greater returns earlier in the life of the investment. If recapturing the investment as early as possible is of primary interest to you, you may prefer to lend the money to your friend.

The above discussion illustrates several quantitative factors that may be considered in choosing from among capital projects. These factors are briefly summarized below.

1. *Amount of Capital Investment*—The amount of the investment is the initial cost of the capital project. In the above illustration, the cost of the investment is important because it provides a benchmark for use in selecting a capital investment. For example, if you felt that the stock could be sold for only $200 at the end of the fourth year, it is unlikely that you would invest in the stock; doing so would provide a total return of only $500 ($300 in dividends + $200 in proceeds from the sale of stock), which is less than the cost of the investment ($1,000).

2. *Cash Inflows (Returns)*—In the above example, the amount of future cash inflows from dividends, interest, and return on the principal provide some indication of the relative desirability of the two investments. As shown in Illustration 1, the overall cash inflows associated with purchasing the stock exceed those associated with making the loan. In most capital budgeting situations, the cash inflows are realized in the form of operating cost savings. For example, when replacing an existing machine with another machine, the replacement machine normally has some technological improvements that reduce operating costs.

3. *Timing of Cash Inflows*—In addition to the amount of future cash inflows, the timing of future cash inflows is an important consideration. As noted in the previous example, the fact that lending the money to your friend would provide greater returns early in the life of the investment may make this alternative more desirable. This desirability results from the fact that the money would be available to you for your use at an earlier point in time.

4. *Cost of Capital*—The final quantitative factor considered in capital budgeting decisions is the cost of capital (also known as the hurdle rate). The cost of capital is simply the cost incurred by the organization to obtain the funds used for the investment. In the above example, assume that you could invest the $1,000 in a bank account and earn interest of 4 percent. If so, the cost of choosing either investment alternative would be the 4 percent interest that is forgone by selecting that alternative.

In other situations, corporations must borrow funds or issue additional stock to obtain funding for capital investments. These sources result in costs incurred for interest (on borrowed funds) or dividends (on stock issued to investors) and should be considered by the organization.

How does the cost of capital affect capital budgeting decisions? Simply stated, capital budgeting decisions should not be selected unless they can earn at least the cost of capital. In the above example, if you could only earn 2 percent lending to a friend and 3 percent from investing in stock, would you give up the 4 percent return from the bank account? Based strictly on quantitative factors, you would be spending 4 percent to earn 2 or 3 percent. Viewed in a similar light, it is unlikely that corporations would borrow funds at 8 percent interest to invest in machinery that would provide a return of only 5 percent.

The effect of these factors on capital budgeting decisions is illustrated below.

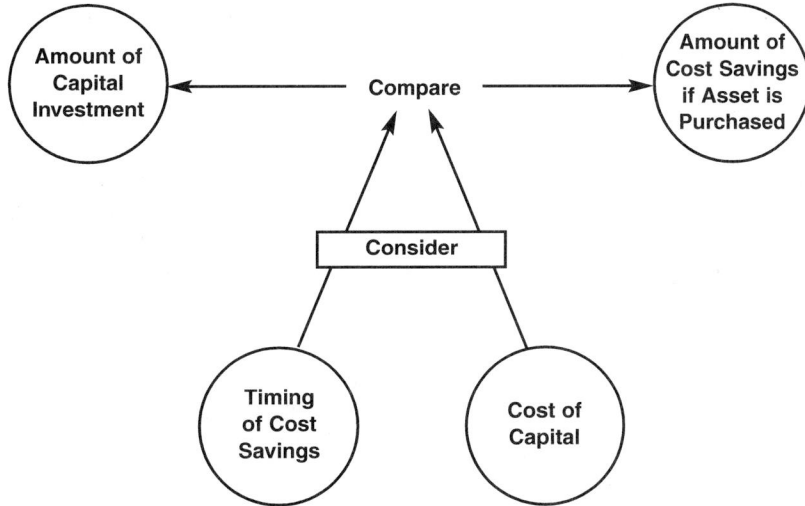

Capital Budgeting–Qualitative Factors

In addition to quantitative factors, qualitative (nonfinancial) factors may also be considered in capital budgeting decisions. In the above example, any special risks associated with the two investment opportunities (for example, the risk of nonpayment if the money is loaned) should be considered. In addition, the awkwardness of loaning money to a friend and possibly risking the loss of a friendship would undoubtedly be a factor. On the other hand, you may be willing to accept a lesser return on your investment in order to provide assistance to a friend. While factors such as these are undoubtedly considered in capital budgeting decisions, they are often difficult to formally incorporate into the decision process. Accordingly, in the remainder of this chapter, the focus is on quantitative factors in capital budgeting decisions.

CAPITAL BUDGETING TECHNIQUES THAT IGNORE THE TIME VALUE OF MONEY

In certain circumstances, the organization is more concerned with the amount of cash inflows earned from a given capital investment rather than the timing of these cash inflows. For example, comparing the two alternatives presented in Illustration 1, you may be more interested in the additional $200 that could be earned by investing in stock than in the fact that most of the cash inflows from this investment will not be received until the later years of the investment. A preference of this sort does not consider the concept of the time value of money (or present value) discussed in the Appendix to this chapter.

Despite the importance of present value in the capital budgeting process, some commonly used capital budgeting techniques do not consider the time value of future cash inflows and future cash outflows. Two of these methods (the payback period and the average rate of return) are discussed in the remainder of this section.

Payback Period

A simple method frequently used to evaluate various capital investment alternatives is the *payback period*. Calculating the payback period allows the organization to determine the length of time necessary to recover its capital investment. The payback period provides the answer to the following question: "At what point do the total cash inflows of a capital project equal the initial investment?" The payback period is stated in terms of an element of time, most frequently the number of years necessary to recover the initial investment.

A limitation of the payback method is that this method does not consider when the cash inflows are actually received by the organization (i.e., the time value of money is ignored). This technique is merely a simple calculation which provides a rough estimate of the time required for an organization to recover its capital investment.

Payback Period with Uniform Cash Inflows. To illustrate the use of the payback period method, we will consider an investment decision facing Clothes by Order, a clothing company that sells to customers on a mail-order basis. Clothes by Order is a manufacturer of menswear that features both business and casual lines of clothing. While Clothes by Order has established a small number of retail outlets, most of its business is through catalog sales. Upon receipt of a customer's order, Clothes by Order locates the merchandise ordered through its warehouse operations and provides delivery to customers within five business days. Because of high start-up costs and an uncertain market for its product, Clothes by Order initially relied on external carriers (such as FedEx and other delivery services) to deliver its products to customers, located mostly in the southwest United States. Because of its recent expansion, as well as increased rates charged by external carriers, Clothes by Order is considering the purchase of its own fleet of delivery trucks. These trucks would cost $180,000 and have a useful life of six years. Clothes by Order does not anticipate any salvage value at the end of the life of the trucks. Based on estimates made by management, maintenance, insurance, and other costs of operating the delivery trucks would average $10,000 per year. However, Clothes by Order estimates that it would save $70,000 per year in fees paid to carriers. Thus, the net savings per year would be $60,000 ($70,000 − $10,000 = $60,000).

In this example, the net cash inflows and outflows associated with the investment in delivery trucks are as follows:

- Cash Inflows: Net cost savings provided by delivery trucks ($60,000 per year)
- Cash Outflows: Cost of purchasing delivery trucks ($180,000)

Since the cash inflows are uniform and are realized annually, the payback period can be determined by dividing the cost of the investment (cost of purchasing the delivery trucks) by the net cost savings per year. Using a simple payback period calculation, Clothes by Order would recover its investment in three years, as shown below:

$$\text{Payback Period} = \frac{\text{Original Investment}}{\text{Average Annual Cash Inflow}}$$

$$= \frac{\$180,000}{\$60,000}$$

$$= 3 \text{ years}$$

Based on the above analysis, Clothes by Order would evaluate this investment opportunity as follows:

1. If Clothes by Order has established organization-wide guidelines for payback periods and recovery of capital investments, the investment in delivery trucks can be evaluated to determine whether it meets these guidelines. This comparison allows investment opportunities to be screened prior to formal action and discussion regarding these projects. This represents an acceptance decision, since only a single potential capital investment is considered. For example, if Clothes by order has a policy which requires a maximum payback period of two years, it is unlikely that the investment in delivery trucks would be considered further because the payback period for the delivery trucks (three years) exceeds the organization's maximum guideline (two years).

2. In deciding between alternative investment opportunities, Clothes by Order could compare the payback period for this project with that of other projects (for example, a less costly fleet of delivery trucks with a shorter useful life). These decisions are referred to as capital rationing decisions and involve allocating scarce resources to the most desirable projects. Based on this comparison, the project with the shortest

payback period would be selected (assuming that Clothes by Order is limited to only one of the two alternatives). For example, if purchasing a less costly fleet of delivery trucks with a shorter useful life provided a payback period of four years, Clothes by Order would likely select the initial investment opportunity with the three-year payback period (assuming that it meets all other stated criteria).

The payback method can use either before-tax cash inflows (as in the Clothes by Order example) or after-tax cash inflows in determining the desirability of an investment opportunity. Because cost savings result in increased net income, the income taxes paid by Clothes by Order would also increase. Thus, organizations would normally expect longer payback periods when after-tax cash inflows are evaluated.

Payback Period with Unequal Cash Flows. The above analysis assumes that the cash inflows (operating cost savings) were uniform throughout the entire life of the capital project. In other cases, greater cash inflows may occur later or earlier in the life of the project. Considering the Clothes by Order example presented above, it seems logical that the cost savings for the delivery trucks purchased by Clothes by Order would increase in later years as external carriers would likely raise their rates. In addition, if capital assets are purchased, the maintenance costs for these assets would ordinarily increase in the later years of an asset's life. If so, it may be more appropriate to perform a year-by-year analysis in determining the payback period. Assume that Alvin Irvin, the manager of delivery services for Clothes by Order, carefully analyzed the additional cost savings and additional costs incurred by purchasing the delivery trucks and has provided management with the summary in Illustration 2.

Illustration 2
Clothes by Order
Annual Cost Savings and Estimated Maintenance
Costs for Investment in Delivery Trucks

Year	Operating Savings	Maintenance Costs	Net Operating Savings
1	$ 80,000	$ 20,000	$ 60,000
2	80,000	20,000	60,000
3	85,000	60,000	25,000
4	90,000	20,000	70,000
5	90,000	20,000	70,000
6	95,000	20,000	75,000
Totals	$520,000	$160,000	$360,000

As shown in Illustration 2, the operating cost savings are expected to be highest in the later years of the project. Note that in years 1 and 2, Clothes by Order would save $80,000, with an expected increase to $85,000 in year 3, $90,000 in years 4 and 5, and $95,000 in year 6. These differences represent the anticipated rate increases that will be charged by Clothes by Order's current carriers in the future. In addition, maintenance costs are expected to be highest in year 3, reflecting Alvin Irvin's estimates that the delivery trucks will require major repairs about halfway through their expected service lives. It is important to note, however, that the average net cost savings are expected to be the same as before ($60,000). That is, a total of $360,000 of cost savings will be realized over the six-year life of the investment. Given the above information, the year-by-year analysis of this proposed investment is shown below:

Year	Beginning Balance of Investment	Cash Inflow	Ending Balance of Investment	
0	$(180,000)		$(180,000)	
1	(180,000)	$60,000	(120,000)	
2	(120,000)	60,000	(60,000)	
3	(60,000)	25,000	(35,000)	← Payback = 3.5 years
4	(35,000)	70,000	35,000	
5	35,000	70,000	105,000	
6	105,000	75,000	180,000	

Based on the above analysis, it appears that the payback period for the investment occurs between years 3 and 4 (note that at the conclusion of year 4, the net cumulative operating savings exceed the cost of the investment). In other words, the net balance in the investment becomes positive. If Clothes by Order assumes that the cash flows occur uniformly throughout the year, the net operating savings would equal the net cost of the investment after savings of $35,000 had been realized during year 4. Since the net savings during year 4 totaled $70,000, it is assumed that the recovery occurred half way through that year ($35,000 ÷ $70,000 = 0.50). Thus, the payback period using a year-by-year analysis is 3.5 years.

Limitations of the Payback Period. Two obvious limitations of the payback period method are important to note. First, this method ignores the timing of the cash receipts in certain instances. For example, consider the analysis conducted by Clothes by Order for the investment in delivery trucks discussed above. Assume that Alvin Irvin prepared his original analysis based on bids from one vendor (AllState). Since this analysis was prepared, the management of Clothes by Order has received two additional bids to supply it with delivery trucks for the same price ($150,000). While these bids do not affect the operating savings of costs paid to external delivery services, the expected maintenance cost of these trucks is slightly different than the trucks supplied by AllState. These differences are summarized below:

- RedDot's vehicles have been shown to have lower annual maintenance costs than those supplied by AllState. However, Alvin Irvin estimates that the engines in these trucks will need to be replaced in the third year. The type of engine in RedDot's vehicles is more expensive than that in AllState's. The net effect of these differences is lower maintenance costs (and higher cost savings) in the first two years and higher maintenance costs (and lower cost savings) in the third year. After the third year, the cost savings are approximately the same.

- BlueLine's vehicles are expected to have the same annual maintenance costs as the vehicles offered by RedDot in the years preceding engine replacement. An advantage of the vehicles sold by BlueLine is that the engine replacement comes with a warranty for all maintenance costs incurred for three years following the engine replacement. Therefore, the only additional costs incurred after engine replacement will be for insurance, gasoline, and other routine charges. As a result, the operating cost savings associated with these trucks are higher than those associated with the trucks supplied by AllState or RedDot.

After meeting with Clothes by Order's management, Alvin Irvin performed a thorough analysis of the three capital investment alternatives (purchase trucks from AllState, RedDot, or BlueLine). His analysis of the net cash inflows generated by these cost savings for the three alternatives are summarized below:

Year	AllState	RedDot	BlueLine
1	$ 60,000	$ 70,000	$ 70,000
2	60,000	70,000	70,000
3	25,000	10,000	10,000
4	70,000	60,000	60,000
5	70,000	75,000	90,000
6	75,000	75,000	95,000
Total	$360,000	$360,000	$395,000

Comparing the cash inflows of the original purchase of delivery trucks from AllState to those purchasing trucks from RedDot, it is evident that both projects achieve a payback period of 3.5 years. However, notice that the cash inflows from purchasing delivery trucks from RedDot are greater earlier in the life of the project than those from purchasing trucks from AllState. Since these cash flows could be invested to earn a return, Clothes by Order would find it desirable to have the cash savings occur earlier in the life of the project. This comparison illustrates how the time value of money may impact an organization's decision. Methods of capital budgeting that explicitly consider the time value of money are discussed in a subsequent section of this chapter.

A second limitation of the payback method is that it fails to consider cash inflows over the entire life of the project. To illustrate this limitation, compare the cash flows associated with purchasing the delivery trucks from AllState, RedDot, and BlueLine. Just as with purchases from AllState and RedDot, the payback period if trucks are purchased from BlueLine is 3.5 years. As a result, based strictly on the payback criterion, Clothes by Order would rank all three projects as equally desirable. However, it is apparent that purchasing the trucks from BlueLine is the superior investment. This conclusion is based on the fact that: (1) the cash inflows by purchasing the trucks from BlueLine occur early in the life of the project and (2) the total cash inflows by purchasing the trucks from BlueLine ($395,000) are greater than those from purchasing trucks from AllState or RedDot ($360,000).

> In 1988, the Chicago Bears (a National Football League team) evaluated the condition of the playing surface at their stadium (Soldier Field). After considering various factors, the Bears decided to switch from an AstroTurf surface to a grass surface. While their primary motive for changing surfaces was to reduce injuries, they also considered the cost of new AstroTurf ($1 million) and the cost of installing natural grass ($700,000). Given that the maintenance costs associated with a grass field are $25,000 to $40,000 per year and that AstroTurf lasts about ten years, Tim LeFevour (the Bears' director of administration) noted that "[o]ver ten years, the cost of the grass will even out with the cost of the AstroTurf." This suggests a payback period of ten years if an AstroTurf field is installed.[2]

Average Rate of Return (Accounting Rate of Return)

A capital budgeting technique which evaluates alternative investment projects based on the profitability of those projects is the average rate of return. The *average rate of return* (also called the *"accounting" rate of return*) is calculated by dividing the average annual increase in net income (after taxes) from the capital investment by the cost of the investment. The formula used to calculate the average rate of return is shown below:

$$\text{Average Rate of Return} = \frac{\text{Average Annual Increase in Net Income}}{\text{Cost of the Investment}}$$

A unique aspect of the average rate of return method is that it focuses on expected future net income, not cash flows. Initially, cash flows and income may seem to be identical. After all, if maintenance costs are reduced, wouldn't net income be increased by the same amount? However, some cash flows do not affect net income while other non-cash flow items do affect net income. For example, referring to the Clothes by Order example, the purchase of the delivery trucks will result in the recognition of depreciation expense. Because depreciation is a non-cash expense, it was not considered in evaluating the purchase of delivery trucks under the payback method. However, because depreciation is an expense that is deducted in determining net income, it will be considered in evaluating the capital investment under the average rate of return method. Thus, the average rate of return equation could be restated as follows:

$$\text{Average Rate of Return} = \frac{\text{Average Annual Cost Savings} - \text{Depreciation Expense}}{\text{Cost of the Investment}}$$

To illustrate the calculation and use of the average rate of return technique, refer to the Clothes by Order example discussed in the previous section. Assume that Clothes by Order has decided to only consider purchasing the trucks from AllState. Recall that the delivery trucks considered for purchase will provide a total of $360,000 in cost savings over a six-year period. Therefore, the average cost savings per year is $60,000 ($360,000 ÷ 6 years = $60,000). Also recall that the delivery trucks have an initial cost of $180,000, a useful life of six years, and a zero salvage value. Assuming the use of straight-line depreciation, the depreciation expense per year would be $30,000 ($180,000 ÷ 6 years = $30,000) per year. If the effective income tax rate is anticipated to be 40 percent, the average increase in net income (after taxes) is $18,000, as shown below:

Increase in Net Income (cost savings) by Purchasing Delivery Trucks	$60,000
Depreciation Expense on Delivery Trucks	(30,000)
Net Increase in Income (before taxes)	$30,000
Less: Income Taxes ($30,000 x 0.40)	(12,000)
Annual Increase in Net Income	$18,000

Once the annual increase in net income has been determined, the average rate of return may be calculated as follows:

$$\text{Average Rate of Return} = \frac{\$18,000}{\$180,000} = 0.10 \text{ or } 10 \text{ percent}$$

---

[2] "A Fight Over Turf," *Sports Illustrated* (November 1, 1993), 39.

Average Rate of Return Using Average Investment. An alternative to the above analysis is using the average level of the investment (rather than the initial investment) in the denominator of the average rate of return ratio. The average level of investment is determined by averaging the book value (cost minus accumulated depreciation) over the life of the investment. The level of the average investment for the delivery trucks considered by Clothes by Order is shown below:

(1) Year	(2) Beginning Book Value	(3) Depreciation Expense	(4) Ending Book Value	(5) Average Book Value
1	$180,000	$30,000	$150,000	$165,000
2	150,000	30,000	120,000	135,000
3	120,000	30,000	90,000	105,000
4	90,000	30,000	60,000	75,000
5	60,000	30,000	30,000	45,000
6	30,000	30,000	0	15,000
Total				$540,000
				÷6
				$ 90,000

The average book value in any year (column 5) is determined by averaging the beginning book value (column 2) and the ending book value (column 4). The average book value over the life of the investment is determined by averaging the book values over the life of the capital project (column 5). Once this has been determined, the average rate of return (based on average investment) is calculated as follows:

$$\text{Average Rate of Return} = \frac{\$18,000}{\$90,000} = 0.20 \text{ or } 20 \text{ percent}$$

The primary advantage of the average rate of return method is the simplicity of its calculation; it utilizes accounting information that is readily available. Similar to the payback period method, the use of the average rate of return allows management to determine a "ranking" of projects based on their return. In addition, projects can be compared to a minimum acceptable rate of return established by the organization to provide a rough approximation of the desirability of one or more alternative project(s). However, like the payback period, the average rate of return method is deficient in that it fails to consider the time value of money.

CAPITAL BUDGETING TECHNIQUES THAT CONSIDER THE TIME VALUE OF MONEY

Both of the capital budgeting techniques discussed above (the payback period and average rate of return) assume that Clothes by Order is indifferent about the time period during which the cash inflows (or cost savings) occur. However, it is unlikely that the timing of the cash inflows will be unimportant. For example, once again consider the cash flow information for two capital projects evaluated by Clothes by Order (purchasing the trucks from AllState or from RedDot). For purposes of this example, recall that both purchases would provide a net cost savings of $360,000 over the six-year life of the investment. However, while the purchase from AllState is expected to provide a $60,000 cash inflow in the first year, purchasing the trucks from RedDot would provide a net cash inflow of $70,000 in that same year.

Using the payback period and average rate of return techniques, it could be shown that Clothes by Order would be indifferent as to the desirability of these two capital investment alternatives. In both cases, the payback period is 3.5 years and the average rate of return is 10 percent. However, Clothes by Order might prefer purchasing trucks from RedDot for one simple reason: doing so would return greater cash inflows earlier in the life of the project. While there may be several reasons for this preference (expected future inflation, cash shortages, or lower expected risk in a future period), when cash is received earlier it can be invested to earn an additional return. Considering only the first year's cost savings for the two alternatives and assuming that Clothes by Order could earn interest at a rate of 10 percent per year compounded annually, Illustration 3 shows the amount of interest earned on the cash inflow (cost savings) attributable to year 1 under the two alternatives.

As shown in Illustration 3, the $60,000 cash inflow in year 1 for the purchase of trucks from AllState earns a total return of $36,630.60 over the six-year period. Notice that this return includes interest on both the original cash inflow of $60,000 (the principal) and interest earned in previous years. For example, the $6,000 of interest earned in year 2 relates solely to the principal of $60,000 ($60,000 x 0.10 = $6,000). In year 3, a total of $6,600

Illustration 3
Clothes by Order
Total Return on Cost Savings in
First Year for Two Alternative Investments

AllState:	Year	(1) Beginning Balance	(2) = (1) x 0.10 Interest Earned	(3) = (1) + (2) Ending Balance
	1			$60,000.00
	2	$60,000.00	$ 6,000.00	66,000.00
	3	66,000.00	6,600.00	72,600.00
	4	72,600.00	7,260.00	79,860.00
	5	79,860.00	7,986.00	87,846.00
	6	87,846.00	8,784.60	96,630.60
			$36,630.60	
RedDot:				
	1			$ 70,000.00
	2	$70,000.00	$ 7,000.00	77,000.00
	3	77,000.00	7,700.00	84,700.00
	4	84,700.00	8,470.00	93,170.00
	5	93,170.00	9,317.00	102,487.00
	6	102,487.00	10,248.70	112,735.70
			$42,735.70	

of interest is earned. This amount is calculated by multiplying the interest rate (10%) by the sum of the principal amount of $60,000 and previous interest earned in year 2 of $6,000. That is, $6,600 = [($60,000 + $6,000) x 0.10].

A similar calculation can be made for the remaining years of the purchase of delivery trucks from AllState. Note that the interest earned each year increases as the total balance on deposit (beginning principal plus interest earned in previous years) increases. This increase in interest earned over the life of a deposit is a feature associated with compound interest.

Illustration 3 also summarizes the interest earned assuming that $70,000 was saved in the first year of the project (purchase of delivery trucks from RedDot). For the first year's cost savings, total interest earned over the life of that investment would be $42,735.70. While some of this interest earned is attributable to the larger principal placed on deposit in year 1 ($70,000 versus $60,000), additional returns are earned each year on the increasing interest received in previous years. Therefore, despite the fact that the original investment will yield higher cash inflows in later years than the purchase of trucks from RedDot, the total interest earned from the cost savings of purchasing from RedDot will exceed that earned from the cost savings by purchasing from AllState. This relationship between the interest earned on these two investments occurs because purchasing from RedDot provides greater cost savings earlier in the life of the project. The inflows resulting from these cost savings remain on deposit for longer periods of time, generating a greater amount of interest.

The above discussion introduces two important concepts: present value (the time value of money) and compound interest. These concepts are discussed further in the Appendix to this chapter. It is critical that the student be familiar with present value concepts before proceeding with the following section of this chapter. It may be helpful for you to review the Appendix as well as some of the selected end-of-chapter questions, exercises, and problems before studying the remaining capital budgeting techniques in this chapter in further detail.

NET PRESENT VALUE

The net present value technique evaluates capital investments based on the net present value (discounted present value) of the expected future cash inflows and cash outflows associated with the investment. These future cash inflows and outflows are discounted to the present period using a discount (interest) rate referred to as the cost of capital. As noted earlier, the cost of capital represents the cost (in the form of an interest rate) of obtaining funds for capital investments. The net present value of a capital investment is defined as the difference between the present value of the future cash inflows and the present value of the future cash outflows.

While calculating the net present value of a capital investment may become somewhat cumbersome, the analysis of capital investment alternatives under the net present value method is fairly straightforward. If the present value of the future cash inflows exceeds the present value of the future cash outflows (i.e., the net present value is positive), the organization can conclude that the return on the proposed capital investment exceeds the cost of capital and, thus, the project should be accepted. If the present value of the future cash outflows exceeds the present value of the future cash inflows (i.e., the net present value is negative), the organization can conclude that the return on the proposed investment is less than the cost of capital. In this case, the organization would usually decide to reject the capital investment.

To illustrate the use of the net present value technique, recall the original example related to the purchase of delivery trucks by Clothes by Order. As described earlier, Clothes by Order is considering the purchase of a fleet of delivery trucks for $180,000 from AllState. These trucks have a useful life of six years, and no salvage value is anticipated. Because of uncertainties concerning future rate increases from its current external carriers, the management of Clothes by Order has decided to assume equal cost savings of $60,000 per year as a result of purchasing the trucks. As discussed earlier, these net cost savings consist of the following components:

➤ Savings of $70,000 per year in fees which were paid to external carriers
➤ Additional maintenance, insurance, and other costs of $10,000 per year

Clothes by Order has determined its cost of capital to be 10 percent. Thus, unless a capital investment can earn a return of at least 10 percent, management does not wish to consider this project. For purposes of clarity, we will not consider income taxes and other factors at this point. These issues will be addressed, one at a time, in the following subsections to highlight how various factors affect capital budgeting decisions using the net present value method.

Future Cash Inflows and Outflows–Basic

The above data indicate that the project considered by Clothes by Order consists of a single cash outflow (the $180,000 cost of the machine) and a single cash inflow (the annual operating savings of $60,000 per year for the next six years). The cash outflow for the cost of the machine of $180,000 would occur upon acceptance of the capital investment (time period 0, which is assumed to be the current year). The cash inflows (cost savings) of $60,000 per year^3 are expected to occur each year at the end of years 1 through 6. These inflows and outflows are graphically illustrated below:

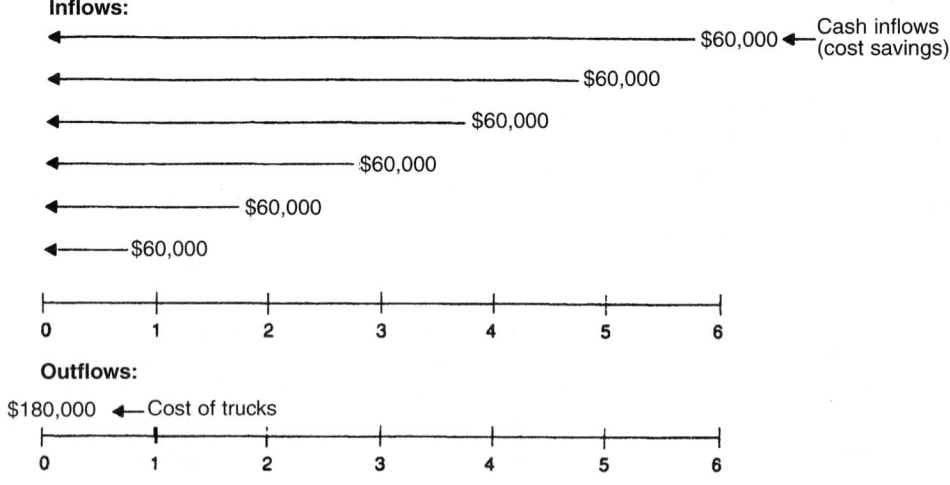

Ignoring income taxes and other factors (which are discussed later in this chapter), future cash inflows may be discounted to the present period using the cost of capital as the discount rate. Once this has been done, the

---

^{3} Alternatively, the net cash inflow of $60,000 could be considered as two separate amounts: (1) an inflow (cost savings) of fees paid to external carriers of $70,000 per year and (2) a cash outflow for maintenance, insurance, and other costs of $10,000 per year. Since these amounts are assumed to be equal in all years, the results of all subsequent analyses would be identical regardless of whether these amounts are considered separately or combined.

present value of the inflows is compared to the present value of the cash outflows to determine the desirability of investing in this project. This discounting, based on both single sum inflows (Table 1 in the Appendix) and annuity inflows (Table 2 in the Appendix), is presented in Illustration 4.

Illustration 4
Clothes by Order
Net Present Value for Investment in Delivery Trucks

Part A: Using Single Sum Discounting

		Year	Amount	Factor From Table 1 (10%)	Present Value
Inflows:	Operating Cost Savings	1	$ 60,000	0.9091	$ 54,546
	Operating Cost Savings	2	60,000	0.8264	49,584
	Operating Cost Savings	3	60,000	0.7513	45,078
	Operating Cost Savings	4	60,000	0.6830	40,980
	Operating Cost Savings	5	60,000	0.6209	37,254
	Operating Cost Savings	6	60,000	0.5645	33,870
	Total Inflows			4.3552	$261,312
Outflows:	Amount of Investment	0	$180,000	1.0000	(180,000)
Total Net Present Value:					$ 81,312

Part B: Using Annuity Discounting

		Year	Amount	Factor From Table 2 (10%)	Present Value
Inflows:	Operating Cost Savings	1-6	$60,000	4.3553	$261,318
Outflows:	Amount of Investment	0	(180,000)	1.0000	(180,000)
Total Net Present Value:					$ 81,318[a]

[a] Difference between this amount and that calculated using the single sum tables is due to rounding.

As shown in Illustration 4, the proposed capital investment has a positive net present value of $81,312. Therefore, this capital investment earns a return greater than the cost of capital (10%) and should be accepted by Clothes by Order based on the use of the net present value technique.[4]

It is important to emphasize certain points with respect to the calculations summarized in Illustration 4. First, since the amounts of the cash inflows (cost savings) are equal for each of the years of the capital investment, the present value of these inflows can be calculated based on either a single sum or an annuity discounting. While the sum of the present value factors presented in part A of Illustration 4 has no real meaning to Clothes by Order, note that, except for rounding, this sum (4.3552) is equal to the annuity factor extracted from Table 2 in the Appendix. This fact clearly indicates that the use of either the single sum or annuity method of discounting equal future cash inflows or outflows will yield the identical result. Also, since the outlay of $180,000 would be required at the present date (upon acceptance of the capital investment), the appropriate factor used to discount this outflow is 1.000 (that is, the present value of this immediate outflow is equal to the amount of cash required to purchase the asset).

Evaluating Competing Projects Using Net Present Value

Comparing the Net Present Value. In many cases, the decision under consideration is more complicated than that illustrated above for Clothes by Order. For example, what if Clothes by Order received another bid for providing it with delivery trucks? In this case, the management of Clothes by Order should evaluate the two alternatives based on the present value of the future cash inflows and outflows associated with each alternative. As noted earlier, this is an example of a *capital rationing decision*. In these cases, Clothes by Order would determine the net present value of each alternative. Assuming that all other factors are equal, management would

---

[4] Had the present value of the inflows and outflows been equal, the capital investment would have earned a return of exactly 10 percent.

select the alternative having the greatest net present value. Thus, similar to the payback method and the average rate of return method, net present value can be used to evaluate an individual project or the relative desirability of two or more competing projects.

To illustrate the evaluation of competing investment projects, assume that a new manufacturer (North-South) offers to sell Clothes by Order a similar fleet of delivery trucks for $225,000. While this price is greater than that charged by AllState, North-South offers a warranty that reimburses purchasers for all maintenance costs. As a result, Clothes by Order expects the total costs of operating the delivery trucks sold by North-South to be $2,000 per year. Since purchasing the delivery trucks will allow Clothes by Order to save $70,000 annually in fees paid to external carriers, the net cost savings associated with the trucks sold by North-South would be $68,000 annually ($70,000 − $2,000 = $68,000). Two methods of comparing these projects are shown in Illustration 5.

Illustration 5
Comparison of Alternative Capital Investment Projects

		Year	Amount	Factor From Table 2 (10%)	Present Value
Part A:	**Total Present Value**				
	AllState:				
	Inflows	1-6	$ 60,000	4.3553	$261,318.00
	Outflows	0	(180,000)		(180,000.00)
					$ 81,318.00
	North-South:				
	Inflows	1-6	$ 68,000	4.3553	$296,160.40
	Outflows	0	(225,000)	1.0000	(225,000.00)
					$ 71,160.40
	Net Present Value in Favor of Purchasing from AllState:				$ 10,157.60
Part B:	**Incremental Present Value**				
	Additional Cash Inflows from North-South:	1-6	$ 8,000	4.3553	$ 34,842.40
	Additional Cost of Trucks Purchased from North-South:	0	(45,000)	1.0000	(45,000.00)
	Net Disadvantage of Purchasing Trucks from North-South:				$ 10,157.60

In Part A of Illustration 5, the total present value approach is used. Under this approach, the total net present value of each of the two (or more) capital investments is determined, and the project with the highest net present value is normally selected. As shown in Part A of Illustration 5, the net present value of purchasing trucks from AllState is $10,157.60 higher than that of purchasing the trucks from North-South. Accordingly, under the total net present value approach, Clothes by Order would purchase the delivery trucks from AllState.

Alternatively, Clothes by Order could focus on the incremental cash flows (i.e., the difference in cash flows under the two alternatives). Under this approach, the incremental cash flows associated with one alternative are compared with the other(s). In this case if Clothes by Order decided to purchase the trucks from North-South, the incremental cash flows would be:

- The additional $8,000 ($68,000 - $60,000 = $8,000) operating savings realized if the trucks were purchased from North-South.

- The additional cost of $45,000 ($225,000 - $180,000 = $45,000) for purchasing the trucks from North-South.

As shown in Part B of Illustration 5, the final conclusion is the same under either approach. This is not surprising, because the analysis in Part B of Illustration 5 merely summarizes the differences between the cash flows associated with the two alternatives shown in Part A. In any case, it appears that Clothes by Order should purchase its delivery trucks from AllState. Under the net present value criterion, this approach will result in an additional net present value of $10,157.60.

Profitability Index. Another method commonly used to rank alternative capital investments is the *profitability index* which is calculated as:

$$\text{Profitability index} = \frac{\text{Present Value of Net Cash Inflows}}{\text{Present Value of Initial Investment}}$$

The present value of the future cash inflows and the amount of the investments for the two alternatives are summarized in Illustration 5. Using this information, the profitability indices associated with Clothes by Order's two investment opportunities would be:

$$\text{AllState} = \frac{\$261,318.00}{180,000.00} = 1.45$$

$$\text{North-South} = \frac{\$296,160.40}{225,000.00} = 1.32$$

Since the profitability index provides another indication of the relationship between the present value of the future cash inflows and the cost of the initial investment, a higher profitability index represents a more desirable investment. Thus, in this situation, Clothes by Order would purchase delivery trucks from AllState.

Additional Complexities Using Net Present Value

Income Tax Effects and Depreciation. The above example which considers only basic cash inflows and outflows does not completely reflect reality because income taxes are ignored. For example, remember that the cash inflows (cost savings) before income taxes from the proposed capital investment are $60,000 per year. As a result, Clothes by Order's net income will be increased each year by this amount. This increase in net income will result in Clothes by Order paying additional income taxes. To illustrate, if net income before taxes increased from $90,000 per year to $150,000 per year because of the cost savings associated with the proposed capital investment and Clothes by Order's tax rate was 40 percent, the net income with and without the capital investment can be determined as shown below:

	With Capital Investment	Without Capital Investment
Net Income Before Taxes	$150,000	$90,000
Income Taxes (at 40%)	(60,000)	(36,000)
Net Income After Taxes	$ 90,000	$54,000

Note that the net cash inflow to Clothes by Order after considering the impact of the additional income taxes is $36,000 ($90,000 - $54,000 = $36,000). This net inflow may also be calculated by comparing the amount of income taxes paid under the two alternatives. While the capital investment will provide cost savings of $60,000 per year before taxes, an extra $24,000 ($60,000 - $36,000 = $24,000) of income taxes must be paid each year on the additional income provided by these cost savings. Thus, the after-tax cost savings can be expressed as $36,000. After-tax cost savings can be conveniently calculated by multiplying the before-tax cost savings by 1.00 minus the tax rate, as follows:

Before-Tax Cost Savings				After-Tax Cost Savings
	x	(1 − tax rate)	=	
$ 60,000	x	(1.00 − 0.40)	=	$ 36,000

An additional factor which must be considered when income taxes are involved is the *depreciation tax shield*. While depreciation expense itself does not result in a cash inflow (cost savings) or cash outflow, the depreciation associated with a given capital investment provides a tax deductible expense to the organization. For example, assuming that Clothes by Order uses the straight-line method of depreciation for its trucks, and no salvage value is expected at the end of the trucks' useful lives, the annual depreciation expense for the proposed capital investment would be $30,000 per year ($180,000 ÷ 6 years = $30,000). Since depreciation expense reduces net income, the amount of tax savings can be calculated as the amount of the depreciation expense multiplied by the tax rate. In this example, the annual tax savings (and cash inflow) resulting from the depreciation expense associated with the proposed capital investment is $12,000 as calculated below:

Tax Savings	=	Depreciation Expense x Tax Rate
	=	$30,000 x 0.40
	=	$12,000

After calculating the above modifications to our earlier analysis, we can illustrate the cash inflows and outflows as follows:

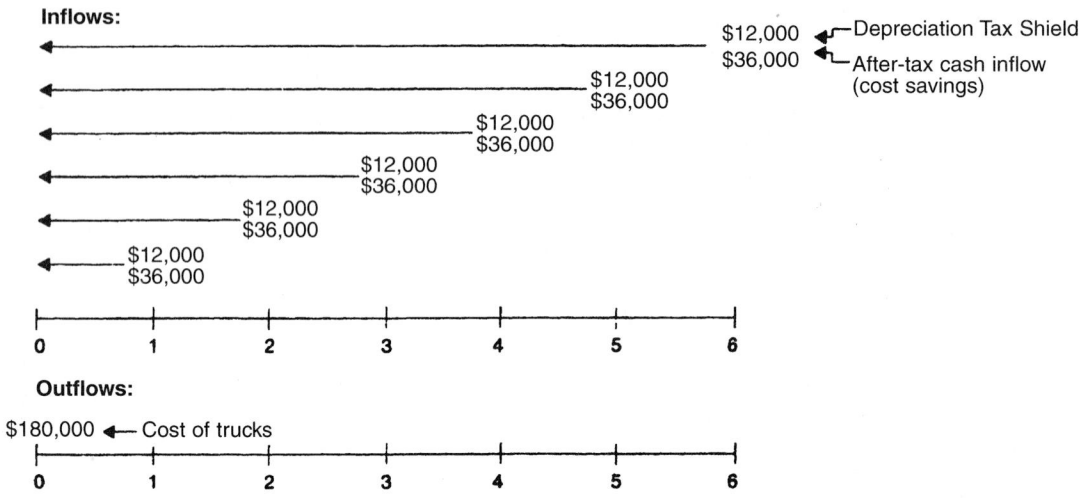

After considering the effects of income taxes and depreciation[5], the net present value of this project is calculated in Illustration 6. Because the straight-line method of depreciation results in an equal amount of depreciation expense each year, the annual tax savings are also equal and can be discounted as an annuity. While the analysis in Illustration 6 could also be performed using single sum tables (as in Part A of Illustration 4), Illustration 6 uses factors from the annuity tables to more clearly focus on the effect of income taxes. It is important to note that considering income tax effects impacts our previous analysis in two primary ways: (1) the before-tax cost savings must be reduced by the additional income taxes that must be paid as a result of those savings, and (2) an additional cost savings results from the tax shield provided by the depreciation associated with the capital investment. As shown in Illustration 6, the net present value of this project is $29,054.40; as a result, the return on this project is higher than the cost of capital (10%). Based on the net present value criterion, Clothes by Order would find this investment to be desirable, since its return is greater than the company's cost of capital.

Illustration 6
Clothes by Order
Net Present Value for Investment in Delivery Trucks
(Including Income Taxes)

		Year	Amount	Factor From Table 2 (10%)	Present Value
Inflows:	Operating Cost Savings	1-6	$36,000[a]	4.3553	$156,790.80
	Depreciation Tax Savings	1-6	12,000[b]	4.3553	52,263.60
	Total Inflows				$209,054.40
Outflows:	Amount of Investment	0	$180,000	1.0000	(180,000.00)
Total Net Present Value:					$ 29,054.40

[a] $60,000 x (1 − 0.40)
[b] $30,000 x 0.40

---

[5] While the Modified Accelerated Cost Recovery System (MACRS) method of depreciation is required for income tax purposes, we will focus on the use of straight-line depreciation in discussing capital budgeting to emphasize the net present value technique rather than the calculation of depreciation expense. The straight-line method of depreciation is the easiest to consider for capital budgeting purposes, since the amount of depreciation expense and tax savings each year is equal. As a result, the tax savings can be discounted using the annuity tables (Table 2 in the Appendix). If an accelerated method of depreciation were used, Table 1 (the present value of a single sum) would be used for each year.

Other Future Inflows and Outflows. In addition to the savings in operating costs and taxes (resulting from depreciation), other future cash inflows and outflows are often associated with capital investments. For example, most fixed assets require future maintenance (and therefore cash outflows) in order to keep the asset in good operating order. In addition, at the end of the asset's useful life, the company may receive cash from the sale of the asset. Similar to the cash inflows and outflows discussed above, the effect of these future inflows and outflows of cash should be considered when calculating the net present value of a capital investment.

To illustrate the effect of other future cash inflows and outflows on capital budgeting decisions using the net present value method, let us modify the previous example as follows. First, in addition to the routine scheduled maintenance on the delivery trucks, assume that Clothes by Order expects to incur additional costs of $10,000 in the third year to replace the tires on the delivery trucks. In addition, also assume that Clothes by Order believes that a salvage value of $15,000 will be realized upon disposal of the trucks at the end of year 6.

These facts modify the previous analysis in two ways. First, the additional cash outflow of $10,000 in year 3 must be incorporated into the analysis of the net present value of this project. While the cost of these tires will require a future cash outflow by Clothes by Order, this outflow will be partially offset by tax savings. These tax savings occur because Clothes by Order can deduct the cost of tires for income tax purposes. Remember that Clothes by Order's income tax rate was 40 percent. Thus, the net cash outflows (after taxes) for year 3 would be $6,000, as shown below:

Cost of Tires for Delivery Trucks	$10,000
Tax Savings ($10,000 x 0.40)	(4,000)
Net Outflow	$ 6,000

Introducing a salvage value of $15,000 at the end of the life of the trucks modifies the existing analysis as follows:

1. The salvage value represents a future cash inflow which must be considered in the capital budgeting decision. If the company receives the expected amount of salvage value upon disposal of the asset at the end of its useful life, no gain or loss is recognized, and thus there is no income tax impact related to this future cash receipt. Therefore, the $15,000 future cash receipt is merely discounted back to the present period to determine its effect on the net present value of the capital investment.

2. The salvage value should be considered by Clothes by Order in determining its depreciation expense. If Clothes by Order expects to receive $15,000 at the end of the life of the trucks, the annual depreciation expense using the straight-line method is recalculated at $27,500:

$$\text{Depreciation Expense} = \frac{\$180,000 - \$15,000}{6 \text{ years}} = \$27,500$$

The tax savings resulting from this depreciation are $11,000 per year ($27,500 x 0.40 = $11,000). Thus our previous analysis is also modified to reflect the lower tax savings resulting from the decrease in depreciation expense. The net cash inflows and outflows given this new set of facts is graphically illustrated below:

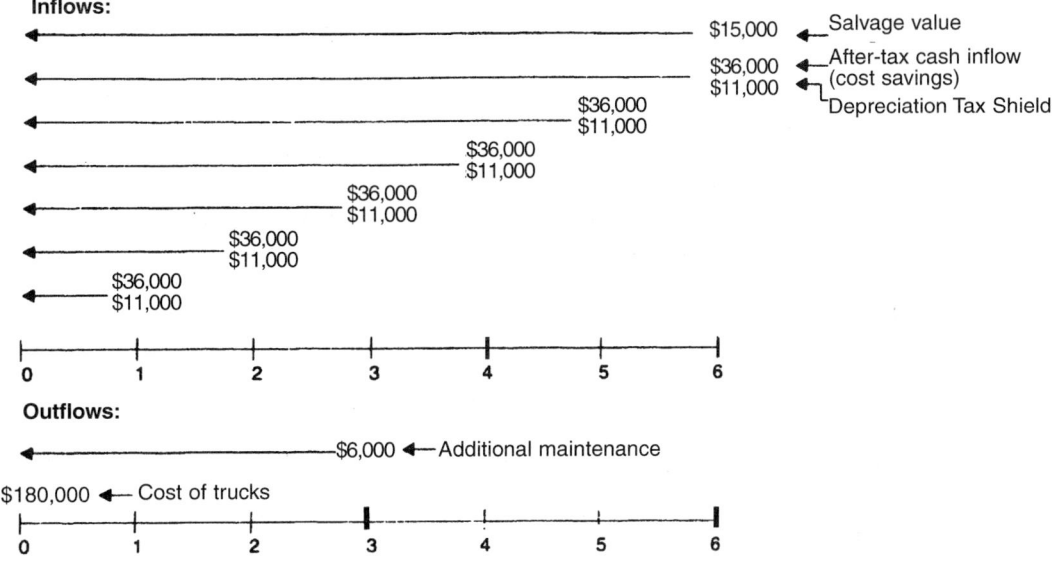

The modified net present value analysis which incorporates these "other" future cash inflows and outflows is presented in Illustration 7. A few changes from the previous analysis presented earlier in Illustration 6 are noticeable. First, additional cash inflows (receipt of the salvage value in year 6) and cash outflows (costs of replacing tires in year 3) are also considered in evaluating this project. Notice that these cash flows are single events, not annuities. As a result, values from the single sum table (Table 1 in the Appendix) are used to discount them to the present period. The only other change reflected in Illustration 7 is that the amount of tax savings from depreciation is reduced from $12,000 per year to $11,000 per year. This reduction is caused by the salvage value. In this particular case, notice that the net present value of this investment is $28,658.80. This implies that the investment earns a return greater than the 10 percent cost of capital. Based on the net present value criterion, Clothes by Order would accept this capital investment.

Illustration 7
Clothes by Order
Net Present Value for Investment in Delivery Trucks
(Including Income Taxes and Additional Cash Inflows and Outflows)

		Year	Amount	Factor From Table 2 (10%)	Present Value
Inflows:	Operating Cost Savings	1-6	$ 36,000[a]	4.3553[c]	$ 156,790.80
	Depreciation Tax Savings	1-6	11,000[b]	4.3553[c]	47,908.30
	Salvage Value	6	15,000	0.5645[d]	8,467.50
	Total Inflows				$ 213,166.60
Outflows:	Amount of Investment	0	$180,000	1.0000	$(180,000.00)
	Cost of Tires	3	6,000	0.7513[d]	(4,507.80)
	Total Outflows				$(184,507.80)
Total Net Present Value:					$ 28,658.80

a $60,000 x (1 − 0.40)
b $27,500 x 0.40
c Factor from the Annuity Table (Table 2 in the Appendix)
d Factor from the Single Sum Table (Table 1 in the Appendix)

Limitations of the Net Present Value Method

Once again, there are certain limitations and unstated assumptions that are inherent in the use of the net present value model. At this point, it may be useful to reiterate these assumptions and limitations. First, the model assumes that the cash inflows and outflows are known with certainty. That is, projections have not considered unforeseen changes in the amount or timing of cash flows. For example, if Clothes by Order performed a present value analysis and decided to purchase the fleet of delivery trucks based on the above assumptions, a large increase in insurance costs or unforeseen repairs could make much of its analysis invalid. A method of dealing with this uncertainty in practice is to use higher discount rates for later cash flows, and in so doing, produce a more conservative (i.e., smaller) measure of net present value.

Second, there is an implicit assumption that the cost of capital considered at the beginning of the analysis remains constant throughout the life of the project. Reflect for a moment on this assumption. Fluctuations in interest rates during the 1970s, from about 6 percent at the beginning of the period, up above 10 percent and back down to 9 percent at the end of the period, indicate that the average investor would have faced significantly different opportunities for investing funds during that period. Similarly, opportunities differ over longer periods of time. If a decision-maker has excess funds and limited investment opportunities, he or she may well accept lower expected returns than when greater investment opportunities are available. Conversely, if a wide variety of investment opportunities exist, higher expected returns would normally be demanded.

A third assumption of the net present value model is that cash flows occur at equal intervals, usually at the end of the year. However, if expected cash flows were projected for six-month intervals in the future, the model could be adjusted by considering each row of the tables presented in the Appendix as a six-month period instead of a year and reducing the interest rate to half the annual rate. For example, recall that Clothes by Order expected cash savings of $60,000 per year. In our previous analysis, we made the assumption that this cash flow occurred at the end of each year. If cash inflows were assumed to occur twice a year ($30,000 for each six-month period) and Clothes by Order's cost of capital was 10 percent, a rough approximation would discount these two inflows as a single sum of $60,000 at the 10 percent rate. This would yield a present value of $54,546 for the operating savings in year 1 ($60,000 x 0.9091= $54,546). More appropriately, we could treat the $30,000 amounts as an annuity discounted at a 5 percent rate, producing a present value of $55,782 for the first year's operating savings ($30,000 x 1.8594 = $55,782). The difference between the two present value calculations is due to compounding earlier returns. Obviously, if cash flows were estimated on a daily basis, the above analysis would be complicated considerably. In most cases, the assumption that cash flows are realized on an annual basis does not introduce a significant error into the analysis.

Advantages of the Net Present Value Method

The primary advantage of the net present value method is its focus on the timing of expected future cash flows. Neither the payback method nor the average (accounting) rate of return distinguish between capital projects based upon the expected timing of future cash flows. If two capital projects have identical total cash flows over their lives, but one of these projects has greater cash inflows earlier in the life of the project, these earlier cash inflows are beneficial to the organization and should be considered.

To illustrate how the timing of cash flows is considered in applying the net present value method, refer to our earlier analysis of future cash inflows and outflows for Clothes by Order (shown in Illustration 4). The net present value of the capital investment providing annual cash inflows of $60,000 per year is $81,312. Compare this net present value to that determined if the delivery trucks were purchased from RedDot. This alternative capital investment was introduced earlier in this chapter. The net cash flows provided by purchasing the trucks from RedDot, along with the net present value of this capital investment, are summarized in Illustration 8.

Illustration 8
RedDot Trucking
Calculation of Net Present Value of Alternative Project with Different Cash Flow Pattern

	Year	Amount	Present Value Factor From Table 1 (10%)	Present Value
Inflows:	1	$ 70,000	0.9091	$ 63,637
	2	70,000	0.8264	57,848
	3	10,000	0.7513	7,513
	4	60,000	0.6830	40,980
	5	75,000	0.6209	46,568
	6	75,000	0.5645	42,338
		$360,000		$258,884
Outflows:	0	$180,000	1.0000	$(180,000)
Net Present Value:				$ 78,884

Illustration 8 reveals that the net present value of purchasing the trucks from RedDot ($78,884) is less than the net present value of purchasing the trucks from AllState ($81,312—see Illustration 4). It is important to note that the total undiscounted cash inflows of these projects are identical ($360,000). The higher net present value for the purchase from AllState occurs because this project has higher cash flows earlier in the life of the project and lower cash flows later in the life of the project. For example, the net cost savings in the first three years for AllState are $180,000, whereas, for RedDot, the cost savings in these same years are $150,000. It is important to reiterate that, as shown in previous sections, neither the payback period method nor the average (accounting) rate of return method distinguished between these two projects. The fact that the net present value method considers the timing of future cash flows is an important advantage associated with this method.

Summary—Net Present Value

The above discussion has illustrated the use of the net present value method to analyze a potential capital investment project. To review, the following major steps are performed when analyzing capital investments using the net present value method:

1. Estimate the amount and timing of all future cash inflows and outflows.
2. Specify the interest rate (cost of capital) used to discount future cash inflows and outflows.
3. Calculate the present value of each cash inflow and outflow.
4. Aggregate the present values of all inflows and outflows (determined in step 3 above).
5. If the net present value is positive, the project's return exceeds the cost of capital and the project should be considered. If the net present value is negative, the return is less than the cost of capital and the project should not be considered further.

In addition to evaluating a single project, the net present value technique can be used to select from among alternative projects. In this case, the five steps enumerated above are repeated for each investment opportunity. When evaluating competing investment projects, the project with the highest net present value (assuming that factors such as quality and serviceability are constant) should be selected.

Illustration 9 summarizes how the various factors discussed in this section are utilized in the net present value analysis.

Illustration 9
Effect of Various Factors on Net Present Value of Capital Investments

Cost of Investment	Cash outflow in period 0 which must be recovered through future operating cost savings.
Operating Cost Savings	Cash inflows over the life of the capital investment. These cash inflows would be discounted to period 0 using the cost of capital.
Income Taxes	Cash inflows from operating cost savings should be reduced by the applicable income taxes prior to discounting.
	Depreciation expense will provide an additional cash inflow through a savings of income taxes.
Other Inflows and Outflows	Other cash inflows and outflows should be discounted to period 0 using the cost of capital.

INTERNAL TIME-ADJUSTED RATE OF RETURN

The *internal time-adjusted rate of return (internal rate of return)* represents the actual return earned by a given capital investment after considering the time value of money. Operationally, the internal rate of return is calculated by finding the discount (interest) rate which equates the present value of the future cash inflows and the present value of the future cash outflows associated with a particular capital investment. While the use of the net present value technique (discussed in the previous section) can reveal only whether the internal rate of return for a given capital investment was greater than the cost of capital, equal to the cost of capital, or less than the cost of capital, the use of the internal rate of return allows the organization to calculate an approximation of the actual return earned with a given capital investment. Since the internal rate of return considers the time value of money, it provides more information to the organization than the average rate of return (discussed earlier in this chapter).

To illustrate the use of the time-adjusted rate of return method, let us consider the Clothes by Order example discussed throughout this chapter. For simplicity, we will ignore the effect of income taxes and any additional future cash inflows from the salvage value and outflows for replacing the tires on the delivery trucks. Thus we will evaluate the future cash inflows and outflows shown earlier in Illustration 4. As shown therein, this involves two cash flows:

> ► The net cost savings of $60,000 per year from purchasing the delivery trucks
>
> ► The purchase price of the delivery trucks ($180,000)

From Illustration 4, we can see that the net present value using a 10 percent interest rate (cost of capital) is $81,312. While this does not provide the actual internal rate of return, it does provide information to Clothes by Order about its internal rate of return. Since the net present value is positive, the purchase of delivery trucks from AllState has a greater rate of return than the cost of capital used to determine that net present value Thus, the internal rate of return on this capital project must be greater than 10 percent. Using a trial-and-error approach, the net present value for various discount rates could be determined. Trying 24 percent, we determine a net present value of $1,200, as shown below:

```
                                    Factor
                                    n = 6
                                    i = 24
                                      ↓
Inflows:
    Operating Savings ($60,000 x 3.020) ................   $181,200
Outflows..................................................   (180,000)
Net Present Value.....................................      $  1,200
```

At this point, we know the internal rate of return is slightly greater than 24 percent, since the net present value at this discount rate is positive. Using 25 percent, we determine a negative net present value of $2,940 as shown below:

```
                                    Factor
                                    n = 6
                                    i = 25
                                      ↓
Inflows:
    Operating Savings ($60,000 x 2.951) ................   $177,060
Outflows..................................................   (180,000)
Net Present Value.....................................      $  2,940
```

Thus, the internal rate of return for purchasing trucks from AllState is between 24 and 25 percent. Clearly, at some point between 24 and 25 percent, the net present value of this capital project is zero. This point represents Clothes by Order's exact internal rate of return on the purchase of delivery trucks.

Rather than a trial-and-error approach, we could use a shortcut in the above calculation. Since the $60,000 cash savings occur at equal intervals and at equal amounts, we could determine the appropriate annuity factor that equates the future cash inflows with the future cash outflows. As shown below, the present value factor is 3.00.

Amount of Inflow	x	Factor From Table 2	=	Cash Outflow
$60,000	x	Factor From Table 2	=	$180,000
		Factor From Table 2	=	3.00

Reading across the n = 6 line of Table 2, we would attempt to find the factor most closely approximating 3.00. As shown below in the excerpt from Table 2, at 24 percent the factor is 3.020; at 25 percent, 2.951. Thus, the appropriate factor (and internal rate of return) lies somewhere between 24 and 25 percent.

	Interest (Discount) Rate		
	22%	24%	25%
n = 6	3.167	3.020	2.951

Desired Factor

Notice that the above calculation does not provide the exact internal rate of return. In most cases, the organization would be satisfied knowing that the internal rate of return is between 24 and 25 percent.[6]

Unequal Cash Flows. The above example makes the assumption that cash inflows and outflows are equal each year and, therefore, can be discounted as annuities. If cash flows are not equal, the use of the internal rate of return method is more cumbersome. The additional complexity arises since the unequal cash flows (i.e., a cash inflow or outflow in a future period that is not uniform for all future periods) must also be considered in calculating the internal rate of return. To illustrate the complexity introduced when cash flows are unequal, assume that the management of Clothes by Order wishes to determine the internal rate of return on an after-tax basis assuming the receipt of a $15,000 salvage value at the end of the investment and the purchase of new tires for $10,000 at the end of the third year. These cash flows (along with the net present value) were shown earlier in Illustration 7. Since the net present value using a 10 percent discount rate is positive, Clothes by Order knows that the internal rate of return is greater than 10 percent. At this point, a trial-and-error basis can be used to determine the discount rate where the net present value is zero. Assume that the following three-step process is used (see Illustration 10):

1. Using a discount rate of 18 percent, a negative net present value of $13,698.00 is calculated (see Part A of Illustration 10). Thus Clothes by Order's internal rate of return would be less than 18 percent.

2. Using a discount rate of 15 percent, a positive net present value of $380.00 is determined (see Part B of Illustration 10). Thus the internal rate of return is greater than 15 percent.

3. Using a discount rate of 16 percent, a negative net present value of $4,501.00 is calculated (see Part C of Illustration 10). Thus we can conclude that the net present value is between 15 and 16 percent.

While the above calculations are straightforward, the process illustrates the difficulty of calculating an internal rate of return when expected future cash flows are not equal. In practice, computer software packages can be used to determine the internal rate of return in lieu of the trial-and-error process shown above. However, it is important to understand that the internal rate of return is that discount rate where the net present value of a capital investment is zero.

Making the Decision. The following process is used in making an investment decision using the internal rate of return method:

> ➤ If the internal rate of return > cost of capital => the investment should be considered
> ➤ If the internal rate of return < cost of capital => the investment should not be considered further

The decision made using the internal rate of return method is identical to that made using the net present value method. This is because when the internal rate of return is greater than the cost of capital, the net present value is positive. In addition, when the internal rate of return is less than the cost of capital, the net present value is negative. As noted earlier, using the net present value method, capital investments with a positive net present value should be considered further, while those with a negative net present value should not be considered further.

Summary—Techniques that Consider the Time Value of Money

The internal rate of return is calculated by determining the set of discount factors that will equate the future cash inflows associated with a particular capital investment with the future cash outflows associated with that investment. This process is often one of trial-and-error, since unequal cash flows are common. Once determined,

---

[6] If more exact information is needed, interpolation or mathematical calculation of the internal rate of return can be used. The exact internal rate of return is 24.29 percent and can be determined through interpolation, as shown below:

	Factor From Table 2	
Factor at 24%............................	3.020	3.020
Internal Rate of Return	3.000	
Factor at 25%............................		2.951
Difference................................	0.020	0.069

Internal Rate of Return = 24% + (0.020/0.069)(1%) = 24.29%

the internal rate of return is then compared to a minimum desired rate of return. If the internal rate of return exceeds this minimum desired rate of return (the cost of capital), the organization would generally accept the proposed capital investment.

In contrast, the net present value method uses the cost of capital as the interest rate to discount expected future cash inflows and outflows to the current period. The present value of these future inflows and outflows are then aggregated, yielding a single total (the net present value). If the net present value is positive or zero, the organization will generally decide to accept the proposed capital investment, since it earns the minimum desired return (the cost of capital). However, if the net present value is negative, the organization will generally not accept the proposed capital investment, since it earns a return lower than the cost of capital. The net present value method of analysis is often easier to apply than the internal time-adjusted rate of return since it does not require searching for present value factors which will produce a "true" rate of return.

SUMMARY OF CAPITAL BUDGETING TECHNIQUES

Illustration 11 summarizes the four major capital budgeting techniques discussed in this chapter (payback period, average rate of return, net present value, and internal rate of return). In addition, the decision criteria employed in using these techniques are also presented.

Illustration 10
Clothes by Order
Internal Time-Adjusted Rate of Return
(Unequal Cash Flows)

Part A: 18 Percent Discount Rate

Inflows:
Operating Savings ($36,000 x 3.498)	$ 125,928.00
Depreciation Tax Savings ($11,000 x 3.498)	38,478.00
Salvage Value ($15,000 x 0.370)	5,550.00
Total Inflows	$ 169,956.00

Outflows:
Cost of Delivery Trucks	$ (180,000.00)
Cost of Tires in Year 3 ($6,000 x 0.609)	(3,654.00)
Total Outflows	$ 183,654.00

Net Present Value .... $ (13,698.00)

Part B: 15 Percent Discount Rate

Inflows:
Operating Savings ($36,000 x 3.784)	$ 136,224.00
Depreciation Tax Savings ($11,000 x 3.784)	41,624.00
Salvage Value ($15,000 x 0.432)	6,480.00
Total Inflows	$ 184,328.00

Outflows:
Cost of Delivery Trucks	$ (180,000.00)
Cost of Tires in Year 3 ($6,000 x 0.658)	(3,948.00)
Total Outflows	$ (183,948.00)

Net Present Value .... $ 380.00

Part C: 16 Percent Discount Rate

Inflows:
Operating Savings ($36,000 x 3.685)	$ 132,660.00
Depreciation Tax Savings ($11,000 x 3.685)	40,535.00
Salvage Value ($15,000 x 0.410)	6,150.00
Total Inflows	$ 179,345.00

Outflows:
Cost of Delivery Trucks	$ (180,000.00)
Cost of Tires in Year 3 ($6,000 x 0.641)	(3,846.00)
Total Outflows	$ (183,846.00)

Net Present Value .... $ (4,501.00)

Illustration 11
Summary of Capital Budgeting Techniques

Method	Definition	Decision Criterion
Payback Period	Length of time required until the organization recovers its initial capital investment	Select the capital investment if its payback period is shorter than organizational guidelines or that of other capital investments
Average (Accounting) Rate of Return	Average increase in net income from capital investment divided by the initial investment (or average investment)	Select the capital investment if its average rate of return is greater than organizational guidelines or that of other capital investments
Net Present Value	Difference between the present value of future cash inflows and future cash outflows	Select the capital investment if its net present value is positive or greater than that of other capital investments
Internal (time-adjusted) Rate of Return	Discount rate at which the present value of the cash inflows equals the present value of the cash outflows	Select the capital investment if its internal rate of return exceeds the cost of capital or the rate of return on other investments

POSTAUDIT OF CAPITAL INVESTMENTS

Once managers have decided to invest in a particular capital project, the capital budgeting process still is not complete. The organization should continually monitor and evaluate the success or failure of that capital project throughout its life. This continual evaluation is referred to as a postaudit and serves as an integral component of the capital budgeting process. In a postaudit, information is obtained about the actual cash inflows and cash outflows of the project. This actual information is then compared to the projections used in making the investment decision. The postaudit can be used to improve the process through which cost savings are estimated on future capital projects. While the postaudit can also be used to evaluate the performance of the individual(s) responsible for selecting the capital project, any punitive action should be exercised with caution. Recall that all capital budgeting decisions are surrounded by a tremendous amount of uncertainty.

In the Clothes by Order example discussed throughout the chapter, a postaudit would determine the actual cost savings associated with the purchase of the delivery trucks. Recall that Clothes by Order estimated an increase in maintenance, insurance, and other costs of $10,000 per year. If these costs averaged $20,000 per year for the first three years of the project, it is evident that the investment in delivery trucks would not be as desirable as initially thought. While Clothes by Order obviously cannot change its decision to purchase the delivery trucks from AllState, the maintenance, insurance, and other costs incurred in operating these delivery trucks should be considered in future investment decisions for other trucks.

CAPITAL BUDGETING FOR HIGH-TECHNOLOGY ASSETS

A recent phenomenon faced by decision-makers is the need to consider investments in high-technology capital assets. For example, many processes previously performed by humans are now automated and are performed by robots or other advanced production processes. While an extensive discussion of automated production processes is beyond the scope of this text, considering capital investments in high-technology assets introduces a number of additional complexities. These complexities are summarized below.

1. **Large initial dollar investments.** When a company initially automates a portion of its production processes, the cost is ordinarily substantial. This large initial cost may make it difficult to justify automation using traditional capital budgeting techniques. When evaluating the possibility of automation, the use of the payback method, average rate of return, net present value, or internal rate of return may suggest that older

production equipment should be replaced with less expensive equipment, as opposed to robots or other advanced production processes.

2. **Longer time horizons.** Automated manufacturing equipment normally provides benefits to the organization over an extremely long time horizon. Thus while a method such as the payback period could indicate that a capital investment in automated equipment is not desirable, cost savings that are realized over an extremely long time horizon may increase the desirability of this investment to management.

3. **Difficulty in quantifying cash inflows.** The cash inflows (cost savings) associated with automated production processes can be quite difficult for management to quantify. First, the complexity of the assets and the lack of previous experience with high-technology assets may make it difficult for managers to accurately estimate the cost savings associated with automated manufacturing equipment. Also, many benefits of automated production processes are not easy to quantify. For example, these processes normally are characterized by faster throughput time, increased manufacturing flexibility, and increased response to changes in customer demand. While these benefits should obviously be considered, they are very difficult to quantify and may be ignored if the company is not careful in conducting its analysis.

THE USE OF CAPITAL BUDGETING TECHNIQUES IN PRACTICE

It should be apparent that a wide range of capital budgeting techniques are available to assist management in making long-term investment decisions. Many companies use a combination of capital budgeting techniques and evaluate the evidence provided by multiple techniques. A survey of Fortune 1000 companies reveals the following use of capital budgeting techniques:[7]

	Primary Technique	Secondary Technique
Payback Period	12%	39%
Accounting Rate of Return	8	3
Internal Rate of Return	49	8
Net Present Value	19	8

Based on the above data, it appears that most companies use some combination of internal rate of return and payback period in evaluating capital investments.

SUMMARY

This chapter introduces the concept of capital budgeting and illustrates techniques used by organizations to evaluate the desirability of alternative capital investments. Some of the major points discussed include:

1. Investment decisions which involve relatively large amounts of money over longer periods of time are referred to as capital budgeting decisions. Capital budgeting decisions include purchasing fixed assets and other types of property, plant and equipment.

2. Two types of capital budgeting decisions are acceptance decisions and capital rationing decisions. An *acceptance decision* occurs when the organization is evaluating the desirability of a single capital investment and has sufficient funds to undertake that investment. *Capital rationing decisions* involve selecting from among alternative capital projects to best employ limited resources.

3. Because of the long periods of time involved with capital investment decisions, the organization may wish to consider the time value of money in making these decisions. The *time value of money concept* is based on the premise that an individual would prefer to receive an amount of money in the current period rather than receiving the same amount of money in a future period. This preference exists because, if received in a current period, the money could be invested to earn a return.

4. Two capital budgeting techniques which ignore the time value of money are the payback period and the average rate of return (accounting rate of return). The payback period is a rough approximation of the length of time necessary for the organization to recover its investment. The average rate of return is a measure of the average profitability associated with a capital investment over its life expressed as a percentage of the cost of the capital investment.

---

[7] S.H. Kim and D.J. Parragher, "Current Capital Budgeting Practices," *Management Accounting* (June 1981), 26–30.

5. When using the above capital budgeting techniques, management can compare the computed payback period and average rate of return to organizational guidelines to determine whether the calculated measures meet minimum desired standards. In addition, if alternative capital investment opportunities exist, these measures can be computed for each opportunity and compared to identify the most desirable investment.

6. Because of the length of most capital investments, it is important for the organization to consider both the amounts and timing of future cash inflows. As a result, many organizations utilize capital budgeting techniques which consider the *time value of money*. These methods include the net present value method and the internal time-adjusted rate of return method.

7. When using the *net present value method*, expected future cash inflows and outflows are discounted to the current period using an interest (discount) rate which represents the organization's cost of capital. Common cash inflows (cost savings) associated with capital investments include operating cost savings, the tax savings from recognizing depreciation expense, and salvage values received upon disposal of the asset. Cash outflows include the initial outlay for the capital investment and any maintenance expenditures expected during the life of the capital investment.

8. The *internal time-adjusted rate of return* represents that interest rate which equates the present value of the future cash inflows with the present value of the future cash outflows. This rate can be calculated with the use of present values tables (if future cash inflows and outflows are uniform each year) or by trial-and-error (if future cash inflows and outflows are not uniform). If the internal time-adjusted rate of return exceeds the cost of capital, the organization will generally consider accepting the proposed capital investment.

KEY DEFINITIONS

Acceptance decision—a capital budgeting decision in which a single investment is considered.

Annuity—a series of equal payments or receipts of cash that occur at equal time intervals

Average rate of return (Accounting rate of return)—a measure of the profitability of a capital investment which expresses the increases in net income attributed to the capital investment as a percentage of the cost of the capital investment.

Capital budgeting—investment decisions which involve relatively large amounts of money over long periods of time.

Capital rationing decision—a capital budgeting decision that involves allocating scarce resources among a set of alternative capital investments.

Cost of capital—the minimum acceptable rate of return required to be earned on a capital investment. The cost of capital also represents the interest rate used to discount future cash inflows and outflows using the net present value method.

Internal time-adjusted rate of return—the interest rate which equates the present value of the future cash inflows with the present value of the future cash outflows.

Net present value method—a capital budgetin g technique which discounts future cash inflows and outflows to the present period using an interest rate equal to the cost of capital.

Payback period—a technique which calculates the length of time necessary for the organization to recover its capital investment.

QUESTIONS

1. How does capital budgeting differ from other forms of budgeting?

2. Which of the following capital budgeting techniques ignore the time value of money?

   a. Payback period.
   b. Average rate of return.
   c. Net present value.
   d. Internal time-adjusted rate of return.

3. What are cash outflows compared to in capital budgeting decisions?

4. A capital budgeting analysis that evaluates investments solely on the basis of total returns is ignoring what crucial factors?

5. Evaluate the following statement: "All firms of similar size will always have the same time value preference rate (time value of money)."

6. A firm may alter its time value preference rate from year to year. What environmental factors could affect the firm's evaluation of the time value of money?

7. "The discounted net present value model weighs early receipts of cash much more heavily than late receipts of cash." Relate this timing sensitivity to the concept of compound interest.

8. What limitations are implicit in the net present value method?

9. Compare and contrast the net present value model with the time-adjusted rate of return method.

10. How does depreciation expense affect the capital budgeting analysis using the net present value method?

EXERCISES AND PROBLEMS

11. *Basic Present Value—Single Sum.* Determine the total present value in year zero of the following expected series of future cash outflows using a discount rate of: (a) 8 percent, (b) 12 percent, and (c) 15 percent.

Year	Cash Outflow
1	$4,000
2	6,000
3	2,000
4	7,000

12. *Present Value—Single Sum.* Determine the present value of $1,000 due in five years at each of the following interest rates:

    a. 6 percent
    b. 8 percent
    c. 10 percent

13. *Present Value—Single Sum.* An investor wishes to have $5,000 available at the end of five years. Determine the amount that must be invested at the present time if the interest rate is:

    a. 6 percent
    b. 8 percent
    c. 12 percent

14. *Present Value—Single Sum.* Compute the net present value of these three individual cases at a rate of 10 percent.

	Outlay 0	Future Period Inflows 1	2	3	4
A	$(2,000)	$1,150		$1,150	
B	$(2,000)	$1,150			$1,150
C	$(2,000)		$1,150	$1,150	

    Required:

    a. Which of these three investments is the most desirable?
    b. Which is more desirable using 6% interest?

15. **Basic Present Value—Annuities.** An investor wishes to receive $12,000 at the end of each of the next six years. How much total money must he invest at the present time (assuming the following interest rates) to achieve his goal?

    a. 10 percent
    b. 13 percent
    c. 14 percent

16. **Basic Present Value—Single Sums and Annuities.** Assume that you have an opportunity to purchase an annuity which will yield $10,000 per year at the end of each of the next six years. Also assume that your cost of capital (interest rate) is 6 percent.

    Required:

    a. Using the annuity tables (Table 2 in the Appendix), how much would you be willing to pay for this privilege?
    b. Repeat (a) using the single sum tables (Table 1 in the Appendix).

17. **Basic Present Value—Various.** Below are four independent cases that explore the relationship between present values, interest rates, length of the investment period, and future values. In each case, one element is missing. Determine the number that corresponds to each missing element, A through D.

	Case 1	Case 2	Case 3	Case 4
Present Value	$5,000	$ 3,050	$2,000	D
Interest Rate	12%	16%	C	11%
Number of Years	8	B	10	15
Future Value	A	$10,000	$4,318	$4,180

18. **Present Value—Annuity.** You are considering an outlay of X dollars, which will produce an annual benefit of Y dollars per year for Z years. Your cost of capital is 10 percent.

    Required:

    Use the following alternative choices to answer A to C below:

    1. 0%
    2. exactly 10%
    3. equal to or greater than 10%
    4. equal to or less than 10%
    5. greater than 10%
    6. less than 10%
    7. none of the above
    8. cannot determine from the data given

    a. If the present value of the Y dollars per year for Z years is X dollars, the return from the investment is _____.
    b. If the present value of the Y dollars per year for Z years is X + 1 dollars, the return from the investment is _____.
    c. If the present value of the Y dollars per year for Z years is X − 1 dollars, the return from the investment is _____.

19. *Present Value—Annuity.* You have a choice of $19 today or two payments of $10 each to be received exactly one year and two years from today. Assume that you can always earn 5% per year.

    Required:

    Answer the following questions:

    a. The present value of the $19 received today is _____.
    b. The total present value of the two $10 payments is _____.
    c. The approximate rate of return earned if the two-payment alternative is selected is between _____ and _____.
    d. Which alternative would you select:
        1. the $19 single payment or
        2. the two $10 payments?

20. *Payback Method.* Determine the payback period for each of the following three capital investment alternatives, based on both a year-by-year analysis of cash inflows and the average cash inflows per year.

	Cash Inflows From Investment				
	0	1	2	3	4
A	$(50,000)	$20,000	$15,000	$10,000	$7,500
B	(50,000)	17,500	20,000	15,000	
C	(50,000)	30,000	15,000		5,000

    Required:

    Based upon your payback period calculation, which investment would be selected if you were restricted to choosing only one of these alternatives?

21. *Payback Method.* Calculate the payback period for the following independent investments using both: average cash inflows per year and a year-by-year analysis of cash inflows. Assuming that only one investment may be selected, which opportunity would be chosen based on these methods?

	Cash Inflows From Investment			
	0	1	2	3
A	$(50,000)	$35,000	$30,000	$25,000
B	(50,000)	35,000	15,000	10,000
C	(65,000)	25,000	25,000	25,000

22. *Payback Method.* The Rogers Corporation uses payback analysis to evaluate its investments. This year, three alternatives are considered, each requiring an outlay of $50,000. The first returns $10,000 for the first four years and $5,000 for five years following. The second returns $6,000 per year for ten years. The third returns $5,000 for the first eight years and $10,000 for the next seven years.

    Required:

    a. Calculate the payback period for each of the three alternatives.
    b. What are the drawbacks of the payback method of capital budgeting analysis?
    c. On the basis of simple payback, which of the three alternatives would be selected?

23. *Average Rate of Return.* The Stevens Company, a processor of whole milk, uses the average rate of return method for computing rate of return. They have two alternatives to consider. The first requires an investment of $25,000 and earns an average after-tax profit of $5,000 for each of ten years. The second also necessitates an investment of $25,000 but produces an average after-tax profit of $4,000 for each of ten years.

    Required:

    a. Compute the average rate of return for both projects.
    b. What essential considerations are not taken into account by the average rate of return method?
    c. In which of the two processes would you invest if you were using the average rate of return? Why?

24. *Average Rate of Return.* The Center Company is contemplating an investment in a new machine. This machine would cost $25,000 and would provide the following net future cash inflows (before taxes):

Year	Cash Inflows
1	$10,000
2	8,500
3	7,000
4	7,000
5	4,000

The Center Company estimates that expenditures for repairs and maintenance for this machine in each year would be $150 (year 1), $200 (year 2), $350 (year 3), $500 (year 4), and $800 (year 5). The machine will be depreciated using the straight-line method with a salvage value of $3,000. The average income tax rate for Center Company is 50 percent.

Required:

Determine the average rate of return before taxes and after taxes. If Center requires a minimum rate of return of 20 percent (after taxes), should this investment be selected?

25. *Average Rate of Return.* Your Company is considering investing in a new machine for use in its factory. The cost of Machine A is $20,000 and the cost of Machine B is $30,000. Both Machine A and Machine B would perform the task required by the company equally well. The net cash inflows (before taxes) from both machines are as follows:

Year	Machine A	Machine B
1	$ 5,000	$ 6,500
2	7,000	9,000
3	10,000	13,000
4	8,000	14,500
5	5,000	7,000
6	4,000	4,000
Total	$39,000	$54,000

Both machines are depreciated on a straight-line basis over their six-year useful lives. Machine A has a $5,000 salvage value and Machine B has a $6,000 salvage value. The average corporate income tax rate is 45 percent for the six-year time period.

Required:

Determine the average rate of return for both machines before income taxes are considered and after income taxes are considered. Based on this method, which investment would be selected?

26. *Average Rate of Return.* The Kicker Corporation is currently faced with a decision on the purchase of a new machine. An old machine, which has a zero salvage value, needs to be replaced. The replacement machine under consideration has forecast cash inflows and outflows as shown below:

Year	Cash Flow
0	$(45,000)
1	10,000
2	15,000
3	22,500
4	12,500
5	7,000

If purchased, the new machine would be depreciated over its five-year useful life using the straight-line method. Kicker estimates that the salvage value of the new machine would be $5,000 (this amount is not included in the year 5 net inflows). Ignore income taxes in your calculation.

Required:

Determine the average rate of return for this investment. If Kicker Corporation requires a minimum average rate of return of 12 percent, should this machine be purchased?

27. *Net Present Value—Unequal Cash Flows Without Taxes.* Joe Grogin has identified four projects as having investment potential. Expected cash flows on each project are described below:

Year	Flow	Project A	Project B	Project C	Project D
0	out	$(4,000)	$(3,500)	$(4,500)	$(3,000)
1	in				
2	in			1,000	3,993
3	in	6,100	1,000	2,000	
4	in		4,000	4,000	

Required:

a. What is the net present value of each project at a 10 percent time preference?
b. Which should Joe accept if he can invest in only one?

28. *Net Present Value—Equal Cash Flows Without Taxes.* Toolco is considering the acquisition of a $60,000 machine that has a four-year life. The machine will do the work of four men, and the resulting cost savings (net of additional machine-related costs) are expected to amount to $20,000 per year. Ignore tax considerations.

Required:

What is the net present value of the proposed project, assuming that Toolco has a 15 percent time value of money?

29. *Net Present Value—Unequal Cash Flows Without Taxes.* Ajax Company has identified three investment opportunities that are summarized below:

Year	Flow	Project A	Project B	Project C
0	out	$(20,000)	$(20,000)	$(20,000)
1	in	10,000	15,000	5,000
2	in	10,000	10,000	10,000
3	in	10,000	5,000	15,000
	Net	$10,000	$10,000	$10,000

Required:

Rank the projects in terms of desirability, assuming a 10 percent time value of money.

30. *Net Present Value—Unequal Cash Flows Without Taxes.* Shown below are the expected cash inflows (outflows) associated with three capital investments. Determine the net present value of each alternative using a cost of capital of 10 percent. Ignore income taxes.

	Investment		
Year	A	B	C
0	$(5,000)	$(2,500)	$(3,000)
1	2,000	1,000	1,000
2	5,000	500	1,500
3	1,000	2,000	1,000
4	3,000	700	3,000

31. *Net Present Value—Equal Cash Flows With Taxes.* The James Company is considering investing in a new machine to increase its productive capacity. The purchase price of this new machine is $45,000, and it has an expected life of eight years and an estimated salvage value of $5,000. This machine would be depreciated using the straight-line method. James Company estimates that the acquisition of the new machine will decrease repair and maintenance expenditures by $15,000 per year, but it will increase insurance and utilities expenditures by $2,000 and $1,500 per year, respectively. James' cost of capital is 12 percent and its expected tax rate is 50 percent.

Required:

Based on the use of the net present value method, should James Company purchase the machine?

32. *Net Present Value—Equal Cash Flows with Taxes.* The Bastrop Company has an old asset with a historical cost of $20,000 and a net book value of zero. Bastrop is considering replacing this old asset with a similar asset having a cost of $45,000. This new asset would be depreciated over its estimated useful life of five years using the straight-line method with a salvage value of $5,000. The company can currently acquire capital to purchase the new asset at an interest rate of 10 percent. The estimated net increase in before-tax cash flows is expected to be $15,000 per year. Bastrop's income tax rate is 40 percent.

Required:

Using the net present value method, determine whether Bastrop should purchase this asset.

33. *Net Present Value—Equal Cash Flows with Taxes.* Ames Company is trying to determine whether it should purchase a new machine or continue using the one it currently owns. The new machine has a cost of $30,000 and will be depreciated using the straight-line method over its useful life of five years with an estimated salvage value of $5,000. The current machine is expected to be used for five more years; the depreciation expense associated with this machine is $2,000 per year with a zero salvage value. It is expected that no proceeds could be received through the sale of the machine currently owned.

While the acquisition of the new machine will not increase future cash inflows, it will avoid future cash expenditures for repairs and maintenance to the old machine of $16,000 per year. Ames' cost of capital is 12 percent and its income tax rate is 45 percent.

Required:

Advise Ames as to whether or not it should buy this machine using the net present value method.

34. *Net Present Value.* Jess, Inc. is considering purchasing a new machine for $18,000. It will have a useful life of 10 years, a salvage value of $3,000 and will be depreciated on a straight-line basis.

The old machine, which cost $15,000, has been depreciated for 5 of its 15-year useful life. It is not expected to have any salvage value at the end of 15 years. It is being depreciated using the straight-line method. At the present time, the machine can be sold for $9,000. Any gain or loss on the sale can be considered ordinary income. The company's cost of capital is 12 percent. The tax rate is 40 percent. The new machine will save the company $2,500 per year.

Required:

Using the net present value method, decide whether the company should purchase the new machine.

35. *Net Present Value.* A company is considering purchasing a new machine for $12,000. The new machine will have a useful life of 10 years and a salvage value of $2,000. It will be depreciated on a straight-line basis.

The old machine, which cost $10,000, also has a useful life of 10 more years but has been fully depreciated for tax purposes. It can be sold for $500 at the present time.

The company's cost of capital is 6%, and the tax rate is 50 percent. The new machine will save the company $2,000 per year.

Required:

Using the net present value method, decide whether the company should purchase the new machine.

36. *Net Present Value—Unequal Cash Flows with Taxes.* The Sue Company is considering the purchase of a new machine to replace a machine it is currently using. The old machine has a current salvage (and book) value of $5,000. The new machine has an expected useful life of ten years, a salvage value of $10,000, and a cost of $60,000. Assume that Sue plans to use the straight-line method of depreciation.

   If purchased, the new machine will increase productivity in such a way that cash inflows will increase by $10,000 per year in the first five years and $18,000 per year in years 6 through 10 (the last five years of the capital investment). Sue has a cost of capital of 12 percent and an income tax rate of 45 percent.

Required:

Using the net present value method, determine whether Sue Company should purchase the new machine. [Hint: Discount the annuity for years 6 through 10 (n = 5) to a single sum at year 5. This single sum can then be discounted to year 0 using Table 1 of the Appendix.]

37. *Net Present Value—Unequal Cash Flows with Taxes.* The Loafer Corporation must make a decision on whether or not to expand its operating capacity. The expansion would require the acquisition of an additional building and equipment. The new building, which would have an expected useful life of forty years, costs $200,000 and would be constructed on property already owned by Loafer Corporation. At the end of its useful life, Loafer does not expect to receive any proceeds from disposal of the building.

    The new machinery would cost $150,000. The expected useful life of this machinery is ten years with an expected salvage value of $20,000. The straight-line method of depreciation will be used for both the building and the machinery.

    If the expansion is undertaken, it is expected that Loafer's cash receipts will increase by $80,000 per year for the first ten years. In the remaining thirty years (after the machine's disposal), it is expected that the net increase in cash receipts provided by the building will be $25,000 per year. The plant expansion will cost an additional $30,000 a year in wages, salaries, maintenance, etc. for the first ten years with the additional costs decreasing to $15,000 per year for the remaining life of the building (30 years).

    Loafer's cost of capital is 10 percent, and its income tax rate is 40 percent.

Required:

Based on the use of the net present value method, should Loafer perform the plant expansion? Explain. [Hint: Discount the annuity for years 11 through 40 (n = 30) to a single sum at year 10. This single sum can then be discounted to year 0 using Table 1 in the Appendix.]

38. *Net Present Value—Unequal Cash Flows with Taxes.* Davis, Inc. is considering purchasing a new machine that has an expected life of ten years. Using the data below, determine whether this venture will be profitable. (Round cents to the nearest dollar.)

    1. The new machine, which will cost $40,000, will have a useful life of six years. At the end of that time, it is expected to have a salvage value of $1,000. The depreciation schedule is:

Year	Depreciation
1	$6,000
2	8,800
3	8,400
4	8,400
5	8,400
6	0

    2. The new machine will not be replacing an old machine. It will be used to handle an increase in demand for the company's product.

    3. Net cash inflows from operations before depreciation and taxes will be $9,500 in years 1 through 3, $12,000 in years 4 and 5, and $8,000 in year 6.

    4. The company's tax rate is 40 percent, and its cost of capital is 10 percent.

39. Internal Time-Adjusted Rate of Return—Equal Cash Flows. Shown below are six capital investment opportunities available to your company, Aints, Inc. The annual cost savings are expected to be realized for the following three years, the life of the capital investment.

	Cash Outflow	Annual Cost Savings
A	$(1,000)	$ 700
B	(5,000)	4,200
C	(3,000)	2,200
D	(3,000)	1,900
E	(6,000)	5,000
F	(1,000)	800

Required:

a. Calculate the internal time-adjusted rate of return for each of these capital investments. Assume a 45 percent income tax rate. Ignore any effects of depreciation in your calculations.
b. Based on (a), which investment(s) should Aints accept if it has $6,000 to invest?

40. Internal Time-Adjusted Rate of Return—Unequal Cash Flows. Shown below are the net cash inflows and outflows associated with three capital investments available to Maris, Inc.

	Cash Outflow 0	Future Cash Inflows 1	2	3
1	$(5,000)	$2,000	$1,700	$2,400
2	(5,000)	3,000	2,000	1,100
3	(5,000)	1,500	600	4,000

Required:

a. Calculate the internal time-adjusted rate of return for each of these three capital investments. Ignore income taxes and do not include any effects of depreciation. (Hint: Begin your analysis using a 10% rate of return and, based on your results, use other rates as considered necessary.)
b. Assume that Maris, Inc. can only accept one of these alternatives, which one should it choose?

41. Internal Time-Adjusted Rate of Return. A local delicatessen owner was considering the purchase of a new meat case to replace the one he had used for fifteen years. The cost of the new case was $2,400, payable in two equal annual payments. The store owner, Mr. Spendlow, felt that the new case would reduce refrigeration and spoilage costs by $800 per year and have a useful life of five years with no salvage value.

Required:

What is the internal rate of return for this investment?

42. Internal Time-Adjusted Rate of Return. A firm is considering the purchase of a new piece of equipment. Below are the basic data relevant to this purchase:

Initial cost—$24,000
Life—8 years
Salvage value—$2,000
Straight-line depreciation
Overhaul at the end of year four—$6,000
Operating cost savings—$7,000 per year
Tax Rate—50%

Required:

Determine this equipment's internal rate of return. Round to the nearest dollar.

43. *Internal Time-Adjusted Rate of Return—Equal Cash Flows.* Fritz Company is considering an investment in a new machine to improve the production of one of its products. The old machine requires a great deal of maintenance because of its age, so the company feels it will save about $10,000 per year in maintenance costs if it purchases the new machine. The power bill will increase by $0.06 per unit, but the company will also be saving $0.48 per unit in labor costs. The machine will cost $375,000 and has a useful life of ten years with no salvage value at that time. It will be depreciated on the straight-line basis. Production will equal sales in all years. In years 1 through 5 production will be 90,000 units, but it will increase by 20,000 units in each of the remaining years. The old machine is fully depreciated and will be abandoned in a field behind the factory.

Required:

If the company's minimum rate of return is 12 percent and its tax rate is 40 percent, should the investment be undertaken? Find the internal rate of return for the investment rounding to the nearest cent.

44. *Net Present Value and Payback Method: Unequal Cash Flows.* The Grahm Company is considering three mutually exclusive proposals, all of which would require an initial cash outlay of $90,000. The company has estimated that the net cash proceeds from each proposal would be:

End-of-Year	Proposal A	Proposal B	Proposal C
1	$50,000	$30,000	$30,000
2	40,000	30,000	30,000
3	30,000	30,000	60,000
4	20,000	30,000	20,000
5	20,000	30,000	20,000
6	20,000	30,000	20,000

Since only one of the three proposals can be accepted, the president of the company has argued that the decision should be made on the basis of a present value analysis. However, the treasurer of the company believes that the decision should be made on the basis of a payback analysis.

Required:

Without considering taxes, rank the three proposals as to their desirability by the present value method (cost of capital is 12%) and the payback method.

45. *Payback Method, Average Rate of Return, and Net Present Value—Unequal Cash Flows.* Able Corporation is considering the purchase of a new asset for $25,000. This asset has an estimated useful life of five years and will be depreciated using the straight-line method with no salvage value. The estimated increase in cash flows resulting from this capital investment over the life of the asset is $7,500, $9,000, $10,000, $8,500, and $5,000 for years 1 through 5, respectively. The desired discount rate for this asset is 15 percent and the average annual income tax rate is 40 percent.

Required:

a. Based on average annual inflows, what is the payback period (ignore income taxes)?
b. What is the average rate of return (after taxes)?
c. What is the net present value of the investment?

46. *Payback Method and Net Present Value—Equal Cash Flows.* Baxter Corporation is currently trying to decide whether or not to buy a new machine for a purchase price of $40,000. This new machine would be depreciated over its eight-year useful life using the straight-line method with a zero estimated salvage value. The incremental cash inflows resulting from the purchase of this machine would be approximately $8,500 per year. Also, an additional $1,500 per year in cost savings related to repairs to Baxter's old machine is expected to be realized if the new machine is purchased.

Baxter has fully depreciated its old machine and does not anticipate receiving any proceeds from the disposal of that machine. Baxter's annual income tax rate is 40 percent, and its cost of capital is 12 percent.

Required:

Determine the following information with respect to Baxter's purchase of the new machine.

a. Net cash inflows (outflows) per year.
b. Present value of the net outlay in year 0.
c. Payback period using average annual cash inflows (ignore income taxes).
d. Advantage (or disadvantage) of the new machine using the net present value method.

47. *Payback Method and Net Present Value: Equal Cash Flows.* The Active Corporation is currently using a machine which was purchased four years ago for a cost of $40,000. This machine has been depreciated over its six-year useful life using the straight-line method with a salvage value of $4,000. Management is currently trying to decide if they should replace this machine. The estimated proceeds received from the sale of this machine are $9,000.

The new machine considered by Active Corporation would cost $65,000. This machine would be depreciated over its six-year useful life using the straight-line method of depreciation assuming a salvage value of $5,000. It is estimated that the purchase of the new machine would lower the annual repair and maintenance expenditures by an average of $19,000 per year; however, it is estimated that the new machine will cost an additional $1,000 per year in increased insurance premiums.

Assume that Active's cost of capital is 10 percent, and its income tax rate is 45 percent.

Required:

Determine the following as they relate to the purchase of the new machine:

a. Net cash inflows (outflows) by year.
b. Present value of the net outlay in year 0.
c. Payback period using average annual cash inflows (ignore income taxes).
d. Advantage (or disadvantage) of the new machine using the net present value method.

48. *Payback Method and Net Present Value: Unequal Cash Flows.* The Ape Company has $60,000 of cash that it wants to invest immediately. It has the following investment alternatives and corresponding cash outflows and inflows:

Year	Investment A	Investment B	Investment C	Investment D
0	$(30,000)	$(60,000)	$(60,000)	$(30,000)
1	14,000	14,000	20,000	8,000
2	12,000	16,500	19,000	8,000
3	9,500	20,000	17,500	8,000
4	5,500	20,000	15,000	8,000
5	4,500	15,000	11,000	8,000

For purposes of this problem, ignore income taxes and assume a cost of capital of 14 percent.

Required:

Rank the investment alternatives in order of desirability based upon the results of the following methods:

a. The net present value method.
b. The payback method (using a year-by-year analysis).

49. *Payback Method and Net Present Value—Unequal Cash Flows Ignoring Income Taxes.* The Jolly Corporation has four investment proposals that require a net outlay of $50,000 in year 0. Jolly's cost of capital is 12 percent. Information on the estimated cash inflows and outflows is as follows:

Year	Investment A	Investment B	Investment C	Investment D
0	$(50,000)	$(50,000)	$(50,000)	$(50,000)
1	14,000	18,400	22,000	30,000
2	15,000	18,400	21,500	25,000
3	18,500	18,400	19,500	16,000
4	20,500	18,400	17,000	10,000
5	19,000	18,400	15,000	10,000

Required:

Ignoring income taxes, rank these four alternative capital investments in order of desirability based on:

a. The net present value method.
b. The payback method (average cash inflows per year).

50. *Average Rate of Return and Net Present Value.* The Dollar-Wise Corporation has hired you as a consultant to help it make a decision on the acquisition of new machinery. The company has given you the following information for two opportunities it is currently considering:

	Machine X	Machine Y
Annual Cost Savings	$45,000	$37,500
Annual Increase in Operating Expenses	30,000	20,000
Annual Increase in Repairs and Maintenance	3,000	5,000
Useful Life	8 years	6 years
Cost of Machine	68,000	57,500
Salvage Value	4,000	3,750

Dollar-Wise has a cost of capital of 12 percent, uses the straight-line method of depreciation, and has a 45 percent income tax rate.

Required:

Which investment should be selected based on the use of: (a) the average rate of return and (b) the net present value method?

51. *Internal Time-Adjusted Rate of Return and Net Present Value—Equal Cash Flows.* Your Company wants to purchase a new machine. The vital information on two possible choices is as follows:

	Machine 1	Machine 2
Purchase Price	$45,000	$55,000
Useful Life	9 years	10 years
Annual Cost Savings	$12,000	$15,000
Salvage Value	9,000	5,000

The annual corporate income tax rate is 40 percent, and the cost of capital is 12 percent. Assume the use of the straight-line method of depreciation.

Required:

Make a recommendation to your employer using both the net present value method and the internal time-adjusted rate of return method. Why would your decision using these two methods be the same?

52. *Comprehensive.* The Acme Company is currently using a machine that was purchased on January 1, 20x1 at a cost of $8,600. It was assigned a useful life of 8 years and a salvage value of $600. The straight-line method of depreciation is used. The company is considering replacing this machine on January 1, 20x4 with a new machine that would cost $9,000. The new machine would have a useful life of 5 years and a salvage value of $1,000. The straight-line method of depreciation would be used.

With the new machine, expected direct labor savings would be $1,250 per year for the five years. The old machine can be sold immediately for $3,500. Assume that the tax impact from the sale of the old machine occurs immediately when the sale is made.

The tax rate is 40 percent. The cost of capital (or rate of discount) is 16 percent.

Required:

Determine the following as they relate to the purchase of the new machine:

a. Net cash flow per year.
b. Present value of the net outlay.
c. Payback period.
d. Advantage (or disadvantage) of the new machine in terms of present value.

Appendix
Interest and Present Value Concepts

If you were given an opportunity to receive $1,000 today or $1,000 a year from today, you would no doubt choose to receive the money immediately. Conversely, if you owed someone $1,000 and were given the option of paying today or paying a year from today, you would elect to pay in a year rather than today. What rationale underlies such behavior? That is, why do most individuals prefer having cash in hand now rather than at a later time? The answer seems to be obvious. By having cash in hand, an individual simply has more options. For example, cash in hand might be used as a cushion against unforeseen events that require immediate attention. Or, the money could be used to satisfy current needs; that is, it can be spent today on consumer goods or services. Also, cash in hand can be invested to produce income as well as to maintain its original balance. This final reason is often referred to as the time value of money.

The concept of present value implies that an individual would prefer to receive a sum of money in the current period as opposed to receiving that same sum in a future period. This preference arises because the sum of money received today could be invested to earn a return (interest). For example, assume that you had a choice between receiving $1,000 today or $1,000 in one year. If you could earn a 10 percent annual return on your money, $1,000 today would increase to $1,100 in a year (interest = $1,000 × 0.10 × 1 year = $100). As a result, you are better off if you choose to receive the $1,000 today than if you choose to receive this same amount in a year.

Similarly, businesses and other organizations must consider the time value of money in evaluating the cash inflows and outflows associated with a given investment. Timing of cash flows is important because of the following principle: *an amount of cash to be received in the future is not equivalent to the same amount of cash held at the present time.* This statement is true because money has a time value—it can be invested to earn a return (i.e., interest or dividends). For this reason, in both borrowing and investing decisions, consideration must be given to the time values of the various cash inflows and outflows.

In order to understand and consider the implications of such decisions, the decision-maker must be able to determine the *present value* of future cash flows. There are a number of important applications of present value concepts in both financial and managerial accounting This Appendix discusses the basic concepts associated with present value and the time value of money and illustrates the calculation of the present value of cash flows.

Interest

Interest is the amount received by the lender and paid by the borrower for the use of money for a given period of time. Thus, upon payment of a debt, interest is the excess of the cash paid over the amount originally borrowed (referred to as the *principal amount*). Interest is normally stated as a rate for a one-year (annual) period.

Simple interest is the amount of interest that is computed on the principal *only* for a given period of time. Simple interest is computed as follows:

$$\text{Interest} = \text{Principal} \times \text{Rate} \times \text{Time}$$
$$\text{Interest} = P \times I \times T \qquad (1)$$

To illustrate, interest on $1,000 borrowed for six months at an annual interest rate of 10 percent is:

$$\$50 = \$1{,}000 \times .10 \times {}^{6}/_{12}$$

Compound interest is interest that is computed on both the principal amount and the interest that has been earned but not paid. That is, interest is compounded when the interest earned in each period is added to the principal amount and both principal and interest will earn interest in all subsequent periods. To illustrate, assume that $1,000 is deposited in a bank that pays interest at a rate of 10 percent annually. If the interest is withdrawn each year (simple interest), the depositor collects $100 in interest each year (or a total of $300 in interest over a three-year period):

$$\begin{aligned}\text{Interest per year} &= \$1,000 \times .10 \times 1 = \$100 \\ \text{Total interest for 3 years} &= \$\ 100 \times 3 = \$300\end{aligned}$$

However, if the interest earned at the end of each period is not withdrawn but, rather, is added to the principal sum (compound interest), the amount earned over the three-year period is computed as follows:

Original investment		$1,000
Balance at the end of year:	1: $1,000 + (.10 × $1,000 × 1)	1,100
	2: $1,100 + (.10 × $1,100 × 1)	1,210
	3: $1,210 + (.10 × $1,210 × 1)	1,331

Compound interest for the three-year period is $331 ($1,331 − $1,000), the difference between the balance at the end of the three-year period and the original investment of $1,000. The amount of compound interest exceeds simple interest because interest is earned each year on both the principal and the interest earned but not withdrawn.

Since compounding occurs when interest is earned on previously accumulated interest amounts, a formula can be developed for computing the compound amount at which the principal sum will increase over a given time period. To develop this formula, consider the compound interest on one dollar invested at an interest rate (I) of 10 percent. The amount accumulated at the end of the first year is $[1 + (1 \times I)]$ or $(1 + I)$. If this amount is allowed to accumulate and earn interest for the second year, the amount accumulated is $(1 + I)(1 + I)$ which may be stated as $(1 + I)^2$. Similarly, the amount at the end of n periods is $(1 + I)^n$. Consequently, the amount (A) to which a principal amount (P) will accumulate over a time period (n) at an interest rate (I) is expressed as:

$$A = P(1 + I)^n \tag{2}$$

For example, if $1,000 is invested for three years at 10 percent interest per year, the amount accumulated at the end of the three-year period is computed as follows:

$$\begin{aligned} A &= \$1,000\,(1 + .10)^3 \\ A &= \$1,000\,(1.331) \\ A &= \$1,331 \end{aligned}$$

This computation of the sum for a single principal amount and the compound interest at a specified future time may be illustrated as follows:

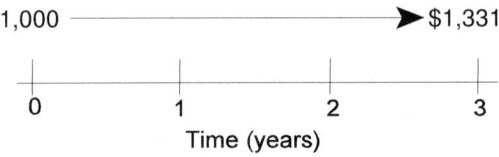
Time (years)

Present Values of a Future Sum

The present value of a given amount at a specified future time is the sum that must be invested at the present time (today) in order to accumulate that future amount at the specified time at a given interest rate. To determine the present value of a single future cash inflow or outflow, the following formula may be used:

$$\text{Present Value} = \frac{\text{Future Value}}{(1 + \text{Interest Rate})^n}$$

In this formula, n is equal to the number of periods remaining until the receipt or payment of cash occurs. For example, to calculate the present value of $1,000 to be received in one year, we substitute the known factors into the above equation:

$$\text{Present Value} = \frac{\$1,000}{(1 + .10)^1}$$
$$= \$909.10$$

Graphically, this relationship can be expressed as:

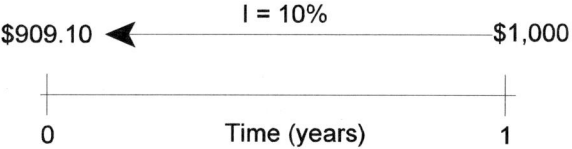

The pictorial illustration shown above summarizes the relationship as follows: "if $1,000 is *discounted* for a period of one year at an interest rate of 10 percent, the present value would be $909.10." The term discounted refers to determining the present value of a future sum of money.

To verify the above, assume that we had $909.10 on hand today. If we invested this $909.10 in a savings account or other investment opportunity earning a return (interest rate) of 10 percent, at the end of one year a total of $1,000 (future value) would be on hand. This calculation is shown below:

Year	(1) Principal	(2) Interest	(1) + (2) Ending Balance
0	$909.10		$ 909.10
1	$909.10	$90.90	$1,000.00

The above calculation illustrates basic present value analysis. The present value represents the amount of money which is needed at the current time to accumulate to a specified amount in a future period (future value) based on a given rate of interest and number of periods (n). Year 0 refers to the date of deposit, and interest in year 1 is equal to the principal amount ($909.10) multiplied by the interest rate (10%) multiplied by time (1 year), or $90.90 ($909.10 × 0.10 × 1 year = $90.90). Based on the above analysis, we can make the following statements:

1. If $909.10 (present value) were invested today at 10 percent (interest), a total of $1,000 (future value) would be available at the end of one year (n).
2. In order to have $1,000 (future value) at the end of Year 1, we must deposit $909.10 today (present value) at 10 percent (interest).

With sufficient additional information, the above formula may be used to solve for the future value, interest rate, or number of periods (n) necessary for a sum to earn a return (time that the funds must remain on deposit). However, in many applications, the analysis is generally restricted to determining the present value of future cash inflows and outflows associated with a particular investment alternative.

A second method of calculating present value is through the use of tables which are constructed to simplify the above formula. We can decompose the above formula as shown below:

$$\text{Present Value} = \text{Future Value} \times \frac{1}{(1 + \text{Interest Rate})^n}$$

Present value tables have been prepared which provide a numerical measure of $[1 \div (1 + \text{interest})^n]$ for a given number of periods and given rates of interest. These factors can greatly simplify present value calculations. Table 1 presents the present value factors used to discount a single sum of $1 to the present time period. This factor incorporates both the appropriate interest rate as well as the number of time periods until the receipt or payment of cash occurs.

To illustrate the use of the formula and table approach, assume that we wish to find the present value of an expected inflow of $1,000 to be received in exactly four years. If the appropriate annual interest rate is 10 percent, the formula approach would yield the following result:

$$\text{Present Value} = \frac{\text{Future Value}}{(1 + \text{Interest Rate})^n}$$

$$= \frac{\$1,000}{(1 + .10)^n} = \$683$$

Using Table 1, we first locate the row corresponding to the appropriate number of periods (n = 4). Next, we read across the row until we reach the column corresponding to the appropriate interest rate (10%). The factor appearing in the intersection of the (n = 4) row and the (interest = 10%) column is 0.6830. This factor is then used to find the present value as shown below:

$$\text{Present Value} = \text{Future Value} \times \text{Factor from Table 1}$$

$$= \$1,000 \times 0.6830 = \$683$$

This calculation implies that we would be indifferent between receiving $683 today or $1,000 in four years assuming that we could earn a return of 10 percent. To verify the above calculations, assume that we place a hypothetical deposit of $683 in a bank account paying interest at an annual rate of 10 percent for four years. As shown below, a total of $1,000 (future value) is on hand at the end of four years (the difference of 10 cents is due to rounding).

Year	(1) Beginning Balance	(2) Deposit	(3) = (1) x .10 Interest	(4) = (1) + (2) + (3) Ending Balance
0		$683.00		$683.00
1	$683.00		$68.30	751.30
2	751.30		75.10	826.40
3	826.40		82.60	909.00
4	909.00		90.90	999.90

TABLE 1
Present Value of $1.00

Periods (n)	1%	1½%	2%	2½%	3%	3½%	4%	4½%	5%	6%	7%	8%	10%
1	0.9901	0.9852	0.9804	0.9756	0.9709	0.9662	0.9615	0.9569	0.9524	0.9434	0.9346	0.9259	0.9091
2	0.9803	0.9707	0.9612	0.9518	0.9426	0.9335	0.9246	0.9157	0.9070	0.8900	0.8734	0.8573	0.8264
3	0.9706	0.9563	0.9423	0.9286	0.9151	0.9019	0.8890	0.8763	0.8638	0.8396	0.8163	0.7938	0.7513
4	0.9610	0.9422	0.9238	0.9060	0.8885	0.8714	0.8548	0.8386	0.8227	0.7921	0.7629	0.7350	0.6830
5	0.9515	0.9283	0.9057	0.8839	0.8626	0.8420	0.8219	0.8025	0.7835	0.7473	0.7130	0.6806	0.6209
6	0.9420	0.9145	0.8880	0.8623	0.8375	0.8135	0.7903	0.7679	0.7462	0.7050	0.6663	0.6302	0.5645
7	0.9327	0.9010	0.8706	0.8413	0.8131	0.7860	0.7599	0.7348	0.7107	0.6651	0.6227	0.5835	0.5132
8	0.9235	0.8877	0.8535	0.8207	0.7894	0.7594	0.7307	0.7032	0.6768	0.6274	0.5820	0.5403	0.4665
9	0.9143	0.8746	0.8368	0.8007	0.7664	0.7337	0.7026	0.6729	0.6446	0.5919	0.5439	0.5002	0.4241
10	0.9053	0.8617	0.8203	0.7812	0.7441	0.7089	0.6756	0.6439	0.6139	0.5584	0.5083	0.4632	0.3855
11	0.8963	0.8489	0.8043	0.7621	0.7224	0.6849	0.6496	0.6162	0.5847	0.5268	0.4751	0.4289	0.3505
12	0.8874	0.8364	0.7885	0.7436	0.7014	0.6618	0.6246	0.5897	0.5568	0.4970	0.4440	0.3971	0.3186
13	0.8787	0.8240	0.7730	0.7254	0.6810	0.6394	0.6006	0.5643	0.5303	0.4688	0.4150	0.3677	0.2897
14	0.8700	0.8118	0.7579	0.7077	0.6611	0.6178	0.5775	0.5400	0.5051	0.4423	0.3878	0.3405	0.2633
15	0.8613	0.7999	0.7430	0.6905	0.6419	0.5969	0.5553	0.5167	0.4810	0.4173	0.3624	0.3153	0.2394
16	0.8528	0.7880	0.7284	0.6736	0.6232	0.5767	0.5339	0.4945	0.4581	0.3936	0.3387	0.2919	0.2176
17	0.8444	0.7764	0.7142	0.6572	0.6050	0.5572	0.5134	0.4732	0.4363	0.3714	0.3166	0.2703	0.1978
18	0.8360	0.7649	0.7002	0.6412	0.5874	0.5384	0.4936	0.4528	0.4155	0.3503	0.2959	0.2502	0.1799
19	0.8277	0.7536	0.6864	0.6255	0.5703	0.5202	0.4746	0.4333	0.3957	0.3305	0.2765	0.2317	0.1635
20	0.8195	0.7425	0.6730	0.6103	0.5537	0.5026	0.4564	0.4146	0.3769	0.3118	0.2584	0.2145	0.4186
21	0.8114	0.7315	0.6598	0.5954	0.5375	0.4856	0.4388	0.3968	0.3589	0.2942	0.2415	0.1987	0.1351
22	0.8034	0.7207	0.6468	0.5809	0.5219	0.4692	0.4220	0.3797	0.3418	0.2775	0.2257	0.1839	0.1228
23	0.7954	0.7100	0.6342	0.5667	0.5067	0.4533	0.4057	0.3634	0.3256	0.2618	0.2109	0.1703	0.1117
24	0.7876	0.6995	0.6217	0.5529	0.4919	0.4380	0.3901	0.3477	0.3101	0.2470	0.1971	0.1577	0.1015
25	0.7798	0.6892	0.6095	0.5394	0.4776	0.4231	0.3751	0.3327	0.2953	0.2330	0.1842	0.1460	0.0923
26	0.7720	0.6790	0.5976	0.5262	0.4637	0.4088	0.3607	0.3184	0.2812	0.2198	0.1722	0.1352	0.0839
27	0.7644	0.6690	0.5859	0.5134	0.4502	0.3950	0.3468	0.3047	0.2678	0.2074	0.1609	0.1252	0.0763
28	0.7568	0.6591	0.5744	0.5009	0.4371	0.3817	0.3335	0.2916	0.2551	0.1956	0.1504	0.1159	0.0693
29	0.7493	0.6494	0.5631	0.4887	0.4243	0.3687	0.3207	0.2790	0.2429	0.1846	0.1406	0.1073	0.0630
30	0.7419	0.6398	0.5521	0.4767	0.4120	0.3563	0.3083	0.2670	0.2314	0.1741	0.1314	0.0994	0.0573
40	0.6717	0.5513	0.4529	0.3724	0.3066	0.2526	0.2083	0.1719	0.1420	0.0972	0.0668	0.0460	0.0221
50	0.6080	0.4750	0.3715	0.2909	0.2281	0.1791	0.1407	0.1107	0.0872	0.0543	0.0339	0.0213	0.0085

TABLE 1 (Continued)
Present Value of $1.00

Periods (n)	12%	14%	15%	16%	18%	20%	22%	24%	25%	26%	28%	30%	40%	50%
1	0.893	0.877	0.870	0.862	0.847	0.833	0.820	0.806	0.800	0.794	0.781	0.769	0.714	0.667
2	0.797	0.769	0.756	0.743	0.718	0.694	0.672	0.650	0.640	0.630	0.610	0.592	0.510	0.444
3	0.712	0.675	0.658	0.641	0.609	0.579	0.551	0.524	0.512	0.500	0.477	0.455	0.364	0.296
4	0.636	0.592	0.572	0.552	0.516	0.482	0.451	0.423	0.410	0.397	0.373	0.350	0.260	0.198
5	0.567	0.519	0.497	0.476	0.437	0.402	0.370	0.341	0.328	0.315	0.291	0.269	0.186	0.132
6	0.507	0.456	0.432	0.410	0.370	0.335	0.303	0.275	0.262	0.250	0.227	0.207	0.133	0.088
7	0.452	0.400	0.376	0.354	0.314	0.279	0.249	0.222	0.210	0.198	0.178	0.159	0.095	0.059
8	0.404	0.351	0.327	0.305	0.266	0.233	0.204	0.179	0.168	0.157	0.139	0.123	0.068	0.039
9	0.361	0.308	0.284	0.263	0.225	0.194	0.167	0.144	0.134	0.125	0.108	0.094	0.048	0.026
10	0.322	0.270	0.247	0.227	0.191	0.162	0.137	0.116	0.107	0.099	0.085	0.073	0.035	0.017
11	0.287	0.237	0.215	0.195	0.162	0.135	0.112	0.094	0.086	0.079	0.066	0.056	0.025	0.012
12	0.257	0.208	0.187	0.168	0.137	0.112	0.092	0.076	0.069	0.062	0.052	0.043	0.018	0.008
13	0.229	0.182	0.163	0.145	0.116	0.093	0.075	0.061	0.055	0.050	0.040	0.033	0.013	0.005
14	0.205	0.160	0.141	0.125	0.099	0.078	0.062	0.049	0.044	0.039	0.032	0.025	0.009	0.003
15	0.183	0.140	0.123	0.108	0.084	0.065	0.051	0.040	0.035	0.031	0.025	0.020	0.006	0.002
16	0.163	0.123	0.107	0.093	0.071	0.054	0.042	0.032	0.028	0.025	0.019	0.015	0.005	0.002
17	0.146	0.108	0.093	0.080	0.060	0.045	0.034	0.026	0.023	0.020	0.015	0.012	0.003	0.001
18	0.130	0.095	0.081	0.069	0.051	0.038	0.028	0.021	0.018	0.016	0.012	0.009	0.002	0.001
19	0.116	0.083	0.070	0.060	0.043	0.031	0.023	0.017	0.014	0.012	0.009	0.007	0.002	
20	0.104	0.073	0.061	0.051	0.037	0.026	0.019	0.014	0.012	0.010	0.007	0.005	0.001	
21	0.093	0.064	0.053	0.044	0.031	0.022	0.015	0.011	0.009	0.008	0.006	0.004	0.001	
22	0.083	0.056	0.046	0.038	0.026	0.018	0.013	0.009	0.007	0.006	0.004	0.003	0.001	
23	0.074	0.049	0.040	0.033	0.022	0.015	0.010	0.007	0.006	0.005	0.003	0.002		
24	0.066	0.043	0.035	0.028	0.019	0.013	0.008	0.006	0.005	0.004	0.003	0.002		
25	0.059	0.038	0.030	0.024	0.016	0.010	0.007	0.005	0.004	0.003	0.002	0.001		
26	0.053	0.033	0.026	0.021	0.014	0.009	0.006	0.004	0.003	0.002	0.002	0.001		
27	0.047	0.029	0.023	0.018	0.011	0.007	0.005	0.003	0.002	0.002	0.001	0.001		
28	0.042	0.026	0.020	0.016	0.010	0.006	0.004	0.002	0.002	0.002	0.001	0.001		
29	0.037	0.022	0.017	0.014	0.008	0.005	0.003	0.002	0.002	0.001	0.001	0.001		
30	0.033	0.020	0.015	0.012	0.007	0.004	0.003	0.002	0.001	0.001	0.001	0.001		
40	0.011	0.005	0.004	0.003	0.001	0.001								
50	0.003	0.001	0.001	0.001										

Note that, assuming that any return is earned, the present value of a sum will always be less than its future value. It is important to emphasize that the concept of present value relates only to the ability of a sum of money to earn a return (by earning interest).

As indicated above, the present value of a given amount at a specified future time is the sum that must be invested at the present time in order to accumulate that future amount at a given rate of interest. To illustrate compound interest, we will use the example of $1,000 invested at 10 percent compound interest which will accumulate to a total of $1,331 in three years. Therefore, $1,000 is the present value of $1,331 three years from the present time (given a 10% annual rate of interest). That is, if we an earn 10 percent on a bank deposit, we are indifferent between receiving $1,000 today (which can be deposited to accumulate to $1,331 in 3 years) or $1,331 three years from now, all other factors being equal.

Recall that the value of a future amount (A) is determined by computing the amount that a principal sum (P) will accumulate to over a specified period of time. Consequently, by dividing the compound interest equation (2) by $(1 + I)^n$, we obtain the formula for computing the present value of a future amount:

$$P = \frac{A}{(1 + I)^n} \tag{3}$$

For example, the present value of $1,331 three years from now is computed as follows:

$$P = \frac{\$1,331}{(1 + .10)^3}$$

$$P = \$1,000$$

Because of the number and variety of decisions based on the present value of future cash flows, tables have been developed from the formula to give the present value of $1 for various interest rates and for various periods of time. These values may be multiplied by any future amount to determine its present value. The factors for the present value of $1 are listed in Table 1.

To again illustrate the use of this table, let us compute the present value of $1,331 to be received three years from now at an interest rate of 10 percent. The value from the table for three years at 10 percent is .7513. This is the present value of $1. Accordingly, the present value of $1,331 is computed as $1,331 x .7513 = $999.80 (this amount is not exactly equal to $1,000 because of rounding in the present value factors included in the table). The computation of the present value of a simple payment due in the future may be illustrated graphically as follows:

Compound Interest and Present Value of a Series of Equal Payments

Business decisions involving a series of cash flows to be paid or received periodically are more common than decisions involving the accumulation of a single principal sum. It is possible to determine the present value of a series of payments (or receipts) by computing the present value of each individual payment or receipt and suming these values to obtain the present value for the entire series. However, if all the payments are equal, formulas or tables may be used to compute the present value of the series of payments. Such a series of equal periodic payments is referred to as an *annuity*. If the payments are made at the end of each period, the annuity is referred to as an *ordinary annuity*.

An annuity is a series of equal future payments or receipts of cash (cash inflows or outflows). An annuity has two characteristics: (1) the amounts of the cash inflows or outflows are equal for all future time periods, and (2) the interval between the future cash inflows or outflows also is equal. While the basic mechanics of calculating the present value of an annuity are similar to those for calculating the present value of a single sum, annuities introduce certain additional issues which require some explanation.

The present value of annuity can be calculated in a manner similar to the present value of a single sum. For example, assume that we expect to receive cash inflows of $1,000 per year at the end of each year for the next four years. One method of determining the present value of these inflows is to treat them as four separate single sums. Using an interest rate of 10 percent, we would extract factors from Table 1 (present value of a single sum of $1) and can calculate the present value of these future cash receipts as shown below:

Year	Amount		Factor		Present Value
1	$1,000	x	0.9091	=	$ 909.10
2	$1,000	x	0.8264	=	826.40
3	$1,000	x	0.7513	=	751.30
4	$1,000	x	0.6830	=	683.00
			3.1698		$3,169.80

Graphically, this situation can be expressed as:

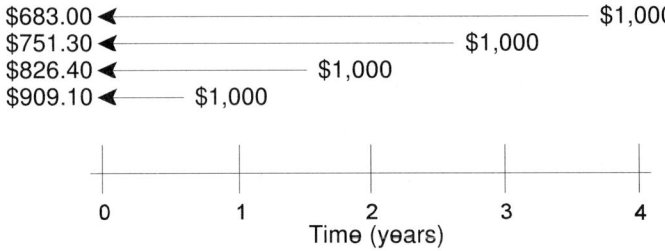

Obviously, if the annuity extends over a relatively long period of time (large number of future periods), calculating the present value using the above method could become somewhat cumbersome. An alternative method of calculation would be using factors from a table prepared to simplify the calculation of present values involving an annuity. Such a table (Table 2) can be used in this problem. Based on the interest rate (10%) and the number of future receipts and payments (4), the factor 3.1699 can be extracted from Table 2. Notice that, except for rounding, this factor is equal to the sum of the individual factors from Table 1 from our earlier calculation. Using this factor, we can calculate the present value of the annuity as follows:

$$\begin{aligned} \text{Present Value} &= \text{Annuity} \times \text{Factor from Table 2} \\ &= \$1{,}000 \times 3.1699 \\ &= \$3{,}169.90 \end{aligned}$$

The above calculation indicates that we would be indifferent between receiving $3,169.90 today or $1,000 per year for each of the next four years, assuming an annual return of 10 percent could be earned. To illustrate this point, if we deposit $3,169.90 now (present value), we can withdraw $1,000 per year at the end of each year for the next four years. To verify the above calculations, refer to the following schedule:

Year	(1) Beginning Balance	(2) Deposit	(3) = (1) x .10 Interest	(4) Withdrawal	(5) = (1) + (2) + (3) + (4) Ending Balance
0		$3,169.90			$3,169.90
1	$3,169.90		$317.00	$(1000.00)	2,486.90
2	2,486.90		248.70	(1000.00)	1,735.60
3	1,735.60		173.60	(1000.00)	909.20
4	909.20		90.90	(1000.00)	0

TABLE 2
Present Value of Annuity of $1.00 per Period

Periods (n)	1%	1½%	2%	2½%	3%	3½%	4%	4½%	5%	6%	7%
1	0.9901	0.9852	0.9804	0.9756	0.9709	0.9662	0.9615	0.9569	0.9524	0.9434	0.9346
2	1.9704	1.9559	1.9416	1.9274	1.9135	1.8997	1.8861	1.8727	1.8594	1.8334	1.8080
3	2.9410	2.9122	2.8839	2.8560	2.8286	2.8016	2.7751	2.7490	2.7232	2.6730	2.6243
4	3.9020	3.8544	3.8077	3.7620	3.7171	3.6731	3.6299	3.5875	3.5460	3.4651	3.3872
5	4.8534	4.7826	4.7135	4.6458	4.5797	4.5151	4.4518	4.3900	4.3295	4.2124	4.1002
6	5.7955	5.6972	5.6014	5.5081	5.4172	5.3286	5.2421	5.1579	5.0757	4.9173	4.7665
7	6.7282	6.5982	6.4720	6.3494	6.2303	6.1145	6.0021	5.8927	5.7864	5.5824	5.3893
8	7.6517	7.4859	7.3255	7.1701	7.0197	6.8740	6.7327	6.5959	6.4632	6.2098	5.9713
9	8.5660	8.3605	8.1622	7.9709	7.7861	7.6077	7.4353	7.2688	7.1078	6.8017	6.5152
10	9.4713	9.2222	8.9826	8.7521	8.5302	8.3166	8.1109	7.9127	7.7217	7.3601	7.0236
11	10.3676	10.0711	9.7868	9.5142	9.2526	9.0016	8.7605	8.5289	8.3064	7.8869	7.4987
12	11.2551	10.9075	10.5753	10.2578	9.9540	9.6633	9.3851	9.1186	8.8633	8.3838	7.9427
13	12.1337	11.7315	11.3484	10.9832	10.6350	10.3027	9.9856	9.6829	8.9936	8.8527	8.3577
14	13.0037	12.5434	12.1062	11.6909	11.2961	10.9205	10.5631	10.2228	9.8986	9.2950	8.7455
15	13.8651	13.3432	12.8493	12.3814	11.9379	11.5174	11.1184	10.7395	10.3797	9.7122	9.1079
16	14.7179	14.1313	13.5777	13.0550	12.5611	12.0941	11.6523	11.2340	10.8378	10.1059	9.4466
17	15.5623	14.9076	14.2919	13.7122	13.1661	12.6513	12.1657	11.7072	11.2741	10.4773	9.7632
18	16.3983	15.6726	14.9920	14.3534	13.7535	13.1897	12.6593	12.1600	11.6896	10.8276	10.0591
19	17.2260	16.4262	15.6785	14.9789	14.3238	13.7098	13.1339	12.5933	12.0853	11.1581	10.3356
20	18.0456	17.1686	16.3514	15.5892	14.8775	14.2124	13.5903	13.0079	12.4622	11.4699	10.5940
21	18.8570	17.9001	17.0112	16.1845	15.4150	14.6980	14.0292	13.4047	12.8212	11.7640	10.8355
22	19.6604	18.6208	17.6580	16.7654	15.9369	15.1671	14.4511	13.7844	13.1630	12.0416	11.0612
23	20.4558	19.3309	18.2922	17.3321	16.4436	15.6204	14.8568	14.1478	13.4886	12.3034	11.2722
24	21.2434	20.0304	18.9139	17.8850	16.9355	16.0584	15.2470	14.4955	13.7986	12.5504	11.4693
25	22.0232	20.7196	19.5235	18.4244	17.4131	16.4815	15.6221	14.8282	14.0939	12.7834	11.6536
26	22.7952	21.3986	20.1210	18.9506	17.8768	16.8904	15.9828	15.1466	14.3752	13.0032	11.8258
27	23.5596	22.0676	20.7069	19.4640	18.3270	17.2854	16.3296	15.4513	14.6430	13.2105	11.9867
28	24.3164	22.7267	21.2813	19.9649	18.7641	17.6670	16.6631	15.7429	14.8981	13.4062	12.1371
29	25.0658	23.3761	21.8444	20.4535	19.1885	18.0358	16.9837	16.0219	15.1411	13.5907	12.2777
30	25.8077	24.0158	22.3965	20.9303	19.6004	18.3920	17.2920	16.2889	15.3725	13.7648	12.4090
40	32.8347	29.9158	27.3555	25.1028	23.1148	21.3551	19.7928	18.4016	17.1591	15.0463	13.3317
50	39.1961	34.9997	31.4236	28.3623	25.7298	23.4556	21.4822	19.7620	18.2559	15.7619	13.8007

TABLE 2 (Continued)
Present Value of Annuity of $1.00 per Period

Periods (n)	8%	10%	12%	14%	15%	16%	18%	20%	22%	24%	25%	26%	28%	30%	40%	50%
1	0.9259	0.9091	0.893	0.877	0.870	0.862	0.847	0.833	0.820	0.806	0.800	0.794	0.781	0.769	0.714	0.667
2	1.7833	1.7355	1.690	1.647	1.626	1.605	1.566	1.528	1.492	1.457	1.440	1.424	1.392	1.361	1.224	1.111
3	2.5771	2.4869	2.402	2.322	2.283	2.246	2.174	2.106	2.042	1.981	1.952	1.923	1.868	1.816	1.589	1.407
4	3.3121	3.1699	3.037	2.914	2.855	2.798	2.690	2.589	2.494	2.404	2.362	2.320	2.241	2.166	1.849	1.605
5	3.9927	3.7908	3.605	3.433	3.352	3.274	3.127	2.991	2.864	2.745	2.689	2.635	2.532	2.436	2.035	1.737
6	4.6229	4.3553	4.111	3.889	3.784	3.685	3.498	3.326	3.167	3.020	2.951	2.885	2.759	2.643	2.168	1.824
7	5.2064	4.8684	4.564	4.288	4.160	4.039	3.812	3.605	3.416	3.242	3.161	3.083	2.937	2.802	2.263	1.883
8	5.7466	5.3349	4.968	4.639	4.487	4.344	4.078	3.837	3.619	3.421	3.329	3.241	3.076	2.925	2.331	1.922
9	6.2469	5.7590	5.328	4.946	4.772	4.607	4.303	4.031	3.786	3.566	3.463	3.366	3.184	3.019	2.379	1.948
10	6.7101	6.1446	5.650	5.216	5.019	4.833	4.494	4.192	3.923	3.682	3.571	3.465	3.269	3.092	2.414	1.965
11	7.1390	6.4951	5.988	5.453	5.234	5.029	4.656	4.327	4.035	3.776	3.656	3.544	3.335	3.147	2.438	1.977
12	7.5361	6.8137	6.194	5.660	5.421	5.197	4.793	4.439	4.127	3.851	3.725	3.606	3.387	3.190	2.456	1.985
13	7.9038	7.1034	6.424	5.842	5.583	5.342	4.910	4.533	4.203	3.912	3.780	3.656	3.427	3.223	2.468	1.990
14	8.2442	7.3667	6.628	6.002	5.724	5.468	5.008	4.611	4.265	3.962	3.824	3.695	3.459	3.249	2.477	1.993
15	8.5595	7.6061	6.811	6.142	5.847	5.575	5.092	4.675	4.315	4.001	3.859	3.726	3.483	3.268	2.484	1.995
16	8.8514	7.8237	6.974	6.265	5.954	5.669	5.162	4.730	4.357	4.033	3.887	3.751	3.503	3.283	2.489	1.997
17	9.1216	8.0216	7.120	6.373	6.047	5.749	5.222	4.775	4.391	4.059	3.910	3.771	3.518	3.295	2.492	1.998
18	9.3719	8.2014	7.250	6.467	6.128	5.818	5.273	4.812	4.419	4.080	3.928	3.786	3.529	3.304	2.494	1.999
19	9.6036	8.3649	7.366	6.550	6.198	5.877	5.316	4.844	4.442	4.097	3.942	3.799	3.539	3.311	2.496	1.999
20	9.8181	8.5136	7.469	6.623	6.259	5.929	5.353	4.870	4.460	4.110	3.954	3.808	3.546	3.316	2.497	1.999
21	10.0168	8.6487	7.562	6.687	6.312	5.973	5.384	4.891	4.476	4.121	3.963	3.816	3.551	3.320	2.498	2.000
22	10.2007	8.7715	7.645	6.743	6.359	6.011	5.410	4.909	4.488	4.130	3.970	3.822	5.556	3.323	2.498	2.000
23	10.3711	8.8832	7.718	6.792	6.399	6.044	5.432	4.925	4.499	4.137	3.976	3.827	3.559	3.325	2.499	2.000
24	10.5288	8.9847	7.784	6.835	6.434	6.073	5.451	4.937	4.507	4.143	3.981	3.831	3.562	3.327	2.499	2.000
25	10.6748	9.0770	7.843	6.873	6.464	6.097	5.467	4.948	4.514	4.147	3.985	3.834	3.564	3.329	2.499	2.000
26	10.8100	9.1609	7.896	6.906	6.491	6.118	5.480	4.956	4.520	4.151	3.988	3.837	3.566	3.330	2.500	2.000
27	10.9352	9.2372	7.943	6.935	6.514	6.136	5.492	4.964	4.524	4.154	3.990	3.839	3.567	3.331	2.500	2.000
28	11.0511	9.3066	7.984	6.961	6.534	6.152	5.502	4.970	4.528	4.157	3.992	3.840	3.568	3.331	2.500	2.000
29	11.1584	9.3696	8.022	6.983	6.551	6.166	5.510	4.975	4.531	4.159	3.994	3.841	3.569	3.332	2.500	2.000
30	11.2578	9.4269	8.055	7.003	6.566	6.177	5.517	4.979	4.534	4.160	3.995	3.842	3.569	3.332	2.500	2.000
40	11.9246	9.7791	8.244	7.105	6.642	6.234	5.548	4.997	4.544	4.166	3.999	3.846	3.571	3.333	2.500	2.000
50	12.2335	9.9148	8.304	7.133	6.661	6.246	5.554	4.999	4.545	4.167	4.000	3.846	3.571	3.333	2.500	2.000

The accumulated amount (future value) of an ordinary annuity is the sum of the periodic payments and the compound interest on these payments. For example, the future value of an annuity of $1,000 per year (at the end of each year) for three years at 10 percent interest can be determined as follows:

The initial payment accumulates at 10% for 2 years to	$1,210
The second payment accumulates at 10% for 1 year to	1,100
The third payment is due at the end of the third year	1,000
Amount of an ordinary annuity of $1,000 for 3 years at 10%	$3,310

The computation of the future value of a series of payments may be expressed as follows:

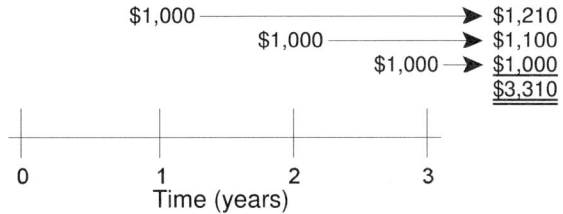

The present value of an ordinary annuity is the amount that, if invested at the present time at a compound rate of interest, provides for a series of equal withdrawals at the end of a certain number of periods. As previously indicated, the present value of an ordinary annuity may be computed as the present values of each of the individual payments. For example, the present value of an ordinary annuity of $1,000 per year for three years at 10 percent can be computed as follows (see Table 1):

Present value of $1,000 in 1 year	.9091	×	$1,000	=	$ 909.10
Present value of $1,000 in 2 years	.8264	×	$1,000	=	826.40
Present value of $1,000 in 3 years	.7513	×	$1,000	=	751.30
Present value of an annuity of $1,000 for 3 periods at 10%					$2,486.80

This computation indicates that if $2,486.80 is invested at an annual interest rate of 10 percent, it will be possible to withdraw $1,000 at the end of each year for three years.

The formula for the present value of an ordinary annuity of $R per period for n periods at I rate of interest may be stated as follows:

$$P = R \left[\frac{1 - \frac{1}{(1 + I)^n}}{I} \right]$$

Table 2 gives the present value of an ordinary annuity of $1 per period for various periods at varying rates of interest. By multiplying the appropriate value from the table by the dollar amount of the periodic payment, the present value of the payments may be calculated. For example, the present value of three annual cash payments of $1,000 made at the end of the next three years at a 10 percent interest rate is computed as follows:

$$\$1,000 \times 2.4869 = \$2,486.90^{[8]}$$

---

[8] Difference of $.10 due to rounding in tables.

This amount may be interpreted as the present cash payment which is exactly equivalent to the three future installments of $1,000 if money earns interest at an annual rate of 10 percent and is compounded annually. The computation of the present value of a series of future payments may be graphically illustrated as follows:

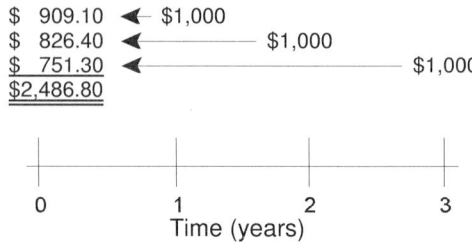

An Example

In order to illustrate an application of the concept of the time value of money, we will use the following example:

> We have a choice of receiving either: (1) $250 in cash today or (2) three payments of $100 each to be received exactly one year, two years, and three years from today. Further, assume that we can always earn interest on any funds we hold at a rate of 10 percent per year.

Obviously, we would prefer to receive a total of $300 rather than a total of $250, given the choice, if all monies were to be received at the same time. This is not the case, however, in this example so it is necessary to somehow consider the two alternatives within the same time frame.

A technique for placing the two choices in the same time frame is to determine the total amount or accumulated value of each alternative at the end of a three-year period, after all monies have been received under both choices. These calculations are as follows:

	Alternative 1	Alternative 2
Payment	$250.00	—
Interest for year 1	25.00	—
Payment	—	$100.00
Balance at end of year 1	$275.00	$100,00
Interest for year 2	27.50	10.00
Payment	—	100.00
Balance at end of year 2	$302.50	$210.00
Interest for year 3	30.25	21.00
Payment	—	100.00
	$332.75	$331.00

As indicated above, under Alternative 1 we would have accumulated $332.75 at the end of the three-year period, $1.75 more than the $331.00 we would have accumulated under Alternative 2. These amounts are the *future values* of these two alternatives and the ultimate difference between the two choices. Future value may be defined as the future equivalent of a present sum, given a stated time period and a given rate of return.

Using these procedures, in order to make a choice, we were required to convert both alternatives to their future values in order to make our selection. Another technique would be to compare the two alternatives in terms of the present value of each. This would require converting Alternative 2 to its present value. (Alternative 1, the sum of $250 received today, is already stated in terms of its present value, since if chosen, it will be received immediately.) These calculations are as follows:

Alternative 1	Alternative 2	
$250 received today	Payment 1... 100 x .9091* =	$ 90.91
	Payment 2... 100 x .8264* =	$ 82.64
$250	Payment 3... 100 x .7513* =	$ 75.13
		$248.68

*From Table 1, Present Value of $1.00, 1, 2, and 3 periods, at 10 percent

Note that in converting the three payments to be received under Alternative 2, each payment of $100 is multiplied by the present value of $1, given the assumed interest rate of 10 percent, for years 1, 2, and 3. These factors are the amounts that would have to be held *now* in order to have *exactly* $1 at the end of each year, 1, 2, and 3. This may be illustrated as follows:

	At the End of Year		
	1	2	3
Factor from Table 1 (at 10%)	.9091	.8264	.7513
Interest, year 1	.09091	.08264	.07513
	1.00001	.90904	.82643
Interest, year 2		.090904	.082643
		.999944	.909073
			.0909073
Interest, year 3			.9999803

As indicated above, under Alternative 1, we have $250.00 on hand today, $1.32 more than the $248.68 we would have accumulated under Alternative 2. These amounts are the *present value* of each alternative and the difference between the two choices. Present value may be defined as the present equivalent of a future sum, given a stated time period and a given rate of return.

Note that the choice made would be the same, whether made on the basis of future values or present values. The advantage, of course, differs depending upon the technique used—$1.75 is the future value of the difference and $1.32 is the present value of the difference. These amounts are, in fact, exactly equivalent, as indicated below:

Future value difference	$ 1.75
Multiply by present value 3 years, 10% interest (Table 1)	x .7513
	$ 1.32
Present value difference	$ 1.32
Interest for year 1	.132
	$ 1.452
Interest for year 2	.1452
	$ 1.5972
Interest for year 3	.15972
	$ 1.75692

Note that in calculating the present value of Alternative 2, each of the $100 payments is multiplied by the appropriate present value factor for years 1, 2, and 3. A "shortcut" method would be to sum the three factors and multiply the $100 by this sum of the factors, as follows:

$100 x (.9091 + .8264 + .7513) =
$100 x 2.4868 = $248.68

which of course, is the identical answer obtained when each individual factor is multiplied by 100 and totaled.

It is not necessary, however, to sum the three individual factors. This sum of the factors may be obtained directly from Table 2, the present value of an annuity of $1.

$$\$100 \times 2.4869 = \underline{\$248.68}[9]$$

Perhaps the most direct approach which can be used to make this decision is to determine the rate of return which would be obtained if the $250 alternative is forgone and the three payments of $100 choice is selected.

Recall that the choice is between $250 received today or $100 each year for three years. If the three-payment alternative is selected, the "cost" of this choice is $250, the alternative not selected. Thus for each of the 100 dollars received each year, the cost is $2.50 ($250/$100) the amount forgone immediately for each dollar.

To determine the rate of return which will be earned if the three-payment alternative is selected, we would refer to Table 2, The Present Value of an Annuity of $1, and go to three periods and look for the cost of $2.50. We would locate factors of 2.5771 (at 8%) and 2.4869 (at 10%), thus the choice of the three-payment alternative would earn a rate of return of more than 8 percent but less than 10 percent. Since this rate is less than the 10 percent we can earn on any funds that we hold, we would reject the three payments of $100 and select the $250 payment.

Exercises and Problems

1. *Future value calculations-Single sum.* Determine the amount that $1,000 will accumulate to in three years at an 8 percent annual interest rate.

2. *Present value calculation-Single sum.* Determine the present value of $1,000 due in five years at each of the following interest rates:

    a. 6 percent
    b. 8 percent
    c. 10 percent

3. *Present value calculation-Single sum.* An investor wishes to have $5,000 available at the end of five years. Determine the amount that must be invested at the present time if the interest rate is:

    a. 6 percent
    b. 8 percent
    c. 12 percent

4. *Present value calculation-Annuity.* Determine the present value of an ordinary annuity for a period of five years with annual payments of $2,000, assuming that the interest rate is:

    a. 7 percent
    b. 10 percent
    c. 12 percent

5. *Present value calculation-Annuity.* What is the maximum amount you would be willing to pay at the present time in order to receive 10 annual payments of $1,000 beginning one year from now? The current interest rate is 10 percent.

---

[9] Factor in Table 2 differs because of rounding.

6. *Present value calculation-Annuity.* Hays Company leases a building at an annual rental of $2,000 paid at the end of each year. The company has the alternative of paying the remaining 10 years of the lease in advance on January 1, 20x0. Assuming an interest rate of 8 percent, what is the maximum amount that should be paid now for the advance rent?

7. *Present value calculations.* You have a choice of $19 today or two payments of $10 each to be received exactly one year and two years from today. Assume that you can always earn 5 percent per year.

Required:

Answer the following:

   a. The present value of the $19 received today is _____ .
   b. The total present value of the two $10 payments is _____ .
   c. The approximate rate of return earned if the two-payment alternative is selected is between _____ and _____ .
   d. Which alternative would you select:

      1. the $19 single payment or
      2. the two $10 payments?

8. *Present value calculations.* You have a choice of $18 today or two payments of $10 each to be received exactly one year and two years from today. Assume that you can always earn 5 percent per year.

Required:

Answer the following questions:

   a. The present value of the $18 received today is _____ .
   b. The total present value of the two $10 payments is _____ .
   c. The approximate rate of return earned if the two-payment alternative is selected is between _____ and _____ .
   d. Which alternative would you select:

      1. the $18 single payment or
      2. the two $10 payments?

LEARNING Objectives

Chapter 12 illustrates the procedures used in preparing the statement of cash flows. Studying this chapter should enable you to:

1. Understand and give examples of the types of information an analysis of cash flows provides.
2. Identify the primary sources and uses of cash.
3. Describe the procedures involved in preparing the statement of cash flows.
4. Prepare a statement of cash flows using both the indirect and the direct methods of computing net cash flows from operating activities.

Chapter 12
The Statement of Cash Flows

Introduction

Ultimately, every business transaction will impact the cash flows of a business. An important consideration in the decision processes of many users of financial statements is the amount of, and the changes which take place in, the cash available to a business. Comparative balance sheets indicate the cash available at the beginning and the end of an accounting period. These balance sheets do not, however, explain the causes of any changes in cash balances. While some of the change in cash may result from the operations of the business, the net income as reported in the income statement may not be accompanied by an equivalent increase in cash. PepsiCo's net income in 2002 was $3,313 million, but the net cash provided by its operating activities was almost one and a half times that amount, at $4,627 million. The increase in its cash balance for the year was $955 million. Consequently, even the combination of the balance sheet and income statement may not provide an adequate indication of the cash flows that take place during the business cycle. For this reason, a statement that discloses the analysis of the cash flows of a firm is required along with the balance sheet, income statement, statement of stockholders' equity, and related notes to the financial statements to complete the required basic financial statements for a firm.

Importance of Cash Flows

Investors are interested in receiving dividends on their investments. Creditors are concerned with receiving periodic interest payments and principal payments on their loans. Suppliers want to be assured that they will receive payments for merchandise sold to the business. Employees depend on receiving their paychecks when they are earned and become due. The critical issue for all of these groups is the cash flow of the business.

Although some information about cash flows can be derived from comparative balance sheets and income statements, neither of these statements provides a complete and detailed picture of a company's cash flows. An income statement discloses the results of operations for the accounting period, but does not indicate either the cash provided by operations or the cash provided by other activities. An income statement is based on the accrual method of accounting, because this method provides a much better indication of future cash inflows and outflows than an income statement based only on cash receipts and cash payments. Comparative balance sheets show net changes in assets, liabilities, and owners' equity, but do not indicate the specific causes of these changes. For example, comparative balance sheets may disclose that property, plant and equipment increased, but do not indicate how the increase was financed. Even if short-term or long-term debt increased, comparative balance sheets do not explain whether the increase was due to only new debt or whether maturing debt was repaid and new debt issued. A third statement is needed—a statement of cash flows.

The statement of cash flows explains in detail the causes of changes in cash and provides a summary of the operating, investing, and financing activities of the business for the accounting period during a period of time. While the basic purpose of this statement is to provide information concerning the cash receipts and payments of a company, the statement also is useful in appraising other factors such as the firm's financing policies, dividend policies, ability to expand productive capacity, and ability to satisfy its future debt requirements.

A Brief History

Prior to the 1960s, many firms voluntarily prepared statements of changes in financial position for inclusion in their annual reports. These statements of changes in financial position usually provided information as to the sources and uses of working capital (current assets minus current liabilities) which took place during the accounting period. The statement of changes in financial position was provided to supplement, not replace the balance sheet and income statement. It was intended to provide information that was not available directly from these other financial statements.

While the basic objective of the statement of changes in financial position was to summarize the financing and investing activities of the firm, in practice the form and content of these statements varied considerably. The statement was designed to allow users to analyze the flow of funds. Funds were usually defined as working capital, but some companies chose to define funds as cash, rather than working capital.

Due to increasing attention placed on funds-flow analysis, the AICPA published *Accounting Research Study No. 2*, "'Cash Flow' Analysis and the Funds Statement," in 1961.[1] This study recommended that the funds statement be presented in all annual reports. In 1963, *APB Opinion No. 3*, "The Statement of Source and Application of Funds," recommended, but did not require, that a statement of sources and applications of funds be presented as supplementary information in financial reports.[2] After the issuance of *APB Opinion No. 3*, there was a substantial increase in the number of firms presenting funds-flow data; however, the nature of these funds statements varied widely in practice, because *APB Opinion No. 3* allowed considerable latitude as to the form, content, and terminology used in the statement.

In 1971, the APB issued its *Opinion No. 19*,[3] which required the presentation of funds flow in all annual reports. In this Opinion, the APB stated that a statement of changes in financial position is essential for the use of financial statement readers and must be presented as a basic financial statement for each period for which an income statement is presented.

The objective of the statement of changes in financial position was to provide information regarding all of the financing and investing activities that occurred during an accounting period. This statement did not replace the income statement or balance sheet. Rather, it was intended to provide information that these other statements did not provide concerning the flow of funds and changes in financial position.

Many companies switched from defining funds as working capital to defining funds as cash or cash plus cash equivalents (such as treasury bills, commercial paper, and money market funds). These changes can be seen in data provided in the 1989 edition of *Accounting Trends & Techniques* for its survey of 600 companies. In 1985, 587 of the 600 companies presented a statement of changes in financial position, and only one company included a statement of cash flows in their annual report. In 1988, only 58 companies presented a statement of changes in financial position and 540 companies included a cash flow statement.

In 1987, the FASB issued *Statement of Financial Accounting Standards No. 95, "Statement of Cash Flows*," requiring a statement of cash flows when both a balance sheet and an income statement are presented. The statement of cash flows should present the net cash flows from operating, investing, and financing activities.[4]

Cash Flow Concept

FASB Statement No. 95 permits preparation of the cash flow statement using either a "pure cash" concept or a "cash and cash equivalents" concept. The pure cash concept reports on the cash flow statement only those transactions that involve a direct inflow or outflow of cash. The cash and cash equivalents is a broader concept, reflecting as cash flow both cash transactions and those transactions involving highly liquid assets

---

[1] Perry Mason, " 'Cash' Flow Analysis and the Funds Statement," Accounting Research Study No. 2 (New York: AICPA, 1961).
[2] *APB Opinion No. 3*, "The Statement of Source and Application of Funds" (New York: AICPA, 1963).
[3] *APB Opinion No. 19*, "Reporting Changes in Financial Position" (New York: AICPA, 1971), para. 7.
[4] *FASB Statement No. 95*, "Cash Flow Statement" (Norwalk, CT: FASB, 1987).

with very short maturity dates (usually three or fewer months). Cash equivalents include U.S. treasury bills (due in three or fewer months), commercial paper, and money market funds. If the cash equivalent concept is used, this fact must be disclosed in the notes to the financial statements as an accounting policy.

The Statement of Cash Flows

The statement of cash flows consists of three major sections: the cash effects of an entity's operations, its investing activities, and its financing activities. Classifying cash flows into these categories enables significant relationships within and among these activities to be disclosed and analyzed and provides useful information to the users of financial statements. The statement of cash flows can provide answers to questions such as the following:

Why does net income differ from net cash flows from operations?

Why were dividend payments low (high) when income was high (low)?

How were acquisitions of plant and equipment paid for or financed?

How much of an increase (decrease) in cash during the year was due to new borrowing (the payment of debt)?

How much cash was used to buy treasury stock?

How much cash was received from selling noncurrent assets?

Previously, the statement of changes in financial position (prepared on either a cash or working capital basis) was presented in the format of a listing of the sources followed by the uses of cash or working capital. However, sources may include such dissimilar transactions as the issuance of bonds and the proceeds from the sale of plant and equipment; similarly, uses can include transactions such as the payment of dividends and the repayment of long-term debt. The new format required by the FASB is more useful and understandable.

The three sections of the statement of cash flows are as follows:

1. *Operating activities*—Operating activities include providing services; paying suppliers and employees; selling, purchasing, and producing goods; and interest income.

2. *Investing activities*—Investing activities include acquiring and disposing of assets used in the business; receipts from loans, acquiring and selling securities (except for cash equivalents) and acquiring and selling plant assets and land.

3. *Financing activities*—Financing activities include proceeds from the issuance of the entity's long-term bonds or the sale of stock, reductions of long-term debt prior to its maturity, outlays to pay the maturity value of bonds, outlays to purchase the entity's stock (treasury stock), and the payment of dividends.

In addition, there may be a separate schedule for noncash investing and financing activities (for example, acquiring land by issuing common stock).

In preparing the statement of cash flows, cash flows from operating activities may be reported by either the *direct* or the *indirect* method. Using the direct method, cash flows from operations are computed by subtracting cash disbursements from operations directly from cash receipts from operations. Alternatively, the indirect method computes net cash flow from operations by adjusting the net income for the period for noncash items (such as depreciation) included in the computation of net income. The cash impact of any extraordinary items should be disclosed separately under either method.

A format for the statement of cash flows using the direct method is presented in Illustration 1 while a format using the indirect method is presented in Illustration 2. Note that the only difference between the direct and the indirect methods is in presentation of net cash flow from operating activities. The remaining two sections of the statement, cash flows from investing activities and cash flows from financing activities, are identical under either the direct or the indirect method.

Illustration 1
*Statement of Cash Flows Using
the Direct Method*

Cash flows from operating activities:		
Cash received from customers	$ X	
Dividends received	X	
Cash provided by operating activities		$ X
Cash paid to suppliers	(X)	
Cash paid to employees	(X)	
Cash paid for interest and taxes	(X)	
Cash paid for operating activities		(X)
Net cash provided (used) by operating activities		$ X
Cash flows from investing activities:		
Proceeds from sale of plant assets	$ X	
Purchase of plant assets	(X)	
Net cash provided (used) by investing activities		X
Cash flows from financing activities:		
Proceeds from issuance of bonds payable	$ X	
Proceeds from issuance of common stock	X	
Payment of cash dividends	(X)	
Net cash provided (used) by financing activities		X
Net increase (decrease) in cash		$ X
Cash—beginning of the year		X
Cash—end of year		$ X

Illustration 2
*Statement of Cash Flows Using
the Indirect Method*

Cash flows from operating activities:		
Net income	$ X	
Noncash expenses, revenues, losses,		
and gains included in income:		
Depreciation and amortization	X	
Increase in receivables	(X)	
Increase in inventories	(X)	
Increase in payables	X	
Net cash provided (used) by operating activities		$ X
Cash flows from investing activities:		
Proceeds from sale of plant assets	$ X	
Purchase of plant assets	(X)	
Net cash provided (used) by investing activities		X
Cash flows from financing activities:		
Proceeds from issuance of bonds payable	$ X	
Proceeds from issuance of common stock	X	
Payment of cash dividends	(X)	
Net cash provided (used) by financing activities		X
Net increase (decrease) in cash		$ X
Cash—beginning of the year		X
Cash—end of year		$ X

When the direct method is used, a supplemental schedule reconciling the reported net income to net cash flows from operating activities must be provided. The format for this schedule is presented in Illustration 3. Note that this schedule, the reconciliation of reported net income to net cash provided by operating activities, is almost identical to the initial section of the cash flow statement prepared using the indirect method, cash flows from operating activities. This is because the indirect method normally provides a reconciliation of net income to net cash flows from operating activities for all noncash expenses, revenues, losses, and gains within the statement itself. The identical amount of net cash from operating activities is reported under the direct and indirect methods, only the format used in each differs.

Illustration 3
*Reconciliation of Net Income
to Net Cash Provided by Operating Activities*

Net income	$ X
Adjustments to reconcile net income to net cash provided by operating activities:	
Depreciation and amortization	X
Increase in receivables	(X)
Increase in inventories	(X)
Increase in payables	X
Net cash provided by operating activities	$ X

While the FASB permits the use of either method, it encourages the use of the direct method because the Board believes that it provides more useful information. The indirect method is used by over 95 percent of companies presenting a statement of cash flows, however. Both methods are presented and illustrated in this chapter.

Cash from Operations

The net income of a firm for an accounting period is defined as the excess of its revenues and gains over its expenses and losses. Revenues generally result in an increase in cash or other current assets. For example, sales usually result in an increase in either cash or accounts receivable. Accounts receivable are subsequently collected, increasing cash. Similarly, most expenses require either that a current outlay of cash be made or that a current liability (which will subsequently require the payment of cash) be incurred.

Direct Method

Under the direct method, the statement of cash flows may show cash receipts and payments from operations directly. Such a format appears in Illustration 1.

Cash received from customers is equal to net sales on an accrual basis adjusted for the change in accounts receivable from customers—sales plus beginning accounts receivable is the total amount which could be collected from customers. Subtracting the ending accounts receivable (the amount which was not collected) from this total provides the amount which was collected. Thus a decrease in net accounts receivable is added or an increase in net accounts receivable is subtracted from net sales to convert sales on an accrual basis to sales on a cash basis. Assume that sales on an accrual basis are $50,000, beginning accounts receivable are $10,000, and ending accounts receivable are $8,000. Then cash collections from customers may be determined as follows:

Sales on an accrual basis	$50,000
Add: Beginning accounts receivable	10,000
	$60,000
Less: Ending accounts receivable	8,000
Cash received from customers	$52,000

The decrease in accounts receivable ($10,000 − $8,000 = $2,000) results in cash received from customers exceeding sales on an accrual basis by $2,000.

Cash paid to the suppliers of merchandise is equal to cost of goods sold less beginning inventory (already on hand from the prior period) plus ending inventory (acquired and on hand but not sold at the close of the current period) plus beginning accounts payable (owed for prior purchases) equals purchases. Purchases less ending accounts payable (not paid but still owed at the end of the current period). In other words, cost of goods sold plus the increase in inventories or minus the decrease in inventories converts cost of goods sold to purchases. Adding the decrease or subtracting the increase in accounts payable and other short-term liabilities to suppliers for merchandise acquired provides the total cash paid to suppliers. For example, assume that cost of goods sold is $40,000, beginning inventories are $7,000, ending inventories are $9,000, beginning accounts payable for inventories are $6,000, and ending accounts payable for inventories are $5,000. Then cash paid to suppliers is determined as follows:

Cost of goods sold	$40,000
Add: Ending inventories	9,000
Cost of goods available	$49,000
Less: Beginning inventories	7,000
Purchases	$42,000
Add: Beginning accounts payable (for merchandise)	6,000
	$48,000
Less: Ending accounts payable (for merchandise)	5,000
Cash paid to suppliers	$43,000

Cash paid for other expenses is equal to the expense reported on an accrual basis plus the beginning accrued expenses payable (owed from the prior period) less the ending accrued expenses payable (not paid but still owed at the end of the current period) less the beginning prepaid expenses (already paid in the prior period) plus the ending prepaid expenses (paid but not used in the current period). In other words, the expenses reported on an accrual basis plus the decrease or minus the increase in the related payable and plus the increase or minus the decrease in any prepayments of expenses provides the total cash paid for other expenses. For example, cash paid to employees is equal to salaries expense reported on an accrual basis plus the beginning salaries payable (which is the total cash which could be paid to employees) minus the ending in salaries payable.

Indirect Method

As indicated above, the reported net income of a firm is not always equal to the net cash flow from operating activities. Not all expenses or revenues result in an inflow or outflow of cash. Certain types of expenses enter into the determination of net income but do not affect cash. For example, depreciation on plant assets is an expense that reduces income but does not require an outlay of cash during the current period. Therefore, depreciation expense does not affect cash. Consequently, to determine the net cash flow from operating activities, it is necessary to include only those expenses that required an outflow of cash during the period. An important factor in determining net cash flow from operating activities under the indirect method is to add back to (or subtract from) net income all those items that did not result in an outflow (inflow) of cash.

Examples of items that are added to net income include depreciation expense, amortization expense, the portion of bond interest expense due to the amortization of bond discount, and the reduction in interest revenue due to the amortization of a premium on a bond investment since none of these items require current period cash expenditures. Examples of items that are subtracted from net income include the reduction in interest expense due to the amortization of bond premium (which does not affect the cash paid for interest) and the portion of interest revenue due to the amortization of a discount on a bond investment since this does not provide cash.

Additional adjustments are required to convert revenues and expenses to cash receipts and disbursements, because income statement data are based on the accrual method of accounting. To determine net cash flow from operating activities using the indirect method, net income must be adjusted for changes in current assets (other than cash) and for changes in current liabilities (other than those not related to operations, such as nontrade notes payable and dividends payable).

These additional adjustments essentially convert income from operations from the accrual to the cash basis. Some of the more common adjustments to net income under the indirect method to obtain net cash flow from operating activities are as follows:

Add	Subtract
Decrease in net accounts receivable	Increase in net accounts receivable
Decreases in inventories and prepaid expenses	Increases in inventories and prepaid expenses
Increases in accounts payable, trade notes payable, and accrued liabilities	Decreases in accounts payable, trade notes payable, and accrued liabilities

A decrease in accounts receivable results in sales on a cash basis exceeding sales on an accrual basis by the amount of the decrease. For example, if sales on an accrual basis are $100,000, beginning accounts receivable are $15,000, and ending accounts receivable are $14,000, then sales on a cash basis are $101,000.

Beginning accounts receivable	$ 15,000
Sales on an accrual basis	100,000
Cash that could have been collected	$115,000
Ending accounts receivable	14,000
Sales on a cash basis	$101,000

Therefore, a decrease in accounts receivable is added to net income in determining net cash flow from operations. Conversely, an increase in accounts receivable is subtracted from net income in determining net cash flow from operations.

In a similar fashion, net income is adjusted by the changes in accounts payable, short-term notes payable, and accrued liabilities to convert expenses on an accrual basis to expenses on a cash basis. A decrease in these current payables results in expenses on a cash basis being higher than expenses on an accrual basis. Therefore, a decrease in these payables is subtracted from net income in determining net cash flow from operations. Conversely, an increase in these payables is added to net income in determining net cash flow from operations.

The change in inventories is an adjustment made to net income in order to convert cost of goods sold to purchases. Cost of goods sold less beginning inventory (already on hand from the prior period) plus ending inventory (acquired and on hand but not sold at the close of the current period) equals purchases. An increase in inventories means that purchases exceed cost of goods sold. For example, if the beginning inventory is $7,000, the ending inventory is $8,000, and cost of goods sold is $80,000, then purchases are $81,000. A decrease in inventories means that purchases are less than cost of goods sold. Therefore, an increase in inventories is subtracted from net income to obtain net cash flow from operations and a decrease in inventories is added to net income to obtain net cash flow from operations.

A firm that experiences a net loss during a period still may generate cash from its operations if the total expenses that did not require the use of cash exceed the amount of the loss, or adjustments for current assets (other than cash and cash equivalents) and current liabilities convert a net loss on an accrual basis to net income on a cash basis. For example, a firm may have a net loss of $10,000 and have depreciation expense of $15,000 among its expenses, so its cash basis income was $5,000.

Additional adjustments may be required in order to obtain net cash flow from operating activities if net income includes extraordinary gains or losses. The disclosure of cash provided by operations is most useful if the effects of extraordinary items, net of tax, are reported separately from the effects of normal items. The net cash flow from operating activities may begin with the net income or loss from continuing operations. Any items that did not use or provide cash during the period and were included in the net income or loss from continuing operations should be added or deducted. Cash provided or used by extraordinary items, net of tax, should be reported immediately following cash provided or used in operations. Adjustments are necessary for any of these extraordinary items that did not provide or use cash during the period.

Similarly, other nonoperating gains or losses should be excluded from cash provided by operations. These amounts should be included as a part of the investing or financing activities. For example, if land that had an original cost of $10,000 is sold for $9,000 in cash, a $1,000 loss on the sale of land is reported and included in the net income for the period. The $9,000 received from the sale represents the cash provided and is shown in the statement of cash flows under investing activities as a separate item. The $9,000 proceeds received in cash is, of course, equal to the $10,000 cost of the land minus the $1,000 loss. Therefore, to avoid double-counting, the $1,000 loss should not be included in determining the net cash flow from operating activities. Thus, to determine the net cash flow from operating activities, it is necessary to add back any nonoperating losses and to deduct any nonoperating gains.

Both the indirect and the direct methods will be used in this chapter to illustrate the calculation of net cash flow from operating activities.

Preparation of the Statement of Cash Flows

The change in cash (including cash equivalents) during the period must be exactly equal to the net change in all of the noncash accounts during the period, because the accounting equation (A = L + SE) must, by definition, always remain in balances.[5] Based on this basic relationship, the increase or decrease in cash may be explained by examining the changes in all of the noncash accounts for the period.

The primary sources of information used in preparing the statement of cash flows are comparative balance sheets, the income statement, the statement of stockholders' equity or retained earnings, and certain supplementary data concerning the transactions affecting specific noncash accounts during the period. The basic data that will be used to present the required steps for the preparation of a statement of cash flows are shown in the financial statements of the Kraton Company (Illustrations 4-6).

Illustration 4
Kraton Company
Income Statement
for the Year Ended December 31, 20X1

Net sales		$1,000
Cost of goods sold		400
Gross profit		$ 600
Operating expenses:		
Depreciation	$100	
Wage expense	100	
Other expenses	200	400
Net income from operations		$ 200
Gain on sale of land		100
Net income		$ 300

---

[5] A = L + SE or
Cash + (other) A = L + SE, therefore
Δ Cash + Δ (other) A = Δ L + Δ SE, or
Δ Cash = Δ L + Δ SE − Δ (other) A

Illustration 5
Kraton Company
Retained Earnings Statement
for the Year Ended December 31, 20X1

Retained earnings at beginning of year	$250
Add: Net income	300
	$550
Subtract: Cash dividends	100
Retained earnings at end of year	$450

Illustration 6
Kraton Company
Comparative Balance Sheet

	December 31 20X1	December 31 20X0	Change
Assets:			
Cash	$ 250	$ 100	+ 150
Accounts receivable—net	350	200	+ 150
Inventories	200	250	− 50
Building	600	400	+ 200
Accumulated depreciation—building	(200)	(100)	+ 100
Land	100	200	− 100
Total assets	$1,300	$1,050	
Liabilities and Stockholders' Equity:			
Accounts payable	$ 300	$ 200	+ 100
Accrued wages payable	50	100	− 50
Bonds payable—long-term	100	200	− 100
Common stock	400	300	+ 100
Retained earnings	450	250	+ 200
Total liabilities and equities	$1,300	$1,050	

Assume that the following additional information is available:

1. During the year, a building was purchased for $200 and land was purchased at a cost of $100.
2. Land with a cost of $200 was sold for $300, resulting in a gain of $100.
3. All common stock was issued for cash.
4. A long-term bond was retired by an outlay of $100 in cash.
5. A $100 dividend was paid during the year.
6. The other expenses of $200 were paid in cash.

Change in Cash

The change in the cash account is an increase of $150 (see Illustration 6). The cash balance was $100 at the end of 20X0, but increased to $250 at the end of 20X1.

Changes in Noncash Accounts

Once the change in cash has been determined, the next step is to compute the changes in all of the noncash accounts (see Illustration 6). All changes in the noncash accounts of Kraton Company from December 31, 20X0, to December 31, 20X1, are summarized below:

Kraton Company
Changes in Noncash Accounts

	December 31 20X1	December 31 20X0	Increase	Decrease
Accounts receivable—net	$350	$200	$150	
Inventories	200	250		$50
Buildings	600	400	200	
Accumulated depreciation—buildings	200	100	100	
Land	100	200		100
Accounts payable	300	200	100	
Accrued wages payable	50	100		50
Bonds payable—long-term	100	200		100
Capital stock	400	300	100	
Retained earnings	450	250	200	

Once the amount of these changes has been determined, it is necessary to consider the effect that each change had on cash. If more than one transaction caused the change in a particular account, the effect of each individual transaction must be analyzed separately. Let us consider the changes in the noncash accounts of Kraton Company.

Retained Earnings. An examination of the comparative balance sheets reveals that retained earnings increased by $200 during 20X1. An analysis of the statement of retained earnings (Illustration 5) indicates that net income for 20X1 was $300 and that dividends of $100 were declared and paid to stockholders during the year. These two transactions account for the net change in retained earnings. The payment of the cash dividend affected cash as follows:

> Cash flow from financing activity:
> Cash dividend .... ($100)

Under the direct method, net cash flow from operating activities is equal to cash receipts from operations minus cash payments from operations. Cash receipts from customers are equal to net sales less the increase in accounts receivables. Cash payments to suppliers are equal to cost of goods sold less the decrease in inventories less the increase in accounts payable. Cash payments to employees are equal to wage expense plus the decrease in accrued wages payable. Cash payments for other expenses during 20X1 was $200. Therefore, net cash flow from operating activities using the direct method is as follows:

> Cash flows from operating activities:
> Cash receipts from customers ($1,000 − $150) $850
> Cash paid to suppliers ($400 − $50 − $100) $250
> Cash paid to employees ($100 + $50) 150
> Cash paid for other expenses 200
> Cash paid for other operating activities 600
> Net cash provided by operating activities $250

Using the indirect method, the effect of the net income of the period on cash is included in the calculation of net cash flow from operating activities. As previously indicated, the net income of Kraton Company ($300) is not equivalent to net cash flow from operating activities ($250). Depreciation expense that is included in the income statement did not require an outflow of cash during 20X1. Therefore, it is necessary to add back depreciation expense of $100 to the net income of the period in computing net cash flow from operating activities for 20X1 under the indirect method.

A second adjustment is required to eliminate the gain on the sale of land from net income. The $100 gain is embedded in the proceeds from the sale of land and is included as an investing activity and must be excluded from net cash flow from operating activities.

The increase in accounts receivable of $150 must be subtracted from net income in calculating net cash flow from operating activities. The decrease in inventories of $50 must be added to net income in calculating net cash flow from operating activities. The increase in accounts payable of $100 must be added to net income in calculating net cash flow from operating activities. The decrease in accrued wages payable of $50 must be subtracted from net income in calculating net cash flow from operating activities. Therefore, using the indirect method the net cash flow from operating activities is determined as follows:

```
Cash flows from operating activities:
  Net Income .......................................... $300
  Noncash expenses, revenues, losses,
      and gains included in income:
    Depreciation ......................................  100
    Gain on sale of land ..............................  (100)
    Increase in accounts receivable ...................  (150)
    Decrease in inventories ...........................   50
    Increase in accounts payable ......................  100
    Decrease In accrued wages payable .................  (50)
  Net cash provided by operating activities ...........  $250
```

Accumulated Depreciation. The $100 increase in accumulated depreciation—buildings resulted from recording the depreciation expense for the year. The amount of depreciation expense is added to net income in determining net cash flow from operating activities under the indirect method and is not considered under the direct method because it does not result in a decrease in cash.

Buildings. The increase in the buildings account was the result of a single transaction in which a building was acquired at a cost of $200. The effect of this purchase on cash is as follows:

```
Cash flow from investing activity:
  Purchase of building ............................... ($200)
```

Land. The comparative balance sheet indicates that the land account decreased by a net amount of $100 during 20X1. This decrease was a result of the sale of land during the year exceeding the purchase of land made during the year. The cash flow from the sale of land is the total proceeds received from the sale. To record the sale, cash was increased by $300, a gain on sale of land of $100 was recorded, and land was decreased by the cost of $200. Thus, $300 of cash was provided by the sale. As indicated previously, the $100 gain on the sale must be subtracted from net income in the calculation of net cash flow from operating activities under the indirect method to avoid "double" counting. The gain is not considered under the direct method. The effect of the sale on cash is as follows:

```
Cash flow from investing activity:
  Sale of land ........................  $300
```

The purchase of land for $100 affected cash as follows:

```
Cash flow from investing activity:
  Purchase of land ....................  ($100)
```

Bonds Payable. Bonds payable decreased by $100 during the year. An analysis of the additional information provided indicates that this decrease resulted from the retirement of the bonds for $100. The effect on cash is as follows:

> Cash flow from financing activity:
> Retirement of bonds payable .... ($100)

Common Stock. The increase in the common stock account resulted from the sale and issuance of additional stock for $100 in cash during the year. This amount is included in the statement as follows:

> Cash flow from financing activity:
> Issuance of common stock $100

Statement of Cash Flows

All of the information that is necessary to prepare the statement of cash flows now has been analyzed. Kraton Company's statement of cash flows for the year ended December 31, 20X1, is shown using the direct method (in Illustration 7) and the indirect method (in Illustration 8). Again, note that net cash flow from operating activities is the same, regardless of the method used.

Illustration 7
Statement of Cash Flows
Using the Direct Method

Kraton Company
Statement of Cash Flows
for the Year Ended December 31, 20X1

Cash flows from operating activities:		
Cash receipts from operations		$ 850
Cash paid to suppliers	$ 250	
Cash paid to employees	150	
Cash paid for other expenses	200	
Cash paid for operating expenses		600
Net cash flow provided by operating activities		$ 250
Cash flows from investing activities:		
Sale of land	$ 300	
Acquisition of land	(100)	
Acquisition of building	(200)	
Net cash used by investing activities		0
Cash flows from financing activities:		
Sale of common stock	$ 100	
Retirement of long-term bonds	(100)	
Payment of dividends	(100)	
Net cash used by financing activities		(100)
Net increase in cash		$ 150
Cash—beginning of year		100
Cash—end of year		$ 250

> **Illustration 8**
> Statement of Cash Flows
> Using the Indirect Method
>
> **Kraton Company**
> Statement of Cash Flows
> for the Year Ended December 31, 20X1
>
> | | | |
> |---|---:|---:|
> | Cash flows from operating activities: | | |
> | Net income | $ 300 | |
> | Noncash expenses, revenues, losses, and gains included in income: | | |
> | Depreciation | 100 | |
> | Gain on sale of land | (100) | |
> | Increase in accounts receivable | (150) | |
> | Decrease in inventories | 50 | |
> | Increase in accounts payable | 100 | |
> | Decrease in accrued wages payable | (50) | |
> | Net cash flow provided by operating activities | | $ 250 |
> | Cash flows from investing activities: | | |
> | Sale of land | $ 300 | |
> | Acquisition of land | (100) | |
> | Acquisition of building | (200) | |
> | Net cash used by investing activities | | 0 |
> | Cash flows from financing activities: | | |
> | Sale of common stock | $ 100 | |
> | Retirement of long-term bonds | (100) | |
> | Payment of dividends | (100) | |
> | Net cash used by financing activities | | (100) |
> | Net increase in cash | | $ 150 |
> | Cash—beginning of year | | 100 |
> | Cash—end of year | | $ 250 |

Additional Problems in the Analysis of the Statement of Cash Flows

Many of the procedures normally used in the preparation of the statement of cash flows were discussed in the preceding sections of this chapter. However, additional problems may arise that require special analysis to determine the effect on cash of a change in an asset (excluding cash and cash equivalents), a liability, or an stockholders' equity account. Some of these special problems are illustrated and examined in the following paragraphs.

Uncollectible Accounts

Under the direct method, in addition to the adjustment for the change in the receivable account, the total of accounts receivable written off as uncollectible during the period must be deducted from sales because the decrease in accounts receivable due to the write-off is not because of collections on credit sales. Under the indirect method, a change in the balance in the allowance for bad debts account resulting from either bad debt expense for the current period or the write-off of uncollectible accounts does not require any adjustment to net income. The allowance for bad debt account is a contra account to a current asset, accounts receivable. Therefore, the change in the allowance account is a part of the increase or decrease to net accounts receivable for the period. The increase in bad debt expense represents a deduction from revenues in determining net income. The decrease in net accounts receivable resulting from the increase in the allowance account is added to net income in determining net cash flow from operating activities under the indirect method. Therefore, the bad debt expense is a deduction in determining net income and the corresponding decrease in net accounts receivable is added to net income so that there is no effect on cash. A write-off of an uncollectible account reduces both the receivable and the related allowance account; it does not affect the balance of net accounts receivable. Accordingly, the write-off has no effect on cash.

Dividends

A reduction in retained earnings resulting from the declaration of a cash dividend to be paid during a subsequent period has no effect on cash. Only the payment of the dividend affects cash and is reported as a financing activity in the period in which the cash payment is made.

Income Tax Expense

Income tax expense must be adjusted for changes in income taxes payable. Under the direct method, income tax expense is increased (decreased) for a decrease (increase) in income taxes payable to determine cash paid for taxes. Under the indirect method, net income is increased (decreased) for an increase (decrease) in income taxes payable.

Stock Dividends and Conversions

When a corporation declares a stock dividend, a transfer is made from retained earnings to one or more contributed capital accounts. Such a transfer does not affect either total stockholders' equity or assets. Therefore, the resulting changes in stockholders' equity do not affect and are not included on the statement of cash flows.

Changes of substance in the individual components of owners' equity should be reported in the statement of cash flows even though these changes do not involve either a receipt or disbursement of cash. Accordingly, the conversion of long-term debt or preferred stock to common stock should be reflected in a supplementary schedule of noncash transactions to the statement of cash flows.

Significant Noncash Transactions

The statement of cash flows should report all financing and investing activities, including those that do not actually involve either a current receipt or disbursement of cash. Among the most common of these transactions are the following:

1. The issuance of noncurrent debt or capital stock for noncurrent assets.
2. The issuance of capital stock to retire noncurrent debt.
3. Refinancing of long-term debt.
4. Conversion of long-term debt or preferred stock to common stock.

To illustrate, assume that a firm issues 50,000 shares of its $5 par value common stock in exchange for land with a fair market value of $380,000. This transaction is recorded as increases in land of $380,000, common stock of $250,000, and additional paid-in capital of $130,000. Although this transaction did not affect cash, the transaction should be viewed as if it were composed of two parts—the sale of stock for $380,000, and the purchase of a building for the same amount. Thus, the transaction is reported in the statement of cash flows as follows:

> Schedule of noncash investing and financing activities:
> Issuance of common stock to purchase a building $380,000

Multiple Changes Affecting Specific Accounts

Frequently, there may be several transactions that cause a net change in a noncurrent account. In these circumstances, it normally is helpful to analyze the individual transactions affecting the account in order to identify the effect of each on cash.

For example, assume that the following information is available regarding the equipment account:

	End of Year	Beginning of Year
Equipment	$212,000	$200,000
Accumulated depreciation	55,000	90,000
Depreciation expense	15,000	
Gain on sale of equipment	7,000	

Equipment with a cost of $70,000 and a book value (cost less accumulated depreciation) of $20,000 was sold for $27,000 during the year. Equipment was acquired at a cost of $82,000. The individual transactions that caused the changes in the equipment and the accumulated depreciation accounts may be summarized as follows:

	Equipment	Accumulated Depreciation
Beginning of year	$200,000	$ 90,000
Acquisition of equipment	82,000	
Sale of equipment	(70,000)	(50,000)
Depreciation expense		$ 15,000
End of year	$212,000	$ 55,000

The amounts recorded at the time of each event and the resulting effect on cash are summarized below:

Sale of equipment:
> Cash increased by $27,000, accumulated depreciation decreased by $50,000, equipment by $70,000, and a gain on sale of equipment of $7,000 was recorded. Cash inflow of $27,000 is reported as an investing activity; the $7,000 gain is subtracted from net income in determining net cash flow from operations under the indirect method and is not considered under the direct method.

Acquisition of equipment:
> Equipment increased and cash decreased by $82,000, the cash outflow of $82,000 is reported as an investing activity.

Depreciation:
> Depreciation expense and accumulated depreciation are each increased by $15,000. Depreciation expense is added to net income in determining net cash flow from operations under the indirect method and is not considered under the direct method.

Cash Flow Information for Analysis

Cash flow from operations is an important indicator of a company's ability to pay its debts on a timely basis. Some analysts believe that cash flow from operations is more useful than net income in this regard, because accrual accounting can sometimes temporarily conceal cash flow problems.

Free cash flow measures the cash available after capital expenditures to at least maintain the current level of production and dividend payments.

Free Cash Flow = Net Cash Flow from Operating Activities − Capital Expenditures − Dividends

For PepsiCo in 2002, free cash flow is computed as follows (dollars are in millions):

Free Cash Flow = $4,267 − $1,437 − $1,046

Free Cash Flow = $1,784

The free cash flow can be used to acquire new equipment, pay debts, or for other business purposes. The free cash flow figure may be understated, because not all of the $1,437 of capital expenditures was used to acquire property, plant and equipment to simply maintain current levels of production. Some (or all) could have been used for expansion purposes.

Cash flow adequacy is a measure of a company's debt-paying ability. Cash flow adequacy can be computed as follows:

$$\text{Cash Flow Adequacy} = \frac{\text{Free Cash Flow}}{\text{Average Amount of Debt Maturing over Next Five Years}}$$

The amount of debt maturing over the next five years is normally disclosed in the note pertaining to long-term debt and, if not already included, the note pertaining to lease obligations. PepsiCo's cash flow adequacy cannot be computed, because the amount of debt maturing over the next five years is not separately disclosed.

Neither free cash flow nor cash flow adequacy should be examined in isolation. They should be compared with past performance of the company, with other companies in the same industry and with industry averages.

Summary

The statement of cash flows is included as one of the major financial statements in corporate annual reports. This statement may be prepared using a "pure cash" or a "cash and cash equivalents" basis and provides a summary of the operating, investing, and financing activities of an enterprise during a period of time. The statement may be prepared using the direct or the indirect method. In addition, all significant transactions involving changes in noncash accounts must be disclosed in the statement of cash flows.

The sections of the statement of cash flows are: (1) cash flows from operating activities, (2) cash flows from investing activities, and (3) cash flows from financing activities. Investing activities include collections on loans, proceeds from the sale of plant assets, and purchases of plant assets; financing activities include proceeds from the issuance of bonds and stock and the payment of cash dividends.

Key Definitions

"Cash and cash equivalents" concept—reflects as cash flow both cash transactions and those transactions involving highly liquid assets with very short maturity dates.
Cash equivalents—include U.S. treasury bills (due in three months or less), commercial paper, and money market funds.
Cash disbursement—any outflow of cash by the firm.
Cash flow—any transaction that increases or decreases the cash balance of the firm.
Cash receipt—any transaction that increases the cash account of the firm.
Direct method—computing net cash flow from operations as the difference between cash receipts from operating activities and cash disbursements from operating activities.

Financing activities—the statement of cash flows section that includes proceeds from the issuance of the entity's bonds or stocks, outlays to pay the maturity value of bonds, outlays to purchase the entity's stock, and the payment of dividends.
Free cash flow—cash available after capital expenditures to at least maintain current production and dividend levels.
Funds—according to *APB Opinion No. 19*, funds were defined as either cash, near-cash, or working capital.
Indirect method—computing net cash flow from operations by adjusting net income for noncash items included in income.
Investing activities—the statement of cash flows section that includes receipts from loans, acquiring and selling securities (except for cash equivalents), and acquiring and selling plant assets and land.
Operating activities—statement of cash flows section that includes selling, purchasing, and producing goods; providing services; and paying suppliers and employees.
"Pure cash" concept—includes on the cash flow statement only those transactions that involve the direct inflow or outflow of cash.
Statement of cash flows—a statement which explains the causes of changes in cash plus highly liquid marketable securities and provides a summary of the investing and financing activities of an enterprise during a period of time.
Working capital—the excess of current assets over current liabilities.

QUESTIONS

1. Why is a statement of cash flows necessary?

2. What are the three major sections of a statement of cash flows?

3. Give examples of items included in each of the three major sections of a statement of cash flows.

4. Explain how income affects cash. Is reported net income always equal to the amount of cash flows from operations?

5. List items that may be included in the determination of net income but that have no effect on cash.

6. Compare and contrast the direct and indirect methods of preparing the statement of cash flows.

7. What steps are needed in preparing a statement of cash flows?

8. What is the purpose of a worksheet in preparing a statement of cash flows?

9. State how the following are presented on a statement of cash flows.

    a. Dividends paid.
    b. Conversions of bonds to common stock.
    c. Amortization of discount on bonds payable.
    d. Loss on the sale of equipment.

10. Explain how each of the following are treated in a statement of cash flows.

    a. Bad debt expense.
    b. Purchasing land by issuing common stock.
    c. Reclassifying a note payable from long-term to current.
    d. Loss on sale of current marketable equity securities.
    e. Increase in inventories.
    f. Amortization of patents.
    g. Increase in accounts payable.
    h. Conversion of bonds to common stock.

11. Is it possible for a company to report a loss and an increase in cash for the same period? Explain.

Exercises and Problems

12. *Statement of Cash Flows—General Classification.* Indicate how each of the items presented below would appear in a statement of cash flows.

   a. Declaration of a cash dividend.
   b. Payment of cash dividend after above declaration.
   c. Depreciation expense for the year.
   d. Fully depreciated equipment written off the books.
   e. Amortization of premium on long-term bonds payable.
   f. Semiannual coupon payments on bonds mentioned in (e) above.
   g. Sale of common stock at a discount.
   h. Purchase of treasury stock at a price above the original issue price.
   i. Payment of wages accrued at the end of the prior year.
   j. Sale of fixed assets at a loss.
   k. Issuance of a 90-day note.
   l. Sale of ten-year bonds at a discount.
   m. Three for one (3-1) split of the preferred stock.
   n. Sale of machinery at a price in excess of its book value.
   o. Amortization of goodwill.

13. *Cash Flow From Operations.* Below is the income statement for Lopes Company for the year ending December 31, 20X2.

Lopes Company
Income Statement
for the Year Ended December 31, 20X2

Sales (net)		$500,000
Cost of goods sold:		
Beginning inventory	$ 50,000	
Purchases	300,000	
Goods available for sale	$350,000	
Ending inventory	40,000	
Cost of goods sold		310,000
Gross profit		$190,000
Expenses:		
Wages	$ 35,000	
Depreciation	30,000	
Advertising	15,000	
Administrative	5,000	85,000
Income from operations		$105,000
Gain on sale of equipment		50,000
Net income		$155,000

The following balances were derived from the balance sheet.

	December 31	
	20X2	20X1
Accounts receivable	$100,000	$ 90,000
Accounts payable	30,000	50,000
Prepaid advertising expense	5,000	3,000
Wages payable	5,000	4,000

Required:

Prepare a schedule showing cash flows from operating activities.

14. *Cash Flows From Operations.* Determine the amount of purchases, the cash disbursements for rent expense, and the cash dividends paid for the Maple Leaf Company for the month of March from the information given below.

Cost of goods sold	$2,579
Increase in prepaid rent	864
Dividends	4,953
Rent expense	970
Increase in inventory	1,240
Decrease in dividends payable	691

15. *Calculation of cash from operating activities.* Milton Company reported net income of $30,000 for 20X1. During the year, accounts receivable increased by $7,000, accounts payable decreased by $3,000 and depreciation expense of $5,000 was recorded. Calculate the net cash provided by operating activities for the year.

16. *Preparation of statement of cash flows using direct and indirect methods.* Below are comparative financial statements for WAC Company for the years 20X4 and 20X3.

WAC Company
Balance Sheet and Income Statements
For the Years Ending December 31, 20X4 and 20X3

	December 31	
	20X4	20X3
Cash	$ 6,000	$ 5,000
Accounts Receivable	14,000	18,000
Inventory	23,000	20,000
Prepaid Interest	2,000	1,000
Land	3,000	2,000
Equipment	73,000	66,000
Less: Accumulated Depreciation	(28,000)	(26,000)
Total Assets	$93,000	$86,000
Accounts Payable	$13,000	$7,000
Wages Payable	3,000	4,000
Income Tax Payable	5,000	4,500
Long-Term Bonds Payable	20,000	23,000
Common Stock ($10 Par)	29,500	27,500
Additional Paid in Capital	500	0
Retained Earnings	22,000	20,000
Total Liabilities and Stockholders Equity	$93,000	$86,000
Sales (all credit sales)	$95,000	$89,000
Less: Cost of Goods Sold	43,000	43,000
Gross Profit	$52,000	$46,000
Less: Operating Expenses—		
Depreciation	$ 9,000	$8,000
Wages	23,000	21,000
Interest	2,000	2,000
Loss on Sale of Equipment	1,0 00	0
	35,000	31,000
Net Income Before Taxes	$17,000	$15,000
Less: Income Taxes	7,000	6,000
Net Income	$10,000	$ 9,000

Additional Information:

Sold equipment with an original cost of $9,000 and accumulated depreciation of $7,000 and purchased new equipment during 20X4.

Required:

Prepare a cash flow statement for the year ended December 31, 20X4, using both the direct and indirect methods.

17. *Cash flow from operations.* The following information is available from Aubrey Company's financial statements for the year ending 20X1:

Accounts payable decreased by	$ 5,000
Accounts receivable increased by	12,000
Bonds payable increased by	50,000
Common stock issued	25,000
Depreciation expense	7,500
Dividends paid	10,500
Gain on the sale of building	5,000
Inventory decreased	11,000
Loss on sale of equipment	3,000
Net income	122,000
Prepaid insurance increased by	4,000
Purchase of land	30,000
Salaries payable increased by	8,000
Sold building (cash proceeds)	45,000
Sold equipment (cash proceeds)	27,000
Supplies decreased by	500
Unearned fees increased by	3,000

From the above information prepare the operating section of the statement of cash flows using the indirect method.

18. *Cash flow from operations.* Duvall Corporation is preparing the operating section of its statement of cash flows. Duvall has decided to use the direct method in preparing this statement. In past years, Duvall has always used the indirect method and the accountant is unsure of what he is doing. He has asked for your assistance and has presented you with the following information:

	Beginning Balance	Ending Balance
Accounts receivable	$10,000	$18,000
Inventories	25,000	20,000
Prepaid expenses	12,000	10,000
Accounts payable for inventories	33,000	35,000
Unearned fees	5,000	4,000
Salaries payable	7,000	12,000
Net sales		$130,000
Cost of goods sold		88,000
Operating expenses (excluding depreciation)		65,000
Depreciation expense		5,000

Prepare the operating section of the statement of cash flows using the direct method.

The Statement of Cash Flows 12-21

19. *Cash Flow From Operations.* Consider the following income statement for Wills Company.

Sales		$1,000,000
Cost of goods sold		750,000
Gross profit		$ 250,000
Selling and administrative expenses:		
Salary expense	$50,000	
Depreciation expense	25,000	
Administrative expense	25,000	100,000
Net Income		$ 150,000

Additional information:

Decrease in inventories	9,000
Increase in accounts receivable	5,000
Increase in accounts payable	6,000

Required:

Compute the cash flows from operating activities using both the direct and indirect methods.

20. *Cash Flow From Operations.* Consider the following information for the period ending December 31, 20X1, concerning the Cey Company.

   1. Net income for 20X1 was $250,000.
   2. Depreciation expense on its buildings was $25,000. Accumulated depreciation on the buildings is $200,000.
   3. Extraordinary (non-operating) gains and losses included a loss of $50,000 on an uninsured building destroyed by fire.
   4. Cash dividends paid during the year were $50,000.

Required:

Compute the cash flows from operating activities, using the indirect method.

21. *Calculation of cash flows using indirect method.* The following balance sheets apply to Kleocyk Company. Prepare a statement of cash flow using the indirect method.

Assets:	20X7	20X6
Cash	$1,200	$ 800
Accounts Receivable	400	440
Inventory	1,220	740
Land	820	500
Equipment	4,600	4,140
Accumulated Depreciation	(800)	(620)
Total Assets	$7,440	$6,000
Liabilities and Stockholders' Equity:		
Accounts Payable	$1,000	$1,600
Long-term Borrowings	1,440	1,800
Common Stock, no par	2,000	1,200
Retained Earnings	3,000	1,400
Total Liabilities and Stockholders' Equity	$7,440	$6,000

Additional data:

a. Net income for 20X7 was $2,200.
b. During 20X7 the company sold equipment that cost $740 and had a book value of $600 for $740.
c. The company sold land for $400, resulting in a loss of $80. The remaining land change was due to the acquisition of land for common stock.

22. *Calculation of cash flows using indirect method.* Following are the comparative balance sheets for Marvin Corporation. Additional information is also provided. Prepare a statement of cash flows using the indirect method.

	20X4	20X3
Assets:		
Cash	$ 89,800	$ 82,400
Accounts Receivable	110,000	101,000
Marketable Securities	11,200	9,900
Inventory	154,500	175,500
Equipment	800,000	620,000
Accumulated Depreciation—Equipment	(228,000)	(250,000)
Total Assets	$937,500	$738,800
Liabilities and Stockholders' Equity:		
Accounts Payable	$110,500	$ 58,800
Long-term Note Payable	0	120,000
Preferred Stock	70,000	20,000
Common Stock	500,000	400,000
Retained Earnings	257,000	140,000
Total Liabilities and Stockholders' Equity	$937,500	$738,800

Additional Data:

a. Net income, $157,000.
b. Depreciation expense, $48,000.
c. Additional equipment was purchased for $250,000 and fully depreciated equipment of $70,000 was scrapped.
d. The long-term note was paid early.

23. *Cash Flow From Operations.* Your examination of the financial statements of Russell Company reveals the following data:

	20X2		20X1	
Sales (net)		$100,000		$75,000
Cost of goods sold:				
Beginning inventory	$17,000		$12,000	
Purchases (net)	58,000		55,000	
Goods available for sale	$75,000		$67,000	
Ending inventory	15,000		17,000	
Cost of goods sold		60,000		50,000
Accounts payable		20,000		25,000
Accounts receivable		50,000		45,000

Required:

Compute the following for 20X2:

a. Cash receipts from sales.
b. Cash disbursements for purchases.

24. *Calculation of general cash flows.* Account balances for Bangor Company for 20X8 and 20X7 follow:

	20X8	20X7
Cash	$20,000	$25,000
Accounts Receivable	42,000	31,000
Marketable Securities (current)	40,000	35,000
Patent	15,000	13,000
Inventory	80,000	70,000
Prepaid Rent	15,000	16,000
Accounts Payable (inventory)	90,000	85,000
Dividends Payable	12,000	10,000
Salaries Payable	41,000	38,000

Consider each separately:

a. If net income before depreciation was $21,000, how much cash was generated from operations?
b. If the income statement had included a loss on inventory of $5,000, how much cash was expended for purchases? (Cost of goods sold was $65,000.)
c. If dividends of $15,000 were declared, how much cash was expended for dividends?
d. If net income before depreciation was $3,000, how much cash was generated from operations?
e. If there were patent amortization of $2,000, how much cash was expended this year for the patent?

25. *Calculation of general cash flows.* The following data is available for Aggie Company:

	May 31	April 30
Accounts payable (for inventories)	$ 3	$ 2
Accounts receivable	6	5
Accumulated depreciation	7	6
Building	9	7
Cash	6	5
Common stock	8	7
Cost of goods sold	6	7
Depreciation expense	1	2
Dividends	2	2
Fees earned	2	3
Inventories	4	3
Land	8	8
Note payable (long-term)	10	5
Prepaid wages	3	2
Retained earnings	6	5
Sales	13	14
Supplies	2	1
Supplies expense	2	3
Unearned fees	2	3
Wages expense	3	4
Wages payable	1	2

Required:

Complete the following:

Cash received from customers during May is .... $_____
Cash paid to suppliers for inventories during May is .... $_____
Cash paid for all expenses
  (other than cost of goods sold) during May is .... $_____

In Aggie's statement of cash flows for May:

Cash from operating activities is .... $_____
Cash from investing activities is .... $_____
Cash from financing activities is .... $_____

26. *Statement of Cash Flows—Preparation.* Wynn, Inc., hired you as an independent accountant to analyze the reasons for their unsatisfactory cash position. The company earned $42,000 during 20X1 but, their cash balance is lower than ever. Your assistant prepared a worksheet providing you with the following information:

1. For 20X1, sales were $207,000, cost of goods sold was $70,000 and all other expenses totaled $98,000.
2. Additional capital stock was sold in 20X1; the proceeds of the sale were $40,000.
3. Vacant land purchased in 20X0 at a cost of $27,000 was sold in 20X1 for $30,000.
4. A payment of $22,000 was made in 20X1 on a long-term mortgage.
5. Equipment costing $89,000 was purchased during the year.
6. Included in the firm's expenses for 20X1 were depreciation charges of $7,500.
7. The firm's accounts receivable increased by $4,000, inventories decreased by $2,400 and accounts payable decreased by $4,500 during the year.

Required:

Prepare a statement of cash flows for the year ended December 31, 20X1, to explain the reasons for the firm's unsatisfactory cash position. Prepare the statement using both the direct and indirect methods.

27. *Statement of Cash Flows—Preparation.* Condensed financial statements for the Billy Company are as follows:

Billy Company
Comparative Balance Sheets
December 31, 20X2 and 20X1

	December 31	
	20X2	20X1
Cash	$ 7,500	$ 6,000
Accounts receivable	9,000	11,000
Inventories	15,000	12,500
Buildings	30,000	25,000
Accumulated depreciation	(12,500)	(10,000)
	$49,000	$44,500
Accounts payable	$18,000	$15,000
Bonds payable	10,000	15,000
Common stock	15,000	10,000
Retained earnings	6,000	4,500
	$49,000	$44,500

Billy Company
Income Statement
for the Year Ending December 31, 20X2

Sales		$35,000
Cost of goods sold		17,000
Gross profit		$18,000
Depreciation	$ 2,500	
Operating expenses	11,000	13,500
Net income		$ 4,500

Required:

Prepare a statement of cash flows for 20X2 using both the direct and indirect methods.

28. *Statement of Cash Flows—Preparation.* The condensed financial statements of Buckner Corporation are as follows:

Buckner Corporation
Comparative Balance Sheets
December 31, 20X2 and 20X1

	20X2	20X1
Assets:		
Current assets:		
Cash	$ 50,000	$ 35,000
Accounts receivable	100,000	90,000
Inventory	60,000	65,000
Prepaid expenses	10,000	8,000
Total current assets	$220,000	$198,000
Long-term assets:		
Building and equipment (net)	200,000	220,000
Land	50,000	50,000
Total assets	$470,000	$468,000
Liabilities and Stockholders' Equity:		
Accounts payable	$100,000	$ 80,000
Interest payable	10,000	10,000
Note payable (current)	50,000	40,000
Common stock	200,000	200,000
Retained earnings	110,000	138,000
Total liabilities and stockholders' equity	$470,000	$468,000

Buckner Corporation
Income Statement
for the Year Ending December 31, 20X2

Sales		$250,000
Less: Cost of goods sold		184,000
Gross profit		$ 66,000
Operating expenses	$ 64,000	
Depreciation	20,000	84,000
Net loss		($ 18,000)

Required:

Prepare a statement of cash flows for 20X2 using both the direct and indirect methods.

29. *Statement of Cash Flows—Preparation (Indirect).* Consider the following selected account balances for Messerschmidt, Inc.

	December 31 20X2	December 31 20X1	Increase	Decrease
Accounts receivable	$ 600	$ 400	$200	
Inventories	550	700		$150
Buildings	1,000	800	200	
Accumulated depreciation— Building	175	150	25	
Land	300	200	100	
Accounts payable	100	150		50
Bonds payable—long-term	200	100	100	
Capital stock	200	300		100
Retained earnings	300	150	150	
Sales	1,100	1,200		
Cost of goods sold	400	450		
Expenses	500	575		

Required:

Prepare a statement of cash flows for Messerschmidt, Inc. for the period ending December 31, 20X2. Use the *indirect* method and assume that the changes in the accounts are the result of cash transactions.

30. *Statement of Cash Flows—Preparation.* Given below are the balance sheets for Zahn Company for 20X1 and 20X2.

Zahn Company
Comparative Balance Sheets
December 31, 20X1 and 20X2

	20X1	20X2
Cash	$ 100	$ 300
Accounts receivable	400	350
Inventories	300	500
Long-term assets	900	1,000
Less: Accumulated depreciation	(100)	(200)
	$1,600	$1,950
Accounts payable	$ 400	$ 600
Bonds payable (due in 19X7)	400	200
Capital stock	500	700
Retained earnings	300	450
	$1,600	$1,950

Additional information:

The corporation paid a 10 percent stock dividend on January 2, 20X2, when its capital stock was selling at par. For 20X2, sales were $1,200, cost of goods sold was $550 and all other expenses totaled $450. During the year, the company sold a long-term asset with an original cost of $100 (and a book value of $25 at the date of sale) for $50. All other changes in the accounts are the results of transactions typically recorded in such accounts.

Required:

Prepare a statement of cash flows for 20X2.

31. *Statement of Cash Flows—Preparation.* The condensed comparative balance sheet for Marshall Company is presented below.

	December 31	
	20X2	20X1
Assets:		
Cash	$ 80,000	$ 65,000
Accounts receivable (net)	100,000	90,000
Inventory	40,000	45,000
Prepaid expenses	12,000	10,000
Long-term assets	173,000	150,000
Accumulated depreciation—		
Long-term assets	(35,000)	(30,000)
Total assets	$370,000	$330,000
Liabilities and Stockholders' Equity:		
Accounts payable	$ 80,000	$ 60,000
Bonds payable	150,000	150,000
Capital stock	100,000	100,000
Retained earnings	40,000	20,000
Total liabilities and stockholders' equity	$370,000	$330,000

Supplemental data for 20X2:

Sales	$175,000
Cost of goods sold	70,000
Expenses (other than depreciation)	80,000
Depreciation expense	5,000

A building was purchased for $23,000 cash.

Required:

Prepare a statement of cash flows for 20X2 using both the direct and indirect methods.

32. *Statement of Cash Flows—Preparation.* Financial statements for Brewer, Inc. are as follows:

Brewer, Inc.
Comparative Balance Sheets
December 31, 20X2 and 20X1

	20X2	20X1	Increase (Decrease)
Assets:			
Current assets:			
Cash	$ 5,000	$ 45,000	$ (40,000)
Accounts receivable	100,000	75,000	25,000
Inventories	50,000	45,000	5,000
Prepaid expenses	30,000	35,000	(5,000)
Total current assets	$185,000	$200,000	$ (15,000)
Noncurrent assets:			
Land	$100,000	$ 75,000	$ 25,000
Buildings	200,000	175,000	25,000
Accumulated depreciation—buildings	(50,000)	(40,000)	(10,000)
Equipment	100,000	75,000	25,000
Accumulated depreciation—equipment	(35,000)	(15,000)	(20,000)
Patents	20,000	30,000	(10,000)
Total noncurrent assets	$335,000	$300,000	$ 35,000
Total assets	$520,000	$500,000	$ 20,000
Liabilities and Stockholders' Equity:			
Current liabilities:			
Accounts payable	$ 50,000	$ 40,000	$ 10,000
Notes payable	25,000	25,000	0
Accrued expenses	40,000	35,000	$ 5,000
Total current liabilities	$115,000	$100,000	$ 15,000
Long-term liabilities:			
Bonds payable	$100,000	$140,000	$ (40,000)
Stockholders' equity:			
Common stock ($100 par value)	$230,000	$200,000	$ 30,000
Additional paid-in capital	40,000	30,000	10,000
Retained earnings	35,000	30,000	5,000
Total stockholders' equity	$305,000	$260,000	$ 45,000
Total liabilities and stockholders' equity	$520,000	$500,000	$ 20,000

Brewer, Inc.
Income Statement
for the Year Ended December 31, 20X2

Sales		$2,000,000
Cost of goods sold		1,500,000
Gross profit		$ 500,000
Operating expenses:		
Depreciation and amortization expense	$ 50,000	
Selling and administrative expense	265,000	
Miscellaneous expense	170,000	
Total operating expenses		485,000
Net income from operations		$ 15,000
Other revenue and expense		
Add: Gain on sale of building		20,000
		$ 35,000
Less: Loss on sale of land	$ 10,000	
Interest expense	15,000	25,000
Net income before income taxes		$ 10,000
Less: Income taxes		5,000
Net income		$ 5,000

Supplementary data:

1. Depreciation and amortization of patents were as follows:

Building	$20,000
Equipment	20,000
Patents	10,000
Total	$50,000

2. A building that cost $50,000 and had accumulated depreciation of $10,000 was sold for $60,000.
3. Common stock with $30,000 par value was sold for $40,000.
4. Land with a cost of $25,000 was sold for $15,000.
5. Land was purchased for $50,000.
6. Bonds of $40,000 were retired.
7. A building was purchased for $75,000.
8. Equipment was acquired for $25,000 cash.

Required:

Prepare a statement of cash flows for 20X2, using both the direct and indirect methods.

33. *Statement of Cash Flows—Preparation.* The trial balances of Canuck Company revealed the following information:

	December 31	
	20X1	20X2
Cash	$ 14,000	$ 15,400
Accounts receivable (net)	26,600	33,600
Inventory	72,800	70,000
Prepaid expenses	4,200	5,600
Long-term investments	14,000	0
Buildings	126,000	168,000
Machinery	56,000	86,800
Patents	7,000	5,600
	$320,600	$385,000
Accounts payable	$ 16,800	$ 11,200
Notes payable—short-term (nontrade)	12,600	18,200
Accrued wages	4,200	2,800
Accumulated depreciation	56,000	54,600
Notes payable—long-term	42,000	49,000
Common stock	168,000	210,000
Retained earnings	21,000	39,200
	$320,600	$385,000

    Additional data:

    1. For 20X2, sales were $157,200, cost of goods sold was $65,000 and all other expenses totaled $58,600.
    2. Recorded depreciation on buildings and machinery was $11,200.
    3. Amortization of patents was $1,400.
    4. Machinery was purchased for $21,000; one-third was paid in cash and an interest-bearing note was given for the balance.
    5. Common stock was issued to purchase machinery costing $35,000.
    6. Old machinery which originally cost $25,200 (one-half depreciated) was sold for $9,800. The gain or loss was reported on the income statement.
    7. Cash was paid for the building addition—$42,000.
    8. Common stock was issued to retire a $7,000 long-term note.
    9. Cash was received for the sale of long-term investment—$16,800.
    10. Paid cash dividends.

Required:

Prepare a statement of cash flows for 20X2, using both the direct and indirect methods.

34. *Statement of Cash Flows—Preparation.* The trial balances of Islander Company revealed the following information.

	December 31	
	20X1	20X2
Cash	$ 3,200	$ 4,000
Accounts receivable (net)	4,000	7,200
Inventory	8,000	9,600
Long-term investments	1,600	0
Machinery	24,000	37,600
	$40,800	$58,400
Accumulated depreciation	$ 4,000	$ 5,600
Accounts payable	2,400	4,000
Notes payable—short-term	3,200	2,400
Notes payable—long-term	8,000	14,400
Common stock	20,000	23,200
Retained earnings	3,200	8,800
	$40,800	$58,400

Additional data:

1. For 20X2, sales were $75,000, cost of goods sold was $30,200 and all other expenses totaled $33,600.
2. Depreciation was $1,600.
3. Long-term investments were sold at cost.
4. Dividends of $5,600 were paid.
5. Machinery was purchased for $4,000 cash.
6. A long-term note payable for $9,600 was given in exchange for machinery.
7. Common stock was issued to retire a $3,200 long-term note payable.

Required:

Prepare a statement of cash flows for the year ended December 31, 20X2 using both the direct and indirect methods.

35. *Statement of Cash Flows—Preparation.* The 20X1 financial statements for the Alston Company are:

Alston Company
Income Statement
for the Year Ended December 31, 20X1

Net sales		$50,000
Cost of goods sold		30,000
Gross profit		$20,000
Operating expenses:		
Depreciation	$2,000	
Wage expense	7,000	
Other expenses	1,000	10,000
Net income from operations		$10,000
Gain on sale of land		5,000
Net income		$15,000

Alston Company
Retained Earnings Statement
for the Year Ended December 31, 20X1

Retained earnings at beginning of year	$25,000
Add: Net income	15,000
	$40,000
Subtract: Dividends	5,000
Retained earnings at end of year	$35,000

Alston Company
Comparative Balance Sheets
December 31, 20X1 and 20X0

	December 31	
	20X1	20X0
Assets:		
Cash	$ 69,000	$ 60,000
Accounts receivable	25,000	20,000
Inventories	15,000	10,000
Building	100,000	100,000
Accumulated depreciation—building	(27,000)	(25,000)
Land	125,000	100,000
Total assets	$307,000	$265,000
Liabilities and Stockholders' Equity:		
Accounts payable	$ 35,000	$ 15,000
Accrued wages payable	7,000	5,000
Bonds payable—long-term	130,000	120,000
Capital stock	100,000	100,000
Retained earnings	35,000	25,000
Total liabilities and stockholders' equity	$307,000	$265,000

The following information is also available:

1. Land with a cost of $25,000 was sold for $30,000.
2. Additional land was purchased for $50,000.
3. A long-term bond was issued for $10,000.
4. $5,000 cash dividends were paid during the year.

Required:

Prepare a statement of cash flows for the Alston Company for the year ending December 31, 20X1 using both the direct and indirect methods.

36. *Statement of Cash Flows—Preparation.* The trial balance of Canadiens Company revealed the following information:

	December 31	
	20X0	20X1
Cash	$ 20,400	$ 20,700
Accounts receivable (net)	7,200	10,200
Inventory	9,600	8,400
Long-term investments	3,600	0
Machinery	48,000	55,800
Treasury stock	0	6,900
	$ 88,800	$102,000
Accumulated depreciation	$ 28,800	$ 23,400
Accounts payable	11,400	7,200
Bonds payable	6,000	18,000
Common stock	30,000	36,600
Retained earnings	12,600	16,800
	$ 88,800	$102,000

Additional information:

1. Sales were $42,000.
2. Cost of goods sold was $27,600.
3. The total of all expenses was $11,400.
4. Depreciation was $3,000.
5. Machinery was sold for $3,600. Its original cost was $12,600 and two-thirds of this cost had been depreciated.
6. Machinery was purchased for $2,400.
7. Bonds payable were issued for $18,000 to purchase machinery.
8. Long-term investments were sold for $5,400.
9. Treasury stock was purchased for $6,900.
10. Bonds payable of $6,000 were retired by issuing common stock.
11. Unissued common stock was sold for $600.

Required:

Prepare a statement of cash flows for the year ended December 31, 20X2 using both the direct and indirect methods.

37. *Statement of Cash Flows—Preparation.* From the following information prepare a statement of cash flows for the Sabre Company for 20X1 using both the direct and indirect methods.

1. For 20X1, sales were $24,000, cost of goods sold was $9,000 and all other expenses totaled $10,000.
2. Dividends paid during 20X1 were $1,000.
3. Capital stock was sold for $2,500.
4. Depreciation for the year was $1,500.
5. Long-term bonds of $1,000 were retired at par.
6. Land was purchased for $3,000.
7. Land was sold for $6,000, resulting in a gain of $1,000.
8. A building was purchased for $4,000.
9. Accounts receivable decreased by $1,200, inventories increased by $1,600 and accounts payable increased by $800.

38. *Cash flow from investing and financing activities.* From the information below prepare the investing and financing sections of the statement of cash flows.

Cash paid for interest	$ 5,000
Cash paid to suppliers	50,000
Cash received from customers	40,000
Issued common stock (at par)	75,000
Paid dividends	25,000
Purchased building	70,000
Purchased long-term investments	33,000
Purchased treasury stock	12,000
Retired bonds	30,000
Sold land at cost	20,000

39. *Statement of cash flows.*

Keller Company
Comparative Balance Sheets
for Years Ending December 31

	20X2	20X1
Cash	$ 92	$ 67
Accounts receivable	140	105
Inventories	151	193
Prepaid expenses	10	20
Buildings and equipment	2,250	2,000
Accumulated depreciation	(1,400)	(1,000)
Land	500	250
	$1,743	$1,635
Accounts payable	$ 33	$ 25
Accrued expenses	30	50
Bonds payable (due in 20X7)	200	480
Common stock ($20 par)	1,100	800
Paid in capital	100	0
Retained earnings	280	280
	$1,743	$1,635

Keller Company
Income Statement
For the Year Ended 1995

Net sales		$1,150
Cost of goods sold		400
Gross margin		$ 750
Less: Selling expense	$ 100	
Depreciation expense	500	600
Operating income		$ 150
Add: Gain on sale of building	$ 150	
Less: Loss on sale of land	(100)	50
Net income		$ 200

Additional information:

a. A building which cost $500 and had accumulated depreciation of $100 was sold.
b. Common stock with a par value of $300 was issued.
c. Land with a cost of $250 was sold for $150.

Required:

1. Cash from operating activities for 20X2.
2. Cash from investing activities for 20X2.
3. Cash from financing activities for 20X2.

Appendix to Chapter 12

Worksheet Approach

In a relatively uncomplicated situation, such as that of the Kraton Company described above, it is possible to prepare a statement of cash flows by simply sequentially examining the changes in each account. In a more realistic situation, however, a worksheet is often used to facilitate the analysis and preparation of the statement. Although it is not necessary to use a worksheet, it normally aids in the preparation of the statement when there are a large number of transactions and various complicating factors.

Illustration 9 presents a worksheet for Kraton Company. The direct method is used to obtain net cash flow from operating activities.

Illustration 9
Worksheet Using the Direct Method

Kraton Company
Worksheet for Statement of Cash Flows
for the Year Ended December 31, 20X1

	Balance December 31, 20X0	Adjustments Debit	Adjustments Credit	Balance December 31, 20X1
Debits:				
Cash	$ 100			$ 250
Accounts receivable (net)	200	$ 150 (3)		350
Inventories	250		$ 50 (11)	200
Buildings	400	200 (5)		600
Land	200	100 (8)	200 (6)	100
	$1,150			$1,500
Credits:				
Accumulated depreciation	$ 100		100 (4)	$ 200
Accounts payable	200		100 (12)	300
Accrued wages payable	100	50 (14)		50
Bonds payable	200	100 (7)		100
Common stock	300		100 (9)	400
Retained earnings	250	100 (1)	1,000 (2)	450
		100 (4)	100 (6)	
		400 (10)		
		100 (13)		
		200 (15)		
	$1,150			$1,500
Statement of cash flows:				
Cash flows from operations:				
Net sales		1,000 (2)		
Increase in accounts receivable			150 (3)	
Cost of goods sold			400 (10)	
Decrease in inventories		50 (11)		
Increase in accounts payable		100 (12)		
Wages expense			100 (13)	
Decrease in accrued wages payable			50 (14)	
Other expenses			200 (15)	
Sale of land		300 (6)		
Purchase of land			100 (8)	
Sale of common stock		100 (9)		
Purchase of building			200 (5)	
Retirement of bonds payable			100 (7)	
Payment of dividends			100 (1)	
		$3,050	$3,050	

The explanations of the adjustments are as follows:

1. The payment of a cash dividend ($100) that decreased retained earnings is recorded as a financing activity.
2. Net sales ($1,000) are included in net income, retained earnings, and as a component of net cash flow from operating activities.
3. The increase in accounts receivable ($150) is subtracted from net sales in determining cash received from customers.
4. The increase in accumulated depreciation ($100) is due to depreciation expense, which is included as a negative element in net income and retained earnings but is not considered in determining net cash flow from operating activities.
5. The purchase of the building for $200 is recorded as an investing activity.
6. The sale of land for $300 is shown as an investing activity. The $100 gain is included in net income and retained earnings but is not considered in determining net cash flow from operating activities.
7. The retirement of long-term bonds payable ($100) at face value is recorded as a financing activity.
8. The purchase of land for $100 is recorded as an investing activity.
9. The sale of common stock for cash is recorded as a financing activity.
10. Cost of goods sold is a negative element in net income and retained earnings and is a negative component of net cash flow from operating activities.
11. The decrease in inventories ($50) is an adjustment to cost of goods sold to determine purchases.
12. The increase in accounts payable ($100) is subtracted from purchases in determining cash paid to suppliers.
13. Wage expense is a negative element in net income and retained earnings and is a negative component in net cash flow from operating activities.
14. The decrease in accrued wages payable ($50) is added to wage expense in determining cash paid to employees.
15. Other expenses are a negative element in net income and retained earnings and are a negative component in net cash flow from operating activities.

Illustration 10 presents an alternative worksheet for Kraton Company. The indirect method is used to obtain net cash flow from operating activities. The explanations of the adjustments are as follows:

1. The payment of a cash dividend ($100) that decreased retained earnings is recorded as a financing activity.
2. Net income included in the ending retained earnings balance is reported as the initial component of net cash flow from operating activities. This amount is adjusted below in determining the net cash flow from operating activities.
3. The increase in accumulated depreciation ($100) is added to net income in determining the net cash flow from operating activities because the depreciation expense did not decrease cash.
4. The purchase of the building for $200 is recorded as an investing activity.
5. The sale of land for $300 is shown as an investing activity. The $100 gain is subtracted from net income in determining net cash flow from operating activities.
6. The retirement of long-term bonds payable ($100) at face value is recorded as a financing activity.
7. The purchase of land for $100 is recorded as an investing activity.
8. The sale of common stock for cash is recorded as a financing activity.
9. The increase in accounts receivable ($150) is subtracted from net income in determining net cash flow from operating activities.

10. The decrease in inventories ($50) is added to net income in determining net cash flow from operating activities.
11. The increase in accounts payable ($100) is added to net income in determining net cash flow from operating activities.
12. The decrease in accrued wages payable ($50) is subtracted from net income in determining net cash flow from operating activities.

Illustration 10
Worksheet Using the Indirect Method

Kraton Company
Worksheet for Statement of Cash Flows
for the Year Ended December 31, 20X1

	Balance December 31, 20X0	Adjustments Debit	Adjustments Credit	Balance December 31, 20X1
Debits:				
Cash	$ 100			$ 250
Accounts receivable (net)	200	$ 150 (9)		350
Inventories	250		$ 50 (10)	200
Buildings	400	200 (4)		600
Land	200	100 (7)	200 (5)	100
	$1,150			$1,500
Credits:				
Accumulated depreciation	$ 100		100 (3)	$ 200
Accounts payable	200		100 (11)	300
Accrued wages payable	100	50 (12)		50
Bonds payable	200	100 (6)		100
Common stock	300		100 (8)	400
Retained earnings	250	100 (1)	300 (2)	450
	$1,150			$1,500
Statement of cash flows:				
Cash flows from operations:				
Net income		300 (2)		
Adjustments:				
Depreciation expense		100 (3)		
Gain on sale of land			100 (5)	
Increase in accounts receivable			150 (9)	
Decrease in inventories		50 (10)		
Increase in accounts payable		100 (11)		
Decrease in accrued wages payable			50 (12)	
Sale of land		300 (5)		
Purchase of land			100 (7)	
Sale of common stock		100 (8)		
Purchase of building			200 (4)	
Retirement of bonds payable			100 (6)	
Payment of dividends			100 (1)	
		$1,650	$1,650	

The procedures used in preparing a worksheet for the statement of cash flows are summarized below:

1. The account balances appearing on the previous year's balance sheet are entered in the first column of the worksheet. All accounts with debit balances are listed first, followed by all accounts with credit balances.

2. Adjustments are entered into the adjustment columns to account for all noncash items from the upper section and to list all of the separate increases and decreases to cash in the lower section of the worksheet. The worksheet adjustments are not entered in any journal; their purpose is solely to facilitate the analysis and classification of the data for the statement of cash flows.

3. The account balances appearing on the current year's balance sheet are entered in the last column of the worksheet. These account balances are used as a check to determine whether the change in the balance of each noncash item has been explained completely—that is, whether the beginning balance plus or minus the change equals the ending balance.

Learning Objectives

Chapter 13 discusses common techniques of analyzing information presented in financial statements. Studying this chapter should enable you to:

1. Distinguish between horizontal and vertical analyses and discuss the type of information that is provided by each method.

2. Discuss the concept of ratio analysis and identify the problems that may be inherent in its use.

3. List the most commonly-used standards against which a firm may be compared and explain the strengths and limitations associated with the use of these standards.

4. Describe and apply the basic techniques of financial analysis as they are used by common stockholders, long-term creditors, and short-term creditors.

CHAPTER 13
Financial Statement Analysis

Introduction

The end result of the financial accounting process is a set of financial statements and footnotes to those financial statements. The major financial statements prepared as a result of the financial accounting process are:

1. The income statement, which shows the results of operations (revenues earned and expenses incurred) of the company over a period of time.
2. The statement of cash flows, which shows the net change in cash and cash equivalents held by the company over a period of time. In addition, the statement of cash flows discloses the major sources (net increases in cash) and uses (net decreases in cash) of cash during that period of time.
3. The balance sheet, which shows the financial condition (assets owned, liabilities owed and shareholders' equity) of the company at a specific point in time.
4. The statement of shareholders' equity, which shows the net change in the assets held by the company that belong to the owners (shareholders) of the company.

The financial statements of a business enterprise are intended to provide much of the basic data used in decision-making and, in general, the evaluation of performance by various groups such as current owners, potential investors, creditors, government agencies, and in some instances, competitors. Because general-purpose published financial statements are by their very nature issued for a wide variety of users, it is often necessary for particular user groups to extract the information in which they are particularly interested from these statements. For example, owners and potential investors are normally interested in the present earnings and future earnings prospects of a business. Similarly, short-term creditors are primarily concerned with the ability of a firm to meet its short-term obligations as they become due and payable. Consequently, a somewhat detailed analysis and interpretation of financial statements is usually required to obtain the information that may be relevant for the specific purposes of a particular user. In this chapter, the major components of each financial statement will be reviewed. Then, a number of selected techniques that are useful in financial analysis will be described, illustrated, and discussed.

The Income Statement

The income statement is the financial statement that provides data concerning the results of operations of a company for a specified period of time. Income is determined by the firm's revenues, expenses, gains, and losses. Revenues and expenses result from the firm's primary operations (e.g., a furniture company selling furniture and incurring expenses in this activity); gains and losses result from peripheral operations or events such as a gain on the sale of an operating asset that is no longer needed or a loss due to a fire.

Revenues normally result in increased assets such as cash or accounts receivable (promises to pay cash to the company). If cash is received in advance of providing goods or services, this is not revenue—a liability (unearned revenues) is assumed and recorded for the amount of cash received. Revenue is recorded as it is earned—when the goods or services are provided. The liability is thereby reduced as the revenue is earned.

Expenses result from outflows of cash or merchandise, the use of assets (e.g., supplies and insurance coverage), and the incurrence of liabilities for services provided to the firm (e.g., electricity).

13-2

The income statements for PepsiCo are presented in Illustration 1. These are comparative statements; income statements are shown for three years, not just the most recent year.[1] The title "statement of income" is a commonly-used alternative title to "income statement." Note that the dollar amounts in the income statements (except for the bottom figure for net income per share) are stated in millions of dollars; therefore, PepsiCo's net sales for 2002 are over $25 billion, not $25 thousand.

PepsiCo's revenues consist mainly of net sales to customers. The cost of sales is the cost of the merchandise sold to PepsiCo customers. If PepsiCo produced an item for $21 and sold it for $26, the company would earn a gross profit of $5 on the sale—the difference between the selling price and the cost of the item sold. The total gross profit must be large enough to cover the firm's other expenses in order for income to be earned. Comparing the gross profit or gross profit percentage (gross profit divided by net sales) of the current year with those of past years is an indication on the effectiveness of the company in its manufacturing and selling activities. PepsiCo's income before income taxes is $4,868 million in 2002. After taxes, income is reduced to $3,313 million. Recall that, unlike a sole proprietorship or partnership, a corporation must pay income taxes on the income it earns.

PepsiCo sells many items of merchandise. Included in PepsiCo's operating, selling, and general administrative expenses are hundreds of expense categories (e.g., salaries, advertising, accounting, shipping, and electricity).

PepsiCo reports a net income per share figure, which is computed by dividing net income by the average number of shares of stock outstanding (owned by stockholders) for the year.

The accounting concept of income assumes that various rules and principles are followed. These principles require the accountant to exercise his or her professional judgment in their application since the accounting concept of income measurement stresses the fair determination of income. Note that fair determination of income does not mean precise determination. Accounting is an estimating process that requires the accountant to view transactions as objectively as possible in calculating both the financial position of a firm and its income for the period but estimates are more susceptible to errors.

Since the income statement presents the results of operations for an accounting period such as a year, information included in this statement is usually considered to be among the most important data provided by the company. This is because profitability is a major concern of those interested in the economic activities of a business. For those who invest in a company's stock, decisions to buy and sell securities are based on their assessment or analysis as to whether the company will be more or less successful in future years. Investors attempt to ascertain whether a company's stock price is likely to increase or decrease in future periods. Creditors, those who loan money to a company, make lending decisions based on their analysis as to whether the company will be able to repay its loans. The company's profitability is a key consideration in these decisions.

Classifications that appear in the income statement are intended to be descriptive, functional categories of revenues, expenses, gains, and losses; there are many different formats employed for income statements. Variations among industries are substantial and, to compound this problem, variations among firms in the same industry can also be significant.

The Statement of Cash Flows

A company reports information pertaining to its cash receipts and cash payments in a statement of cash flows. This statement explains the causes of changes in cash plus cash equivalents (highly-liquid marketable securities) and provides a summary of the operating, investing and financing activities of an enterprise during a period of time. Operating activities pertain to the firm's income-producing activities such as buying and selling inventories, providing services, and incurring expenses for salaries and advertising. An income statement reports revenues as they are earned and expenses as they are incurred, regardless of when cash is received and paid. On the other hand, cash flows from operating activities report revenues when cash is received and expenses when

---

[1] PepsiCo has refocused its business in recent years. Some of these changes are that PepsiCo: (1) consolidated its bottling business, (2) launched new products (e.g., Pepsi Blue and Propel Fitness Water), (3) divested itself of restaurants (e.g., Pizza Hut, Taco Bell, and KFC), (4) merged with Quaker Oats, (5) launched the WOW! line of fat-free snacks, (6) acquired Cracker Jack, and (7) its Frito-Lay division opened its first plant in Russia.

Illustration 1
*PepsiCo
Consolidated Income Statement*

OUR FINANCIAL RESULTS

CONSOLIDATED STATEMENT OF INCOME
PepsiCo, Inc. and Subsidiaries
Fiscal years ended December 28, 2002, December 29, 2001 and December 30, 2000

(in millions except per share amounts)	2002	2001	2000
Net Sales	$25,112	$23,512	$22,337
Cost of sales	11,497	10,750	10,226
Selling, general and administrative expenses	8,523	8,189	7,962
Amortization of intangible assets	138	165	147
Merger-related costs	224	356	–
Other impairment and restructuring charges	–	31	184
Operating Profit	4,730	4,021	3,818
Bottling equity income	280	160	130
Interest expense	(178)	(219)	(272)
Interest income	36	67	85
Income before Income Taxes	4,868	4,029	3,761
Provision for Income Taxes	1,555	1,367	1,218
Net Income	$ 3,313	$ 2,662	$ 2,543
Net Income per Common Share			
Basic	$1.89	$1.51	$1.45
Diluted	$1.85	$1.47	$1.42

See accompanying notes to consolidated financial statements.

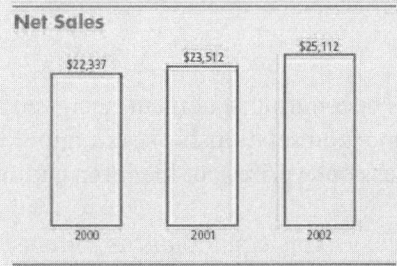

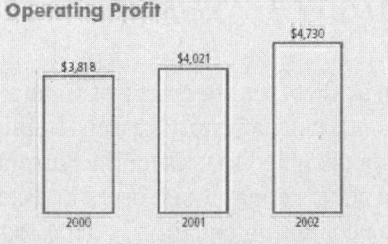

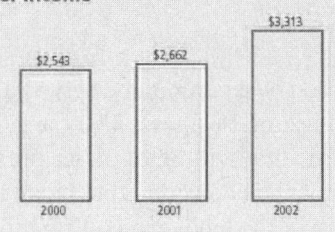

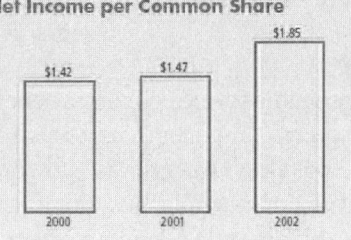

cash is paid. Investing activities are concerned with the purchase and sale of noncurrent assets used in the business such as plant and equipment. Financing activities pertain to issuing stocks or debt (both short and long-term), repaying debt, and paying dividends.

The statement of cash flows is useful in appraising factors such as the firm's financing policies, dividend policies, ability to expand productive capacity, and ability to satisfy future debt requirements. Numerous questions can be answered using the statement of cash flows, for example:

- How much cash did the company generate from its operations?
- What is(are) the main source(s) of the company's cash?
- Does the company rely too little or too heavily on nonoperating sources of cash?
- How much cash has been expended on increasing the productive capacity of the company?
- How much debt has the company incurred or repaid?

While certain information concerning changes in cash plus cash equivalents can be obtained from an analysis of comparative balance sheets and income statements, neither of these statements provides complete disclosure of the financing and investing activities of an enterprise over a period of time. An income statement discloses the results of operations for a period of time but does not indicate the amount of resources provided by other activities. Further, reported revenues and expenses may not represent actual increases or decreases in cash during the period. Comparative balance sheets show net changes in assets and equities but do not indicate the specific causes of these changes. Therefore, while some information concerning changes in cash plus cash equivalents may be obtained from comparative balance sheets and income statements, a complete analysis of the financial activities of a business can be derived only from the statement of cash flows.

The statement of cash flows for PepsiCo is presented in Illustration 2. The company generated cash from operations in all three years presented. Purchase of short-term investments is the primary reason for the outflow of cash in 2000 and 2001. Capital spending is the primary reason for investing outflow in 2002. Cash outflows for financing activities are due to payments of debt, payments of cash dividends, and share repurchases (treasury stock).

The Balance Sheet

The balance sheet, or statement of financial position, is the accounting statement designed to provide information concerning an entity's assets, liabilities, and equity and their relationship to one another at a point in time. It is not designed to present the current value of a business enterprise, but the information provided in the balance sheet should assist users in assessing this value.

The basic accounting equation is depicted by the balance sheet. This equation is as follows:

$$\text{Assets} = \text{Liabilities} + \text{Stockholders' Equity}$$

Assets are probable future economic benefits obtained or controlled by a particular entity as a result of past transactions or events. In general, assets are items of value owned by the business. They are the economic resources of the business. An asset is an economic right or a resource that will be of either present or future benefit to the firm. For example, an acre of land purchased by a company is considered to be an asset because the company can obtain future economic benefits from the ownership of the land, can control others' access to these benefits, and has completed the transaction for the purchase of the land. If access to the land cannot be controlled by the company, for example, because the city can use it as a right-of-way or if the transaction has not yet occurred, but will take place in the future, then the land is not considered to be an asset. The assets of a business may take various forms. Examples of assets include: cash, inventory (merchandise held for sale to

Illustration 2
PepsiCo
Statement of Cash Flows

CONSOLIDATED STATEMENT OF CASH FLOWS
PepsiCo, Inc. and Subsidiaries
Fiscal years ended December 28, 2002, December 29, 2001 and December 30, 2000

(in millions)	2002	2001	2000
Operating Activities			
Net income	$ 3,313	$ 2,662	$ 2,543
Adjustments to reconcile net income to net cash provided by operating activities			
Depreciation and amortization	1,112	1,082	1,093
Merger-related costs	224	356	–
Other impairment and restructuring charges	–	31	184
Cash payments for merger-related costs and other restructuring charges	(123)	(273)	(38)
Pension plan contributions	(820)	(446)	(103)
Bottling equity income, net of dividends	(222)	(103)	(74)
Deferred income taxes	288	162	33
Deferred compensation – ESOP	–	48	36
Other noncash charges and credits, net	263	209	303
Changes in operating working capital, excluding effects of acquisitions and dispositions			
Accounts and notes receivable	(260)	7	(52)
Inventories	(53)	(75)	(51)
Prepaid expenses and other current assets	(78)	(6)	(35)
Accounts payable and other current liabilities	426	(236)	219
Income taxes payable	278	394	335
Net change in operating working capital	313	84	416
Other	279	8	(215)
Net Cash Provided by Operating Activities	**4,627**	**3,820**	**4,178**
Investing Activities			
Capital spending	(1,437)	(1,324)	(1,352)
Sales of property, plant and equipment	89	–	57
Acquisitions and investments in noncontrolled affiliates	(351)	(432)	(98)
Divestitures	376	–	33
Short-term investments, by original maturity			
More than three months – purchases	(62)	(2,537)	(4,950)
More than three months – maturities	833	2,078	4,585
Three months or less, net	(14)	(41)	(9)
Snack Ventures Europe consolidation	39	–	–
Net Cash Used for Investing Activities	**(527)**	**(2,256)**	**(1,734)**
Financing Activities			
Proceeds from issuances of long-term debt	11	324	130
Payments of long-term debt	(353)	(573)	(879)
Short-term borrowings, by original maturity			
More than three months – proceeds	707	788	198
More than three months – payments	(809)	(483)	(155)
Three months or less, net	40	(397)	1
Cash dividends paid	(1,041)	(994)	(949)
Share repurchases – common	(2,158)	(1,716)	(1,430)
Share repurchases – preferred	(32)	(10)	–
Quaker share repurchases	–	(5)	(254)
Proceeds from reissuance of shares	–	524	–
Proceeds from exercises of stock options	456	623	690
Net Cash Used for Financing Activities	**(3,179)**	**(1,919)**	**(2,648)**
Effect of exchange rate changes on cash and cash equivalents	34	–	(4)
Net Increase/(Decrease) in Cash and Cash Equivalents	955	(355)	(208)
Cash and Cash Equivalents, Beginning of Year	683	1,038	1,246
Cash and Cash Equivalents, End of Year	$ 1,638	$ 683	$ 1,038

See accompanying notes to consolidated financial statements.

customers), land, buildings, and equipment. In other words, assets are the resources used by a business to continue its operations.

At any point in time, the total of the assets of a business are, by definition, equal to the total of the sources of these assets, liabilities and equity. In other words, every asset has a source; everything comes from somewhere. A business obtains its assets from two basic sources: its owners and its creditors.

Creditors lend resources to the firm. These debts, referred to as liabilities, must be repaid at some specified date. Liabilities may be defined as probable future sacrifices of economic benefits arising from present obligations of a particular entity to transfer assets or provide services to other entities in the future as a result of past transactions or events. Examples of liabilities include payments owed to suppliers of merchandise held for sale, salaries owed to employees, and amounts owed to public utilities.

Owners invest their personal resources in the firm. Investments by owners are increases in the net assets of an enterprise resulting from transfers to the company from other entities (including individual people) of something of value in exchange for ownership interests (or equity). Assets are by far the most common investments made by owners, but a business may also receive services or payments of its liabilities. The investments of owners in the firm and any profits retained in the business are its equity (or capital). Equity is the residual interest that remains in an entity's assets after deducting its liabilities (i.e., Equity is equal to Assets minus Liabilities). In a business enterprise, the equity is the ownership interest. Thus, the sources of a firm's assets are its liabilities and owners' equity.

The balance sheet for PepsiCo is presented in Illustration 3. It is structured in a manner to enhance its understandability by the users of the financial statements.

The various classifications included in the balance sheet are intended to assist the users of the statement in acquiring as much information as possible concerning the assets, liabilities, and owners' equity of the business. The individual elements of the financial statements are the building blocks with which financial statements are constructed—the classes of items that comprise the financial statements. The items included in financial statements represent in words and numbers business resources, claims to those resources, and the effects of transactions and other events and circumstances that result in changes in these resources and claims.

It might appear that if a firm desires to provide the users of its statements with as much information as possible, it can supply them with a listing of all transactions which took place during the period so that the users can perform their own analysis. However, large firms routinely enter into hundreds of thousands or even millions of transactions during any given period. It is therefore highly unlikely that any user would have either sufficient time, the inclination, or the ability to analyze this type of listing. To simplify the analysis of financial statements, firms group similar items in order to reduce the number of classifications which appear on the balance sheet. For example, a chain store may own many buildings of different sizes, at various locations and serving different functions, but rather than listing these assets separately, all buildings are normally grouped together and presented as a single amount on the balance sheet.

ASSETS

When assets are acquired by a business, they are initially recorded at the cost of their acquisition, or original purchase price. This is true even if the business pays only a part of the initial cost in cash at the time of acquisition and owes the remaining balance (a liability that will be paid to the seller of the asset). .

Assets vary in such characteristics as their useful life, physical attributes, and frequency of use. Accountants attempt to describe certain characteristics of assets on the balance sheet by the use of general classifications such as current assets; property, plant and equipment; and other assets. Within these broad categories there are also several sub-classifications. The usual ordering of assets on the balance sheet is in terms of their liquidity—the order in which the assets are normally converted into cash or used up in the operations of the business.

CURRENT ASSETS. Generally, current assets include cash and those assets that are expected to be converted into cash, sold, or used in operations or production during the next year. For most companies, the year encompasses

Illustration 3
PepsiCo
Consolidated Balance Sheet

CONSOLIDATED BALANCE SHEET

PepsiCo, Inc. and Subsidiaries
December 28, 2002 and December 29, 2001

(in millions except per share amounts)	2002	2001
ASSETS		
Current Assets		
Cash and cash equivalents	$ 1,638	$ 683
Short-term investments, at cost	207	966
	1,845	1,649
Accounts and notes receivable, net	2,531	2,142
Inventories	1,342	1,310
Prepaid expenses and other current assets	695	752
Total Current Assets	6,413	5,853
Property, Plant and Equipment, net	7,390	6,876
Amortizable Intangible Assets, net	801	875
Nonamortizable Intangible Assets	4,418	3,966
Investments in Noncontrolled Affiliates	2,611	2,871
Other Assets	1,841	1,254
Total Assets	$23,474	$21,695
LIABILITIES AND SHAREHOLDERS' EQUITY		
Current Liabilities		
Short-term obligations	$ 562	$ 354
Accounts payable and other current liabilities	4,998	4,461
Income taxes payable	492	183
Total Current Liabilities	6,052	4,998
Long-Term Debt Obligations	2,187	2,651
Other Liabilities	4,226	3,876
Deferred Income Taxes	1,718	1,496
Preferred Stock, no par value	41	41
Repurchased Preferred Stock	(48)	(15)
Common Shareholders' Equity		
Common stock, par value 1 2/3¢ per share (issued 1,782 shares)	30	30
Capital in excess of par value	–	13
Retained earnings	13,464	11,519
Accumulated other comprehensive loss	(1,672)	(1,646)
	11,822	9,916
Less: repurchased common stock, at cost (60 and 26 shares, respectively)	(2,524)	(1,268)
Total Common Shareholders' Equity	9,298	8,648
Total Liabilities and Shareholders' Equity	$23,474	$21,695

See accompanying notes to consolidated financial statements.

several operating cycles. For a retailer (manufacturer), the operating cycle is the amount of time needed to buy (produce) the inventory, sell the item to a customer, and collect the cash.

The general subclassifications of current assets normally found in the balance sheet include cash, marketable securities, accounts receivable, inventories, and prepaid expenses. These individual asset categories are briefly described below:

Cash. Cash includes all cash that is immediately available for use in the business, including cash on hand, in cash registers, and in checking accounts (demand deposits).

Marketable Securities. Marketable securities are temporary investments in stocks, bonds, and other securities that can be sold readily and that management intends to hold for only a relatively short period of time. If these investments have a maturity (i.e., they become due or will be converted into cash) of three months or less, they are considered to be cash equivalents. Note in Illustration 6 that the first item under current assets for PepsiCo is cash and cash equivalents. The second item is short-term investments.

Receivables. The accounts receivable balance represents the amount owed to the business by its customers. If a business has a significant amount of receivables from sources other than its normal trade customers, the receivables from customers are normally classified as trade accounts receivable and the amounts owed by others are classified as other receivables. A balance sheet may also include notes receivable, which are receivables (from customers or others) for which a business has received written documentation of the debtors' intent to pay.

Inventories. Inventories represent the cost of goods or materials held for sale to customers in the ordinary course of business, in the process of production for such sale, or for use in the production of goods or services to be available for sale at some future date.

Prepaid Expenses. Prepaid expenses represent expenditures that were made by the company in either the current or a prior period and that will provide benefits to the firm at some future time. Prepaid expenses result from paying expenses in advance. For example, a fire insurance policy that protects the assets of a firm for a year may be purchased during the current year. Although the policy was paid for and a portion of the protection was used during the current year, the firm benefits from the insurance protection in the upcoming year as well. A portion of the cost of the policy is applicable to the coming year and should be considered a prepaid expense.

PepsiCo has current assets of $6,413 million in 2002. These current assets consist of cash and cash equivalents, short-term investments, accounts and notes receivable, inventories, and prepaid expenses. Inventories constituted 20.9 percent ($1,342/$6,413) of PepsiCo's current assets.

Property, Plant and Equipment. Property, plant and equipment are those assets acquired for use in the business rather than for resale to customers. They are assets from which the business expects to receive benefits over a number of future accounting periods. Examples of these assets include land, buildings, machinery, and equipment. Since property, plant and equipment are used in the operations of the firm and benefits are derived from their use, the cost of these assets (except for land as explained in a later chapter) is allocated to depreciation expense during all periods that benefit from their use.

PepsiCo has land, buildings and improvements, machinery and equipment, and construction in progress classified as property, plant and equipment. The accumulated depreciation account balance is equal to the total amount of depreciation expense that has been allocated to these assets owned. Depreciation expense is recorded over the useful lives of these assets.

Other Assets. The classification, other assets, includes those assets that are not appropriately classified under either the current or the property, plant and equipment categories described above. This classification may include both tangible and intangible assets. Tangible assets are those assets that have physical substance, such as land held for investment purposes. Intangibles are assets without physical substance, such as patents, copyrights, and trademarks. The cost of intangible assets is allocated to expense over their useful lives by a process called amortization. Another asset that may be classified as an other asset is a long-term investment. Long-term investments include purchases of stock of another company. Such stock may be acquired to exercise influence or control over the operations of the other company. PepsiCo classifies intangible assets and investments in affiliates separately, rather than including these assets under the "other assets" heading.

Liabilities

Liabilities are debts. They represent the claims of creditors against the assets of a business. Creditors have a prior legal claim over the owners of a business. In the event a business is liquidated, creditors will be paid the amounts owed them before any payments are made to the owners of the business. Creditors are very concerned with the ability of a business to repay its debts. In certain instances, creditors may earn interest on the amounts due them. Normally, a liability has a maturity or due date, at which time it must be paid.

Liabilities, like assets, fall into descriptive categories. The two basic classifications usually employed in the balance sheet are current liabilities and long-term liabilities. Each of these general classes may also have sub-classifications.

Current Liabilities. Current liabilities include those obligations that are expected to require the use of current assets (usually cash) or the provision of services within one year. Examples of current liabilities include accounts payable, notes payable, taxes payable, and unearned revenues. These are described in the following paragraphs.

Accounts Payable. Accounts payable are the claims of vendors who sell goods and services to the company on a credit basis. Accounts payable are usually not evidenced by a formal, written document such as is the case with a note. PepsiCo's accounts payable on December 29, 2002 totaled $1,543 million out of the $4,998 million listed in the balance sheet as accounts payable and other current liabilities.

Notes Payable. Notes payable normally arise from borrowing or, on occasion, from purchases of assets and are evidenced by a formal written document. Notes payable may or may not be interest bearing. Notes usually have a fixed or determinable due date

Taxes Payable. This liability includes any local, state, and federal taxes owed by the business at the end of the accounting period but payable in the next period. PepsiCo has accrued income taxes payable of $492 million on December 28, 2002.

Unearned Revenues. Unearned revenues are amounts received from customers for goods that have not been shipped or services that have not yet been performed. Unearned revenues arise when customers make prepayments for goods and services.

Long-term Liabilities. Long-term liabilities generally represent claims that will be paid or satisfied in a future accounting period (or periods) beyond one year. Examples of long-term liabilities are bonds payable, mortgages payable, long-term notes payable, and obligations under certain types of lease contracts, called "capital leases," that give the company the right to use specified properties in exchange for future cash payments. PepsiCo reports long-term debt as a total on the balance sheet ($2,187 million at December 28, 2002), with the details being reported in a note to the financial statements.

Long-term liabilities are reclassified and reported as current liabilities when they become due within one year. For example, a note payable classified as a long-term liability in 20X1 because it is due in 20X3 is reclassified to a current liability at the end of 20X2. Part of short-term borrowings on PepsiCo's balance sheet consists of the portion of long-term debt due within one year.

Stockholders' Equity

Owners' equity (also referred to as capital for a proprietorship or partnership and stockholders' equity for a corporation) represents the claims of the owners against the net assets of the firm. Owners normally assume risks that are greater than those of creditors, because the return on investment to the owners is usually uncertain or undefined. In the event of bankruptcy, claims of creditors take priority over those of owners and must be satisfied first. After all creditors have been paid, any assets that remain are then available for distribution to the owners of the firm.

Accounting for owners' equity is influenced by the legal status of the company—the form of its organization. The most extensively used legal forms of business in the United States are the sole proprietorship, the partnership, and the corporation. There are certain legal differences associated with these types of organizations; these will be considered in later chapters of this text. Basically, the owners' equity of a business comes from two major sources: direct investments made by the owners from their personal resources and profits retained in the business. Owners' equity accounts will be discussed in detail in later chapters.

Investments by Owners. Investments by owners are increases in the equity of a particular business enterprise resulting from transfers of something of value to the enterprise in exchange for ownership interests (or equity) in the business. Investments by owners are most commonly made in the form of assets (e.g., cash); investments may also include services performed or the payment of the enterprise's liabilities.

Approximately 220,000 shareholders who have invested in PepsiCo are represented by common stock and capital in excess of par value. These terms will be explained later in this book. The stockholders' investment in PepsiCo on December 28, 2002 is $30 million for common stock. Basically, this indicates that the stockholders contributed $30 million to the company in exchange for their ownership interests.

The retained earnings account for a corporation reports the profits retained in the business over its lifetime. Retained earnings are increased (decreased) by profits (losses) and decreased by dividends. The retained earnings balance for PepsiCo is $13,464 million on December 28, 2002.

The Statement of Stockholders' Equity

The statement of stockholders' equity for PepsiCo is presented in Illustration 4. The owners' investment in a corporation is evidenced by shares of stock. The net change in stockholders' equity due to income and due to dividends, is represented by the retained earnings account. There may be other accounts also included as part of the statement of stockholders' equity for a corporation.

In a statement of stockholders' equity (or statement of shareholders' equity) for a corporation, elements of stockholders' equity are shown across the top of the statement to form columns; the changes in these elements during each year are listed down the left side of the statement. As in the case of PepsiCo's income statement, these are comparative statements for three years. All amounts included in this statement are stated in millions.

On December 30, 2000, PepsiCo had 2,029 million shares of its stock outstanding (2,038 million shares issued (2,030 million + 8 million) minus 9 million treasury shares). Due to purchases of PepsiCo stock by the company in 2001 (for reasons to be discussed later in this text), there were only 1,782 million shares of stock outstanding on December 28, 2002.

Look at the retained earnings column. The amount of retained earnings on December 25, 1999 (which is, of course, the beginning balance for 2000) is $14,921 million. The net income for the year ended December 20, 2000 is $2,543 million. You can also find this number at the bottom of the 2000 column on PepsiCo's

Illustration 4
PepsiCo
Consolidated Statement of Shareholders' Equity

CONSOLIDATED STATEMENT OF COMMON SHAREHOLDERS' EQUITY

PepsiCo, Inc. and Subsidiaries
Fiscal years ended December 28, 2002, December 29, 2001 and December 30, 2000

(in millions)	2002 Shares	2002 Amount	2001 Shares	2001 Amount	2000 Shares	2000 Amount
Common Stock						
Balance, beginning of year	1,782	$ 30	2,029	$ 34	2,030	$ 34
Quaker share repurchases	–	–	–	–	(9)	–
Stock option exercises	–	–	6	–	–	–
Quaker stock option exercises	–	–	3	–	8	–
Shares issued to effect merger	–	–	(256)	(4)	–	–
Balance, end of year	1,782	30	1,782	30	2,029	34
Capital in Excess of Par Value						
Balance, beginning of year		13		375		559
Quaker share repurchases		–		–		(236)
Stock option exercises(a)		(9)		82		52
Reissued shares		–		150		–
Shares issued to effect merger		–		(595)		–
Other		(4)		1		–
Balance, end of year		–		13		375
Deferred Compensation						
Balance, beginning of year		–		(21)		(45)
Net activity		–		21		24
Balance, end of year		–		–		(21)
Retained Earnings						
Balance, beginning of year		11,519		16,510		14,921
Net income(b)		3,313		2,662		2,543
Shares issued to effect merger		–		(6,644)		–
Cash dividends declared – common		(1,042)		(1,005)		(950)
Cash dividends declared – preferred		(4)		(4)		(4)
Stock option exercises(a)		(322)		–		–
Balance, end of year		13,464		11,519		16,510
Accumulated Other Comprehensive Loss						
Balance, beginning of year		(1,646)		(1,374)		(1,085)
Currency translation adjustment(b)		56		(218)		(289)
Cash flow hedges, net of tax(b)		18		(18)		–
Minimum pension liability adjustment, net of tax(b)		(99)		(38)		(2)
Other(b)		(1)		2		2
Balance, end of year		(1,672)		(1,646)		(1,374)
Repurchased Common Stock						
Balance, beginning of year	(26)	(1,268)	(280)	(7,920)	(271)	(7,306)
Share repurchases	(53)	(2,192)	(35)	(1,716)	(38)	(1,430)
Stock option exercises	19	931	20	751	29	816
Reissued shares	–	–	13	374	–	–
Shares issued to effect merger	–	–	256	7,243	–	–
Other	–	5	–	–	–	–
Balance, end of year	(60)	(2,524)	(26)	(1,268)	(280)	(7,920)
Total Common Shareholders' Equity		$ 9,298		$ 8,648		$ 7,604

(a) Includes total tax benefit of $143 million in 2002, $212 million in 2001 and $177 million in 2000.
(b) Combined these amounts represent total comprehensive income of $3,287 million in 2002, $2,390 million in 2001 and $2,254 million in 2000.
See accompanying notes to consolidated financial statements.

income statement in Illustration 2. The net income for the year is added to retained earnings. The cash dividends of $954 million, which consist of both preferred and common dividends, are subtracted from retained earnings. These dividends are not an expense that is reported in the income statement, but instead are considered to be a distribution of earnings. The ending retained earnings balance on December 30, 2000 is $16,510 million. Similarly, net income is added and dividends are subtracted in computing the retained earnings amounts for 2001 and 2002.

The relationship between income and dividends can be seen in the retained earnings column of PepsiCo's statement of shareholders' equity. Some companies believe their shareholders wish to receive high dividends and attempt to please them. Other companies distribute little or no dividends but instead use the money for growth purposes, which hopefully will provide a return to shareholders by increasing the market value of its shares of stock. PepsiCo's cash dividends increased from $954 million to $1,009 million to $1,046 million. Cash dividends as a percentage of net income increased from 37.5 percent ($954/$2,543) in 2000 to 37.9 percent ($1,009/$2,662) in 2001 and then decreased to 31.6 percent ($1,046/$3,313) in 2002.

Comparative Financial Statements

In general, the usefulness of financial information is increased when it can be compared with related data. Comparison may be internal (i.e., within one firm) or external (i.e., with another firm). External comparisons may be difficult to make in practice since financial statements of firms may not be readily comparable because of the use of different generally accepted accounting principles. However, some useful information may be obtained by comparison with industry averages, ratios, etc. (such as those compiled by *Moody's* and *Standard and Poor's*) or by direct comparison with the statements of another firm. Considerable caution must be exercised when making this type of analysis, however.

The financial statements of a firm are most useful when they can be compared with related data from within the current period, information from prior periods, or with budgets or forecasts. Comparative statements are useful in providing a standard that facilitates the analysis and interpretation of changes and trends that have occurred in the various elements of the financial statements. Generally, published annual reports of corporations provide comparative accounting statements from the previous period and often also include selected historical information for the firm for a longer period of time, such as ten years.

Assume, for example, that the income statement of a firm for the year ended December 31, 20X2, reports net income of $100,000. This information, in and of itself, provides a user with only a single indicator of the absolute amount of income earned for the year. If an income statement for 20X1, disclosing net income of $80,000 is also presented, 20X2 net income becomes much more meaningful information to the user. The 25 percent increase of 20X2 income over that for 20X1 indicates a significant improvement in performance that cannot be determined from the 20X2 statements alone.

Basic Analytical Procedures

Comparisons of financial statement data are frequently expressed as percentages or ratios. These comparisons may represent:

1. Percentage increases and decreases in individual items included in comparative financial statements.
2. Percentage relationships of individual components to an aggregate total in a single financial statement.
3. Ratios of one amount to another in the financial statements.

Application of each of these three methods will be illustrated by the use of the comparative financial statements of Dolbey Company. A comparative balance sheet is presented in Illustration 5, a comparative

Illustration 5
Dolbey Company
Comparative Balance Sheet
December 31, 20X2 and 20X1

	20X2 Dollars	20X2 Percent of Total Assets	20X1 Dollars	20X1 Percent of Total Assets	Increase (Decrease) Dollars	Increase (Decrease) Percent
Assets:						
Current assets:						
Cash	$ 80,000	5.0	$ 40,000	2.8	$ 40,000	100.0
Net accounts receivable	100,000	6.3	80,000	5.5	20,000	25.0
Inventories	200,000	12.5	160,000	11.1	40,000	25.0
Prepaid expenses	20,000	1.2	8,000	.6	12,000	150.0
Total current assets	$ 400,000	25.0	$ 288,000	20.0	$112,000	38.9
Land, buildings, and equipment (net)	1,200,000	75.0	1,152,000	80.0	48,000	4.2
Total assets	$1,600,000	100.0	$1,440,000	100.0	$160,000	11.1
Liabilities:						
Current liabilities:						
Accounts payable	$ 200,000	12.5	$ 130,000	9.0	$ 70,000	53.8
Notes payable	100,000	6.3	60,000	4.2	40,000	66.7
Total current liabilities	$ 300,000	18.8	$ 190,000	13.2	$110,000	57.9
Bonds payable	200,000	12.5	200,000	13.9	0	0
Total liabilities	$ 500,000	31.3	$ 390,000	27.1	$110,000	28.2
Stockholders' Equity:						
Common stock ($30 par)	$ 900,000	56.2	$ 900,000	62.5	0	0
Retained earnings	200,000	12.5	150,000	10.4	$ 50,000	33.3
Total liabilities and stockholders' equity	$1,600,000	100.0	$1,440,000	100.0	$160,000	11.1

income statement in Illustration 6, and a comparative statement of retained earnings in Illustration 7. Selected data from the 20X0 statements are also included in Illustration 7.

Horizontal Analysis

Analysis of increases or decreases in a given financial statement item over two or more accounting periods is often referred to as horizontal analysis. Generally, this type of analysis discloses both the dollar and percentage changes for the corresponding items in comparative statements. An example of horizontal analysis is included in the comparative financial statements presented for Dolbey Company. These statements include data with regard to income, retained earnings, and financial position for a two-year period with the dollar and percentage changes for each item listed in the final two columns.

Interpretation of the increases or decreases in individual statement items cannot be completely evaluated and understood without additional information. For example, the comparative balance sheet discloses an increase in inventory during 20X2 of $40,000, an amount 25 percent greater than in 20X1. This increase may have been required in order to support a higher sales volume as net sales increased by one-third during 20X2. Alternatively, this increase could have resulted from a build-up of obsolete inventories. The point to be made

Illustration 6
Dolbey Company
Comparative Income Statement
for the Years Ended December 31, 20X2 and 20X1

	20X2		20X1		Increase (Decrease)	
	Dollars	Percent of Sales	Dollars	Percent of Sales	Dollars	Percent
Net sales	$2,000,000	100.0	$1,500,000	100.0	$500,000	33.3
Cost of goods sold	1,400,000	70.0	1,080,000	72.0	320,000	29.6
Gross profit on sales	$ 600,000	30.0	$ 420,000	28.0	$180,000	42.9
Operating expenses:						
Selling expenses	$ 300,000	15.0	$ 240,000	16.0	$ 60,000	25.0
Administrative expenses	180,000	9.0	129,000	8.6	51,000	39.5
Total operating expenses	$ 480,000	24.0	$ 369,000	24.6	$111,000	30.1
Operating income	$ 120,000	6.0	$ 51,000	3.4	$ 69,000	135.3
Interest expense	10,000	.5	9,000	.6	1,000	11.1
Income before income taxes	$ 110,000	5.5	$ 42,000	2.8	$ 68,000	161.9
Income taxes	30,000	1.5	12,000	.8	18,000	150.0
Net income	$ 80,000	4.0	$ 30,000	2.0	$ 50,000	166.7

here is that additional information is often useful and sometimes absolutely necessary for meaningful interpretation of financial statements.

Illustration 7
Dolbey Company
Comparative Statement of Retained Earnings
for the Years Ended December 31, 20X2 and 20X1

	20X2	20X1	Increase (Decrease) Dollars	Percent
Retained earnings (January)	$150,000	$135,000	$15,000	11.1
Net income	80,000	30,000	50,000	166.7
	$230,000	$165,000	$65,000	39.4
Less: Dividends	30,000	15,000	15,000	100.0
Retained earnings (December 31)	$200,000	$150,000	$50,000	33.3

Data from the 20X0 financial statements:
    Total assets (December 31, 20X0) $1,160,000
    Stockholders' equity (December 31, 20X0) 1,035,000
    Net receivables (December 31, 20X0) 70,000
    Inventory (December 31, 20X0) 110,000

Accounts payable increased by $70,000, more than the $40,000 increase in inventories. Selling expenses increased by $60,000; administrative expenses increased by $51,000. But these increased expenses may have been necessary because net sales increased by $500,000. Operating income rose by $69,000, an increase of

135.3 percent. The increase in operating expenses and cost of goods sold (29.6%) may have been justified by the increased sales.

Percentage changes included in the statements for Dolbey Company are stated in terms of the data for two years. When a comparison is made between statements of two periods, the earlier statement is normally used as a base in computing percentage changes. For statements that include more than two years, there are two methods that may be used in selecting a base year. One alternative is to use the earliest year as a base. If this alternative is selected, each amount on all succeeding statements is expressed as a percentage of the base year amount. Since this procedure results in a constant base, percentage changes for more than two years can be interpreted as trend values for individual components of the financial statements. A second alternative is to compare each statement with the statement that immediately precedes it (the prior year's). Adoption of this procedure results in a changing base that may make comparisons of percentage changes over a period of several years somewhat more difficult.

Vertical Analysis

The percentage relationship of an individual item or component of a single financial statement to an aggregate total in the same statement often discloses significant relationships. These relationships may be useful information for decision-making purposes. For example, in reporting income data, it may be useful to indicate the relationship between sales and other elements of the income statement for a period. This analysis of the elements included in the financial statements of a single period is often referred to as vertical analysis.

Vertical analysis is illustrated in the financial statements presented for Dolbey Company. In the comparative balance sheets, the total assets and the total liabilities and stockholders' equity for each year are used as a base. Each item in the statement is then expressed as a percentage of this base. For example, the statements indicate that current assets increased from 20 percent of total assets in 20X1 to 25 percent at the end of 20X2. An analysis of the composition of the current asset balance provides additional details of the changes in various individual categories of current assets. Liabilities increased as a percent of total assets from 20X1 to 20X2. Current liabilities are 18.8 percent of total assets in 20X2, an increase from 13.2 percent in 20X1.

Vertical analysis may also be employed in presenting a comparative income statement. In the Dolbey Company comparative income statement illustration, each individual item is stated as a percent of net sales for the period. Net income for 20X2 is 4 percent of sales whereas net income for 20X1 is only 2 percent of sales. Gross profit is a higher percentage of sales in 20X2 than in 20X1 (30% to 28%); operating expenses are a lower percentage of sales in 20X2 than in 20X1 (24% to 24.6%). These favorable percentage comparisons are offset somewhat by the higher percentage of income taxes to sales in 20X2 than in 20X1 (1.5% to 0.8%).

Common-size Statements

Horizontal and vertical analyses are frequently useful in disclosing certain relationships and trends in individual elements included in the financial statements. The analysis of these relationships may be facilitated by the use of common-size statements (i.e., statements in which all items are stated in terms of percentages or ratios). Common-size statements may be prepared in order to compare data from the current period with those from one or more past periods for a firm. These statements may also be used to compare data of two or more business firms for the same period or periods, subject to the limitations mentioned previously.

A common-size statement comparing income statement data of Dolbey Company and Nutt Company is presented in Illustration 8. The column for Dolbey Company is prepared by using the percentage figures that are included in the comparative income statement in Illustration 6. Net sales of each firm are set as a base of 100 percent and each individual item included in the statement is shown as a percentage of net sales. Consequently, use of this statement format provides a comparison of the relationships of the income statement items for the two firms regardless of the absolute dollar amount of sales and expenses of either company. It can be seen, for example, that Dolbey Company obtained $.30 of gross profit and $.04 of net income from

Illustration 8
Dolbey Company and Nutt Company
*Condensed Common-Size Income Statement
for the Year Ended December 31, 20X2*

	Dolbey Company	Nutt Company
Net sales	100.0%	100.0%
Cost of goods sold	70.0	72.5
Gross profit on sales	30.0%	27.5%
Operating expenses:		
Selling expense	15.0%	17.5%
Administrative expense	9.0	7.5
Total operating expenses	24.0%	25.0%
Operating income	6.0%	2.5%
Interest expense	.5	1.0
Income before income taxes	5.5%	1.5%
Income taxes	1.5	.5
Net income	4.0%	1.0%

each dollar of net sales, while Nutt Company netted only $.275 of gross profit and $.01 of net income from each sales dollar.

Ratio Analysis

A ratio is an expression of the relationship of one numerical item to another. Significant interrelationships that may be present in financial statements are often identified and highlighted by the use of ratio analysis. A simple example of such a relationship is the ratio of cash to current liabilities for Dolbey Company at the end of 20X2. The ratio is computed as follows:

$$\text{Ratio of Cash to Current Liabilities} = \frac{\text{Cash}}{\text{Current Liabilities}}$$

$$.27 = \frac{\$80,000}{\$300,000}$$

Ratios may be expressed in several different ways. Generally, ratios are stated in relation to a base of one. For example, for the ratio computed above, it can be stated that the ratio of cash to current liabilities is .27 to 1 (which is sometimes simply stated as .27 with the "to 1" omitted). In any case, a ratio is a method used to describe a relationship between two financial statement amounts. The meaningful use of ratio analysis requires that there be a logical relationship between the figures compared, and that this relationship be clearly understood by the user.

Comparison with Standards

The analytical procedures employed in computing percentage changes (horizontal analysis), component percentages (vertical analysis) and ratios convert financial statement items into a form that may be compared to various standards. Comparisons made among the relationships derived from the financial statements and selected standards allow the user to draw meaningful conclusions concerning the firm. Among the most commonly-used standards of comparison against which the position of a particular firm may be measured are the following:

1. Past performance of the firm.
2. Financial data of similar or competing firms.
3. Average performance of a number of firms in an industry.

A major deficiency of comparison with the past performance of the firm is that there is no indication of what *should* have occurred given the nature of the firm, the economy of the period, etc. For example, the fact that the net income of a firm increases by 3 percent from the previous year may appear to be favorable; however, if there is evidence that net income *should* have increased by 6 percent, the performance for the current year is regarded as unfavorable.

The weakness of comparisons with the past performance of the firm may be overcome somewhat by using the performance of a similar firm or firms or an industry average as an additional standard for comparison. A problem with this approach, however, is that it is often difficult to identify firms that are truly comparable, both because of the nature of the firms themselves and because of the use of alternative "generally accepted accounting principles." In spite of these limitations, a careful analysis of comparative performance, both internal and external, often provides meaningful input for use in decision-making.

Users of Financial Statements

Recall that the purpose of financial accounting is to summarize, classify, record, and interpret events and transactions to provide information to users in making economic decisions about a company. In financial accounting, the focus is on users *outside* (or *external* to) the company. The main types of external users and information of interest to these users are:

1. *Lenders* provide resources to the company, usually in the form of cash. In exchange for these resources, lenders accept a written promise by the company to repay the funds over time. Lenders charge companies interest for the use of funds. Several important questions that lenders and creditors use accounting information to answer are:

    - Should a loan be made to the company?
    - What interest rate should be charged for the loan?
    - What collateral requirements should be placed on this loan?
    - What repayment period should be specified for the loan?

2. *Investors* are individuals who purchase shares of the company's stock directly from the company (in an initial public offering) or in trading through the stock exchanges. Investors are interested in answers to the following types of questions:

    - Will the price of the stock increase or decrease in the future?
    - What is the company's ability to pay dividends in the future?

3. *Short-term creditors* provide goods or services to the company in exchange for a promise to repay these creditors for these goods and services at a later date. In most cases, the repayment period for short-term creditors is a month or less; because of their relatively short duration, short-term credit obligations are

typically non interest-bearing. Short-term creditors are interested in answers to the following types of questions:

- Should the company be provided short-term credit?
- What types of credit terms should be granted to the company?
- How long of a repayment period should the company be permitted?

Several major types of ratios provide these users with the information necessary to make their economic decisions with respect to the company. These ratios are described and illustrated in the following sections of this chapter.

Analysis for Common Stockholders

Common stockholders and potential investors purchase the securities of a firm to earn a return on their investment through increases in the market price of the stock and by dividends. Because each of these factors is influenced by net income, the analysis of financial statements made by, or on behalf of, an investor is focused primarily on the company's earnings. Certain of the more important relationships that are of interest to the stockholder-investor are discussed in the following sections of this chapter.

Profitability ratios provide an indication of a company's success in generating income. A limitation in evaluating a company's ability to generate income is that larger companies should be able to earn greater income than smaller companies. To allow the net income earned by companies to be compared across companies of different sizes, profitability ratios divide net income (or some variation of net income) by a measure of size (such as total assets or total common shareholders' equity). Dividing net income (or some variation of net income) by a measure of size provides a percentage that can be compared easily across companies to identify their relative abilities to generate income.

Two common ratios used to evaluate a company's profitability are the rate of return on total assets (ROA) and the rate of return on common shareholders' equity (ROCE). These ratios are discussed below.

Rate of Return on Total Assets

The rate of return on total assets (ROA) expresses the net income earned by a company as a percentage of the total assets available for use by that company. ROA suggests that companies with higher amounts of assets should be able to earn higher levels of income. The measure of "net income" used in calculating ROA is the net income (after taxes) from the continuing operations of the company. To focus on ongoing activities, the income statement effects of such items as discontinued operations, extraordinary items, and the cumulative effect of a change in accounting principles are typically not considered in calculating ROA. The net income from continuing operations is a subtotal that normally is readily available from the company's income statement.

The numerator of the ROA formula adjusts net income for interest expense. The rationale for this adjustment is that while dividends paid to shareholders are not deducted in determining net income; interest expense is deducted. In a sense, interest and dividends are similar, as both represent amounts paid by the company to individual(s) providing capital to it. This inconsistent treatment of interest expense and dividends penalizes companies that raise capital by borrowing funds or issuing debt as opposed to issuing stock. The adjustment for interest expense makes the net income earned by companies using debt and equity financing comparable.

The average total assets used in the denominator of the ROA formula is obtained by dividing the sum of the beginning and ending total assets by two. This averaging is consistent with the nature of the numerator, since net income is earned throughout the period(s). A reasonable estimate of the average level of assets available to the company during the year is the average of its beginning and ending total assets. This averaging also reduces the impact of year-end transactions (such as purchases of property, plant and equipment) on ROA. Average total assets can be readily determined using information from the company's balance sheet, as follows:

$$\frac{\text{Beginning Total Assets + Ending Total Assets}}{2}$$

There is no "magic" benchmark for determining whether a company's ROA is good or bad. Typically, the ROA earned by a company in a given year is compared to the ROA earned by that company in previous years or the ROA for other companies in the same industry.

To summarize, ROA provides a measure of management's ability to earn a return on the firm's resources—its assets. The income amount used in this computation is income before the deduction of interest expense, since interest is the return to creditors for the resources that they provide to the firm. The resulting adjusted income amount is thereby the income before any distributions (interest or dividends) to those who provided funds to the company. Thus, ROA is computed by dividing net income plus interest expense by the company's average investment in assets during the year.

$$\frac{\text{Rate of Return}}{\text{on Total Assets}} = \frac{\text{Net Income (after taxes) + Interest Expense}}{\text{Average Total Assets During the Year}}$$

Although assets are continually acquired and disposed of throughout a period, an average of asset balances at the beginning and end of the period is generally used for this calculation. The calculation for Dolbey Company is as follows:

	20X2	20X1
Net income	$ 80,000	$ 30,000
Add: Interest expense	10,000	9,000
Net income before interest expense	$ 90,000	$ 39,000
Total assets:		
Beginning of year	$1,440,000	$1,160,000
End of year	1,600,000	1,440,000
Total	$3,040,000	$2,600,000
Average total assets	$1,520,000	$1,300,000
Rate of return on assets (ROA)	5.9%	3.0%

This ratio indicates that the earnings per dollar of assets invested have almost doubled in 20X2. It appears that the management of Dolbey Company has increased its efficiency in the use of the firm's assets to generate income.

The ROA for PepsiCo and Coca-Cola is as follows:

Year	PepsiCo	Coca-Cola
2002:	$\frac{\$3{,}313 \text{ million} + \$178 \text{ million}}{(\$23{,}474 \text{ million} + \$21{,}695 \text{ million})/2} = 15.5\%$	$\frac{\$3{,}050 \text{ million} + \$199 \text{ million}}{(\$24{,}501 + \$22{,}417)/2} = 13.9\%$
2001:	$\frac{\$2{,}662 \text{ million} + \$219 \text{ million}}{(\$21{,}695 \text{ millioon} + \$20{,}757 \text{ million})/2} = 13.6\%$	$\frac{\$3{,}969 \text{ million} + \$289 \text{ million}}{(\$22{,}417 + \$20{,}834)/2} = 19.7\%$

The rate of return on total assets can be decomposed into the two components, the *asset turnover* and *return on sales* ratios as follows:

$$\text{Rate of Return on Total Assets} = \underbrace{\frac{\text{Net Sales}}{\text{Average Total Assets During the Year}}}_{\text{Asset Turnover}} \times \underbrace{\frac{\text{Net Income (after taxes)} + \text{Interest Expense}}{\text{Net Sales}}}_{\text{Return on Sales}}$$

Asset Turnover. The first factor of ROA is the company's ability to utilize assets to generate revenues. This factor is represented by the asset turnover, which equals the total sales (or total revenues, for service-oriented organizations) divided by the average total assets. Asset turnover provides an indication of the amount of sales (or revenues) generated from each dollar of total assets.

Return on Sales. The second factor that influences a company's ROA is its profitability relative to the sales (or revenues) it generates. This is referred to as its return on sales or profit margin. Companies which are able to control their costs more effectively will generate greater amounts of net income from each dollar of sales (or revenue) than those not able to control their costs effectively. The ability of a company to control its costs is reflected in the profit margin. The profit margin provides an indication of the amount of net income that is generated from each dollar of sales (or revenues).

ROA, Asset Turnover, and Profit Margin. ROA can be calculated by multiplying the company's asset turnover by its profit margin. The "sales" in the numerator of the asset turnover and denominator of the profit margin cancel, leaving ROA. The decomposition of ROA indicates that enhancing ROA is a function of (1) effectively using assets to generate sales or revenues (asset turnover) and (2) controlling costs (profit margin). Companies having higher levels of asset turnover and companies with higher profit margins will have higher ROAs.

Gross Profit. A factor that affects the profitability of companies whose primary form of revenue-generating activity is through the sale of inventory is their ability to "mark up" their inventories (or control the costs of purchasing or producing their inventories). A ratio that provides this type of information is the **gross profit ratio** (or **gross margin ratio**). Gross margin (profit) is the difference between the sales revenue and cost of goods sold and can be determined from the income statement. The gross profit ratio is calculated as:

$$\text{Gross Profit Ratio} = \frac{\text{Gross Profit}}{\text{Sales Revenue}}$$

The gross profit ratio of Dolbey Company is:

$$20X2: \quad \frac{\$600,000}{\$2,000,000} = 30.0\%$$

$$20X1: \quad \frac{\$420,000}{\$1,500,000} = 28.0\%$$

The gross profit ratios of PepsiCo and Coca-Cola are as follows:

Year	PepsiCo		Coca-Cola	
2002:	$\frac{\$25{,}112 \text{ million} - \$11{,}497 \text{ million}}{\$25{,}112 \text{ million}}$	= 54.2%	$\frac{\$19{,}564 \text{ million} - \$7{,}105 \text{ million}}{\$19{,}564 \text{ million}}$	= 63.7%
2001:	$\frac{\$23{,}512 \text{ million} - \$10{,}750 \text{ million}}{\$23{,}512 \text{ million}}$	= 54.3%	$\frac{\$17{,}545 \text{ million} - \$6{,}044 \text{ million}}{\$17{,}545 \text{ million}}$	= 65.6%

Rate of Return on Common Stockholders' Equity

A second useful measure of a company's profitability is the amount of net income it generates for its common stockholders (owners). The *rate of return on common stockholders' equity* (or *ROCE*) measures the amount of net income earned by the company that could be distributed to its common stockholders as a percentage of the assets provided to the company by these common stockholders. Stated another way, ROCE provides an answer to the following question: "How much income that could be distributed to common stockholders' is earned for each dollar provided by the common stockholders?" ROCE is calculated using the following formula:

$$\text{Rate of Return on Common Stockholders' Equity (ROCE)} = \frac{\text{Net Income} - \text{Preferred Dividends}}{\text{Average Common Stockholders' Equity}}$$

The ROCE numerator represents the amount of net income earned by the company that is available for distribution to common stockholders (*i.e.*, the amount that "belongs" to the common stockholders). Two important items are excluded from the numerator:

1. Interest, which is contractually required to be paid to lenders. Unlike the ROA formula, interest is not added back to net income. The net income used in the numerator of the ROCE formula has already considered (and excluded) interest since it was deducted as an expense.

2. Preferred dividends, which must be paid to preferred stockholders prior to the distribution of any amounts to common stockholders. Preferred dividends can be found by examining the statement of stockholders' equity.

The denominator of the ROCE formula reflects average common stockholders' equity. Like the use of average total assets in the ROA formula, the average common stockholders' equity is determined by dividing the sum of beginning and ending common stockholders' equity by 2. This averaging lessens the influence of year-end transactions (such as the issuance of common stock) on ROCE. In addition, it is consistent with the measurement of the numerator, since net income is earned throughout the period under consideration.

The items included in average common stockholders' equity include the following and can be readily obtained from the company's balance sheet:

1. Common stock and additional paid-in capital (which represents the total amounts invested by owners/common stockholders in the organization).

2. Retained earnings (which represents net income earned by the organization that has not been distributed to the owners of the organization) (common stockholders).

3. Other items (with the exception of preferred stock accounts) that influence the organization's total stockholders' equity. These items include increases and decreases in the market values of foreign currency, investments, and derivative financial instruments.

Like ROA, there is no "magic" benchmark for determining whether a company's ROCE is acceptable. Typically, the ROCE earned by a company in a given year is compared to the ROCE earned by that company in previous years or the ROCE of other companies in the same industry.

ROCE is a measure of a firm's ability to earn a profit for its residual owners, the common stockholders. Because interest paid to creditors and dividends paid to preferred stockholders are normally fixed in amount, ROCE may not be equal to the return on total assets (ROA). If management is able to earn a higher return on assets than the cost (i.e., interest expense) of assets contributed by the creditors, the excess benefits the owners. This is often referred to as using debt as favorable "leverage" in order to increase the owners' rate of return or as "trading on equity." If the cost of borrowing funds exceeds ROA, leverage is unfavorable and reduces ROCE.

Since Dolbey Company has no preferred stock, ROCE on common stockholders' equity would be computed as follows:

	20X2	20X1
Net income	$ 80,000	$ 30,000
Common stockholders' equity:		
Beginning of the year	$1,050,000	$1,035,000
End of the year	1,100,000	1,050,000
Total	$2,150,000	$2,085,000
Average common stockholders' equity	$1,075,000	$1,042,500
Rate of return on common stockholders' equity (ROCE)	7.4%	2.9%

ROCE is higher than ROA for 20X2 because the cost of the funds contributed by creditors is less than the rate earned on assets. Thus the company is experiencing favorable "leverage," using borrowed funds to earn a return in excess of their cost.

ROCE for PepsiCo and Coca-Cola is as follows:

Year	PepsiCo	Coca-Cola
2002:	$\dfrac{\$3{,}313 \text{ million} - \$4 \text{ million}}{(\$9{,}298 \text{ million} + \$8{,}648 \text{ million})/2} = 36.9\%$	$\dfrac{\$3{,}050 \text{ million}}{(\$11{,}800 \text{ million} + \$11{,}366 \text{ million})/2} = 26.3\%$
2001:	$\dfrac{\$2{,}662 \text{ million} - \$4 \text{ million}}{(\$8{,}648 \text{ million} + \$7{,}604 \text{ million})/2} = 32.7\%$	$\dfrac{\$3{,}969 \text{ million}}{(\$11{,}366 \text{ million} + \$9{,}316 \text{ million})/2} = 38.4\%$

Financial Structure Leverage. Financial structure leverage provides a measure of the relative source of funds provided to the company. Recalling the basic accounting equation (assets = liabilities + stockholders' equity), a company receives its assets from one of two sources: lenders (liabilities) and stockholders' (equity). The financial structure leverage measures the relative proportion of assets received from these sources by dividing average total assets by average common shareholders' equity, as follows:

$$\text{Financial Structure Leverage} = \frac{\text{Average Total Assets}}{\text{Average Common Shareholders' Equity}}$$

Higher levels of financial structure leverage indicate that companies obtain a relatively higher proportion of their assets from lenders as opposed to shareholders (owners). Since asset equals liabilities plus equity, when liabilities are used extensively to finance activities, common shareholders' equity will be a relatively low proportion of total assets, resulting in a higher financial structure leverage.

The financial structure leverage for Dolbey Company is as follows:

$$20X2: \quad \frac{(\$1{,}440{,}000 + \$1{,}600{,}000)/2}{(\$1{,}050{,}000 + \$1{,}100{,}000)2} = 1.41$$

$$20X1: \quad \frac{(\$1{,}160{,}000 + \$1{,}440{,}000)/2}{(\$1{,}035{,}000 + \$1{,}050{,}000)2} = 1.25$$

The financial structure leverage for PesiCo and Coca-Cola is:

Year	PepsiCo		Coca-Cola	
2002:	$\dfrac{(\$23{,}474 \text{ million} + \$21{,}695 \text{ million})/2}{(\$9{,}298 \text{ million} + \$8{,}648 \text{ million})/2}$	= 2.52	$\dfrac{(\$24{,}501 \text{ million} + \$22{,}417 \text{ million})/2}{(\$11{,}800 \text{ million} + \$11{,}366 \text{ million})/2}$	= 2.03
2001:	$\dfrac{(\$21{,}695 \text{ million} + \$20{,}757 \text{ million})/2}{(\$8{,}648 \text{ million} + \$7{,}604 \text{ million})/2}$	= 2.61	$\dfrac{(\$22{,}417 \text{ million} + \$20{,}834 \text{ million})/2}{(\$11{,}366 \text{ million} + \$9{,}316 \text{ million})/2}$	= 2.09

Common Earnings Leverage. Common earnings leverage provides an indication of the percentage of net income earned by the company that is available for distribution to its common shareholders after payments are made to lenders for interest and preferred shareholders for preferred dividends. Companies with higher levels of common earnings leverage have lower commitments to lenders and preferred shareholders than those with lower levels of common earnings leverage. Common earnings leverage is determined as follows:

$$\text{Common Earnings Leverage} = \frac{\text{Net Income} - \text{Preferred Dividends}}{\text{Net Income} + \text{Interest Expense}}$$

The numerator of the above formula represents the remaining net income available for distribution to common shareholders after dividends have been paid to preferred shareholders. This amount represents the net income earned by the company after paying interest expense (which is deducted in determining net income) and deducting preferred dividends. The denominator of the common earnings leverage formula represents the total net income earned by the company prior to paying interest to lenders or preferred dividends to preferred shareholders. Viewed from another standpoint, common earnings leverage answers the following question: "What percentage of a company's net income is available for distribution to common shareholders after considering obligations for interest and preferred dividends?"

The common earnings leverage for Dolbey Company is as follows:

$$20X2: \quad \frac{\$80{,}000}{\$80{,}000 + \$10{,}000} = 88.9\%$$

$$20X1: \quad \frac{\$30{,}000}{\$30{,}000 + \$9{,}000} = 76.9\%$$

The common earnings leverage for PepsiCo and Coca-Cola is:

Year	PepsiCo		Coca-Cola	
2002:	$\dfrac{\$3{,}313 \text{ million} - \$4 \text{ million}}{\$3{,}313 \text{ million} + \$178 \text{ million}}$	= 94.8%	$\dfrac{\$3{,}050 \text{ million}}{\$3{,}050 \text{ million} + \$199 \text{ million}}$	= 93.9%
2001:	$\dfrac{\$2{,}662 \text{ million} - \$4 \text{ million}}{\$2{,}662 \text{ million} + \$219 \text{ million}}$	= 92.3%	$\dfrac{\$3{,}969 \text{ million}}{\$3{,}969 \text{ million} + \$289 \text{ million}}$	= 93.2%

(None of these companies have preferred stock so there was no adjustment for preferred dividends.)

ROCE, ROA, Capital Structure Leverage, and Common Earnings Leverage. ROCE can be expressed as the product of ROA, financial structure leverage, and common earnings leverage.

$$\begin{aligned}
\text{ROCE} &= \text{ROA} \times \text{Financial Structure Leverage} \times \text{Common Earnings Leverage} \\
&= \frac{\text{NI} + \text{Int Exp}(1 - \text{Tax Rate})}{\text{Average Total Assets}} \times \frac{\text{Average Total Assets}}{\text{Average CS Equity}} \times \frac{\text{Net Income} - \text{Preferred Divs}}{\text{NI} + \text{Int Exp}(1 - \text{Tax Rate})} \\
&= \frac{\text{Net Income} - \text{Preferred Dividends}}{\text{Average CS Equity}}
\end{aligned}$$

The above depiction indicates that ROCE is enhanced by:

1. Using assets effectively to generate net income (ROA)
2. Obtaining assets from lenders as opposed to owners (financial structure leverage). These assets can then be used in the operations of the company to generate income for the company's owners (common shareholders).
3. Having a relatively high percentage of net income available for distribution to common shareholders (common earnings leverage).

The Relationship between ROA and ROCE

Once ROA and ROCE have been calculated, comparing these two measures of profitability allows financial statement users to assess the company's ability to effectively utilize sources of funds other than common shareholders (funds from lenders and preferred shareholders) in generating income.

From the common shareholders' perspective, if a company can obtain funds from lenders and preferred shareholders at a certain cost (say 8 percent) and utilize those funds to earn a higher return (say an ROA of 10 percent), common shareholders benefit. This benefit results from the fact that assets obtained from non-common shareholders (at a relatively low cost) are being used to generate income for common shareholders.

If ROCE exceeds ROA, financial leverage is being used to the advantage of common shareholders. In this case, the ROA earned by the organization exceeds the cost of obtaining capital from parties other than common shareholders. The cost of capital can be determined as follows:

$$\text{Cost of Capital} = \frac{\text{Interest Expense} + \text{Preferred Dividends}}{\text{Average Liabilities} + \text{Average Preferred Equity}}$$

The above cost of capital calculation reveals that the net cost of obtaining funds from lenders (liabilities) is the after-tax interest expense and the net cost of obtaining funds from preferred shareholders (preferred equity) is the dividends that must be paid to these shareholders.

In contrast, if ROCE is less than ROA, financial leverage is being used to the detriment of common shareholders. In situations such as this, the organization is paying more for the use of capital than it earns by using this capital in its operating activities. This situation reflects the fact that the cost of capital exceeds the ROA earned by the organization.

These relationships are summarized below:

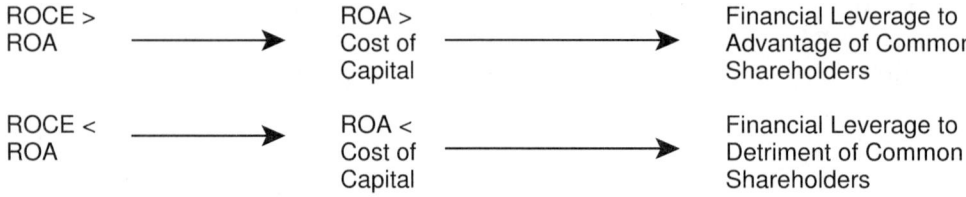

Earnings Quality

ROA and ROCE measure the profitability of the organization (based on its relationship with either total assets or common shareholders' equity). A major limitation of any net income-based measure is that income is recognized under the accrual basis; that is, revenues are recognized as they are *earned* (and not necessarily collected) and expenses are recognized as they are *incurred* (and not necessarily paid). While net income is an important measure, it has little meaning unless the organization will actually be in position to collect the revenues it earns.

A measure that attempts to provide a clearer picture of the quality (collectibility) of an organization's net income is referred to as *earnings quality*. Earnings quality may be expressed in many ways, but the most straightforward is the ratio of cash flow from operating activities (taken from the Statement of Cash Flows) to net income (as reported in the Income Statement). This ratio provides an indication as to whether:

1. High levels of revenue may reflect uncollectible or aggressively-recognized sales.
2. Low levels of cost of goods sold may reflect inventories that are accumulating to excessive amounts.
3. Net income may be dependent upon nonoperating activities, such as the disposal of property, plant and equipment or investments.

Generally speaking, the higher the level of earnings quality, the more reliable the organization's measure of net income in reflecting the true operating activities of the organization. Instances where earnings quality is below 1.0 (*i.e.,* net income exceeds cash flow from operating activities) should raise suspicions on the part of the financial statement reader.

"Earnings quality" for PepsiCo and Coca-Cola is:

Year	PepsiCo		Coca-Cola	
2002:	$\dfrac{\$4{,}627 \text{ million}}{\$3{,}313 \text{ million}}$	= 1.40	$\dfrac{\$4{,}742 \text{ million}}{\$3{,}050 \text{ million}}$	= 1.56
2001:	$\dfrac{\$3{,}820 \text{ million}}{\$2{,}662 \text{ million}}$	= 1.44	$\dfrac{\$4{,}110 \text{ million}}{\$3{,}969 \text{ million}}$	= 1.04

Earnings per Share of Common Stock

Since the owners of a business invest in shares of stock, they are usually interested in an expression of earnings in terms of a per share amount. If a company has only a single class of common stock outstanding, earnings per share is computed by dividing net income for the period by the average number of common shares outstanding.[2] If the firm has other securities outstanding that have certain characteristics similar to those of common stock (such as convertible bonds), the usefulness of earnings per share data is enhanced if these other securities are also considered in the computation of earnings per share. These securities are often referred to as potentially dilutive securities. While a discussion of the inclusion of potentially dilutive securities in the computation of earnings per share is beyond the scope of this text, the basic principle involved is that earnings per share is calculated so as to indicate the effects of the conversion of these securities into common stock.

---

[2] The calculation of earnings per share was discussed in Chapter 11.

When there is both common and preferred stock outstanding, net income must be reduced by preferred dividend requirements in order to determine net income available to common stockholders.

$$\text{Earnings per Share} = \frac{\text{Net Income} - \text{Preferred Dividends}}{\text{Weighted Average Number of Common Stock Shares Outstanding}}$$

In the case of Dolbey Company, which has no preferred stock and 30,000 shares ($900,000 of common stock divided by the $30 par value per share) outstanding throughout 20X1 and 20X2, the earnings per share of common stock is calculated as follows:

	20X2	20X1
Net income	$80,000	$30,000
Number of common shares outstanding	30,000	30,000
Earnings per share of common stock	$ 2.67	$ 1.00

Earnings per share is frequently mentioned in the financial press in relation to the earnings performance of business firms. In addition, earnings per share data are reported on the income statement and usually in various other sections of corporate annual reports. Although the concept of earnings per share has received a great deal of attention, particularly in recent years, it should be viewed with some caution. As a minimum, it should be recognized that all of the significant aspects of a firm's performance simply cannot be reduced to a single figure. This point cannot be overemphasized.

The earnings per share of common stock for PepsiCo and Coca-Cola is as follows:

Year	PepsiCo	Coca-Cola
2002:	$\frac{\$3{,}313 \text{ million} - \$4 \text{ million}}{1{,}782 \text{ million}} = \$1.86$	$\frac{\$3{,}050 \text{ million}}{2{,}470 \text{ million}} = \$1.24$
2001:	$\frac{\$2{,}662 \text{ million} - \$4 \text{ million}}{1{,}906 \text{ million}} = \$1.40$	$\frac{\$3{,}969 \text{ million}}{2{,}486 \text{ million}} = \$1.60$

Price-earnings Ratio on Common Stock

Each investor must allocate his or her limited resources among various investment opportunities available to him or her. For this reason, the rate of earnings relative to the current market price of his or her investment often provides a useful basis for comparing alternative investment opportunities. This ratio is commonly referred to as the price-earnings (PE) ratio. It is computed by dividing the current market price per share of common stock by earnings per share.

$$\text{Price-earnings Ratio} = \frac{\text{Market Price per Share of Common Stock}}{\text{Earnings per Share}}$$

Assuming that the market price per common share of Dolbey Company at the end of 20X2 is $24 and at the end of 20X1 is $8, PE ratios are calculated as follows:

	20X2	20X1
Market price per share at the end of the year	$24.00	$8.00
Earnings per share	$ 2.67	$1.00
Price-earnings ratio	9	8

The PE ratio may be interpreted as the value that investors in the stock market place on every dollar of earnings for a particular firm. An investor may compare the PE ratio of a firm to that of other companies in an attempt to estimate whether a firm's stock is overpriced or underpriced. A high PE ratio may indicate that the stock price is too high, but not always; a low PE ratio may indicate that the stock price is too low, but, again, not always. PE ratios differ among industries. Generalizations are not easy.

The PE ratio on common stock for PepsiCo and Coca-Cola is as follows:

Year	PepsiCo		Coca-Cola	
2002:	$\dfrac{\$41.67}{\$1.86}$	= 22.4	$\dfrac{\$43.84}{\$1.24}$	= 35.4
2001:	$\dfrac{\$49.05}{\$1.40}$	= 35.0	$\dfrac{\$47.15}{\$1.60}$	= 29.5

Other Investor Ratios

Investor ratios provide two important types of information to potential investors in a company's stock. First, one set of ratios provide a measure of the price of a company's stock in relationship to its earnings, book value of net assets, sales, or operating cash flows. Second, the dividend yield ratio provides an indication as to the extent to which dividends declared by the company's board of directors provide a return to shareholders.

"*Price*" ratios express a company's stock price (on a per share basis) in terms of its earnings, book value of net assets, sales, or operating cash flows (on a per share basis). These ratios provide an approximate measure of how much investors are willing to pay for a dollar of earnings, net assets, sales, or operating cash flows. Higher price ratios may be indicative of one of: (1) a share price which is overvalued by the market or (2) earnings, net assets, sales, or operating cash flows which are perceived to be understated by the market (as measured by traditional accounting principles).

The general formula for price ratios is:

$$\frac{\text{Market Price per Share}}{\text{"Measure" per Share}}$$

The "measure" per share can be determined by dividing a subtotal from the income statement (net income, sales), balance sheet (net assets), or statement of cash flows (cash flow from operating activities) by the number of shares outstanding. The company's net assets are calculated as the difference between its assets and liabilities, which is also equal to its shareholders' equity.

The number of shares outstanding can be determined in a number of ways:

1. From the income statement, as part of the disclosure of earnings per share.
2. From a footnote to the financial statements discussing earnings per share.
3. From the balance sheet or statement of shareholders' equity.

Typically, the analyst uses the "average" number of shares outstanding during the period. This number is usually provided in either the income statement or footnotes to the financial statements. If an average number is not available, an approximation to this average can be obtained by averaging the beginning and ending shares outstanding.

The *dividend yield* expresses the dividend per share of a company's common stock as a percentage of the market price of that stock. This ratio provides an indication of the return provided to investors in the form of dividends. The dividend yield is calculated as:

$$\text{Dividend Yield} = \frac{\text{Common Dividends per Share}}{\text{Market Price per Share}}$$

Dividends per share are frequently disclosed in the Statement of Shareholders' Equity or in other areas of the company's annual report. If not disclosed on a per share basis, the total common dividends declared by the corporation can be found in the Statement of Shareholders' Equity. This total can then be divided by the average number of common shares outstanding, which is disclosed in the income statement, footnotes to the financial statements, balance sheet, or statement of shareholders' equity.

Analysis for Long-term Creditors

Long-term solvency is a company's long-run financial viability and its ability to repay its long-term obligations (debt). Common ratios used in analyzing a company's long-term solvency provide the answer to the following major questions.

1. How much long-term debt does the company currently have?
2. Does the company have the capability to assume additional long-term debt?
3. Has the company's financial condition reached such a stage that its continued existence is questionable?

How Much Long-term Debt?

To evaluate the level of long-term debt held by the company, analysts express the company's long-term debt as a percentage of other balance sheet subtotals. Three common subtotals used for this purpose are: total assets, total tangible assets (which exclude goodwill and other intangible assets), and total shareholders' equity. While the percentage of long-term debt will differ depending upon the denominator used, the relative comparisons of the long-term debt held by companies will be the same. The most common measure of long-term debt is the ratio of long-term debt to assets ratio (commonly referred to as the *long-term debt ratio*), as follows:

$$\text{Long-term Debt Ratio} = \frac{\text{Long-term Debt}}{\text{Total Assets}}$$

The PE ratio acknowledges that an organization's long-term financing comes from one of two sources: lenders and shareholders (owners). This ratio provides information as to the relative proportion of long-term financing that is received from lenders. Higher levels of the PE ratio are indicative of companies with higher levels of debt. While the elements included in "long-term debt" are somewhat controversial, this subtotal typically includes:

1. Contractual obligations, such as notes and bonds payable (labeled as "long-term debt" on the balance sheet).
2. Capital lease obligations.

An additional measure of the extent of long-term debt held by companies is the ratio of cash flow from operations to the total of current liabilities and long-term contractual liabilities. As with the long-term debt ratio, long-term contractual liabilities typically include notes and bonds payable as well as capital lease obligations. Liabilities such as deferred taxes and "other" liabilities are typically not included.

This ratio provides an indication of the length of time required for a company to repay its existing liabilities, given the level of cash flow from operating activities that it is able to generate. The ratio of cash flow from operations to "contractual liabilities" is:

$$\text{Cash Flow from Operations to "Contractual Liabilities"} = \frac{\text{Cash Flow from Operating Activities}}{\text{Average Current Liabilities} + \text{Average Long-term Contractual Liabilities}}$$

The reciprocal of this ratio provides an indication as to the length of time required for the company to repay its liabilities. For example, if the ratio of cash flows from operating activities to "contractual liabilities" is 0.5, this implies that the company could repay all of its existing liabilities in 2 years (1 ÷ 0.5 = 2), assuming that:

1. No additional liabilities are incurred.
2. Cash flow from operations continue at current levels.

Debt-to-equity Ratio

The debt-to-equity ratio measures the proportion of funds supplied to the firm by its stockholders as opposed to the funds provided by its creditors. It is computed by dividing total debt by total stockholders' equity.

$$\text{Debt-to-equity Ratio} = \frac{\text{Total Debt}}{\text{Stockholders' Equity}}$$

The debt-to-equity ratio provides a measure of the risk incurred by creditors and common stockholders. Since debt consists of fixed obligations, the larger the debt-to-equity ratio, the greater is the chance that a firm may face a situation in which it is unable to meet its obligations to its creditors. At the same time, however, a high debt-to-equity ratio can increase the rate of return on stockholders' equity through the use of favorable financial leverage. This can occur because interest on debt is fixed in amount, regardless of the amount of earnings. Consequently there is no ideal debt-to-equity ratio. Rather, each investor must define a satisfactory debt-to-equity ratio based on his or her desired degree of risk.

For Dolbey Company the debt-to-equity ratios are calculated as follows:

	20X2	20X1
Total debt	$ 500,000	$ 390,000
Stockholders' equity	$1,100,000	$1,050,000
Debt-to-equity ratio	45.5%	37.1%

The debt-to-equity ratio for PepsiCo and Coca-Cola is as follows:

Year	PepsiCo	Coca-Cola
2002:	$\frac{\$14{,}183 \text{ million}}{\$9{,}291 \text{ million}} = 152.7\%$	$\frac{\$12{,}701 \text{ million}}{\$11{,}800 \text{ million}} = 107.6\%$
2001:	$\frac{\$13{,}021 \text{ million}}{\$8{,}674 \text{ million}} = 150.1\%$	$\frac{\$11{,}051 \text{ million}}{\$11{,}366 \text{ million}} = 97.2\%$

INTEREST COVERAGE RATIOS

The long-term debt ratio and ratio of cash flow from operating activities to "contractual" liabilities (discussed above) provide an indication of the amount of long-term debt held by the company. However, neither provides an indication of the company's ability to assume additional debt. Typically, companies can assume additional debt when:

1. Income is sufficient to repay interest costs incurred during the year as well as other obligations maturing during the year.
2. Cash flows from operating activities are sufficient to repay interest costs incurred during the year as well as other obligations maturing during the year.

Interest coverage ratios measure the company's ability to generate sufficient pre-tax income or cash flows to repay interest costs. Two adjustments are made to net income in determining the numerator of the interest coverage ratio:

1. Interest expense is added back to net income. The purpose of this adjustment is to provide an indication as to what proportion of a company's net income prior to interest expense must be paid to lenders as interest.
2. Income tax expense is added back to net income. This adjustment acknowledges that income taxes are not incurred until the company is profitable after considering interest expense (which, of course, is deductible for income tax purposes).

A limitation of the interest coverage ratio is that it is based on accounting net income. Obviously, the ability to repay interest (and assume additional debt) is based on the organization's ability to generate sufficient cash flows. The interest coverage ratio can also be evaluated using cash flows as opposed to accounting net income, as follows:

$$\frac{\text{Cash Flow from Operations + Cash Paid for Interest + Cash Paid for Taxes}}{\text{Cash Paid for Interest}}$$

Cash paid for taxes and interest can either be obtained from the company's statement of cash flows or supplemental footnote disclosures. As with the accounting net income versions of this ratio, higher levels of the ratio suggest instances where companies have the ability to assume additional debt. A common rule of thumb for interest coverage ratios is that any interest coverage ratio above 2.0 indicates that companies have the capability to assume additional long-term debt.

Like stockholders and investors, bondholders and other long-term creditors are concerned with measures of the profitability of a business. In addition, however, long-term creditors are particularly interested in a firm's ability to meet its interest requirements as they become due and payable. A good indicator of a firm's ability to pay interest is the margin between income and interest payments. A common measure of this margin is the ratio of net income available for interest payments to annual interest expense. This interest coverage ratio, which is referred to as the number of times interest earned, is computed by dividing net income before interest expense and income taxes by the interest requirement for the period. As indicated above, income taxes are added back to net income because interest charges are an expense which is deducted in computing income taxes. Similarly, interest charges are deducted in determining net income that must be added back because the ratio provides a measure of the ability of the firm to pay its fixed interest charges.

$$\frac{\text{Number of Times}}{\text{Interest Earned}} = \frac{\text{Net Income + Interest Expense + Income Taxes}}{\text{Interest Expense}}$$

The computations for Dolbey Company are as follows:

	20X2	20X1
Net income	$ 80,000	$30,000
Add back:		
Income taxes	30,000	12,000
Interest expense	10,000	9,000
Amount available for interest requirements	$120,000	$51,000
Number of times interest earned	12.0	5.7

The increase in the ratio from 5.7 times in 20X1 to 12.0 times in 20X2 appears to be favorable with respect to a long-term creditor of Dolbey Company.

The number of times interest earned for PepsiCo and Coca-Cola is as follows:

Year	PepsiCo	Coca-Cola
2002:	$\dfrac{\$3{,}313 \text{ million} + \$178 \text{ million} + \$1{,}555 \text{ million}}{\$178} = 28.4$ times	$\dfrac{\$3{,}050 \text{ million} + \$199 \text{ million} + \$1{,}523 \text{ million}}{\$199 \text{ million}} = 24.0$ times
2001:	$\dfrac{\$2{,}662 \text{ million} + \$1{,}367 \text{ million} + \$219 \text{ million}}{\$219 \text{ million}} = 19.4$ times	$\dfrac{\$3{,}969 \text{ million} + \$1{,}691 \text{ million} + \$289 \text{ million}}{\$289 \text{ million}} = 20.6$ times

Continued Existence of the Company

A final consideration in evaluating the long-term solvency of a company is whether the company's financial condition has reached such a state that its continued existence is questionable. Altman's Z utilizes various financial statement subtotals to determine an overall score that is used to classify the company in terms of its likelihood of bankruptcy. This score was developed based on the profile of a wide variety of both bankrupt and nonbankrupt companies. The formula for Altman's Z is shown below:

$$\left(0.717 \times \frac{\text{Working Capital}}{\text{Total Assets}}\right) + \left(0.847 \times \frac{\text{Retained Earnings}}{\text{Total Assets}}\right)$$

$$+ \left(3.107 \times \frac{\text{NI before Interest and Taxes}}{\text{Total Assets}}\right)$$

$$+ \left(0.420 \times \frac{\text{Shareholders' Equity}}{\text{Total Liabilities}}\right) + \left(0.998 \times \frac{\text{Sales}}{\text{Total Assets}}\right)$$

Once calculated, Altman's Z scores are assessed as follows:

1. Scores below 1.23 indicate that a company is susceptible to the possibility of bankruptcy.
2. Scores between 1.23 and 2.91 indicate that some uncertainty exists about the ability of the company to continue in existence.
3. Scores above 2.91 indicate that little concerns regarding bankruptcy exist.

Based on the components of Altman's Z, companies are less likely to be susceptible to bankruptcy if they have: (1) higher levels of working capital, retained earnings, net income before interest and taxes, and sales and (2) lower levels of total liabilities.

Analysis for Short-term Creditors

Short-term creditors are concerned with the earnings prospects of a firm. Of primary importance to the short-term creditor, however, is a firm's ability to pay its current debts on a timely basis and to meet its current operating needs. This is often referred to as the current position of the firm.

The Nature of Short-term Liquidity Analysis

Short-term liquidity focuses on the organization's ability to meet its short-term (those due in less than one year) obligations on a timely basis. Short-term liquidity focuses on items classified as current assets and current liabilities. *Current assets* are those items that exist in the form of cash (or will be converted to cash) within a year or the operating cycle, whichever is longer (typically, a year is used). Examples of current assets include:

1. Cash and cash equivalents (short-term investments with a maturity of three months or less, such as Treasury bills).
2. Accounts receivable (sales made to customers for which payment has not been received).
3. Inventories (items held for sale by the organization in the ordinary course of business).
4. Prepayments (situations where expenses such as insurance or rent have been paid in advance for services to be received in the future).

Current liabilities represent obligations that will be paid by the organization within one year or the operating cycle, whichever is longer. Like current assets, the typical benchmark is whether the item will require an outflow of cash within a year. Examples of current liabilities include:

1. Accounts payable (purchases made by the organization from vendors for inventory or supplies that will be paid in the future).
2. Accrued liabilities (amounts owed to employees for salaries and wages, lenders for interest, and taxing authorities for income taxes).
3. Payments required during the current year for long-term debt or capital leases.

Working Capital

An overall measure of the short-term liquidity of the organization is the amount of *working capital* it maintains. *Working capital* is the difference between current assets and current liabilities. Positive working capital indicates that the organization will collect more cash from its current assets during the upcoming year than it must pay for its current liabilities. In contrast, negative working capital indicates that the payments to be made by the organization for current liabilities exceed the collections expected from its current assets.

The ability of a firm to pay its current debts as they fall due depends largely upon the relationship between its current assets and current liabilities. The excess of a firm's current assets over its current liabilities is its working capital.

$$\text{Working Capital} = \text{Current Assets} - \text{Current Liabilities}$$

Adequate working capital enables a firm to meet its current needs and obligations on a timely basis. Excessive working capital may indicate that the firm is not investing sufficiently in productive assets such as new equipment; too little working capital may indicate that the firm may not be able to pay its current bills as these obligations become due. However, an analysis of the components of working capital and the flow of working capital is necessary in order to determine the adequacy of the working capital position of a specific firm.

The working capital for PepsiCo and Coca-Cola is as follows:

Year	PepsiCo	Coca-Cola
2002:	$6,413 million – $6,052 million = $361 million	$7,352 million – $7,341 million = $11 million
2001:	$5,853 million – $4,998 million = $855 million	$7,171 million – $8,429 million = ($1,258) million

CURRENT RATIO

The absolute amount of working capital may be an inadequate measure of a firm's ability to meet its current obligations. As an illustration, consider the following data for two companies:

	Bryant Company	Iverson Company
Current assets	$20,000	$50,000
Current liabilities	10,000	40,000
Working capital	$10,000	$10,000

In this example, both companies have $10,000 of working capital. However, the current assets of Bryant Company can be reduced by 50 percent and still be equal to the current liabilities, while the current assets of Iverson Company can shrink by only 20 percent and remain equal to current liabilities.

Another means of evaluating working capital is to evaluate the relationship between current assets and current liabilities. This ratio is referred to as the *current ratio*.

$$\text{Current Ratio} = \frac{\text{Current Assets}}{\text{Current Liabilities}}$$

The use of the current ratio for the example given above discloses a ratio of 2 to 1 for Bryant Company and 1.25 to 1 for Iverson Company. This clearly indicates the stronger current position of Bryant Company.

The current ratio measures the number of dollars of current assets available to satisfy current liabilities. A basic rule of thumb is that a current ratio of 2.0 or greater (*i.e.,* the organization has two dollars of current assets for each dollar of current liabilities) indicates that the organization is quite healthy (from a short-term liquidity perspective). However, as indicated previously, higher current ratios may indicate the inefficient use of resources, since current assets do not normally generate returns for the organization. For example, accounts receivable and inventories represent "investments" that do not provide a return of interest. Similarly, accounts payable represent liabilities that do not result in a cost to the company for the use of funds. Current ratios less than 1.0 are indicative of potential problems regarding short-term liquidity.

A satisfactory current ratio for a particular firm depends upon the nature of its business. Although short-term creditors generally feel safer as the current ratio increases in amount, this may not be efficient from a business standpoint. For example, a firm with excess cash in relation to its current needs is inefficient since cash is a nonproductive asset. A good measure of the adequacy of a firm's current ratio is often a comparison with the current ratios of similar firms or industry averages.

The current ratios for Dolbey Company are calculated as follows:

	20X2	20X1
Current assets	$400,000	$288,000
Current liabilities	300,000	190,000
Current ratio	1.3 to 1	1.5 to 1

Although the working capital of Dolbey Company increased from $98,000 in 20X1 to $100,000 in 20X2, current assets per dollar of current liabilities declined from $1.50 to $1.30. This is an unfavorable trend from the viewpoint of short-term creditors because the margin of safety has declined.

The current ratio for PepsiCo and Coca-Cola is as follows:

Year	PepsiCo		Coca-Cola	
2002:	$\frac{\$6,413 \text{ million}}{\$6,052 \text{ million}}$	= 1.06 to 1	$\frac{\$7,352 \text{ million}}{\$7,341 \text{ million}}$	= 1.00 to 1
2001:	$\frac{\$5,853 \text{ million}}{\$4,998 \text{ million}}$	= 1.17 to 1	$\frac{\$7,171 \text{ million}}{\$8,429 \text{ million}}$	= 0.85 to 1

Acid-test or Quick Ratio

A limitation of the current ratio is that the collection of cash from some current assets is not always certain. For example, some organizations' inventories may not be easily sold, particularly if subject to obsolescence and spoilage. The *quick* (or *acid-test*) ratio presents a more stringent test of a company's short-term liquidity by including only the most liquid of current assets in the numerator. Quick assets are limited to:

1. Cash and cash equivalents.
2. Accounts receivable.
3. Investments in debt or equity securities with a ready market.

In analyzing the ability of a firm to meet its obligations, the distribution of current assets is important. For example, a firm with a large proportion of cash to current assets is better able to meet its current debts than a firm with a larger proportion of inventories. This is because inventories usually require more time for conversion into cash than do other current assets. Assets with a longer conversion period are usually referred to as less liquid. For this reason, a ratio that excludes the less liquid assets is often used as a supplement to the current ratio. The ratio of the highly liquid current assets—cash, marketable securities, and receivables—to current liabilities is known as the acid-test or quick ratio.

$$\text{Acid-test Ratio} = \frac{\text{Cash + Marketable Securities + Receivables}}{\text{Current Liabilities}}$$

Since Dolbey Company owns no marketable securities, its acid-test ratio is calculated as follows:

	20X2	20X1
Cash	$ 80,000	$ 40,000
Net accounts receivable	100,000	80,000
Total	$180,000	$120,000
Current liabilities	$300,000	$190,000
Acid-test ratio	0.60 to 1	0.63 to 1

In evaluating the acid-test ratio, again the nature of the business must be considered. The 0.60 to 1 acid-test ratio for Dolbey Company in 20X2 may indicate a serious problem as there may not be sufficient liquid assets to meet current liabilities as they become due.

The acid-test ratio for PepsiCo and Coca-Cola is as follows:

Year	PepsiCo		Coca-Cola	
2002:	$\dfrac{\$1{,}638 \text{ million} + \$207 \text{ million} + \$2{,}531 \text{ million}}{\$6{,}052 \text{ million}}$	= 0.72 to 1	$\dfrac{\$2{,}126 \text{ million} + \$219 \text{ million} + \$2{,}097 \text{ million}}{\$7{,}341 \text{ million}}$	= 0.61 to 1
2001:	$\dfrac{\$683 \text{ million} + \$966 \text{ million} + \$2{,}142 \text{ million}}{\$4{,}998 \text{ million}}$	= 0.76 to 1	$\dfrac{\$1{,}866 \text{ million} + \$68 \text{ million} + \$1{,}882 \text{ million}}{\$8{,}429 \text{ million}}$	= 0.45 to 1

Like the current ratio, the quick ratio has a benchmark level that can be used to assess a company's short-term liquidity. Generally, quick ratios of 1 or greater indicate that the organization is healthy from a short-term liquidity perspective; on the other hand, quick ratios of less than 0.50 suggest concern regarding the organization's short-term liquidity.

Both the current and quick ratios provide a "snapshot" of the relative amounts of current assets and current liabilities held by the organization at year-end. However, these ratios do not indicate whether cash flows earned during the upcoming year will be sufficient to allow the organization to meet its current obligations. The *cash flow ratio* (or *ratio of operating cash flows to current liabilities*) provides such an indication and is calculated as follows:

$$\text{Cash Flow Ratio} = \frac{\text{Cash Flow from Operating Activities}}{\text{Current Liabilities}}$$

The cash flow from operations is obtained from the organization's statement of cash flows and should focus exclusively on the organization's operating activities (and not investing or financing activities). A cash flow ratio of 0.40 or greater is characteristic of financially-healthy organizations.

Cash flow ratios for PepsiCo and Coca-Cola are:

Year	PepsiCo		Coca-Cola	
2002:	$\dfrac{\$4{,}627 \text{ million}}{\$6{,}052 \text{ million}}$	= 0.765	$\dfrac{\$4{,}742 \text{ million}}{\$7{,}341 \text{ million}}$	= 0.646
2001:	$\dfrac{\$3{,}820 \text{ million}}{\$4{,}998 \text{ million}}$	= 0.764	$\dfrac{\$4{,}110 \text{ million}}{\$8{,}429 \text{ million}}$	= 0.488

Benchmark levels of these ratios are summarized below:

	Healthy	Adequate	Questionable
Current Ratio	2.00	1.01 - 1.99	1.00 or below
Quick Ratio	1.00	0.51 - 0.99	0.50 or below
Cash Flow Ratio	0.40	0.20 - 0.40	0.20 or below

Analysis of Key Current Assets and Liabilities

The above analyses focus on the level of current assets and liabilities held by the organization but do not address the liquidity of those assets and liabilities. For example, the amount of accounts receivable held by the organization at year-end was included in the current and quick ratios; however, these ratios did not consider the speed at which accounts receivable are collected by the organization from its customers. Similar statements can be made for inventories (how quickly does the organization sell its inventories?) and accounts payable (how quickly does the organization pay its vendors for purchases?).

Analysis of Accounts Receivable

Days of accounts receivable (or *days' sales outstanding*) represent the number of days of sales (or revenues) that is included in the organization's accounts receivable at year-end. Higher levels of days of accounts receivable reflect instances where the collection of accounts receivable is delayed (and *vice versa*). Days of accounts receivable is calculated by dividing average accounts receivable by the average daily sales:

$$\text{Days of Accounts Receivable} = \frac{\text{Average Accounts Receivable}}{\text{Average Daily Sales}}$$

As with average total assets and average common shareholders' equity, average accounts receivable is determined by dividing the sum of beginning accounts receivable and ending accounts receivable by 2. The average daily sales is determined by dividing total sales (or total revenues) by 365 (the number of days in a year).

The rate at which non-cash current assets may be converted into cash is an important determinant of the firm's ability to meet its current obligations. Because neither the current nor the acid-test ratio considers this movement in current assets, short-term creditors should use additional tests in considering the liquidity of significant working capital items.

An approximation of the average time required by a firm to collect its receivables may be determined by first computing the turnover of accounts receivable. Receivables turnover is computed by dividing net credit sales by the average accounts receivable balance. Ideally, a monthly average of receivables should be used, but generally only the balances at the beginning and end-of-the-year are available to the users of the financial statements.

$$\frac{\text{Accounts Receivable}}{\text{Turnover}} = \frac{\text{Net Sales on Account}}{\text{Average Accounts Receivable}}$$

The accounts receivable turnover is an approximation of the number of times accounts receivable were converted into cash during the period. Therefore, the higher the turnover, the more liquid are the firm's receivables.

Accounts receivable turnover of Dolbey Company is computed below. Assume that all sales were made on a credit basis and that only the beginning and end-of-the-year balances of receivables are available.

	20X2	20X1
Net sales on account	$2,000,000	$1,500,000
Net receivables:		
Beginning of year	$ 80,000	$ 70,000
End-of-the-year	100,000	80,000
Total	$ 180,000	$ 150,000
Average	$ 90,000	$ 75,000
Accounts receivable turnover per year	22.2 times	20.0 times

This increase in the receivables turnover for Dolbey Company during 20X2 indicates that the average collection period for receivables has decreased as a result of more successful collection practices or a change in credit policies, or a combination of both factors.

The accounts receivable turnover for PepsiCo and Coca-Cola is as follows:

Year	PepsiCo		Coca-Cola	
2002:	$\dfrac{\$25{,}112 \text{ million}}{(\$2{,}531 \text{ million} + \$2{,}142 \text{ million})/2}$	= 10.8 times	$\dfrac{\$19{,}564 \text{ million}}{(\$2{,}097 \text{ million} + \$1{,}882 \text{ million})/2}$	= 9.8 times
2001:	$\dfrac{\$23{,}512 \text{ million}}{(\$2{,}129 \text{ million} + \$2{,}142 \text{ million})/2}$	= 11.0 times	$\dfrac{\$17{,}545 \text{ million}}{(\$1{,}882 \text{ million} + \$1{,}757 \text{ million})/2}$	= 9.6 times

The receivables turnover may be used to determine the average collection period, which can be readily compared with the firm's credit terms. The average number of days to collect receivables is computed by dividing 365 days by the receivables turnover.

$$\text{Average Number of Days to Collect Receivables} = \frac{365 \text{ Days}}{\text{Accounts Receivable Turnover}}$$

If the average number of days required to collect receivables significantly exceeds the credit terms of the firm, the credit department may be ineffective in its credit granting and collecting activities.

The average number of days to collect receivables is calculated for the Dolbey Company as follows:

	20X1	20X2
Days in year	365 days	365 days
Receivables turnover	22.2 times	20.0 times
Average number of days to collect receivables	16.4 days	18.3 days

The average collection period for PepsiCo and Coca-Cola is as follows:

Year	PepsiCo	Coca-Cola
2002:	$\dfrac{365}{10.8}$ = 33.8 days	$\dfrac{365}{9.8}$ = 37.3 days
2001:	$\dfrac{365}{11.0}$ = 33.2 days	$\dfrac{365}{9.6}$ = 38.0 days

Analysis of Inventories

Procedures similar to those used for evaluating receivables may be employed in evaluating the inventories of a firm. An indication of the liquidity of inventories is obtained by determining the relationship between the cost of goods sold and the average balance of inventories on hand during a period. Cost of goods sold is used because it represents the cost (rather than the selling price) of goods that have been sold from the inventories which were available for sale during the period.

Days of inventory represents the number of days of sales that is included in the organization's inventory. From a theoretical perspective, days of inventory provides the organization with an indication of how many days they could continue in operation without purchasing additional inventory. Higher days of inventory reflect instances where the organization has a higher amount of cash invested in its inventories. Days of inventory is calculated by dividing average inventories by the average daily cost of goods sold. Average inventories and average daily cost of goods sold are calculated in much the same manner as average accounts receivable and average sales in the calculation of days of accounts receivable.

Inventory turnover is calculated by dividing cost of goods sold by the average inventory. Again, if possible, monthly figures should be used to determine average inventory. Usually, however, only the beginning and end-of-the-year inventory balances are available.

$$\text{Inventory Turnover} = \frac{\text{Cost of Goods Sold}}{\text{Average Inventory}}$$

A low inventory turnover may indicate management inefficiency in that excess cash has been committed to the company's investment in inventory. Although inventories are necessary to meet the demands of a firm, there are advantages in maintaining the investment in inventory at the minimum levels necessary to service customers, thus minimizing carrying costs, risks of loss, and obsolescence.

Assuming that only the beginning and ending inventories are available, the computation of inventory turnover for Dolbey Company is as follows:

	20X2	20X1
Cost of goods sold	$1,400,000	$1,080,000
Inventory:		
Beginning of the year	$ 160,000	$ 110,000
End-of-the-year	200,000	160,000
Total	$ 360,000	$ 270,000
Average inventory	$ 180,000	$ 135,000
Inventory turnover	7.8 times	8 times

It appears that the trend of the inventory turnover for Dolbey Company is somewhat unfavorable, since inventories were turned over more slowly in 20X2 than in 20X1. Again, the analyst would obtain additional information before making a definitive judgment.

The inventory turnover for PepsiCo and Coca-Cola is as follows:

Year	PepsiCo		Coca-Cola	
2002:	$\frac{\$11{,}497 \text{ million}}{(\$1{,}342 \text{ million} + \$1{,}310 \text{ million})/2}$	= 8.7 times	$\frac{\$7{,}105 \text{ million}}{(\$1{,}294 \text{ million} + \$1{,}055 \text{ million})/2}$	= 6.1 times
2001:	$\frac{\$10{,}750 \text{ million}}{(\$1{,}310 \text{ million} + \$1{,}192 \text{ million})/2}$	= 8.6 times	$\frac{\$6{,}044 \text{ million}}{(\$1{,}055 \text{ million} + \$1{,}066 \text{ million})/2}$	= 5.7 times

The inventory turnover may be used to determine the number of days' supply in inventory.

$$\frac{\text{Average Number of Days'}}{\text{Supply in Inventory}} = \frac{365 \text{ Days}}{\text{Inventory Turnover}}$$

The average number of days' supply in inventory is calculated for the Dolbey Company as follows:

	20X2	20X1
Days in year	365 days	365 days
Inventory turnover	7.8 times	8 times
Average number of days' supply in inventory	46.8 days	45.6 days

The number of day's supply in inventory for PepsiCo and Coca-Cola is as follows:

Year	PepsiCo	Coca-Cola
2002:	$\frac{365}{8.7}$ = 42.0 days	$\frac{365}{6.1}$ = 59.8 days
2001:	$\frac{365}{8.6}$ = 42.4 days	$\frac{365}{5.7}$ = 64.0 days

Days of accounts payable indicates the speed with which the organization pays its vendors for purchases made on a credit basis. Higher levels of days of accounts payable indicate that the organization is effectively utilizing interest-free financing by delaying the payment of its obligations (assuming, of course, that the organization is not past due on its payments). Days of accounts payable is determined by dividing average accounts payable by average daily purchases.

$$\text{Days of Accounts Payable} = \frac{\text{Average Accounts Payable}}{\text{Average Daily Purchases}}$$

Average accounts payable and average daily purchases are calculated in much the same manner as average accounts receivable and average sales in the calculation of days of accounts receivable. A difficulty in calculating average purchases is that a total amount of "purchases" is not provided in the organization's financial statements. Recall that the basic inventory equation can be stated as:

Beginning Inventory + Purchases − Ending Inventory = Cost of Goods Sold

Restating this equation, purchases can be calculated as:

Purchases = Cost of Goods Sold + Ending Inventory − Beginning Inventory

As with days of accounts receivable and days of inventory, an alternative calculation of days accounts payable begins by calculating the number of times a company "turns over" (or pays) its accounts payable. *Accounts payable turnover* is calculated by dividing purchases by average accounts payable, as shown below:

$$\text{Accounts Payable Turnover} = \frac{\text{Purchases}}{\text{Average Accounts Payable}}$$

Then, the days of accounts payable is calculated by dividing 365 (the number of days in a year) by the accounts payable turnover calculated as above.

The *cash conversion cycle* represents the organization's net position as an interest free lender or interest-free borrower. This measure is determined as follows:

Days of Accounts Receivable
+ Days of Inventory
− Days of Accounts Payable
= Cash Conversion Cycle

Longer cash conversion cycles indicate that the organization has higher working capital requirements, since more working capital is tied up in accounts receivable and inventory. If the cash conversion cycle is positive, the organization is a net interest-free lender. In contrast, a negative cash conversion cycle indicates that the organization is holding a greater level of accounts payable than the combined level of accounts receivable and inventory and is a net interest-free borrower.

A final measure of an organization's short-term liquidity is the extent of working capital (current assets minus current liabilities) it maintains. A way of measuring the sufficiency of an organization's working capital is by expressing it in terms of the number of *days of cash needs* represented by this working capital. This involves a two-step process. First, the average daily cash needs are determined by dividing operating expenses (other than depreciation) by 365. Depreciation is excluded, since this expense does not require an outlay of cash. This measure is referred to as the *cash burn rate* and is calculated as follows:

$$\text{Cash Burn Rate} = \frac{\text{Operating Expenses (Other than Depreciation)}}{365 \text{ days}}$$

Then, the extent of working capital is determined by dividing the net working capital by the cash burn rate. This measure indicates the number of days of expenses that could be paid by the organization's current level of working capital. Typically, organizations attempt to maintain sufficient working capital to meet two weeks (14 days) of expenses. The days of working capital is calculated as follows:

$$\text{Days of Expenses} = \frac{\text{Current Assets} - \text{Current Liabilities}}{\text{Cash Burn Rate}}$$

Operating Cycle

The average period from the purchase of inventory to the collection of sales of the product to customers may be calculated by adding together the average number of days' supply in inventory and the average number of days to collect receivables. For Dolbey Company, this calculation is as follows:

	20X2	20X1
Average number of days' supply in inventory	46.8 days	45.6 days
Average number of days to collect receivables	16.4 days	18.3 days
Operating cycle	63.2 days	63.9 days

Year	PepsiCo	Coca-Cola
2002:	33.8 days + 42.0 days = 75.8 days	37.3 days + 59.8 days = 97.1 days
2001:	33.2 days + 42.4 days = 75.6 days	38.0 days + 64.0 days = 102.0 days

Interpretation of Analyses

The user must exercise considerable caution in the use of ratios in order to analyze the financial statements of a business enterprise. Some of the problems inherent in ratio analysis are summarized below:

1. Comparisons of items for different periods or for different companies may not be valid if different accounting practices have been used. For example, one firm may use straight-line depreciation and the FIFO inventory method while a similar company may use accelerated depreciation and LIFO for its inventories.

2. Financial statements represent only one source of financial information concerning a firm and its environment. Consequently, other information not disclosed in financial statements may have an impact on the evaluation of the statements.

3. Financial statements are not adjusted either for changes in market values or in the general price level. This may seriously affect comparability of firms over time.

4. As ratio analysis has increased in popularity, there has sometimes been a tendency to develop ratios that have little or no significance. A meaningful ratio can be developed only from items which have a logical relationship.

All of the ratios and measurements developed in this chapter need not be used as input in a particular decision. In determining the financial strengths and weaknesses of a particular firm, relevant measurements must be selected, developed, and interpreted in view of the conditions relating to the business.

SUMMARY

Financial statements provide a variety of external users with essential data regarding a firm's financial position and the results of its operations. However, most users of financial statements must make a detailed analysis and interpretation of the data presented to obtain evaluative information which is useful in making decisions.

The actual evaluative techniques used by an individual vary according to personal preference and the nature of the individual's relationship to the reporting firm. Most techniques involve some type of comparison with related data. The data may relate to the firm's past performance, to similar or competing firms, or to an industry average. Comparisons are often expressed in terms of percentage or ratios, although there are certain problems inherent in ratio analysis.

Firms may present a horizontal or vertical analysis of relevant data along with their regular financial statements. Horizontal analysis usually presents both the dollar and percentage changes for corresponding items for two or more accounting periods. Vertical analysis discloses the percentage relationship of an individual item or component of a single financial statement to an aggregate total included in the same statement. Presentation of these analyses may be facilitated by the use of common-size statements in which all items are stated in terms of percentages and ratios.

Since current and potential stockholders are primarily interested in earning an acceptable return on their investments through increases in the market price of the stock and by dividends, their analyses focus on the company's record of earnings. Examples of earnings relationships of interest to the stockholder-investor are the rate of return on total assets, the rate of return on common stockholders' equity, the earnings per share of common stock, and the price-earnings ratio on common stock.

Stockholders and creditors may be interested in the debt-to-equity ratio as a measure of the risk incurred by both. In addition, bondholders and other long-term creditors are concerned with the firm's ability to meet its interest requirements as they become payable. A common measure of such ability is the ratio of net income available for interest payments to annual interest expense. This measure is generally referred to as the number of times interest is earned.

Short-term creditors are primarily interested in the firm's ability to pay its current debt on a timely basis and to meet its current operating needs. Although the absolute amount of working capital available to a firm may provide useful information to a creditor, the ratio of current assets to current liabilities (referred to as the current ratio) is generally thought to provide better evaluative data. If only the more liquid current assets are used in ratio, it is referred to as an acid-test ratio. Other evaluation methods used by short-term creditors include the analysis of accounts receivable and the analysis of inventories. A summary of the financial ratios discussed in the chapter are presented in Illustration 9.

Illustration 9
Summary of Financial Ratios

Ratio	Method of Computation	Meaning
1. Analysis for Common Stockholders		
a. Rate of return on total assets (ROA)	$\dfrac{\text{Net Income (after taxes)} + \text{Interest Expense}}{\text{Average Total Assets During the Year}}$	Measures management's ability to earn a return on the firm's assets
b. Asset turnover	$\dfrac{\text{Net Sales}}{\text{Average Total Assets During the Year}}$	Measures the efficiency of use of the firm's assets
c. Return on sales	$\dfrac{\text{Net Income (after taxes)} + \text{Interest Expense}}{\text{Net Sales}}$	Measures the rate of earnings on each dollar of net sales
d. Gross profit ratio	$\dfrac{\text{Gross Profit}}{\text{Sales Revenues}}$	Measures the rate of profit on net sales
e. Rate of return on common stockholders' equity (ROCE)	$\dfrac{\text{Net Income (after taxes)} - \text{Preferred Dividends}}{\text{Average Common Stockholders' Equity}}$	Measures the firm's ability to earn a profit for the common stockholders
f. Financial structure leverage	$\dfrac{\text{Average Total Assets}}{\text{Average Common Shareholders' Equity}}$	Measures the relative proportion of assets from shareholders
g. Common earnings leverage	$\dfrac{\text{Net Income} - \text{Preferred Dividends}}{\text{Net Income} + \text{Interest Expense}}$	Measures the percentage of net income available for distribution to common shareholders
h. Earnings quality	$\dfrac{\text{Cash Flow from Operating Activities}}{\text{Net Income}}$	Measures the collectibility of net income
i. Earnings per share	$\dfrac{\text{Net Income} - \text{Preferred Dividends}}{\text{Weighted Average Number of Common Stock Shares Outstanding}}$	Measures the earnings of each share of common stock
j. Price-earnings (PE) ratio	$\dfrac{\text{Market Price per Share of Common Stock}}{\text{Earnings per Share}}$	Measures the relationship of the market value of common stock to the earnings of the firm on a per share basis
k. Price ratios	$\dfrac{\text{Market Price per Share of Common Stock}}{\text{"Measure" per Share}}$	Expresses stock price in terms of measures (earnings, book value, sales, operating cash flows) on a per share basis
l. Dividend yield	$\dfrac{\text{Common Dividends per Share}}{\text{Market Price per Share}}$	Measures return provided to investors in dividends
2. Analysis for Long-term Creditors		
a. Long-term debt ratio	$\dfrac{\text{Long-Term Debt}}{\text{Total Assets}}$	Measures relationship of long-term debt to assets
b. Cash flow from operations to "contractual liabilities"	$\dfrac{\text{Cash Flow from Operating Activities}}{\text{Average Current Liabilities} + \text{Average Long-term "Contractual Liabilities"}}$	Measures the extent of long-term debt
c. Debt-to-equity ratio	$\dfrac{\text{Total Debt}}{\text{Stockholders' Equity}}$	Measures the relative amount of total resources provided by creditors and owners
d. Cash interest coverage ratio	$\dfrac{\text{Cash Flow from Operations} + \text{Cash Paid for Interest} + \text{Cash Paid for Taxes}}{\text{Cash Paid for Interest}}$	Measures the ability of the firm to pay fixed interest charges in cash
e. Number of times interest earned	$\dfrac{\text{Net Income} + \text{Interest Expense} + \text{Income Taxes}}{\text{Interest Expense}}$	Measures the ability of a firm to pay fixed interest charges from pretax earnings
f. Altman's Z Score	See page 12-20	Measures the firm's susceptibility to bankruptcy

Illustration 9
continued

Ratio	Method of Computation	Meaning
3. Analysis for Short-term Creditors		
a. Working capital	Current Assets − Current Liabilities	Measures the ability to pay short-term debt from current assets
b. Current ratio	$\dfrac{\text{Current Assets}}{\text{Current Liabilities}}$	Measures the ability to pay short-term debt from current assets
c. Acid-test (quick) ratio	$\dfrac{\text{Cash + Marketable Securities + Receivables}}{\text{Current Liabilities}}$	Measures the ability to pay short-term debt from a firm's most liquid assets
d. Cash flow ratio	$\dfrac{\text{Cash Flow from Operating Activities}}{\text{Current Liabilities}}$	Measures whether cash flows from operations will be sufficient to meet current obligations
e. Days of accounts receivable	$\dfrac{\text{Average Accounts Receivable}}{\text{Average Daily Sales}}$	Measures the number of days of sales in receivables
f. Accounts receivable turnover	$\dfrac{\text{Net Sales on Account}}{\text{Average Accounts Receivable}}$	Measures the number of times accounts receivable were converted into cash during the period
g. Average number of days to collect receivables	$\dfrac{365 \text{ Days}}{\text{Accounts Receivable Turnover}}$	Measures the average collection period of receivables
h. Days of inventory	$\dfrac{\text{Average Inventory}}{\text{Average Daily Cost of Goods Sold}}$	Measures the number of days sales in inventories
i. Inventory turnover	$\dfrac{\text{Cost of Goods Sold}}{\text{Average Inventory}}$	Measures the liquidity of inventory
j. Average number of days' supply in inventory	$\dfrac{365 \text{ Days}}{\text{Inventory Turnover}}$	Measures the average days' supply in inventory
k. Days of accounts payable	$\dfrac{\text{Average Accounts Payable}}{\text{Average Daily Purchases}}$	Measures the speed with which the firm pays its vendors
l. Accounts payable turnover	$\dfrac{\text{Purchases}}{\text{Average Accounts Payable}}$	Measures the number of times accounts payable are paid annually
m. Cash conversion cycle	Days of Accounts Receivable + Days of Inventory − Days of Accounts Payable	Measures the firm's position as an interest free borrower or lender
n. Cash burn rate	$\dfrac{\text{Operating Expenses (Other than Depreciation)}}{365}$	Measures the daily cash requirement for operating expenses
o. Days of expenses	$\dfrac{\text{Current Assets − Current Liabilities}}{\text{Cash Burn Rate}}$	Measures the number of days of cash needs in working capital
p. Operating cycle	Average number of days to collect receivables + average number of days' supply in inventory	Measures the time from the purchase of inventory to the collection of the proceeds from its sale

Key Definitions

Accounts payable turnover—purchases divided by average accounts payable. Measures the number of times accounts payable were paid.

Accounts receivable turnover—an approximation of the number of times accounts receivable were converted into cash during the period. It is defined as net sales on account divided by average accounts receivable.

Acid-test ratio—a measure of a firm's ability to pay its current liabilities as they become due with its more liquid current assets. It is usually the ratio of cash, marketable securities, and receivables to total current liabilities.

Altman's Z—classifies a company's likelihood of bankruptcy.

Asset turnover—sales divided by average total assets. A measure of the firm's ability to utilize assets in generating revenues.

Average collection period—a measure of the average time required by a firm to collect a receivable. The collection period is computed by dividing 365 days by the receivables turnover.

Average number of days' supply in inventory—an approximation of the number of days' supply in the inventories held.

Cash burn rate—operating expenses (other than depreciation) divided by 365. Measures the average daily cash needs.

Cash conversion cycle—days of accounts receivable plus days of inventories minus days of accounts payable. Measures the firm's net position as interest-free lender or borrower.

Cash flow from operations to "contractual liabilities"—cash flow from operating activities divided by average current liabilities plus average long-term contractual liabilities. An indication of the ability to repay existing liabilities from operating cash.

Cash flow ratio—cash flow from operating activities divided by current liabilities. Measures the ability to meet current obligations from current operating cash flows.

Common earnings leverage—net income less preferred dividends divided by net income plus interest expense. Measures income available for distribution to common shareholders.

Common-size statements—in common-size financial statements, all items are stated in terms of percentages or ratios.

Current ratio—measures a firm's ability to pay current liabilities as they become due. It is defined as the ratio of current assets to current liabilities.

Days of accounts payable—average accounts payable divided by average daily purchases. Also, 365 divided by the accounts payable turnover indicates the speed in which vendors are paid for purchases.

Days of accounts receivable—average accounts receivable divided by average daily sales. Measures the number of days' revenues in year-end receivables.

Days of expense—working capital (current assets less current liabilities) divided by the cash burn rate. Measures the sufficiency of working capital.

Debt-to-equity ratio—measures the proportion of funds supplied by stockholders as opposed to the funds provided by creditors. It is computed by dividing total debt by total stockholders' equity.

Dividend yield—common dividends per share divided by the market price per share. Measures the return to investors in the form of dividends.

Earnings quality—cash flow from operating activities divided by net income. Measures the collectibility of net income.

Earnings per share—net income less preferred dividends divided by the average number of common shares outstanding. Measures each common share of stock's "share" of net income.

Financial structure leverage—average total assets divided by average common shareholders' equity. A measure of the relative sources of funds provided to the entity.

Gross profit (margin)—sales less cost of goods sold.

Gross profit (margin) ratio—gross profit divided by sales revenue. Measures the ability to "mark up" inventory for sale.

Horizontal analysis—the analysis of the increase or decrease in a given financial statement item over two or more accounting periods..

Interest coverage ratios—measures the ability to pay interest expense. Uses income or cash flows as a basis.

Inventory turnover—gives an indication of the liquidity of inventories. Its computation involves dividing cost of goods sold by the average inventory.

Long-term debt ratio—long-term debt divided by total assets. A measure of the company's long-term debt.

Number of times interest earned—this measure of a firm's ability to pay interest is computed by dividing net income before interest expense and income taxes by the interest expense.

Operating cycle—the time from the purchase of inventory to the collection of the proceeds from the sale.

Price-earnings (PE) ratio—the current market price of a share of stock divided by the earnings per share.

Price ratio—market price per share divided by a "measure" (net income, sales, net assets, cash flow from operating activities, etc.). An approximate measure of what investors are willing to pay for each dollar of the "measure."

Rate of return on common stockholders' equity (ROCE)—this measure of the firm's ability to earn a profit for its common stockholders is computed by dividing net income after taxes and preferred dividends by the average common stockholders' equity.

Rate of return on total assets (ROA)—this measure of the ability of the firm's management to earn a return on the assets without regard to variations in the method of financing is computed by dividing net income plus interest expense by the average investment in assets during the year.

Ratio—an expression of the relationship of one numerical item to another.

Ratio analysis—the analysis of items in financial statements expressing the relationship of one numerical item to another.

Return on sales—net income plus interest expense divided by net sales. Measures profitability relative to sales.

Users of financial statements—lenders, investors and short-term creditors.

Vertical analysis—the percentage relationship between an individual item or a component of a single financial statement to an aggregate total in that statement.

Working capital—current assets less current liabilities. Measures the ability to pay current debt as it becomes due.

QUESTIONS

1. How is financial statement analysis related to the needs of the various users of financial statements?

2. Distinguish between vertical analysis and horizontal analysis. What are common-size statements?

3. What is the Altman's Z score used for?

4. How are each of the following computed?

    a. Rate of Return on Total Assets.
    b. Rate of Return on Common Stockholders' Equity.
    c. Earnings per Share of Common Stock.
    d. Price-earnings Ratio on Common Stock.
    e. Debt-to-equity Ratio.
    f. Number of Times Interest Earned.
    g. Current Ratio.
    h. Acid-test Ratio.
    i. Accounts Receivable Turnover.
    j. Average Number of Days to Collect Receivables.
    k. Inventory Turnover.

5. Each of the ratios (in Question 4 above) are utilized by one user group more than others. Indicate the group each item is utilized most by (1) common shareholders (or investors), (2) long-term creditors, or (3) short-term creditors.

6. What are the principal limitations that should be considered in evaluating ratios? What are the most commonly used standards against which to measure the position of a particular firm? What are the weaknesses inherent in these standards?

7. Business corporations usually provide comparative statements in their annual reports. What is a comparative statement? How do they enhance the usefulness of financial information?

8. What will be the effect (increase, decrease, none) on the rate of return on assets of each of the following?

    a. Cash purchase of a new machine.
    b. Increase in the tax rate.
    c. Cash payment of an account payable.
    d. Cash sale of a fully depreciated machine.

9. What is indicated if the average number of days to collect receivables significantly exceeds the credit terms of the firm? What is earnings quality?

10. What is financial structure leverage? What does common earnings leverage measure?

11. When percentage changes are given in comparative statements for more than two years, there are two methods for selecting the base year. What are they? Which of these methods makes comparison of percentage changes over several years more difficult? Why?

12. What is a "cash burn" rate? How is it used?

Exercises and Problems

13. *Preparation of common size income statement.* The comparative income statement for Joe Company and John Company is presented below.

Joe Company and John Company
*Comparative Income Statement
for the Year Ending December 31, 20X1*

	Joe Company	John Company
Net sales	$500,000	$250,000
Cost of goods sold	350,000	150,000
Gross profit on sales	$150,000	$100,000
Operating expenses:		
Selling expense	$ 50,000	$ 10,000
Administrative expense	10,000	7,000
Total operating expenses	$ 60,000	$ 17,000
Operating income	$ 90,000	$ 83,000
Interest expense	30,000	5,000
Income before taxes	$ 60,000	$ 78,000
Income taxes	20,000	25,000
Net income	$ 40,000	$ 53,000

Required:

Using the above information, prepare a common-size statement comparing income data for Joe Company and John Company.

14. *Preparation of income statement.* Following is the condensed common-size income statement for Francis Co.:

Francis Company
Condensed Common-Size Income Statement
for the Year Ended December 31, 20X2

Net sales	100.0%
Cost of goods sold	68.0
Gross profit on sales	32.0%
Operating expenses:	
Selling expense	16.0%
Administrative expense	6.0
Total operating expense	22.0%
Operating income	10.0%
Interest expense	0.5
Income before income taxes	9.5%
Income taxes	2.0
Net income	7.5%

Net sales for the period were $3,000,000.

Required:

Prepare the income statement for Francis Company.

15. *Balance sheet preparation.* Using the information given, complete the balance sheet below.

   a. The "quick" ratio is 2:1.
   b. Note payable are long-term liabilities and are four times the dollar amount of the marketable securities.
   c. Accounts receivable are $2,000 and are one-half of the "quick" assets, one-fourth of the current assets, and equal to plant and equipment.
   d. Total stockholders' equity is equal to the working capital and contributed capital is twice the dollar amount of the net accumulation of earnings.

Assets		Liabilities and Stockholders' Equity	
Cash	_____	Accounts payable	_____
Marketable securities	_____	Note payable	_____
Accounts receivable	_____		
Inventories	_____	Capital stock	_____
Plant and equipment	_____	Retained earnings	_____

16. *Horizontal and vertical balance sheet analysis.* Given below are the balance sheets for Meyers, Inc., for 20X1 and 20X2.

Meyers, Inc.
Comparative Balance Sheet
December 31, 20X2 and 20X1

	20X2	20X1
Assets:		
Current assets:		
Cash	$ 20,000	$ 17,000
Accounts receivable (net)	45,000	60,000
Inventory	8,000	6,000
Prepaid expenses	7,000	5,000
Total current assets	$ 80,000	$ 88,000
Land	120,000	70,000
Buildings (net)	200,000	100,000
Total assets	$400,000	$258,000
Liabilities:		
Current liabilities:		
Accounts payable	$ 10,000	$ 7,000
Taxes payable	9,000	3,000
Total current liabilities	$ 19,000	$ 10,000
Bonds payable	115,000	70,000
Total liabilities	$134,000	$ 80,000
Stockholders' Equity:		
Common stock ($5 par)	$ 50,000	$ 45,000
Additional paid-in capital	125,000	80,000
Retained earnings	91,000	53,000
Total liabilities and stockholders' equity	$400,000	$258,000

Required:

Prepare a horizontal and vertical analysis of the balance sheets of Meyers, Inc. for 20X1 and 20X2.

17. *Calculation of general financial ratios.* Strider Company is attempting to measure the efficiency of its operations for the year 20X1. Strider's accountant has asked you to assist her in making this determination. The following information is available from the financial records of the company:

Cash inflow from operating activities	$ 85,000
Interest expense	12,000
Net income	60,000
Net sales	160,000
Stockholders' equity, January 1	300,000
Stockholders' equity, December 31	240,000
Total assets, January 1	480,000
Total assets, December 31	360,000

Strider Company has no preferred stock. Calculate and comment on each of the following ratios:

   a. Asset turnover
   b. Return on sales
   c. Financial structure leverage
   d. Common earnings leverage
   e. Earnings quality
   f. Rate of return on total assets

18. *Calculation of general financial ratios.* Dante Corporation is concerned with its cash flows and has decided to analyze its current operations. The following information is available from the financial statements of Dante for the year ending 20X0:

Cash inflow from operating activities	$ 65,000
Cash paid for interest	8,000
Cash paid for taxes	38,000
Current assets	140,000
Current liabilities	95,000
Depreciation expense	4,000
Inventories	20,000
Operating expenses	34,000
Prepaid expenses	12,000

Calculate and comment on each of the following ratios:

a. Cash interest coverage
b. Cash burn rate
c. Days of expenses
d. Current ratio
e. Acid-test ratio
f. Working capital

19. *Calculation of general financial ratios.* Tundra Corporation is analyzing its current assets and current liabilities to determine if there are any areas in which improvements can be made for 20X2. The following information is available from the financial statements of Tundra for the year ending 20X1:

Accounts payable, December 31	$ 25,000
Accounts payable, January 1	32,000
Accounts receivable, December 31	42,000
Accounts receivable, January 1	35,000
Current assets	400,000
Current liabilities	300,000
Cost of goods sold	270,000
Net sales	345,000
Purchases	300,000
Inventory, December 31	72,000
Inventory, January 1	60,000

Calculate and comment on each of the following ratios:

a. Current ratio
b. Days of accounts receivable
c. Accounts receivable turnover
d. Average number of days to collect receivables
e. Days of accounts payable
f. Accounts payable turnover
g. Days of inventory
h. Inventory turnover
i. Average number of days supply in inventory
j. Cash conversion cycle
k. Operating cycle

20. *Effect of liability payment on working capital and current ratio.* Carol Company pays a current liability.

Required:

How will this cash payment affect Carol's:

a. Working capital
b. Current ratio

21. *Calculation of general financial ratios.* The following information was taken from the financial statements of Maker Company on December 31, 20X2.

Cash	$ 75,000
Accounts receivable	125,000
Inventory	100,000
Fixed assets (net)	500,000
	$800,000
Accounts payable	$100,000
Bond payable (due December 31, 20X2)	300,000
Common stock ($10 par)	300,000
Retained earnings	100,000
	$800,000

Net income for 20X2 was $50,000.

Required:

Compute the following:

a. Current ratio
b. Working capital
c. Acid-test ratio
d. Earnings per share
e. Debt-to-equity ratio
f. Long-term debt ratio

22. *Calculation of general financial ratios.* The following are financial statements of ZYX Corporation for 20X1.

ZYX Corporation
Balance Sheet
December 31, 20X1

Assets:

Current assets:		
Cash	$100,000	
Accounts receivable (net)	200,000	
Prepaid expenses	50,000	
Inventory	110,000	
Total current assets		$460,000
Fixed assets:		
Land	$ 50,000	
Machinery (net)	100,000	
Building (net)	250,000	
Total fixed assets		400,000
Total assets		$860,000

Liabilities and Stockholders' Equity:

Current liabilities:		
Accounts payable	$ 50,000	
Wages payable	5,000	
Interest payable	2,000	
Total current liabilities		$ 57,000
Bonds payable (due December 31, 20X6)		200,000
Total liabilities		$257,000
Common stock ($2 par value)		400,000
Retained earnings		203,000
Total liabilities and stockholders' equity		$860,000

ZYX Corporation
Income Statement
for the Year Ended December 31, 20X1

Sales (net)		$1,000,000
Cost of goods sold:		
Beginning inventory	$ 90,000	
Purchases	600,000	
Goods available for sale	$690,000	
Ending inventory	110,000	
Cost of goods sold		580,000
Gross profit on sales		$ 420,000
Operating expenses:		
Sales salaries expense	$ 75,000	
Depreciation expense	20,000	
Insurance expense	5,000	
Interest expense	10,000	
Total operating expense		110,000
Income before taxes		$ 310,000
Income taxes		100,000
Net income		$ 210,000
January 1, 20X0 data:		
Common shares outstanding	200,000	

Required:

Compute the following:

a. Earnings per Share of Common Stock
b. Debt-to-equity Ratio
c. Number of Times Interest Earned
d. Current Ratio
e. Acid-test (Quick) Ratio
f. Inventory Turnover
g. Gross Profit Ratio
h. Financial Structure Leverage
i. Cash Burn Rate
j. Days of Expenses

23. *Calculation of general financial ratios.* The following information applies to River Road Products.

	20X5	20X4
Net Sales	$1,260,000	$780,000
Net Income before Interest and Taxes	330,000	255,000
Net Income after Taxes	166,500	189,000
Bond Interest Expense	27,000	24,000
Stockholders' Equity, December 31		
(20X3: $600,000)	915,000	705,000
Common Stock, Par $50, December 31	780,000	690,000

Average number of shares outstanding were 15,600 for 20X5 and 13,800 for 20X4.

Required:

Compute the following ratios for River Road for 20X5 and 20X4.

a. Number of times bond interest was earned.
b. Earnings per share based on the number of shares outstanding on December 31.
c. Price-earnings ratio (Market prices: 20X5 – $96 per share; 20X4 – $ 116 per share).
d. Return on common stockholders' equity.

24. *Calculation of general financial ratios.* Below are the financial statements of McKeown Company.

	20X2	20X1
Revenues:		
Net Sales	$315,000	$262,500
Other Revenues	6,000	7,000
Total Revenues	$321,000	$269,500
Expenses:		
Cost of Goods Sold	$189,000	$154,875
Selling Expenses	27,000	24,000
General and Administrative Expenses	16,000	15,000
Depreciation Expense	5,000	5,000
Interest Expense	4,000	4,500
Income Tax Expense (40%)	32,000	26,450
Total Expenses	$273,000	$229,825
Earnings from Continuing Operations before Extraordinary Items	$ 48,000	$ 39,675
Extraordinary Gain (net of $8,000 tax)	6,000	0
Net Earnings	$ 54,000	$ 39,675
Assets:		
Current Assets:		
Cash	$ 6,500	$ 11,500
Marketable Securities	1,000	1,500
Accounts Receivable	50,000	47,500
Inventories	150,000	145,000
Prepaid Expenses	5,000	2,500
Total Current Assets	$212,500	$208,000
Plant and Equipment (net)	157,000	157,000
Intangibles	30,500	0
Total Assets	$400,000	$365,000
Liabilities and Stockholders' Equity:		
Liabilities:		
Current Liabilities		
Accounts Payable	$ 60,000	$ 81,500
Other	25,000	22,500
Total Current Liabilities	$ 85,000	$104,000
Bonds Payable	100,000	100,000
Total Liabilities	$185,000	$204,000
Stockholders' Equity:		
Common Stock ($3 par)	$150,000	$150,000
Paid-In Capital in Excess of Par	20,000	20,000
Retained Earnings	45,000	(9,000)
Total Stockholders' Equity	$215,000	$161,000
Total Liabilities and Stockholders' Equity	$400,000	$365,000

Required:

Calculate the following ratios for 20X1 and 20X2. When insufficient data prohibits the computation of averages, year-end balances should be used in the calculations.

a. Return on equity
b. Earnings per share
c. Price-earnings ratio (market price at end of 20X2 and 20X1 was $5.94 and $4.77, respectively)
d. Book value per share of common stock
e. Times interest earned
f. Working capital
g. Current ratio
h. Acid-test ratio

i. Accounts receivable turnover
   j. Inventory turnover
   k. Debt to equity ratio
   l. Gross profit ratio
   m. Financial structure leverage
   n. Common earnings leverage
   o. Cash burn rate
   p. Days of expenses

25. *Calculation of working capital.* Sam Company has working capital of $400,000 and a current ratio of 2.5 on May 31. On June 1, Sam pays a $50,000 account payable. What is the amount of Sam's working capital immediately after the June 1 payment?

26. *Effects of borrowing on working capital and current ratio.* Sweney Company had $250,000 of current assets and $90,000 of current liabilities before borrowing $60,000 from the bank with a 3-month note payable.

    a. What effect did the borrowing transaction have on the amount of Sweney Company's working capital?
    b. What effect did the borrowing transaction have on Sweney Company's current ratio?

27. *Effect of transactions on current ratio.* Wilbur Manufacturing has a current ratio of three to one on December 31, 20X8. The following are examples of transactions the company could engage in. Indicate whether each transaction would (+) increase, (-) decrease, or (0) no effect on Wilbur's current ratio. Do the same for the effect on Wilbur's working capital.

    a. Collected accounts receivable
    b. Invested in current marketable securities
    c. Paid cash for a trademark
    d. Wrote-off an uncollectable account receivable
    e. Sold equipment for cash
    f. Sold merchandise for a profit (cash)
    g. Collected a long-term note receivable
    h. Declared a cash dividend
    i. Purchased inventory on account
    j. Scrapped a fully depreciated machine (no gain or loss)
    k. Issued a stock dividend
    l. Purchased a machine by issuing a long-term note payable
    m. Paid a previously declared cash dividend

28. *Effects of transactions on acid-test ratio.* The acid-test ratio at the beginning of 20X0 was 2 to 1 for the Gilly Company.

    Required:

    How would the following transactions affect the acid-test or quick ratio?

    a. Collection of note receivable from Silly Co. The note was due in 20X3.
    b. Collection of accounts receivable.
    c. Sales on account.
    d. Purchase of inventory on account.
    e. Payment of accounts payable.
    f. Cash purchase of common stock of ABC Co. as a temporary investment.
    g. Purchase of a new machine on a credit basis, the purchase price payable in 6 months.

29. *Calculation of current ratio, acid-test ratio, and working capital.* The December 31, 20X1 financial statement of Flunkart Company included the following data:

Cash	$ 60,000
Accounts Receivable	200,000
Marketable Securities	100,000
Prepaid Expenses	25,000
Accounts Payable	200,000
Notes Payable (current)	85,000
Inventory	115,000
Bonds Payable (due in five years)	300,000
Wages Payable	15,000

Required:

a. What is the current ratio? Acid-test ratio? Working capital?
b. Comment on the significance of this current ratio.

30. *Calculation of current ratio, acid-test ratio, and working capital.* The current ratio of Lap Co. on December 31, 20X1 was 2 to 1 ($200,000 to $100,000). In 20X2 the following transactions occurred:

a. Payment of accounts payable, $125,000.
b. Collection of accounts receivable, $50,000.
c. Sales of $200,000, ¾ of which was cash; cost of goods sold was $125,000.
d. Purchase of goods, all on credit, $150,000.
e. A loan for $100,000, due in 5 years.
f. Cash purchase of marketable securities, $10,000.

Required:

On the basis of the preceding information, compute the current ratio at December 31, 20X2.

31. *Analysis of inventory turnover.* The ending inventory for each month of 20X1 is listed below for the Expo Company:

1/31	$21,998	7/31	$35,000
2/28	33,000	8/31	40,000
3/31	28,000	9/30	47,000
4/30	29,500	10/31	48,600
5/31	34,200	11/30	47,300
6/30	29,000	12/31	49,100

During the last half of the year, the company decided to order inventory in larger quantities to take advantage of a quantity discount. The company was able to pass this discount on to its customers in the form of a price decrease. Cost of goods sold for the first half of the year was $224,000 and for the last half of the year was $410,000, reflecting an increase in demand.

Required:

Compute inventory turnover for both halves of the year and decide whether this new inventory policy is beneficial.

32. *Determination of appropriate ratio usage.* Joe Stockholder is contemplating investing in one of the following companies, both in the same industry. Below is financial data relating to each company (income statement amounts are for the most recent year; balance sheet figures are the weighted average amount for that year):

	Pirate Company	Cardinal Company
Sales	$ 6,000	$18,000
Cost of Goods Sold	3,800	13,884
Depreciation Expense	800	1,400
Interest Expense	200	800
Other Expenses	44	110
Income Taxes	480	600
Cash	1,000	4,000
Accounts Receivable	3,500	10,000
Inventory	800	1,900
Fixed Assets	10,000	38,000
Accumulated Depreciation	4,000	14,000
Accounts Payable	1,800	4,000
Income Taxes Payable	480	600
Bonds Payable	200	3,600
Common Stock ($20 par value)	6,000	36,000
Retained Earnings	2,820	(4,300)
Current Market per Share	$ 33	$ 5.35

Required:

Compute the ratio that would best answer each of the following questions, then answer the question. State all necessary assumptions.

a. Which company has the best current position?
b. Which company has the most effective credit department?
c. Which company is doing the best job at keeping the most appropriate inventory level?
d. Which firm has the best ability to make their interest payments?
e. Which firm is earning the best return on the firm's assets?
f. Which stock is the best buy?

33. *Preparation of balance sheet and income statement and general ratios.* Shown below are partially completed comparative financial statements of Neil Company.

Required:

a. Complete the statements.
b. Compute the following for 20X2:

1. Rate of Return on Total Assets
2. Rate of Return on Common Stockholders' Equity
3. Earnings per Share of Common Stock
4. Debt-to-Equity Ratio
5. Number of Times Interest Earned
6. Working Capital
7. Current Ratio
8. Acid-Test Ratio
9. Inventory Turnover
10. Average Number of Days to Collect Receivables
11. Gross Profit Ratio
12. Financial Structure Leverage

13. Common Earnings Leverage
14. Dividend Yield (assume a market value of $50 at December 31, 20X2)
15. Long-Term Debt Ratio
16. Cash Burn Rate
17. Days of Expenses

Neil Company
Comparative Balance Sheet
December 31, 20X2 and 20X1

	20X2		20X1		Increase (Decrease)	
	Dollars	Percent of Total Assets	Dollars	Percent of Total Assets	Dollars	Percent
ASSETS						
Current assets:						
Cash	$ 55,000		$ 50,000			
Net accounts receivable	200,000		175,000			
Inventories	300,000		225,000			
Prepaid expenses	45,000		50,000			
Total current assets	$ 600,000		$ 500,000			
Land, buildings, and equipment (net)	1,400,000		1,250,000			
Total assets	$2,000,000		$1,750,000			
LIABILITIES						
Current liabilities:						
Accounts payable	$ 300,000		$ 350,000			
Note payable	200,000		100,000			
Total current liabilities	$ 500,000		$ 450,000			
Bonds payable	500,000		500,000			
Total liabilities	$1,000,000		$ 950,000			
STOCKHOLDERS' EQUITY						
Common stock ($20 par)	$ 600,000		$ 600,000			
Retained earnings	400,000		200,000			
Total liabilities and stockholders' equity	$2,000,000		$1,750,000			

Neil Company
Comparative Income Statement
for Years Ended December 31, 20X2 and 20X1

	20X2 Dollars	20X2 Percent of Net Sales	20X1 Dollars	20X1 Percent of Net Sales	Increase (Decrease) Dollars	Increase (Decrease) Percent
Net sales	$3,000,000		$2,000,000			
Cost of goods sold	2,100,000		1,500,000			
Gross profit on sales	$ 900,000		$ 500,000			
Operating expenses:						
Selling expenses	$ 300,000		$ 100,000			
Administrative expenses	100,000		50,000			
Depreciation expense	100,000		100,000			
Total operating expenses	$ 500,000		$ 250,000			
Operating income	$ 400,000		$ 250,000			
Interest expense	40,000		30,000			
Income before income taxes	$ 360,000		$ 220,000			
Income taxes	90,000		45,000			
Net income	$ 270,000		$ 175,000			

34. *General ratios.*

Carol Company
Balance Sheet
December 31

	20X1	20X2
Cash	$ 2	$ 6
Marketable securities	4	9
Receivables	1	3
Inventories	13	20
Prepaid expenses	4	4
Property, plant and equipment	3	2
Other assets	0	1
	$27	$45
Accounts payable	$ 6	$ 5
Notes payable	2	3
Taxes payable	3	4
Unearned revenues	1	2
Long-term liabilities	6	16
Common stock ($1 par value)	2	6
Retained earnings	7	9
	$27	$45

Carol Company
Income Statement
For the Year Ending December 31

	20X1	20X2
Net sales	$15	$16
Cost of goods sold	4	4
Gross profit on sales	$11	$12
Operating expenses:		
Selling expenses	$ 2	$ 3
Administrative expenses	1	1
Depreciation expense	2	2
Total operating expenses	$ 5	$ 6
Operating income	$ 6	$ 6
Interest expense	1	1
Income before income taxes	$ 5	$ 5
Income taxes	1	1
Net income	$ 4	$ 4

Compute the following for 20X2:

1. Rate of return on common stockholders' equity, ____%
2. Earnings per share of common stock, $_____.
3. Average number of days to collect receivables, ____ days.
4. Gross profit ratio, ____%
5. Financial structure leverage, ____ to 1.
6. Common earnings leverage, ____%.
7. Dividend yield (assume a market value of $10 at December 31, 20X2, ____%.
8. Current ratio, ____ to 1.
9. Days of expenses, ____ days.

Index

A

Accountants, Role of in the Management Process 1-8
Accounting Function, Location 1-9
Accounting Systems 1-4
Additional Processing 10-17
American Vegetable Company 4-5, 4-19
    Account for Units Produced 4-5
    Accumulate Costs with Inventory Units 4-9
    Calculate the Cost per Unit 4-8
    Determine Equivalent Units of Production 4-7
    Determine Total Manufacturing Costs 4-6
    Transfer and Completion of Production 4-10
Analysis,
    Common Stockholders 13-18
        Earnings per Share of Common Stock 13-25
        Earnings Quality 13-25
        Rate of Return
            on Total Assets 13-18
            on Common Stockholders' Equity 13-21
        Relationship, ROA and ROCE
        Price to Earnings Ratio 13-26
        Other Ratios 13-27
    Long-term Creditors 13-28
        Amount of Debt 13-28
        Continued Existence 13-31
        Debt-to-Equity Ratio 13-29
        Interest Coverage Ratios 13-30
    Short-Term Creditors 13-32
        Accounts Receivable 13-36
        Acid Test (Quick Ratio) 13-34
        Current Ratio 13-33
        Intrepetation 13-40
        Inventories 13-37
        Key Current Assets and Liabilities 13-35
        Nature 13-32
        Working Capital 13-32
    Interpretation 13-40
Analytical Procedure, Basic 13-12
    Vertical Analysis 13-15
    Common-size Statements 13-15
Assets 13-6
    Cash 13-8
    Marketable Securities 13-8
    Recievables 13-8
    Inventories 13-8
    Prepaid Expenses 13-8
    Property, Plant, and Equipment 13-8
    Other Assets 13-8

B

Balance Sheet 13-4
Balanced Scorecard 9-23
BLAST! Snack Foods 9-3, 9-23
Budget 1-10, 8-4, 8-5, 8-6, 8-7, 8-8, 8-11, 8-20
    Comparing Actual Activity 1-11
    Financial and Resource 8-11
        Accounts Payable Budget 8-16
        Accounts Receivable Budget 8-14
        Budgeted Shareholders' Equity 8-17
        Cash Budget 8-11
        Inventory Budgets 8-14
        Notes Payable Budget 8-17
        Property, Plant, and Equipment Budget 8-15
    Manufacturing Overhead and Direct Labor 8-8
    Merchandising and Service Organizations 8-20
    Operating 8-4
        Comprehensive Example 8-4
    Preparing 1-10
    Production 8-6
    Sales 8-5
    Standards 1-10
    Usage 8-7
        Direct Materials Purchases 8-7
Budgeting 8-2, 8-3, 8-18
    Nonquantitative Aspects 8-18
        Budget Standards, Difficulty 8-18
        Participative Budgeting and Slack 8-20
    Process 8-3
    Purposes 8-2

C

Capital Budgeting 11-2
    Decisions, Types 11-3
    High-Technology Assets 11-24
    Introduction 11-2
    Qualitative Factors 11-5
    Quantitative Factors 11-3
    Summary 11-23
    Techniques in Practice 11-25

Techniques that Consider the Time Value of Money 11-10
    Summary 11-22
Techniques That Ignore the Time Value of Money 11-5
    Average Rate of Return (Accounting Rate of Return) 11-9
        Average Rate of Return Using Average Investment 11-10
    Payback Period 11-6
        Limitations of the Payback Period 11-8
        Payback Period with Unequal Cash Flows 11-7
        Payback Period with Uniform Cash Inflows 11-6

Cash
    from Operations 12-5
        Direct 12-5
        Indirect 12-6

Cash Flows
    Analysis, Information 12-15
    Analysis, Problems 12-13
        Uncollectible Accounts 12-13
        Dividends 12-14
        Income Tax Expense 12-14
        Stock Dividends and Conversions 12-14
        Noncash Transactions 12-14
        Multiple Changes 12-15
    Brief History 12-2
    Concept 12-2
    Importance 12-1
    Statement of 12-3, 13-2
        Preparation 12-8
            Change in Cash 12-9
            Changes in Noncash 12-10

Compound Interest 11-43
Continuation of a Segment or Production Line 10-14
    Resource Constraints 10-16
    Summary 10-17

Cost Accumulation 3-2, 4-14, 7-11
    Accumulation of Direct Labor Costs with Production 7-12
    Closing Variance Accounts and Adjusting for Differences Between Standard and Actual Costs 7-12
    Completion of Production 7-12
    Decision-Making Process 3-3
    Importance 3-2
    Issuance of Direct Materials to Production 7-11
    Purchase of Direct Materials 7-11
    Sale of Inventory 7-12

Cost Behavior 2-5, 2-13
    Activity Level 2-6
    Analyzing 2-13
        Graphical Method 2-13
        Least Squares Regression Method 2-16
        Semi-Averages Methods 2-15
        Two-Point Method 2-14
    Cost Driver 2-6
    Illustration 2-8
    Overview 2-5
    Relevant Range 2-7
    Retail and Service Companies 2-17

Cost Centers 9-5
Costing 5-14, 7-15
    Activity-Based 5-14
        ABC 5-20
        Allocate Costs to Inventory Items 5-17
        Batch-Level Activities 5-18
        Cost Drivers. 5-21
        Facility-Level Activities 5-18
        Identify Cost Drivers 5-16
        Identify Overhead Cost Pools 5-15
        Non-Manufacturing Costs 5-20
        Other Issues 5-20
        Product-Level Activities 5-18
        Service Organizations 5-21
        Unit-Level Activities 5-17
    Standard 7-15

Costs 2-2, 5-2, 5-6
    Allocations 5-6
        Departmental Overhead Rates 5-7
        Direct Method 5-9
        Operating Departments 5-8
        Other 5-14
        Step-Down Method 5-11
    Fixed Costs 2-9
    Manufacturing Overhead 5-2
    Overhead Costs, Applying 5-3
    Overhead Costs, Recording 5-5
    Semi-Variable (Mixed) Costs 2-12
    Step Costs 2-11
    Types 2-2
        Direct Labor 2-3
        Direct Materials 2-2
        Manufacturing Overhead 2-4
    Variable Costs 2-10

Costs and Profits 1-11
    Accumulating Data 1-11

CVP Analysis 6-3
    Assumptions 6-15
    Equation Approaches 6-6

Contribution Margin Ratio Approach 6-7
General Equation Approach 6-6
Unit Contribution Margin Approach 6-7
Graphical Approach 6-3
Other Uses 6-8
Contribution Margin 6-10
Desired Level of Profit 6-8
Desired Profit 6-9
Fixed Costs 6-10
Multiple Products 6-11
Selling Prices 6-10
Variable Costs 6-9
Variable Levels of Profit 6-9
Practical Application 6-15

F

Feedback 1-7
Financial Statements 3-2, 8-9
Comparative 13-12
Operations 8-9
Budgeted 8-9
Preparation 3-2, 3-11
Cost of Goods Manufactured Statement 3-11
Cost of Goods Sold Statement 3-12
Users 13-17

I

Income Determination 6-16
Absorption (Full) Costing 6-16
Comparing 6-18
Variable (Direct) Costing 6-18
Income Statement 13-1
Interest 11-39
Internal Time-adjusted Rate of Return 11-20
Making the Decision 11-22
Unequal Cash Flows 11-22
Investment Centers 9-11
Evaluating, Issues in 9-16
Life of Investment 9-17
Net Income 9-17
Transfer Pricing 9-18
Cost 9-19
Dual Pricing 9-20
Market Price 9-20
Negotiated Transfer Prices 9-20
Other Transfer Pricing Incentives 9-21
Summary 9-21

J

Job-Order Costing 3-3
Ace Construction Company 3-3, 3-16
Summary 3-14
Incur Manufacturing Costs 3-5
Direct Labor, Use 3-6
Direct Materials, Use 3-5
Overhead Costs, Applying 3-7
Introduction 3-3
Obtain Direct Materials 3-4
Production, Completion 3-9
Sale of Inventory 3-10
Joint Manufacturing Processes 4-10
Just-in-Time Inventory 4-14

L

Liabilities 13-9
Current Liabilities 13-9
Accounts Payable 13-9
Notes Payable 13-9
Unearned Revenue 13-9
Long-term Liabilities 13-9

M

Make-or-Buy Decisions 10-18
Alternative Use of Capacity 10-19
Other Considerations 10-21
Qualitative Considerations 10-19
Management Control Systems 9-1
Management Process 1-4
Managerial Accouting Information 1-3
Decisions 1-11
Need 1-3
Overview of Function 1-10
Manufacturing, recent developments 7-13
Activity-Based Costing (ABC) 7-15
Highly Automated Manufacturing Processes 7-13
Just-in-Time (JIT) Manufacturing 7-13
Total Quality Management (TQM) 7-14
Value- and Non-Value-Added Activities 7-14

N

Net Present Value 11-11
Additional Complexities 11-15
Advantages 11-19
Income Tax Effects and Depreciation 11-15

Limitations 11-18
Other Future Inflows and Outflows 11-17
Evaluating Competing Projects 11-13
Comparing the Net Present Value 11-13
Profitability Index 11-15
Future Cash Inflows and Outflows–Basic 11-12
Summary 11-20
Nonfinancial Performance 9-23

O

Operating Leverage 6-13
Automated Manufacturing Processes 6-13

P

Performance Standards 7-1, 7-15
Direct Materials and Direct Labor Costs 7-2
Manufacturing Overhead Costs 7-4
Postaudit of Capital Investments 11-24
Present Value of a Series of Equal Payments 11-43
Present Values of a Future Sum 11-40
Process Costing 4-2
Overview 4-2
Product Pricing Decisions 10-7
Contribution Margin (Variable) Approach 10-8
Elasticity of Demand 10-10
Full-Cost (Absorption) Approach 10-8
Setting Prices to Earn a Profit 10-9
Profit Centers 9-7

R

Ratio Analysis 13-16
Comparison with Standards 13-16
Reports 1-6
Preparing 1-6
Using for Decisions and Activities 1-6
Residual Income 9-15
Disadvantage 9-16
Responsibility Centers 9-2
Responsibility Accounting 9-3
Return on Investment (ROI) 9-11
Decomposing ROI 9-13
Weaknesses of ROI 9-14

S

Short-term Decisions, Terminology 10-2
Decisions 10-2
Managerial Accounting Data, use of 10-6
Opportunity Costs 10-5

Relevant Costs 10-2
Qualitative Considerations 10-4
Summary 10-6
Sunk Costs 10-5
Special Orders 10-11
No Excess Capacity 10-12
Qualitative Considerations 10-13
Summary 10-14
Stockholders' Equity 13-10
Statement of 13-10

T

Total Quality Management 9-21
Transactions 1-5
Identifying and Gathering Information 1-5

U

Using Managerial Accounting Information
Ace Construction Company 3-16
American Vegetable Company 4-19, 5-22
Better Books 2-17
Blast! Snack Foods 9-23
Golden Music Producers 6-21
Sportsworld 7-16
Toy Concepts, Inc. 8-20

V

Variance Analysis 7-6
Direct Labor 7-6, 7-9
Direct Material 7-6, 7-7